Reframing the Danish Renaissance
Problems and Prospects
in a European Perspective

Papers from an International Conference in Copenhagen
28 September - 1 October 2006

Reframing the Danish Renaissance Problems and Prospects in a European Perspective

Papers from an International Conference in Copenhagen
28 September - 1 October 2006

*Edited by
Michael Andersen,
Birgitte Bøggild Johannsen
and Hugo Johannsen*

PNM

Publications from the National Museum

Studies in Archaeology & History Vol. 16

Copenhagen 2011

Publications from the National Museum, Studies in Archaeology & History Vol. 16
Reframing the Danish Renaissance

Edited by Michael Andersen, Birgitte Bøggild Johannsen and Hugo Johannsen

Copyright © The National Museum of Denmark and the authors 2011
All rights reserved

University Press of Southern Denmark 2011
Cover Design by the National Museum and Unisats ApS
Printed by Special-Trykkeriet Viborg a-s

Published by The National Museum of Denmark
Danish Middle Ages and Renaissance
12 Frederiksholms Kanal, DK-1220 Copenhagen K.

On commission at University Press of Southern Denmark
ISBN: 978-87-7602-129-0

Funded by:
Farumgaard-Fonden
Heritage Agency of Denmark
Ny Carlsbergfondet

Cover front: Christiansstad (Scania). Holy Trinity Church, interior facing east (Photo Ole Akhøj).
Cover back: Christian I. Medal struck by Bartolomeo Melioli 1474. The National Museum of Denmark, Copenhagen (Photo National Museum).

CONTENTS

Preface by Michael Andersen, Birgitte Bøggild Johannsen and Hugo Johannsen   7

Introduction by Birgitte Bøggild Johannsen   11

REFRAMING THE FRAMES
Thomas DaCosta Kaufmann: The European Perspective   32
Birgitte Bøggild Johannsen: The Danish Perspective.   51
Claire Farago: Reframing the Renaissance Problem Today   71
Keith Moxey: Do We Still Need a Renaissance?.   79
Jacob Wamberg: The Renaissance: The Origin of Modernity or Its First Resistance?   89
Maria Fabricius Hansen: Renaissance Art and Art History in Denmark: Some Remarks on the Conference. .   99

LUTHERAN RHETORICS
Jan Harasimowicz: Wort-Bild-Wort. Die Rhetorik der lutherischen Kirchenkunst Nordeuropas im
16. und 17. Jahrhundert   104
Margit Thøfner: Imported Patterns and Homegrown Virtues: Hendrick Goltzius's *Exemplar Virtutum*
Prints and the Altarpieces of St Nicholas in Kolding and St Mary in Flensburg   117
Krista Kodres: Denmark in Estonia. Import and Domestic Renaissances?   126
Hanne Kolind Poulsen: A Tribute to the Reformation: Hesselagergård in a Lutheran Perspective.   137

CATALYSTS TO CHANGE
Marianne Marcussen: Implementing Perspective in Danish Renaissance Sculpture: Claus Berg as a Pioneer . .   152
Mikael Bøgh Rasmussen: Melchior Lorck's Portrait of Sultan Süleyman the Magnificent (1562):
A Double-Coded View   165
Angelica Dülberg: Die künstlerische Ausstattung des Dresdner Residenzschlosses in der zweiten Hälfte
des 16. Jahrhunderts als Ausdruck der neu gewonnenen Kurwürde   171
Mario Titze: Annaburg und Lichtenburg. Schloßbauten des Kurfürsten August von Sachsen und
seiner Gemahlin Anna von Dänemark   183

Uwe Albrecht: Deutsche, französische und niederländische Einflüsse als Wegbereiter und Katalysatoren der dänischen Renaissance-Architektur in der zweiten Hälfte des 16. Jahrhunderts:
Das Beispiel des Herrenhauses 197
Krista de Jonge: A Netherlandish Model? Reframing the Danish Royal Residences in a European Perspective   219

REX TRIUMPHANS: THE UNSURPASSED PARADIGM OF CHRISTIAN IV

Juliette Roding: King Solomon and the Imperial Paradigm of Christian IV (1588-1648)   234
Mara R. Wade: Duke Ulrik (1578-1624) as Agent, Patron, Artist: Reframing Danish Court Culture
in the International Perspective c. 1600   243
Barbara Uppenkamp: Wolfenbüttel and Copenhagen: The Exchange of Architectural Ideas
in the Time of Christian IV   263
Badeloch Vera Noldus: Art and Music on Demand – A Portrait of the Danish Diplomat Jonas Charisius
and his Mission to the Dutch Republic   279
Heiner Borggrefe and Thomas Fusenig: Pieter Isaacsz., Jacob van der Doordt, Hans Rottenhammer
and their Artistic Networks   301
Konrad Ottenheym: Hendrick de Keyser and Denmark.   313
Mogens Bencard: Ebony and Silver Furniture at Frederiksborg Castle   325
Kristoffer Neville: Christian IV's Italianates. Sculpture at the Danish Court   335
Dirk van der Vijver: Claiming Danish Renaissance. The Historiography of the Architectural Relations
between the Low Countries and the Balticum/Denmark   347

List of authors   361

Bibliography.   367

Index.   399

PREFACE

Michael Andersen, Birgitte Bøggild Johannsen and Hugo Johannsen

This collection of essays represents the fruits harvested from the international conference, "Reframing the Danish Renaissance. Problems and Prospects in a European Perspective", held during the days 28 September – 1 October 2006 at the National Museum in Copenhagen and at the castles of Kronborg and Frederiksborg in Northern Zealand. The conference took place within the frameworks of the Danish cultural festival of the Renaissance (Fig. 1, *Renæssance 2006*), subsidized by the Danish Ministry of Culture, and it was supported by a large number of enthusiastic cultural institutions, private foundations and individual groups of professionals and amateurs. The festival in itself developed as an open, composite project in the wake of related cultural jubilees, during recent years memorializing the Middle Ages (*Middelalderåret 1999*) and the world famous Danish author, Hans Christian Andersen (*H. C. Andersen-året 2005*). Basically, the aim of the 2006-campaign was to profit by the synergy and attentions, national as well as international, bestowed upon the previous ventures, equally following up their superior mission of communicating to a wider audience an understanding of a specific period in the past or an individual personality, regarded in the conceptual framework of an existing, dynamic cultural encounter between Denmark and the World. For 2006, the Renaissance was chosen as a subject, not only representing a moment of major importance in history, but also regarded as a foundation for the present society, at the same time seeking a coherent, multifaceted dissemination of the past, and through this venture boosting Denmark, commercially as well, as a cultural nation of significance in the indicative epoch (cf. Nicolai Gjessing & Jens Vellev (eds.), *Renæssance 2006*, Århus 2008).

Aims and objectives of the conference "Reframing the Danish Renaissance" were no less ambitious. Focus was placed upon a number of specific targets as defined in the preliminary programme (Fig. 2). Of overriding importance was the wish to establish a frame or forum for open discussions between national and international art historians, to which should be added the final goal of communicating the various contributions in a well-illustrated volume with a detailed bibliography, to be published, not in 'inaccessible' Danish, but in the *linguae francae* of English and German. Attention was moreover directed towards a re-evaluation of Danish Renaissance art in its European context in the light of recent research and of current theoretical or methodological discourses, no less taking into account the results of Danish art historians, mainly disseminated in native language and in domestic contexts. Of further significance was the endeavour

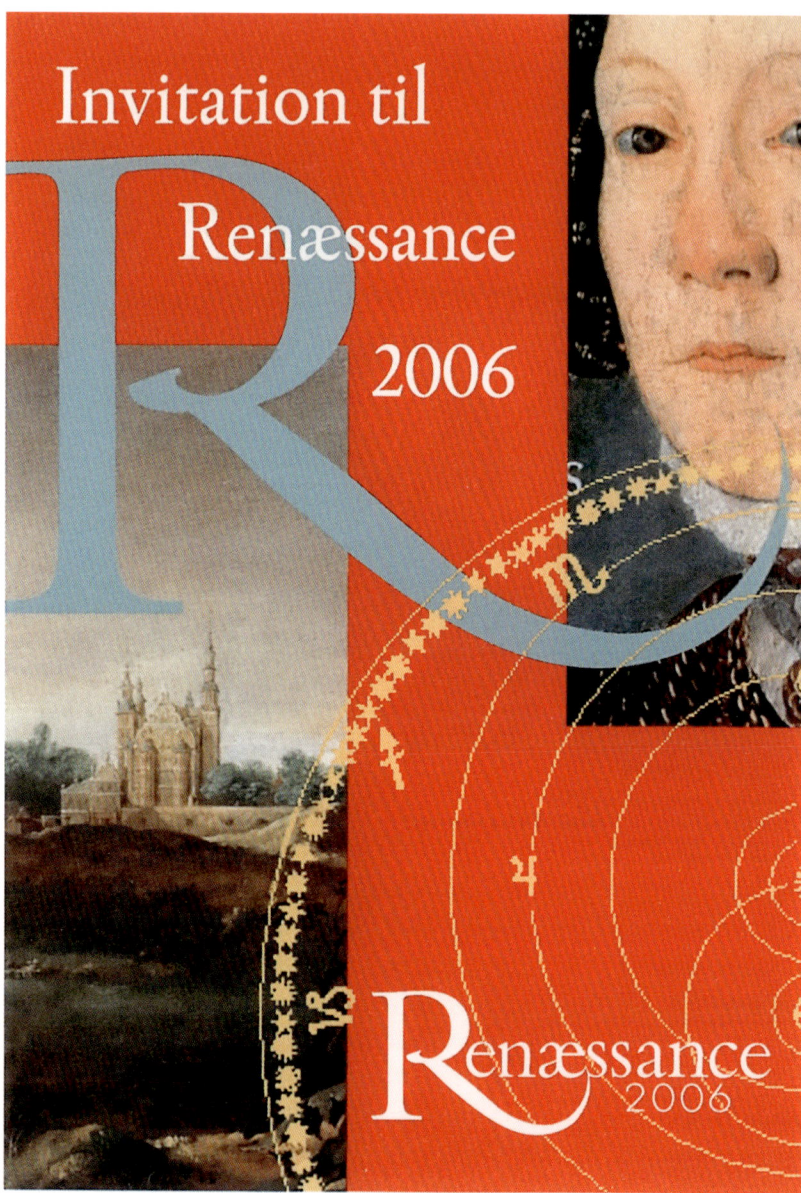

Fig. 1. Poster of The Renaissance Year 2006.

to contribute to debates in international fora, introducing lesser known Danish monuments and manners of approaching general problems. Last, but definitely not least was cherished a wish to create new networks and stimulate collaboration between colleagues across established institutional, professional and national borders. Regarding the outcome with the wisdom of hindsight, the editors of the present publication sincerely hope that at least some of these aspirations have been fulfilled.

In particular, it is of imperative importance to acknowledge the conference's debts to former, related initiatives. Special attention deserve two previous international conferences in Copenhagen in 1975 and 2003, the CIHA-conference, "Pays du Nord et l'Europe. Art et Architecture au XVIe siècle" (published in *Hafnia. Copenhagen Papers in the History of Art*, 3 (1976)) and "Cultural Traffic and Cultural Transformation around the Baltic Sea, 1450-1720" (published in *Scandinavian Journal of History* 28, 3-4 (2003), 151-283), introducing still challenging issues of integrating regions or places, or bringing into discussion the multifarious processes of diffusion and reception with the inclusion of Danish cases, though leaving out more theoretical or methodological discussions of the Renaissance in general.

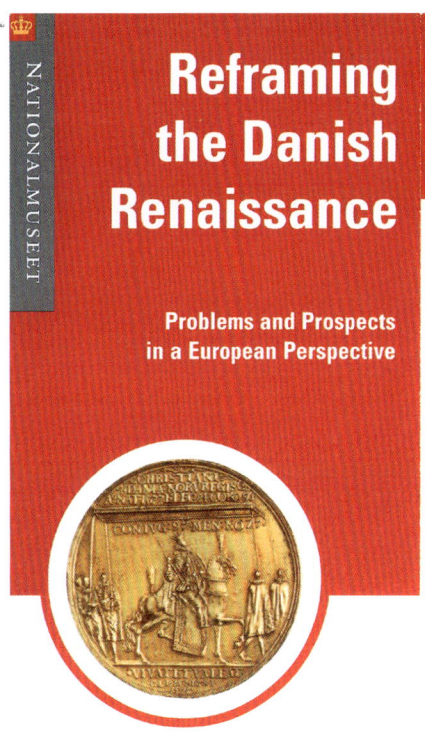

Fig. 2. Flyer of The Copenhagen Conference 2006.

No less inspirational as point of departure was the wide range of exhibitions in 1988, organized in Denmark by the Council of Europe and extolling the reign of Christian IV (1588-1648) and its European relations. Though not followed up by any colloquies, the image communicated in the richly illustrated exhibition catalogue, *Christian IV and Europe* still to a large extent has dominated the international vision of the Renaissance in Denmark.

The planning of the conference developed during the years 2003-2006. Active participants during the preparations were Maria Fabricius Hansen, Marianne Marcussen, Badeloch Noldus and Hanne Kolind Poulsen together with the editors, in practical matters during the carrying out of the symposium in 2006 assisted by Heidi Lykke Petersen and Susanne Gottlieb Aasted. During work on the conference publication, the readings of proofs and the composition of the bibliography, important assistance has been given by the last mentioned as well as by Michael Märcher and Lasse Jonas Bendtsen. We owe our sincere thanks to everyone involved.

The generous funding of the conference was due to *Carlsbergs Mindelegat for Brygger J. C. Jacobsen, Danish Agency for Science, Technology and Innovation, Elsass Fonden, Farumgaard-Fonden* and *Tuborgfondet*. Invaluable support, finally allowing us to communicate the results to a wider public, was given by *Farumgaard-Fonden, Heritage Agency of Denmark* and *Ny Carlsbergfondet*. All financial supporters mentioned deserve our deepest gratitude.

Michael Andersen, Birgitte Bøggild Johannsen and Hugo Johannsen
The National Museum of Denmark in May 2011

INTRODUCTION

Birgitte Bøggild Johannsen

Reflexions on Frames and Names, Contexts and Concepts

"Die geistigen Umrisse einer Kulturepoche geben vielleicht für jedes Auge ein verschiedenes Bild, und wenn es sich vollends um eine Zivilisation handelt, welche als nächtes Muster der unsrigen noch jetzt fortwirkt, so muss sich das subjective Urteilen und Empfinden jeden Augenblick beim Darsteller und beim Leser einmischen".[1]

This admonitory verdict on the subjectivity, temporality and frame-bound nature of any judgments on past civilizations, uttered by Jacob Burckhardt in the introduction to his seminal *Die Kultur der Renaissance in Italien*, deserves once more to be considered in relation to the present collection of essays, aiming at 'Reframing the Danish Renaissance in a European Context'. The self-imposed challenge, as defined by the conference's working group, was basically inspired from the anthology by Claire Farago (ed.), *Reframing the Renaissance: Visual Culture in Europe and Latin America, 1450-1650*, New Haven 1995. In the wake of postmodern and postcolonial critical research this important work has for recent generations opened to a renewed vision of traditional notions on frames, centres and peripheries in relation to the fundamental issue of cultural exchange during the historical period, defined as 'the Renaissance' - in fact pretty close covering the chronological space, taken as point of departure for the Danish conference as well.

As demonstrated by research during the latest decades, the very strategy of using 'a reframing rhetoric', i.e. framing anew, reorienting or re-presenting certain areas of debate, has incessantly generated new meanings.[2] Questioned have been hegemonic and time bound concepts in relation to paradigms of centre and periphery or to issues of frames, margins, frontiers, limits and borders, all of these - whether mental or material, factual or fictious – basically to be regarded as social and cultural constructions.[3] Indeed, the very psychological process of reframing has since the 1970s been a current issue in the field of alternative therapy and neuro-linguistic programming (NLP),[4] implying a positive behavioural attitude and interpersonal communication, resetting or reformulating adapted and negative frameworks into positive and successful ditto, thus achieving a believed improved change of matters. The issue represents in itself the nucleus of the Renaissance's utopian message of rebirth, innovation and improvement, continuously being reactivated for ideological purposes. This agenda was valid for the Danish cultural festival, *Renæssance 2006* as well.[5]

A few general remarks should be premised, relevant to the positioning of the conceptual frameworks for the contributions presented. A succeeding survey will focus upon the national historiography of Danish Renaissance art and architecture, while a third section presents arguments and results of the 25 papers. Accordingly, the editors have chosen to follow the classical principle, "*Generalia præcedunt, specialia sequuntur*", thus restructuring the original disposition of lectures, cf. also below. Basically however, the general notion of the 'Renaissance' has been maintained, notwithstanding current inclinations for replacing this by the term 'Early Modern', depending upon, as Leah S. Marcus has suggested, whether you orient retrospectively, with focus upon questions of origin, influence and filiations, rebirth and renewal – with a certain aura of elitism in the choice of subject – or instead interpret prospectively, taking into account concepts associated with modernity or with lower and more egalitarian connotations.[6] In short, being defined as a historical period, a movement, a mentality or simply "a fantasy, a dream" (Guido Ruggiero),[7] the Renaissance consequently in this context remains "something that we all understand" (Rebecca Zorach).[8] And, as it recently has been emphasized: "Rumours of the Renaissance's death have been greatly exaggerated" (Jonathan Woolfson).[9] However, it should at the same time not be disguised either, that 'The Renaissance is not what it used to be', meaning that the field of research and the issues judged relevant have considerably expanded during these last decades, with evident repercussions for the present venture as well.

As to the geopolitical frames, the perspectives in Renaissance studies have continuously been re-oriented from a national to a regional, European or further, to a Trans-European or Global vision.[10] Shift in weight from a unilateral emphasis on Italy, Southern or Central Europe into a more even, pan-European focus, including Northern Europe and the Baltic region,[11] has contributed to reset a proper balance. However, prejudices, based upon one-sidedly judgments on nation states, formed during the latest centuries without the necessary consciousness of past, composite political entities, still often leave Denmark (or Scandinavia in general) in the blind spot of interest (cf. also the contributions by Da Costa Kaufmann and Bøggild Johannsen).[12] On the other hand, the conference's reference to 'the Danish Renaissance' hopefully should not lead to an accusation of untrendy, biased and anachronistic nationalism, when debating social, political and religious issues, patterns or activities, referring to moments and monuments of the 16th and 17th centuries in this area.[13] In fact, as demonstrated by several of the contributions, a keen awareness of the complex nature of this very question should be a necessary equipment for further discussions.

This leads to another pressing task, the imperative need to revalue the chronological and qualitative frames defined for the Renaissance era in the Danish Realms, particularly taking into account the principal 'Renaissance Agenda', the transformation and assimilation of forms and ideas, into a local context well beyond the Roman *limes*, reflecting the canonical paradigm of Antiquity, preferably through Italian, Netherlandish and German intermediary. From a superficial glance, the fixed definitions of period styles might contribute to marginalize the Danish efforts, during the first part of the 16th century exposing 'untrendy' Gothic, when High Renaissance was at stake and jumping into Mannerism and Early Baroque in the first half of the 17th century, almost before a sense of 'proper Renaissance' was demonstrated! In fact, the question invites for a renewed evaluation, including further reflexions on concepts of 'modernity', 'innovation', 'rebirth' or 'discontinuity' versus 'tradition' and 'continuity' – all basically fluent denominators. Of equal concern should be discourses on 'othering' or 'alterity', as well as on 'purity' or 'hybridity'.[14] These issues, exactly relating to crossing boundaries in time and space, have for the last decades been eagerly discussed in the cultural sciences with focus upon the fundamental crisis of losing oneself by shaping a hybrid 'third language or space', appropriating and selectively assimilating with the unfamiliar or - on the contrary - alienating from it and clinging to tradition and the well-known.[15]

Acknowledging the experience of a pluralism or the horizontal co-existence of cultures as a determinant aspect of the Renaissance,[16] the deliberate dialogue or dispute with foreign ages, areas and aesthetics was an issue in Northern as well as in Southern European 'hybrid',[17] 'eccentric' or 'bastard' renaissances since the early 16th century. This would also include Denmark, reflecting stylistic pluralism (comprising the notion of 'Renaissance Gothic', "Gothique de la Renaissance" or 'Gothic Renaissance')[18] or creative anachronism as alternatives to the unreserved assimilation of Antiquity in its 'pure' version. These phenomena should in all be regarded as pan- or even trans-European phenomena, not one-sidedly as the characteristics of a province or a decentred region.[19] Options to reckon with as well were the positive meanings, given to retrospective references to tradition or to the common past, whether native or antique, constituting at the same time valuable means for creating status and identity.[20] In this field, the Danish power elite without any reservations or delays[21] since c. 1500 followed the prevailing European development, each kingdom or political entity - in terms of *cujus regio, ejus renovatio* - cultivating its individual and indigenous history for new purposes in discourse with the Grand Narrative of Antiquity.[22]

Accordingly, a re-reading of the Danish developments should not one-sidedly take its point of departure in the age of Christian IV (1588-1648), still to a large extent dominating the international vision of the Renaissance in Denmark.[23] Also the previous decades deserve attention, whether you define its birth from c. 1550, associate the beginnings in a monocausal explanation with the confessional change in 1536, the official introduction of the Lutheran Reformation, or track its origin further back in time, to c. 1500, or even to c. 1450, as recent attempts to describe the phenomena in their embryonic state ('Renæssancen i svøb') have proposed.[24]

Influential to the renewed discourse on 'the state of Denmark' would also be the expanding inclusion of visual objects or media, comprising not only 'the great monuments', but also 'minor' genres or 'peripheral' subjects such as cartography, Neo-Latin epitaphs and epigraphy, heraldry, ornaments, textiles, furniture, ceramics, jewellery, medals and prints. Crucial should as well be the increasing focus upon cultural processes, referring to multiple ways of exchange, transfer and traffic, or - more specifically - to complex patterns of authors, agents and audiences of production, performance, patronage, consumption, communication and visual reception.[25] Reflecting a dynamic intercourse, where influences were spread i.a. via different dynastic, cultural, confessional or commercial networks, the economic and sociological approaches are of vital importance when debating artistic centres and regions, reckoning with the co-existence of more centres, even within a 'minor' region as Denmark. Or, when you take into account the option of 'occasionalism', relating to different modes of expression, chosen in various contexts by individual artists or patrons.[26]

In short, the agenda of breaking the traditional frames in relation to the conference's principal theme seems more urgent than ever.

Reconsidering the National Historiography

Marking out new boundaries and aiming at re-defined issues should not, however, exclude interaction with past cognitions, preferably established within an indigenous framework. Indeed, each national area has its own historiography to consider, transcend or to supply. Accordingly, any discourse, deconstructing historical constructions or meta-narratives should take its point of reference in the no-nonsense questions, posed by Peter Burke (2004): "Who is doing the construction?", "Under what constraints?" and "Out of what?".[27]

With focus upon the formative years during the 19th and early 20th century of Danish art history as a scientific discipline, the institutional status, occupation and nationality of the agents involved should be commented upon in relation to the first issue, the political and social contexts named in the second case and the state of known research material dwelled upon, pertaining to the last. During this period, the still current image of the Renaissance in a Danish context was in the main established, including a definition of the Renaissance concept and of the chronological

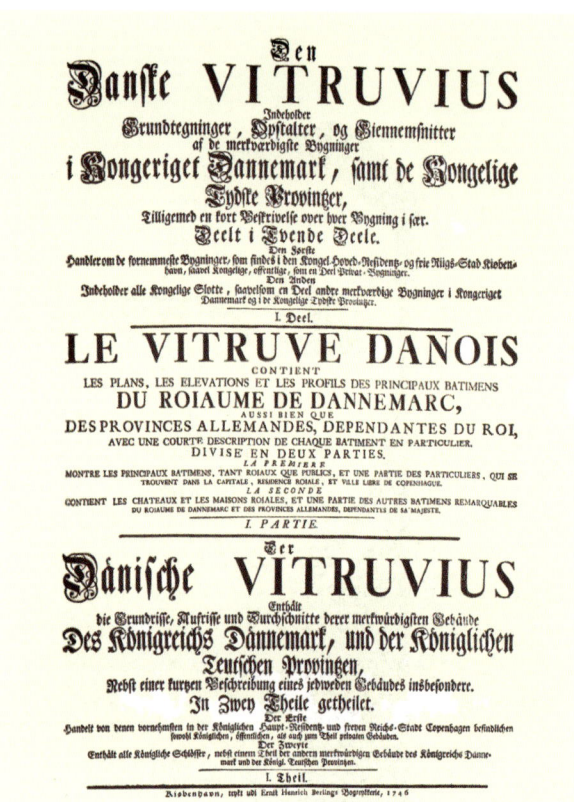

Fig. 1. Lauritz de Thurah, *Den Danske Vitruvius*. Frontispiece of volume I, Copenhagen 1746.

frame involved, evaluating the products in terms of novelty, originality (made in Denmark or by Danes versus foreigners) and quality (referring in particular to the closeness or distance to the unrivalled paradigm of the Italian Renaissance). The following survey, however, is bound to take into account that the field still is not yet fully explored. Neither should it be concealed however that the vision of the author is biased, anchored in the object-centred and antiquarian tradition of a museum of cultural history. The National Museum of Denmark.[28]

Contrary f.i. to Sweden,[29] the early Danish literature on art and architecture is characterized by a considerable lack of theoretical works. Before c. 1750 the antiquarian literature dominates, i.e. registrations of collections, inscriptions or monuments, structured according to a philological approach, produced by historians, topographers or linguists, i.a. since the early 17th century following royal commands of systematic inventorying Danish antiquities.[30] Exceptions are a few examples of artistic biographies, f.i. the survey by the German vicar Johannes Dauw (1721), who in particular pointed out Melchior Lorck as the period's only Danish painter of European renown.[31]

The enterprising mercantilism during the reign of Frederik V (1746-66), actively promoting the patriotic discourse,[32] witnessed the first editions of sources to the Danish history and culture, followed by an ambitious, though never accomplished, plan in 1746 to publish i.a. a historical survey of arts and the crafts "of our nation", a biographical encyclopaedia and an overview of Danish antiquities.[33] Of far greater implications, however, was the (partial) publication 1746-49 by the architect Lauritz de Thurah of *Den Danske Vitruvius*, a topographical presentation of Danish monuments, originally planned in 10 illustrated folio volumes, (with parallel texts in French and German) (Fig. 1). This was supplied by the description of the metropolis, *Hafnia Hodierna* (1748) and by *Den Danske Atlas*, a likewise illustrated topographical edition in seven volumes, launched by the historians Erik Pontoppidan and Hans de Hofman (1763-1781).[34] All three editions, aiming at describing both profane and religious monuments from the Middle Ages up to present times from the Danish realms *in toto*, were of paramount importance to the national self-esteem, even (in the case of Thurah) including a few architects of the Renaissance era (i.e. Jørgen Friborg), though eliminating any theoretical discussions or more detailed analyses. However, these works would represent the literary foundation (together with a reedition in 1755 of Dauw's work) for the education, since 1754 situated in the reorganized Royal Academy of Fine Arts in Copenhagen, of future generations of native artists during the Absolutist government, following the guiding principles of classical antiquity, "le bon goût" (in contrast to the Gothic taste) and nature.[35] The growing specialisation and reorganization, partly according to chronological and nationalistic criteria, of the royal and various private collections during the late 18th and early 19th centuries equally resulted in a still more openly

Fig. 2. Portrait of Niels Lauritz Høyen. After J. L. Ussing (ed.), *N. L. Høyens Skrifter*, I-III, Copenhagen 1871-76.

exposed knowledge of older Danish art and architecture.[36]

The recently codified concept of the Renaissance, defined during the second third of the 19th century as a period, a style and a mentality with reference to the cultural rebirths in 16th century Italy and France, was in Denmark earliest confronted with the increasingly activist nationalism of the liberal political opposition. This happened during the years of change and crisis, when a democratic constitution replaced Absolutism (in 1849), and the small nation-state during the Schleswig-Holstein Wars (1848-50, 1864) had to defend its independency. An equally fatal hour of collective despair represented the burning of Frederiksborg Castle in 1859 (see also p. 51). The different tensions were particularly reflected in the writings of Niels Lauritz Høyen (1798-1870), professor at the Royal Academy (1829) and at the University of Copenhagen (1856). Høyen (Fig. 2), glorified as 'Father of Danish Art Historical Science',[37] was governed by a vision of promoting a genuine Danish art in form and content as one among several instruments for furthering the democratic education and feeling of identity of the common citizenry. Further, he acknowledged the influence of moderating factors, indigenous to each individual nation or tribe, such as "dens naturlige Forhold, dens Erhvervskilder, dens Opholdssted" (its natural conditions, sources of commerce, whereabouts), combined with "Tiden, den fjerne Afstand, de højst forskellige Stammeudtryk" (Time, the far distance, the most different tribal expressions).[38] Evaluated with the standards of national stereotypes,[39] i.e. "vor ejendommelige Nationalitet" (our singular nationality), impaired by "Sindighed, med Beskedenhed, men med Fasthed" (steadiness, with modesty, yet with constancy), as reflected in the creations of his own time, Danish art and architecture of the 16th and early 17th century however, were judged as 'not-Danish', dominated by foreign influences or artists, preferably from Germany and the Netherlands.[40] Accordingly, even Christian IV's Frederiksborg Castle should be characterized as a heterogeneous and bizarre synthesis of mixed Gothic-Italian style.[41]

The open approval of the Renaissance, defined as a paradigm for contemporary architecture, arts and crafts, in its Italian as well as its native version, became a current issue for the succeeding generations of practicing artists, architects and art historians. Already previously to the rebuilding of Frederiksborg Castle (1860-1906), painters and architects had studied the castles of Frederiksborg and Kronborg and with growing enthusiasm introduced the decorative vocabulary into contemporary architecture, the 'Netherlandish-North-German style' of the architecture of Christian IV's reign actually in 1855 being recommended by the historian and antiquarian, Christian Molbech (1783-1857) as a model for a national style.[42] In parallel to the increasing scientific research and awareness of the indigenous values of the late 16th and early 17th century Danish art and architecture, the 'Dutch or Netherlandish Renaissance', 'Christian IV-Style', 'Frederiksborg-'

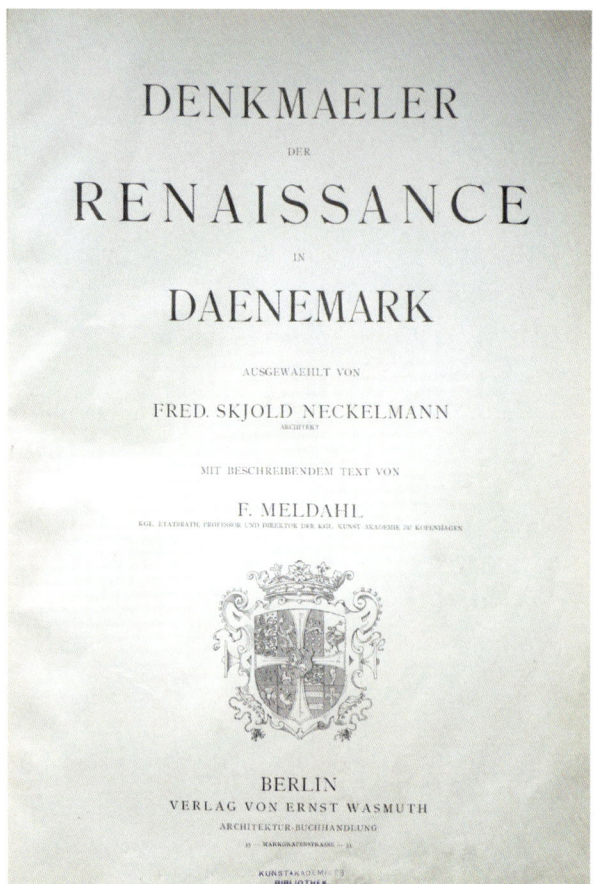

Fig. 3. F. Meldahl & Fred. Skjold Neckelmann, *Denkmäler der Renaissance in Dänemark*, Berlin 1888.

or 'Rosenborg-Style' flourished in public and private enterprises in the second half of the 19th century.[43] Following in the wake of the period's economic boom in agriculture, several country houses were restored or rebuilt in the native renaissance style in a deliberate revival of the aristocracy's heydays during the so-called Age of the Nobility ("Adelsvælden", c. 1536-1660), prior to Absolutism.[44] Ferdinand Meldahl (1827-1908), the main person responsible for the restoration of Frederiksborg Castle, became a highly influential key figure in this context, combining his architectural practice with the teaching profession at the Royal Academy and an art historical activity, particularly displayed in the folio corpus, *Denkmäler der Renaissance in Dänemark* (1888) (Fig. 3), internationally propagating the knowledge of Renaissance Architecture in Denmark, i.e. exclusively the architecture from the age of Frederik II and Christian IV.[45] Following in the wake of the publications on German, Dutch and Belgian Renaissance art and architecture by Wilhelm Lübke, August Ortwein and August Scheffer, as well as of Franz Ewerbeck and his cooperators (cf. also Dirk van der Vijver, pp. 347 ff), Meldahl's image of the indigenous Danish or Nordic contributions to Renaissance architecture, conditioned by climate, materials and local building traditions, was further disseminated by Gustav von Bezold.[46]

The advocacy for a particular national 'standard style', was however, opposed by the art historian Julius Lange (1838-96), emphatically warning against one-sidedly taking departure in objects from the reign of Frederik II and Christian IV.[47] Yet, in Lange's general outline of the history of art in Denmark (1895), the authentic Danishness, i.e. art, emanating from active and productive forces in the people itself, whether or not resuscitating by foreign influences, was still his yardstick of quality, thus in the main derogating art before the 19th century as not-Danish in its essence, and emphasizing nationality's negative effect upon the cultural life during moments of crisis, i.e. in the aftermaths of the fateful year 1864. Accordingly, the 'socalled Renaissance' in Denmark, earliest reflected – though coincidentally – in 1536, the year of the Lutheran Reformation in the tomb slab of Archbishop Absalon in Sorø (cf. Fig. 11, p. 63), was described as an unharmonious mixture of medieval, classical, Italian, German and Netherlandish elements, transformed into a certain "kækt og brovtende, barokt og forsorent Væsen" (bold and boastful, baroque and jaunty manner), in summary characterized as the "gothiske Renæssance" (Gothic Renaissance).[48] This term was in parenthesis used at the same time in a decidedly positive meaning (though in modern ears with unpleasant racist undertones) by the author Johannes V. Jensen (1901), characterizing the new and 'heathen' technological breakthrough, initiated by the blond 'Goths' of his own age from Britain, America, Germany and Scandinavia.[49]

Lange's narrative of the Danish development, the establishment of the chronological frames (c. 1536-c.1650) and the use of the term, "Gothic Renaissance" for the hybridisms of the period[50]

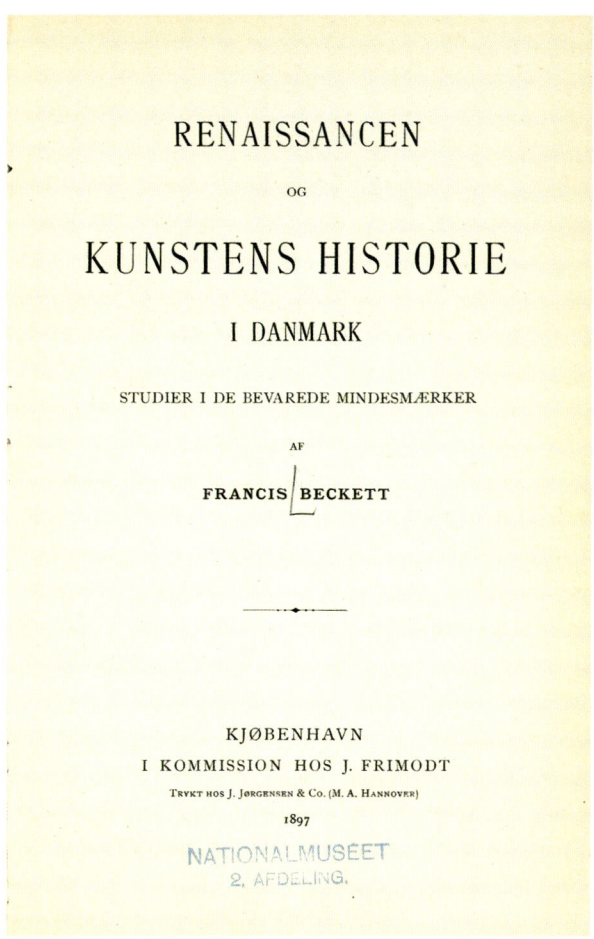

Fig. 4. Francis Beckett, *Renaissancen og Kunstens Historie i Danmark*, Copenhagen 1897.

were for the next century to become paradigmatic for the subsequent major surveys of Danish art and architecture during the 20th century, as earliest reflected by Francis Beckett (1868-1943), follower of Lange as an associate professor in art history at the University of Copenhagen, former assistant at the Rosenborg Collection and simultaneously keeper at the Royal Collection of Casts.[51] Though representing a giant stride forward as to his intimate empirical and documentary knowledge of the period's artistic culture, including the decorative arts, Beckett still in his pioneering doctoral dissertation, *Renaissancen og Kunstens Historie i Danmark* (1897) (Fig. 4), stated – particularly focusing upon the 16th century, previous to the reign of Christian IV(a subject to be explored by him at a later moment) – that the arts, immediately succeeding Gothic art, neither in Denmark nor anywhere else to the North of the Alps could in any way be considered as an artistic break-through, compared to the Italian Renaissance. Yet, he now tentatively included some of the foreign-born individuals as Danes, i. a. the sculptor and painter Claus Berg of Lübeck, working here for a generation. While admitting the existence of a singular Danish profane architecture, represented by the period's manor houses,[52] the conclusion nevertheless became self-evident: Upon a pair of scales of originality, innovation and a well-informed adaptation of Italian and antique decorative designs, it could be argued that the Renaissance only superficially influenced Denmark, the architectural decorations from the era of Christian IV already having extensively adopted Baroque elements to the consequence that "Renaissance-Ornamentikens Historie i Danmark (…) saaledes i det væsentligste (er) forbi med Frederik II" (the history of Renaissance ornamentation in Denmark thus in the main came to an end with Frederik II).[53]

Since Beckett's dissertation, the perspectives have incessantly widened, the antiquarian and documentary knowledge of objects, monuments and artists deepened and the arguments sharpened,not in the least during recent fertile discussions and interchange of ideas in international contexts, breaking a certain indigenous reservation for several decades in the Danish academia of art history.[54] I refer in particular to the two major conferences in Copenhagen 1975 and 2003, already mentioned in the preface. Important new cognitions, i.a. the introduction of the concept of Mannerism in a Danish context, was discussed in detail in 1978 by Kirsten Agerbæk with reference to the architecture of Christian IV.[55] Yet, a number of 'ghosts' still haunt the field, reflected i.a. by the current social fragmentation among native researchers,[56] estranging the 'object fetishists' or empirically anchored scientists at the museums, libraries and archives from their university colleagues, preferably cultivating theoretical issues and contemporary visual media (on this problem, cf. also Claire Farago, pp. 71-78; Keith Moxey, pp. 79-87, Maria Fabricius Hansen, pp. 99-103). Indeed, the different approaches should generally be regarded as equally indispensable, and neither deserves marginalizing in any future debates on 'Whose Renaissance?', whether giving priority to the philosophical frameworks or to the visual enchantment of the physical items present.

A Minority Report – Or Towards New Visions?

The papers from the Renaissance conference in 2006, collected in this volume, have critically, inquisitively and with original new observations approached and further developed the themes suggested in the preliminary programme. The contributions represent different perspectives and scientific traditions, exploring more general theoretical and methodological issues, or elaborating selected subjects and problem areas in reference to individual artists, patrons, agents and monuments, often reflecting cases of cultural exchange or cultural transfer and thus exemplifying that "Micro-historical perspectives offer an especially promising approach" to this field, "making it possible to unpack a variety of influences and way of perception".[57] Point of departure has equally been taken in material from the former Danish Realms or from abroad, subsidized by Danes (i.a. by Danish princesses, married to foreign spouses) or presenting solutions to matters, to be paralleled with related, though less documented, topics in Denmark.

The introductory papers by *Thomas DaCosta Kaufmann* and *Birgitte Bøggild Johannsen* focus upon the superior issue of 'The Danish Renaissance', regarded through the eyes of an 'outsider' and an 'insider'. Both contributions point to the essential ambiguity of the Danish Renaissance, considered as a moment in history during the 16th and early 17th century, or equally developed as an art historical concept and a paradigm for artistic production during the 19th century. As stressed by Thomas DaCosta Kaufmann, Denmark's geographical position in itself may be termed ambiguous, positioned at the margins between different regions in Northern Europe and Balticum, distant to the paradigmatic cultural centres of the Continent, leading to a relative indifference to Danish monuments in international research and to a comparative belatedness of the reception of Renaissance, defined as the implementation of classical forms, orders and content. Though apparently giving way for conclusions on singularity and provinciality, the author in particular stresses the importance of cultural transfer, represented i.a. in the conscious choice not only of an influence, but also reflected in resistance. While following as to royal patronage the examples of other European courts, not in the least the Imperial court at Prague, a predominant characteristic of the Danish Renaissance – or as it more properly should be named 'The Renaissance in Denmark' – was its singularly Netherlandish cast, due to the remarkable presence of Netherlanders, even different from contemporary Sweden. As a conclusion Thomas DaCosta Kaufmann proposes a new model for the study of the Renaissance in Denmark, pointing to the advantages of exploring a periphery or rather a 'frontier land', where cultures meet, leading to cultural production, and appealing for a renewed rethinking of the Renaissance in Denmark in a European or even wider global setting. The paper by Birgitte Bøggild Johannsen frames the description of the Danish Renaissance in terms, basically associated with concepts of cultural memory studies. Like Thomas DaCosta Kaufmann, the analysis is approached via a re-reading of the geopolitical and historiographical status (the last-mentioned being presented above). In her survey, she advocates for the inclusion of Denmark into the "Renaissance *familia*" already from the first half of the 16th century, challenging the traditional notion of belatedness and equally arguing for a disregard of the traditional chronological watersheds, placed at the Lutheran Reformation (c. 1536) or c. 1550. Examples are mentioned of cultural traffic (or deliberate resistance) between North and South, contemporary to and intermediated through individuals or cultural 'emporias' in Northern Europe, in particular in the Netherlands and Germany, appropriating, though partly in 'marginal' or 'peripheral' issues, forms and ideas of basically classical origin and Italian transmission. As a counterpart to the revival of classical Antiquity is emphasized the memory cult of the power elite (comprising not only the royal court, but also the aristocracy and the upper clergy), directed towards the national *antiquitas*, though expressing the 'otherness' of time with the use of a Renaissance vocabulary of Italian derivation, combined with 'antiquated' forms of medieval stamp. This invites for a reconsideration of the eccentricity of a geographically distant realm, taking into account a horizontal approach with focus upon a pluralism of styles and meanings. The image of the early 'hybrid or bastard Danish Renaissance' (cf. above) deserves reconsideration, allowing for the inherent Danish elements of the products, i.e. the locally determined social, political and religious contexts, as well as the predominant local materials and masters, yet as to the more prestigious or 'high-quality' monuments and objects displaying a polyphony of foreign voices, preferably of German and Netherlandish stamp. However, as emphasized in relation to the artistic situation of Naples during the Late Middle Ages and Early Modern Time, the import of foreign artists and works of art should not one-sidedly be regarded as a sign of cultural weakness, but probably ought as well to be evaluated as an expression of intentional enrichment and a foundation for freedom of choice, essentially defining a centre. Indeed, even within the narrow borders of the former Danish realms, it appears relevant to operate with polycentricity, defined not only geographically, but socially as well.

The following four papers, presented by *Claire Farago*, *Keith Moxey*, *Jacob Wamberg* and *Maria Fabricius Hansen*, were in the conference program included in the final session, "The Renaissance: Period, Problems, and Potentials", the last-mentioned paper in itself having the status as an epilogue or comment to the conference. However, in view of the universality of the contributions, offering meta-reflections on issues of relevance to the general debate of the Renaissance, nor limited only to Danish matters, these articles are in the present context deliberately reframed as important parts of the *introitus*.[58] In the wake of her seminal anthology from 1995, Claire Farago's paper revisits 'the Renaissance Problem'. Taking point of departure in the essential debate on centers and peripheries, founded in anachronistic categories and past generations' constructions of 'nationality' as illustrated by a view of Denmark's history in the version, presented by the website of The Foreign Ministry, she underlines the still urgent need for integrated accounts, allowing disparate voices to be heard, equally important as contributors to European conceptions of art. In this context, a renewed evaluation of Danish (or Italian, European, American etc.) responses to concepts of national identity and to representational systems and cultural conditions, developed at the confrontation with the unfamiliar, is seen as an ethical responsibility as well. Acknowledging the field of present art history as expanded and de-centered or the discourses as dialogic, the rethinking of art history with attention to cross-cultural dimensions, fundamental to the discipline's scope, method and vision, should in her opinion be regarded as the 'Renaissance Problem of Our Time'. In his paper, Keith Moxey takes point of departure in the well-known strategy of annihilation, posing the provocative, yet pertinent question: "Do we still need a Renaissance?", given the impossible distance in time and space to its very source and to its later interpretations, or considering its out-dated dominating status in the university curriculum, when confronted with current obsessions with contemporary art. Despite the basic dilemma of imposing order to chaos in visions of the past, when rooted in the time-bound agendas of one's own position or confronted with the concerns and concepts of the Renaissance's 'founding fathers' and their followers (burdened i.a. with Hegelian teleological principles and canonical notions of periodization, style or rebirth), Moxey points to illuminating recent approaches to 15th and 16th century art (i.e. Joseph Koerner and Georges Didi-Huberman), taking into account a synchronic aesthetic encounter between the work of art and the present beholder, while at the same time respecting the larger historical frameworks. Accordingly, his basic question should be answered in affirmative, though with certain reservations.[59]

Jacob Wamberg follows in his contribution a related agenda of revisionism, challenging the common identification of the Renaissance as synonymous with modernity. In his view, the Renaissance should instead be regarded as counter-productive to modernity, a subset or 'a later pocket of time which offers modernity its first resistance", in its reactionary or 'conservative' approach to time, space and representation of nature, emulating antique ideals and being anchored "in a closed and supra-temporal body". True modernity, reflected in variability, subjectivity and infinity of time, body and space, is according to him incarnated in Gothic art, since 1000-1400 equally distributed in Europe between North and South, yet in its Northern version from the middle of the 15th century repressed or muted down by the Italian Renaissance. Wamberg finds support to his arguments a.o. in Oswald Spengler's *Der Untergang des Abendlandes. Umrisse einer Morphologie der Weltgeschichte* (1918-22, 1923) and his organological reconstruction of World History. Maria Fabricius Hansen, who as mentioned above presented her paper at the *exordium* of the conference, like the previous speakers deplores the "boredom" of younger art historians to confront the study of the Renaissance and points to the general reluctance of embracing new methodologies in this field. As she stresses, a particular problem represents the onomastic dilemma, how to name the current venture and the – to her opinion – marginal material, enfolded in a Danish context within an a priori defined frame of chronology and geography, i.e. the 'Renaissance period of 1500-1650' and the Danish realms. When referring to art and culture of around 1600, the period designation 'Renaissance' could appear even harmful (instead of f.i. Mannerism). A more neutral designation of the period might be given by its century, comprising i.a. marvellous manifestations of eclecticism, artistic invention and the fascination with originality, as well as the crucial transformation of image perception and use in the wake of the Reformation – as a consequence muting down issues, relating to the more or less belated or transformed reception of elements of Italian stamp and of ultimately Roman antique origin.

The paradigm of the Reformation, established as a common confessional and mental frame for major parts of Northern Europe since the second third of the 16th century, forms the basis for four contributions, focused upon issues, pertaining to a specific Lutheran rhetoric of form and meaning, yet with important off-shoots to the superior debate of 'the Danish Renaissance'. *Jan Harasimowicz* in his general survey of Lutheran church art in Northern Europe of the 16th and 17th centuries, including examples from Denmark, takes his point of departure in the cathartic purification of the Lutheran creed, directly founded upon the Word of God, as revealed in the Holy Scriptures. This element of unlimited and timeless eternity was visually translated into church art in a subtle interplay of words and images, framing in wall decorations and the different furnishings the community during the service as an accompaniment to the spoken words and the music. While emphasizing the *a priori* supremacy of the eternal Word, he gives in his paper attention to the 'subjective' and 'objective' uses of images, at times subdued, though never totally banished from a Lutheran context, displaying 'witnesses' of Christ (i.e. evangelists, apostles, prophets and chosen saints) or narrative representations from the Bible, in both cases being self-referential and explanatory through the – almost - indispensible component of inscriptions. Through a closereading of two late 16th century altarpieces from Denmark or former Danish realms, in St Nicholas in Kolding, belonging to the Kingdom of Denmark and at St. Mary in Flensburg in the Duchies, *Margit Thøfner* discusses four central topics, to her opinion to be reframed or regarded in context: 1) The issue of a 'Danish Renaissance', preferably to be approached in the plural rather than in singularis; 2) The predominance given to the art of the Oldenburg court, in reality to be paralleled with cultural activities by the civic elite in major cities, belonging to various parts of the Danish realms; 3) The question of import and domestication, related to different approaches to a common pictorial source (the allegorical prints from 1578 by the Netherlandish artist, Hendrick Goltzius) and 4) The importance of frames, through placement, inscriptions and ornaments explored as speaking signs of meaning in relation to the pictures represented. *Krista Kodres* in her paper equally tackles the very notion of 'Danish' and the issue of import vs. domestication in relation to selected late

16th century and early 17th century church furnitures, produced in the Estonian island, Saarema/Ösel during the period of Danish colonization (1559-1645). The remarkably un-Estonian predilection in single cases of catechism altarpieces and the use of Latin inscriptions may in a certain sense be regarded as 'Danish' elements, transmitted through Danes, temporarily residing at Saarema, or by local lords, loyal to the Danish king. However, more dominant is the hybridism of the products (only in one case, possibly, executed by a Dane), mediating a Lutheran imagery in a visual vocabulary, displaying Netherlandish influences or in general, Mannerist style. This invites for differentiation and further reflectivity on the notion of peripheral or provincial, regional Renaissances of the Baltics, though according to Kodres – however - not leading to the excess of completely denying the use of the term "Renaissance", actually referring to a certain visual strategy of common relevance.

Hanne Kolind Poulsen's contribution focuses upon a distinct Lutheran approach in form, content and visual strategy, as illustrated by the decorations of the round-arched gables and of the so-called Stag Hall in the manor house of Hesselagergård, the prominent entailed seat of the powerful Chancellor to King Christian III, Johan Friis. Kolind Poulsen takes point of departure in the Stag Hall, by far the best preserved (though not in every detail, cf. also p. 64) of Danish profane interior decorations from c. 1550. In a discourse with earlier interpretations, she places her main emphasis upon three, so-called 'misfit' images, placed in the peripheral zone of the window recesses (Bathsheba and David, three doves in a birdcage and a devil upon horseback), regarding these in a reactivated Lutheran perspective, functioning as illustrations of "the human conditions in relation to God" or as commemorative signs, in parallel to the mass-produced *Merkbilder*, mentioned by Luther 1529 in the seventh sermon on the Deuteronomy. Of sign value or as a meaning-laden message, propagating Friis' Lutheran creed is equally interpreted the round-arched gables of the manor house and the neighbouring church, to be paralleled with the 'antique' gables at Philip Melanchthon's residence in Wittenberg, in all cases in her opinion communicating the buildings as seats of "pure, orginal faith" through their deliberate architectural references to the age of the Early Church.

The current issue of cultural exchange or cultural transfer forms a prevailing Leitmotif for several of the contributions. As exemplified, the moving cultures and the catalysts to change were brought about during encounters between different courts, dynastically related, they were mediated through travelling artists or patrons or caused at confrontation with circulating printed media. The case-studies by *Marianne Marcussen* and *Mikael Bøgh Rasmussen* take their points of departure in the works of two 'Danish' artists, the sculptor and painter Claus Berg from Lübeck, documented and active in Denmark during the first three decades of the 16th century, part of the time as a court artist to Queen Christine, and the internationally renowned painter, Melchior Lorck of Flenburg, *antiqvitatis stvdiosissim(vs)*, whose major works however were produced in a non-Danish cultural milieu, during his engagement to the Imperial court, i.a. as member of an embassy, sent to Turkey. Incentives to change for both artists were effectuated through cultural clashes with 'otherness'. In the case of Berg, the changed aesthetics or convention for rendering visual space in pictorial arts, following the newly invented one-eyed linear perspective, was reflected in his *opus major*, the altar of Odense Cathedral (formerly Greyfriar's Church). Knowledge of the changed methods were transferred to Northern Europe during the early 16th century via direct (i.e. workshop practices) as well as indirect channels (in graphics and printed treatises), one important *emporia* of exchange between Italy and Denmark being the Saxon court, the origin of his patroness, Queen Christine. As argued by Marianne Marcussen through analysis, in particular of the reliefs at the side wings, Claus Berg may actually have had knowledge of technical methods to convey three-dimensional space in sculpture – in the affirmative an early example of assimilation with a Renaissance paradigm. Mikael Bøgh Rasmussen presents in his paper the portrait of Sultan Süleyman the Magnificent (published in 1562 and 1574), executed during his previous stay at Constantinople. In particular, Bøgh Rasmussen points to the important issue of frames in context or to the ambivalent double-coded view, as reflected in the medial transmission of the seemingly neutral, objective and descriptive portrait of the Sultan. In the framing texts, however, the powerful ruler is presented to the European public in a biased way, in the version of 1562 striking a more benevolent tone in the commentary to Süleyman, almost as the epitome of an ideal ruler, while the second version of 1574 communicates a decidedly negative image of the Sultan's barbaric wildness in accordance with the current turkophobia, the very epitome of evil or Antichrist.

The emphatic will to self-representation and magnificent display of a changed political status as crucial incentives to modernity is analyzed in the articles by *Angelica Dülberg* and *Mario Titze*, both pointing to the examples of the Electors of Saxony, belonging to the newly created Albertine line, in particular the brothers Moritz and August, the latter married in 1548 to Anna of Denmark, daughter of King Christian III. In her paper, Angelica Dülberg focuses upon the fascinating interplay of different cultural influences, reflected in the renovation and high-quality decoration of the Residence Palace at Dresden during the second half of the 16th century. In Dresden – in contrast to the contemporary situation of Denmark – Italian artists (first and foremost the brothers, Gabriele and Benedetto Tola of Brescia) in dialogue with local masters embellished the exteriors and interiors, in the pictorial programme of narrative and allegorical motifs displaying a multifaceted iconography of Roman or Biblical subjects, mixed with genre or historical issues. The strategic boosting of the Albertine dynasty was furthermore reflected in the wide-ranging architectural policy during the reign of August of Saxony, as described by Mario Titze, revising the former image of the Elector as a miser of modest and patriarchal inclinations. To the contrary, August of Saxony exposes his distinctive awareness of dynastic status (markedly improved through his direct affiliation to the Royal Danish court) in his more than 50 building projects, reflecting various European examples of the highest rank and typologically in his residences showing an impressive differentiation, ranging from palaces, hunting seats and *villae suburbanae*, following antique and Italian models, to prodigy houses or refugees, administrative centres and "Denkmalarchitektur" - in summa, in their variety almost anticipating the Baroque. The article's focus upon Annaburg and Lichtenburg in particular pays tribute to the Danish connections, both residences of Anna and later of Hedwig, daughter of King Frederik II and since 1611 dowager of the Elector Christian II.

Shifting the perspective from the specific approach to a more general vision, sociological as well giving priority to the building activities of the Danish nobility, *Uwe Albrecht* presents a genealogy of the architecture of manor houses in Denmark during the second half of the 16th century, reflecting a broad wave of multiple influences, deriving from German, French and Netherlandish prototypes. Albrecht takes his point of departure in early examples from the third decades of the 16th century, rebuilt or innovated in the wake of the Civil War in 1534-36. In spite of traditional elements, influenced by local half-timbered houses and with respect to still impending needs for fortifications, he stresses innovating dispositions in plans and decorations, i.e. the increasing differentiation of rooms, regularity, representative decorations and a heightened consideration of comfort and communication, all resulting from foreign influences (and foreign, not native masters (?)). The very breakthrough of the Renaissance c. 1570 (after the Seven Years' War with Sweden) in civil architecture is reflected in the exteriors and plans, now liberated from the last remnants of medieval elements, embellished with rich ornaments *all' antica* to be contrasted with red-whitish brickwork (with the characteristic "Speklagen") of Brabantine derivation, with axiality, symmetry and increasing variation in the disposition of the interiors. In his conclusion, Albrecht characterizes the manor houses of Southern Scandinavia as a specific contribution to the issue of identity shaping by way of architecture, reflecting the builders' zest for social ascent as well as their humanistic education and international orientation. Of particular value is mentioned the harmonious symbiosis between country and court, buildings and landscape, in short to be regarded as one of the most successful creations of profane architecture at the beginnings of Early Modern Time. In her contribution *Krista de Jonge* moves the focus to Danish royal residences from the 16th and early 17th century, discussing in particular the Netherlandish content of the so-called Danish Renaissance. Her conclusion matches the abovementioned, considering the architecture of the Danish court from the indicative period as "a uniquely Danish phenomenon, not in the sense of being purely home-grown, but as a characteristic assimilation of "local" manners of building with elements consciously taken from elsewhere". Central in her argumentation is the demonstration of phenomena (i.e. the fashion of brick and stone, the predilection for architectural fantasies or prodigy houses and the close interrelation between court ceremonials and the architectural lay-out - this last important topic still awaiting a closer scrutiny in a Danish context), to be commonly diffused through Netherlandish agency during the 16th century among various European courts, independent of current political conflicts or confessional incompatibilities. This particular 'Netherlandish component', with great versatility transferring the latest fashions in forms and technique, whether of Italian or French off-spring, was openly welcomed in Denmark as well, as a sign of courtly prestige and sophistication.

The unsurpassed paradigm of court patronage from the reign of Christian IV, for several generations of art historians having taken up attention due to the magnificent monuments, the openly exposed internationalism and the relatively better status of preservation of items and documentary sources, constitutes, no wonder, *le grand finale* in the last section's papers, exploring further issues of cultural transmission with focus as well upon the frames, centers and peripheries. In her penetrating analysis, *Juliette Roding* draws attention to the imperial paradigm of King Solomon as a universal identity model for kings and princes during the 16th and 17th centuries, even including the Turkish Sultan. This ideal vision of a powerful ruler of global range and a master builder, ordained by God and incarnating as an *alter deus* the highest wisdom, should in her opinion be regarded as a superior code of meaning, with obvious implications also for the development of Absolutism, yet still not sufficiently explored. In relation to Christian IV, the Solomon paradigm is several times directly emphasized in contemporary literature and festivals. Furthermore, a closereading of the Stock Exchange, the Castles of Rosenborg and Frederiksborg, as well as the Trinitatis Complex, including the Round Tower, in this manner opens for a deepened understanding of architectural structures and pictorial programs, subtly reflecting the ruler's mastering of universal wisdom, to be understood as an all-embracing symbiosis between mystical-religious, utopian-political, alchemistic and cabbalistic ideas. In relation to Christian IV's town planning in Copenhagen, Roding convincingly links together the visions of the Heavenly Jerusalem, symbolizing the Stone of Wisdom, with the recurrent attempts, to be followed well into the 18th century, to create an ideal city of circular ground plan, the perfect centre for the global-ranging enterprises of any new world leader.

Mara R. Wade explores in her richly documented study on Duke Ulrik of Denmark an illustrative example of cultural agency, focusing upon the virtually unknown, highly accomplished younger brother of Christian IV, who during the late 16th and early 17th centuries played a pivotal role as mediator, patron and artist (or performer) in his unremitting activities, in a kind of cultural diplomatic shuttle moving between Denmark and the courts of his sisters in Wolfenbüttel, Edinburgh, London, Gottorf and Dresden. During this process various impulses, also emanating from the Danish court, were spread and transformed in the indicative contexts. The article points in particular to the culture-generating force of more mobile members of the royal court, while emphasizing in general the promising potentials, relating to the powerful network of multidirectional exchange among the Protestant elites, for further investigations on the Danish Renaissance and its European contexts. The close dynastic relation between the ducal court of Brunswick-Wolfenbüttel during the reign of Henrich Julius, married to the sister of Christian IV, Elisabeth, also forms the point of departure for the contribution by *Barbara Uppenkamp*, discussing in particular the interchange of forms and meanings, relating to the Protestant Churches of Wolfenbüttel and Christiansstad. Notwithstanding the obvious similarities in dimensions, rational design, plans and decorations between two monuments, both centres of *urbes novae* and the Wolfenbütteler Beatae Mariae Virginis Church evidently serving as a model to Holy Trinity Church in Christiansstad, Uppenkamp debates their common off-spring in German and Netherlandish treatises on ideal cities. Further, from a superior perspective, she points to the influencing importance of political theory, reflected in the works of a number of eminent political theorists (active later at the Danish and Swedish courts), attached to the University of Helmstedt and developing ideas of Aristotelian origin, i.a. with emphasis on the value of architecture as a political practice and on the elevated status of the sovereign, virtually anticipating, like the previously mentioned Solomon paradigm, notions of absolutist monarchy.

Creating cultural dynamism through clever manoeuvering of agents, artists and international networks appears as a predominant asset of Christian IV's reign in general and of the king's personal qualifications in particular. *Badeloch Vera Noldus* presents the illustrative *exemplum*, hitherto overlooked, of the Danish diplomat Jonas Charisius, during his missions, especially the well-documented visit to the Dutch Republic in 1607-08, acting as an important middleman in cultural affairs or in fact as the centre of the spider's web in relation to the mediation of several major artists. As participant in the embassy, numbering also the Councillor of the Realm, Jacob Ulfeldt, Charisius actively contributed in various areas, working as a talent spotter, inducing craftsmen, artists and merchants to travel to Denmark, or buying art and musical instruments from different contractors, in all serving the superior goal of developing the frames, in particular Frederiksborg Castle, for the representational staging of Christian IV. In her detailed account, Noldus also discusses the cultural implication of the increasing Scandinavian representation in the Dutch Republic, mentioning, too, the novelty of permanent national agency as an aspect of the growing internationalization. In a broader aspect, the very symbiosis of art and politics is underlined as well, reflected not only in prestigious building enterprises and decorations, but no less in the activity of collecting, the collections equally serving as codes to exclusivity and princely *Magnificentia*. Networking in relation to contacts between various courts or artistic centers in North and Central Europe is also illustrated by *Heiner Borggrefe* and *Thomas Fusenig*, focusing upon the international interactions of the painters Pieter Isaacz., Jacob van der Doordt and Hans Rottenhammer. Comparing the basically mismatched, small court of Count Ernest of Holstein-Schaumburg and his embellishment of the castle of Bückeburg, with the far greater court of Christian IV and the contemporary decorations of Frederiksborg and Rosenborg, the authors point to the obvious parallelism in regard to the political ambitions and aesthetic predilections of the patrons. In fact, the 'peripheral' examples from Bückeburg apparently even served as inspiration to the Danish 'centre', as mediated by the versatile artists, constantly shuttling between the different cultural emporia and being well-equipped with a basic mastery of an up-to-date Italian artistic language of Roman or Venetian derivation and Netherlandish translation. In a relation to the given 'Reframing the Renaissance Agenda' this case illuminates a further observance, when approaching questions of styles, of the socio-symbolic factor, incessantly crossing geo-political borders and cultural milieus.

The topics of cross cultural exchange in Europe and the co-existence of several minor centers, not limited to the main Northern European regions of the Low Countries, Scandinavia or the Baltic countries, are equally addressed in *Konrad Ottenheym*'s article. Illuminating his arguments by a close-reading of The Marble Gallery of Frederiksborg (1619-22), Ottenheym discusses the fluid meanings of 'Netherlandish influence upon Danish Renaissance Architecture', for several generations being adopted as the canonic meta-narrative of this issue. In fact, the turnkey task involved a multiplicity of actors, first of all the internationally engaged and broadly oriented sculptor, architect and entrepreneur, Hendrick de Keyser in Amsterdam and his Danish-born (though of Netherlandish extraction) colleagues, the brothers Lourens and Hans van Steenwinckel, both equally well-informed and updated. Each of them thriving towards the ideal of innovation and individual inventiveness, the van Steenwinckel brothers (or their royal patron) presented their personal version of a *modern antique*, preferring, however, in the ornamental details, the German model of Wenzel Dietterlin's *Architectura* (1598), to the other paradigmatic novelties, in particular reflected in Michelangelo's Porta Pia in Rome (1563). The extraordinary and demonstrative (almost verging on barbarity (!)) use at Frederiksborg Castle of sumptuous furnishings with items, made of ebony and silver, is described by *Mogens Bencard*, equally underlining the internationality of Christian IV's court. During the king's long reign, his main residence was equipped with various extravagant items of luxury, several of German fabrication (from Jacob and Hans Mores of Hamburg and Matthäus Wallbaum of Augsburg), yet like the castle's framing architecture also displaying models of forms and iconography of Netherlandish, Central European or basically Italian origin. Of particular interest is the author's conclusion, pointing to the fact that Christian IV in this area apparently set the example for many other princely residences in Europe, his initiative only to be compared, intentionally or not, to "Die Reiche Kapelle" at the Residence at Munich, furnished in a similar way c. 1607-15 by Maximilian I of Bavaria. A critical revision of Christian IV's consumption of Netherlandish art (in particular sculpture) is presented by *Kristoffer Neville*, who points to the king's apparent predilection for high-quality artists like Adrian de Vries and François Dieussart, who, however – notwithstanding their origin – to a higher degree would be appreciated for their Italianate stamp and for their versatility in an international court milieu, willingly changing their visual modes according to local contexts. These qualifications apparently were highly estimated and regarded as just as valid as the 'genuine article'. In this matter as well, Christian IV followed his fellow peers in Northern Europe, i.a. Charles I of England, engaging 'Italianates' instead of Italians, whether out of sheer necessity or due to a natural and rather pragmatic inclination. The implementation of the desirable Italian models would in parenthesis also be directly obtained through royal subvention to study tours for young Danish talents or at the import of art works, as can be documented in details with reference to music.[60]

The overriding question of the Netherlandish (Belgian/Dutch) impact upon Danish architecture during the 16th and 17th centuries is finally debated in a historiographic perspective by *Dirk van den Vijver*, analyzing the so-called 'style Christian IV' and its reception in Belgium and the Netherlands, the art historians' interest being initiated by Auguste Schoy and his reflections at the presentation in 1878 at the Paris World Exhibition of various projects in national styles, the Danish pavilion, inspired from the Stock Exchange in Copenhagen, being of a strikingly similarity to the Belgian, Dutch and English examples. While the theme 'Netherlandish architecture abroad' during the following period recurrently became instrumentalized in national discourses on Belgian and Dutch architectural history, this eye-opener of the close cultural relations between Denmark, Belgium and the Netherlands has since generated a fertile and rich research, incessantly opening new perspectives through deepened archive research and the introduction of more elaborated methodological frames.

The final outcome of the 2006 conference evidently cannot be formulated in one superior statement, nor can the simplistic question, "Did Denmark have a Renaissance?", paraphrasing Alice T. Friedman's classical, rhetoric inquiry as to the status of England (1989) or the previous (1977) utterance by Joan Kelly, "Did Women have a Renaissance?", both placing their arguments within the extremes of denial.[61] As abundantly demonstrated by the present contributions, simple questions never – alas – give rise to simple answers, neither can a single, though highly inspirational, *convivium* of fellow researchers, commenting from various backgrounds and methodological traditions upon selected themes, aspire to find the Stone of Wisdom, when – due to natural causes, not to deliberate omissions - several other issues, equally relevant, had to be left out, i.a. memorial culture and funerary art, religious and civil art and architecture of the 'minorities' outside the aloof circle of the power elite, or a close-reading of the different approaches to the Renaissance, displayed by the sister countries (and former arch-enemies) Sweden and Denmark, just to name a few.

Nevertheless, previous mental frames and established concepts of national vs. period styles, or of centers and peripheries have hopefully been changed, due to the many illuminating inputs, leading to the safe conclusion that henceforward the image of 'The Danish Renaissance' or 'The Renaissance in Denmark', as it probably should more properly be named, will never be the same!

Notes

1 Jacob Burckhardt, *Die Kultur der Renaissance in Italien. Ein Versuch* (1860), Leipzig 1925, 3.

2 On discussions of the Renaissance in national context and the fluent values of centres vs. peripheries, cf. a.o. Roy Porter & Mikulas Teich (eds.), *The Renaissance in National Context*, Cambridge 1992; Claire Farago (ed.), *Reframing the Renaissance. Visual Culture in Europe and Latin America 1450-1650*, New Haven & London 1995; Peter Burke, *The European Renaissance: Centres and Peripheries*, Oxford 1998; Thomas daCosta Kaufmann, *Toward a Geography of* Art, Chicago 2004; Thomas DaCosta Kaufmann & Elizabeth Pilliod (eds.), *Time and Place. The Geohistory of Art*, Aldershot 2005; Gerald MacLean (ed.), *Re-Orienting the Renaissance. Cultural Exchanges with the East*, Basingstoke & New York 2005; Brenda Deen Schildgen et al. (eds.), *Other Renaissances. A New Approach to World Literature*, Basingstoke & New York 2006; Peter Burke, "Decentering the Italian Renaissance: The Challenge of Postmodernism", in: Stephen Milner (ed.), *At the Margins. Minority Groups in Premodern Italy*, Minneapolis & London 2005, 36-49.

3 See Florin Curta, "Introduction", in: Florin Curta (ed.), *Borders, Barriers, and Ethnogenesis. Frontiers in Late Antiquity and the Middle Ages*, Turnhout 2005 (Studies in the Early Middle Ages, 12), 1-9.

4 Cf. the definition in *Oxford English Dictionary Online* (http://dictionary.oed.com.bib), draft revision Sept. 2009.

5 On the mission of *Renæssance 2006*, cf. Nicolai Gjessing, "Renæssanceårets arbejde og organisation", in: Nicolai Gjessing & Jens Vellev (eds.), *Renæssance 2006*, Aarhus 2008, 21-32, espec. 24f.

6 Leah S. Marcus, "Renaissance / Early Modern Studies", in: Stephen Greenblatt & Giles Gunn (eds.), *Redrawing the Boundaries: The Transformation of English and American Literary Studies*, New York 1992, 41-63. For Peter Erickson f.i., the use of Early Modern instead of Renaissance, has obvious advantages, shifting "the attention from isolated art objects to cultural systems in their social, historical and political contexts", and changing "the operating stance from aesthetic reverence to an analytic, critical mode", see Peter Erickson, "Review of Lucy Gent (ed.), *Albion's Classicism: The Visual Arts in Britain, 1550-1660*, New Haven 1995, and of Claire Farago (ed.), *Reframing the Renaissance: Visual Culture in Europe and Latin America, 1450-1650*, New Haven 1995", *Art Bulletin*, 87,4 (1996), 736-738.

7 Guido Ruggiero, "Renaissance Dreaming: In Search of a Paradigm", in: Gudio Ruggiero (ed.), *A Companion to the Worlds of the Renaissance*, Oxford 2007 (Blackwell Companions to European History), 1-20, espec. 1.

8 Rebecca Zorach, "Renaissance Theory: A Selective Introduction", in: Elkins & Williams (eds.) 2008, 3-36, spec. 4.

9 Jonathan Woolfson, "Introduction" in: Jonathan Woolfson (ed.), *Renaissance Historiography*, Basingstoke 2005 (Palgrave Advances), 1-5, spec. 3. A recent broad, critical reappraisal of the Renaissance, taking into account also economical, political, religious, social and ethnological issues is Ruggiero (ed.) 2007.

10 Cf. quite recently James Elkins (ed.), *Is Art History Global?*, New York and London 2007, in particular the introduction by the same, "Art History as a Global Discipline", 3-23, commenting in his advocacy for the global vision i.e. upon the "patent nationalism of individual art histories"(…) working "against the current interest in transnationality, multiculturalism, and postcolonial theory". Elkins, however, admitted the universal relevance of methods, forms of texts and questions raised in local contexts (though not necessarily dwelling upon the individual subject matters). The challenge of a global or world art history was equally in the zenith of the debate at the 32nd Congress of the International Committee of the History of Art (CIHA) at Melbourne in 2008, cf. Jaynie Anderson (ed.), *Crossing Cultures: Conflict, Migration and Convergence*, Melbourne 2009.

11 For a rehabilitation of the Northern Renaissance, including the Baltic region, cf. i.e. Marina Belozerskaya, *Rethinking the Renaissance. Burgundian Arts across Europe*, Cambridge 2002; Krista Kodres et al. (eds.), *The Problem of Classical Ideal in the Art and Architecture of the Countries around the Baltic Sea*, Tallinn 2003; Jeffrey Chipps Smith, *The Northern Renaissance*, London & New York 2004; Jan Harasimowicz, Piotr Oszczanowski & Marcin Wisłocki (eds.), *On the Opposite*

posite Sides of the Baltic Sea, 1-2, Wrocław 2006; Krista Kodres & Merike Kurisoo (eds.), *Art and the Church. Religious Art and Architecture in the Baltic Region in the 13th-18th Centuries*, Tallinn 2008 (Estonian Academy of Arts, Proceedings 18); Gordon Campbell (ed.), *The Grove Encyclopedia of Northern Renaissance Art*, I-III, Oxford 2009. See also the Danish conferences of 1975 and 2003, mentioned above and note 5. For a recent highly stimulating discussion of cultural exchange in Europe and beyond during the Renaissance period, see the various contributions in Robert Muchembled & William Monter (eds.), *Cultural Exchange in Early Modern Europe*, I-IV, Cambridge 2006-2007.

12 As recently observed by Paul Douglas Lockhart, *Denmark, 1513-1660. The Rise and Decline of a Renaissance Monarchy*, Oxford 2007, 1: "Perhaps more than any other region of Europe, Scandinavia is written off as being peripheral and marginal." The exclusion of Denmark or Scandinavia in general art historical surveys on the Renaissance is also remarked a.o. by Craig Harbison, *The Mirror of the Artist. Northern Renaissance and its historical Context,* New York 1995, 8, by Thomas DaCosta Kaufmann, "Christian IV and Europe. The 19th Art Exhibition of the Council of Europe, Denmark 1988", *Konsthistorisk Tidskrift* 58, 1 (1989), 19-22 (reissued with an addendum in Thomas DaCosta Kaufmann, *The Eloquent Artist. Essays on Art, Art Theory and Architecture, Sixteenth to Nineteenth Century*, London 2004, 227-235, 465-466); see also Larry Silver in his review of the recent status of research on Early Modern art in Northern Europe, "Arts and Minds: Scholarship on Early Modern Art History (Northern Europe)", *Renaissance Quarterly* LIX,2 (2006), 331-373, in particular 366 (with note 27). Silence, due to a qualitative verdict, is present in Byron J. Nordstrom, *Scandinavia since 1500*, Minneapolis 2000, 48, derogating in particular the late reception of the Renaissance in Scandinavia in general: "Art, reflected in the portraits of monarchs and nobles of the period, was primitive. Native artists were almost nonexistent, and there were few resources to spend on importing talents from the south." Cf. equally Chipps Smith 2004, taking his geographical point of departure in Erhard Etzlaub's roadmap of central Europe (locating Denmark (without Sweden and Norway) at the bottom margin) and underlining, 7: "Although the cultural patrimonies of Britain, Scandinavia and Eastern Europe are significant, these lands contributed less frequently to the broad artistic innovations (…) c. 1380-1580 (…)".

13 A remarkable, counter-productive case of nationalism, a "nostalgic metonymy for lost territory" or an example of "blatant colonialism" was demonstrated by the Danish Cultural Ministry in the socalled "Canon of Danish Art and Culture" (Den Danske Kulturkanon) from 2006, including the "Bordesholmer Altar" by Hans Brüggemann from 1521, created for the memorial of Duke Frederick (Frederick I) in the previous Augustine monastery church of Bordesholm (since the mid-17th century in Schleswig Cathedral), geographically belonging to the domain of the former Duchies, not to the old Kingdom of Denmark. On this example, cf. Jan von Bonsdorff, "The Inertia of the Canon: Nationalist Projections onto the Works of Hans Brüggemann and Bernt Notke", in: James Elkins & Robert Williams (eds.), *Renaissance Theory*, New York & London, 2008 (The Art Seminar 5), 278-286, espec. 280. Left out, however, were the 'great' monuments from the Renaissance, f.i. Claus Berg's Odense retable, the castles of Kronborg, Rosenborg and Frederiksborg or other examples from the age of Frederick II and Christian IV.

14 The still diffuse concepts in 15th and early 16th century Italy of Antiquity, preferably relating - though never consequentially correct from an archaeological perspective - to artistic products from classical Rome, have been emphasized by several, see i.a. Maria Fabricius Hansen, "Representing the Past : The Concept and Study of Antique Architecture in 15th-century Italy", *Analecta Romana Instituti Danici* XXIII (1996), 83-116.

15 On the crises at encounters with alterity, cf. i.a. Sanford Budick, "Crises of Alterity. Cultural Untranslatability and the Experience of Secondary Otherness", in: Sanford Budick & Wolfgang Iser (eds.), *The Translatability of Cultures. Figurations of the Space Between*, Stanford 1996, 1-22. Cf. also recently, Peter Burke, *Cultural Hybridity*, Cambridge 2009, espec. 65, emphasizing the awareness of human agency, when using the terms of 'appropriation' and 'cultural translation', while concepts of 'hybridization' or 'creolization' more reflect considerations of changes, of which the agents are unaware.

16 Karlheinz Stierle,"Translatio Studio and Renaissance: From Vertical to Horizontal Translation", in Budick & Iser (eds.) 1996, 55-67.

17 Cf. the section on "Hybrid Renaissances in Europe and Beyond", in Anderson (ed.) 2009, 180-238, with the introductory remarks by Luke Morgen & Philippe Sénechal, "Introduction", 180-181.

18 Cf. Ethan Matt Kavaler, "Renaissance Gothic: Picture of Geometry and Narratives of Ornament", *Art History* 29,1 (2006), 1-46, in particular 1, further elaborated in the author's "Gothic as Renaissance: Ornament, Excess, and Identity, Circa 1500", in: Elkins & Williams (eds.) 2008, 115-158; cf. also the discussion paper by Monique Chatenet, Ethan Matt Kavaler, Krista de Jonge & Norbert Nussbaum, "Architecture européenne du XVIe siècle: un "gothique de la Renaissance"?", *Perspective* 2 (2006), 290-299, a prelude to the conference "La Gothique de la Renaissance", IVe

Rencontres d'Architecture Européenne at Paris, Centre André Chastel, 12 - 16 June 2007. I am grateful to Krista de Jonge for having informed me of the contents of the volume, edited by the four involved participants and published in 2011, after the conclusion of this essay.

19 On the discussion of the pluralism of styles in the early phases of the Renaissance, integrating as well the particular Northern European or extra-Italian contributions, cf. i.e. Jean Guillaume (ed.), *L'invention de la Renaissance. La reception des forms "à l'antique" au début de la Renaissance*, Paris 2003; Norbert Nussbaum, Claudia Euskirchen & Stephan Hoppe (eds.), *Wege zur Renaissance. Beobachtungen zu den Anfängen neuzeitlicher Kunstauffassung im Rheinland und den Nachbargebieten um 1500*, Cologne 2003, cf. here Dagmar Eichberger, "Stilpluralismus und Internationalität am Hofe Margaretes von Österreich", in Nussbaum, Eusskirchen & Hoppe (eds.) 2003, 261-283; further Stephan Hoppe, Matthias Müller & Norbert Nussbaum (eds.), *Stil als Bedeutung in der nordalpinen Renaissance: Wiederentdeckung einer methodischen Nachbarschaft*, Cologne 2008, cf. here in particular Ariane Mensger, "Jan Gossaert und der Niederländische Stilpluralismus zu Beginn der 16. Jahrhunderts – eine Annäherung", 188-211; Krista de Jonge, "Style and Manner in Early Modern Netherlandish Architecture (1450-1600). Contemporary Sources and Historiographical Tradition", 2008, 264-285. Even in an Italian perspective, the fluent values of regional identities and the ideological importance given to traditions have recently been analysed by Stephen J. Campbell & Stephen J. Milner (eds.), *Artistic Exchange and Cultural Translation in the Italian Renaissance City*, Cambridge 2004. On anachronism as constitutive element of the Renaissance, see also the debate in *The Art Bulletin*, 87,3 (2005) raised by Alexander Nagel & Christopher S. Wood, "Interventions: Towards a New Model of Renaissance Anachronism", 403-415, with responses by Charles Dempsey, "*Historia* and Anachronism in Renaissance Art", 416-421, Michael Cole, "*Nihil sub Sole Novum*", 421-424, and Claire Farago, "Time Out of Joint", 424-429, followed by the authors' reply, 429-432. Further Christopher S. Wood, *Forgery, Replica, Fiction. Temporalities of German Renaissance Art*, Chicago & London 2008.

20 Cf. in particular Klaus Graf, "Stil als Erinnerung. Retrospektive Tendenzen in der deutschen Kunst um 1500", in Nussbaum, Euskirchen & Hoppe (eds.) 2003, 19-29.

21 The issue of a specific Danish sense of identity during the Middle Ages and Early Modern Times has been intensively discussed among Danish historians, cf. in particular Harald Ilsøe, "Danskerne og deres fædreland. Holdninger og opfattelser ca. 1550-1700", in: Ole Feldbæk (ed.), *Fædreland og Modersmål 1536-1789*, Copenhagen 1991 (Dansk identitetshistorie 1), 27-88; Troels Dahlerup, "Danish National Identity, c. 700-1700", in: Claus Bjørn et al. (eds.), *Nations, Nationalism and Patriotism in the European Past*, Copenhagen 1994, 56-67; Ole Feldbæk, "Is there Such a Thing as a Medieval Danish Identity?", in: Brian Patrick McGuire (ed.), *The Birth of Identities. Denmark and Europe in the Middle Ages*, Copenhagen 1996, 127-134. Recently Mette Brønserud Larsen, "National identitet i dansk senmiddelalder?", *Historie* (1998) 2, 320-332, has challenged the theories of Benedict Anderson, Eric Hobsbawm and Ernest Gellner on the rather late birth of nation-states and nationalism, with reference to Adrian Hastings's concept of pre-modern ethnicities. The basic work on Danish historiography, focusing upon the reign of Christian IV, but including as well the preceding period from c. 1536, is Karen Skovgaard-Petersen, *Historiography at the Court of Christian IV (1588-1648). Studies in the Latin Histories of Denmark by Johannes Pontanus and Johannes Meursius*, Copenhagen 2002; on the previous development, cf. Karsten Friis-Jensen, "Humanism and Politics: The Paris Edition of Saxo Grammaticus's Gesta Danorum 1514", *Analecta Romana Instituti Danici* 17-18 (1988-89) 149-162; Karsten Friis-Jensen, "Historiography and Humanism in Early Sixteenth-century Scandinavia", in: Alexander Dalzel et al. (eds.), *Acta Conventus Neo-Latini Torontonensis*, Binghamton & New York 1991, 325-333; Nanna Damsholt, "Tiden indtil 1560", in: Søren Mørch (ed.) *Historiens historie*, Copenhagen 1992 (Aksel E. Christensen et al. (eds.), *Danmarks historie* 10), 34-51.

22 Recently Carola Fey, Steffen Krieb & Werner Rösener (eds.), *Mittelalterliche Fürstenhöfe und ihre Erinnerungskulturen* (*Formen der Erinnerung*, 27), Göttingen 2007.

23 Cf. Steffen Heiberg (ed.), *Christian IV and Europe. The 19th Art Exhibition of the Council of Europe*, Copenhagen 1988. An important evaluation of this 'eye-opener' towards Danish art and architecture during the period defined is DaCosta Kaufmann 1989, 19-22 (reissued in DaCosta Kaufmann 2004, 227-235, 465-466). The predominant focus on Christian IV is a topic as well in Peter Burke, "State-Making, King-Making and Image-Making from Renaissance to Baroque: Scandinavia in a European Context", *Scandinavian Journal of History* 22 (1997), 1-8.

24 The watershed of the year 1536 was in the main still upheld by the editors of *Den Store Danske Encyclopædi* 4, Copenhagen 1996, 505-506 ("Danmark. Kultur", see Birgitte Bøggild Johannsen og Hugo Johannsen, "Renæssancen"); equally in vol. 16, Copenhagen 2000, 120 ("Renæssancen", see Lise Bek, "Billedkunst og arkitektur", though a previous limit for decorative art to c. 1520 was allowed for in Ulla Houkjær, "Kunsthåndværk"). Cf. equally the entrances on Danish archi-

tecture, painting, the graphic arts, sculpture and interior decoration, in Jane Turner (ed.), *The Dictionary of Art*, 8, London & New York 1996, 724-725, 732-735, 739-741, 742-743 (Hugo Johannsen, "Architecture 1540-1840", Birgitte Bøggild Johannsen, "Painting and Graphic Arts" and "Sculpture 1540-1840" and Mirjam Gelfer-Jørgensen, "Interior Decoration before 1750). The articles from the Dictionary were updated and revised in Campbell (ed.) 2009, I, 479-484 ("Denmark"), yet with a preliminary survey of medieval antecedents. In Maria Fabricius Hansen, "Renæssancens grotesker", in: Ole Høiris & Jens Vellev (eds.), *Renæssancens verden. Tænkning, kulturliv, dagligliv og efterliv*, Aarhus 2006, 323-349, espec. 323, the Danish Renaissance is limited to the age of Frederick II and Christian IV. The chronological demarcation of the Renaissance in Denmark c. 1500-1650, "for practical reasons" was stated in the introductory paper for "Renæssance 2006" and repeated in the official publication of the Renaissance Year, cf. Carsten Bach-Nielsen et al. (eds.), *Danmark og renæssancen 1500-1650*, Copenhagen 2006, 5. Arguments for moving the chronological limits back to c. 1450, due a.o. to early developments of cartography, ventures of expeditions to distant regions overseas and of humanistic studies, including Neo-Latin literature and epigraphy, were presented at two conferences at Odense University in 2006, cf. Lars Bisgaard, Jacob Isager & Janus Møller Jensen (eds.), *Renæssancen i svøb. Dansk renæssance i europæisk belysning 1450-1550*, Odense 2008.

25 Cf. Bernd Roeck, "Introduction", in: Herman Roodenburg (ed.), *Forging European Identities, 1400-1700*, Cambridge 2007 (Cultural Exchange in Early Modern Europe, IV), 1-29.

26 On 'occasionalism', cf. Peter Burke 2005, espec. 41; on the sociological approach, cf. i.a. Donat Grueninger, "Die kunsthistorische Regionalisierung.Grundsätzliches zu einem neuen Forschungsansatz", *Concilium medii aevi* 7 (2004), 21-44; Nicolas Bock, "Patronage, Standards and *Transfert culturel*: Naples between Art History and Social Science Theory", *Art History* 31,4 (2008), 574-597 (special issue, Cordelia Warr & Janis Elliott (eds.), *Import/Export: Painting, Sculpture and Architecture in Naples, 1266-1713*).

27 Peter Burke, *What is Cultural History?*, Cambridge 2004, 97.

28 In general, Else Kai Sass, "Kunsthistorie", in: Povl Johs. Jensen (ed.), *Det filosofiske Fakultet*, Copenhagen 1979 (Svend Ellehøj et al. (eds.), Københavns Universitet 1479-1979 XI, 4), 199-344; Erik Mortensen, *Kunstkritikkens og kunstopfattelsens historie i Danmark*, 1-2, Copenhagen 1990; Hans Dam Christensen & Louise C. Larsen (eds.), *Det kunsthistoriske studieapparat. Hånd- og debatbog fra den videnskabelige hverdag*, Copenhagen 2004. A brief sketch to a Renaissance historiography is Otto Norn, "Serlio and Denmark", *Analecta Romana Instituti Danici* 1 (1960), 105-121, in particular 106-107; a quite recent survey of general overviews, monographs and specialized analyses, by Danish and international scholars, is Hugo Johannsen, "Renaissance Art and Architecture in Denmark", in: Michael Andersen, Ebbe Nyborg & Mogens Vedsø (eds.), *Masters, Meanings & Models. Studies in the Art and Architecture of the Renaissance in Denmark. Essays published in Honour of Hugo Johannsen,* Copenhagen 2010, 22-31. The basic account on Danish Historicism is Mette Bligaard, *Frederiksborgs genrejsning. Historicisme i teori og praksis*, 1-2, Copenhagen 2008. Regarded from foreigners' perspective are important contributions by DaCosta Kaufmann 1989, 19-22; DaCosta Kaufmann 2004, 227-235, 465-466; Juliette Roding, "The Myth of the 'Dutch Renaissance' in Denmark. Dutch Influence on Danish Architecture in the 17th Century", in: J. Ph. S. Lemmink & J. S. A. M. Koningsbrugge (eds.), *Baltic Affairs. Relations between the Netherlands and North-Eastern Europe 1500-1800*, Nijmegen 1990 (Baltic Studies 1), 343-353; see also Dirk van der Vijver, below p. xxx.

29 Cf. Allan Ellenius, *De arte pingendi. Latin Art Literature in Seventeenth-century Sweden and its International Background*, Uppsala 1960; Solfrid Söderlind, "Konsthistorieämnets förhistorie", in: Peter Gillgren, Britt-Inger Johansson & Hans Pettersson (eds.), *Åtta kapitel om konsthistoriens historia i Sverige*, Stockholm 2000, 9-38; Thomas DaCosta Kaufmann, "The Baltic Area as an Artistic Region. Historiography, State of Research, Perspectives for Further Study", in: Harasimowicz, Oszczanowsi & Wisłocki (eds.) 2006, 1, 33-39, spec. 34-35.

30 In general, Torben Damsholt, "Den nationale magtstat 1560-1760", in: Mørch (ed.) 1992, 61-69; on private or royal collections, cf. H. D. Schepelern, *Museum Wormianum*, Århus 1971; Bente Gundestrup (ed.), *Det kongelige danske Kunstkammer 1737*, 1-3, Copenhagen 1991-1995; Camilla Mordhorst, *Genstandsfortællinger. Fra Museum Wormianum til de moderne museer*, Copenhagen 2009*;* Jørgen Hein, *The Treasury Collection of Rosenborg Castle: Royal Heritage and Collecting in Denmark-Norway 1500-1900*, 1-3, Copenhagen 2009. A recent survey, with particular focus upon research on antiquities and epigraphy, is Birgitte Bøggild Johannsen, "Epigraphik im dänischen Inventar *Danmarks Kirker* –Paradigmen, Potentiale und Perspektiven – Mit einem Exkurs über das frühe neulateinische Epitaph in Dänemark", in: Christine Magin et al. (eds.), *Traditionen, Zäsuren, Umbrüche. Inschriften des späten Mittelalters und der frühen Neuzeit im historischen Kontext*, Wiesbaden 2008, 349-367.

31 *Der Kunst-Erfahrne curieuse, galante (…) Nachricht von*

der Edlen Schilder-Kunst, Copenhagen 1721.

32 Ole Feldbæk, "Fædreland og Indfødsret. 1700-tallets danske identitet", and Karin Kryger, "Dansk identitet i nyklassicistisk kunst. Nationale tendenser og nationalt særpræg 1750-1800", both in: Feldbæk (ed.) 1991, 111-230 and 231-424.

33 Damsholt 1991, 68-69.

34 Lauritz de Thurah, *Den Danske Vitruvius*, I-II, Copenhagen 1746-1749, reedited, together with a third volume, by Hakon Lund (ed.), Copenhagen 1966-1967; Lauritz de Thurah, *Hafnia Hodierna*, Copenhagen 1748; Erich Pontoppidan & Hans de Hofman, *Den Danske Atlas*, Copenhagen 1763-1781 (reedited 1968-1972).

35 Emma Salling & Claus M. Smidt, "Fundamentet. De første hundrede år", in: Anneli Fuchs & Emma Salling (eds.), *Kunstakademiet 1754-2004*, 1-3, Copenhagen 2004, 1, 23-117.

36 Cf. Villads Villadsen, *Statens Museum for Kunst 1827-1952*, Copenhagen 1998; Tove Benedikt Jakobsen, *Birth of a World Museum*, Oxford 2007 (Acta Archaeologica 78:1, suppl. VIII); Hein 2009. Further the librarian Niels Henrich Weinwich's survey on Danish art and architecture, starting from the reign of Christian I (1449-81), *Maler-, Billedhugger-, Kobberstik-, Bygnings- og Stempelskiærer-Kunstens Historie* (..), Copenhagen 1811, in particular 25-68, followed by his biographical encyclopaedia of *Dansk, Norsk og Svensk Kunstner-Lexicon*, Copenhagen 1829.

37 Kirsten Agerbæk, *Høyen mellem klassicisme og romantik. Om idegrundlaget for N. L. Høyens virke for kunsten i fortid og samtid*, Esbjerg 1984; recently, Hans Dam Christensen, "Billedkunsten. Om kunsthistorien, N. L. Høyen og folkets billedkunst", in: Palle Ove Christiansen (ed.), *Veje til danskheden. Bidrag til den moderne nationale selvforståelse*, Copenhagen 2005, 66-94. Høyen included the term 'Renaissance' in his vocabulary from 1836 and had since the 1860s used Jacob Burckhardt's *Die Kultur der Renaissance in Italien* (1860) in his *curriculum*, cf. Agerbæk 1984, 271, 387.

38 N. L. Høyen, "Om Konstens Væsen og Opgave, særligt med Hensyn til Danmark (1851)", in: J. L. Ussing (ed.), *Niels Laurits Høyens Skrifter* , I-III, Copenhagen 1871-1876, III, 1-159, esp. 66-67.

39 Cf. generally Thomas DaCosta Kaufmann, "National Stereotypes, Prejudice, and Aesthetic Judgments in the Historiography of Art", in: Michael Ann Holly & Keith Moxey (eds.), *Art History, Aesthetics, Visual Studies*, New Haven & London 2002, 71-84.

40 Cf. N. L. Høyen, "Om national Konst" (1863), in: Ussing (ed.) 1871-76, III, 160-182; Høyen 1851, 100-111.

41 N. L. Høyen, "Frederiksborg Slot" (1831), in: Ussing (ed.) 1871-1876, I, 160 ff.; cf. also Bligaard 2008, 1, 244-246.

42 Christian Molbech, *Anmærkninger over nyere Tiders Architektur* (…), Copenhagen 1855, cf. Bligaard 2008, 1, 86-87, 244-256, in particular 247.

43 Bligaard 2008, I, 256-263.

44 Cf. Rikke Tønnes, "Sidste blomstring", in: John Erichsen & Mikkel Venborg Pedersen (eds.), *Herregården. Menneske-samfund-landskab-bygninger*, I-IV, Copenhagen 2004-06, II, 225-298.

45 Ferdinand Meldahl & Fred. Skjold Neckelmann, *Denkmäler der Renaissance in Dänemark*, Berlin 1888.

46 Gustav von Bezold, *Baukunst der Renaissance in Deutschland, Holland, Belgien und Dänemark*, Stuttgart 1900 (Handbuch der Architektur 2,VII).

47 Julius Lange, "Nogle Sætninger om Kunstindustri i vor Tid" (1885), reprinted in: Georg Brandes & P. Købke (eds.), *Udvalgte Skrifter af Julius Lange*, I-III, Copenhagen 1900-03, III, 192-199; cf. Jørgen Guldberg & Hans Christian Jensen, " "Kulturen af Tingene". Julius Lange og kunstindustrien", in: Hanne Kolind Poulsen et al. (eds.), *Viljen til det menneskelige. Tekster omkring Julius Lange*, Copenhagen 1999, 281-303; Bligaard 2008, 1, 90; Marianne Marcussen, "The Danish Art Historian Julius Lange, His Attitude to Trends in Art History in Europe and his Collaboration with Scandinavian Colleagues", in: Johanna Vakkari (ed.), *Towards a Science of Art History. J. J. Tikkanen and Art Historical Scholarship in Europe*, Helsinki 2009 (Taidehistoriallisia tutkimuksia – Konsthistoriska Studier/Studies in Art History 38), 71-83.

48 Julius Lange, "Udsigt over Kunstens Historie i Danmark", in: *Salmonsens Konversationslexikon*, Copenhagen 1895, reprinted in Brandes & Købke (eds.) 1900-1903, 1, 1-87, in particular 1-2, 16-22, 77.

49 Johannes V. Jensen, *Den gotiske Renaissance*, Copenhagen 1901 (reprint 2000).

50 Cf. a.o. Vilh. Lorenzen, *Studier i Dansk Herregaards Arkitektur i 16. og 17. Aarhundrede*, Copenhagen 1921.

51 In his article on Danish art in *Salmonsens Konversationslexikon*,[2] Copenhagen 1916, V, 662-664, Beckett repeated almost verbatim Lange's verdicts.

52 Francis Beckett, *Renaissancen og Kunstens Historie i Danmark*, Copenhagen 1897, 219, 221.

53 Beckett 1897, 222.

54 See i.a. the volume, *Art in Denmark 1600-1750*, in: Leids Kunsthistorisch Jaarboek 2 (1983). For a brief historiography of antiquarian literature, referring to the study of religious art and architecture, previous to the publication since 1933 of *Danmarks Kirker*, cf. Bøggild

Johannsen 2008; further on the Renaissance research in general Johannsen 2010; see also the currently updated internet version of the National Bibliography of Danish Art and Architecture (BDK) in www.kunstbib.dk.

55 Cf. Kirsten Agerbæk, "Børsen og Sparepenge. Eksempler på manieristisk arkitektur i Danmark?", in: Hakon Lund (ed.), *En bog om kunst til Else Kai Sass*, Copenhagen 1978, 174-185; see also in general Thomas DaCosta Kaufmann, "The Problem of Northern 'Mannerism': A Critical Review", in: S. E. Murray & Ruth I. Weidner (eds.), *Mannerism: Essays in Music and the Arts*, West Chester, Pennsylvania 1980, 89-115.

56 On the well-acknowledged dilemma, cf. i.a. Silver 2006, 351-373; Thomas Crow, "The Practice of Art History in America", *Daedalus* (2006), 70-90.

57 Cf. Roeck 2007, 14.

58 Since 2006, the arguments of Claire Farago and Keith Moxey have been further elaborated as contributions to the session "Hybrid Renaissances in Europe and Beyond" at the CIHA conference in Melbourne 2008, cf. Anderson (ed.) 2009, 227-232 (Claire Farago, "Reframing the Renaissance Problem Today. Developing a Pluralistic Historical Vision") and 233-238 (Keith Moxey, "Do we still need a Renaissance?").

59 Cf. Moxey 2009, 237.

60 On Danish musicians, during the period 1599-1622 studying in Italy (in particular Venice), see recently Ole Kongsted, "Herlufsholm-samlingen: R 121-125 og danskere i Italien omkring 1600", in: John T. Lauridsen & Olaf Olsen (eds.), *Umisteligt. Festskrift til Erland Kolding Nielsen*, Copenhagen 2007, 101-118 focusing in particular upon the first wave (1599-1600) and the related import of – brand-new – Italian music.

61 Alice T. Friedman, "Did England Have a Renaissance? Classical and Anticlassical Themes in Elizabethan Culture", in: Susan J. Barnes & Walter S. Melion, *Cultural Differentiation and Cultural Identity in the Visual Arts*, Hanover & London 1989 (Studies in the History of Arts, 27), 95-111; Joan Kelly, "Did Women have a Renaissance?", in: Joan Kelly, *Women, History and Theory. The Essays of Joan Kelly*, Chicago & London 1984, 19-50.

Fig. 1. Hillerød, Frederiksborg Castle, 1602-1623 (Photo Hillerød, The Museum of National History, Frederiksborg Castle).

THE EUROPEAN PERSPECTIVE[1]

Thomas DaCosta Kaufmann

It is difficult to find a single European, better supranational, perspective on the Danish Renaissance. One may even wonder if any definitive view of the Danish Renaissance exists. This paper does not however intend to propose some sort of post-modern thesis which denies the possibility of an objective approach to argue that everything always depends on the point of view of the observer. Even though it may seem ironic that a North American has been called upon to offer the European perspective, this introductory essay will offer some interpretations of the historiographical, geographical, and historical position of the Danish Renaissance, compare it to the Renaissance in other sites, and to suggest not only how it is different from but how it also may be related to them. Nevertheless, the issues involved do seem to suggest the existence of a multiplicity of possible standpoints, which depend on and also determine the questions framed to consider them. They may even cause reconsideration of what is meant by the Renaissance in general.

To put it briefly, the concept of the Danish Renaissance is ambiguous in several respects. Previous reception of the period of the Renaissance in Danish history points to a basic dichotomy in interpretations.[2] In the history of art or more generally of culture (notably music) the Danish Renaissance signifies roughly speaking a century of accomplishment from 1550 to 1650. This era is often considered to be a Golden Age in the cultural history of Denmark, a time in which many of the most famous monuments in the country were constructed or decorated. Kronborg, Frederiksborg, and Rosenborg castles were put up and adorned, major tomb monuments were installed in the cathedral at Roskilde, and several important churches and the Stock Exchange were designed and erected in Copenhagen (Fig. 1, 9). Danish architects and artists of later epochs also regarded architecture and art of the late sixteenth and early seventeenth centuries as exemplary: in the nineteenth century there originated the *Rosenborg-style*, what might be called the Christian IV revival style in architecture, which still marks much of the built landscape of Copenhagen and other places in Denmark, and nineteenth-century painters celebrated the monarch and his deeds (Fig. 2, 3).[3]

Yet from the point of view of political or territorial history, the period of the Danish Renaissance, and notably the long reign, 1588-1648, of Christian IV, also marks the start of what is often called the tragedy of Denmark. This is the sequence of events by which Denmark, once a regional power, became a small and secondary European state. Once the ruler over large stretches of Scandinavia, Greenland, Iceland, the Faroe Is-

Fig. 2. Copenhagen, 'New Rosenborg', 1893, by Ludvig Clausen and H. O. Hagemann (Photo Hugo Johannsen).

lands, and Schleswig-Holstein, as well as a good part of what is now modern Estonia, the lands of the Danish crown have now been reduced to the present rump state of Jutland and the sound islands (Funen, Lolland-Falster and Zeland), with Greenland and the Faroe Islands as quasi-autonomous dependencies. This process was set in motion during the period of the Danish Renaissance. At the beginning of the period Sweden split off from the realm of the three crowns; during the sixteenth century it asserted and maintained its independence, and began to challenge Denmark for domination of the Baltic. The struggle for supremacy continued into the seventeenth century. In the 1620's Christian IV intervened unsuccessfully in the Thirty Years' War on the continent. By mid-century Denmark had lost its place in Livonia and Estonia, as well as substantial portions of what is now Sweden, along with Gotland. The rest of its holdings across the sound were to be lost in the 1650's. The royal treasury was in shambles. Thus by the end of the period, Denmark's perennial claim to exercise the *dominium maris baltici*, to dominate the Baltic Sea, had also dissipated.

To be sure, disjunctions between political importance and cultural accomplishments are often encountered in history. Along with contemporaneous phenomena elsewhere in Europe, the cultural efflorescence of some Danish regions in the second quarter of the seventeenth century may also provoke the question, in the manner of Jean Baudrillard or Jean Cocteau, if the Thirty Years' War ever took place.[4] But there remains a marked distinction between the role that Denmark receives in the political history of the Early Modern period and its neglect in a broader history of European culture of the time; if Denmark enters into European history books, it is precisely mainly in regard to the Thirty Years' War and other conflicts with Sweden.

While the artistic and architectural monuments of the Danish Renaissance are no doubt worthy of broad attention, recognition of their importance is not widespread. A series of publications and major exhibitions of the 1970's and 1980's, which culminated in the 1988 exhibitions devoted to Christian IV and Europe, brought some more interest to the period, but no major symposium was held at the time.[5] And the exhibitions of 1988 did not evoke the kind of lasting resonance one might have expected. Although notable exceptions exist,[6] the period continues to gain little interest outside Denmark. Thus even though some more attention has begun to be paid in the past few decades to the Danish Renaissance, it still does not command much mention from more than a few specialists in other countries. Significantly, the Danish Renaissance still does not appear in most handbooks or surveys of art history.[7]

There are many reasons the Danish Renaissance may not have gained a more prominent position in European historiography. The geo-

Fig. 3. Roskilde Cathedral, interior of the funerary chapel of Christian IV, 1614-1620, by Lourens II and Hans II van Steenwinckel with paintings 1863-66 by Vilh. Marstand celebrating the deeds of the king (Photo Henrik Wichmann).

graphical situation affects everything. Within its immediate surroundings of the Sound and Kattegat in its position between the North and Baltic Seas Denmark may appear central, but from many other geographical perspectives its status is ambiguous, as is even this location. The word surroundings is deliberately chosen instead of region, since one might even wonder to which region Denmark belongs. Traditionally, and by affinity and at times enmity, Denmark is of course included with Sweden, Norway, and Finland in Scandinavia. But because of its position between the North and Baltic seas, Denmark may also be considered to belong to either of these regions as well. In fact, Denmark has been included recently in discussions of both of them.[8] Until 1864 the Duchies of Schleswig-Holstein were annexed to the Danish kingdom, so that historic Denmark might also be related to Central Europe. From another standpoint, this multiplicity of affiliations might have had advantages for gaining a variety of perspectives on Denmark (Fig. 4).

However, from another point of view, Denmark might be regarded as liminal to all of these regions; and more important, regardless of the region for which it has been claimed, Denmark has largely been left on the margins of European cultural as well as political geography. With the possible if problematic exception of Central Europe, all the regions mentioned: the North Sea, even more the Baltic and Scandinavia, are distant from the paradigmatic cultural centers of the continent, in relation to which the place of Denmark seems peripheral. The lands of historic Denmark, especially Norway and the Faroe Islands, are located to the far north of Europe. They are relatively remote from Greece or Rome, and other centers of classical antiquity, as well as from the Near East,

THE EUROPEAN PERSPECTIVE   35

the cradle of western civilization. While it is true that Roman coins and products have been found in Denmark, and that slaves and other goods were traded south, the Romans never penetrated this far beyond the *limes*. Rome's successor states such as Byzantium were far away, and even the Carolingian and Ottonian empires at best reached only the borders of historic Denmark. Denmark's physical location has also had obvious cultural consequences, starting with issues of religion: for example, although Christianity came earlier to Denmark than to some areas of northern and northeastern Europe, it also came relatively late.

Distance has often meant exclusion. Art historical studies of the Renaissance traditionally concentrate on the Italian peninsula, from which Denmark is far distant. In art history the concept of the Northern Renaissance has been constructed as a counterweight to deal with phenomena which were deemed worthy of the same kind of consideration that the Italian Renaissance has received, but this notion has also not included Denmark. Even today in Anglophone countries the concept of the Northern Renaissance applies mainly to the study of Early Netherlandish painting from Van Eyck to Brueghel, with German painters of the period of Dürer, and now perhaps the work of the limewood sculptors included.[9] Moreover, while the art of other countries such as France and Spain which lie on the Mediterranean have also gained international recognition, Denmark clearly has not enjoyed similar favor.

The expansion of art history to cover other European regions has also not included Denmark. As suggested, Denmark might have been included in accounts of art in Central Europe. As duke of Holstein the king of Denmark was considered the leader of the North German circle, an admin-

Fig. 4. 'The Kingedome of Denmarke', by John Speed, 1626. For other parts of the Danish realm, cf. map on p. 54. Copenhagen, The Danish Royal Library (Photo Royal Library).

istrative division of the Holy Roman Empire, and it was as such that Christian IV found a pretext to intervene in the Thirty Years' War. Yet even treatments of art in Central Europe which have covered the period after that of Dürer and the limewood sculptors have not dealt with Denmark.[10]

Geographical distance has also meant chronological disjunction for Danish culture. As is the case with other geographically liminal or remote regions, remote not only in terms of physical geography but in the sense that they are far from the centers in which the major currents of European art and culture originated, many European cultural phenomena, not just Christianity, but aspects of art, and specifically the concern here, the Renaissance, come comparatively belated. If one thinks of the advent of the Renaissance in other lands, and mean by the Renaissance art with classical forms or content, or architecture employing in one way or another the classical orders, then the Renaissance was a tardy arrival in Denmark. Take Central Europe in comparison. Already in the late fifteenth century Florentine sculptors and craftsmen were working at Matthias Corvinus' court in Buda, where they made such fine pieces as Christoforo Romano's relief bust of that ruler. In the early sixteenth century Florentines designed and carved the Bakocz Chapel in Esztergom Cathedral. By the end of the fifteenth century Florentines were also present in Poland. In Kraków, the Polish capital, artists such as Francesco Fiorentino designed the arcaded courtyard in the Wawel, and Bartolommeo Berrecci planned and saw the construction of the Sigismund Chapel in Wawel Cathedral. In the Czech lands, traces of the Renaissance are also visible in Moravia and in the capital of Prague already by the end of the fifteenth century. By the 1530s the Belvedere, a splendid Italianate villa, was being erected in the palace gardens on the Hradčany hill in Prague. Even in other German-speaking lands, art and architecture which was remarkably Italianate could be seen already by the 1540s. Here there may be mentioned as exemplary the important monument of the Stadtresidenz in Landshut, an urban palazzo in Bavaria which some have even gone so far as to attribute to Giulio Romano (Fig. 5). Illusionistic ceiling paintings, depicting subjects *di sotto in su*, which were inspired by Italian prototypes, were also to be seen, most remarkably in the Protestant chapel in Neuburg an der Donau.[11] Nothing like these phenomena is to be encountered in early modern Denmark.

Comparisons of places like Neuburg with Denmark may be hard to make, because some of the

Fig. 5. Landshut, city palace of Duke Louis X of Bavaria, courtyard of the 'Italian house', 1537-43 (Photo Krista de Jonge).

Fig. 6. Hans Gudewerdt the Younger, Altarpiece, 1640. Eckernförde, St. Nicolas' Church (Photo Landesamt für Denkmalpflege, Kiel).

major monuments in Denmark are not paintings, but sculpture or architecture, but that is only part of the problem. The Danish monuments of sculpture and architecture which are usually taken into account might be termed works of at best the very late Renaissance, or "Mannerist". It is not necessary to enter in the vexed question of Northern Mannerism,[12] to see how the possible applicability of this notion also points to the relative belatedness of the Danish Renaissance. Even supposedly Mannerist forms are found in their latest manifestations in the lands of historic Denmark. This pertains both to seemingly indigenous creations found in wood altarpieces and epitaphs made by the Eckernförde school of Hans Gudewerdt and his followers in Schleswig-Holstein (Fig. 6).[13] The term also may pertain to the bronze fountain sculpture at Frederiksborg, an important work by Adriaen De Vries. De Vries was a pupil of Giambologna, the very late Renaissance or Mannerist sculptor, making him a sculptor of the seventh generation of the Renaissance. Furthermore, the fountain for Frederiksborg postdates all the work done by De Vries for that supposedly most Mannerist of monarchs, Rudolf II (Fig. 7).[14]

Moreover, if one really wishes to speak about major monuments of painting, and to expand the notion of the Danish Renaissance to cover the reign of Christian IV, as is common, then one may even actually be talking about painters or artists who in most other contexts are usually considered to be 'baroque'. For example, some of the most important commissions for paintings in Denmark went to artists in Amsterdam and Utrecht. In the early seventeenth century Pieter Lastman and other Amsterdam painters were commissioned to supply works for the royal oratory at Frederiksborg.[15] Other pictures depicting episodes from Danish history were meant to pro-

Fig. 7. Adriaen de Vries, Neptune, 1615-18, from the Frederiksborg fountain, dismantled and taken to Sweden as war booty 1659. Erected in front of Drottningholm Palace, Stockholm (Photo Per Magnus Persson, Nationalmuseum, Stockholm).

Fig. 8. Gerrit van Honthorst, Frederik I at the siege of Copenhagen 1623, c. 1640. Hillerød, The Museum of National History, Frederiksborg Castle (Photo Frederiksborg).

vide decoration for a hall at Kronborg, and were commissioned from Gerrit van Honthorst and other major artists active in Utrecht (Fig. 8).[16] However, Honthorst is perhaps best known as an Utrecht Caravaggist, and Lastman as the teacher of Rembrandt; neither may be rightly considered a 'Renaissance' painter, in the sense of traditional style history.

In any event, mention of Adriaen De Vries, Honthorst, and others of their like indicates another important aspect of the ambiguity of the Danish Renaissance. This collection is gathered under the rubric that this essay has heretofore employed, namely the Danish Renaissance. But it would probably be best to choose another term, since if what is meant by Danish those from Denmark, then very few native-born Danes were involved in designing or creating the major monuments of the period. To be sure, many stone or wood workers, limners and joiners may have been indigenous, and there are important local schools of sculpture in the period like that at Eckernförde. The printmaker and painter Melchior Lorck, from Flensburg, may occupy a special place in considerations of art, but his activity in the Danish crown lands was limited. Other painters like Pieter Isaacsz. (Fig. 14), were born at Helsingør, and so were Søren Kiær and probably. Reinhold Thim.[17]

But just as many important works were imported, the preponderance of major artists came from abroad. In addition to paintings and sculpture already mentioned, imports include large works of sculpture, like the tomb monuments by Cornelis Floris in Schleswig, Roskilde (fig. 9), and elsewhere, the monument by Willem Van den Blocke in Odense, or statues from the De Keyser workshop for Frederiksborg.[18] Even the beautiful silvered altarpiece in Frederiksborg castle came from the workshop of Jakob Mores in Hamburg. Paintings were bought *en masse* in Amsterdam. Moreover, many painters, sculptors, and architects who worked physically in the Danish lands were in effect originally foreigners. A few, like the painter Franz Cleyn (Fig. 10), hailed from relatively nearby in northern Germany (Cleyn was from Rostock), but many came from the Low Countries. Netherlanders like Hans Steenwin-

THE EUROPEAN PERSPECTIVE   39

Fig. 9. Cornelis II Floris, Funerary Monument for Christian III, 1574-75, erected 1580 in Roskilde Cathedral, Chapel of the Magi (Photo The National Museum of Denmark, Copenhagen).

kel from Antwerp and Anthonis van Opbergen from Mechelen/Malines played important roles in architecture, in sculpture, as exemplified by Jan Joris van der Schardt from Nijmegen, and in painting by many court artists starting with Hans Knieper from Brabant and continuing to the Delft-born Karel van Mander III.[19] Rather than the Danish Renaissance, it is perhaps thus better to speak about the Renaissance in Denmark (Fig. 11, 12).

The presence of so many Netherlanders also provides a reminder that the Renaissance in Denmark is a Renaissance of a singularly Netherlandish cast. It is important to emphasize this characteristic, because Denmark is even different from Sweden in this regard. Netherlanders were also abundant in Sweden, but there the Italian or Italianate presence was also much more direct. In the 1570s Johan III of Sweden called the Parr (or Pahr) family of architects and masons into Swedish royal service. The Parrs, originally from Lombardy, had introduced an arcaded courtyard in Brzeg, and worked elsewhere in Silesia, whereafter they had gone on to Mecklenburg. In Sweden they were involved in the construction of the castles at Borgholm, Stockholm, Uppsala, and Kalmar, where their efforts are still visible not just in the general disposition of the building and the shape of the towers, but in the decoration of sever-

Fig. 10. Frantz Clein, A nursery, c. 1620. Hillerød, The Museum of National History, Frederiksborg Castle (Photo Frederiksborg).

Fig. 11. Johan Gregor van der Schardt, Frederik II, 1577-78. Hillerød, The Museum of National History, Frederiksborg Castle (Photo Frederiksborg).

al rooms and the chapel in the interior (Fig. 13).[20] Along with Netherlanders, the relative impact of Germanic artists and architects may also have been greater in Sweden. This does not mean that some particularly Germanic character was adopted, but it does indicate the possibility of a wider variety of sources and references. Nicodemus Tessin the Elder, the leading architect in Sweden in the mid-seventeenth century, the end of our period, had a broad multi-national orientation: Tessin, who came from Pomerania, brought to Sweden experiences and knowledge not just of local German and Netherlandish sources and models, but also of French architecture and experience in Italy: he had been to Rome, and the effects of this experience are also seen in his designs.[21]

Therefore, in contrast even with the situation with the Parrs in Sweden, if we are to think first of the Renaissance in Italianate terms, the Renaissance came only in mediated forms (and content) to Denmark. In painting it has long been recognized that Netherlanders, or Netherlandish-related artists came as intermediaries or indeed as surrogates for Italians or for the Italian art which the Danes could not get. However, it might again be said that this mediation came only belatedly, and in late or Mannerist forms, and furthermore that it occurred not just at second but at third hand. This process is exemplified by the fascinating figure of Pieter Isaacsz.. Isaacsz. became royal painter to Christian IV, and in addition to making portraits was responsible among other things for the part of the decoration of the Winter Room at Rosenborg. He was also a sort of art merchant, mediating painting purchases in Holland. Under Christian he became master of the sound tolls. However, he was also a spy in Swedish service (and maybe Danish counterintelligence). Isaacsz. had received some of his artistic training in Italy. But the clear stylistic formation of his art did not come merely through his own direct experience, but what he learned while he was working there in the atelier of Hans von Aachen, later court painter to Rudolf II, who the historian Karel van Mander says was his teacher. A drawing by Isaacsz. from this Italian period confirms as much: Isaacsz. signs himself as a *discipulus* of Von Aachen (Fig. 14). And both this drawing and a slightly later painting of 1602 (Basel, Museum) show his adaptation of that northern amalgamation effected by the German-born Von Aachen of both Venetian motifs (the nude with the lute player), northern handling, and Florentine forms, perhaps seen through the Vasari circle and such artists as Frederik/Friedrich Sustris, himself a Netherlander who had worked before in Italy. In this painting these elements are combined with a characteristically Rudolfine erotic charge.[22]

The picture drawn so far might give an impression not only of the ambiguity of the Renaissance in Denmark, but of Danish singularity, even provinciality. Yet this would not be correct, for there are several ways in which Denmark shares features more positively with other places and regions, and other perspectives by which the Danish Renaissance may be interpreted.

One of these is as the result of cultural transfer.[23] This means the ways in which not only ideas or in the present case spiritual culture, but also its

THE EUROPEAN PERSPECTIVE   41

products, namely elements of material culture, in more traditional language, art and architecture, may be passed from one place to another. This happens very frequently in the spread of the Renaissance: what is encountered in Denmark is often met elsewhere.

The phenomenon by which, for example, Netherlanders stand in for Italians, and spread the Renaissance to other countries, is broadly familiar. In the past I have pointed to a remarkable offer made by the sculptor (and mason) Paul van't Hofe, who later worked in Wolgast and elsewhere in Pomerania. Van't Hofe announced himself in Lübeck in the 1540s by advertising that he could work in the antique manner, which was not yet present there. He thus offered himself as a surro-

Fig. 13. Kalmar, Chapel of the Castle, 1586, by Domenicus Pahr (Photo Kalmar Castle).

Fig. 14. Pieter Isaacsz., Holy Family with St Catherine, late 1580s. Dresden, Staatliche Kunstsammlungen, Kupferstich-Kabinett (Photo Staatliche Kunstsammlungen).

gate Italian. Similarly, the disciples of Giambologna, having trained in Tuscany, spread this sculptor's gospel over much of Europe: Pietro Tacca in Spain, Pierre Franqueville in France, Hans Reichle in Augsburg, De Vries in Augsburg and then Prague.[24] Sustris, who has been mentioned as having been part of Vasari's equipe in Florence, was along with the Bruges-born Pieter de Witte, known as Candid, one of the Italo-Netherlanders who were responsible for directing and creating much of the flowering of architecture, palace decoration, and painting associated with the Renaissance under William V and Maximilian II in Bavaria.[25] The same situation may be traced in many other places, not the least of which was Prague. In addition to a few Italians like Giuseppe Arcimboldo, most of the figures who served Rudolf II had either been Germanophones like Von Aachen and his pupil Joseph Heintz who had been in Italy, or Netherlanders who had also been there like the sculptors De Vries or Hans Mont, or more significantly, Bartolomeus Spranger, the painter who served the imperial court longest of all. Spranger had imbibed art in Parma, Rome, and Florence (Fig. 15).[26]

As far as architecture or sculpture are concerned, the Netherlandish impact made the Baltic sea area during the late sixteenth and early seventeenth century in many ways a Netherlandish lake. Masons, architects, and sculptors who were active in Denmark appear in the major Baltic emporium of Danzig/Gdańsk. For example Peter Husen designed the Neptune fountain before the Artus Hof in Gdansk before he was called to Denmark, where he modeled sculpture we may still see in the grounds of Rosenborg. Opbergen, whether or not he was the architect of the Arsenal in Gdańsk, was certainly involved with the fortifications there; earlier he had helped in their design at Kronborg castle. Other Netherlanders worked in many other Baltic centers (Fig. 16, 17).[27]

Fig. 12. Hans Knieper, Frederik II and Prince Christian (IV), 1581-85, tapestry from the series of Danish kings, originally in the Great Hall of Kronborg Castle. Copenhagen, The National Museum of Denmark (Photo National Museum).

THE EUROPEAN PERSPECTIVE 43

Fig. 15 Bartholomeus Spranger, Venus and Adonis, c. 1595. Vienna, Kunsthistorisches Museum (Photo KHM).

But Denmark does not need to be grouped exclusively with the Baltic area. Munich and Prague, where similar things occurred, do not lie on the Baltic, but in Central Europe. If the North Sea region be taken into account, then in both sculpture and painting other phenomena like those in Denmark may also be found elsewhere. In England for example Netherlandish painters such as Isaac Oliver (or later, but still contemporary with Christian IV, Rubens and Van Dyck) and Gerard Johnson were active, as were many sculptors.[28]

Cultural transfer is also not merely a matter of influence: it may also involve resistance, bringing up the issue of conscious choice. It has been suggested that the choice of or affinity for Netherlandish art was one such decision. This may help explain why at least in building Netherlandish designs, and the plans of Vredeman de Vries, were preferred over many others.[29]

In any case, as far as Netherlandism is concerned, the use of materials may also have led to a predisposition, at least in architecture, for this choice. Because of a lack of much good stone outside Jutland, from early on brick has long been a predominant material used for building in Denmark. Brick is the material used for castles, like Frederiksborg, for civic structures, like the Copenhagen Stock Exchange, and for churches, like that in Christiansstad, now in Sweden. Brick is moreover certainly not exclusive to Denmark: it has been noted as a common material throughout the Baltic (Fig. 18). However, we may also extend the range in which this material is used to include not only the Low Countries, but England making this not just a regional marker. And of course other choices could also be made: significant monuments like Kronborg were eventually clad with sandstone ashlars.[30]

Religion might be a category which links Denmark with other regions.[31] However, neither the Netherlands nor England is Lutheran, so it is better to focus on other aspects of culture, including the social milieu. Here it is noticeable that much of what is thought of as the Renaissance in Denmark is either the direct result of court patronage and collecting, or made in emulation of the court. Just to recall: the palaces of Kronborg, Rosenborg, Frederiksborg, and Copenhagen itself, along with many others, were all royal residences. The royal chapels at Roskilde, the Round Tower and Trinity Church, and several other ecclesiastical foundations were also paid for by the crown.[32] Major tombs, fountains, and other monuments were also royal commissions. The main painters were in royal employ. And finally the biggest collection was that of the king; others formed by men such as Ole Worm emulated him. The king of Denmark was in a particularly favorable position to call this activity forth, for he owned huge amounts of land, when land was the source of wealth, as it was in early modern Denmark, and the royal purse also benefited from the immense income derived from tolls on ships passing through the sound (Fig. 19).

Fig. 16. Elsinore, Kronborg Castle, Dormer 1585 on the western façade of the west wing. Drawing by A. Krog 1876. Copenhagen, National Danish Art Library.

Royal renaissances are by no means exclusive to Denmark. Jan Białostocki once said that the Renaissance came to Eastern Europe as a royal fancy. By this he meant that the places such as Kraków, Buda, and Prague where the first Italian Renaissance monuments were to be seen were brought there because of the desire of the king.[33] *Mutatis mutandis*, much the same could be said about many other areas of Europe. Florentine sculptors appear first in England at Hampton Court, and in France already in the fifteenth century Francesco Laurana was working in Marseilles and Aix en Provence at the behest of René d'Anjou. Francis I brought Leonardo da Vinci and Andrea del Sarto to France, and later Primaticcio and Rosso Fiorentino, where they founded the school of Fontainebleau. In Spain there are a number of different foci, but the concentrated presence of Italians both in the royal palace at Granada, and in making the tombs there, is due to the crown, as is the collecting and patronage, by the way, of early Netherlandish paintings.[34] Closer to Denmark, many Renaissance sites both in the Low Countries and certainly in the Germanic parts of Central Europe were due to court patronage.[35]

In this connection it is important to consider one main reason why Christian IV might not only be regarded as having emulated earlier and contemporaneous monarchs in using patronage and collecting as an expression of magnificence,

Fig. 17. Gdańsk, Armory, 1600-1612 (Photo Hugo Johannsen).

THE EUROPEAN PERSPECTIVE   45

but also to have acted in an environment where monarchs and princes were encouraged to be collectors and patrons. His predecessor, Frederick II, had already followed Emperor Maximilian II in taking the sculptor Johann Gregor van der Schardt into his employ. In Christian IV's time the leading monarch in protocol was Emperor Rudolf II. Rudolf acceded to the imperial dignity in 1576, twelve years before Christian became king, and for the next quarter century of Christian's reign ruled from Prague, where he amassed the biggest and best *Kunstkammer* and painting collection in all of Europe, and brought scores of artists to his court. Rudolfine Prague was the cynosure of the contemporary German courts, and we may also recall that the emperor was also sovereign over the Duke of Holstein, one of Christian's titles.

Many of the German courts were inspired by the imperial court, and emulated it. They had artistic contacts both direct and indirect with Prague. The German princes gave and received gifts from the emperor, helped the Prague court acquire objects and acquired them on commissions from court artists. In some instances they exchanged servants with the court, sent their own court artists to Prague for training, as did the duke of Saxony, or picked as court artists, as in Wolfenbüttel, artists who had been trained by Prague court artists. They also acquired or had made objects that imitated those created by Rudolfine painters and craftsmen.[36]

In many respects the Danish court followed this pattern. Christian IV commissioned sculpture from the imperial bronze caster Adriaen de Vries. Pieter Isaacsz., Christian IV's court painter, had, as remarked, been the pupil of Hans von Aachen, Rudolf II's court painter. Isaacsz. remained in contact with Von Aachen and with other artists like Vredeman de Vries, who had served Rudolf II, long after he had left Von Aachen's atelier. Copies of compositions by Arcimboldo and the

Fig. 19. Hendrick Cornelisz. Vroom, View of Elsinore and Kronborg Castle, between 1615 and 1629. Cambridge, Fitzwilliam Museum (Photo © Fitzwilliam Museum).

Fig. 18. Hillerød, Frederiksborg Castle, Bathhouse, c.1580 (Photo Hugo Johannsen).

Prague painter Savery are in Rosenborg. Compositions by Spranger provided models for Danish painters. A Danish letter written twenty-five years after Rudolf II's death, and thirty-seven after that of Joris Hoefnagel, refers to that artist as imperial court painter. This suggests something of the continuing cachet that the Prague court enjoyed in Denmark.[37] It may have been this kind of cachet that inspired or at least stimulated the assemblage of the *Kunstkammer* in Copenhagen, as of the dukes of Holstein at Gottorp. The decoration of the rooms in Gottorp which housed the *Kunstkammer* have a noticeably cosmic theme, which was also imparted to and by the *Kunstkammer* in Prague. It is of course also possible that these collections were also stimulated by the general competitive atmosphere of the German princely courts.[38]

Central Europe was the home of many princely houses with which Denmark had close connections. Of these courts Christian was related by marriage and family ties to the rulers in Wolfenbüttel, Dresden, and Brandenburg. These were all ruled by Lutherans (until the conversion of the margrave of Brandenburg to Calvinism), as was Denmark. The leadership of the Protestant cause was important. However, it might also be noted that the dukes of Brunswick-Wolfenbüttel and Saxony were also the rulers who were closest to Habsburg emperors in their politics and love of art. It may well be that interchanges between these courts and Prague created a broader community of interest into which Christian IV also fits.[39] For example, Giammaria Nosseni, the Italian impresario, who was active at the Dresden court, designed a mount of virtue for the coronation of Christian IV in 1596, which was assembled in Dresden, and brought to Copenhagen.[40]

Court relations expanded in other directions, too. Christian IV's sister, Anne of Denmark, was James I's queen. This may have had important consequences for the arts. It might be useful to examine the inspiration that British court painters, most of them Netherlanders, may have had on Christian, who visited England in 1606 and again in 1614, when he was painted by them.

In conclusion, another model may be proposed for considerations of Denmark. In response to the much discussed issue of centers and peripheries, Jan Białostocki saw that the periphery might have a positive advantage for developments in the arts.[41] However, other scholars such as Enrico Castelnuovo have advanced another cultural model which might also be applied to the Danish situation.[42] This is the idea of frontiers, both geographical and cultural. Rather than limiting regions, frontiers may be regarded as sites where cultures meet and contact takes place. Encounters may lead to various forms of cultural production, like those in Denmark. Culturally liminal, Denmark might thus be conceived not just as peripheral, but as having a productive position, productive because it lies on the frontiers of various cultural zones.

In posing this model for consideration, this paper wishes to suggest some new ways to think

Fig. 20. Artist unknown, Tranquebar (India) with Dansborg, c.1650. Skokloster Castle, Sweden (Photo Jens Mohr, Skokloster).

about the Renaissance in Denmark. But one need not stop with Europe. Denmark was also linked with the wider world: it traded in the Indian Ocean, and established a settlement in Tranquebar, on the east coast of India, whose mercantile and artistic relations with the Danish homeland have been well studied (Fig. 20).[43] With this connection in mind (and Denmark was also later present in Africa, and the Americas, in the Virgin Islands), it is useful to remember that the Renaissance was a phenomenon with a compass broader than Europe. When the globe is taken into account, issues of marginality and liminality become problematic. The place of Denmark in the European perspective of the Renaissance might thus well be rethought in terms of the wider questioning of art in a global setting, which is a pressing concern today.

Notes

1. In this essay I have tried to retain the flavor of the original introductory lecture on which it is based, hence the more personal tone. Similarly, I have restricted references; many arguments touched upon here are documented in the other essays in this volume.

2. The historiography of Danish Renaissance art is discussed in the paper by Birgitte Bøggild Johannsen in this volume.

3. The latter subject was the topic of an exhibition in Aarhus which was one of the series devoted to Christian IV in 1988; see Steffen Heiberg (ed.), *Christian IV and Europe. The 19th Art Exhibition of the Council of Europe, Denmark 1988,* Herning 1988, 507-543.

4. Thomas DaCosta Kaufmann, "La guerre de trente ans a-t-elle eu lieu? Continuities and Discontinuities during the Thirty Years' War", in: Jacques Thuillier et al. (eds.), *Paix de Westphalie. L'art entre la guerre et la paix en Europe/ Westfälischer Friede. Die Kunst zwischen Krieg und Frieden.* Actes du colloque organisé par le Westfälischer Landesmuseum le 19 novembre 1998 à Münster et à Osnabrück et le Service culturel du musée du Louvre les 20 et 21 novembre 1990 à Paris, Paris 1999, 141-167.

5. See Heiberg (ed.) 1988. The notes and catalogue entries refer to much of the literature of the previous decades.

6. I had in mind the work of such scholars as Juliette Rod-

ing and Mara Wade, both represented in the present collection.

7   The present collection, and the sequence of exhibitions to which it was related, remedy this situation. I have not referred to these most recent contributions, which of course will alter the situation to which I am referring *en gros et en detail*.

8   See Juliette Roding & Lex Heerma van Voss (eds.), *The North Sea and Culture (1550-1800)*, Verloren, 1996; Krista Kodres et al. (eds.), *Religious Art and Architecture in the Baltic Region in the 13th -18th Centuries*, Tallinn 2008.

9   For an overview of the bibliography and historiography of the question, especially in regard to the period of the Danish Renaissance, see Thomas DaCosta Kaufmann (ed.), *Art and Architecture in Central Europe, 1550-1620. An Annotated Bibliography,* Marburg 2003 (Revised and updated edition with Heiner Borggrefe and Thomas Fusenig), especially the preface and introduction, 11-23. It may be remarked parenthetically that the category of limewood sculpture has left Denmark out of the picture, as exemplified by Michael Baxandall, *The Limewood Sculptors of Renaissance Germany*, New Haven & London, 1980, which pointedly excludes Claus Berg, who carved in oak, and also does not mention Bernt Notke.

10 I have to confess that my *Court, Cloister and City. The Art and Culture of Central Europe, 1450-1800, Chicago 1995* was also guilty of this oversight. See however Kristoffer Neville, *Nicodemus Tessin the Elder: Architecture in Sweden in the Age of Great Power,* Turnhout 2009 (Architectura Moderna 7), which argues for the inclusion of Sweden in a Central European context, and in passing, also for Denmark.

11 For a general account of these monuments see Kaufmann 1995.

12 See Thomas DaCosta Kaufmann, "The Problem of Northern 'Mannerism': A Critical Review", in: S. E. Murray & Ruth I. Weidner (eds.), *Mannerism: Essays in Music and the Arts*, West Chester, Pennsylvania 1980, 89-115.

13 For which see Holger Behling, *Hans Gudwerdt. Bildschnitzer zu Eckernförde*, Neumünster 1990.

14 For De Vries see most thoroughly Frits Scholten (ed.), *Adriaen de Vries 1556-1626. Exhibition catalogue*, Zwolle 1998. The Frederiksborg fountain is also treated most recently by Charlotte Christensen and Magnus Olausson in Steffen Heiberg (ed.), *Christian 4. og Frederiksborg*, Copenhagen 2006, 153-183.

15 Hugo Johannsen, "Christian IV's Private Oratory in Frederiksborg Castle Chapel – Reconstruction and Interpretation", in: Badeloch Noldus & Juliette Roding (eds.), *Pieter Isaacsz (1568-1625). Court Painter, Art Dealer and Spy*, Turnhout 2007, 164-179; see also Heiberg (ed.) 2006.

16 For these see H. D. Schepelern & Ulla Houkjær, *The Kronborg Series. King Christian IV and his Pictures of Early Danish History*, Copenhagen 1988.

17 Isaacsz. and his contemporaries were the topic of a recent exhibition at Frederiksborg, see Noldus & Roding (eds.) 2007.

18 For works of the Floris school see most recently Hugo Johannsen, "Willem van den Blocke and his monument (1585-86) for Christoph von Dohna in the Cathedral of Odense. An Example of the Spread of the Style of Cornelis Floris in the Baltic", in: Małgorzata Ruszkowska-Macur (ed.), *Netherlandish Artists in Gdańsk in the Time of Hans Vredeman de Vries*, Gdańsk & Lemgo 2006, 111-115. Activity of the De Keyser workshop is considered in the essay by Konrad Ottenheym in this collection.

19 Some of these figures are considered in the papers by Krista de Jonge and Kristoffer Neville within. The painters however deserve more attention, as does the rather contested oeuvre of Johan Gregor van der Schardt.

20 See August Hahr, *Die Architektenfamilie Pahr. Eine für Renaissancekunst Schlesiens, Mecklenburgs und Schwedens bedeutende Künstlerfamilie*, Strasbourg 1908 (Studien zur deutschen Kunstgeschichte 97); Marius Karpowicz, "La conquista delle corti", in: Cesare Mozzarelli (ed.), '*Familia*' *del principe e famiglia aristocratica*, Rome 1988, 745-751.

21 These issues are treated in Neville 2007.

22 Isaacsz. is treated in Noldus & Roding (eds.) 2007. For these works and a general discussion see further Juliette Roding & Marja Stompé, *Pieter Isaacsz. (1569-1625). Een Nederlandse schilder, kunsthandelaar en diplomat aan het Deense hof*, Verloren 1997.

23 For perspectives on the application of this notion to the early modern period see Wolfgang Schmale (ed.), *Kulturtransfer*, Innsbruck 2003 (Wiener Schriften zur Geschichte der Neuzeit 2).

24 See in general Thomas DaCosta Kaufmann, "Italian Sculptors and Sculpture outside of Italy (chiefly in Central Europe): Problems of Approach, Possibilities of Reception", in: Claire Farago (ed.), *Reframing the Renaissance*, New Haven and London 1995, 47-66.

25 See Thea Wilberg-Vignau, *In Europa zu Hause: Niederländer in München um 1600/Citizens of Europe. Dutch and Flemish Artists in Munich c. 1600,* Munich, 2005.

26 See Eliška Fučíková et al. (eds.), *Rudolf II and Prague. The Court and the City*, London 1997; Thomas DaCosta Kaufmann, *The School of Prague. Painting at the Court of Rudolf II*, Chicago and London 1988.

27 For a general introduction to this subject see Thomas DaCosta Kaufmann, "Påverkan västerifrån: nederländsk

konst och arkitektur", in: Janis Kreslins, Steven A. Mansbach & Robert Schweitzer (eds.), *Gränsländer. Östersjön in ny gestalt*, Stockholm 2003, 17-41 (also published as "Ietekme no rietumiem: Nīderlandes māksla un arhitektūra", in: *Baltija: jauns skatīums*, Riga 2003, 29-48). See also Thomas DaCosta Kaufmann, "Ways of Transfer of Netherlandish Art", in: Ruszkowska-Macur (ed.) 2006, 13-21. The other essays in this volume also pertain to this theme; see further Krista Kodres, "Der Vredeman de Vries-Stil als Markenzeichen Arent Passers in Reval/Tallinn", and Arnold Bartetzky, "Hans Vredeman de Vries' geschwifte Beschlagwerkgiebel. Zu ihrer Herkunft, Aneignung und Verbreitung in der Architektur Mittel-und Nordeuropas", in: Heiner Borggrefe & Vera Lüpkes (eds.), *Hans Vredeman de Vries und die Folgen*, Marburg 2005 (Studien zur Kultur der Renaissance 3), 50-57, 73-82.

28 See Christopher Brown, "Artistic Relations between Britain and the Low Countries (1532-1632)", in: Roding & Van Voss (eds.) 1996, 340-354, and Christopher Brown, "British Painting and the Low Countries", in: Karen Hearn (ed.), *Dynasties. Painting in Tudor and Jacobean England 1530-1630*, London 1995, 27-31; Juliette Roding (ed.), *Dutch and Flemish Artists in Britain 1550-1800* (Leids Kunsthistorisch Jaarboek 13), 2003.

29 See in general for this circumstance Borggrefe & Lüpkes 2005; Heiner Borggrefe et al. (ed.), *Hans Vredeman de Vries und die Renaissance in Norden*, Munich 2002.

30 For more on the choice of brick as a material see Thomas DaCosta Kaufmann, "Art and the Church in the Early Modern Era: The Baltic in Comparative Perspective", in: Kodres (ed.) 2008, 20-40. See also Hugo Johannsen, "Kronborg", in: Carsten Bach-Nielsen et al. (eds.), *Danmark og renæssancen 1500-1650*, Copenhagen 2006, 290-299.

31 More is said about this issue in other essays in this collection, for instance that by Jan Harasimowicz.

32 See Juliette Roding, *Christiaan IV van Denemarken (1588-1648). Architectuur en stedebouw van een Luthers vorst*, Alkmaar 1991.

33 Jan Białostocki, *The Art of the Renaissance in Eastern Europe*, Oxford & Ithaca 1976.

34 See Earl Rosenthal, "The Diffusion of the Italian Renaissance Style in Western European Art", *Sixteenth Century Journal* 9 (1978), 33-45.

35 For Central Europe see in general Kaufmann 1995; the continuing publications of Krista de Jonge address this topic in the Low Countries.

36 See Thomas DaCosta Kaufmann, "Planeten im kaiserlichen Universum. Prag und die Kunst an den deutschen Fürstenhöfen zur Zeit Rudolfs II.," in: *Hofkunst der Spätrenaissance. Braunschweig-Wolfenbüttel und das kaiserliche Prag um 1600*, Braunschweig 1998, 9-19.

37 This information was pointed out in Thomas DaCosta Kaufmann, review article,"*Christian IV and Europe. The 19th Art Exhibition of the Council of Europe*, Copenhagen, 1988", *Konsthistorisk Tidskrift* 58 (1989),19-22. Of course, it might be remembered that Tycho Brahe, after being in Christian IV's favor, went to Prague to become imperial astronomer, and died there.

38 See Mogens Bencard, „Idee und Entstehung der Kunstkammer", in: Heinz Spielmann & Jan Drees (eds.), *Gottorf im Glanz des Barock. Kunst und Kultur am Schleswiger Hof 1544-1713*, Schleswig 1997, 261-267.

39 For the relation with Brunswick-Wolfenbuttel see the essay by Barbara Uppenkamp.

40 See Heiberg (ed.) 1988, 130, cat. 445. The topic of Danish-Saxon relations is the subject of an exhibition with catalogue, see Jutta Kappel & Claudia Brink (eds.), *Mit Fortuna übers Meer. Sachsen und Dänemark – Ehen und Allianzen im Spiegel der Kunst (1548-1709)*, Dresden 2009.

41 Jan Białostocki, "Some Values of Artistic Periphery," in: Irving Lavin et al. (eds.) *World Art: Themes of Unity in Diversity*, London 1989, 1, 49-58.

42 Enrico Castelnuovo, "La frontiera nella storia dell'arte", and "Le Alpi, crocevia e punto d'incontro delle tendenze artistiche nel XV secolo", in: *La cattedrale tascabile. Scritti di storia dell'arte*, Livorno 2000, 15-45.

43 See most comprehensively Martin Krieger, *Kaufleute, Seeräuber und Diplomaten. Der dänische Handel auf dem Indischen Ozean (1620-1868)*, Cologne, Weimar & Vienna 1998.

THE DANISH PERSPECTIVE[1]

Birgitte Bøggild Johannsen

"*Eximium humani generis memoria donum, quæ præterita, præsentia ac futura bilance librat*" (Memory is an excellent gift for humanity, weighting upon her pair of scales the past, the present and the posterity). [2]

Between Past, Present and Posterity: Redrawing the Lines

Among the several lost monuments or ruined *disjecta membra* from 16th and early 17th century Denmark, giving to-day only a limited image of the period's artistic scenery,[3] one of the more regrettable losses is the original interior decorations and furnishing of Frederiksborg Castle. Temporarily renovated by King Frederik II from a former manor house, the complex was radically transformed during the early 17th century by his son and follower, Christian IV, into a monument of princely magnificence, quite on par - to the opinion of a contemporary - with other European highlights, i.e. the palaces and collections at Escorial, Fontainebleau, Dresden and Venice. Or virtually surpassing "der Schlösser und Gebäw in allen Ländern", including as well the wonders of Antique Greece and Rome (!), according to another enthusiastic advocate, almost bursting with national self-esteem.[4]

The subsequent destiny of Frederiksborg's splendours is well-known. Plundered during the Swedish Wars in 1658-60 and since dramatically ravaged by fire in 1859, leaving – except for the chapel – only the architectural framework, the castle was due to private initiative respectfully restored in the second part of the 19th century, transforming the previous royal residence into a museum for the national history, a *lieu de mémoire* of past glory and present accomplishments.[5] Yet, even in modern times, the architecture of Christian IV's Frederiksborg including the still extant decorations has justly maintained a canon status as one of the most prominent embodiments of 'the Danish Renaissance'. Indeed, as recently stated (by a Dane): "Only in a few places outside Italy has the Renaissance's dream of Antiquity been so intensely manifested",[6] translating the idioms of Classical Antiquity through Italian, Netherlandish, French and German mediation into a synthesis of unique standing.

In its previous totality of expressions, the castle was an illustrative example of a "relay station" of interchanging cultures,[7] equally reflecting foreign influences and local ingenuity. At the same time, the complex represented "la figure du roi",[8] embodying in a proper as well as in a figurative sense the Danish king and his realms. The fundamental discourses on royal power were particularly re-

Fig. 1. Hillerød, Frederiksborg Castle, 'Memoria', detail from the reconstructed ceiling of the Great Hall, 1874-80 (Photo Hugo Johannsen).

flected in the main settings for the king's appearance, the Palace Church and the Great Hall ("Riddersalen" or "Dansesalen"). This last room, in its modern status a recreation from 1874-80, was c. 1620 embellished i.a. with a profusely carved, painted and gilded ceiling, in images presenting a pictorial Mirror of Princes, which in addition to the architectural structure itself displayed an almost encyclopaedian assembly of subjects or a *mixtum compositum* of classical, biblical, medieval and modern ideas.[9]

In particular, one of the images from the peripheral decorative area of the ceiling may serve as point of reference to the present venture, reframing 'the Danish Renaissance' in a Danish perspective. Confronting *Humilitas*, and flanked by *Pax* (opposite *Sinceritas*) and *Religio* (opposite *Misericordia*) was the image of *Memoria*, shown with a tablet hanging around her shoulders, whereupon were three golden balls with the words: "*Præterita, Præsentia, Futura*" (cf. Fig. 1). The *inscriptio* beneath the picture read the text, quoted above. The exact literary or pictorial sources of the emblem have not yet been revealed.[10] Equally disputed is the code to the inner meanings of the pictorial programme *in toto* (see also Juliette Roding, pp. 238 ff.).[11] Yet, the message of the creative qualities of memory, constructed in the present with equal regards to the past and the posterity, was unmistakable and had its parallel in the allegory of Memory in the Palace Church after Frans Floris and Cornelis Cort (Fig. 2-3).[12] Both were of obvious relevance to the Danish king's comprehensive enterprises, ensuring his immortality and hindering oblivion, assisted as well "durch beyspringen der Feder" (i.e. the contemporary descriptions).[13]

In their very essence, the acts of memory or oblivion are vital culture-generating forces, constructing remembrance or erasure of the past, freely organizing or eliminating chosen elements - material, verbal, symbolical or performative - into patterns of meaning, strategically designed to create legitimacy, power and status. Accordingly, any construction of the past reflects the values and agendas of the present, represented with a view to the future. During the recent

Fig. 2. Hillerød, Frederiksborg Castle, 'Memoria', spandrel relief on the gallery of the Chapel, 1606-1617 (Photo Hugo Johannsen).

Fig. 3. Cornelis Cort, 'Memoria', engraving after Frans Floris, 1560. Copenhagen, The National Gallery of Denmark, Print Room (Photo National Gallery).

decades, research on this continually topical issue has developed into an all-embracing field, a "Leitbegriff der Kulturwissenschaften" (Aleida Assmann),[14] equally promoting the 'constructivist turn' and the interdisciplinarity of postmodern cultural history. Shared memory or oblivion of a community contributes to shape its identity, involving the mythic discourse on the reconstruction or deconstruction of a society or nation in moments of change, "manifesting the consequences of violations or observances of the rule of propriety".[15]

Accordingly, *Memoria* shall be also our guiding star, equally relevant to reflections on the historiographical construction of the 'Danish Renaissance' (see the introduction), on the geopolitical position of Denmark, past and present, and on the state of art and architecture in Denmark during the 16th and early 17th century. In this context, emphasis shall be placed upon the period, prior to 'The Golden Age of Christian IV' (1588-1648), in particular internationally boosted in 1988 at the 19th Art Exhibition of the Council of Europe, *Christian IV and Europe*.[16] The narrative of the last issue will reflect the author's own agenda, advocating for the necessity of reconsidering the early beginnings, i.e. the artistic culture of the previous decades of the 16th century, into the general image of Renaissance Europe, with particular focus upon the first half of the century, before as well as after the confessional watershed of the Lutheran Reformation. Within this frame of thinking, it shall further be argued that the Danish ways, also comprising 'peripheral' or 'marginal' subjects (a.o. cartography, Neo-Latin epitaphs and epigraphy, heraldry, ornaments, textiles, furniture, ceramics, jewellery, medals and prints) should not be one-sidedly deprecated for distance or estrangement in time, scope, form and content to the European mainstream. Rather, they may invite for a renewed evaluation as equally valid contributions to the debate on cultural diversity and the 'decentering' of the Renaissance.

Ultima Thule or *In Medias Res*: Re-presenting the Geopolitical Framework

"*Scoti, dani, sveti, norvegii in ultimis orbis oris siti, nihil est quod extra donum queant*" (The Scots, Danes, Swedes, Norwegians are situated at the end of the world, and they are not capable of doing anything outside their native soil"). This harsh verdict was uttered by the Italian humanist, Aeneas Silvius Piccolomini (later Pope Pius II (1405-64)) in an anti-Turkish oration, held at the *Reichstag* in Frankfurt in October 1454, after having in vain appealed for Danish support to a forthcoming crusade.[17] A thought-provoking contrast represented the enthusiastic eulogy, presented only 20 years later, by another Italian, the Mantuan courtier and humanist, Filippo Nuvoloni, praising in 1474 the "*regnum large et magnifice*" of the Danish King Christian I during a visit to his brother- and sister-in law, Ludovico Gonzaga and Barbara of Brandenburg, at the court of Mantua. Nuvoloni furthermore acclaimed the king as "*Caesar Augustus*", a "*sol inter stellas fulgendo*" and a Prince of Peace in contrast to his belligerent ancestors, the Goths.[18] The political and personal agenda behind Nuvoloni's outburst was of course no less biased. This represented a renewed appeal for Danish intervention in another crusade, mixed with the author's private expectations for his own career.

In reality, during these years Denmark should be considered a political actor of more than inferior status, presiding as the leader of the Calmar Union (1397-1523), a pretentional co-regency of Denmark, Norway and Sweden under the Danish crown. Even after the dissolution of the union, the double monarchy of Denmark-Norway (Fig. 4) still during the 16th and the first part of the 17th century retained government of Iceland, Greenland, parts of Southern and Eastern Sweden, the Duchies of Schleswig and Holstein (though remaining fiefs under the German Emperor), the recently conquered or acquired areas of the Ditmarshes in Northern Germany and the Estonian island of Saaremaa (Øsel), islands in the North-Atlantic archipelago and, from 1620, even comprising colonies in India (Tranquebar). A recent account by Paul Douglas Lockhart (2007) of Danish history 1513-1660 with the speaking subtitle: *The Rise and Decline of a Renaissance Monarchy*, aptly characterizes Denmark, not as a 'superpower', yet undeniably as a "great *regional* power", being Europe's largest polity in terms of sheer land mass next to the Spanish Empire (according to Piccolomini, Denmark for this very reason should be called an "*archiregnum*"),[19] the dominating power in the Baltic Sea region for more than a century and "Europe's first truly Protestant kingdom", which accordingly would play a leading role in European affairs, not in the

Fig. 5. Christiern Pedersen, World map, 1521. Copenhagen, The Danish Royal Library (Photo Royal Library).

least in religious matters.[20] As indicated above, the Danish kings showed an increasing involvement during the late 15th and early 16th centuries in international planning for Crusades or for the discovery and conquest of foreign realms, such as Greenland and India, to be propagated in printing as well as in paintings and cartography.[21] Indeed, the central placement of Denmark in the map by Christiern Pedersen from 1521 (Fig. 5) probably tells more than words of the contemporary Danish self-image. Denmark, of course, is placed in the 'fine company' of Europe in "den anden partt aff Werden" (the second part of the world), between Rome, Germany, France and Spain, all affronting the enchanting first part of the universe, comprising India, Asia, Jerusalem – and Paradise![22]

As to constitution, Denmark since the Early Middle Ages was an electoral monarchy, the organization of authority and power being divided between the King and the aristocratic Council, which in a consensual *monarchia mixta* constituted the Crown of Denmark until the *coup d'état* of Hereditary Absolutism in 1660. Indeed, this construction, antiquated as it may seem, proved effective and constant until the end of the period, contributing from the early 16th century to transform Denmark from a backward, parochial state with only limited participation in European matters, into an integrated and dedicated actor, within politics, economy, religion and culture being in the main track of European civilization. As to learning, a qualified verdict by Erasmus Rotero-

Fig. 4. Map of Northern Europe c. 1570. After Gerard de Jode, *Speculum Orbis Terrarum*, Antwerpen 1578. Copenhagen, The Danish Royal Library (Photo Royal Library).

THE DANISH PERSPECTIVE   55

damus already in 1517 included the Danes (together with the Scots and Irishmen (!)) into the erudite society, now cultivating 'polite letters'.[23] However, it should not be overlooked that current internal, political instabilities, in particular in the wake of the expulsion of Christian II in 1523, the Civil Wars in 1534-36 and the gradual implementation of Lutheran Reformation during the same period, set certain limits to an unreserved cultural expansion.

Three factors, two of these of geopolitical nature, in particular furthered the Danish 'integration' into Europe, as emphasized by Lockhart:[24] The holding of the key to the Baltic Sea (the *dominium Maris Baltici*) and the possession of the rich duchies of Schleswig-Holstein, though at the same time being fiefs to the Holy Roman Empire, a fact which necessitated the Danish kings, willingly or not, to be involved in German politics. Lastly, the Lutheran Reformation from its official start in 1536, being officially univocal in Denmark in contrast to Sweden (though not in every respect monolithic in practice),[25] strengthened the economical and political power of the king as leader of the national Church. However, the advocacy for the Protestant case currently forced the Danish king to involvement in religious wars or confessional debates on the Continent.

To these factors, with particular relevance to the period prior to 1536, should be added the crucial importance of dynastic alliances, the royal marriages of King John (in 1478) with Christine (1461-1521), daughter of Ernst, the Elector of Saxony and of King Christian II (in 1514/1515) with Isabella (Elisabeth) of Austria (1501-26), granddaughter of the German Emperor Maximilian. Both matches in several respects furthered contacts with prominent cultural centres of the Renaissance, Saxony, the Netherlands, Austria and Spain. Admittedly, the Protestant predilections would dominate in royal marriage policy after the 1530s – in contrast to Sweden - avoiding dynastic alliances with Roman Catholics.[26] Yet, diplomatic, cultural and commercial relations with the Roman Catholic world would never be cut off, even after the Reformation (see also below). Determinative as well was the topic of hereditary enmity or the status of an almost permanent 'cold war' with Sweden since the 16th century – in itself a major site of memory, influencing cultural predilections and the construction of national myths of origin.[27]

Accordingly, the biased vision of 16th and early 17th century Denmark as a distanced and closed, self-sufficient entity, marked by conservatism and xenophobia, should be reframed or partly regarded as a later construction - an offshoot of the considerable territorial reductions of the nation-state from the second half of the 17th till the 19th centuries. Even in modern times, the current self-perception of the present Danish 'midget' state is dominated by minority feelings and a sense of humility, though often paired with an ambivalent and probably disproportionate self-esteem of uniqueness, typical to a small state, feeling a moral right to exercise influence, because of its strong and coherent society.[28]

Probably, Renaissance Denmark should rather be seen as an open, composite geopolitical entity, upholding interaction with various European regions (cf. Fig. 6.), including the Oriental world as well,[29] equally exposing a pluralism of networks between different centres or groups. In fact, the impression of the extrovert nation and its inhabitants is quite in accordance with the contemporary (1588) description of the Danes in Braunius and Hogenberg, *Civitates Orbis Terrarum*, emphasizing the natives' "lust zu (…) reysen" and "zu freien künsten und geschickligkeit", as well as their docility in several languages.[30] By the way, this moment might partly be an explanation behind the very low activity of translations from foreign tongues into Danish, not only as a consequence to the peripheral location upon the map, as maintained by Peter Burke (2007), pointing to the virtually non-existent export of Danish literary works - a postulate, which, however, remains to be explored.[31] Indeed, the above mentioned picture of the open-minded and easily impressionable region to a certain degree matches the image, outlined much later by Julius Lange (1895), according to whom, Denmark, due to the geographical placement at "a public highway" in confrontation with the outer world and freed from nature-born fortifications, "has been easily flown over by all foreign, open to every shifting

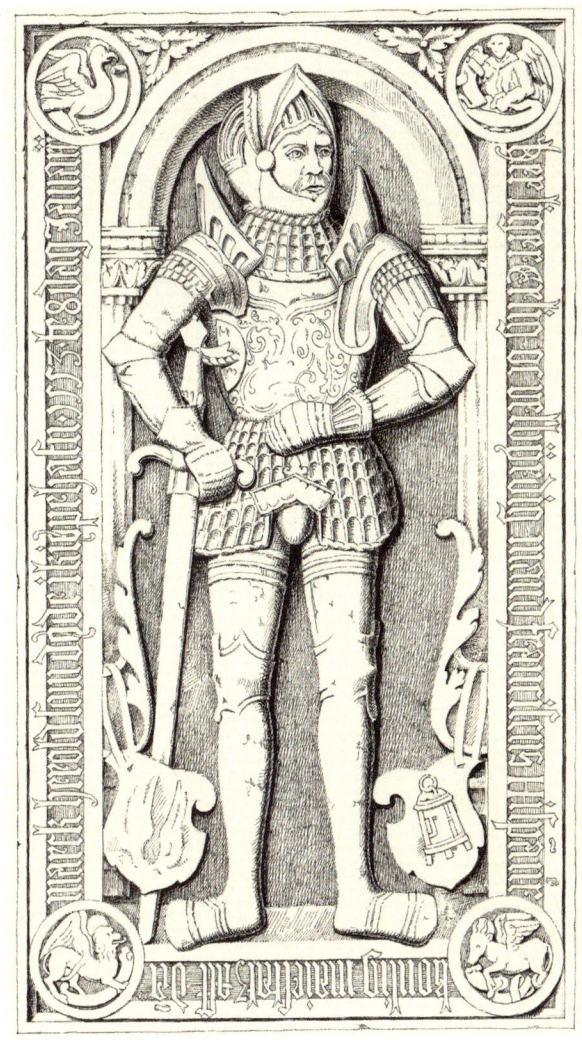

Fig. 6. Roskilde Cathedral, Tomb slab of the Spanish herald Franciscus da Medina, †1553, represented in a traditional Northern cuirass. Drawing by Heinrich Heeger. Copenhagen, The National Museum of Denmark.

winds". Nevertheless, these characteristics according to Lange should be counterbalanced by "a certain closed independence", distinctive to the nation, fostering the peculiarities of its culture,[32] a verdict, still open to challenge.

Appropriating Alterity: Confronting Classical Antiquity and the Native Past

Whenever transgressing cultural frames in time and space or confronting alterity, a necessary prerequisite should be to state one's own central position, or rather this act will be given indirectly, always defining the point of origin in relation to something else. As to the questions of modernity or innovation vs. tradition and continuity, a contemporary testimonial, related to the Danish king, exactly extolled the virtues of traditionalism, outright characterised as a code to 'nativeness'. In his biography from 1560 of King Hans (1455-1513), the historian Hans Svaning praised the king for his conservatism, simplicity and Danish predilections. Though keeping his royal dignity, he was always modest in appearance, detested every kind of luxury in travels, armours, eating and dressing and preferred the native customs ("*patriæ mores*") to foreign ones, so that no one could accuse him of spurning the traditions.[33]

The verdict should, however, be regarded in context as a marking of status in opposition to non-Danes, in particular related to the current attacks upon contemporary Swedish (and anti-Danish) historiography, and probably as well an indirect assault upon the *homines novi*, the uprising Vasa dynasty in Sweden, already during the reign of Gustav Vasa and Erik XIV displaying more ostentatious and internationally oriented ways of self-presentation.[34] A similar broadside, addressed in 1528 to King Gustav, was let off by the Carmelite historian and humanist, Paulus Helie (c. 1485-c. 1535), derogating superfluous princely consumption, including drinking, games, clothing, palaces and other kinds of luxurious living, these predilections, as well to be found among the rich upper class, i.a. decorating their houses with abominable female idols such as Pallas, Juno and Venus (!).[35]

Programmatic utterances of the virtues of native man-power in contrast to scepticism towards the import of foreigners were – no wonder – brought forward, up till and following the dethronement in 1523 of the enterprising Christian II (see below). His target-oriented use of experts and labourers, in particular from the Netherlands, was together with his openness towards new customs (now judged unnecessary) stigmatized as leading "the Kingdom of Denmark to eternal damage, slavery and ruin".[36] A similar biased verdict of national self-sufficiency, uttered

THE DANISH PERSPECTIVE 57

Fig. 7a-b. Bartolomeo Melioli, Christian I, medal struck on occasion of the Danish King's visit to Mantua 1474, a. averse, b. reverse. Copenhagen, The National Museum of Denmark (Photo National Museum).

however not during any exaggerated moment of crisis like the above-mentioned, was the rejection in 1557 by Christian III of the project drawings for a baptismal font, ordered by the king in the west ("vester paa") by the master who had made the tomb for his father, i.e. Cornelis Floris of Antwerp, arguing that 'the king himself had artists, who could do the work'. From a distance, this comment appears pretty unfounded, and apparently the king soon regretted his rebuff, as witnessed by the magnificent imported font, ascribed to Floris, and installed in the Royal Chapel at Sønderborg Castle.[37] In reality, during the whole period migrating artists and art works should prove to be the very incentive for the implementation of alterity. Admittedly, direct employment of Italian know-how (i.e. Giovanni Maria Nosseni and Johan Baptista Pahr) is only witnessed from the end of the century. However, since the 1520s the Danish court and the nobility had engaged different foreigners, preferably from Germany and the Netherlands, the most important being the versatile, itinerant Jacob Binck from Cologne, from the late 1540s to be followed by the distinguished 'star' of Northern European Renaissance, the abovementioned Cornelis Floris (though never personally in Denmark). In reverse, it should neither be forgotten, that Christian III actively supported young Danish talents, including musicians and the painter Melchior Lorck, to pursue their studies in foreign countries, i.a. in Italy.[38]

The prejudices or predilections towards 'the others' would in particular be tested at direct encounters with 'emporias' of new developments. Two cases of Royal confrontations with the Early Italian Renaissance during the 15th century should, however, turn out to have no apparent consequences to visual arts and architecture in Denmark. King Erik of Pomerania (c. 1382-1459) upon his pilgrimage for Jerusalem 1423-25 was graciously received by the Doge in Venice, yet suffered the negative experience of having his portrait secretly depicted at the instigation of the son of the Greek Emperor (John VIII Palaiologos), subsequently to be passed on to the Sultan of Damascus as a stratagem for a planned kidnapping.[39] Christian I's above-mentioned, combined diplomatic mission and pilgrimage to Italy in 1474 seems not to have been exploited in this context either. Triumphantly greeted at the courts and cities of Milan, Mantua, Bologna, Florence and Rome, and even portrayed *all'antica* upon a medal by the Mantuan artist, Bartolomeo Melioli (Fig. 7a-b) in concordance with the eulogy of Nuvoloni, this representational modus had no visual repercussions in general to his other portraits, the

Fig. 8. Jacob Binck, Christian II, engraving after Jan Gossaert. Copenhagen, The National Gallery of Denmark, Print Room (Photo National Gallery).

king being shown in civil dress (cf. i.a. Fig. 7b) or in royal attire with crown and a long 'pilgrimage' beard.[40] Notwithstanding the apparent political and cultural outcome, i.e. the papal support to the establishment in 1479 of the University in Copenhagen (previously applied for by King Erick in 1419),[41] the potentials of the Italian sojourns of Christian I's and his Queen Dorothea of Brandenburg's later (1475 and 1488) did not lead to any more focused consumption of Italian art in Denmark, except from the import of luxury items, in particular textiles and jewellery, in exchange for fish and furs.[42] In parenthesis, this pattern was later followed by Christian II, ordering in 1515 costly jewellery for his bride from the Florentine goldsmith "Jacob Twriszani" (probably Jacopo Torrigiani), yet including diamonds from Constantinople, reportedly of a far better quality than deliveries from Florence and Venice.[43] In general, these early cases of cultural traffic between North and South, promoted as well by Danish representatives at the Curia in Rome,[44] at the universities in Northern Italy and in Venice, still await a more detailed scrutiny.

This goes also for the cultural implications of the dynastic relations, previous to the Reformation, with the Saxon court in the wake of the marriage in 1478 between King Hans and Christine of Saxony, great sister to the Elector, Frederick the Wise, the Queen's political and cultural activities, not in the least during her widowhood (1513-21), deserving comparison with those of Margaret of Austria, Regent of the Netherlands.[45] Though never visiting the home country after her marriage, Christine upheld a close contact with her Saxon family and may, i.a., well have been a mediator for the early dissemination of Albrecht Dürer's and Lucas Cranach the Elder's prints from the first two decades of the 16th century in Denmark, including their sporadic references to motifs in a hybrid Renaissance vocabulary, as reflected in the sculptures and paintings by her court artist, Claus Berg of Lübeck (cf. also below).[46]

A far more well-documented and targeted, though only temporary (1513-23), case of intense cultural exchange with the Netherlands resulted from Christian II's inclusion into the Habsburg *familia* at his marriage with the Emperor Maximilian I's granddaughter, Elisabeth, the match being highlighted as well c. 1515-18 in the printed Arch of Honor by Albrecht Dürer.[47] Apparently from the very first moment, the king grasped this rare opportunity to benefit from the open access to the dynamic political, economic and cultural melting pot, importing technical and scientific know-how and materials for minting, arms production and building, in particular boosting Copenhagen as a forthcoming international centre of commerce and culture. With no less enthusiasm, Christian II embraced the visual and mental models for the ostentatious parading of princely magnificence, following the standards of the 'Imperial style' - in its essence a pluralism of modes, combining Gothic in its modern Brabantine or Flamboyant versions with the Renaissance's classicizing repertoire of Italian stamp.[48] During his official visit to the Netherlands in 1521, the king and his retinue were even visually transformed, redressed in status-laden at-

Fig. 9. Frontispiece from the edition by Christiern Pedersen and Jodocus Badius Ascensius of Saxo Grammaticus, *Gesta Danorum*, Paris 1514. Copenhagen, The Danish Royal Library (Photo Royal Library).

tires of the latest local fashion. At the same time, Christian II was the object of a number of triumphal entries, while his features were perpetuated in paintings, drawings, sculptures and medals.[49] The king's involuntary exile in spring 1523 became a hindrance to his promising enterprises in Denmark, which in several respects might have anticipated the cultural blooming of Frederik II's reign by almost half a century. This includes in particular his targeted import of foreign experts, as mentioned above an issue of no criticism half a century later.[50] Also Christian II's subsequent use of Netherlandish and German prints during the exile for propaganda purposes, i.a. distributing his own portraits framed by a triumphant arch (Fig. 8), and his open predilection for the refined classizing vocabulary of Jan Gossaert for the funeral monument in St. Peter's in Ghent for Queen Elisabeth (d. 1526),[51] leaves no doubts as to his tastes and ambitions – for political purposes at this early stage to appropriate the Renaissance in its North European version into Denmark.

The Imperial impact upon the cultural policy of Christian II not only implied an inspiration from Maximilian I's strategic campaigns of 'marketing' through public media, but gained no less momentum from the Emperor's vital concern for the 'gedechtnus'. In the quest for political status, his lobbyists diligently promoted the myth of the superiority of *Germania*, the Holy Roman Empire, as the true follower to *Imperium Romanum* through the cultivation - heavily relying upon inspirations from Italian humanists - of the national *antiquitas*, as reflected in historiography, the visual arts, heraldry and genealogy.[52] Also in Denmark, a similar target-oriented obsession with the native past formed during the first decades of the 16th century a symbiosis with activities, equally directed towards the future, including humanistic studies, Neo-Latin literature and classicizing epigraphy as well as the introduction of a Renaissance vocabulary in visual arts and architecture, particularly in ornamentation.[53]

Of great ideological importance and obviously directly related to the Habsburg marriage was the *editio princeps* in Paris 1514 of Saxo Grammaticus' *Gesta Danorum* from c. 1200, published as a joint venture by Lage Urne, Bishop at Roskilde, the humanist Christiern Pedersen and the Flemish-born editor, Jodocus Badius Ascensius, the latter praising this initiative as "an omen (*praesagio*) of a better and more learned century in Denmark".[54] As previously indicated, this work not only earned Erasmus' and his contemporaries' praise of the Danes' literacy and spurned the competitive spirit of Swedish historians, but it also became a major impetus to the creative approach to the past. The frontispiece of the volume (Fig. 9) combines in an intriguing way the visual languages of tradition and innovation, the main image of a Danish king, clad in a traditional cuirass (probably a hidden portrait of Christian II) and the text in Gothic minuscule being framed by an architectural border with 'antique' arabesque ornaments, medallions and figures, possibly of North Italian

Fig. 10. Claus Berg (attr.), Wall monument King John and Queen Christine, including Prince Frans, c. 1513-1523, formerly in Odense, Greyfriars' Church, now in Odense Cathedral (Photo National Museum, Copenhagen).

extraction, though with the inclusion of 'unclassical' dragons, maybe a deliberate reference to Old Norse Antiquity.[55] These framing references to past and present would be repeated for new purposes the following year in Pedersen's Danish edition of biblical texts and sermons, *Jærtegns Postil*, also printed in Paris.[56]

The rhetoric messages of diachronicity and of frames – subordinated, yet illuminating and commenting the main image[57] – are also reflected in the great wall monument, ascribed to Claus Berg, for King Hans and Queen Christine from c. 1513-21 (Fig. 10), formerly in the royal funerary chancel of Greyfriars' Church in Odense. The central representation of the royal couple with their minor son, prince Frans, is encircled by a heraldic border and accompanied by a narrow frieze with a hybrid mixture of grotesque figures and candelabra motifs of classical and medieval origin, in fact one of the earliest incidents in Denmark of decoration in 'antique' manner, though in single details copied from a contemporary (1513) South German print.[58] Equally reflecting the patroness' (Queen Christine) pluralistic preferences, the monument should be regarded in context with the mausoleum's furnishings, in particular with the lavishly gilded and ornamented retable by Claus Berg, according to the verdict of Sebastian Münster, a "*mirabile & artificiosissimum opus (…), cuius simile in Europa non invenitur*".[59] The sporadic inclusion of classical decorative motifs and a sense of perspective space (cf. Marianne Marcussen, pp. 153 ff.), equally mediated through printings, was however subordinated to a rich, vegetal ornamentation, to be paralleled with other contemporary examples (retables and wall paintings), covering the architectural structures with a visually vibrant texture of Paradisian exuberance, eventually reflecting as well the *renovatio* aspirations of Reform Catholicism.[60] At the same time, the examples might be brought in common with Continental monuments of 'Renaissance Gothic' or 'La Gothique de la Renaissance',[61] though it should not be concealed that Danish architecture lacks more sophisticated specimens of tracery decorations or intricate patterns of vault and tower designs. A potential example, though, alas, never erected, might have been the project drawing from 1521 by the architect, Master Michiel from Haarlem, for a tree-storied spire upon the so-called Bakery Tower at Copenhagen Castle, made 'according to the art of geometry'.[62]

Cultivating tradition and retrospection in relation to the national past were issues, in particular reflected in the funeral culture of the power elite, restoring or renewing burial spaces or monuments.[63] An early incident of apparent antiquarianism was witnessed in 1512 in relation to the Cathedral of Lund, where the Archbishop Birger Gunnersen had planned to erect a private funerary chapel to the north of the building. Confronted with the project, King Hans however, ordered the Archbishop to stop his works and to restore the walls of the church, equally respecting the previous structure and the building's visual appearance and firmness ("Som hon førsthe sinnæ bygdh war meth, baadæ for synlighett och fasthedh"),[64] giving, though probably at random, associations towards two basic Vitruvian terms of *Venustas* and *Firmitas*.[65] Instead the Archbishop was recommended to reform ("reformeræ") the crypt. The freestanding tumba for Birger Gunnarson (d.1519), of a type hitherto being a royal prerogative, was erected during the following years by the probably Westphalian sculptor, Adam van Düren, in a remarkably simplified manner, possibly in deliberate harmony with the surrounding architecture of early 12th century Romanesque.[66]

The wish to confront and commemorate individual 'heroes' of the distant past in respect to the national history in general or to related sites of memory in particular, became an incentive to early cultivators of Humanism already during the first decades of the 16th century. Descriptions of the Danish mythic figure, Holger Danske (Ogier le Danois), paladin at the court of Charlemagne and according to the legends conqueror of India as well, were issued 1521 (1534) at the instigation of Christian II by Christiern Pedersen, to be accompanied by retrospective wall-paintings in Skævinge, a parish church close to Helsinge, the domicile of Pedersen, and possibly also in Aarhus Cathedral.[67] The visual translation of anachronism was particularly expressed in the former case through the hybrid language of contemporary and 'antique' dress, the accompanying inscriptions displaying a mixture of Romanesque majuscules and Early Humanistic capitals. The activities, centred around this Danish role model, deserves comparison with the contemporary cult of Roland, Siegfried and King Arthur in France, Germany and England, constructing historic 'credulity' (or forgery) in the service of a superior political agenda.[68] A similar case of creativity was reflected in the establishment of funeral memorials in Roskilde Cathedral for the historian Saxo Grammaticus, as previously mentioned a canon figure in the Danish *renovatio* movement. At the initiative of Bishop Lage Urne (d. 1529), a painted wall tablet (renovated in 1728) with a flowering epitaph in Neo-Latin elegiac distichs, written in Humanistic italics, was placed in the northern crossing, referring to the tomb of Saxo in the floor beneath. A worn-off medieval slab of grey-blue limestone from Öland, covering a burial of dubious contents, was apparently the Bishop's 'archaeological' evidence to his – highly questionably – advocacy for the historian's affiliation to Roskilde.[69]

A commemorative performance of related programmatic status, yet based upon much firmer grounds was the reburial in the former Cistercian Monastery Church of Sorø, of Archbishop Absalon (c. 1128-1201), immediately in the wake of the official introduction of Lutheran Reformation in 1536. Venerating the great Danish *primarius* and politician, Christian III ordered an opening of his burial in the choir, followed by a symbolic translation of power from the old Roman Catholic to the new Lutheran Church, at the placement of Absalon's ring upon the finger of his successor in office, Bishop Peder Palladius. In memory of the act, a former wooden monument was replaced by a modern tomb slab of limestone from Gotland, ascribed to the sculptor Morten Bussert and displaying the magic year of 1536. The slab showed the portrait of Absalon and his two relatives (in hierarchical diminutive) (Fig. 11) set in an architectural 'antique' frame with candelabra and putti, comparable to the former examples, illustrating, too, the strategic readiness of the Lutheran church to adapt forms of (Early Christian) Antiquity (see also Hanne Kolind Poulsen, p. 147). In this case, however, it was anticipated by a few years older, now lost, Neo-Latin epitaph, composed by Lage Urne, presenting an eulogy in classical mode of Absalon, 'the Sun of Denmark', comparable even to Achilles and Plato.[70]

A major approval of the visual language of classicism, equally denoting venerable age and modernity, is reflected in Christian III's large Seal of Majesty from 1546, ascribed to Jacob Binck of Cologne, showing for the first time the king framed by a classical triumphal arch, while surrounded by traditional emblems of territorial coats-of-arms.[71] Yet, the Danish kings, who as previously mentioned at least since the late 15th century had been familiar with this particular distinction of honor and princely power *all' an-*

Fig. 11. Morten Bussert (attr.), Tomb slab of Archbishop Absalon, c. 1536, Sorø Abbey church (Photo National Museum, Copenhagen).

tica, apparently till the late 16th century abstained in actual ceremonial contexts from exploiting its potentials, contrary to (and maybe even deliberately adverse to) the example of the Swedish 'archenemy', Erik XIV having already introducing the motif in 1563 (and 1568).[72] However, the monumentalizing in stone of the triumphal arch in the funeral monument of Christian III by Cornelis Floris (1574-75), virtually demonstrated, not only the increasing powers of the classical language, already given an official blue-print in the sculptor's funeral monument in Schleswig for Frederik I (1549-55), but even was the occasion for Frederik II's open creed to innovation and princely magnificence, the king boasting of the tomb to his sister Anna, the Electress of Saxony, to be of a standard "that hitherto no other king in Denmark had got the like", nor could its similar even be found in Germany according to Henrik Rantzau, Governor of the Duchies.[73] Nevertheless, the respect to continuity and the past was equally expressed through Frederik II's choice of his grave, though not respecting his father's wish to be buried in Odense Cathedral, the pantheon of Denmark's distinguished Royal saint, St. Canute,[74] but instead preferring a similar venerable locus, the cathedral of Roskilde in Zeeland, since the Early Middle Ages containing the tombs of a number of Danish kings and queens. Accordingly, Christian III's *gisant* was presented in the cuirass of medieval tradition, not 'dressed up' in antique fashion.

Concluding Remarks

Presenting in 1571 a retrospective picture of the period, regarded from the perspective of the 76-year old Johan Friis (1494-1570), the young historian and author of Friis' funeral sermon, Anders Sørensen Vedel pointed out that the great statesman, actively serving no less than four kings, had witnessed an age of 'strange changes (…) never before experienced in living memory in the spiritual as well as in the secular regime'.[75]

Taking his point of departure in this illustrating statement, the art historian Otto Norn in 1961 gave a pertinent analysis of Friis' activity as patron of architecture and the arts with particular emphasis on his main residence in Funen, Hesselagergaard, 'erected (from) anew' as strategically proclaimed by the building tablet, dated 1538, at the entrance (Fig. 12a-b).[76] Novelty, in particular represented by the semi-circular gables of Italian off-spring, added c. 1550 during a second building campaign and repeated upon the local church, are indeed conspicuous codes of meaning in this, the most prominent among Friis' three manor houses (cf. Hanne Kolind

Fig. 12a-b. Hesselagergaard, Building tablets, 1538, a. averse, b. reverse of the lowest part with an unidentified (profane?) representation (Photo National Museum, Copenhagen).

Poulsen and Uwe Albrecht, pp. 146 ff., 202).[77] Yet, no less prominent is the pluralism of interchanging visual models and meanings, representing a composite product of the patron's personal preferences and the contributions of the involved artists' whether natives or foreigners. Indeed, this extraordinary micro-historical case deserves mention as a concluding marker as well, illuminating as a *pars pro toto* the multifarious approach to alterity or to 'the Renaissance idiom' in the first half of the 16th century Denmark, at one and the same time looking back to the past and forward to posterity, taking point of departure in local materials and manners, while in an unorthodox way selecting and appropriating a polyphony of stylistic or iconographical motifs into the decorative frameworks.

Like Frederiksborg Castle, Hesselagergaard virtually represented its originator, his political status and cultural horizon. Johan Friis was a versatile 'man of all seasons', in writing and actions furthering the Lutheran Reformation, well-educated and cosmopolitan in his outlook, due to travels and contacts abroad (including Italy), and during a life-long administrative career building up his singular political position from a comparatively modest basis. A particular incentive to innovation and self-expression was the respect for dynastic tradition and historical continuity. Originally erecting his entailed estate upon, almost, virginal ground in traditional forms, architectural references to the past was not left out, while 'modern' dispositions of plan and decorative details mingled with reused *spolia* (cf. fig. 12b), i.a. from demolished parish churches. The 'speaking' interiors, so far only explored in detail for the western part of the house, combined instructing inscriptions from the Bible, classical and contemporary (Erasmus) authors with allegories, heraldry, historical or religious motifs and genre scenes. Of special status was the impressive frieze of life-size male and female stags, typologically referring like genealogical representations to dynastic fertility.[78] In equal mood was Johan Friis' care for the memory of his ancestors in Odense Greyfriars' Church and Hesselager Church, for the benefit of the descendants also prospectively modernizing the buildings with wall paintings and new furnishings.

The glorification of *patriæ mores* and the learning of older generations runs as a red line through the funeral sermon as well, firing a broadside at the example of present times and the new generations, who praised 'unvirtuousnesss, barbarity and every obscene, evil, new inventions'.[79] Indeed, retrospection towards the native past and the respect for continuity, reflected in every strata of society, in particular at the royal court as well as among members of the nobility and the higher clergy, should until the second half of the 16th century represent a strong contra-productive force – as one among several other hindrances against the unconditional or more 'pure' embracement of the Renaissance in Denmark, yet not in certain areas excluding an openness to recent developments.

Indeed, the example of Danish art and architecture, already from the first part of the century should be paralleled with other 'hybrid' or 'bastard' renaissances' (cf. Introduction, p. 13), displaying a horizontal co-existence of cultural diversity or of multiple styles and meanings. Admittedly, economical, political and religious factors up to a certain extent were obstacles during this early period to the unbridled will to modernity and magnificence, as reflected during the later reigns of Frederik II and Christian IV. Yet, as indicated, up-to-date patterns (or projects) and cases of cultural traffic between North and South can be detected already under Christian II, Frederik I and Christian III. A polyphony of foreign voices, preferably of German and Netherlandish origin, were equally present at the early stages, yet counterbalanced by indigenously conditioned social, political and religious contexts, as well as by local materials and native masters. This endows 'The Danish Renaissance', also in its first moments, with a multifaceted physiognomy of its own, yet to some degree in comparison admittedly being piecemeal, provincial or of limited aesthetic quality. At the same time the accusation for 'peripherization' or 'un-Danishness', due to the not-native artistic representation, should be reconsidered. As emphasized in relation to the artistic status at Naples during the Late Middle Ages and Early Modern Time, the prominent presence of foreign artists and works of art in a particular area should not one-sidedly be regarded as an expression of cultural weakness. Instead, this element might as well be evaluated as a sign of intentional enrichment and a foundation for freedom of choice,

essentially defining a centre.[80] At the end, the Danish 'periphery', in itself constituting 'a centre' (or even a number of co-existing centers, when regarded in a socio-symbolic context), also in this connection displayed a composite picture, not so very different to other parts of contemporary Europe.

Notes

1 Following in the main the disposition of the introductory paper, the author in the present essay has deliberately given references in more details, exploiting this opportunity to include literature on Danish issues, probably not familiar to an international audience.

2 Cf. Johan Adam Berg, *Kurtze und eigentliche Beschreibung Des fürtrefflichen und weitberühmten Königlichen Hauses Friedrichsburg in Seeland gelegen (…),* Copenhagen 1646, HivB; Lauritz de Thurah, *Den Danske Vitruvius* II, Copenhagen 1749, 47; Johan Peter Rasbech, *Frederiksborg Slots Beskrivelse*, Copenhagen 1832, 167.

3 Among lost monuments from this period, not to mention the rich material of drawings and documentary sources, all eliminated through active or passive acts of forgetting, including renovating, in this context considered equally destructive, are several royal residences, a.o. Copenhagen Castle (torn down c. 1731), Kronborg Castle (burned in 1629 and plundered 1659-60), the castles of Lundehave (Marienlyst) and Jægersborg in Northern Zealand, Nykøbing in Falster, Skanderborghus and Koldinghus in East Jutland and of Hansborg, Grøngård and Tønderhus in Schleswig-Holstein. Several aristocratic manor houses have equally suffered destruction or reconstruction, the most grievous loss being the astronomer Tycho Brahe's Temple of Wisdom, Uraniborg, at the island of Hven, already demolished at royal instigation as an act of *damnatio memoriae* in the 17th century. Urban architecture from the period, in particular in the metropolis of Copenhagen, is today only sparsely represented, in the last case a.o. due to the city fires of 1728 and 1795, and the English bombardment of 1807. In contrast, the majority of Danish parish and city churches still to a large extent reflect the multifaceted image of the period's religious art and architecture, comprising not only new items, acquired in the wake of the Lutheran Reformation since the 1530's, but also several remnants from the Catholic era.

4 Berg 1646, Biij v- Biv r., Miv r (poem by Joachim Gerdes).

5 Recently, Steffen Heiberg (ed.), *Christian 4. og Fre-*

deriksborg, Copenhagen 2006; Mette Bligaard, *Frederiksborgs genrejsning. Historicisme i teori og praksis*, 1-2, Copenhagen 2008.

6   Steffen Heiberg, "Introduction", in: Heiberg (ed.) 2006, 7.

7   For the expression, cf. Bernd Roeck, "Introduction", in: Herman Roodenburg (ed.), *Forging European Identities, 1400-1700*, Cambridge 2007 (Robert Muchembled & William Monter (eds.), *Cultural Exchange in Early Modern Europe* IV), 23.

8   Cf. also Gérard Sabatier, *Versailles ou la figure du roi*, Paris 1999; Matthias Müller, *Das Schloß als Bild des Fürsten. Herrschaftliche Metaphorik in der Residenzarchitektur des Alten Reiches*, Göttingen 2004.

9   A preliminary analysis of the decorations in these rooms as well as the so-called Summer Room, is Sebastian Olden-Jørgensen, "Sommerstuen, Slotskirken og Dansesalen", in: Heiberg (ed.) 2006, 115-131, spec. 121-131; on the Palace Church, cf. Hugo Johannsen, "Slotskirken", in: Heiberg (ed.) 2006, 133-151. On the restoration of the Great Hall, cf. Bligaard 2008, 2, 99-110.

10 The figure of *Memoria* with a pair of scales is represented in a contemporary print by the Flemish engraver, Martin Baes in his and Charles Musart, *Adolescens academicus seu institutionis Salomonis*, Douai 1633, though illustrating a different message of *Memento Mori*.

11 Olden-Jørgensen 2006, 124-128, points to the inconsistency of previous descriptions of the cycle from the 17th-19th centuries and numbers *Memoria* together with *Pietas*, *Sinceritas*, *Virtus* and *Intelligentia* as representations of virtues and intellectual forces of common human relevance.

12 Cf. the motto: "*Præteri(t)os memori et prudens si respicis actus ad res præsentes hinc erit utilitas*".

13 Berg 1646, BiiA-B.

14 Aleida Assmann, "Gedächtnis als Leitbegriff der Kulturwissenschaften", in: Lutz Musner & Gotthart Wunberg (eds.), *Kulturwissenschaften: Forschung – Praxis – Positionen*, Vienna 2002, 27-45.

15 Hayden White, "Catastrophe, Communal Memory and Mythic Discourse: The Uses of Myth in the Reconstruction of Society", in: Bo Stråth (ed.), *Myth and Memory in the Construction of Community*, Brussels 2000, 49-74, spec. 51.

16 Steffen Heiberg (ed.), *Christian IV and Europe. The 19th Art Exhibition of the Council of Europe*, Copenhagen 1988. See also "Introduction", 9, 13.

17 Quoted from Vilho Niitema, *Der Kaiser und die Nordische Union bis zu den Burgunderkriegen* (*Annales Academiae Scientiarum Fennicae*, B 116), Helsinki 1960, 228. On Piccolomini's descriptions of Denmark, cf. most recently Michael von Cotta-Schønberg, "De Daniae regno aliqua non indigna cognitu: Danmarksbilledet hos en italiensk renæsssancehumanist, Æneas Silvius Piccolomini (Pius II)", in: Lars Bisgaard, Jacob Isager & Janus Møller Jensen (eds.), *Renæssancen i svøb. Dansk renæssance i europæisk belysning 1450-1550*, Odense 2008, 83-110.

18 Filippo Nuvoloni, *Oratio ad Serenissium Dominum Christiernum Datiae, Norvegiae, Suetiae, Gothorum Slavorumque Regem*, (Mantua) 1474, here quoted after: Vivian Etting, Rodolfo Signorini & Birgitte Werdelin (eds.), *Fra Christian I's Italiensrejse 1474*, Copenhagen 1984, 76, 82. In 1526, the Danish humanist, Christiern Pedersen in his vernacular version of the speech, translated 'the Goths' into 'the Danes', a possible biased plea in the Dano-Swedish 'Gothicist controversy', cf. 51-52, 55-56, 58-65 and below.

19 Cf. von Cotta-Schönberg 2008, 90.

20 Lockhart 2007, 1, with bibliography, 261-268. An authoritative introduction in English by a Danish historian is Knud J. V. Jespersen, *A History of Denmark*, Basingstoke 2004, proffering as well as Lockhart from recent Danish and international research from the latest decades. In the following survey, Denmark should be used as a super ordinate for the composite communion of territories.

21 Cf. in particular Janus Møller Jensen, *Denmark and the Crusades 1400-1650*, Leiden & Boston 2007 (Barbara Crawford et al. (eds.), *The Northern World. North Europe and the Baltic c. 400-1700 A. D. Peoples, Economics and Cultures* 30). Further Janus Møller Jensen, "Humanister, korstog og kortlægningen af det yderste nord", in: Bisgaard, Isager & Møller Jensen (eds.) 2008, 215-244; Lars Bisgaard, „Kampen om enhjørningen. Christian IIs planlagte Grønlandstogt 1514-22 i danske kalkmalerier", in: Bisgaard, Isager & Møller Jensen (eds.) 2008, 245-278.

22 Axel Bjørnbo, "Adam af Bremens Nordensopfattelse", *Aarbøger for nordisk Oldkyndighed og Historie* 2, XXIV (1909), 120-244, in particular 191-193; Møller Jensen 2008, 236. On the representative value of cartography as a reflection on and an instrument of power, cf. i.a. Karl Schlögel, *Im Raume lessen wir die Zeit. Über Zivilisationsgeschichte und Geopolitik*, Munich and Vienna 2003, in particular 81ff.

23 Here quoted after Peter Burke, *The European Renaissance: Centres and Peripheries*, Oxford 1998, 97.

24 Lockhart 2007, 2-4.

25 A coming survey of art and architecture of the Early Lutheran church in Denmark is Birgitte Bøggild Johannsen & Hugo Johannsen, "Re-forming the Confessional Space: Early Lutheran Churches in Denmark

c. 1536-1600", in: Andrew Spicer & Margit Thøfner (eds.), *Lutheran Churches in Early Modern Europe*, Oxford (forthcoming).

26 The dilemma was discussed in reference to the marriage plans of Frederik II, cf. Joh. Grundtvig, "Et Frieri af Kong Frederik II. i 1566-68", *Meddelelser fra Rentekammerarchivet* I (1871-1876), 100-113.

27 Étienne François & Hagen Schulze (eds.) *Deutsche Erinnerungsorte*, 1-3, Munich 2001, I, 389ff.; a recent survey of the Danish-Swedish rivalry 1563-1720 is Knud J. V. Jespersen, „Kappestrid uden sejrherre. Den dansk-svenske rivalisering 1563-1720", in: Janus Møller Jensen (ed.), *Slaget ved Nyborg 1659. Historie, arkæologi og erindring*, Nyborg 2009, 18-30.

28 Uffe Østergård, "The Geopolitics of Nordic Identity – From Composite States to Nation-States", in: Øystein Sørensen & Bo Stråth (eds.), *The Cultural Construction of Norden*, Oxford et al. 1997, 25-71, pointing equally to the tendency in the 19th century Scandinavian countries, to downplay the Baltic and the European component of their national identifications, forming a transnational common Nordic identity.

29 The intensified cultural, commercial and political contacts with Europe and the Orient during the Late Middle Ages (ranging to c. 1550) have been analysed in Per Ingesman and Bjørn Poulsen (eds.), *Danmark og Europa i senmiddelalderen*, Aarhus 2000; equally in Bisgaard, Isager & Møller Jensen (eds.) 2008. On the educational travels of Danes, generally Vello Helk, *Dansk-norske studierejser fra reformationen til enevælden 1536-1660. Med en matrikel over studerende i udlandet*, Copenhagen 1987; Vello Helk, "Den danske adels dannelsesrejser i Europa 1536-1660", in: Per Ingesman & Jens Villiam Jensen (eds.), *Riget, magten og æren. Den danske adel 1350-1660*, Århus 2001, 524-556, espec. 541, on Danish noblemen, venturing yearlong travels to Asia Minor, Constantinople, Palestine and Egypt. Yet, the Near-Eastern expeditions in the last decades of the 16th century of the Councillor Jacob Ulfeldt and the nobleman Christian Barnekow apparently did not have marked consequences to their private consumption of art. On the singular case of the Danish painter, Melchior Lorck and his travels to Constantiople, see the article by Mikael Bøgh Rasmussen, p. 165 ff. Contact with the Muslim world, motivated by projects of crusades and pilgrimages, was also a reality to be reckoned with after the Lutheran Reformation, see Møller Jensen 2007. On Danish colonial art and architecture in Tranquebar, India, cf. a.o. Karin Kryger, "Kirkerne i Tranquebar i den danske periode 1620-1845, *Architectura* 29 (2007), 57-90. Royal ceremonials equally gave occasion to exchange between the European courts. Several royal heralds, serving as cultural agents as well during the 16th century, were foreigners, the Scottish born David Kock (d. c. 1529), the Spanish Franciscus de Medina (d. 1553, cf. Fig. 6), the French Claus Fontein (d.1566) and the probably Italian-born Johannes Baptista Giudeti (d. before 1580), cf. Ernst Verwohlt, "Kongelige danske heroldér", *Heraldisk Tidsskrift* 3, 25 (1972), 201-229. Master of ceremonies was also the Danish nobleman, Jørgen Lykke, 1532-43/44 serving at the court of the King Francis I, contemporary to the diplomatic mission here of Frants Brockenhuus. On the international (though not mentioning the royal heralds) or preferably German influences on Danish court culture, in particular from the age of Christian IV, cf. basically Mara R. Wade, *Triumphus nuptialis Danicus. German Court Culture and Denmark. The Great Wedding of 1634,* Wiesbaden 1996. A case-study on the Polish, Netherlandish and German influences on the funeral ceremonies of Frederik II in 1588 is Birgitte Bøggild Johannsen, "The Polish Paradigm. On the Heraldic Funeral of King Frederik II of Denmark and its European Context, in: Harasimowicz, Oszczanowski & Wisłocki (eds.) 2006, II, 555-568. Cultural exchange through the agency of music and musicians during the reign of Christian III is in particular studied by Ole Kongsted, cf. "'Jeg sender nogle nye messer...'. Om Rasmus Heinssen og repertoiret i Christian 3.s kantori i midten af 1500-tallet", *Fund og Forskning* 46 (2007), 37-55; Ole Kongsted, "Til Guds pris, Majestætens ære og Rigets gavn'. Om Matz Hack og hans virke som kongelig sangmester ved Christian IIIs hof", in: Bisgaard, Isager & Møller Jensen (eds.) 2008, 279-303.

30 Here quoted after Harald Ilsøe, "Danskerne og deres fædreland. Holdninger og opfattelser ca. 1550-1700", in: Ole Feldbæk (ed.), *Fædreland og Modersmål 1536-1789* (*Dansk identitetshistorie* 1), Copenhagen 1991, 71.

31 Peter Burke, "Cultures of Translation in Early Modern Europe" and "Translating Histories" in: Peter Burke & R. Po-Chia Hsia (eds.), *Cultural Translation in Early Modern Europe,* Cambridge 2007, 7-38 and 125-141, numbering (p. 24) only two examples of historical works being translated into Danish.

32 Lange 1895 in Brandes & Købke (eds.) 1900, I, 1.

33 Hans Svaning, *Refutatio calumniarum cuiusdam Ioannis Upsalensis (…) Huic accessit Chronicon sive Historia Joannis Regis Daniæ (…) 1560*, s.l. 1561, 53.

34 Johannes Magnus, *De omnibus gothorum sveonumque regibus*, Rome 1554; on the 'Gothicist controversy', during the 16th and 17th century embodying the political conflicts between Denmark and Sweden, cf. in particular Kurt Johannesson, *The Renaissance of the Goths in Sixteenth-Century Sweden*, Berkeley & Oxford 1991; Skovgaard-Petersen 2002, in particular 93-104; Inge Schmidt-Voges, *De antiqva claritate et clara antiqui-*

tate Gothorum. Gotizismus als Identitätsmodell im frühneuzeitlichen Sweden, Frankfurt 2004; Niels Werner Frederiksen, "Nationale fjendebilleder. Rimkrøniken og de dansk-svenske relationer 1495-1613", in: Henrik Blicher et al. (eds.), *Tænkesedler. 20 fortællinger af fædrelandets litteraturhistorie. Festskrift til Flemming Lundgreen-Nielsen*, Copenhagen 2007, 25-37; Karen Skovgaard-Petersen, "Arguments against Barbarism. Early Native, Literary Culture in three Scandinavian National Histories", *Renæssanceforum* 5 (2008) 1-16; Christoffer Neville, "Gothicism and Early Modern Historical Ethnography", *Journal of the History of Ideas* 70,2 (2009) 213-234. A bias against the demonstrative representation of princely magnificence, referring to classical and contemporary prototypes, expressed at the funeral of Gustav Vasa in 1560 and the coronation of Eric XIV the following year may as well have been at stake, cf. Bøggild Johannsen 2006b; further, Birgitte Bøggild Johannsen, "Conflit, Concurrence et Coévolution. Pratiques autour de la mort des rois et reines danois et suèdois à l'epoque moderne", in Mark Hengerer & Gérard Sabatier (eds.), *Mémoire monarchique et la construction de l'Europe aux XVI-XVIII siècles. Papers from two international conferences at Cracow and Madrid 2007-08* (forthcoming); on the early use of triumphal arches in Sweden, cf. Inga Lena Ångström-Grandien, "The Reception of the Classical Ideal in Swedish 16th Century Art and Architecture", in: Krista Kodres et al. (eds.), *The Problem of Classical Ideal in the Art and Architecture of the Countries around the Baltic Sea*, Tallinn 2003, 32-54, espec. 42.

35 Marius Kristensen (ed.), *Skrifter af Paulus Helie*, 1-7, Copenhagen 1932-38, 2, 179, 270-271.

36 Cf. the verdict from Jutlandish Council members, already uttered in December 1522, quoted in Mikael Venge, *Bondekær eller tyran? Tekster til Christian II's regime, politik og personlighed*, Odense 1975, 7. The opinions were later elaborated in the coronation charter of Frederik I in August 3 (March 26) 1523 and expressed as well by Paulus Helie, cf. Kristensen (ed.),1, 174; see also Birgitte Bøggild Johannsen, "Promising Enterprises and Broken Dreams: Netherlandish Architectural Influences in Denmark during the Early 16th Century", in Krista de Jonge & Konrad Ottenheym (eds.), *The Low Countries at the Crossroads. Netherlandish Architecture as an Export Product in Early Modern Europe (1480-1680). Papers from an international symposium at Heverlee, 2008* (forthcoming, a).

37 Cf. E. C. Werlauff, *De hellige Tre Kongers Kapel (…)*, Copenhagen 1849, 44, note z; *Kancelliets Brevbøger, 1556-1560,* Copenhagen 1887-88, 65. Further Birgitte Bøggild Johannsen, "Til Kongens og Rigets behov. Nogle betragtninger om kunstforbruget ved Frederik II's hof", *Renæssanceforum* 2 (2006), 1-28, in particular 14 f.

38 Cf. note 29. On a number of Danish scholars, studying during the age of Christian III, in Italy, cf. Isak Mouritsen Gilleleje's epitaph for Johannes Pratensis, 1576, quoted in Holger Fr. Rørdam, *Kjøbenhavns Universitets Historie fra 1537-1621*, 4, Copenhagen 1868-74, 111-115.

39 Cf. Heinz Barüske, *Erich von Pommern. Ein nordischer König aus dem Greifengeschlecht*, Rostock 1997, 163-177. On a contemporary portrait drawing of King Erik, with Sigismund, later German Emperor and John VIII Palaeologus, cf. Imre Takács (ed.), *Sigismundus Rex et Imperator. Kunst und Kultur zur Zeit Sigismund von Luxemburg 1387-1437,* Mainz 2006 (Exhibition Catalogue), 452-453.

40 The portraits of Christian I, in particular in Mantova, Malpaga and Rome, are analysed in Rodolfo Signorini, *Opvs hoc tenve. La "architipata" Camera Dipinta detta "degli Sposi" di Andrea Mantegna,* Mantova 2007, 61-78, 228-249. On the medals of the King, cf. also Kirsten Bendixen, "Medailleportrætter af de ældste oldenborgske konger", *Nationalmuseets Arbejdsmark* (1979), 68-69; Filippo Trevisani (ed.), *Andrea Mantegna e i Gonzaga. Rinascimento nel Castello di San Giorgio*, Milan 2006 (Exhibition Catalogue), 140 (cat. no. I,10).

41 Martin Schwarz Lausten, "Københavns Universitet i middelalderen 1479-ca. 1530", in: S. Ellehøj et al. (eds.), *Københavns Universitet 1479-1979*, I, Copenhagen 1991, 1-77, espec. 27-30.

42 Cf. Signorini 2007; previous Danish accounts are C. Paludan-Müller, "Kong Christiern den Førstes Rejser i Tydskland og Italien i Aarene 1474 og 1475", *Historisk Tidsskrift* 5,2 (1880-1881), 241-347; Johannes Lindbæk, "Dorothea, Kristiern den Førstes Dronning, og Familien Gonzaga, *Historisk Tidsskrift* 7,3 (1900-1902), 455-512; more recently Stephen Turk Christensen, "Christian I's promovering af Rom som pilgrimsby", in: Ingesman & Poulsen (eds.) 2000, 134-159; Per Ingesman, "Den danske konges repræsentanter ved renæssancepavernes hof", in: Ingesman & Poulsen (eds.) 2000, 160-182; Stephen Turk Christensen, "Introduction", *Scandinavian Journal of History* 28, 3-4 (2003), 151-164, espec. 152.

43 L. Moltesen et al. (eds.), *Acta Pontificum. Pavelige Aktstykker vedrørende Danmark 1316-1536*, I-VII, Copenhagen 1904-43, VI, nr. 4526 (3 June 1515).

44 See further Per Ingesman, *Provisioner og processer. Den romerske Rota og dens behandling af danske sager i middelalderen*, Aarhus 2003.

45 Cf. Birgitte Bøggild Johannsen,"Genealogical Representation in Gendered Perspective: on a Lost Royal Mausoleum from Early Sixteenth-Century Denmark", in: Truus van Bueren & Andrea van Leerdam (eds.), *Care for the Here and the Hereafter:* Memoria, *Art and Ritual in the Middle Ages*, Turnhout 2005, 79-105.

These connections, alas, never became an issue during the recent exposition of the Danish-Saxon relations in Dresden and Copenhagen, cf. Jutta Kappel & Claudia Brink (eds.), *Mit Fortuna übers Meer. Sachsen und Dänemark – Ehen und Allianzen im Spiegel der Kunst (1548-1709)*, Dresden 2009.

46 See Jan Friedrich Richter, *Claus Berg. Retabelproduktion des Spätmittelalters im Ostseeraum*, Berlin 2007.

47 Cf. Bøggild Johannsen (forthcoming, a).

48 See "Introduction", 13 and note 19. On the 'Imperial style' and its pluralism, cf. also. Bob van der Boogert, "Macht en pracht. Het mecenaat van Maria van Hongarije", in: Bob van den Boogert & Jacqueline Kerhoff (eds.), *Maria van Hongarije, koningin tussen keizers en kunstenaars, 1505-1558*, 's-Hertogenbosch & Utrecht 1993, 269-301; Ariane Mensger, *Jan Gossaert. Die niederländische Kunst zu Beginn der Neuzeit*, Berlin 2002, 95-107.

49 Lars Hendrikman, "Portrait and Politics. Evolution in the Depiction of King Christian II of Denmark during his Reign and Exile (1531-1531)", in: Hanno Brand (ed.), *Trade, Diplomacy and Cultural Exchange*, Hilversum 2005 (Groningen Hanze Studies, 1), 186-210. On his activitiy as a collector, receiving a.o. a collection of prints from Albrecht Dürer, cf. Bøggild Johannsen (forthcoming, a).

50 Cf. Bøggild Johannsen (forthcoming, a). On Frederik II's use of foreign artists, also recently Bøggild Johannsen 2006c.

51 On the portraits, cf. Mària van Berge-Gerbaud, "Some "Background" Information", in: Villads Villadsen et al. (eds.), *Festschrift to Erik Fischer. European Drawings from six Centuries*, Copenhagen 1990, 279-294; on the tomb, cf. Mensger 2002, 104-106; Birgitte Bøggild Johannsen, "Køn, magt og minde. Omkring den rituelle og monumentale iscenesættelse af senmiddelalderens dronningebegravelser", in: Agnes S. Arnórsdottir, Per Ingesman & Bjørn Poulsen (eds.), *Konge, kirke og samfund. De to øvrighedsmagter i dansk senmiddelalder*, Aarhus 2007, 179-218, spec. 214-215; Bøggild Johannsen (forthcoming, a).

52 Cf. recently Larry Silver, *Marketing Maximilian. The visual Ideology of a Holy Roman Emperor*, Princeton & Oxford 2008; Christopher S. Wood, *Forgery, Replica, Fiction. Temporalities of German Renaissance Art*, Chicago & London 2008.

53 Friis-Jensen 1989; Friis-Jensen 1991; Schwarz Lausten 1991, 66-77; Minna Skafte-Jensen, "Denmark. The 16th Century", in: Minna Skafte Jensen (ed.), *A History of Nordic Neo-Latin Literature*, Odense 1995, 19-34; Bøggild Johannsen 2008.

54 Friis-Jensen 1989, 156.

55 Cf. Lars Olof Larsson, "Eine andere Antike und die wilde Natur. Das Bild des Nordens in der bildenden Kunst der frühen Neuzeit", in: Annelore Engel-Braunschmidt et al. (eds.), *Ultima Thule, Bilder des Nordens von der Antike bis zur Gegenwart*, Frankfurt am Main et al. 2001 (Imaginatio Borealis. Bilder des Nordens, 1), 93-105, espec. 94.

56 Johan Møhlenfeldt Jensen, "Den rette vej til Himmeriges Rige", in: Bach-Nielsen et al. (eds.) 2006, 242-259.

57 Lars-Olof Larsson, "Bilder i marginalen som retorisk modus", in: Kersti Markus (ed.), *Bilder i marginalen/ Images in the Margins*, Talinn 2006, 12-25; cf. also Friedrich Teja Bach, "Albrecht Dürer – Figuren des Marginalen", in: Isabelle Frank & Freia Hartung (eds.), *Die Rhetorik des Ornaments*, Munich 2001, 121-145.

58 A male figure in cuirass *all' antica* is copied from a woodcut by Hans Schäufelein in the 1513 Augsburg edition of *Via Felicitatis*, cf. V. Thorlacius-Ussing, *Billedskæreren Claus Berg*, Copenhagen 1922, 10; further, Birgitte Bøggild Johannsen, "Odense Domkirke. Gravminder", in: *Danmarks Kirker. Odense Amt*, 2, Herning 1997, 733-740; Richter 2007, 29-33.

59 Sebastian Münster, *Cosmographia Universalis*, III, Basel 1554, 814.

60 Cf. Søren Kaspersen, "Kirken som en have", in: Paul Svensson (ed.), *Løjttavlen. Et sønderjysk alterskab*, Herning 1983, 129-142.

61 Cf. p.13 and note 18.

62 Cf. Otto Norn, *Mester Michiels to Breve til Christian den Anden. Et Bidrag til Nederlandenes og Danmarks kunstneriske Forbindelse*, Copenhagen 1948, XX-XXI; Bøggild Johannsen (forthcoming, a).

63 A systematic analysis of antiquarianism and the restoration of medieval monuments during 16th century Denmark is still a *desideratum*. On the later activities of Frederik II, cf. Bøggild Johannsen 2006c, 10-11.

64 Cf. P. F. Suhm, "Sanctarium Birgerianum", in: P. F. Suhm (ed.), *Samlinger til den Danske Historie* I,3 (1780), 28; Jan Svanberg,, "Adam van Düren. A German Stone Mason in Scandinavia in the Early Sixteenth Century", *Hafnia* 1976, 125-139, spec. 129 ff.

65 Positive knowledge of Vitruvius in a Danish context is only documented from the last third of the 16th century, cf. Hakon Lund, "Palladianismus zwischen Nord- und Ostsee", in: Jörgen Bracker (ed.), *Bauen nach der Natur- Palladio: Die Erben Palladios in Nordeuropa*, Ostfildern 1997(Exhibition Catalogue), 200-212.

66 In his remarkable self-biographic inscription in the cathedral, cf. Svanberg 1976, 136, the artist combines epigraphy of different ages, Nordic Pre-Medieval runes, Gothic minuscules and Early Humanistic cap-

66 itals. On his use of runes, cf. Carsten Bach-Nielsen, "The Runes: Hieroglyphs of the North", in: Gerhard F. Strasser & Mara R. Wade (eds.), *Die Domänen des Emblems: Ausserliterarische Anwendungen der Emblematik*, Wiesbaden 2004, 157-172.

67 On the cult of Holger Danske during the reign of Christian II, cf. recently Bisgaard 2008, 267-270. On Skævinge, further Kirsten Lading Bidsted, "Holger Danske i Skævinge", *ICO* 1 (1989), 21-31.

68 Wood 2008, 172-184.

69 On Early Humanistic 'Memoriengräber' or 'Retrospective tombs' with epitaphs in Neo-Latin metre, cf. Bøggild Johannsen 2008, 349-367, in particular 364f. ; on Saxo's relation, probably to Lund rather than to Roskilde, cf. Karsten Friis-Jensen,"Introduction", in: Karsten Friis-Jensen & Peter Zeeberg (eds.), *Saxo Grammaticus Gesta Danorum*, Copenhagen 2005, I, 31f.

70 Cf. Bøggild Johannsen 2008, 363-364. Related 'antique' ornaments are represented in the wooden, probably contemporary, reliquary cupboard in Sorø, executed (or renovated) at the instigation of Lage Urne and the prior, Henrik Tornekrans, the latter also restoring the church's late 13th and early 14th century heraldic frieze, while replacing in 1527 an older triumphal crucifix by a modern one by Claus Berg.

71 See Birgitte Bøggild Johannsen & Hugo Johannsen, *Kongens kunst*, Copenhagen 1993 (*Ny dansk kunsthistorie*, 2), 30.

72 Cf. Ångström-Grandien 2003, 42.

73 Cf. Hugo Johannsen, "Dignity and Dynasty. On the History and Meaning of the Royal Funeral Monuments for Christian III, Frederik II and Christian IV in the Cathedral of Roskilde", in: Andersen, Nyborg & Vedsø (eds.) 2010, 116-149; *Descriptio Pompae Funebris (...) Friderici II (...)*, s.l. 1588.

74 Cf. Bøggild Johannsen 1997, 701, 712.

75 "Thi der som wi ville acte den Tid, som hand haffuer leffued udi, da skulle wi i sandhed forfare saa merckelige forandring(er) være skeed, baade i det Aandelige oc Verdslige Regiment, som ey tilforn i nogen Mands minde haffue begiffuet sig", cf. Anders Sørensen Vedel, *En Prediken, som seede udi (…) salige Johan Friisis begraffuelse (…)*, Copenhagen 1571; quoted in Otto Norn, *Hesselagergaard og Jacob Binck*, Copenhagen 1961 (Meddelelser fra Foreningen til gamle Bygningers Bevaring 8, 4), 9f.

76 During a recent restoration an unidentified narrative scene with figures in contemporary (Italianate (?)) dress was revealed upon the reverse of the tablet (Fig. 12b).

77 An open question to debate is the interpretation of the gables as confessional, i.e. Lutheran, signatures, as earliest proposed by Svend Eriksen, *Om vælske gavle og andre problemer i dansk arkitektur i det 16. århundrede*, Copenhagen 1956 (Meddelelser fra Foreningen til gamle Bygningers Bevaring 7, 4), cf. also Kolind Poulsen, p. 146 ff. They might also be regarded as harbingers of 'Italian' ('welsche') influences, transmitting motifs of late 15th century Northern Italian (Venetian) origin via Central Europe and Germany to the north, cf. basically Eyvind Unnerbäck, *Welsche Giebel. Ein italienisches Renaissancemotiv und seiner Verbreitung in Mittel- und Nordeuropa*, Stockholm 1971, further o.a. G. Ulrich Grossmann, "Die Einführung von Architekturformen der frühen Renaissance in Mitteleuropa", in: Nussbaum, Euskirchen & Hoppe (eds.) 2003, 176-179; Birgitte Bøggild Johannsen, "Johan Friis og Hesselagergård", in Bach Nielsen et al. (eds.) 2006, 270-279, espec. 275; Heiner Borggrefe, "Kitchen windows, Italian gables and court ceremonial – ornamentation in early Renaissance castles", in: Michael Bischoff & Hillert Ibbeken (eds.), *Castles of the Weser Renaissance/Schlösser der Weserrenaissance*, Stuttgart & London 2008, 29-35. On the use of the gable types, c. 1550 or even earlier at Gottorp Castle, cf. Uwe Albrecht, "Frührenaissance-Architektur in Norddeutschland und Dänemark (1530-1570), *Nordelbingen* 66 (1997) 25-47, spec. 43,

78 Cf. Bøggild Johannsen 2006a, 277; generally Ralf Weingart,"Der Rotwildfries im Güstrower Schloss – Voraussetzungen und Nachfolge", *Mecklenburgische Jahrbücher* 115 (2000), 119-152.

79 Vedel 1571.

80 Nicolas Bock, "Patronage, Standards and *Transfert culturel*: Naples between Art History and Social Science Theory", *Art History* 31,4 (2008), 574-597, espec. 591-593 (special issue, Cordelia Warr & Janis Elliott (eds.), *Import/Export: Painting, Sculpture and Architecture in Naples, 1266-1713*).

REFRAMING THE RENAISSANCE PROBLEM TODAY

Claire Farago

Seventeen years ago, when I published my collaborative book, *Reframing the Renaissance*, there existed an urgent need for integrated accounts that allow the disparate voices who have contributed to European conceptions of art to be heard – not parallel accounts that represent the same events from mutually exclusive points of view, but integrated attempts to define the issues that produce mutually exclusive narratives in the first place. We still need such accounts.

During the same period that European images and artists were exported on a global scale, works of art and other artifacts entered European collections from other parts of the world, in both cases providing a rich setting for the development of new cultural formations in which artistic production played an important role. In the past decade, studies of early modern patronage and collecting practices have flourished. Yet impressive though this new body of literature is, we still need strategies for studying the contributions of fluctuating sixteenth-century senses of 'art' to later ideas about cultural identity and aesthetic sensibility. We need investigative strategies that undercut anachronistic categories that interfere with our ability to see the complexity of artistic interactions during the early modern period. We need to take up epistemological issues at a sufficiently deep level to address the urgent question of the conditions and practices that enabled the construction of Eurocentric cultural attitudes at the same time that Europeans widened their worldviews. To do this, part of the challenge is to understand how newly emerging nations in the nineteenth century imagined themselves as antique – to ask, as Benedict Anderson asked in his groundbreaking study of nationalism entitled *Imagined Communities* (1983) – why awareness of a radically changed form of consciousness in the nineteenth century led to the construction of a 'nationalist memory' reaching back in time. The challenge is to utilize what feminist art historian Joan Kelly called a "double vision" – to look both 'inside' and 'outside' the frameworks traditionally associated with the Renaissance. This conference has given concrete specificity to the various kinds of collective identity available in the fifteenth, sixteenth, and seventeenth centuries. It is not the case that national identity did not exist before the nineteenth century, but rather that it took different forms. Fluid and dynamic royal alliances, complex religious affiliations, and the civic sphere are three such overlapping forms of "nationality" that conference participants have stressed.

It is not enough to speak in generalities, but it is important to keep the big picture in mind even when undertaking detailed case studies. The challenge of articulating what (and where) the

"Renaissance Problem" has gone today might, in the context of the present volume, begin by examining the language in which this conference is framed. According to the conference program, the first target of our gathering has been to "re-evaluate Danish Renaissance art in its European context in light of recent research and methodological discourses." I cannot present myself as an authority on Danish art history, nor do I want my voice to be heard as that of the expert from abroad telling you what to do. I am myself still struggling to understand why "reframing" and "Danish" are conjoined in the conference title and its agenda – given that reframing "the Renaissance" demands attention to cultural exchange, ethnic difference, heterogeneous societies – as well as looking self-critically at the role of scholars who write national histories. In short, the rhetoric of imperialism played an important role in establishing national histories of art. Our opening keynote speaker Professor Kaufmann, who recently published *Toward a Geography of Art* (2004), a groundbreaking study of the writings of German and east central European writers from the seventeenth through the nineteenth centuries, has made us far more aware than ever before just how enmeshed racial theory is in the foundations of the discipline of art history.

It has often been asked over the past four days – and I want to ask it again - to what does the word "Danish" refer in the phrase "Danish Renaissance"? I do not have to tell this audience that the Denmark of the Renaissance period was not identical to the modern nation-state that was created after the fall of Absolutism in 1848, in the size of its population, extent of its geographical territory, range of its ethnicity, type of government, cultural production, or any of the other categories conventionally used to describe national collective identity.

A virtual tour of Denmark's official website emphasizes that there have been a number of different Denmarks in Danish history, even though the official historians tell the story as if some underlying, essential Denmark existed throughout.[1] For example: the earliest Denmark identified by the website came into existence around 1200, when "Danes were [first] able to read the history of the heroic deeds of their forefathers" in Archbishop Anders Sunesen's Latin poem *Hexaëmeron* and in Saxo Grammaticus's *Gesta Danorum*, which gave "the country a clearer conception of its national identity." Of course, not many in the country were literate, and the literature itself would have been the primary agent for creating a feeling of national identity for those few who did have access to Grammaticus's chronicle or Sunesen's poem. Perhaps printed editions of these works in the sixteenth century created a sense of national identity retrospectively. The thirteenth century was a time, still according to Denmark's official website, when the king's wish to be seen as "the nation's lawgiver" was at odds with the clergy, who created a separate clerical legal system, gained economic independence by acquiring land, introducing tithes, and creating links with European centers of learning.

By the early fourteenth century, the official website tells me, "Denmark" had emerged as a "divided nation made up of a number of estates of the realm" in which only nobles and church leaders had any say. The clergy offered protection to the peasants against the payment of taxes issued by the national assemblies; consisting of nobility, and in return for this protection the peasants provided the means for building so many fortified castles that by 1330 nearly every parish had one. The so-called "divided nation" in this situation is, strictly speaking, the division of a unity that can be imagined as such only from the modern perspective of what Denmark later became. This is history written in the future anterior tense.

To continue with my foreigner's understanding of the Danish Renaissance. Until 1658-60, when the realm was reduced to about a third of its former size after the end of the Second Swedish War, "Denmark" designated a huge and ethnically diverse kingdom. The monarchy of Denmark during the Renaissance period included Scania, Halland, Blekinge, Gotland, Ösel, Norway with its extensive North Atlantic possessions and part of the duchy of Schleswig-Holstein. Moreover, the system of government until 1660 consisted of a king elected by the estates (who always elected the king's oldest son), and the power was divided between the Crown and the Council of the Realm

("Rigsråd), made up of only a dozen members of the high nobility. So whose Renaissance are we talking about when we say "Danish Renaissance"? Certainly not the ancestors of the citizens of the modern nation state. The future anterior tense is only a fiction. It is, I think, difficult to argue that the Danish Renaissance refers to the underprivileged peasant class who managed the country's 60,000 farms and accounted for approximately 75% of the total population. Or rather, included them only in the sense that "the burden of taxation fell solely on those groups who were least able to meet the demands."

Of course, these circumstances could describe many other feudal states in Europe and elsewhere in the world. Only the privileged participated in the Italian Renaissance. And only after the end of the "Renaissance," when Danes were being instructed at state Lutheran schools "in the new creed and turned into loyal subjects," did "a feeling a Danish national identity" begin to emerge – and only then among the "leading strata of society."[2] In the 1740s, still according to the official government website, during a time of economic boom based on overseas trade, "young, well educated sons of the middle class began to identify themselves with their nation, its language, and its history, both in intellectual and emotional terms." It is important to add that this new form of bourgeois class-consciousness was partly a reaction against the presence of foreign aristocracy and native aristocracy who adopted foreign culture. (The 1776 Law of Indigenous Rights made it illegal for foreigners to hold a government post). During the same period, the website tells me, conflicts emerged between Danish, Norwegian, and German members of the population. So even when it did emerge, the "Danish" national identity was a very partial one, limited to one sector of the middle class. Until the late eighteenth century, the predominantly rural population had no way to participate in the state that governed them, tying them to work on the farms where they were born, thus providing landowners with cheap labor. Abolition of adscription (serfdom) in 1788 was the single most important agricultural reform of the State Council, marking a new consciousness of basic human rights that complements the 1792 royal decree banning Danes from taking part in the slave trade. Let me quickly add that these reforms took place 80 years before slavery was abolished in the US.

The modern idea of a nation-state in which the entire population enjoys citizenship and treats foreigners with the same regard for social justice, really begins in the late eighteenth century. The intellectual responsibility of historians today is tied to ethical responsibilities: there still exists an urgent need to formulate integrated accounts which allow the disparate voices that have contributed to Danish, Italian, European, American, and so on conceptions of national identity to be heard – not mono-cultural accounts that speak in one voice for all, nor parallel accounts that represent the same events from mutually exclusive points of view, as nationalist histories conventionally do. The Jewish Museum in the old Royal Library designed by Daniel Libeskind is a model of representational strategies – Christian IV admitted Jews, a point of historical importance – and the installation stresses Denmark's history as a safe haven but without glossing over the history of anti-semitism.[3]

The virtual national identity presented on the national website of Denmark appears unified, but masks an underlying set of contradictions and conflicts. Perhaps the foremost challenge that the "Renaissance Problem" presents today is the institutional one of reconfiguring our inherited understanding of historical structure. To live in history, and to wish to write it, is not a universal anthropological postulate, but is a certain way to conceive of and be in the world, and it is a certain practice of subjectivity.

Connections between foundational critiques of disciplinarity as such and the concrete project of critiquing a given disciplinary practice are often obscure. It may be one thing to critically assess practices that conform to existing disciplinary expectations, but it is often quite another to question the configuration itself. Yet unless the subject position of the critic in the institution is brought into the equation for exactly this purpose, the past will always haunt the present, and the most significant epistemological and ethical issues will remain unarticulated and unaddressed. The specter is invisible in the mirror, as Jacques Derrida put it, and this condition can either haunt us in the manner of the ghost of Hamlet's father reminding us that "time is out of joint," or we can remember our past, learn from it in the present, and use the lessons to devise a better future.[4]

I suggest reframing the Renaissance problem to address a methodological conundrum of long-standing and widespread concern in the humanities: that is, how to account for relationships between "ethnicity" and culture, between collective social identity and artistic production. One of the most demanding theoretical challenges posed by the study of cultural exchange is the self-reflexive one of paying attention to the history of the forms of thought that have been applied to the historical artifact, as well as to the history of the artifact itself. The methodology equal to this challenge, in keeping with an important trend in post-colonial studies worldwide, adopts a relativistic approach to the problem of reconstructing cultural continuity and accepts partial recovery of dispossessed cultural traditions as a valid form of interpretation.

The painstaking process of partial recovery involves identifying the continued presence and transformation of artistic conventions. As such, it implicates historians in the same continuum of cultural events it studies. As scholars supported by powerful institutions, we are not innocent bystanders to the history of cultural interaction. Yet previous generations of scholars were also sensitive to the problem of projecting their cultural values onto alien historical material. The difference between our current position and theirs is more tenuous than some contemporary cultural theorists might like to admit.

Interpretative aims may not have changed, but epistemological underpinnings have. One of our deepest-rooted forms of art historical thought is the assumption that an artwork has a radical unity that reconciles (harmonizes, synthesizes) any surface contradictions. This radical unity purportedly stems from the conscious or unconscious intention of the author who is imagined to be singular and unified, and in turn accounts for the work's power to communicate to audiences. The conditions of production and use of art in heterogeneous societies call into fundamental question the connections among artistic intention, unified meaning, and communicative power. There appears to be no way to resolve the meaning of the certain works of art into a single, stable reading, any more than there appears to be a resolution to the complex agencies involved in their production and use.

Recently I participated in a discussion of the "Renaissance problem" part of a series organized by James Elkins at the University of Cork, Ireland, at which six invited speakers discussed the state of the field of Renaissance art history from theoretical points of view.[5] Elkins and his co-organizer for this seminar Robert Williams urged us to consider a structural problem in the discipline of art history in which "the Renaissance is made to serve both as a starting point for the modern and as something against which modernism reacts".[6] What seems to be at stake is that "Modernism needs legitimization, yet it also seems to require repressing some aspects of how we got to where we are."[7] "Institutions in all fields," seminar participant Ethan Matt Kavaler offered, "tend to attract authority to themselves, and respect authority, and authority is a very conservative force. It is not only a problem of administrators, but of colleagues too, in judging and appreciating their fellow colleagues."[8]

The kind of art historical practice I would like to see in Renaissance studies goes all over the world, and deals with all kinds of practices, representational systems, cultural conditions; not at the level of social history alone, but at deeper epistemological levels, studying what happens when new identities are formed, when new communication occurs, when representational practices that have never been in contact before are suddenly in collision and contention, when the readability of the art changes because of contact, when people's ability to live changes because of their altered material culture.

If those kinds of questions came to be of overriding importance in the field, if they were encouraged at the institutional level, we could have an entirely different kind of art history. It would look genuinely different. We would not just be establishing the canon of old masters in Europe.

We would be looking at colonial and what several speakers at this conference have called regional productions. We would be looking at print culture, the importance of which several conference papers have stressed. We would be looking at things made by artists without training and we would see the production of artists without applying ethnocentric labels like "provincial." And we wouldn't necessarily be spending our time on taxonomies of that material. We would be examining the interesting processes that occur, maybe in terms of the Renaissance definition of art as work, as process.

Yet such a re-construal of art history de-stabilizes the discipline, leading to tremendous anxiety about the loss of disciplinarity. In addition to anxiety about the potential loss of disciplinarity, there is anxiety associated with a certain form of nationalism. In a country that has no tradition of art history, the conviction that art historical research and teaching should remain central to the larger discipline of art history drives research. Elkins gave the specific example of Ireland – our host country which had sponsored his roundtables and the ensuing publications by the way - as taking the position that the western European tradition and Irish art history are the proper focus regardless of student demographics. The Renaissance problem today presents the pertinent challenge of deeply rethinking our identities. What a wonderful challenge it would be, to rethink the world in terms that privilege interaction and the unknown over national culture and pride in the familiar! As Stephen Campbell put it at our roundtable in Cork, this would also mean taking a stand *against* the essentialism of identity politics in university education, where students are expected to identify with certain specializations as being more 'about themselves.'[9]

One only needs to look at studies such as Stephen Campbell and Stephen Milner's edited volume on cultural interactions in the Italian Renaissance City (2004), to see that exchanges taking place in Ferrara, across the street from Florence as it were, can be quite radical if they are looked at in the right way, if their implications are fully analyzed.[10] This kind of approach can certainly be developed for the study of the Danish Renaissance. Many of the papers presented at this conference have stressed the theme of artistic exchange. Let me name only a few that struck me as especially rich in their theoretical implications. On the first day Margit Thøfner spoke about plural Renaissances in a paper dealing with the use of Goltzius's prints in two altarpieces of the 1590s (p. 117). She called attention to the performative aspects of meaning and argued for subtle forms of domestication of print sources by local elites. Kristoffer Neville looked at Danish interest in Dutch culture as a mediated form of interest in Italian Renaissance art – the implications being that the taste of Danish Monarchs Frederik II and Christian IV was not provincial at all, but their access to the latest, most stylish art was limited by circumstance (p. 335). Krista Kodres carefully considered regional complexities, terminology, and models of cultural transmission to explain the local look of Estonian art (p. 127).

However, it is also important to emphasize that intra- and extra-European studies have lagged far behind. By continuing to work within the nationalistic, sub-disciplinary formations we have inherited from the heyday of nation-state formation, we reproduce the same hegemonic schemes. The irony is that in today's world of weakened nation-states, the study of national culture is worth less and less – and in the US, the UK, and elsewhere, that is ultimately why art history departments are not held in higher prestige at our universities. This situation extends to all of the humanities.[11]

What is our responsibility to society as intellectuals? *This* question deserves to be driving our research agendas. The pre-modern period, with its often unstable large dynastic formations and competing religious institutions, is becoming much more interesting to look at in the present era of the decline of the nation state and the rise of transnational corporate capitalism. The current and coming kinds of loyalties and identity formations have analogs in that period. George Kubler, Carlo Ginsburg, Enrico Castelnuovo and Jan Bialostocki, and more recently Thomas DaCosta Kaufmann, John Onians, and other Europeanists have called for recognition of the political dimension of artistic geography in a framework of historical critique. Their central argument is that provincial artistic cultures need not be seen as passively reflecting the influences trickling from the center, but as resisting or critiquing or transforming the art of urban centers.

While these observations allow us to see the local manifestations of classicizing Italianate and other "styles" in a different, more positive light than older, diffusionist theories of stylistic transmission, a major problem is inherent in the center/periphery model of art history itself. The problem is that the structure unavoidably reiterates the historical relations of power that its critical reemployments attempt to dismantle. Words like "provincial," "late," "periphery," have meaning only within a system of values based on an evolutionary theory of progress and normative standards. More objective is the consideration of the differing circumstances of regional reception such as Kaufmann's analysis of the varying expressions of "dynastic identity" that often "blur any sense of place" by stressing the supra-individual characters of ruling families manifested in groupings of tombs, coats of arms, and other forms of artistic expression.[12] These forms of art identified particular families and places with precedents in the Roman Empire. In such circumstances, Kaufmann writes, the expression of national or ethnic identity "seems much less clear—what for example, did it mean to be German, rather than non-German, when an individual's primary fealty was to a ruler first, then perhaps to a dynasty?"[13]

In other cases, however, the positivist assumptions of scholars who do not admit open-ended or multiple readings of the visual monuments, have had the effect of erasing the possible active participation of the indigenous peoples and colonial subjects. Motifs, subjects, and stylistic features held meaning on both sides of the major cultural divide between Italian sources and their local conditions of reception in many settings. There is now an extensive body of scholarship that attempts to recognize the possibility of agency on the part of the colonized and the dispossessed untethered from the category "Renaissance".[14]

For reasons having to do with the asymmetrical relations of power in cultural exchanges and the affiliation of scholars with institutions historically aligned with the dominant power, I suggest we think differently about the operations of power in all situations of cultural interaction. Power operates everywhere. If the term is retained at all we might consider "Renaissance" an open-ended system always under investigation. I am concerned with the ethical dimensions of what we produce as scholars: what do we pass on to future generations? What kinds of political implications are there to the knowledge we produce? Our work can seem a-political when we produce it, but at the same time it excludes other work from taking place, or relegates that work to the margins. Once we start thinking about objects from this broader perspective, we can see inherited paradigms structuring our contemporary practices in fresh ways.

To what extent is it our responsibility as scholars operating in today's social networks to feel responsibility for the effects of the knowledge we produce? What is the relationship of ideology to commerce within the frame of academic practices? Historians commonly argue that scholarly publications are not driven by profit motives in theory or fact. From the standpoint of the intellectual's ethical responsibilities to society, however, it matters not at all whether the profit is going directly into the pockets of publishers or scholars. Today, the entertainment industry and the mass media perpetuate the national and ethnic stereotypes on which the modern discipline of art history was founded in the nineteenth century. The common presence of dated ideas in popular culture may partly explain why art history the discipline and Renaissance art history the subdiscipline continue to rely on categories rooted in theories of cultural evolutionism, but it would be a serious short circuit of logic to blame the current situation solely on the culture industry. There is a pressing need on the part of academics to revise disciplinary practices at a more fundamental epistemological level than has commonly been the case in Renaissance studies.

In drawing this paper to a conclusion, I would briefly like to suggest on a more general level how current research is addressing "the Renaissance problem" differently than it did, when *Reframing the Renaissance* was published. Currently we see a great interest in studying cultural interaction, which is a very good sign, but beyond this, I also see emerging a thoughtful effort to dismantle the most fundamental categories that define Renaissance as a distinct period and place. Why is this necessary? "The degree to which we are able to look back reflectively and appropriately apply post-Kantian ideas of aesthetics to the Renaissance is one of the themes we're all dealing with", which draws together art historians with historians in neighboring fields, notably in the history of religion, literature, anthropology, and the history of science.[15] In this expanded field for the study of material culture, scholars are putting into question the terms in which Enlightenment thinking framed the modern era for us – because the most fundamental categories art, science, and religion no longer adequately frame the questions that challenge us most today.

Historians of science and art are finding that the Enlightenment understanding of art and science hinder our ability to grasp what was going on two hundred years before this system of classification was firmly in place. Mastering nature through technology on an unprecedented scale resulted in the development of various new arts and sciences, new conceptions of nature as well as a new discourse about nature that became a central cultural force in western society. Pamela Smith and Paul Findlen, both historians of science, introduce their anthology, *Merchants and Marvels*, 2002, in these terms.[16]

The term 'scientia' does not conform to its modern meaning – it was primarily used by individuals to give authority to an activity. Rethinking "ars" in a historical context reinforces the same kinds of conclusions: the word was used by scholars to denote a teachable discipline, an epitome or handbook, technical writing about image-making as well as fortification-building, or a process of making things. Such examinations leave historians of art and science struggling with the same basic epistemological questions. What was art, what was science? We could add, what was religion?[17] Modern ideas of the value of artifice and the categorization of objects as either "high art" or "popular religious image" are currently being rethought and this, too, bears on the Renaissance problem.

I can think of no topic more urgent than the need to rethink the Enlightenment categories of art, science, and religion. Not to develop new taxonomies of objects corresponding to these words, but to recognize that these abstractions may be three versions of the same thing – attempts to come to terms with the relation of the material, quotidian world to the immaterial, the spiritual, the noumenal.

But what does it mean to "do history," at this point in time? How we account for cultural transmission is part of the larger question of how we account for collective memory. And to account for our own position in relation to our subjects of study, we must ask, as Derrida said, about what is located in the envelope of the question.[18] With awareness that the field we inherited and the stable epistemological assumptions on which it was built no longer serve contemporary purposes comes a destabilization of the field itself. The field of art history is now expanded, but also de-centered. There is no unified vision, no consensus on a research agenda, if there ever was. The discourse is thus more dialogic in its structure – indeed, an international conference on a focused topic like "Reframing the Danish Renaissance" fosters this kind of intellectual engagement.

Let me conclude with the question raised by the call for papers at the 2008 Congress of the International Committee of the History of Art: "To what extent do we need to rethink the discipline of the history of art in order to establish cross-cultural dimensions as fundamental to its scope, method, and vision?"[19] This is the Renaissance Problem in our time.

Notes

1 http://denmark.dk, accessed September 20, 2006.

2 When these "lower classes" directed their anger at the Council of the Realm ("Rigsråd"), which collapsed amid growing financial crisis in 1660, an absolutist government with a hereditary monarchy was established that created the foundation for a stable bureaucratic state in the eighteenth century, see note 1.

3 See Henrik Sten Møller (ed.), *The Danish Jewish Museum: Daniel Libeskind*, Copenhagen 2004.

4 Jacques Derrida, "Parergon," *The Truth in Painting*, (trans. Geoff Bennington and Ian McLeod), Chicago 1987.

5 James Elkins & Robert Williams (eds.), *Renaissance Theory* (The Art Seminar, 5), New York and London 2008.

6 Citing Robert Williams in: Elkins & Williams (eds.) 2008, 242.

7 How do we structure the intervening centuries? Modernists write as if there were an uncrossable, intervening abyss, as if the present is divided from its founding moment "by a fault-line or rupture, so that the past stands in need of a quieting or even a repression." Citing James Elkins in: Elkins & Williams (eds.) 2008, 241.

8 Citing Ethan Matt Kavaler in: Elkins & Williams (eds.) 2008, 261-262.

9 Citing Stephen Campbell in: Elkins & Williams (eds.) 2008, 257.

10 Stephen Campbell & Stephen Milner (eds.), *Artistic Exchange and Cultural Translation in the Italian City*, Cambridge 2004.

11 See Bill Readings, *The University in Ruins*, Cambridge and London 1996, especially Chapter 2, "The Idea of Excellence," 21-43; and Samuel Weber, *Institution and Interpretation* (1987), expanded edition, Stanford 2001, especially Chapter 2, "The Limits of Professionalism," 18-32; and Chapters 13-15, on the future of the humanities in the University, 207-254.

12 Thomas DaCosta Kaufmann, *Toward a Geography of Art*, Chicago and London 2004, 137.

13 Kaufmann 2004, 143-144. See further, Claire Farago, "Review of Thomas DaCosta Kaufmann, *Toward a Geography of Art*", in: *Renaissance Quarterly* 53 (2005), 279-280.

14 The bibliography is too extensive to cite, but includes Jeanette Peterson & Dana Leibsohn (eds.) *Seeing across Cultures*, (forthcoming, Aldershot 2012), with essays that argue against the term, including my "Understanding Visuality".

15 Citing Kavaler, in: Elkins & Williams (eds.) 2008, 204.

16 Pamela H. Smith and Paula Findlen (eds.), *Merchants and Marvels: Commerce, Science, and Art in Early Modern Europe*, New York and London, 2002. Artist/artisans, medical practitioners, and other investigators of nature helped to lay a new foundation for natural philosophy that emphasized practice and the interrelation of commerce with scientific and artistic representations of nature. Paying attention to the growth of new technologies in this re-reading transforms the conventional account of the Scientific Revolution centered on theoretical advances. The anthology, entitled *Colonial Botany: Science, Commerce, and Politics in the Early Modern World*, Philadelphia 2005, edited by Londa Schiebinger and Claudia Swan, likewise revises received notions of 'encounters' between Europeans and indigenous peoples, emphasizing the role of commerce but also contributions of dispossessed peoples to European cultures, even when our ability to recover the meaning and extent of these contributions is partial and incomplete. Richard Goldthwaite, Lisa Jardine, Evelyn Welch, among others are documenting the intersection between patronage, gift economy, and commodity exchange as key to the amplification of value and cultural significance accorded to certain types of objects. Welch's *Shopping in the Renaissance: Consumer Cultures in Italy 1400-1600*, London and New Haven, 2005; Rebeccah Zorach's *Blood, Milk, Ink, Gold: Abundance and Excess in the French Renaissance*, Chicago 2005; and Stephen Campbell's *The Cabinet of Eros: Renaissance Mythological Painting and the Studiolo of Isabella d'Este*, New Haven and London 2006, are three recent art historical studies with very different methodologies that share an interest in charting the circulation of works of art through gift exchange and commerce, thereby destabilizing the conventional categories of art, national style, and biography that has for so long organized the archive of our field. David Freedberg's study of the Academy of the Linceans, entitled *The Eye of the Lynx: Galileo, His Friends, and the Beginnings of Modern Natural History*, Chicago 2002, argues against classifying scientific illustrations as art or science – because there were no such clear-cut categories during the period under investigation. His study combines European materials with those of the so-called New World because the Linceans did the same.

17 Where does one draw the line between the kinds of visual culture we art historians study and the kinds we don't, and between the ways we study them, and the ways we don't, when the historical record tells us that humble *tavolette* and *boti* and sophisticated altarpieces by leading artists, were venerated in the same way by the same people. Writes Fredrika Jacobs: "Does (or should) the history of Renaissance art accommodate systemic relationships beyond the canonical to include a broad range of aesthetic productions, including those labeled "popular", categorized as "low", and not infrequently segregated from "art" by the rubric "visual imagery"?, citing Fredrika Jacobs, "Rethinking the Divide: Cult Images and the Cult of Images" in: Elkins and Williams 2008, 95f.

18 Derrida 1987, 22.

19 Now available as Jaynie Anderson (ed.), *Crossing Cultures: Conflict/Migration/Convergence*, 32nd Congress of the International Committee of the History of Art, Melbourne 2009.

DO WE STILL NEED A RENAISSANCE?

Keith Moxey

"…this time of African existence is neither linear time nor a simple sequence in which each moment effaces, annuls, and replaces those that preceded it, to the point where a single age exists within society. This time is not a series but an interlocking of presents, pasts and futures that retain their depths of other presents, pasts, and futures, each bearing, altering, and maintaining the previous ones." (Achille Mbembe, *On the Postcolony*, Berkeley 2001, 16.)

Do we still need a Renaissance? When first asked, the question seems nonsensical, even absurd. The idea of the Renaissance is the lodestar, the shining light, around which the history of art until recently revolved. In fact, the concept is so deeply naturalized that it is impossible to conceive our discipline without it. But let us imagine, for a moment, that it is possible to think around the edges of this idea, to analyze critically the work performed by this seemingly indispensable notion. Who is the "we" that may or may not need a Renaissance? And just what is the "Renaissance" we may or may not need? Like the light from distant stars, the gleam that reaches us from works of past art has no fixed pattern. Despite the efforts of many civilizations—from the Greeks to the Inca—to impose order on the swirling turbulence of the starry heavens, no one star ever orders the appearance of the rest. Yet when it comes to art historical writing, the urge to order is paramount, and never more so perhaps than in the exaltation of the Renaissance. The luster of this period and the discoveries of its interpreters for nearly two centuries have often dimmed the brilliance of other stars in the constellation.

Every one of us approaches the study of what has happened in the past for different reasons and out of complex and not always articulable motives. What follows is, in part, a highly personal response. The center of interest for art historical studies in the United States has experienced a remarkable shift during the course of my lifetime. When I first entered the field in the late 1960's, the study of the Renaissance was at the heart of disciplinary activity.[1] Not only were some of the leading art historians of the day committed to this period – Erwin Panofsky, for example, was still alive – but all graduate students passed through or stayed with the study of this pinnacle of the art historical canon. The situation today is remarkably different. University departments of art history in the United States have had to acknowledge that most students, on both undergraduate and graduate levels, are drawn to study only modern and contemporary art. There was a moment in the 1970's and 1980's when the nineteenth century became a magnet for graduate students, in large part because of the work of Robert Herbert and T.J. Clark, but there is little doubt that the twentieth and twenty-first centuries have usurped its place.[2] The most notable scholars and critics of modern and postmodern art, Rosalind Krauss, Benjamin Buchloh, and Hal Foster, for example, now hold the attention of the discipline.[3] Why and how has this transformation taken place?

As an historical field, the Renaissance has been the subject of much debate for at least a couple of decades. First of all, it is associated with a philosophy of history – Hegelian historicism – that has been largely rejected, even though it continues to maintain an active life in our disciplinary unconscious. Much valuable empirical work, of course, still depends on a rarely questioned system of ideas to give it coherence. Scholars who insist that their work addresses works of art directly are sometimes unwilling to acknowledge that their contributions only make sense within the context of a broader conceptual structure. The Renaissance, as an identifiable moment in history, arose in the wake of Hegel's transcendent philosophy, according to which the movement of the "Spirit" through time reached a crucial stage when it shed the superstitious beliefs of the Middle Ages and looked at man and nature with secular eyes. The creation of the Renaissance, in the work of such compelling historians as Jacob Burckhardt and Jules Michelet, became instrumental to the project of carving up time into distinct but sequentially related units.[4] It was a grand scheme, as Ernst Gombrich pointed out long ago, that attributed meaning to the past by suggesting that it had a teleological movement – that it was going somewhere.[5] Periodization functioned as the architecture on which the history of art constructed its imposing edifice.

I do not need to rehearse the criticisms that have shaken this philosophy of history. Critics of Hegelian historicism have been relentless. Philosophers such as Michel Foucault have argued for a vision of the past marked by rupture and discontinuity, rather than continuity and progress, by insisting that the epistemological basis for understanding the world is as uncertain as the chaos of events it seeks to order.[6] Historiographers, such as Michel de Certeau and Hayden White, among others, have emphasized the role of language in historical writing, arguing that the events of the past itself cannot be confused with their interpretation and concluding that the past must remain forever unknowable.[7] The study of historical writing makes it clear, for example, that Burckhardt and Michelet shared the historicist conviction that the Renaissance anticipated their own time.[8] Their exaltation and vilification of Renaissance figures depended on their belief that the period inaugurated both the glories and the miseries of the modern age. Students of these "founding fathers" of the Renaissance, such as Felix Gilbert and Lionel Gossman, continue to reveal the extent to which their writings manifest the concerns of the nineteenth century in the course of their analyses of sixteenth-century affairs. And, most recently, the idea of the Renaissance has been criticized from a variety of postcolonial perspectives on the grounds of its Eurocentrism. Indian historians, such as Partha Chatterjeee and Dipesh Chakrabarty, have pointed out that many of the world's cultures have managed to do very well and exist for thousands of years without having a teleological concept of history, let alone a pivotal moment such as the Renaissance.[9] Other historians have articulated how Western historical narratives fail to capture the nature of the past in different parts of the globe. Writing about the Americas, for example, Anthony Pagden and Walter Mignolo, argue for the incommensurability of different cultures and the impossibility of finding grounds for translating the experiences of one into another.[10]

The study of the Renaissance is, of course, not singular in the way in which its luster has tended to obliterate that of other periods and places. Let me dwell for a moment on the perils of the period that seems to have taken its place in our disciplinary consciousness – the study of the art of modernity. Histories of modern and contemporary art are hardly free of the kind of teleological or progressive thinking that was once associated with the Renaissance. Clement Greenberg once argued very successfully that modern art followed an inevitable course, according to which modern art pursued a necessary trajectory leading to the recognition of the essential formal qualities of each artistic medium.[11] Fortunately, those days are – for the most part – over, but the hegemonic hold of European and American art over that of the rest of the world still holds many in its grip. Interest in contemporary art increasingly includes the fascinating artistic productions of Africa, Asia, the Middle East, and Latin America, but this is not always the case. Some modernists view the products of non-western centers with unease. How are they related to the dominant models of artistic creativity located in the artistic centers of the West? Within academia serious discussions take place, for example, as to whether to hire specialists in contemporary African art or continue to support the study of the traditional work familiar from the nineteenth century moment of European contact. While the idea of contemporaneity might suggest that the art of all cultures are equally susceptible to art historical consideration, the interpretive traditions of the past dictate that time runs at different speeds in different parts of the globe. The time that is accorded the greatest prestige – the time that is said to matter – takes place at the centers of power rather than in the periphery.

It is not the abstract idea of the Renaissance that preoccupies us here, however, but whether or not it is a useful term with which to consider the radically different varieties of artistic production that are characteristic of Europe during the fifteenth and sixteenth centuries. At the Copenhagen conference the question took the following form: to what extent is the concept of the Renaissance, developed to account for transformations experienced by Italian culture during the fourteenth, fifteenth, and sixteenth centuries, appropriate for the discussion of this time frame in Denmark? Can an idea first used to privilege the trans-historical importance of Italy be applied to the understanding of different historical and geographical circumstances? Heinrich Wölfflin and Alois Riegl used the concept of style to track the development of the "spirit" in the arts of the past, a strategy that became the paradigmatic principle on which the history of art was based.[12] Art was the cultural institution in which history's teleological drive was thought to be most clearly discernible. The concept of style, however, inevitably summons two axes of meaning: on the one hand, it refers to a time, and on the other, to a place.[13] When we refer to a Renaissance style, for example, what comes to mind is not only a period in history, but a moment now identified with the European nation of Italy. The fact that the nation state known as Italy did not exist during the period known as the Renaissance, is already an indication that the concept of a "Renaissance style" postdates the political unification of the peninsula during the course of the nineteenth century and that it is not embedded in the order of things. Thus, every time we use this expression we refer not only to a moment in time but also to a particular place.

The consequences of this practice were discussed at the conference and various alternatives with which to avoid the ideological implications associated with the idea of the Renaissance were suggested. Describing the Danish art of the time as "courtly," for example, thereby avoiding the ideological implications of the Renaissance as an identifiable period seemed unsatisfactory. While that adjective might be appropriate to the circumstances in which this art was produced, it yields no sense of how this moment is related to forms or styles of art that preceded or succeeded it. It lacks, in short, situatedness in time.

An unwitting example of the consequences of the enduring prestige accorded to Italian art by the period of the Renaissance was on parade in the introductory banner to the exhibition of the life and work of the Danish astronomer Tycho Brahe which was on view in Copenhagen's National Museum during the conference itself. The large wall hanging informed its visitors:

> "The word Renaissance means rebirth – that is, of the Roman and Greek culture of Antiquity. True, the culture of Antiquity had by no means been forgotten in the Middle Ages. But it was only during the Renaissance that ancient form and ancient content were reunited. Art tried to achieve a harmony that corresponded to an ideal image of ancient society. The development of the sciences formed the basis of many new facets. This also applied to the mathematically correct and logical structure of the human body, of the appearance of the world, and the mathematical rules of perspective. In Italy the

Renaissance flourished in the fifteenth century, while Denmark's Renaissance only began in the sixteenth century".[14]

Quite apart from the lateness attributed to the "Renaissance" in Denmark, one that reduces all its artists to the status of epigones of their Italian forerunners, anyone familiar with Panofsky's brilliant texts *Renaissance and Renascences* and *Perspective as Symbolic Form* will recognize that the historical developments that are said to mark the genius of that period all took place in Florence.[15]

So what happens when we talk of the Danish Renaissance? As we have seen, Denmark becomes the location where something that had its origins in Italy played itself out at "second" or "third" hand in "foreign" soil. Unfortunately, my knowledge of the events, as well as the art, of the Danish Renaissance – much improved though it had been by attending the conference – prevented me from trying to answer this question directly. As a scholar of the Netherlands and Germany in the fifteenth and sixteenth centuries, however, I can approach the question from another angle.

One of the most influential treatises on the "Northern Renaissance" – Erwin Panofsky's *Early Netherlandish Painting* – recounts the rise of pictorial verisimilitude in fifteenth-century Flemish painting as an offshoot of Italian tendencies of the fourteenth century.[16] "Naturalism," in other words, is an Italian invention that gradually wends its compulsive way to other European outposts. On this view, there is one origin for this style, and Italy is its privileged source. According to Panofsky, the papal schism that took Siennese masters to Avignon introduced "naturalistic" motifs that were then spread throughout France and the Lowlands. These motifs were what Aby Warburg called "pathos formulae," devices by which the emotional content of religious images might be made accessible to the faithful, as well as the representation of a greater range of figure and physiognomic types, an interest in the play of light and shade, and a concern with the representation of illusionistic space. Not only does this account fail to address the circumstances in which Flemish illusionism was born – that is, the specific nature and function of images within the context of local cultural, religious, and social practice – but, more importantly, it fails to come to terms with the distinctive qualities of Flemish "naturalism" as opposed to the character of that

Fig. 1. Robert Campin, Annunciation triptych (Merode altarpiece), c. 1425. New York, The Metropolitan Museum of Art (Photo Art Resource, NewYork).

stylistic tendency in Italy.[17] Why is it, for example, that Flemish artists are so much more concerned with the depiction of the "skin" of objects than are the Italian? Rather than extolling the surface textures of, say, Robert Campin's *Merode Altarpiece* (Fig.1), Panofsky discerns a tension between surface and depth, one that leads him to describe it as retrograde. One-point perspective (a Florentine development) is the yardstick used to evaluate Flemish painting. The requirement to relate historical developments to one another and to attribute them to a common source serves to obscure the particularity of the local for the sake of the universal. Time, in other words, is invoked only to denigrate the demands of place.

Panofsky's approach to Albrecht Dürer similarly privileges Italian achievements over those taking place north of the Alps.[18] The artist's career is measured by reference to his Italian contemporaries. The highpoints of his oeuvre coincide with those instants in which he engages most seriously with Italian theory and practice. His knowledge of human proportions and perspective, not to mention his humanist familiarity with ancient mythology and history, are the qualities that rank him the equal of the likes of Leonardo. The work on which Panofsky concentrates most attention, however – the engraving *Melancolia I* (Fig. 2) – becomes an allegory of the struggle between intellectual principles and artisanal know-how that, he says, characterizes the artist's work as a whole. Concluding that the print represents the defeat of reason by unreason serves to identify Dürer as essentially German and as a star-crossed genius whose melancholy led to an artistic impasse. He was in the wrong place at the right time.

How have more recent authors dealt with the problem posed by Renaissance periodization? If we compare Panofsky's fifty-year old account of Dürer with that of a more recent author, Joseph Koerner, we discover less interest in fitting the artist into a pre-established historical and geographical plot.[19] Perhaps it is inevitable, given the problematization of the concept of historical development characteristic of our time, that innovative art historians should emphasize the "lure of the object," the status of the work of art as something that occupies a transhistorical nature above its location within any particular historical structure or sequence. Instead of measuring Dürer against his Italian counterparts in order to show how his northern experience made him different, Koerner focuses on the artist's own achievements.

The key to his thesis is Dürer's *Self-Portrait* of 1500 (Fig. 3), a painting whose artistic self-consciousness provokes a profound transformation of the status and function of the pictorial image. The *Vera Icon* (or "True Likeness") panels that inspired Dürer's portrait are documents of the miraculous transfer of Christ's features to the veil of St. Veronica on the way to Calvary. By equating his own portrait with these records of the face of the divinity allegedly "made without hands," Dürer deliberately calls attention to his own pro-

Fig. 2. Albrecht Dürer, Melancholy, 1514. Paris, Louvre (Photo Art Resource, New York).

Fig. 3. Albrecht Dürer, Self-portrait, 1500. Munich, Alte Pinakothek (Photo Art Resource, NewYork).

digious powers of creation. Where the images of Christ's face depend on the deity whose features they transcribe, the power of Dürer's self-portrait depends on the artist's genius. Even if Koerner's narrative has echoes of Burckhardt's vision of the Renaissance as the "age of the individual," he is less intent on locating him in such a context than finding new grounds for his appreciation. Panofsky's sense of historical progress prevented him from recognizing that cultural incommensurability makes the comparison of Flemish and Italian paintings a violent one, just as his discussion of Dürer is shadowed by his awareness of what he considers the primacy of Italian art. For Koerner, on the other hand, the encounter with the work becomes central. The business of the art historian is now to articulate the distinctive quality of a work or an artist. The need to relativize these insights through reference to a comparative historical framework is either ignored or unrecognized. Time and place are congruent with one another, and their equipoise encourages a presentist appreciation of art on aesthetic terms.

How does such an approach play out with regard to the Italian Renaissance itself? How does a contemporary alternative to a developmental history work there and then? Georges Didi-Huberman, like Koerner, argues that the dialectical relationship between a painting and its beholder outweighs the necessity to relate the artist to a larger historical framework.[20] The physical execution and material substance of Fra Angelico's frescoes in San Marco, he writes, functions as a metaphor of the Christian doctrine of the Incarnation (Fig. 4). The paintings themselves become meditations on the way in which Christ's divine being becomes material, the means by which a transcendent narrative assumes temporal dimensions. Synchrony, the contemporaneity of aesthetic experience, outweighs diachrony, the location of that experience in a historical continuum. Writing of the historian's desire for the past, Didi-Huberman intimates the complexity of the bond:

> "Such a desire names simultaneously the indispensable and the unthinkable of history. Indispensable, because we can comprehend the past … only by surrendering to a kind of hymenal bond: by penetrating the past as well as ourselves, in other words by feeling that we have married it in order to grasp it completely, while in return we are, by this act, gripped by it ourselves; grabbed, clasped, even stupefied. It is difficult to misconstrue, in this empathetic movement, the deeply mimetic character of the historical operation itself".[21]

Didi-Huberman's words capture both the intricate as well as the intimate nature of the historian's encounter with the past. Gendered as his description of the encounter of historical horizons appears to be, it nevertheless suggests that our continuing fascination with what has happened in other ages depends on a process of identification analogous to psychoanalytic processes of transference and counter-transference.[22] While our own assumptions and beliefs today are the basis by which we evaluate those that came before, we also allow ourselves to be molded by those we encounter so as to relativize and even alter our own.

Fig. 4. Fra Angelico, Noli me tangere, c. 1440-1445. Florence, Museo di San Marco (Photo Art Resource, New York).

Just what happens to the Renaissance as a period in the texts of Koerner and Didi-Huberman? Rather than define the context in which the works of art they engage with were produced, they describe the visual structures by which they call forth our response. Works unfold according to their effects on spectators. They reveal themselves through the bonds they establish with viewers. The object or work, rather than the period, becomes the means by which to address the radical incommensurability that separates one moment in time from another. Inverting the Hegelian paradigm, the passage of the "Spirit" through time is no longer recorded by the work of art. Art, rather, provides the channel through which the past encounters the particular quality of our contemporary response. The past acts upon the present as much as the present does on the past, and the subject-object distinction – so long a model for historical interpretation – is replaced by a relation that is more deeply interactive.

Is the attention paid to the specificity of the work, the intensity of the aesthetic bond between work and viewer, a viable solution to a historical enterprise set adrift by the challenges to the historicist account of time? Koerner and Didi-Huberman are just two of many gifted art historians who have set themselves the task of writing history in the absence of the "grand narrative" that animated the discipline for so long. I have selected these scholars because they have found original and effective means of circumventing the historicist dilemma, as well as of making vital the aesthetic dimension of art history. Both Koerner's and Didi-Huberman's texts are enormously learned. Their concentration on individual artworks never fails to offer a rich and complex account of the historical situation in which Dürer and Fra Angelico's careers unfolded, but these historians bring this knowledge to bear on their own response to the works themselves. The concept of period becomes embodied in, rather than serving as the background for, the work of art. The distinction between time and place is avoided. Comparisons – say between North and South fall by the wayside. The individual object initiates the recognition of a difference between historical moments now and then – the gulf is both emphasized and bridged by means of aesthetic experience.

The challenges to evolutionary ideas of history that are ultimately responsible for the question "do we still need a Renaissance?" have made art historians acutely aware of the philosophical stakes involved in the project of representation. The construction of meaning interrupts the chaotic flow of events in order to suggest that they may have a discernible pattern, yet at the same time we know that such interventions are essentializing gestures, fleeting and transitory attempts at stasis, that betray as much about our own attitudes as they afford us access to the past. Periods, therefore, cannot be regarded as a stable framework within which historical interpretation takes place. Jonathan Culler and Norman Bryson have reminded us of the naturalizing power of the idea of the interpretive "context" and the need to reconceptualize it as a constructed "frame."[23] They argue that interpretations that treat the work of art as a problem of interpretation before allegedly stable social circumstances fail to consider how uncertain our understanding of those circumstances may be. We use their analysis of the "context" idea as a means of grasping the role of the period in the history of art. Instead of stabilizing historical interpretation, as is so often the case, periods, like contexts, become part of the arbitrary "frame" placed around any interpretation. Historical writing is inevitably shaped by established philosophies of history, and each contribution to our understanding of the past necessarily betrays the ideological agenda that motivates it. As permanent and foundational as these systems of thought may sometimes appear, they are just as transient as any other aspect of our experience.

The idea of the Renaissance, traditionally used to privilege a particular time and place, the fifteenth and sixteenth centuries in Italy, can no longer support this burden. While its prestige derives from the continuing dominance of Western economic and cultural power in our own time, we now understand that its luster is relative and that its claims to preeminence are not absolute. While definitions of the period have always been subject to renegotiation, its status has only recently begun to be questioned. The myths with which it is associated: that it saw the revival of a glorious antiquity, the birth of modernity, the rise of the individual, and so forth, have served to exalt a vision of the art historical past in which the time that mattered most was distinctly European and specifically Italian. It is becoming more and more apparent that the splendor of this moment can constitute a curse as much as a blessing. The recognition that time matters in places other than in this touchstone of Western identity appears as the increasingly urgent task of our disciplinary future.

Notes

1 See Christopher Wood, "Art History's Normative Renaissance", in: Allen Grieco et al. (eds.), *The Italian Renaissance in the Twentieth Century.* Acts of an International Conference, Florence, Villa I Tatti, June 9-11, Florence 1999, 65-92.

2 See Robert Herbert, *Impressionism: Art, Leisure, and Parisian Society,* New Haven 1988 and T. J. Clark, *Image of the People: Gustave Courbet and the 1848 Revolution*, London 1973.

3 Rosalind Krauss, *The Originality of the Avant-Garde and Other Modernist Myths,* Cambridge, Mass. 1985; Hal Foster, *The Return of the Real: The Avant-Garde at the End of the Century*, Cambridge, Mass. 1995; Benjamin Buchloh, *Neo-Avant-Garde and Culture Industry: Essays on European and American Art from 1955-1975*, Cambridge, Mass. 2000.

4 For the history of the creation of the Renaissance as a historical epoch, see Wallace Ferguson, *The Renaissance in Historical Thought: Five Centuries of Interpretation*, Cambridge Mass. 1948; William Kerrigan & Gordon Braden, *The Idea of the Renaissance*, Baltimore 1989; Peter Burke, *The Renaissance* Atlantic Highlands, New Jersey 1987; Stephen Bann, *Romanticism and the Rise of History,* New York 1995.

5 For a vigorous critique of Hegelianism in art history, see Ernst Gombrich, *In Search of Cultural History*, Oxford 1969.

6 Michel Foucault, *The Order of Things: An Archaeology of the Human Sciences*, New York 1973 (1966).

7 Michel de Certeau, *The Writing of History,* Tom Conley (trans.), New York 1988 (1975); Hayden White, *Tropics of Discourse: Essays in Cultural Criticism*, Baltimore 1978; HaydenWhite, *The Content of the Form: Narrative Discourse and Historical Representation*, Baltimore 1987.

8 Felix Gilbert, *History or Culture? Reflections on Ranke and Burckhardt*, Princeton 1990; Lionel Gossman, *Basel in the Age of Burckhardt*, Chicago 2000; Francis Haskell, *History and Its Images*, New Haven 1993; J. B. Bullen, *The Myth of the Renaissance in Nineteenth Century Writing*, Oxford 1994; Stephen Bann, *Romanticism and the Rise of History*, New York 1995; Jo Tollebeek, "Renaissance and 'Fossilization'", in: Michelet, Burckhardt & Huizinga, *Renaissance Studies* 15 (2001), 354-366.

9 Dipesh Chakrabarty, *Provincializing Europe: Postcolonial Thought and Historical Difference*, Princeton 2000; Partha Chatterjee, *Nationalist Thought and the Colonial World: A Derivative Discourse*, Minneapolis 1993.

10 Anthony Pagden, *European Encounters with the New*

World: From the Renaissance to Romanticism, New Haven 1993; Walter Mignolo, *The Darker Side of the Renaissance*, Ann Arbor 1995. For attempts to relate European history of the Renaissance to that of other cultures see Claire Farago (ed.), *Reframing the Renaissance: Visual Culture in Europe and Latin America 1450-1650*, New Haven 1995; Lisa Jardine & Jerry Brotton, *Global Interests: Renaissance Art between East and West*, Ithaca 2000; Jerry Brotton, *The Renaissance Bazaar: From the Silk Road to Michelangelo*, Oxford 2002.

11 Clement Greenberg, *Art and Culture: Critical Essays*, Boston 1989 (1961).

12 Heinrich Wölfflin, *Principles of Art History: The Problem of the Development of Style in Later Art*, M. D. Hottinger (transl.), London 1932 (1917); Alois Riegl, *The Group Portraiture of Holland*, Evelyn Kain & David Britt (transl.), Los Angeles 1999 (1902).

13 For the indissolubility of the time-space nexus, see Svetlana Boym, *The Future of Nostalgia*, New York 2001.

14 On the exhibition, see further Poul Grinder-Hansen (ed.), *The World of Tycho Brahe*, Copenhagen 2006.

15 Erwin Panofsky, *Perspective as Symbolic Form*, Christopher Wood (transl.), New York 1991 (1927); Erwin Panofsky, *Renaissance and Renascences in Western Art*, Stockholm 1960.

16 Erwin Panofsky, *Early Netherlandish Painting*, 2 vols., Cambridge, Mass. 1953.

17 For a critique of Panofsky's Italo-centric view and for a persuasive theory based on the religious function of Flemish images see Lloyd Benjamin, *The Empathetic Relation of Observer to Image in Fifteenth Century Northern Art*, PhD dissertation, University of North Carolina 1973, Ann Arbor 1975.

18 Erwin Panofsky, *The Life and Art of Albrecht Dürer*, I-II, Princeton 1943.

19 Joseph Koerner, *The Moment of Self-Portraiture in German Renaissance Art*, Chicago 1993.

20 Georges Didi-Huberman, *Confronting Images: Questioning the Ends of a Certain History of Art*, John Goodman (transl.), Pennsylvania 2005 (1990).

21 Didi-Huberman 2005, 37.

22 Dominick La Capra, "History and Psychoanalysis", in: Dominick La Capra, *Soundings in Critical Theory*, Ithaca 1989, 30-66.

23 Jonathan Culler, *The Pursuit of Signs: Semiotics, Literature, Deconstruction*, Ithaca 1981; Norman Bryson, "Art in Context", in: Ralph Cohen (ed.), *Studies in Historical Change*, Charlottesville 1992, 18-42.

THE RENAISSANCE:
THE ORIGIN OF MODERNITY OR ITS FIRST RESISTANCE?

Jacob Wamberg

As the idea of a Renaissance Year in Denmark demonstrated, the concept of the Renaissance has been one of historiography's big success stories, a Dawkinsian meme that is seemingly able to reproduce itself incessantly and without losing any glamour. The Renaissance is a seemingly unfailing object of desire, something radiating and good, true and beautiful, of which it suits any historical period to be in possession. Therefore, jealousy is also felt towards the point of origin of this idea, the Italian Renaissance, and attempts have been made to wrest from it its monopoly on the Renaissance: "So ein Ding müssen wir auch haben!" It is, for instance, a remarkable triumph for the notoriously inferior rival of the Renaissance, the Middle Ages, when it can be shown that a number of renascences also occurred in this period – and that these even occurred first in medieval times.[1]

But why exactly are renascences so amazingly attractive? First, of course, they reproduce another object of desire: antiquity. But this is not the only reason: this reproduction somehow enables a given later period to know what is what, to know that it is less dark Middle Ages – in short, more modern. This connection is for instance still observable in a Copenhagen research network by the name of *Renaissance: The Origins of Modernity*.[2]

Taking my starting point in visual art, however, I would like to raise the question whether this identification of Renaissance and modernity is still historiographically sound.[3] Indeed, in a historiographical perspective the idea of a modernity-creating Renaissance appears to be a special Italian construction which, to be sure, spreads to the North-European cultures but which nonetheless reactualizes the cultural heritage of the Mediterranean area. However, there is an element of *coup d'état* in this construction, for if we trace the etymology of the term 'modern', we will find a late-medieval connection to North European culture. At the same time, if we look at the more mature pictorial art of modernity and try to trace its main ingredients – panoramic views, subjective viewpoints, traces of time and change, prosaic details, cultivated or sublimely deserted terrains – we will encounter these ingredients in the Gothic tradition rather than in the Italian Renaissance (Fig. 1). The pictorial gaze of the Italian Renaissance does not posit its point of gravity in infinite space and variable time; rather, emulating antique ideals, it is anchored in a closed and supra-temporal body (Fig. 2). In contrast, modern pictorial vision more readily moves its attention from this body and out towards the infinite space marked by temporal change, in particular towards landscape.

In other words, Renaissance pictorial space appears as a selective and beautified subset of the paradigm of modernity – a subset which, in accordance with the neo-antique canon, highlights plastic ideality and represses arch-mimetic phenomena such as oblique angles, distant wide expanses, confused compositions, amorphous spots, hyper-definition, fragments, particularities, ugliness: indeed, the prosaic in general. The Renaissance, I will suggest, should not be understood as a period, but rather as a movement *within* a period: the early parts of modernity. The Renaissance does take part in modernity, but it does so in a muted way. Therefore, it is not the origin of modernity, but rather a later pocket of time which offers modernity its first resistance, after the modern movement has grown forth from its Gothic bosom.

According to prevailing art history, infused as it still is with the idea of the Renaissance, the new naturalism of the 1400s emerged through the simultaneous pursuit of two sources: the observation of nature *and* the study of antiquity. By this means an art emerged that was ostensibly both more true to nature and aesthetically more satisfying. But as already suggested by Panofsky, there is a possible divide wrapped up in this dual objective: is the most beautiful and most antique appearance also necessarily the most true to nature? Panofsky states that until the end of the Renaissance, the divide was surmounted by the thesis "that classical art itself, in manifesting what *natura naturans* had intended but *natura naturata* had failed to perform, represented the highest and 'truest' form of naturalism."[4] With his characteristic, strategically placed inverted commas Panofsky suggests that there is something extremely vague about this form of 'true' naturalism – a naturalism that should rather be understood more as its opposite, *idealism*. For does the Late Medieval pursuit of the antique pictorial ideal actually lead to anything which could reasonably be called a

Fig. 1. Pieter Brueghel the Elder, The Way to Calvary, 1564. Vienna, Kunsthistorisches Museum (Photo KHM).

more naturalistic pictorial paradigm, or does the antiquization conversely lead to an idealistic pictorial art which masks or indeed suppresses an already advanced naturalism?

The question leaves us with three options rising in degree of scepticism:

1. When the Renaissance broke through, modernity was so little developed that even a resuscitation of antiquity would look modern;
2. The Renaissance's self-perception is partly self-deception and its 'antique' ingredients a masquerade of a modernity that does not have resuscitation of antiquity as an essential keystone of its existence;
3. The Renaissance is utterly conservative, a reactionary movement the outer forms of which are not just masks, but expressions of inner structures that subdue the emerging modernity.

In the following I shall mainly lean in the direction of 3), albeit a dose of 2) and a gram of 1) are necessary for the sake of nuance. As regards point 1), indeed the pictorial art of antiquity is characterised by a semi-developed perspective with foreshortenings and light-shade representation; and this perspective was deconstructed in the Middle Ages in favour of a flatter, more diagrammatic pictorial space in which propensities to infinity are only expressed symbolically. Based on that observation, there must then be something or other in the pictorial culture of antiquity that is suppressed in the Middle Ages and 'reborn' in early modernity. Broadly speaking, it could be an acknowledgement of the sense of sight as a crucial factor in pictorial representation – even though it should be stressed that antiquity's concept of visibility is based in the corporeal, whereas its modern counterpart looks towards space. It would thus not seem improbable that antique pictorial culture did actually act as a catalyst, since it optically became a guide for the Late Medieval image, albeit we have to be aware that this catalyst also had its limits, if it didn't simply lead to the neo-antique pictorial idiom.

Should the latter be the case, one interpretation is found in point 2), i.e. that we are dealing with an exterior cladding of an otherwise advanced modernity. The German philosopher of culture Oswald Spengler, for example, sees the Renaissance as anti-modern in its attempts to repress the musical-Gothic and depth-seeking in favour of the plastic-corporeal, and yet it has no core substance that can justify these stylistic phenomena as anything other than semblance:

"But the Renaissance, when it had mastered some arts of word and picture, had shot its bolt. It altered the ways of thought and the life-feeling of West Europe not one whit. It could penetrate as far as costume and gesture, but the roots of life it could not touch – even in Italy the world-outlook of the Baroque is essentially a continuation of the Gothic".[5]

So, even though Spengler acknowledges the muted existence of the Gothic in Italy, there is still so much of it that it constitutes a core upon which the neo-antique is merely ornamentation. The Renaissance thereby limits itself to an enterprise in taste, an artificial counter-movement, which might indeed be anxious about modern, what Spengler calls Faustian, supremacy, but at the same time lacks awareness of what it will put in its place.

But is accepting this idea of masquerade not to undervalue the effect of the Renaissance? For if sufficient power is staked behind the masquerade, this power appropriates what there might be of original personality, and we land in point 3), the understanding of the Renaissance as regressive, also in its fundamental structures. According to this model, the Renaissance can still effectively be an illusion at inveterate distance from its antique prototype, and yet the identification with antiquity represents a symptom of a cultural regression that radically changes the cultural structures in the 15th-16th centuries.

If not before, this model made itself felt in Italy after 1850 when the *Risorgimento* was unifying the peninsula under a republican form of government, and democratically-minded historians began searching for national antecedents to republicanism. In this quest writers such as Pasquale

Villari and Alessandro Wesselofsky were seized by bitterness against Renaissance humanism and its promotion of classical culture, as classicism was seen as camouflage for a 14th-15th-century political decline in which the republicanism of the communes was supplanted by the despotism of the *signorie* – antecedents, that is, to the very same mighty nobility which the *Risorgimento* was in the process of neutralising.⁶ According to Villari's argument, for example, the communes were the cradle of European democracy, as they afforded the third estate a stake in power – as is evident from 14th-century chronicles and diaries, the *volgare* of which is full of chaotic, everyday details. As the despotism spreads, however, the writers are seized by Neo-Latin airs and consequently their images of history become synthesised constructions scorning empirical trifles.⁷ It was only with the Dominican monk Savonarola's attempt to re-establish the Florentine republic at the end of the 15th century that the *volgare* culture ostensibly had a final chance to break with the classicist-clad absolute rule, in this instance of the Medici, and the 19th-century Italian school of historians itself was therefore given the name *I savonaroliani* or *I nuovi piagnoni* (after Savonarola's followers, 'the crying').⁸

Apart from the aforementioned nuances – the Renaissance's doses of actual modernity and masquerade – this model of regression corresponds quite precisely to what is my concern here. The wealth of detail in 14th-century chronicles thus correspond with pictorial art's contemporaneous movement towards an unbridled naturalistic paradigm, just like those constructions of history estranged from empirical corpus prevalent in later humanist literature correspond with the focus on the ideal body – the particularity-shy body – prevalent in pictorial art from and including the later 15th century, the epoch in which the High Renaissance came into being – and some times before.

Lynn Thorndike, historian of science, goes to the heart of the issue:

> "The concept of the Italian Renaissance (...) has, in my opinion, done a great deal of harm in the past and may continue to do harm in the future. It has kept men in general from recognizing that our life and thought is based more nearly and actually on the Middle Ages than on a distant Greece and Rome, from whom our heritage is more indirect, bookish and sentimental, less institutional, social, religious, even less economic and experimental".⁹

Fig. 2. Raphael, The School of Athens, 1510-11. Rome, Musei Vaticani, Stanza della Segnatura (Photo Musei Vaticani).

According to Thorndike, then, the Middle Ages paves the way to modernity, whereas the perception of the Italian Renaissance confuses the understanding of both the character and the genesis of modernity. By expanding the Renaissance category from posterity's historiography to a Late Medieval practice seeking to transform this category into reality, we could be even more specific and say: early modernity is curbed and modified by the Italian Renaissance, first regaining its full strength in the 18th century. Modernity could thus be understood as a movement which grows out of the Middle Ages around 1000, reaching first maturation in the 15th century – the century that ushers in the naturalist paradigm of pictorial art – culminating in the 18th-19th centuries and phasing out with the same paradigm after 1900.¹⁰

Whereas the modern movement in the Late Middle Ages, from 1000-1400, is equally distributed between North and South Europe – indeed, in certain respects is most sharply accentuated in Italy – it is, however, muted down here by the Renaissance from the middle of the 15th century, so that the waters are definitively divided from 1500 onwards. In art history, for instance, Svetlana Alpers has expertly revealed the many aspects in which 17th-century Dutch painting, and Northern art altogether, escape the Italian Renaissance aesthetic – an aesthetic which art historians have hitherto elevated to an almost universal instrument in the understanding of all pictorial art produced between the Middle Ages and the 20th century. What Alpers observes in the Netherlanders, going back to Jan van Eyck; is their *descriptive* method – a method which abandons itself to the pure visual process, to the empirical registration of the surroundings in all their diversity. With

its attention to texture and particularity detail, this way of looking is in striking contrast to the Italian, which cultivates *narrative action* in accordance with the antique canon, as revived not least in Alberti's *De pictura*.[11]

Even though there are some problematic details in Alpers' theory, it is enormously profitable in its basic concept. The tendency in Northern art, which Alpers pins down, can be expanded both forward to the 18th-19th centuries and backward to the Gothic, the beginning of modernity. The characteristics of Italian art also have wide-reaching consequences, for they become guidelines for *academic* art. As is well known, the art academies – the new places of education established by the absolutistic princely and royal houses – which from the 16th century onwards replace the Medieval workshops, have *history painting* as their norm, i.e. depiction of the heroic human body in narrative or allegorical situations. The art academies could but look down on genres which let their gaze slide away from the symbol-satiated ideal body and over to its symbol-weak prosaic surroundings. The further one moved out into the chaos of the environment, the lower one was posited in the genre hierarchy. Thus, one was flung centrifugally from portrait to genre to marine and animal painting, in order to land at the outermost – and lowest – point, in the humble landscape and still life.[12] The reason for the inferiority of these genres was therefore no different in modernity than it had been in antiquity. Rather than guiding the intellect towards grand perceptions, they pulled it down into the darkness of sensuality. That the academic view of art in the 18th-19th centuries was increasingly looked

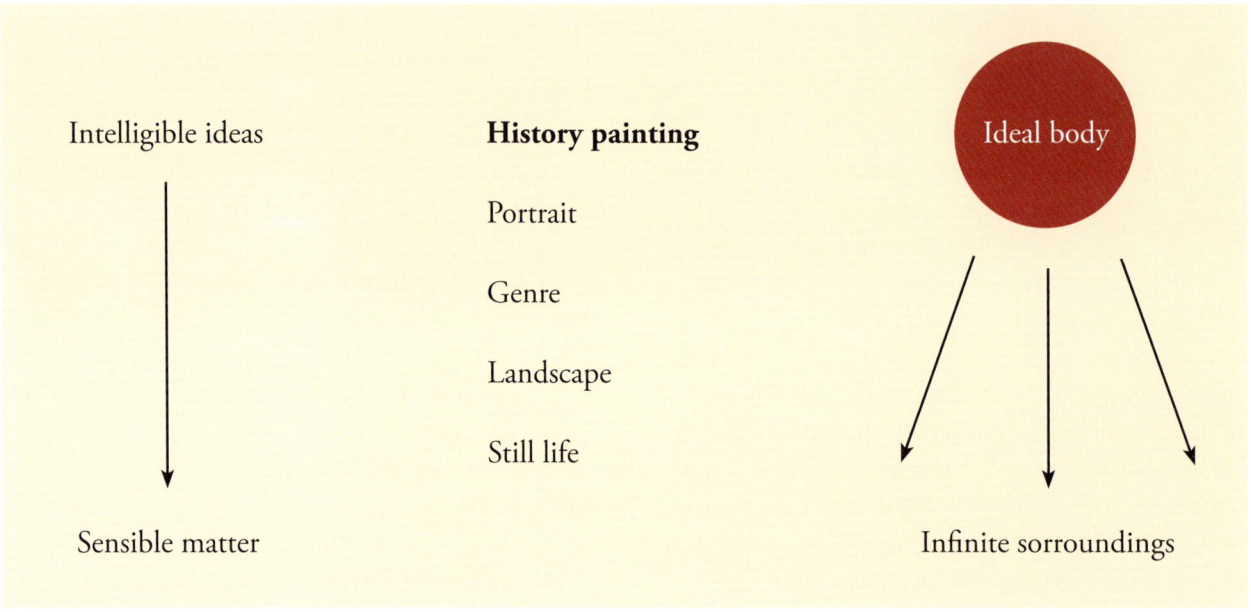

upon as conservative, was therefore due to more than a purely contemporaneous reason. From its very introduction in the 15th-16th centuries, the question could be asked as to how universally it expressed its contemporaries' conception of the world.

The idea that, on the other hand, Gothic culture is heavy with modern tendencies could be sustained, first, by etymological considerations. In fact, within my own area of study, what we now call visual art, the first style to be labelled 'modern' was Gothic in architecture. North of the Alps the modern architectural style is associated with Gothicism right up until the middle of the 17th century. It was, however, an Italian construction to invent the Middle Ages, topple the Gothic in its darkness and then to transfer the Gothic label of 'modern' to the revived antique style. The Goths were the ones who, along with other Northern barbarians, had ravaged the antique culture, the grandiose Italian past. Therefore, their style – however long after the great migrations it might have been developed – must have been primitive. The idea of Northerners who ravage the antique culture and institute their own barbaric building style is presented in Manetti's biography of Brunelleschi (c.1480), and it is further developed in the letter from Raphael and Castiglione to Pope Leo X (c.1519), in which pointed arches are compared with the topos of the wild man who builds bowers.[13]

Although the idea of the dark Middle Ages can be traced back at least to Petrarch, and from then on antiquity was the ideal for Italian intellectuals, it was nonetheless a long time before they spotted the Gothic blunders, and at first only in architecture where the clash with antiquity was more immediately visible than in painting and sculpture. Filarete was possibly the first Italian writer to bemoan the Gothic when, in his *Trattato di architettura* (c.1460-1464), he wrote: "I too was once pleased by modern buildings, but as soon as I began to enjoy the antique ones I grew to despise the modern."[14] It was not until the next century, however, with Vasari's confirmation of Italy as the home and most advanced bastion of modern art that the coup with which we still live with took place: the juxtaposition of *moderno* with *la buona maniera greca antica* in its re-awakened form.[15]

Even though Vasari had an instinctive eye for the classical-oriented painters who were part of the Italian current of modernity from the outset – most obviously Giotto and Masaccio, more problematically Leonardo – he saw no conflict between these painters and their typical, Gothic-dominated environment in the 14th-15th centuries. All were forerunners of the classical, 'modern'

Fig. 3. Diagram of the genre hierarchy.

style culminating with Michelangelo in the 16th century, the classicists just to a more pronounced degree. That Vasari and his predecessors were thus blind to the Gothic features of painting, while at a relatively early stage they were offended by Gothic architecture, can partly be explained by the lack of antique paintings for comparison before the end of the 15th century, the beginning of the Renaissance. Moreover, painting was not scarred by the North-South conflict. While architecture had been ravaged by the Gothic, painting had simply stagnated in *maniera greca*, the Byzantine manner.[16] The style which succeeded *maniera greca* in the 14th-15th centuries was accordingly not associated with the Gothic, but only with the Renaissance. It is therefore not so strange that far into the 1400s the humanists preferred Gothic painters to Masaccio.[17]

However, by the time the Gothic features of early modern painting were finally spotted during the Romantic period and the Gothic revival of the 18th-19th centuries, the Renaissance myth was so well-developed that Gothicism's modern aspects had evaporated. The 15th-century Netherlanders and (to an extent) Italians became 'primitive'. Bruegel was a medieval painter. The argumentation is again the Platonic, which Panofsky went so far as to equip with inverted commas: the 'true' naturalism is that which realises what nature had 'actually' intended, but could not carry out. The beautiful is the true; the ugly is the primitive. In Johann George Sulzer's *Allgemeine Theorie der Schönen Künste* (1792), "Gothische Malerei" is defined, for example, as the painting that precedes the study of nature and antiquity in the late 15th century and which has elongated figures and unnatural movements. "The painters before that time drew according to an ideal that was not a heightened nature, as was the ideal of the Greeks, but according to a nature that was corrupted in proportion and movement."[18]

Both Panofsky and his predecessor Sulzer thus acknowledge that the Renaissance aspires to a 'heightened' nature, a neo-antique nature free of Gothic 'corruption'. And yet it is still the prevailing myth that naturalism *by and large* is a Renaissance invention. But can the same movement embrace nature in its expansive, temporal and particular aspects – all the modern ingredients which literally corrupt beauty – and at the same time aim at beauty with only limited access for these ingredients? It seems far simpler to attribute the new naturalism to the Gothic and instead to look at the Renaissance as a counter- or subsidiary movement to this – a movement which curbs the modern lack of restraint in favour of a more ideal beauty.

This view could be sustained, furthermore, by looking at the infinity, variation and roughness with which the Gothic was equipped by both Romantic and Classically oriented viewers, as all these qualities are core elements of modern, perspectival vision. Around 1800, for instance, John Milner (1752-1826) saw an *artificial infinite* in the Gothic's "aspiring form of the pointed arches, lofty pediments, and the tapering pinnacles", besides the serial repetition of the bays. And when Uvedale Price was seduced by Gothic architecture in his *Essays on the Picturesque* of 1794, it was a consequence of its coarseness, sudden variation and detailed irregularity – all features which were contrary to the classical closed form, and which also made it well-suited to become a picturesque ruin.[19] The feeling of infinity is thus already roused on the microscopic level in the teeming Gothic detail, layer upon layer of tympanum figures, foliage ornamentation, small architectural members etc. In reference to Milan Cathedral, Goethe even speaks of a "multiplied smallness" (*Multiplizierter Kleinheit*), so the thought could, in Speglerian fashion, lead to Leibniz's and Newton's later integral calculus.[20] Bringing together all these observations, it does not seem strange that by *Romantic* Hegel understood post-antiquity in general.

However, this axis from Gothic to Romantic – and bypassing the Renaissance – is made truly tangible by the fact that all the terminology with which the Romantics rehabilitate the Gothic actually goes back to the Gothic's own time. For, although in a judgment reversed 180 degrees, the Italian and French Renaissance writers focus on the same characteristics of the Gothic as those highlighted by their Romantic successors. As the

Italians gradually became convinced of the blessing of the Renaissance and the curse of the Gothic – the hitherto modern style – it was precisely the un-proportional throng of detail that caught the eye. Filarete, one of the first declared adversaries of the Gothic, states in his tract on architecture that the Gothic style was not created by real architects, but rather by painters, stonemasons and especially goldsmiths, who designed their modern works "like tabernacles and thuribles".[21] And in Raphael's and Castiglione's letter to Leo X (c. 1519), offence is taken at the Gothic's badly executed and observed small figures and at the "strange animals and figures and foliage beyond all reason".[22]

Vasari, too, giving *maniera tedesca* the deathblow in the mid-16th century, thinks that these artists made "a curse of tiny tabernacles, one above the other, with so many pyramids and spires and leaves, that (...) it seemed impossible that they could sustain themselves; and they appeared more as if they were made of paper than of stone and marble."[23] Apart from this confusing hotchpotch, then, Vasari is also offended by the Gothic's *incorporeality*, its all too slight appearance. This discourse survives undiminished when, in 1642, Giovanni Baglione defines *Gotico* or *Tedesco* as "particular disorder in art and architecture", (*più tosto disordine dell'arte e dell'architettura*),[24] and also when, in 1681, the art historian Filippo Baldinucci refers to the Gothic "infinity of small tabernacles" and its "extremely subtle columns and long distortions (*smisuratamente lunghe*), turned and in many ways unnatural".[25]

Even though the Italian Renaissance and Baroque writers find the Gothic style repugnant, and not sublime, they still describe it via exactly the same concepts as the Romantics used. Both parties are concerned – whatever the assessment – with Gothic infinity, immeasurability, irregularity, coarseness, myriads of detail and incorporeality. If we also add Gothic naturalism to these properties, we are practically left with a recipe for a landscape image. Only the projection onto a surface is missing. This we find in Michelangelo's alleged comment on Flemish painting, reported in *Four Dialogues on Painting* by the Portuguese Francisco de Hollanda:

"Flemish painting (...) will, generally speaking, (...) please the devout more than any painting from Italy which will never bring him to shed one tear, whereas Flemish painting will cause him to shed many; and this is not because of the strength and goodness of the painting but because of the goodness of the devout person. It will appeal to women, particularly the very old and the very young, and also to monks and nuns, and to certain noblemen without sense of true harmony. For in Flanders they paint in order to bind you to the outer view (*pera enganar a vista exterior*), or such things that may cheer you up, and of which you cannot speak badly, such as for instance saints and prophets. They paint materials and masonry, turf of fields, shadows of trees, and rivers and bridges, which they call landscapes (*paisagens*), and many figures on this side and many on that. And all this, although it appeals to some, is done without reason and art, without symmetry and proportion, without clever choice and boldness, and, finally, without any substance and nerve".[26]

In Michelangelo's view, the Flemish sensory inclusion of pictorial elements impedes the reasoned choice that creates symmetry and proportion, prerequisites of a closed art work in accordance with antiquity's canon. Without closedness, substance cannot be created either, and then we are left with exactly the same objections that the Italian writers had against Gothic architecture: lack of proportions, confusing myriads of detail, incorporeality.

Michelangelo's comments are so much the more striking in that he is himself a sculptor and, moreover, when he paints, the Renaissance expert of the figure par excellence. While the volume of his naked bodies swells to titanic, sometimes grotesque dimensions, the landscape is restricted to an almost forced minimum. Adam and Eve on the ceiling of the Sistine Chapel (1510) are expelled to a green plateau without so much as a blade of grass or a stone. The thought occurs that the closed corporeality required of neo-antique art is a problem in the open space of modernity. It is unlikely to be a coincidence that Gothic human figures are slight, spindly and ethereal, as if the materiality has been dissolved in the expansive surrounding environment.

That post-Hegelian art history has, however,

been blind to the continuity in the Northern tradition is because it has been sliced into at least three parts, each with an isolated discourse: Middle Ages, Renaissance and modernity. As the first two have both done their bit to tie the Gothic solidly to the Middle Ages, the only Gothic-Romantic axis that historians of modernity have been able to spot is the one that turns the Romantics' interest in the Gothic into a question of reception history: the Romantics' view of the Gothic as sublime revealed more about themselves than about the nature of the Gothic. But, as I have shown here, to a surprising extent *the same* properties come to light when a Renaissance commentator and a Romantic discuss the Gothic: i.e. infinity, myriads of detail, coarseness, lack of substance etc. The difference between the two discourses is not due to content, but to the *evaluation* of this content.

In conclusion, having demonstrated that many well-qualified attempts have actually been made to break up the Renaissance monopoly on the definition of early modernity since the 19th century, we have all the more cause to wonder why these attempts are repeatedly silenced and ousted from the general historical consciousness. Perhaps we are at last approaching the state of affairs in which we can join Spengler in stating:

"That close inward relation in which we conceive ourselves to stand towards the Classical, and which leads us to think that we are its pupils and successors (whereas in reality we are simply its adorers), is a venerable prejudice which ought at last to be put aside. The whole religious-philosophical, art-historical and social-critical world of the 19th Century has been necessary to enable us (...) to begin to realize, once and for all, how immeasurably alien and distant these things are (...)".[27]

Notes

1 Erwin Panofsky, *Renaissance and Renascenses in Western Art*, Stockholm 1960.

2 http://www.igl.ku.dk/~pade/modern/Welcome.html, last consulted in June 2010.

3 I initiated this argument in Jacob Wamberg, "Ghiberti, Alberti, and the Modernity of Gothic", *Analecta Romana Instituti Danici* 21 (1993), 173-211, and develop it in more detail in Jacob Wamberg, *Landscape as World Picture: Tracing Cultural Evolution in Images*, Århus 2009 (1st Danish ed. 2005), II, 51-116.

4 Panofsky 1960, 19, 30 (with citation), 36-37, 165.

5 Oswald Spengler, *Der Untergang des Abendlandes. Umrisse einer Morphologie der Weltgeschichte*, Munich 1972 (1923), 277-278, 290, 300-308, 330-366, citation, 300-301: "Die Renaissance bemächtigte sich einiger Künste des Bildes und Wortes, und damit war alles getan. Sie hat die Denkweise Westeuropas, das Lebensgefühl in nichts verändert. Sie drang bis zum Kostüm und zur Gebärde vor, nicht bis zu den Wurzeln des Daseins, denn die Weltanschauung des Barock ist selbst in Italien dem inneren Wesen nach eine Vorsetzung der Gotik." English translation from Spengler, *Decline of the West*, Charles Francis Atkinson (trans.), London 1971, 233.

6 Hans Baron, *The Crisis of the Early Italian Renaissance: Civic Humanism and Republican Liberty in an Age of Classicism and Tyranny*, Princeton 1955, 251-252.

7 See for example, Pasquale Villari, *The Two First Centuries of Florentine History: The Republic and Parties at the Time of Dante*, Linda Villari (trans.), London 1905³, vi, 2-11 and 34. Cf. also Denis E. Cosgrove, *Social Formation and Symbolic Landscape*, Madison (Wisconsin) 1998, 82.

8 See in particular, Pasquale Villari, *The Life and Times of Girolamo Savonarola*, Linda Villari (trans.), New York 1888 (reprint St. Clair Shores (Mi) 1972), especially I, 38-49, 297-305, and II, 418-22; Baron 1955, 251.

9 Here cited from Stanley L. Jaki, *Uneasy Genius: The Life and Work of Pierre Duhem*, Haag, Boston & Lancaster 1984, 423.

10 Spengler 1972, 216, 234, 236.

11 Svetlana Alpers, *The Art of Describing: Dutch Art in the Seventeenth Century*, Chicago 1983, xix-xxv.

12 On the academic genre hierarchy, see for instance Nikolaus Pevsner, *Academies of Art: Past and Present*, Cambridge 1940, 94-95.

13 Antonio di Tuccio Manetti, *Operette istoriche*, G. Milanesi (ed.), Florence 1887, 103-04; Paul Frankl, *The Gothic: Literary Sources and Interpretations through Eight Centuries*, Princeton 1960, 255; letter to Leo X, cited in Ingrid D. Rowland, "Raphael, Angelo Colocci, and the Genesis of the Architectural Orders", *Art Bulletin* 76 (1994) 81-104, 101: "Pur, questa architectura ebbe qualche ragione. Però che naque dalli arbori non anchor tagliati, delli quali, piegati li rami e rilegati insieme, fanno li lor terzi acuti." In this letter it is also claimed that Italy with its glorious past "(...) in vero è patria universale di tutti li cristiani (...) ", 100. On

bowers, see for example Vitruvius, *De architectura*, 2, 1, 2-3.

14 Antonio Filarete, *Trattato di architettura*, A. M. Finoli & L. Grassi (ed.), Milan 1972, 13, 380: "Ancora a me solevano piacere questi moderni, ma poi, ch'io commenciai a gustare questi antichi, mi sone venuti in odio quelli moderni." English translation from *Filarete's Treatise on Architecture*, John Spencer (trans.), New Haven & London, 1965, 175.

15 Giorgio Vasari, *Le vite de'più eccelenti pittori scultori e architettori* (synoptic edition of the versions 1550 and 1568, R. Bettarini & P. Barocchi (ed.), Florence 1966-1987, II, 97, III, 18 and V, 8. See also Panofsky 1960, 34-35.

16 Lorenzo Ghiberti, *Lorenzo Ghibertis Denkwürdigkeiten (I Commentarii)*, Julius von Schlosser (ed.), Berlin 1912, II, 1.

17 Michael Baxandall, *Giotto and the Orators: Humanist Observers of Painting and the Discovery of Pictorial Composition 1350-1450*, Oxford 1971, 91.

18 George Sulzer, *Allgemeine Theorie der Schönen Künste*, II, Leipzig 1792, 434: "Die Mahler vor diesem Zeitpunkt zeichneten nach einem Ideal, das nicht eine erhöhete Natur war, wie das Ideal der Griechen, sondern eine in Verhältniss und Bewegung verdorbene Natur." See also "Gotik" (1910), in Julius von Schlosser, *Präludien. Vorträge und Aufsätze*, Berlin 1927, 289.

19 Frankl 1960, 439-446. Milner states his opinions in *Essays on Gothic Architecture by the Rev. T. Warton, Rev. J. Bentham, Captain Grose and the Rev. J. Milner*, London 1800. Panofsky 1991, 53-54, also remarks on the fundamentally unlimited aspect of the serial repetition in Gothic bays.

20 Goethe, *Über Baukunst*, here cited from Schlosser 1927, 291.

21 Filarete 1972, XIII, 382. English translation from Filarete 1965, 176.

22 My translation from Rowland 1994, Appendix 1, 101: "E li tedeschi, la maniera delli quali in molti luochi ancor dura, spesso per ornamento pongono un qualche figurino ranichiato e mal fatto et peggio inteso per mensola, a sostenere un travo, et altri strani animali e figure et fogliami fuor d'ogni ragione." Rowland, who establishes Colocci as the letterwriter, reproduces the letter with philological accuracy.

23 Vasari 1966-1987 I, 382: "E così per tutte le facce et altri lore ornamanti facevano una maledizione di tabernacolini l'una sopra l'altro, con tante piramidi e punte e foglie, che, non ch'elle possano stare, pare impossibile ch'elle si possino reggere, et hanno più il modo da parer fatte di carta che di pietre o di marmi."

24 In *Le vite de'pittori*, cited in E. S. de Beer, "Gothic: Origin and Diffusion of the Term: The Idea of Style in Architecture", *Journal of the Warburg and Courtauld Institutes* 11 (1948), 143-62, here: 153.

25 "Ordine Gottico" in *Vocabulario toscano dell'arte del disegno*, Florence 1681, 113: "un'infinità di piccoli tabernacoli" (cited in Schlosser 1927, 288) and "sottilisime colonne, e smisuramente lunghe, auuolte, e in più modi snaturate (...)" (cited in Frankl 1960, 343). Baldinucci's judgement is echoed in the classically-oriented Jean-François Félibien des Avaux (1658-1733), the man behind the academic genre hierarchy in France. The foreword to Félibien's collection of biographies of major architects (1687), claims that at least the Late Gothic period, influenced as it was by *délicatesse*, was overwhelmed "dans l'amas confus d'une multitude infinie d'ornements et dans une hardiesse de travail démesurée."

26 Francisco de Hollanda, "*Vier Gespräche über die Malerei geführt zu Rom 1538*", in: Joaquim de Vasconcellos (ed.), *Quellenschriften für Kunstgeschichte und Kunsttechnik des Mittelalters und der Neuzeit*, 9 (1899), 28-29.

27 Spengler 1972, 37: "Es ist ein ehrwürdiges Vorurteil, das wir endlich überwinden sollten, daß die Antike uns innerlich nahesteht, weil wir vermeintlich ihre Schüler und Nachkommen, weil wir tatsächlich ihre Anbeter gewesen sind. Die ganze religionsphilosophische, kunsthistorische, sozialkritische Arbeit des 19. Jahrhunderts war nötig (...) um uns endlich fühlen zu laßen, wie unermeßlich fremd und fern das alles innerlich ist (...) ." English translation from Spengler 1971, 27.

RENAISSANCE ART AND ART HISTORY IN DENMARK: SOME REMARKS ON THE CONFERENCE

Maria Fabricius Hansen

An important impetus for arranging a conference on the Danish art of the Renaissance – or art in Renaissance Denmark – is the curiosity of discovering who is working on what material and how, internationally. The gathering of specialized knowledge is a way of fertilizing the study of the art of this period and region. The conference might thus have contributed to reactivating Renaissance art history, which, in my view, currently lives a languishing existence. Some of us may humbly ascribe the decreasing number of students working on this field to our own inadequacy as teachers, but if we widen our gaze we will soon discover that the problem is of a much more general kind, constituting what could be called an international crisis in Renaissance art history. I will return to this issue below.

The conference presentations were broadly based, both as regards the material dealt with and the methodological approaches involved. We were presented with artist-specific and genre-specific topics, with painting, sculpture, architecture and decorative art, and we had the chance to compare methods and results from micro-historic and empirically oriented presentations with theoretically based analyses addressing general problems or observations. The result was, as I see it, a very enlightening image of how important these basically different art historical approaches are in establishing a contour, although approximate and sketchy, of the field and its potentials. It was encouraging and inspiring to become acquainted with such substantial and rich material so far from a well-established canon, material lying there so temptingly and ready at hand, often amazingly unknown, just waiting to be analyzed. And finally, it was enlightening to hear the meta-reflections on what we are actually doing, to have questions raised concerning the premises so often taken for granted in analyses of Renaissance art, and to have our fundamental and much-too-often preconceived assumptions challenged about how the past is to be understood. Rather than offering specific analyses of individual works of art, this section of papers provided inspiration for further reflection on our endeavours as Renaissance art historians in general. What may be achieved within the discipline – and where lie the possibilities today? What are the dangers? And as always it is fruitful to be particularly attentive and critically minded when dealing with matters that appear most evident and eternally valid, or when dealing with some of the many tacit presuppositions that we so often forget to question. Whether positioned in a traditional understanding of the period and of historical studies or encountering the field from a more deconstructionist angle, it is probably useful to keep in mind Kierkegaard's remark about a private teacher who always went around repeating Descartes's *de omnibus dubitandum est*; according to Kierkegaard, this teacher expressed himself with such firm conviction that it was clear he himself had never suffered from doubt at all.[1]

Offering a mutually enlightening alternation between different art historical approaches, the conference was perhaps especially enriching in making evident how much work there is to be done, and how intriguing the conceptual and methodological framework really is.

Seen from a Danish point of view, the conference was useful in presenting the material as seen from the outside. Some of us have been formed by scholarly traditions and national barriers that are obviously irrelevant as regards the Renaissance. These traditions and barriers mean less or perhaps nothing to foreigners. As I see it, the conference was particularly illuminating in drawing fruitful connections between Danish and non-Danish material and, not least, material that was originally – but is no longer – Danish. We were reminded of how internationalized, not to say globalized, the Renaissance world was, also due to the many direct, personal and family relations between the courts within the European area, as well as to art agency and to the extensive trading and colonizing endeavours. The presentations may help to open up some of the perspectives that were evident at the time but are difficult to grasp today because our image of the period is unavoidably coloured by our own time and its conditions. This is an awareness of the so-called new art history which has gradually been commonly accepted, leaving, however, much revision to be done of our heritage of assumptions.

Parts of twentieth-century Danish art history have undoubtedly been restricted by a strong nationalist sentiment going back to the politically difficult times of the nineteenth century. There has been a tendency to define ourselves in opposition to our great neighbours, resulting in a psychologically very bizarre mixture of an inferiority complex and stubborn self-sufficiency in relation to the rest of the world. In consequence, the sense of the international perspectives in our art has in many cases been restricted. To see everything as national and as Danish as possible has been a generally accepted ideal, and this idealization of the national has taken place at the expense of the profoundly international Renaissance culture, so open to other countries or geographical areas and their cultures. Of course, other barriers existed at the time, mainly social divisions between an aristocratic elite and the large multitudes of farmers, tradesmen and petit bourgeois. But in Denmark we can learn much from the vast international scope of the art-consuming elite at a time when too many people seem to think that Danish identity and nationalism have to go hand in hand with xenophobia, and that it is even supposed to be a valuable quality to cultivate a Danish and national consciousness in terms of such hostility. The Renaissance material and the way it was put into perspective by the speakers at the conference may encourage another way to deal with and behave in the globalized world of today.

It might perhaps have been feared that a conference arranged as part of an official Renaissance Year would consist of a long series of papers glorifying the Renaissance as a very special, groundbreaking and particularly important historical period. We are all highly engaged in this period – probably none of the participants would deny this – yet the speakers managed to keep to sober, factual analyses of the material, without falling back into the period glorification that has characterized much of twentieth-century Renaissance art history. It was a kind of art history which tended to overlook and suppress both old and new insights, for instance of scholars like Aby Warburg, whose respect for the medieval period and consciousness of how important tradition is in the understanding of the Renaissance has too often been forgotten. Now, it seems that a healthy distance to the immensely well-constructed Renaissance myth, perhaps particularly cemented by Vasari in his *Vite,* is finally coming within reach.

If Renaissance art history is in dire straits at present, attracting a regrettably reduced number of students, it may partly be a reaction to the glorification which the period has enjoyed in the past 150 years since Burckhardt and his generation (and ultimately, Vasari and his age). This glorification has probably made the younger generation of art historians feel almost a kind of loathing or perhaps, even worse, boredom, when confronted with the established enthusiasm, and almost reverence, for the Renaissance. Many of the brightest students have tended to choose more marginal subjects and periods as well as approaches, and here marginal is of course to be understood as opposed to a notion of the Italian Renaissance as undeniably central to art history.

We have to admit that even the naming of this conference was problematic, as some of the speakers also touched upon. Thomas DaCosta Kaufmann made a very appropriate adjustment to the title, changing it from 'The Danish Renaissance' to 'The Renaissance in Denmark'; Claire Farago discussed the problem of the national in relation to the concept of the Renaissance; Mogens Bencard was opposed to the use of the term Renaissance for this period of art history, and, finally, Keith Moxey and Jacob Wamberg also pointed to a series of problems in the concept of the Danish Renaissance, questioning the relevance of operating with the Renaissance concept at all; Keith Moxey concluded, however, by very subtly accepting our use of period designations after all.

But why call the art and culture of around 1600 'the Renaissance'?

If we are to use these period designations (and it is not at all evident that we should), the only reasonable thing to do would be to talk about Mannerism. Then why are we not doing that? First, very simply because the conference was part of a larger cultural event called the Renaissance Year. So the name of the period dealt with at the conference was given in advance. Probably, the people who took this cultural initiative very reasonably imagined that the aura of the Renaissance would attract an audience as well as the sponsors needed. And why care – is it not just a word, just an innocent name, the Renaissance?

No, surely it is not. As I see it, the prominence attached to this name is part of the problem. It is rooted in the surprisingly persistent notion of the ideal supremacy of Italian art with its heritage of classical antiquity. Just as there has been a hierarchy within iconographical studies, in which the ultimate success would be to demonstrate the neo-Platonic content of a picture, in general Renaissance art history has been – and sometimes still is – governed by the notion that the ultimate kind of art history is the one that deals with the great canonical (Italian) artists. For those doing research on non-Italian material, demonstrating indebtedness to Italy and ultimately classical antiquity has been the greatest legitimization of scholarly endeavours. This ideal of Italian art and its *all'antica* stylistic idiom distorts our work on other – for instance, northern European – cultures because it is based on criteria that northern art cannot match and that, even more importantly, may not even be as crucial if our project is to characterize the distinctive qualities of the art and the way it was seen and used in this period. When looking at the amazing castles with their architectural ornament (like Kronborg or Frederiksborg, which were visited during the conference), the strange altarpieces and the relation between word and image, the intriguing grotesques and so forth, why not focus on this marvellous manifestation of eclecticism, or on artistic invention and the fascination with originality – as Konrad Ottenheym emphasized in his paper – instead of concentrating on the elements that may be found to go back to the Italian area and ultimately Roman antiquity? Indeed, why not focus on how remarkable the results of the many diverse kinds of cultural interaction are? If Italian art and architecture really were the intended product, why then do the buildings and the pictorial art look so amazingly un-Italian?

It is not my intention to ban the observation of *all'antica* or classical elements that undeniably occur in the art and architecture in ever increasing measure throughout the period. Only, I find the investigation should not stop by describing their presence in the culture north of the Alps. We need to go on analyzing the way Italian or any other cultural idioms were taken over and combined in new ways, and why.

But, evidently, the conventionally high status of the term 'the Renaissance' is the reason why we in Denmark insist on calling both the sixteenth and the seventeenth centuries by this name. In consequence, we bury ourselves in different kinds of more or less irrelevant and self-imposed problems only because we of course have difficulty fabricating a coherent image of the past. If one artist working at a central European court is defined as mannerist or early baroque, then why should his works suddenly turn Renaissance if bought by Christian IV in the beginning of the seventeenth century?

And if Italian art and the renewal of classical antiquity are seen as the measure of the avant-garde innovation of the Renaissance, we are in trouble if we would like to argue that works were produced in Denmark of a quantity and quality comparable to those produced in Italy. If we instead chose to describe the period in other ways, these academic problems would be eliminated. Maybe it is exactly the only too common equation of the Renaissance with modernity that we should reconsider, as Jacob Wamberg suggested in his paper.

One way of framing the art of the period could be in terms of social history, focusing on the economic and political centres of Europe, as many of the papers indeed did. Within a certain set of social conditions, within a certain level of court culture, of sovereign government, of urban development, involving a gradually growing nationalistic consciousness, art covered certain aesthetic and political functions that had quite a lot in common north and south of the Alps. Some important questions, then, would be whether there were cities and major courts or other powerful cultural centres, whether people travelled, and so on.

These conditions are connected to a certain concept of art, and this has nothing to do with formal phenomena like the stylistic similarity of cultural objects to Italian art. This has to do with how human beings in specific living conditions responded to and used art. It also seems clear that the Reformation is related to a crucial transformation in how images were perceived and used. The resulting new concept of the image is a common denominator of much art of the northern European area; also on this level, the extent of an *all'antica* style appears to be less relevant.

We continue to call the era of Frederik II and Christian IV the Renaissance, although the similarities between the artwork produced in Denmark in this period and the art of Raphael and Bramante are not particularly obvious, because we insist on using the conventional period designations and this makes the preceding period hard to explain away as anything but late Gothic. For some reason this is seen as highly disturbing. For if we jump directly from the late Gothic of the fifteenth century to the Mannerism of the sixteenth century, the harsh reality is that we would not have a Renaissance at all in the overall historical account of Danish Art.

Again, we are paralyzed in repressive systems because of the mythic ideal of the Italian Renaissance. Yet, the visual evidence seems to indicate that as soon as the economic and political conditions resembled those in other cultural centres of Europe, there was no delay either as regards the means invested in art on an international level or the general outlook or understanding of the world, including the concept of art. If we adhered to the more neutral designation of the period by its century or even if we insisted on using a period name and consequently talked about Mannerism as a term covering the art produced and used in the cultural centres of the sixteenth and early seventeenth centuries, we would avoid the indeed very curious time loops we have to deal with now, loops that imply, for instance, that Christian IV did not live in the same period as the contemporary French or Italian princes. To sum up, I think using the term Renaissance in reference to the Danish art of the seventeenth century is rather more harmful to the field than is perhaps immediately evident.

Returning to the problem of the decreasing number of students dealing with Renaissance art – or Mannerist art, for that matter: The general upgrading of studies of visual culture and all it implies has apparently encouraged students' involvement in the Middle Ages as well as in the contemporary period or in the non-European world, where the traditional concept of art does not have the status it achieved from the Renaissance to the nineteenth century. At least, in Denmark remarkably few students dare specialize in Renaissance material compared with the many who deal with contemporary visual culture and methodological and theoretical questions. Moreover, seen from my point of view, the art historians working on the medieval period have been able to mobilize new insights in a meaningful and fruitful way to a much larger extent than their colleagues within Renaissance art history.

Allow me to conclude by posing some questions. How may Renaissance art history regain its vitality? Is it relevant and topical today? And why do we see this reluctance to embrace new insights and adopt new methodological approaches to the material precisely within this field? It seems clear that the more heavily canonized the works of art, the more difficult it is to break away from an uncritically reproductive, glorifying and unreflective art history, the kind of art history always focusing on who came first and who was the greatest. Perhaps the high estimation of art historical research dealing with great individual artists, preferably the Italian ones, has resulted in art historians forgetting the necessity of reflecting on why and how we deal with history, and has made Renaissance art history more problematically conventional, self-sufficient and resistant to new ideas and insights than other fields within the discipline.

The conference took its starting point in a framing of the material implied by the Danish context – and allow me to call it *marginal* Danish material, although Thomas DaCosta Kaufmann very convincingly identified the specific circumstances of rich cultural interaction in this small region connecting different parts of Europe. But perhaps exactly because of our starting point in this framing of marginal material, many of the methodological pitfalls of more conventional Renaissance art history were avoided. Evidently, art historians who participate in a conference like this already have a love of dealing with material off the beaten track. Their papers may indicate a future for Renaissance art history, also in the long term, by rejecting an uncritical glorification of the Renaissance – a glorification which younger art historians probably find much too predictable, smooth and unapproachable – and by strengthening an awareness of the interest of this period, perhaps especially from marginal points of view.

Notes

1 Søren Kierkegaard, "Concluding Unscientific Postscript" to *Philosophical Fragments*, in: Edna H. Hong & Howard V. Hong (eds. & trans.), New Jersey 1992, I, 195.

The English text has been revised by Stacey Cozart, University of Aarhus.

WORT-BILD-WORT. DIE RHETORIK DER LUTHERISCHEN KIRCHENKUNST NORDEUROPAS IM 16. UND 17. JAHRHUNDERT

Jan Harasimowicz

Bald nach dem Auftritt Martin Luthers breitete sich in ganz Mittel-, West-, und Nordeuropa der Ruf nach *reinem klaren Wort Gottes* aus. Auf der Heiligen Schrift allein, der einzigen „speysse unser seelen", sollte sich die Lehre der Kirche stützen, denn nur da ist „die Wahrheit Gottes, jeder Wille Gottes und Güte, Gebot und Barmherzigkeit", wie es im Jahre 1544 Jan Seklucjan, der polnische Prediger am Hofe Herzogs Albrecht von Preußen in Königsberg erklärte.[1] „Ich glaube daran stark und halte an den Doktoren der Heiligen Schrift fest – schrieb er weiter in seinem *Bekenntnis des christlichen Glaubens* – dass kein Altertum (nicht das älteste), kein Brauch, keine Concilien, Synode und Anordnungen, kurz, kein Mensch je solche Macht hätte oder haben könne, irgendetwas dem Worte Gottes, welches in der Heiligen Schrift klar offenbart ist, zuwider einzuführen, zuzufügen, zu fassen oder zu ändern. Denn wahrlich ist das Wort Gottes und die Heilige Schrift allen Anordnungen, Bräuchen, mögen sie noch so alt sein, den Synoden, Concilien und Gesetzen übergestellt".[2]

Die besondere Verehrung des offenbarten Wortes, der Heiligen Schrift, durch die Reformatoren resultierte aus seiner völligen zeitlichen und räumlichen Unabhängigkeit „dieser" Welt gegenüber: es gehörte einer „anderen" Welt an, wie es im ersten Apostelbrief des heiligen Petrus zu lesen ist: „Verbum Domini Manet in Aeternum", „Das Wort des Herrn bleibt in Ewigkeit" (1. Pt 1,25). Dieser Bibelvers, der allgemein als Wahlspruch der Reformation angesehen war, und sowohl in der vollen lateinischen Version, wie auch in der Abkürzung VDMIAE auftrat, erschien zum ersten Mal 1522 auf sächsischen Münzen und Gewändern am Hofe des Kurfürsten Friedrich des Weisen in Wittenberg.[3] Im Jahre 1529 trugen ihn die Angehörigen im Gefolge des Landgrafen Philipp von Hessen, die zum Reichstag in Augsburg kamen, auf den Ärmeln ihrer Kleidung auf. Etwa zur gleichen Zeit begann man den Spruch an den Toren von Schlössern oder an den Portalen der Bürgerhäuser, an Fensterumrahmungen und Glockenmänteln anzubringen. Im Jahre 1532 erschien er auch auf dem Titelblatt der ersten vollständigen Ausgabe der Luther-Bibel und wenige Jahre später auf den oberen Schaftstücken der zwei ältesten evangelischen Abendmahlskelche im sächsisch-thüringischen Raum: in der St.-Anna-Kirche in Annaberg (1540) und in der Predigerkirche in Erfurt (1541).[4]

Fig.1. Halle (Saale), Marktkirche Unser Lieben Frauen. Die steinernen Emporen entlang der Umfassungsmauer, 1550-1554. Nach Sabine Kramer und Karsten Eisenmenger (Hg.), *Die Marktkirche Unser Lieben Frauen zu Halle*, Halle (Saale) 2004, 30.

Die Initialen des reformatorischen Wahlspruchs kamen ebenfalls in die Innenräume jener Kirchen, die allmählich den Bedürfnissen des evangelischen Gottesdienstes angepasst wurden. Eines der frühesten Beispiele dieser Adoptierung ist die Marktkirche Unser Lieben Frauen in Halle an der Saale (Fig. 1). In den Jahren 1550-1554, kurz nach der Einführung der Reformation in der Stadt, baute man entlang der Umfassungsmauer steinerne Emporen, dank denen die Zahl der Teilnehmer des Gottesdienstes erweitert werden konnte. Auf den Brüstungen der Emporen wurden zahlreiche Bibelsprüche aufgetragen, welche gemeinsam ein durchdachtes theologisches Programm vermitteln.[5] Es beginnt am nordwestlichen Wendelstein mit Zitaten zu der auf dem Evangelium gestützten „Heilsgewissheit", um weiter zu dem in der Mitte der Ostempore, über dem Altar angebrachten Zitat aus dem Johannes-Evangelium zu führen (Joh 5,24): WAHRLICH WAHRLICH ICH SAGE EUCH WER MEIN WORT HÖRT UND GLAUBET DEM DER MICH GESANDT HAT DER HAT DAS EWIGE LEBEN UND KOMMT NICHT IN DAS GERICHT SONDERN ER IST VOM TODE ZUM LEBEN HINDURCH GEDRUNGEN (Fig. 2). Der Inschrift, die hier eine grundsätzliche Bedeutung hat, geht von der nördlichen Seite der reformatorische Wahlspruch voran, und von der südlichen Seite öffnet sie sich auf die Fortsetzung des Programms in Richtung der südwestlichen Ecke der Kirche und die darin enthaltene Bezeugung der Rolle, welche das Wort Gottes als Grundlage des gegenwärtigen und Verheißung des zukünftigen Heils habe. Auf diese Weise wird der gesamte Innenraum der Kirche und somit die darin versammelte Gemeinde in das überzeitliche Dasein des Wortes Gottes eingebettet. Ins Stein auf den Emporen eingemeißelt und in Predigten, wie im Lobgesang verheißen, sollte es tief in die Herzen geritzt werden, um in ihnen „ewig zu bleiben".

Das Ausschmücken der Wände und Emporenbrüstungen mit Bibelinschriften war in Mittel- und Nordeuropa recht üblich (Fig. 3).[6] Lutherische Pastoren, wie Balthasar Schupp aus Hamburg, der im Jahre 1649 in der dortigen Pfarrkirche St. Jakobi 229 Bibelsprüche angebracht hatte,[7] stan-

Fig. 2. Halle, Marktkirche Unser Lieben Frauen. Biblische Inschrift (Joh. 5,24) an der Brüstung der Empore, 1550-1554. Nach Kramer und Eisenmenger, 26.

den den kalvinischen Geistlichen, die dem alttestamentarischen Bilderverbot verpflichtet waren,[8] nicht nach. Rein inschriftlichen Schmuck bekamen also sowohl die kalvinistischen, als auch die lutherischen Kanzeln,[9] unterdessen das Phänomen der so genannten Schriftaltäre, die die bilderstürmerischen Praktiken, mittelalterliche Altarbilder durch gemalte Inschriften zu ersetzen (Fig. 4), bestimmtermaßen fortführten, sich eigentlich auf jene Gebiete beschränkte, die unter dem deutlichen Einfluss des reformierten Bekenntnisses standen: und zwar sowohl durch längere Zeit, wie die Grafschaft Ostfriesland, Harlingerland, Erzstift und Stadt Bremen,[10] als auch nur einige Jahrzehnte, wie Dänemark und Norwegen unter König Christian IV. zu Beginn seiner Herrschaft. Neben der nordwestdeutschen Schriftaltäre in Norden (1577),[11] Dornum (1590-1594)[12] und Ringstedt (1598)[13] haben wir also dänische in Store-Magleby (1580),[14] Helsingør (1589),[15] Sigersted (1596, Fig. 5)[15a] und Kirke-Saaby (1598)[16] sowie norwegische in Gaupne (1589),[17] Vereide (1604)[18] und Breim (1615).[19] In einigen von ihnen, zum Beispiel in den Altären von Stedesdorf in Harlingerland (1613)[20] und Langwarden in der Grafschaft Oldenburg (1621, Fig. 6),[21] waren die Sprüche von Anfang an mit kleineren biblischen Bildern ergänzt, in anderen, beispielsweise in den Altären in Alsønderup in Dänemark (1599)[22] und in Nedstryn in Norwegen (1610)[23] wurden ähnliche Darstellungen im 18. oder Anfang des 19. Jahrhunderts hinzugefügt.[24]

Die oben angeführten Beispiele zeigen deutlich, das eine rein inschriftliche Ausschmückung der Kirchen nicht immer und nicht vollkommen von evangelischen, besonders lutherischen Gemeinden akzeptiert wurde. Übrigens ist der erwähnte Inschriftenzyklus in Halle nicht ganz frei von Bildlichkeit, denn es befindet sich dort einerseits das so genannte Luther-Wappen, andererseits ein Medaillon mit der Darstellung des von einem Fisch gespienten Propheten Jonas, das sich auf Justus Jonas bezieht, den ersten evangelischen Pfarrer der Marktkirche (1541-1547).[25] Das Medaillon ist eine Art persönlichen Mottos des Reformators und steht den Druckerzeichen des 16. Jahrhunderts sehr nahe: ähnlich, wie diese, schließt es einen geschriebenen und öffentlich bekanntgegebenen Text und autorisiert ihn zugleich.[26] Es ist sicherlich kein Zufall, denn gerade in der reformatorischen Buchdruckkunst, insbesondere in den ersten gedruckten Bibeln und Katechismen Martin Luthers, sind die Quellen der für die evangelische Kirchenkunst des 16. und frühen 17. Jahrhunderts charakteristischen Bild-Wort-Sprache zu suchen.

Martin Luther legte bekanntlich sehr großen Wert auf die Auswahl der Holzschnitte für seine Wittenberger Bibeln: sie sollten „auffs einfeltigst

Fig. 3. Hillerød, Frederiksborg, Schloßkapelle. Biblische Inschrift an der Brüstung der Empore, 1606-1617 (Foto Hugo Johannsen).

Fig. 4. Uthlede bei Wesermünde, Pfarrkirche. Teilfreigelegte Tafel eines gotischen Flügelaltars mit der niederdeutschen Beschriftung aus der Reformationszeit, vor 1595. Nach Dietrich Diederichs-Gottschalk, *Die protestantischen Schriftaltäre des 16. und 17. Jahrhunderts in Nordwestdeutschland*, Regensburg 2005, Abb. 68b.

den inhalt [...] abmalen".[27] Ähnlich war es mit den biblischen „Merkbildern" für die Innenräume der Kirchen und Profanbauten: sie sollten „dem Worte nach" gemalt und „dem Text gemäß" verstanden werden.[28] Einer eben solchen Wirkung halber, empfahl Luther nachdrücklich die Darstellungen mit einem wörtlichem Kommentar zu versehen: mit der Betrachtung der Bilder und mit dem Lesen der dazugehörenden „Sprüche aus der Schrift" werden unsere Augen Gott loben und Ihm Danksagung aussprechen.[29] Das Hauptproblem war demzufolge richtige Formeln für das Nebeneinander von Bildern und Texten zu finden. Noch zu Lebzeiten Luthers, so etwa um das Jahr 1540, unternahm man den Versuch einen reformatorischen Altar in der Form eines monumentalen Buches zu schaffen – ja einer wahren „Laienbibel". Im Umkreis des Herrenberger Malers Heinrich Füllmaurer entstanden zwei beinahe identische Poliptychen, genannt heute der Gothaer Tafelaltar (Schloßmuseum in Gotha) und der Mömpelgarder Tafelaltar (Kunsthistorisches Museum in Wien).[30] Sie enthalten jeweils 157 Szenen aus dem Neuen Testament: beginnend mit der Verkündigung an Zacharias, über Kindheit, Wirken, Passion und Verklärung Christi bis hin zum Pfingstwunder. Jede Tafel besteht aus einem narrativen Bild, einer großen Kartusche mit einem entsprechenden, recht umfangreichen Bibelzitat sowie aus einer kleinen Kartusche, die den biblischen Fundort und die synoptischen Parallelstellen angibt. Man findet hier sowohl Darstellungen mit einer langen ikonographischen Tradition, wie auch vollkommen neue Verbildlichungen biblischer Geschehnisse und Lehren, die für die beiden Altäre geschaffen wurden. Die letztgenannten, wenn es gerade keine „bildhaften" Gleichnisse waren, bereiteten dem Maler und vor allem dem Theologen, Inventor des Programms, mancherlei Schwierigkeiten.

Fig. 5. Sigersted, Pfarrkirche, Schriftaltar, 1596 (Foto Hugo Johannsen).

Die Differenzierung und Belebung der auf ein ähnliches Schema gestützten Kompositionen, wo Christus unter den Jüngern steht und spricht, war mit Sicherheit keine leichte Aufgabe. Man sieht dies sehr gut auf einer Tafel aus dem Mömpelgarder Altar mit der bildlichen Umsetzung des Themas „Jünger ohne Wenn und Aber" nach Mt 8, 18-22 bzw. Lk 9, 57-61 (Fig. 7).

In der weiteren Entwicklung der lutherischen Kirchenkunst trennte man den „subjektiven", die Verfasser der biblischen Bücher betreffenden Aspekt, von dem „objektiven", die Inhalte dieser Bücher betreffenden Aspekt des „ewigen Wortes". Den ersten veranschaulichten Darstellungen der einzelnen „Zeugen Christi": Evangelisten, Apostel, Propheten und ausgewählter Heiligen: der „biblischen", wie Johannes der Täufer, Maria Magdalena oder der Diakon Stephan,[31] und der „allegorischen", wie der Ritter Georg und der Riese Christophorus,[32] den anderen Aspekt führten vor Augen narrative biblische Darstellungen, typische „Historien", an.[33] Die Bilder der Evangelisten wurden gewöhnlich, insbesondere auf den Kanzeln, von Zitaten aus deren Evangelien begleitet,[34] die Bilder der Propheten – von Worten ihrer Prophezeiungen, die Bilder der Apostel – von Artikeln des Apostolischen Glaubensbekenntnisses (Fig. 8).[35] Man könnte viele Programme dieser Art nennen, wie etwa die Malereien auf der Brüstung des Häuptlingsstuhls im Chorraum der Kirche in Resterhafe in Ostfriesland (1624-1629),[36] wo die Bilder Christi als Salvator Mundi und der zwölf Apostel von dem *Apostolicum* und dem Missions- und Taufbefehl (Mt 28,19) auf Niederdeutsch begleitet werden, oder die Gewölbemalereien im Chor und Schiff der Kirche in Tøstrup in Dänemark (1582),[37] wo sich dem „Apostelkolleg" mit Artikeln des Glaubensbekenntnisses auch Propheten anschließen: Jesaja, Jeremia, Hesekiel, Daniel, Micha, Hosea,

Fig. 6. Wiefels bei Jever, Pfarrkirche, Schriftaltar aus der St.-Laurentius-Kirche in Langwarden, 1621. Nach Diederichs-Gottschalk, Abb. 47.

WORT-BILD-WORT 109

Fig. 7. "Jünger ohne Wenn und Aber", Tafel aus dem Mömpelgarder Altar, um 1540. Wien, Kunsthistorisches Museum (Archivalisches Foto aus der Sammlung des Verfassers).

Joel, Habakuk und Sacharja, ergänzt mit den Gestalten König Davids und Johannes des Täufers (Fig. 9). In beiden Fällen sind die Darstellungen der „Zeugen Christi" eine „Beglaubigung" der Bibeltexte, die neben ihnen aufgeschrieben wurden, eine Art „Garantie ihrer Authentizität", wie es zu Beginn des 17. Jahrhunderts einige Autoren der Einweihungspredigten lutherischer Altäre und Kanzeln formuliert haben.[38]

Den „objektiven" Aspekt des göttlichen Wortes macht natürlich die *fides historica*, die biblische Geschichte aus, die seit dem frühen Mittelalter in mannigfaltigen narrativen Darstellungen vor Augen geführt wurde. In der reformatorischen Kunst bildeten sie üblich Zyklen, die sich auf dem zweiten Artikel des Apostolischen Glaubensbekenntnisses in der Auffassung Martin Luthers stützten und das Leben Christi seit dem Moment der Empfängnis (Verkündigung) bis zum Verlassen des Diesseits vor seiner „Wiederkunft in Herrlichkeit" (Himmelfahrt) zeigten.[39] Die Darstellungen einzelner Etappen des irdischen Lebens Christi

Fig. 8. „Apostel Philippus" (mit einem Artikel des Apostolikums), Detail der Deckenmalereien im Schiff der Pfarrkirche in Klępsk/Klemzig in der Neumark Brandenburg, 1613 (Foto Verfasser).

wurden – in größerer oder kleinerer Auswahl – auf Altären, Kanzeln und Emporenbrüstungen aufgetragen, manchmal mit Ergänzung durch alttestamentliche „Typen".[40] Die Bilder wurden in der Regel von längeren bzw. kürzeren Bibelzitaten begleitet, die die einzelnen Geschehnisse durch deren Beschreibung im Evangelium kommentierten. Die Kommentare konnten auch, obwohl viel seltener, das hermeneutisch-homiletische Prinzip *scriptura sui ipsius interpres* verfolgen (Fig. 10).[41]

Beide der erwähnten Varianten der Wort-Bild-Beziehung sind auf den Emporenbrüstungen in der Kapelle des Schlosses Gottorf in Schleswig zu sehen; sie wurden in den Jahren 1590-1592 mit Tafelbildern aus der Werkstatt des niederländischen Malers Marten van Achten ausgestattet.[42] Von den 28 Bildern mit Szenen aus dem Leben Christi sind die meisten mit einem „beschreibenden" Zitat versehen: zum Beispiel ist der Szene der Beschneidung Christi das Zitat Luc. 2,21 zugeordnet: „Und da acht tage umbwaren, das das Kind beschnitten / würde, da ward sein nahme genennet Jesus", bei der Gefangnahme Christi dagegen – das Zitat Joh. 18, 12: „Die schar und der Oberheubtman und die diener / der Juden griffen Jesum und bunden ihn". Wir haben hier aber auch einige Beispiele für die Anwendung der Sprüche aus dem Alten Testament und der Apostolischen Briefe des heiligen Apostel Paulus: die Szene der Kreuzigung Christi kommentiert das Zitat Gal. 3,13: „Christus hat uns erlöset von den fluch des gesetzes, da er wart ein / fluch für uns, da es steht geschriebe, verflucht ist der am Holtz haget", während die Szene der Himmelfahrt Christi mit dem Zitat Ps. 68,19 versehen ist: „Du bist in die höhe gefahren, und hast das gefencknis / gefange, du hast gaben empfange für die mensche". Die Ideenbotschaft dieses Zyklus

Fig. 9. "Prophet Jeremias" (mit den Inschriften Jer. 31,16 und Jer. 31,33), Detail der Gewölbemalereien im Schiff der Pfarrkirche in Tøstrup, 1582 (Foto Nationalmuseum, Kopenhagen).

WORT-BILD-WORT 111

Fig.10. "Elias führt den Himmelfeuer herbei" (mit der Inschrift Sirach 48,1), Relief am Korb der Kanzel in der Pfarrkirche St. Maria Magdalena in Wrocław/Breslau,1579-1580 (Foto Mirosław Łanowiecki, Wrocław).

ist im Wesentlichen eng mit dem verbunden, was wir an den Emporen der Marktkirche Unser Lieben Frau in Halle beobachten konnten: das Wort Gottes „umgibt" auch hier die zum Gottesdienst versammelte Gemeinde, allerdings scheint die multimediale „Aussaat" wirkungsvoller zu sein, als die bescheidene, rein verbale Lehre vom Zeichen Justus Jonas. Die pädagogisch-erbauliche Funktion dieses „ewigen Evangeliums" wusste man in Gottorf besonders zu schätzen, da man nach dem Einbau des Fürstenstuhls an der Nordseite durch Herzog Johann Adolf im Jahre 1610 die zwei ersten und zwei letzten Bilder des Zyklus an neue Stellen setzte, ohne die Integrität des Ganzen zu stören.

Die Einführung der Wort-Bild-Programme in einen symbolisch geprägten Raum betraf nicht nur „geschlossene" Strukturen, die nach Innen konzentriert waren und das ganze Kircheninnere bzw. dessen Teil umfassten, sondern auch „offene", nach außen hin gerichtete Strukturen, wie vor allem Kanzeln mit Schalldeckeln und Taufsteine mit hohen Aufsätzen.[43] Besonders die ersten waren mit der „Botschaft des Wortes" sehr eng verbunden und schufen fast uneingeschränkte Möglichkeiten zur „Beschreibung" und „Auslegung" mit Hilfe des Wortes und Bildes der einzelnen Bestandteile (Korpus, Treppe, Stütze, Schalldeckel, Portal, Rückwand), wie auch aller Verknüpfungen zwischen ihnen.[44] Es wäre unmöglich auch nur eine kurze Übersicht über die reichen, vielseitigen Programme der Kanzeln in den großen Pfarrkirchen zu Danzig, Hamburg, Lübeck, Rostock oder Stralsund darzulegen, daher möge als Beispiel eine weniger komplizierte, dafür aber sehr repräsentative Kanzel dienen: die Kanzel im dänischen Højby, aus dem Jahre 1656, ein Werk des Bildschnitzers Lorentz Jør-

Fig. 11. "Mannalese" (mit der Inschrift *VERBUM*), Relief am Korb der Kanzel in der Pfarrkirche in Højby,1656 (Foto Nationalmuseum, Kopenhagen).

Fig.12. Abendmahlskelch aus der Stiftung der Herzogin Augusta von Holstein-Gottorf, 1632. Kopenhagen, Schloß Rosenborg (Foto Rosenborg).

gensen.[45] Den Korpus schmücken hier Reliefs des Sündenfalls (Untertitel: DESTITUTIO), des Gekreuzigten und der erhöhten ehernen Schlange (Untertitel: RESTITUTIO), der Mannalese (Untertitel: VERBUM, Fig. 11), der Taufe Christi (Untertitel: BAPTISMUS) und des Jüngsten Gerichts (Untertitel: CONSUMMATIO), oben und unten mit zwei Bibelzitaten begleitet: „Meine Schafe hören meine Stimme" (Joh. 10,27) und „Das Evangelium ist eine Kraft Gottes, die selig macht alle, die daran glauben" (Röm. 1,16). Der Schalldeckel, mit der Christusfigur bekrönt, trägt auf dem Fries, über dem Kopf des Predigers, den Spruch Joh. 8,52: „Wer mein Wort hält, der wird den Tod nicht schmecken in Ewigkeit". Auf diese Weise wird das gesamte Programm zu einer inbrünstigen Apotheose des göttlichen Wortes, dieser „himmlischen Manna", die uns von der Todesangst befreit.

Um die Zeitgenossen und Nachkommen an dem unerschütterlichen Glauben und der aus ihm resultierenden „Heilsgewißheit" Anteil haben zu lassen, hat man im 16. und 17. Jahrhundert die Innenräume der lutherischen Kirchen Mittel- und Nordeuropas mit unzähligen bildlich-schriftlichen „Bekenntnissen" erfüllt.[46] Das Wort hatte in ihnen immer Vorrang dem Bild gegenüber, es bediente sich des Bildes, und wenn es nötig war, präzisierte seinen Sinn mit einem zusätzlichen Kommentar. Zu den Ausnahmen gehörten jene

Kunstwerke, bei denen die schriftliche Komponente – so könnte man meinen – vollkommen entfällt. Ist aber der wunderbare Abendmahlskelch von 1632 (Fig. 12), der heute auf dem Schloss Rosenborg in Kopenhagen aufbewahrt wird und eine Stiftung der Herzogin Augusta von Holstein-Gottorf war,[47] der auf der Kuppa Szenen des Abendmahls, der Fußwaschung und des Gebets in Gethsemane, und am Fuß die Kreuzigung in Begleitung von fünf typologischen Szenen aus dem Alten Testament trägt, nicht eine gleiche Exemplifizierung der „ewigen" Existenz des Wortes, wie der Schriftaltar in Norden oder die Kanzel in Højby? Wenn wir den Blick dort anhalten, wo der Totenkopf mit Knochen anstelle des Knaufs, der das Grab des Urvaters Adam symbolisiert, zu sehen ist, werden unsere Gedanken unausweichlich zu den Lehren des heiligen Apostel Paulus aus dem ersten Korintherbrief (1. Kor. 15,21-22) geführt: „Denn da ja durch einen Menschen der Tod kam, so auch durch einen Menschen die Auferstehung der Toten. Denn wie sie in Adam alle sterben, so werden sie in Christus alle lebendig gemacht werden".

Notes

1. Jan Seklucjan, *Wybór pism* (hg. und bearb. v. Stanisław Rospond), Olsztyn 1979, 3-28.
2. Seklucjan 1979, 14.
3. Frederick John Stopp, "Verbum Domini Manet in Aeternum: The Dissemination of a Reformation Slogan, 1522-1904", in: Siegbert Saloman Prawer, Richard Hinton Thomas & Leonard Forster (Hg.), *Essays in German Language, Culture and Society*, London 1969 (London University Institute of Germanic Studies: Publications 12), 123-135.
4. Johann Michael Fritz, *Das evangelische Abendmahlsgerät in Deutschland: Vom Mittelalter bis zum Ende des Alten Reiches*, Leipzig 2004, 365-367, Kat. 58, 62, Abb. 107, 103.
5. Friedrich de Boor, "Die Bibelsprüche an den unteren Emporen der Marktkirche: In Stein gemeisselte Proklamation des reformatorischen Glaubens", in: Sabine Kramer & Karsten Eisenmenger (Hg.), *Die Marktkirche Unser Lieben Frauen zu Halle*, Halle an der Saale 2004, 21-29.
6. Martin Scharfe, *Evangelische Andachtsbilder: Studien zu Intention und Funktion des Bildes in der Frömmigkeitsgeschichte vornehmlich des schwäbischen Raumes*, Stuttgart 1968 (Veröffentlichungen des Staatlichen Amtes für Denkmalpflege Stuttgart. Reihe C: Volkskunde, 5), 320-322; Reinhard Lieske, *Protestantische Frömmigkeit im Spiegel der kirchlichen Kunst des Herzogtums Württemberg*, München & Berlin 1973 (Forschungen und Berichte der Bau- und Kunstdenkmalpflege in Baden-Württemberg 2), 71-74; Hans-Joachim Krause, *Sächsische Schloßkapellen der Renaissance*, Berlin 1982 (Das Christliche Denkmal 80); Reinhard Lieske, „Zur Ikonographie der protestantischen Schloßkapellen des 16. Jahrhunderts", in: Ernst Ullmann (Hg.), *Von der Macht der Bilder: Beiträge des C.I.H.A.-Kolloquiums 'Kunst und Reformation'*, Leipzig 1983, 395-412; Jan Harasimowicz, *Kunst als Glaubensbekenntnis: Beiträge zur Kunst- und Kulturgeschichte der Reformationszeit*, Baden-Baden 1996 (Studien zur deutschen Kunstgeschichte 359), 43-45; Hugo Johannsen, „The Writ on the Wall: Theological and Political Aspects of Biblical Text-Cycles in Evangelical Palace Chapels of the Renaissance", in: Eyolf Østrem, Jens Fleischer & Nils Holger Petersen (Hg.), *The Arts and the Cultural Heritage of Martin Luther*, Copenhagen 2003, 81-97.
7. Scharfe 1968, 321.
8. Margarete Stirm, *Die Bilderfrage in der Reformation*, Gütersloh 1977 (Quellen und Forschungen zur Reformationsgeschichte 45), 130-223; Sergiusz Michalski, *The Reformation and the Visual Arts: The Protestant Image Question in Western and Eastern Europe*, London & New York 1993 (Christianity & Society in the Modern World 246), 59-74.
9. Peter Poscharsky, *Die Kanzel: Erscheinungsform im Protestantismus bis zum Ende des Barocks*, Gütersloh 1963 (Schriftenreihe des Institutes für Kirchenbau und kirchliche Kunst der Gegenwart 1), 88-89, 124, 141-145.
10. Dietrich Diederichs-Gottschalk, *Die protestantischen Schriftaltäre des 16. und 17. Jahrhunderts in Nordwestdeutschland: Eine kirchen- und kunstgeschichtliche Untersuchung zu einer Sonderform liturgischer Ausstattung in der Epoche der Konfessionalisierung*, Regensburg 2005 (Adiaphora: Schriften zur Kunst und Kultur im Protestantismus).
11. Diederichs-Gottschalk 2005, 39-67, Abb. 1-6.
12. Heute in der Ev.-luth. Kirche in Roggenstede, Kirchenkreis Harlingerland. Diederichs-Gottschalk 2005, 108-127, Abb. 16-22.
13. Diederichs-Gottschalk 2005, 227-247, Abb. 49-53.
14. *Danmarks Kirker. Københavns Amt*, 1, Kopenhagen 1944, 310-311.

15 Eva Louise Lillie (Hg.), *Danske Kalkmalerier. Efter reformationen 1536-1700*, Kopenhagen 1992, 42.

15a *Danmarks Kirker. Sorø Amt*, 1, Kopenhagen 1936, 435.

16 *Danmarks Kirker. Københavns Amt*, 2, Kopenhagen 1946, 857-858.

17 Margarethe Henden Aaraas et al., *På kyrkjeferd i Sogn og Fjordane*, 2: *Sogn*, Førde 2000, 220-225.

18 Margarethe Henden Aaraas et al., *På kyrkjeferd i Sogn og Fjordane*, 1: *Nordfjord og Sunnfjord*, Førde 2000, 161-166.

19 Aaraas 2000, 1, 158.

20 Diederichs-Gottschalk 2005, 150-165, Abb. 34-40.

21 Heute in der Ev.-luth. Kirche in Wiefels, Kirchenkreis Jever. Diederichs-Gottschalk 2005, 186-199, Abb. 47.

22 *Danmarks Kirker. Frederiksborg Amt*, 3, Kopenhagen 1970, , 1445-1446.

23 Aaraas 2000, 1, 121-125.

24 Der gesamte Bestand der Schriftaltäre in Dänemark und Norwegen umfasst laut der neuesten Forschung 346 Objekte, davon 268 in Dänemark und 78 in Norwegen. Vgl. Ragne Bugge, "Tekstaltertavlene i Danmark-Norge omkring 1600", in: Ingmar Brohed (Hg.), *Reformationens konsolidering i de nordiska länderna 1540-1610*, Oslo 1990, 306-326; Ragne Bugge, "Ikonoklasmen i Norge og de norske katekisme altertavlene", in: Eva Louise Lillie (Hg.), *Tro og bilde i Norden i Reformationens århundre*, Oslo 1991, 85-92; Joseph Leo Koerner, *The Reformation of the Image*, London 2004, 297-303.

25 Werner Freitag, "Die späte Reformation in der Residenzstadt Halle", in: Kramer & Eisenmenger (Hg.) 2004, 11-19 (auf der Seite 13 die Abbildung des Jonas-Medaillons).

26 Anja Wolkenhauer, *Zu schwer für Apoll: Die Antike in humanistischen Druckerzeichen des 16. Jahrhunderts*, Wiesbaden 2002 (Wolfenbütteler Schriften zur Geschichte des Buchwesens 35).

27 Harasimowicz 1996, 46.

28 Stirm 1977, 90-95; Bengt Arvidsson, *Bildstrid Bildbruk Bildlära: En idéhistorisk undersökning av bildfrågan inom den begynnande lutherska traditionen under 1500-talet*, Lund 1987 (Studia Theologica Lundensia 41), 187-200.

29 Martin Luther, *Werke: Kritische Gesamtausgabe*, Weimar 1883-1983, Bd. 31 I, 415.

30 Harry Kieser, *Das große Gothaer Altarwerk: Ein reiches Werk deutscher Reformationskunst*, Würzburg-Aumühle 1939 (Phil. Dissertation, Königsberg); Herbert von Hintzenstern, *Die Bilderpredigt des Gothaer Tafelaltars*, Berlin 1965; Herbert von Hintzenstern, „Der Gothaer Tafelaltar: Das bilderreichste Kunstwerk aus der Reformationszeit", in: Ullmann (Hg.) 1983, 340-343; Gerhard Faix, „Heinrich Füllmaurer – Maler zu Herrenberg", *Blätter für württembergische Kirchengeschichte* 87 (1987), 153-173; Frank Muller, „Der Mömpelgarder und der Gothaer Altar im Lichte der politisch-konfessionellen Lage Süddeutschlands um 1540", in: Sönke Lorenz & Peter Rückert (Hg.), *Württemberg und Mömpelgard: 600 Jahre Begegnung*, Leinefelden-Echterdingen 1999, 169-190; Thomas Packeiser, „Lehrtafel, Retabel, Fürstenspiegel?", in: Lorenz & Rückert (Hg.) 1999, 191-250.

31 Jan Harasimowicz, "Evangelische Heilige? Die Heiligen in Lehre, Frömmigkeit und Kunst in der evangelischen Kirche Schlesiens", in: Joachim Köhler & Gundolf Keil (Hg.), *Heilige und Heiligenverehrung in Schlesien: Verhandlungen des IX. Symposions in Würzburg vom 28. bis 30. Oktober 1991*, Sigmaringen 1997 (Schlesische Forschungen 7), 171-216, hier 184-191; Jan Harasimowicz, „Die Verehrung der »biblischen Heiligen« in der evangelischen Kirche Schlesiens im 16. und 17. Jahrhundert", in: Marek Derwich & Michel Dmitriev (Hg.), *Fonctions sociales et politiques du culte des saints dans les sociétés de rite grec et latin au Moyen Âge et a l' époque moderne. Approche comparative*, Wrocław 1999 (Opera ad historiam monasticam spectantia. Series I, Colloquia 3), 247-270.

32 Harasimowicz 1997, 191-195.

33 Lieske 1973, 75-87; Jan Harasimowicz, *Treści i funkcje ideowe sztuki śląskiej reformacji 1520-1650*, Wrocław 1986 (Acta Universitatis Wratislaviensis No 819, Historia Sztuki II), 30-37.

34 Poscharsky 1963, 113-115; Harasimowicz 1986, 86.

35 Jan Harasimowicz, "'Non minus sunt credenda, quam ipsi articuli'. La confession de foi apostolique dans la catéchèse et l'art d'église luthériens au siècle de la Réforme", in: Pierre Lacroix, Andrée Renon & Éliane Vergnolle (Hg.), *Pensée, image et communication en Europe médiévale. À propos des stalles de Saint-Claude*, Besançon 1993, 237-246; Harasimowicz 1996, 83-96.

36 Diederichs-Gottschalk 2005, 127-135, Abb. 23-26.

37 Henrik Græbe, "Tøstrup kirke, Djurs Nørre herred. En kalkmaleriudsmykning fra 1582", in: Hugo Johannsen (Hg.), *Synligt og Usynligt: Studier tilegnede Otto Norn på hans 75 års fødselsdag den 13. december 1990*, Herning 1990, 83-94.

38 Harasimowicz 1997, 184.

39 Poscharsky 1963, 165-181; Harasimowicz 1986, 62-65; Marcin Wisłocki, *Sztuka protestancka na Pomorzu 1535-1684*, Szczecin 2005 (Biblioteka Naukowa Muzeum Narodowego w Szczecinie. Seria Historia Sztuki), 74-80.

40 Scharfe 1968, 87-89; Lieske 1973, 88-92; Harasimowicz 1986, 37-39; Wisłocki 2005, 80-83.

41 Jan Harasimowicz, "»Scriptura sui ipsius interpres«. Protestantische Bild-Wort-Sprache des 16. und 17. Jahrhunderts", in: Wolfgang Harms (Hg), *Text und Bild, Bild und Text: DFG-Symposion 1988*, Stuttgart 1990 (Germanistische-Symposien-Berichtsbände 11), 262-282; Harasimowicz 1996, 41-81.

42 Anna Mohrat-Fromm, *Theologie und Frömmigkeit in religiöser Bildkunst um 1600: Eine niederländische Malerwerkstatt in Schleswig-Holstein*, Neumünster 1991 (Schriften des Vereins für Schleswig-Holsteinische Kirchengeschichte, I, 37), 16-27, 111-113; Dietrich Bieber, „Die Kapelle von Schloß Gottorf – ein Sakralraum des Frühabsolutismus", in: Heinz Spielmann & Jan Drees (Hg.), *Gottorf im Glanz des Barock: Kunst und Kultur am Schleswiger Hof 1544-1713. Kataloge der Ausstellung zum 50-jährigen Bestehen des Schleswig-Holsteinischen Landesmuseum auf Schloß Gottorf und zum 400. Geburtstag Herzog Friedrichs III.*, Schleswig 1997, I, 157-177.

43 Jan Harasimowicz, "Evangelische Kirchenräume der frühen Neuzeit", in: Susanne Rau & Gerd Schwerhoff (Hg.), *Zwischen Gotteshaus und Taverne: Öffentliche Räume im Spätmittelalter und Früher Neuzeit*, Köln, Weimar & Wien 2004 (Norm und Struktur: Studien zum sozialen Wandel in Mittelalter und Früher Neuzeit 21), 413-445.

44 Poscharsky 1963, 112-141; Harasimowicz 1986, 85-110; Wisłocki 2005, 95-117.

45 Eva Louise Lillie, "Prædikestolen i Højby kirke – og om forholdet mellem kunstner, lensmand og gejstlig", in: Johannsen 1990, 189-199.

46 Harasimowicz 1996, 25-39, 127-143; Jan Harasimowicz, „Sztuka jako medium nowożytnych konfesjonalizacji", in: Jan Harasimowicz (Hg.), *Sztuka i dialog wyznań w XVI i XVII wieku. Materiały Sesji Stowarzyszenia Historyków Sztuki. Wrocław, listopad 1999*, Warszawa 2000, 51-75.

47 Fritz 2004, 398-400, Kat. 125; Jan Harasimowicz, "Altargerät des 16. und frühen 17. Jahrhundert im konfessionellen Vergleich", in: Carl A. Hoffmann et al. (Hg.), *Als Frieden möglich war: 450 Jahre Augsburger Religionsfrieden. Begleitband zur Ausstellung im Maximilianmuseum Augsburg*, Regensburg 2005, 210-221, hier 216-218.

IMPORTED PATTERNS AND HOMEGROWN VIRTUES: HENDRICK GOLTZIUS'S EXEMPLAR VIRTUTUM PRINTS AND THE ALTARPIECES OF ST NICHOLAS IN KOLDING AND ST MARY IN FLENSBURG

Margit Thøfner

The parish churches of St Nicholas in Kolding and St Mary in Flensburg both possess remarkable altarpieces (Figs. 1 and 2). Both altars are based – at least in part – on a set of complex allegorical prints made in Antwerp in the Low Countries (Figs. 3, 4, 5 and 6). These prints were made in 1578 by Hendrick Goltzius, a promising young Netherlandish print-maker.[1] For this reason alone the two altarpieces constitute two highly appropriate case-studies for the present volume. They manifest, quite literally, how external influences were received, reworked and reframed in the late sixteenth century in the area we now call Denmark. The two altars may help us to map out the exact circumstances which made local individuals receptive to imported artistic forms.

In fact, these altarpieces are doubly important because they serve as a counterweight to many of the papers contained in this volume. It places considerable emphasis on the Oldenburg court. This makes sense: the court – with its far flung international connections – was naturally an important vehicle for artistic exchange. However, it was not the only such vehicle. It is wrong to assume that, in the early modern period, the culture of the Oldenburg court was essentially synonymous with that of Denmark. The small yet busy harbour cities of Denmark and Northern Germany, cities such as Kolding and Flensburg, were also important cultural centres, peculiarly open to external influences. These influences, however, were mediated through trade rather than politics.

Now, it must be acknowledged that only one of these two altar-pieces is truly Danish: that from Kolding (Fig. 1). Flensburg was never Danish. It lies in the Duchy of Schleswig, part of which is in present-day Germany. In the early modern period, the Oldenburgs held this Duchy and also neighbouring Holstein as hereditary fiefs. The twin Duchies were distinct states and each had its own political system, separate from Denmark 'proper'.[2] Yet both states were also components in the larger dynastic federation governed by the Oldenburg kings. It should be noted that several important influences on Danish culture came via the Duchy of Schleswig. For example, it was here that the Lutheran reforms were first implemented by the then Duke Christian, the future King Christian III.[3] This happened already in 1525, more than a decade before Lutheranism became the official religion of Denmark-Norway. The speed with which Luther's reforms spread in Schleswig-Holstein was in part due to the various dialects of this region: a version of Low German was spoken side by side with Danish (the much-vaunted first Lutheran sermon preached in the vernacular within the boundaries of present-day Denmark was probably in Low German).[4]

Fig. 1. Anonymous painter and Matz Christensen, Altarpiece of St Nicholas's Church, 1589, Kolding (Photo The National Museum, Copenhagen).

All of this suggests why it is sensible to compare the Kolding and Flensburg altarpieces. That they come from Denmark and Schleswig respectively is a useful reminder of the inherent complexity of the Oldenburg federation. In such a context, is it not somewhat anachronistic to talk of a Danish Renaissance, as if that part of the Oldenburg realms was somehow uniquely receptive to external influences?

Given their unusual characteristics, it is not surprising that these two altarpieces have already been studied in detail. Besides descriptions in modern inventories, Hanne Honnens de Lichtenberg has reassessed the Kolding altar whilst the Flensburg piece has been analysed by Claudia Meier.[5] Both authors note in passing that there may be a relationship between the two. But neither pursue the issue. In addition, both authors approach the altars in a fairly standard art-historical manner, focusing on authorship, iconography and style and, in the case of the Kolding altar, also on patronage. And finally, like many writers on Lutheran altars of this date, both authors wonder – without adducing any real evidence – whether these altars embody Lutheran orthodoxy or perhaps some form of dissent.

These approaches have certainly yielded results. Even so, they fail to account for several striking characteristics of the two altars. The first of these is about Goltzius's imagery (Figs. 3, 4, 5 and 6). It cannot, in itself, be understood as a clear sign of orthodoxy or dissent. This is because the prints come from a particular religious environment. When Goltzius made them, he was part of a certain intellectual circle in the great mercantile port of Antwerp in the Low Countries.[6] At this point in time, Antwerp was bedevilled by protracted religious conflicts.[7] In response, many of Goltzius's friends cultivated a conciliatory or ecumenical stance on religious matters. The young printmaker would have been particularly receptive to this because his first master, Dirck Volkertsz. Coornhert, had favoured similar views.[8] Accordingly, if Goltzius's prints have any core message, it is that they are conciliatory. They stand for the middle ground, the tolerant and inclusive Christianity advocated by the likes of Desiderius Erasmus.

For example, the image entitled *Exemplar Virtutum* (Fig. 3) puts forth the well-worn point that a good Christian should imitate Jesus. In it *Anima* – the Christian soul – paints into her heart an image of Christ.[9] Similarly, in the print entitled *Miracula Christi* (Fig. 4), an allegorical figure of Faith raises the hand of the *Anima Morbida*, the sick soul.[10] Thus Faith helps the soul to her cure: the redemptory blood flowing from Christ's side. The allegory, as a whole, posits Jesus as the ultimate spiritual healer. There is nothing here to offend the average Christian of the early modern period, whether Catholic or Protestant. This, then, provides an initial answer to why Goltzius's imagery found ready homes in Kolding and Flensburg. The prints are inherently flexible. They are cleverly allusive, polysemic, even vague.

Fig. 2. Johan von Enum, Johan von Bremen and Heinrich Ringerinck (?), Altarpiece of St Mary's Church, 1598, Flensburg. After Claudia A. Meier, *Heinrich Ringerinck und sein Kreis: Eine Flensburger Bildschnitzerwerkstatt um 1600*, Flensburg 1984 (Schriften der Gesellschaft für Flensburger Stadtgeschichte, XXXIV), fig. 56.

In the early modern period, such flexibility seems to have been a crucial facilitator for artistic exchange.

This is not to say that questions of orthodoxy or otherwise are insignificant here. But, in themselves, Goltzius's images offer no clue. Instead one must consider how they were framed, the clearest piece of evidence for how they were received. In fact, to my mind, this is the most intriguing feature of both altarpieces. Even so, nobody so far has considered the relationship between the two-dimensional images, copied from imported prints, and the locally made frames. If one can get to the core of that relationship one may truly begin to understand something about the reception and reframing of these Netherlandish prints within the Oldenburg realms. That is the central aim of this article. It is, however, a complex issue so, for reasons of space, I can only offer some suggestions.

One way of approaching the problem is via function. First and foremost, both altars are pieces of liturgical equipment. They were designed to serve as backdrops to the Eucharist, one of only two sacraments retained in the Lutheran church. So they were looked at under specific conditions. First note that, in the late sixteenth century, Lutheran parishioners could usually not see their altarpiece from the nave: there was normally a roodscreen.[11] One only saw the altarpiece when approaching the altar to take communion. Also note that taking communion in the early Lutheran church did not involve kneeling in front of the altar, as is current practice. Instead, one approached the altar from the left, kneeling first to receive the Eucharistic wafer. Then one walked over to the right, and knelt to receive the wine (Fig. 7). This seems to have been standard practice. The artists and patrons involved in making these two altars must have known that. Most likely, they paid special attention to the sides of each altarpiece and therefore it makes sense to focus on these areas. If one can determine the relationship between frames and images on the sides of each altarpiece, it should be possible to attain some grasp of how artists and patrons engaged with Goltzius's prints.

The Kolding altarpiece is the earliest, dating to 1589 (Fig. 1). Here, the relationship between the frame and Goltzius's imagery works both on a formal and a conceptual level. Approaching the altar from the left, the first image one sees is that entitled *Exemplar Virtutis*. As already noted, is an exhortation to imitate Christ. Below the image, in the space most visible to communicants, the anonymous painter has copied in large golden letters the Biblical passages in Latin that Goltzius appended rather more discreetly to his print. In effect, the textual part of Goltzius's prints has been magnified. This is, in fact, a salient characteristic of the altar: it has a great deal of text on it, mostly in Latin but also some in Danish. As Tove Jørgensen and her colleagues have argued most persuasively, the sum of these inscriptions is

Fig. 3. Hendrick Goltzius, Exemplar Virtutum, 1578. After Walter L. Strauss, *Hendrick Goltzius, 1558-1617: The Complete Engravings and Woodcuts*, 1-2, New York 1977.

Fig. 4. Hendrick Goltzius, Miracula Christi, 1578. After Strauss.

an exhortation to Lutheran orthodoxy in relation to the Eucharist.[12] In other words, here Goltzius's moderate Christianity has been subverted, appropriated for particular doctrinal purposes.

There are also an unusually great number of patronal inscriptions on the altarpiece. At the very top one sees the coat of arms and name of the patron: Caspar Markdanner. There is also the following inscription on the Corinthian frieze above the lower storey: 'Caspar Markdanner of Søgaard who at this time was His Royal Majesty's lieutenant at Koldinghus had this altar piece made at his own expense [and] for the honour of Kolding church: anno 1590.'[13] Finally, Markdanner's initials are included in the strapwork ornament on the lower left and right of the altarpiece, just where a kneeling communicant would have his or her head. This kind of self-promotion is, in part, what one would expect of somebody with Markdanner's colourful history. Possibly a royal bastard, he had spent his youth as a soldier of fortune and was eventually knighted for his services by Maximilian II, the Holy Roman Emperor. Later, he was recalled to Denmark and attained his relatively high office in the Oldenburg administration as a protégé of Peder Oxe, one of the most powerful members of the Danish Council of State.[14]

Even so, to explain fully why Markdanner's identity is reiterated no less than three times on the altarpiece, one must consider certain aspects of local history. First, it may be that, as the local representative of royal power, Markdanner was actively reviving an older tradition: in the pre-Reformation period, the kings of Denmark had maintained an altar in the church of St Nicholas.[15] Secondly, it must also be noted that, like most early modern cities, Kolding was essentially an independent political unit. It was governed by a college of burgomasters and aldermen who constituted a self-perpetuating civic oligarchy. The role of the crown was limited to overseeing the

Fig. 5. Hendrick Goltzius, Passio Christi, 1578. After Strauss.

Fig. 6. Hendrick Goltzius, Resurrectio Christi, 1578. After Strauss.

dispensation of justice and, in return, it received a measure of taxation. This means that, despite his grand title, the lieutenant of the royal castle of Koldinghus had only limited powers within the actual city of Kolding. Nevertheless, in the middle of the sixteenth century, the Oldenburgs had tried to increase their powers in the city by ordering that all elections of burgomasters and aldermen should be attended by the lieutenant.[16] It was now his job to oversee them and guarantee that they were fair. Against this background, the altar takes on a political role. By virtue of all its patronal inscriptions, it proclaims itself to be a grand gift to the city as well as a revival of older ties between the monarchy and the urban community. Perhaps it was an attempt to solicit civic favour and, in particular, civic consent to the lieutenant's relatively new duties.

This certainly tallies with the lowest of the inscriptions on the left side, the one most visible to a kneeling communicant. It proclaims, in Latin:

'For I have given you an example, that ye should do as I have done to you' (John 13;15). The example invoked here is surely not just that of Christ, whose virtues are set out in the image above, but also the peculiar virtues of Markdanner, whose initials are below. The altarpiece embodies his personal generosity towards the citizens of Kolding. Here the response to the imported pattern is a local enactment of a specific virtue. From this one may deduce an important point about this kind of cross-cultural exchange. There has to be some point of congruence. For, although Goltzius's prints are vague and allusive, they are not meaningless. They give form to a general notion of Christ's virtues and this general notion is then made specific, local and immediate in Markdanner's gift of the altarpiece. The frame thus serves to instantiate Christ's generosity and, at the same time, the generosity of its patron.

One can make similar arguments about the right side of the altar but, for reasons of space, these cannot be pursued here. Suffice it to consider the strapwork frame. It is very closely related to the 'internal' frames, the emblematic frames that surround each picture. In Goltzius's originals, these frames comprise a mixture of strapwork and fruit motifs (Figs. 3, 4 and 6). However, in the Kolding altar, in the two side images, the fruit motifs have disappeared. Instead, the strapwork fills all the space between the emblematic images. So Goltzius's original framing has been reframed, changed subtly to fit with the style of the locally carved frame. As a consequence, frame and imagery are extremely tightly integrated. Goltzius's pictures stand for a general and inclusive conception of Christianity, for the broader Christian community. The frame domesticates this concept. It makes it immediate and present, by reference to Markdanner's generosity, his own imitation of Christ. Here, then, the Oldenburg court – or rather, one fairly prominent member of the Oldenburg administration – definitely served as a conduit for external cultural influences. The importance of the court cannot be denied but it should not be overemphasised.

That becomes clear if one considers the altarpiece of the church of St Mary in Flensburg (Fig. 2). It was put up nine years later, in 1598. Indeed, it may be that the Flensburg altar was influenced in some manner by the Kolding piece.

There were close connections between the two cities, which, in any case, are only some seventy kilometres apart.[17] Moreover, on the Flensburg altar, Goltzius's 'internal' frames have been edited in a similar way, the fruit motifs replaced with simple strapwork. But the exact relationship between the two altars has, so far, remained elusive. What is certain is that, despite using the same set of Goltzius prints, the Flensburg altar is substantially different.

Most obviously, the altar is simultaneously more sculptural and more pictorial. Unlike the Kolding altar, it is not full of text. There are only three discreet text-frames: one immediately above the altar-table and two on either side, set so low that they are virtually invisible. Even more notably, the Goltzius images have lost their subscripts; those subscripts which, in Kolding, were writ large in golden letters. In addition, the patrons of the altar are bodied forth rather more discreetly. They appear in cartouches high up on the altar: Catharina Nacke and her husband Diedrich Nacke, for many years burgomaster of that half of Flensburg called the 'Marienspiel'.[18] Again, we are dealing with a civic oligarchy. Even so, the location of these portraits is merely in keeping with Diedrich Nacke's will: he asked his widow to order an altar for St Mary which would double as an epitaph for both of them.[19] Moreover, when the altar was ap-

Fig. 8. Johan von Enum, Johan von Bremen and Heinrich Ringerinck (?), St. Peter (detail), Altarpiece of St Mary's Church, 1598, Flensburg. After Meier, fig. 57.

proached through a rood screen - as was probably originally the case - these portraits would not necessarily have been visible unless one craned one's neck quite indecorously.

Instead, when communicants approached the altar from the left, their focus must have been on the lifesize caryatid of St Peter and then, secondarily, on the image of the *Circumcision of Christ* in the frame immediately to the right (Fig. 8). That picture would be next to the communicants' heads as they knelt down. If they peered up, as they rose up, they would see Goltzius's two images of Christ as the exemplar of virtue and Christ as the healer of sick souls (Figs. 3 and 4). Then, once on the other side, communicants encountered a caryatid of St Paul paired with a painting of the *Baptism of Christ* (Fig. 2). Again, Goltzius's pictures would be visible only if one made the effort to peer up at them. On this side are his allegories of the Passion and the Resurrection of Christ (Figs. 5 and 6).

The two sides of the altar actually constitute a neat typology, a point which has hitherto eluded scholarly notice. First, one takes the bread at the side of St Peter and the *Circumcision*. St Peter, of course, was the apostle to the Jews and thus it is appropriate that he is next to the *Circumcision*, the ritual associated with Jewry, with the Old Covenant, with the era of the Law. Highest above St Peter and the *Circumcision* is the *Exemplar Virtutis*, where Christ is set forth as a pattern for virtuous behaviour. So in this context the picture figures Christ as an embodiment of how to live by the Law. The image below then posits him as a cure for those who fail to do so. Then, at the other side, one takes the wine at the side of St Paul, the apostle to the Gentiles. He stands next to the *Baptism of Christ*, the beginning of the era

Fig. 7. Anonymous engraver, Lutheran Eucharist, in Gothofridus Kilian, Postilla Sacramentalis, Glücksburg 1668. After Danmarks Kirker, Sønderjylland, kunsthistorisk oversigt, Copenhagen 1963, p. 2891.

of Grace, of the New Covenant. The two Goltzius images above allude to the Passion and Resurrection, key moments in the era of Grace.

Taking communion at this altar was a performance of inclusiveness: of linking up *Circumcision* and *Baptism*, the Old and the New Covenant, Jew and Gentile, Peter and Paul. It was, in effect, to enact that most tolerant of Pauline dicta on the nature of the Church: 'There is neither Jew nor Greek, there is neither bond nor free, there is neither male nor female: for ye are all one in Christ Jesus. And if ye be Christ's, then are ye Abraham's seed, and heirs according to the promise' (Galatians 3:28-29). Here, then, the framing serves a very different purpose. It works iconographically rather than formally and it is in close keeping with the conciliatory tenor of Goltzius's prints. The frame both affirms and elaborates on their core messages.

This is probably due to patronal wishes. We know a fair amount about burgomaster Nacke. Most notably, in 1581, a few years before his death, Nacke gave to the city library of Flensburg the complete works of Philip Melanchthon.[20] That would have been a very public statement of Nacke's religious views. Melanchthon was, of course, the inclusive and conciliatory face of the Lutheran reform; his flexible and changing attitudes to Christianity would be particularly evident from a complete anthology of his writings.[21] In other words, there is no great distance between his Christianity and that advocated in Goltzius's prints as well as in the Flensburg altarpiece.

Why, then, should Goltzius's prints be reframed so positively in Flensburg, more positively than in Kolding? It might be because of the nature of that city. Kolding had a royal lieutenant. Flensburg was different, first and foremost a commercial city. In fact, in the late sixteenth century Flensburg was quite simply the most important and most affluent mercantile city in the Oldenburg realms, a city which enjoyed commercial rights and privileges far beyond those of Copenhagen, the nascent capital of Denmark. This was because Flensburg was a vital entrepôt which linked the Oldenburg realms with the extensive trading networks of the Hanseatic cities and beyond.[22] In such a city, a certain tolerance was a prerequisite for doing business. So, despite being very different, the frame of the Flensburg altar still serves to domesticate the general notions of Christianity set forth in Goltzius's prints. For it makes these notions appropriate to the locality; it bodies forth an inclusive version of Christianity; it makes of St Mary's a broad church. Here, however, the external cultural influences were most likely not mediated through the Oldenburg court. Rather, they came through Flensburg's extensive trading links with cities such as Lübeck, Hamburg and Bremen and, via these, the great printing centre of Antwerp.

What broader conclusions should be drawn from all this? First, that there is not much point in talking about a 'Danish Renaissance'. If that term is to have any power, it needs to be in the plural. Moreover, it should be rephrased into something unwieldy and deliberately estranging, like 'the Renaissances of the Oldenburg realms'. For the same external influences – in this case Goltzius's prints – were received very differently in different locations within these realms. Secondly, one has to look beyond the Oldenburg court. It was not the only place receptive to external influences. The cities were too; it is, in fact, in the nature of cities to be so. It would be exceedingly unwise to exclude them from the present enquiry. A third point follows from this: it is not surprising that these prints, with their allusive learnedness, would appeal to well-educated civic elites. Being vague and yet appealingly clever, the prints quite simply lend themselves to borrowing. They were congruent with the needs and views of people as different as Catharina Nacke and Caspar Markdanner, a burgomaster's widow and a retired soldier of fortune. Fourthly, one needs to pay careful attention to frames. Framing can do very subtle as well as very literal things to pictures. It really does matter. Moreover, it is not only in St Nicholas in Kolding and in St Mary in Flensburg that one finds reframings of Goltzius prints. As Hugo Johannsen demonstrated already in 1984, it is hard to underestimate the importance of Goltzius's graphic works when considering the arts of early modern Denmark.[23] His prints were reframed across the Oldenburg domains. But, I would contend, so far we have failed to understand the sheer subtlety with which these imports were domesticated. The frame very much needs to be in the frame.

Notes

1. On Goltzius's period in Antwerp, see Manfred Sellink, "Een teruggevonden *Laatste Oordeel* van Hendrick Goltzius: Goltzius' relatie met de Antwerpse uitgever Philips Galle", *Nederlands Kunsthistorisch Jaarboek/Netherlands Yearbook for History of Art* 42-43 (1991-92), 145-158. On the series of prints, see Walter L. Strauss, *Hendrick Goltzius, 1558-1617: The Complete Engravings and Woodcuts*, New York 1977, 1, 66-77.

2. A good sense of the complex relationship between the twin Duchies and the Danish Crown may be gained from Carsten P. Rasmussen, Inge Adriansen & Lennart S. Madsen (eds.), *De Slesvigske Hertuger*, Aabenraa 2005 (Skrifter udgivet af Historisk Samfund for Sønderjylland, XCII).

3. Hans V. Gregersen, *Reformationen i Sønderjylland*, Aabenraa 1986 (Skrifter udgivet af Historisk Samfund for Sønderjylland, LXII), 63-173.

4   On the importance of Low German in this area, see Gregersen 1986, 39, 95, 108-110.

5   Hanne Honnens de Lichtenberg, *Tro, Håb og Forfængelighed*, Copenhagen 1989 (Renæssancestudier III), 30-31, 172, 349-353; Claudia A. Meier, *Heinrich Ringerink und sein Kreis: Eine Flensburger Bildschnitzerwerkstatt um 1600*, Flensburg 1984 (Schriften der Gesellschaft für Flensburger Stadtgeschichte XXXIV), 72-83, 210-211. The altars are also described in the inventories: *Die Kunstdenkmäler des Landes Schleswig-Holstein. Stadt Flensburg*, Berlin & Munich 1955, 90-96; *Danmarks Kirker. Vejle Amt*, Copenhagen 2009, 661-671. The last description, however, was published after the completion of the present article [editors comment].

6   Sellink, 1991-92, 149-155.

7   The best overview of this situation is Guido Marnef, *Antwerp in the Age of Reformation: Underground Protestantism in a Commercial Metropolis, 1550-1577*, Baltimore and London 1996 (transl. J.C. Grayson).

8   A helpful introduction to Coornhert's views may be found in Mirjam G.K. van Keen, "Spiritualism in the Netherlands: From David Joris to Dirck Volckertsz Coornhert", *The Sixteenth Century Journal* 33 (2002), 129-150.

9   Strauss 1977, 1, 72.

10 Strauss 1977, 1, 70.

11 Tove Jørgensen, Vivi Jensen & Poul Dedenroth-Schou, *Skt. Nikolaj Kirke, Kolding*, Kolding 1987, 111.

12 Jørgensen, Jensen & Dedenroth-Schou 1987 111-112.

13 "Caspar Marckdaner til Siøgaard som de(n) tid war Kong. Matss. Høffuitzmand paa Koldinghuss lod giøre denne Altar Taffle paa sin eigen bekostning Kolding Kircke til ære: ANNO 1590".

14 Honnens de Lichtenberg 1989, 352-353.

15 Jørgensen, Jensen & Dedenroth-Schou, 1987, 27-28.

16 On these aspects of the history of Kolding, see Birgitte Dedenroth-Schou & Jens Å.S. Pedersen, *Rådhus og Bystyre i Kolding 1500-2000*, Kolding 2001, 17-21.

17 One example of such a link is the marriage between the Flensburg woodcarver Anthoni Wulf and one Dorothea Kolding, daughter of Jost von der Heyde from Kolding, see Meier 1984, 25.

18 Meier 1984, 73.

19 The relevant details of the will are published in Meier 1984, 73.

20 Gerhard Kraack & Nis Lorenzen, *Die St.-Nikolai-Bibliothek zu Flensburg*, Flensburg 1984 (Schriften der Gesellschaft für Flensburger Stadtgeschichte XXXV), 224.

21 On Melanchthon's theology, see Carl E. Maxcey, *Bona Opera: A Study in the Development of Doctrine in Philip Melanchthon*, Nieuwkoop 1980 (Bibliotheca Humanistica et Reformatorica, XXXI).

22 Meier 1984, 14-15.

23 Hugo Johannsen, "The Graphic Art of Hendrick Goltzius as Prototype for Danish Art during the Reign of Christian IV", *Leids Kunsthistorisch Jaarboek* 2 (1983), 85-110.

Fig.1. Kuressaare/Arensburg, the Bishop's castle, later residence of the Danish vice-regent (Photo Peeter Säre).

DENMARK IN ESTONIA.
IMPORT AND DOMESTIC RENAISSANCES?

Krista Kodres

The destiny of the Danish state and Estonian territories has crossed on several occasions. In this article I will focus on the so-called second Danish time, the years 1559-1645, when Denmark owned the biggest island of Estonia, Saaremaa/Ösel[1]. The size of the island, together with many small islands around it, is 2 969 sq km, the same as Gotland only 150 km away from Saaremaa.

My main interest lies in art objects that appeared in Saaremaa during the Danish era, primarily church art, because that is all from which we actually have either physical or documental evidence. I will tackle an especially „Danish" altar in a Saaremaa church Kihelkonna/Kielkond dating from 1591 more thoroughly. Considering the topic of the conference "Reframing the Danish Renaissance", I also try to find out to what extent we can use the term "Danish" in church art or in other words – whether we can talk about the late 16th – early 17th century objects of art in Saaremaa in the context of „Danish renaissance". There is also made a reflection on a more general topic – "art and how to name it".

Danish eras in Estonia

Denmark and Estonia have been connected twice in history. The first time in 1219 when Valdemar II, together with Andreas the Archbishop of Lund, bishop Nicolaus and Petrus Jacobi the Bishop of Roskilde arrived in Tallinn/Reval on a military campaign.[2] Valdemar first conquered the Estonians' stronghold and established his own – the Danish stronghold. According to a legend, Denmark acquired its national flag – *Dannebrog* – on the eve of this event when a white cross in the glowing red sky appeared to the king who was preparing to attack on the Tallinn Bay. A few years later Valdemar II arrived at Saaremaa and "started to build a stone stronghold" there as well.[3] Already in 1213, Andreas of Lund had been granted the papal privilege to appoint bishops to Estonia. After the successful crusade in 1238, Denmark was a major landowner in Old Livonia besides the Livonian Order (according to the contract of Stensby, 1238) and the bishops acted as papal legates. The first Danish period in Estonia lasted until 1346, when Valdemar IV Atterdag sold his share (North-Estonia, Tallinn/Reval, Narva and Rakvere/Wesenberg) to the Livonian order master Heinrich Tusmer for 19 000 silver marks according to the Cologne weight. This was a staggering 4.44 tonnes of silver!

The destiny of Estonia crossed the Danish Kingdom for the second time 200 years later, during the Russian-Livonian war starting in 1558. Predicting long warfare, the last Catho-

Fig. 2. Unknown master, altar of Kihelkonna/Kielkond Church, 1591 (Photo Peeter Säre).

lic Bishop of Saare-Lääne /Ösel-Wiek district, Johannes Münchhausen, sold his rights in his area in 1559 to the Danish King Frederik II who then gave them to his brother, the Duke Magnus. Duke Magnus arrived with 400 mercenaries, young Danish noblemen and the court clergyman[4] in Saaremaa in 1560, and was immediately ordained as the bishop of Ösel-Wiek. The Danish power in Saaremaa, however, was not established quite so easily, as part of the island still belonged to the Livonian Order. The Swedes and the Russians also coveted the island, so between 1560 and 1570 the Danes, sword in hand and together with local supporting knights, were busy establishing their total power in Saaremaa. Still, it was only in 1584 when the Saaremaa knighthood pledged loyalty to Frederik II. Sweden made another attempt to conquer the island in 1612, but failed. In 1645 the Kingdom of Sweden finally acquired Saaremaa after the Brömsebro peace treaty.

The second Danish period in Estonia thus lasted 86 years. Folk legends describe this period as a "golden era" in Saaremaa.[5] One reason for glorifying the Danish era was the fact that unlike mainland Estonia, Saaremaa was able to live in peace during most of the period.

Denmark carried out its politics through a vice-regent appointed by the king. In order to win over the local knights, Duke Magnus gave new lands to them, although the majority of land remained in the possession of the state. The Danish church law was established in Saaremaa in 1562, and Magnus provided each church with a so-called plough-land of grace, a right confirmed by all subsequent Danish kings. In 1563, at the beginning of the Danish era, Duke Magnus granted the town rights to the settlement called Arensburg/Kuressaare (Fig. 1). This was a place where various wealthier people had settled from the mainland to escape the Russian-Livonian war. In the late 16th century the grain merchants' profits increased, as Sweden had barred grain trade on the mainland. Life in Saaremaa only really started recovering since the 1590s, which is also evident in the fact that the first major art purchases for adorning the churches were made at that time.

Catechism altar of Kihelkonna Church

In 1591 the medieval church of Kihelkonna/Kielkond got a new altar.[6] The main part of it is a triptych, where the central panel is a painting showing "The Last Supper", and the wings have only texts (Fig. 2). The text is the same on both panels – excerpts from St. Paul's 1st letter to the Corinthians, telling about the preparation for the last supper; the writing on the right wing is in Latin, on the left in German. A smaller panel of painting is on the aedicula with volutes above the central panel, showing "The Resurrection of Christ". The Resurrection scene is flanked by Fides and Spes, and the figure of the third theological virtue, Charitas, at the top. This hierarchy corresponds to St. Paul's claim: „So faith, hope, love remain, these three; but the greatest of these is love (1 Cor 13, 13). The text on the cornice between the triptych and the front doubles the altar's theological message:

> "*Das Brot das wir brechen / ist das nicht die Gemeinschafft des Leibes Christi* and *Das gesegnete Kelch welchen wir segnen / ist des nckt die gemeinschafft des blutes Christi.*" (1 Cor 10, 6)

In its appearance, the Kihelkonna altar is a fairly common type of altarpiece in the 16th century Danish church art, the so-called catechism altarpiece. It should be stressed that the Kihelkonna altar is the only one of this kind not only in Saaremaa but in the whole of Estonia. The Kihelkonna altar is also the oldest known evangelical altar retable survived in Estonian territory.[7] It must have been specially commissioned, because the church of Kihelkonna in fact already had an old, Catholic-era altar that still stood there in 1716 – "*auff der Süder Seiten ein alt steinerne Altar, dabei etliche von Holz geschnitzte Bilder gesehen.*"[8] It must be emphasized that after the Reformation a lot of the big town churches, not to mention the parish churches, in mainland Estonia continued using the Catholic-era main altars without any problem.

The exceptional type of the Kihelkonna altarpiece forces to ask about its origin. It is obvious that this must be sought in Denmark or the territories connected to it. In Denmark (thus also in Scania, Gotland and Norway that were parts of Denmark) the first catechism altars were made in the 1580s. Their concept relied on the peculiarity of the so-called consolidation period of the Danish reformation era: the church did not join the 1577 *Concordienformel*, and was looking for its own path. Despite of the consensus-seeking attitude of Nils Hemmingsen, the leading theologian at the Copenhagen University in 1557-1579, who actually recommended the use of images, the Crypto-Calvinist ideas were standing firm in Denmark.[9]

268 catechism altars have been registered in Denmark, and 78 in Norway.[10] At the same time, there are only 8 Danish and 4 Norwegian altars that really bear an excerpt from Martin Luther's Small Catechism. We can now add the Kihelkonna altar, where the texts precisely repeat the Small Catechism: the altar wings and cornice are adorned with the texts of Luther's Small Catechism, found in the chapter "Das Sacrament des Altars". The chosen excerpt indicates to Crypto-Calvinist attitude.[11] The Kihelkonna altar may also be added to about half the whole number of Danish catechism altars, which besides the text panels have pictures as well.[12]

What other conclusions can be drawn from the altar in Kihelkonna church? One thing that strikes the eye is that the altar texts are written in both Latin and German. The latter was naturally meant for the local nobility. Latin is more difficult to explain, as the noblemen most probably could not read it, to say nothing of the Estonian peasants. However, it is likely that the usage of Latin was connected with evangelical liturgy determined in Denmark. The last, unifying liturgy regulation – "*alle kirckens ceremonier*" – was established in 1568. This stipulated two languages to be used in the service: Danish and Latin, whereas the Credo was followed by the Latin passage of the preparation for the "Last Supper".[13] It seems reasonable to connect the usage of Latin on the altar of Kihelkonna to this liturgy regulation. We cannot find any Latin inscriptions on the liturgical objects in the churches on Estonian mainland that belonged partly to the Swedish, partly to the Polish kingdom.

Like with all altars, the position of whoever commissioned it is always telling. The 1716 church inventory register says that "*Der Altar ist Ao 1591 von Seel H. Reinholdt Anrep und seine Hausfrau Tekla Bähr, deren Namen und Wapen darin zustehen.*"[14] We indeed find the initials R.A. and T. B., as well as the date ANNO 1591 on the Last Supper picture (Fig. 3). Reinholt Anrep was a local manor lord who must have enjoyed considerable authority in Saaremaa as he was one of two noblemen who was invited in 1596 to the coronation of Christian IV in Copenhagen.[15] In the 1596 *Quarti Confirmatio Privilegiorum* the king confirmed all Reinholt Anrep's privileges: "*durch seine liebe getreue Reinholt Anrep und Johann Vietinghoff ersuchen, in Ansehung der seinem Vater Friedrich II u ihm geleisteten, u künfftig noch zu leisteten dienste.*"[16]

Fig. 3. Unknown master, The Last Supper, middle panel of the altar of Kihelkonna/Kielkond Church, 1591 (Photo Peeter Säre).

The above is however only part of the connections and interpretations that the Kihelkonna altar offers. The theological concept behind it points towards "Denmark", but what else?

Examining the form of the altar and its pictures, we have to move away from Denmark. Painted altars in the form of triptych were already widely spread in the Low Countries of the 15th century, but the Kihelkonna altar possesses a strikingly novel element: the aedicula with volutes. The form of aedicule is related to the work of Hans Vredeman de Vries, indicating knowledge of his book, „Dorica und Ionica" published in 1565. The pictures, too, refer to Antwerp: "The Last Supper" of the central panel was made after a 1585 print by Hendrick Goltzius of the same title. That in turn was made after a painting of either Lambert Lombardi or Pieter Coeck van Aelst. The model of the "Resurrection" is still unclear as is the source for figures representing theological virtues.[17]

The "travelling" of models in early modern Europe was nothing extraordinary, and at the era of the printed book it was no longer necessary for a work to be connected with the place where the models were actually made. In the second half of 16th century, Antwerp was the cultural capital of Northern Europe and its artists and architects the successful producers of pictorial and architectural models for the others. Thus the "Netherlandish connection" is obvious in most of the art production in Central Europe and in the countries around the Baltic Sea. It is however impossible to believe that the Kihelkonna altar was made locally. The reason was very simple – at that time Saaremaa did not have a painter of that quality, in fact in the documents there is no indication of active painters at all. We have to conclude that the altar was bought elsewhere.

Where did Anrep order it? I have not managed to find a painter in Denmark or the territories that belonged to the crown who could have completed the altar. The Low Countries cannot be excluded here. The destination of the flourishing grain trade in Saaremaa in the late 16th century, mentioned previously, was Amsterdam.[18]

Import and the domestic

At the end of the Danish era Saaremaa had altogether 12 churches, two of them were erected during the Danish rule; unfortunately they have not remained. As far as we know at least 7 churches were provided with new altars during the Danish period. Four of them have fully or partly survived.

The retable of the Kärla/Kergel church (Fig. 4) dates back to 1591, the same year as the Kihelkonna altar. The quality of woodcarving in Kärla forces us to believe that also this altarpiece was imported to Saaremaa. It was donated by Anna Overläcker whose husband was Otto Buxhövden, *Landrat* of Ösel. The original altar composition was altered in 1642 when the local woodcarver

Fig. 4. Unknown master, altar of Kärla/Kergel Church, 1591, alterations by Balthasar Rascky, 1642 (Photo Peeter Säre).

Balthasar Rascky added two clumsy figures to its front and left a celebratory note to this effect at the back of the altar.[19] When the Saaremaa pastor Martin Körber described the altar in 1915, it still had wings: one with Buxhövden's, and the other with Overläcker's coat-of-arms. This coincides with the 1716 inventory:

"*Im Chor als im erster Gewölbe, stehet ein von Holtz gemachtes mit allerhand farbe gemahltes, und ausgeschnitzten Bilden geziertes Altar, woran 2 flügel, ein jegl. Mit 2. kleinen eisen Hängen, so da könne auff und zu gemacht werden, und sind gleichfalls bemahlet. Dieses altar ist ao 1591, d 24 Mai von sel. Anna Öwerlackn, seel Otto Buxhöweden Wittibe verehret worden.*"[20]

Thus the altar had not originally been of the so-called alabaster type, as it appears to us now, but, *mit allerhand farb gemahlet.*

As for its form, the altar clearly belongs to the Netherlandish mannerism, its architectonics indicating again the so-called Vredeman style, although there is no direct equivalent to it in Vredeman's books. The main scene with the Crucified Christ, Mary, Mary Magdalene and John the Baptist reflects the compositions of "Crucifixion" of Pieter Coecke van Aelst.

The altar wings, with pictures of Adam and Eve on one and with six pictures of the Passion on the other side of the wings, now in the Saaremaa Museum, belonged to an unknown altar that was probably imported as well (Fig. 5). The topic on the altar wings clearly demonstrates evangelical faith – the depicted pictures firmly correspond to Martin Luther's concept of „Law and Grace". The wings are difficult to date. Still, at least in depicting one scene – Christ on the Mount of Olives – the master has used Zacharias Dolendo's engraving after Carel van Mander, made at the end of 16th or in the early 17th century (Dolendo died in 1604); Adam and Eve indicate a model relying on tradition of Lucas Cranach the Elder.[21] This allows us to assume that the altar was acquired during the Danish period. The painter of the wings was obviously not first-class, but it should be stressed again that no painter is known to have worked in Saaremaa at the end of 16th and in the early 17th century.

"The archive sources confirm that an altar was ordered also for Karja/Karris Church at the end of the 16th century:

"*Im ersten Gewölbe als im Chor stehet ein von Holz gemachtes mit allerhand Farben angemahltes Altar vormitten ein vergult gemachtes Crucifix am selber altar zwey Flügell oder thür mit 2 kleinen Eisernen Hängen auff den thüre so können auff und zu gemacht werden und sind gleichtheils bemahlt, das Gatter werck hat der seel. Capitain Niclas von Kramern vermahlen lassen. Vor dem Altar welche H. Landrath Ernst berg Gert von Howen und H. Pastor loci Tunder hat erfertigen lassen...*"[22]

Interestingly enough pastor Tunder, who is mentioned in the text, was earlier priest in Kihelkonna – the church which housed the two-wing catechism altarpiece in 1591. The painted wings with

DENMARK IN ESTONIA 131

Fig. 5. Unknown master, Adam and Eve and Passion, side wings of the altar of Karja Church(?). Museum of Ösel (Photo Emil Urbel).

Adam and Eve and the Passion scenes, just mentioned, may have belonged to the altar of Karja, since their programme requires depiction of the Crucifixion in the middle panel.

In 1604 Landrat Claus von Vietinghoff, the same whose privileges were confirmed by Christian IV, donated to Püha/Pyhha Church "*dass Altar künstlich geschnitzet und vermahlet*".[23] In the visitation protocols of the early 18th century is mentioned that Muhu/Mohn[24] and Anseküla/Anseküll[25] churches had painted altars too, both "*mit einem vermahlten Schranken umbgehen*"; the central panel of the Anseküla altar depicted the Crucifixion, and this picture has survived. The descriptions of both altars in the visitation protocols refer to the triptych type and allow us to assume that they were provided in the late 16th, or the early 17th century.

Besides altars, pulpits were ordered as well. These are mostly simple and – obviously influenced by Danish tradition again – without "pictures", which was quite unseen in mainland Estonia. The earliest, 1604 pulpit, was again donated by the patron of Kihelkonna Church, Anrep whose coat-of-arms, together with those of his two wives can be seen on the pulpit (Fig. 6). The author of pulpits in Muhu (1629) (Fig. 7), Valjala/Valjal (1634)[26] and Karja (1638) has been established. It was Balthasar Raschky, the man who also renovated the afore-mentioned Kärla altar. Raschky was the first master to work locally for years, becoming the head of his guild in Arensburg. His skills in sculpting, however, were not spectacular; as models he probably used the publications of the Cologne cabinetmakers Veit Eck and Jacob Guckeisen from late 16th till early 17th century.[27] Still, he was not the only one to receive commissions. The pulpit donated to Kärla Church in 1623 by Margareta von Tiesen-

Fig. 6. Unknown master, pulpit of Kihelkonna/Kielkond church, 1604 (Photo Peeter Säre).

Fig. 7. Balthasar Rascky, pulpit of Muhu/Mohn Church, 1629 (Photo Peeter Säre).

hausen[28] was most probably ordered from Arent Passer in Tallinn. In the year 1645, the same year when Saaremaa was given to Sweden, one pulpit, quite extraordinary with a larger pictorial programme, was obtained by the church of Kaarma/Karmel (Fig. 8, 9). The name of the carver was Jakob Jakobson,[29] which may indicate a Danish origin. No further works of this master are known in Saaremaa.

In addition to such significant objects for evangelical liturgy as the altar and the pulpit, the churches under the Danish rule acquired other necessary items: various baptismal vessels and chalices have survived. It should be pointed out that several donators were Danish protectors: for example, the widow of the brother of the Danish vice-regent Jürgen von Ungern gave the Jämaja/Jamma Church a baptismal cup (1573-76),[30] the vice-regent Jakob Becke 1614-23 donated a large altar chandelier to the Muhu St Catherine Church,[31] etc.

The wife of the Vice-regent Claus Maltesen Sehested, Anna Lykke, even gave money for the building of the whole chapel, which was then called after her name – Mustjala/Mustel Anna church.[32] Unfortunately the chapel, obviously constructed in wood, was demolished in the 19th century to build a new and bigger one instead.

In conclusion we may be certain that the Danes truly promoted the evangelical faith in Saaremaa, as if fulfilling the hope of pastor Timan v. Brackel, educated in Wittenberg, who wrote in a letter of 1576 that:

> "... Königlicher Majestät des Reiches Dänemarks, Statthalter, Klaus v. Ungern, daselbst neben treuen Predigern alles in Ordnung zu bringen und dem Bösen zu wehren Fleiss, Mühe und Ernst angewendet...."[33]

And the other statement quoted from the contemporary source states:

> "Wollte Gott, ich könnte dazu Hilfe und Rath geben, dass die gottlosen Bischöfe ausgerottet würden; denn wo sie mitregieren, ist es nimmer wohl zugegangen...."[34]

"Regional renaissances"

The church objects as mediators of the "true belief" that were donated for the churches in Saaremaa reflect upon "Danish content", on the one hand, and at the different geographical areas of artistic influence, on the other. How then should we define the Danish period in Saaremaa relying on familiar art historical terminology?

"The Danish Renaissance in Saaremaa" seems insufficient, because the above discussed objects, according to their formal qualities cannot directly or can only partly be connected to Denmark.[35] Thus, very generally spoken we are dealing with the Renaissance of the North or Mannerism of the North.[36] In Estonia, the 16-17th century art has been called "Renaissance/Mannerism in Estonia", which is quite right, as it refers to something imported: in the mainland of Estonia as well as in Saaremaa, we can follow not only the import of

Fig. 8. Jacob Jacobson, pulpit of Kaarma/Karmel Church, 1645 (Photo Peeter Säre).

art works but also the increasing immigration of artists from Northern Europe during the late 16th and in the 17th century. It could be mentioned here that in Estonian art historical historiography since the 19th century, the notion of "Renaissance in Estonia" has had a peculiar connotation: it was used in a way that refers to the ambitions of the self-determination as a "cultured" region (as by the Baltic German authors) or nation (as by Estonian authors of the 20th century): to have a "Renaissance" meant to have participated at the European process of cultural civilization. When we shift the point of view, that kind of construction becomes weirdly ambivalent, as it talks about "self-colonization" that was needed to support the main idea of nation building in Estonia: "Let us stay Estonians, but let us become Europeans!", as sounded the slogan that was raised by young Estonian intellectuals in 1905.[37]

In some way or other, introducing the political and national aspect to the question "how to name art of 16th to 17th century in Saaremaa?" then the valid denomination could be "Danish Colonial Renaissance". This notion, in turn, suggests raising the questions of reception of art objects by the local community.[38] The research has still not come so far.

Another possible denomination can be taken further in the spirit of Jan Białostocki, who in his article "Langsames und schnelles Geschehen in der Geschichte der Kunst"[39] used (following Ljubo Karaman) terms such as *Kunst der Grenzgebiete, Provinzialgebiete, Peripherien*. All these are determined in relation to the centre, the metropolis. Using the given concepts in particular the Saaremaa case we can thus talk about several different arts there at the same time: about art belonging to the centre (as by altars of Kihelkonna and Kärla) and then about the "Peripherial Renaissance" (pulpits made by the local master B.

Fig. 9. Jacob Jacobson, Ascension of Christ, pulpit of Kaarma/Karmel Church, 1645 (Photo Peeter Säre).

Raschky). Incidentally, it seems that describing history through the centre and the periphery has given some headache also to the Danish historians: in the book "Reformationens konsolidering i de nordiska länderna 1540-1610" (1990), Tarald Rasmussen writes about Saxony and Württemberg as centres of Lutheranism, which from there reaches the so-called "nordiske sentrene" (Copenhagen – Stockholm/Uppsala), from where innovations radiated further to the "northern peripheries".[40]

The concept of art of the centre/province/periphery refers to both similarities and differences; it also indicates dynamics and direction. At the same time it also alludes to hierarchy and is somehow evaluative, perhaps more than we would like today. Still, we have to admit that in the 16th and 17th centuries the actual direction of artistic transfer was from centre(s) to the periphery. Our case of Saaremaa is a good proof here.

From the point of view of formal analysis the recently often used term "regional (style)"[41] seems quite appropriate. Speaking of "Regional Renaissance" of the Baltics that includes different local "renaissances" – Danish, Swedish, Estonian etc – allows reference to the common but also indicates at the possible differences and does not sound evaluative. Relying on cultural geography, therefore, looks like a sensible proposal, although it does not solve all the problems.[42]

One of these problems touches the content of the art that we are used to generalise under the term "Renaissance". For example, if determining the objects of church art, as it was done in this article, we certainly cannot avoid the 16th-17th century reality, the process of confessionalisation and its impact on art in Europe. Determining something by style only thus seems to be not enough, because the term does not have the ability to indicate on the content of church art, which in Europe was connected either with Lutheran, Catholic or Calvinist theology. Could we then use: "Evangelical Renaissance (in Saaremaa, in Denmark, in Germany)"?

In sum, we have to conclude that one should be careful in using general terms without referring to the conditions of their validity. We have to "reframe" them with more specific and illuminating notions for the sake of the more correct reflection. However, the term "Renaissance" should not be thrown into the dustbin of history just because it always requires explanations and extensions - after all, "Renaissance" does point to something visually common, to a certain visual strategy.[43] We should not – how could we? – deny its reflexivity, but we should neither deny our possibilities to fulfil it with more specific and adequate international, regional and local content.

Notes

1. The names of the places are first given both in Estonian and German transcription.

2. *Henriku Liivimaa kroonika*, Enn Tarvel (translation and commentaries), Tallinn 2005, 131 (published as *Heinrichs Livländische Chronik (Henrici Chronicon Livoniae)*, ed. by Leonid Arbusow & Albert Bauer, Hannover 1955).

3. Henriku Liivimaa kroonika 2005, 154.

4. Martin Körber, *Bausteine zu einer Geschichte Oesels, fünf Jahrhunderte. Von der heidnischen Vorzeit bis zum Frieden von Nystädt*, Arensburg 1885, 203-204.

5. Martin Körber, *Oesel einst und jetzt*, 1, Arensburg 1887, 4-5.

6. Krista Kodres, "Church and Art in the First Century of the Reformation in Estonia: Towards Lutheran Orthodoxy", *Scandinavian Journal of History* 28 (2003), 194-197.

7. In 1584 the altarpiece for the St. John's church in Tartu/Dorpat was acquired but this was replaced already in the 17th century.

8. Estonian Historical Archives (EHA) 1192, 1, 112, 18p.

9. Hans Jørgen Frederiksen, "Reformationens betydning for den kirkelige kunst i Danmark", *Reformationsperspektiver, Acta Jutlandica LXII:3, Teologisk serie 14*, (1987), 100-126. On Hemmingsen and the images, cf. Anita Hansen & Birgitte Bøggild Johannsen, "IMO LICET. Omkring Niels Hemmingsens billedsyn", in: *Kirkearkeologi og kirkekunst. Studier tilegnet Sigrid og Hakon Christie*, Øvre Eivik 1993, 181-198.

10. Ragne Bugge, "Tekstaltertavlerne i Danmark-Norge omkring 1600", in: Ingmar Brohed (ed.), *Reformationens konsolidering i de nordiska länderna 1540-1610*, Oslo 1990, 306.

11. The author of this article is grateful to Jan Harasimo-

wicz for this remark.

12 The other region where the type of Cathechism altar or "Schriftaltar" was widely spread was the northwestern part of Germany (Ostfriesland, Oldenburg). See Dietrich Diederichs-Gottschalk, *Die protestantischen Schriftaltäre des 16. und 17. Jahrhunderts in Nordwestdeutschland. Eine kirchen- und kunstgeschichtliche Untersuchung zu einer Sonderform liturgischer Ausstattung in der Epoche der Konfessionalisierung,* Regensburg 2005.

13 Knud Ottosen, "Liturgien i Danmark 1540-1610", in: Brohed (ed.) 1990, 271.

14 EHA 1192, 1, 112, 18.

15 Martin Körber, *Oesel einst und jetzt*, 2, Arensburg 1899, 55.

16 EHA 957, 1, 1358 – Osiliana II, 76.

17 There were several series of virtues known in the 16th century of which the ones of Virgil Solis from Nuremberg seem to resemble most the Kihelkonna figures (Eight Virtues. Single engraving. Albertina, Vienna).

18 A. Luha, E. Blumfeldt & A. Tammekann (eds.), *Saaremaa. Maateaduslik, majanduslik ja ajalooline kirjeldus*, Tartu 1934, 307.

19 Martin Körber, *Oesel einst und jetzt*, 3, Arensburg 1915, 103-104.

20 EHA 1291, 1, 31.

21 Reet Rast, "Fragmente Saaremaa sakraalsest interjöörist 17. sajandil", in: Olavi Pesti (ed.), *Saaremaa Muuseum. Kaheaastaraamat 1995-96,* Kuressaare 1997, 49-50.

22 EHA 1192, 1, 112, 7.

23 EHA 1192, 1, 111, 9.

24 EHA 1192, 1, 110, 15.

25 EHA 1192, 1, 113, no page.

26 EHA 957, 1, 1357 – Osiliana, 136.

27 Günter Irmscher, *Kölner Architektur- und Säulenbücher um 1600*, Bonn 1999.

28 Körber 1899, 104.

29 Körber 1915, 77.

30 Körber 1899, 249.

31 Körber 1915, 6.

32 Körber 1899, 27.

33 Körber 1899, 240.

34 Körber 1885, 180.

35 See about the problem: Thomas da Costa Kaufmann, "Italian Sculptors and Sculpture Outside of Italy (Chiefly in Central Europe): Problems of Approach, Possibilities of Reception", in: Claire Farago (ed.), *Reframing the Renaissance*, New Haven & London 1995, 27-66.

36 Jan Białostocki, *The Art of the Renaissance in Eastern Europe: Hungary, Bohemia, Poland*, Ithaca & New York 1976.

37 The notion of "self-colonization" has been used to describe the cultural ambitions of Estonian intellectuals of the 19th and early 20th century in the light of postcolonial theory. See Tiit Hennoste, "Postkolonialism ja Eesti. Väga väike leksikon", *Vikerkaar* 4/5 (2003), 88-89.

38 Claire Farago, "Introduction", in: Farago (ed.) 1995, 8.

39 Jan Białostocki, "Langsames und schnelles Geschehen in der Geschichte der Kunst", in: Friedrich Möbius & Helga Sciurie (eds.), *Stil und Epoche. Periodisierungsfragen*, Dresden 1989, 214.

40 Tarald Rasmussen, "Innledende overveielser med europeisk perspektiv", in: Brohed (ed.) 1990, 11.

41 Thomas da Costa Kaufmann, *Artistic Regions and the Problem of Artistic Metropolises: Questions of (East) Central Europe*, Chicago & London 2004 (Toward a Geography of Art), 154-186.

42 Kaufmann 2004, 186.

43 Jas Elsner, "Style", in: Robert S. Melson, Richard Shiff (eds.), *Critical Terms for Art History*, Chicago & London 2003, 108.

A TRIBUTE TO THE REFORMATION: HESSELAGERGÅRD IN A LUTHERAN PERSPECTIVE

Hanne Kolind Poulsen

Hesselagergård is situated on the eastern side of the island of Funen. It is an important monument in the Danish as well as the European art of the 16th century. The two most extraordinary and spectacular (surviving) aspects of the manor house are the conspicuous round-arched gables of the façades (Fig. 1) and the decoration of one of the main halls, known as the Stag Hall (Fig. 2). Both works are ascribed to Jacob Binck, a German artist working in Denmark, both are dated around 1550, and both were executed for Johan Friis (1494-1570), chancellor to the Danish King, Christian III.

Johan Friis was a learned, humanist nobleman who wielded great power by virtue of his position as the King's chancellor. Furthermore, he was one of the leading figures behind the Lutheran Reformation in Denmark. Being a highly-educated, powerful and self-assured man, Friis must have had a carefully considered rationale behind his projects and choices.[1]

The earlier Hesselagergård was destroyed in the 1534-36 civil war provoked, among other things, by the confessional shift. Friis embarked on the rebuilding of the house in c. 1538 and it was completed in about 1540. Around 1550 he had the house extended by the addition of an extra storey and a large stair tower on the south side. He decorated the east and west facades of the building, as well as the stair tower, with the spectacular round-arched gables. Hesselagergård then appeared, more or less, as we see it today.[2] The decoration of the Stag Hall was also undertaken during this second building phase.[3] This article will focus primarily on the Stag Hall decoration and the round-arched gables, concluding with an interpretation of the monument as such.

The Stag Hall

The Stag Hall is situated on the first floor of the main building. Following the extension work, the private quarters were moved up into the new second floor. The entire first floor was then given over to reception rooms,[4] comprising two big halls separated by a narrow entrance hall, which the guests entered from the stair tower (Fig. 3).[5] While the decoration in the Stag Hall is preserved, the east hall decoration has been lost, although some fragments have been documented in a few sketches and tracings.[6] The decoration in the Stag Hall covers the top half of the walls, stopping just short of two meters above the floor. The section of wall between the floor and the decoration was, in all probability, covered with panels.[7] The key question is, of course, what the hunting motif – which seems so innocent to the

Fig. 1. Hesselagergård, east gable and stair tower gable, c. 1550 (Photo author).

modern eye – may have meant at the time of its execution? First, however, we must ask, what do we actually see?[8]

When entering the Stag Hall (Fig. 2), we are immediately aware of the large animal figures painted on the walls. The male stags originally had sculptured heads with real antlers.[9] Visually, they completely dominate the hall. However, on closer inspection we realise that a lot of smaller-scale activity is going on 'behind' the stags: we see, for example, a horse-drawn carriage with travellers, a boat transporting noble passengers, a fashionable outdoor party, young noblemen practising their fighting skills, towns, castles, ships and landscapes, and hunters with dogs walking among the stags. Furthermore, rich acanthus motifs cover the top bevels of the window recesses, and we know that the ceiling beams were also once decorated with vegetation motifs, although these have not survived.[10]

The east wall is not the original and we have no information as to how it would have been decorated – perhaps there was a continuation of the stags from the other walls? Or perhaps the fragment of a battle scene, found in 1953, was part of a war motif here?[11] The fragment has now been inserted in the new wall.

Besides the paintings on the walls and ceiling, the side bevels of the window recesses are also decorated. Both side walls in each of the six original recesses were probably once painted, making twelve paintings in all, but only seven of these are preserved. In the two western recesses, four of these paintings depict the patron's family coats-of-arms. The remaining three are unquestionably the strangest images of the entire decoration, and they do not seem to fit in with the surrounding imagery at all. These images will be a pivotal point in the following discussion. One of them is a religious motif, namely *King David Watching Bathsheba* (Fig. 4). The two others depict a birdcage with three doves (Fig. 5) and a devil riding a white horse (Fig. 6). The question is, of course, why a religious motif suddenly appears in this otherwise secular context? And what the meaning is of three doves in a birdcage? And a horse-riding devil? How are we to understand these, so to speak, 'misfit' motifs?

The Interpretations

Considering the importance of the monument, surprisingly little research has been undertaken with regard to the images in the Stag Hall and, as we will see, even less with reference to the three 'misfit' motifs. Hesselagergård is primarily discussed in relation to architectural history.[12]

The first, and still most notable, contribution to an understanding of the decoration is a book written by Otto Norn, published in 1961.[13] At the very beginning of this study, Norn stresses that it is impossible to *document* anything concerning either the building of Hesselagergård or its decoration.[14] We have to base any interpretation on our knowledge of the era, of the patron and of art at the time. Norn convincingly attributes the decoration and the gables to Jacob Binck, and he identifies a number of the sources of inspiration on which Binck based his designs for Hesselagergård.[15] Norn is equally persuasive when he

Fig. 2. Hesselagergård, the Stag Hall (Photo The National Museum, Copenhagen).

specifies and dates the two building phases. These results have never been seriously challenged, nor will they be challenged here. It is primarily Norn's *interpretation* of the decoration (and the round-arched gables) that I would like to discuss.

According to Norn, the east hall was decorated with large war scenes, which once included the aforementioned battle scene fragment.[16] He argues that the two halls illustrated the princely sports of hunting and waging war. The various background motifs in the Stag Hall represented the "pleasures and sports of hunting"[17] – e.g. the outdoor hunting party and the young noblemen practising their fighting skills, as seen on either side of the fireplace – whereas the pleasures and sports of waging war were depicted in the east hall. Thus, the meaning of the decoration as a whole, as argued by Norn, was to celebrate the two most fundamental privileges of the aristocracy: hunting and war.

Every other study of Hesselagergård's wall paintings agrees, by and large, with Norn's conclusions – with the exception of two articles, one by Rikke Agnete Olsen (1996) and a recent one by Birgitte Bøggild Johannsen (2006).

Olsen agrees with Norn as to the general understanding of the decoration, namely that it deals with the hunt and with war, but her arguments are somewhat different.[18] Olsen states that Friis' intention was essentially to legitimise his nobility, pointing out that, although he was intensely loyal to the king, he *also* wanted to protect and improve the status, position and power of the nobility.[19] The new social structure in post-Reformation Denmark – a structure in which the estates of the realm were clearly delimited and social status was therefore fixed – meant that from now on the upper classes had to *prove* their noble extraction. Every nobleman or -woman had to produce evidence that sixteen ancestors had held the privileges accorded the former powerful elite; for many, Friis among them, this turned out to be difficult.[20] The privileges of this powerful elite had primarily been hunting and waging war. In depicting these two customs (whether the latter was shown on the east wall of the Stag Hall or in the east hall), which had traditionally defined the free elite who, after 1536, could call themselves noble,[21] the decoration is thus, concludes Olsen, a manifesto for nobility and the nobility's

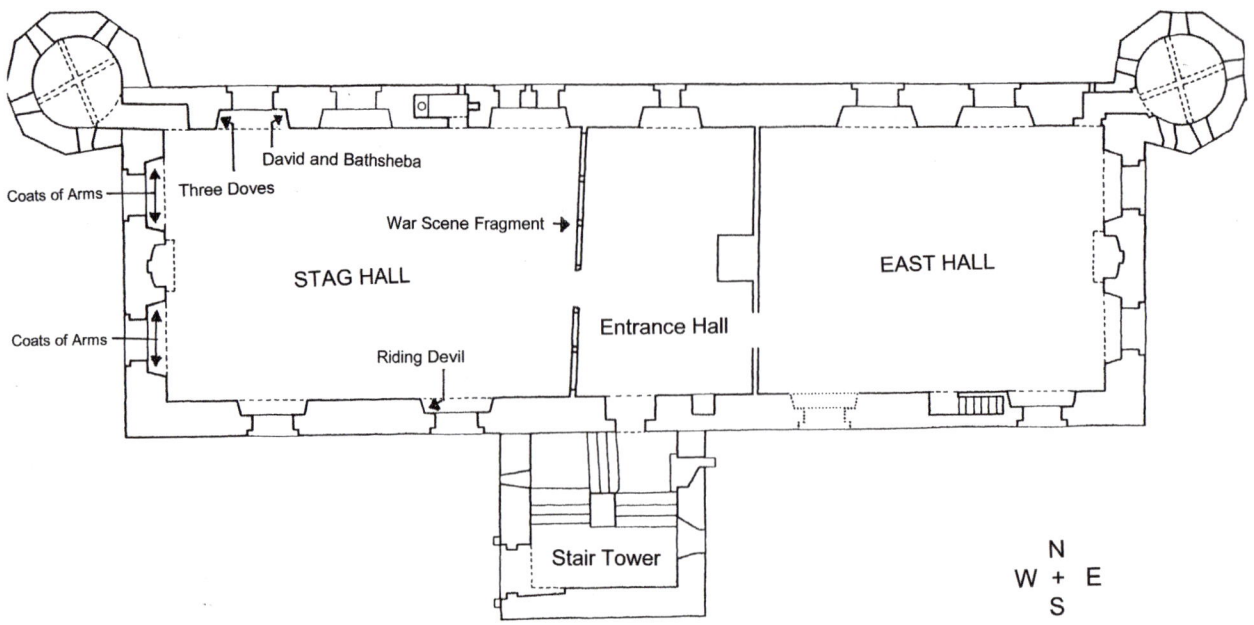

Fig. 3. Hesselagergård. Groundplan of the first floor. The wall-paintings mentioned are indicated by the author. After Engqvist 1996.

rights and privileges.²² Friis provides evidence of his lineage, and thus his claim to nobility, via the four family coats of arms in the side bevels of the two western window recesses. Olsen suggests that the remaining twelve of the prescribed sixteen ancestral coats of arms were placed elsewhere in the Stag Hall. In this way, Friis was able to present himself as a free and privileged nobleman of ancient extraction, and thus entitled to the privileges of hunting and waging war.²³

Bøggild Johannsen weights her interpretation somewhat differently.²⁴ She understands the decoration primarily as an image of a peaceful and well-ordered society – from the nobility's point of view – with entertaining activities such as hunting, hunting parties, excursions, travel and sports. The trophies (i.e. the real antlers on the original stags) refer to the privileges and fighting power of the nobility, but, in Bøggild Johannsen's view, they are also an important motif of fertility. They are symbols of the life-giving procreative force, the quintessence of masculine strength, which was the prerequisite for the continuation of the lineage – for animals as well as for human beings. Therefore, the ancestral heraldry in the window recesses is emphasised, as is a motif of growth in the vegetal ornament on the top bevels of the window recesses and (originally) on the ceiling beams.²⁵ According to Bøggild Johannsen, also the decoration in the east hall was a vision of a peaceful society; in support of this argument, she refers to the (very few) preserved sketches and tracings of the original imagery showing learned men (e.g. a man with a compass) and children with books.²⁶ She does not discuss how the aforementioned battle scene fragment fits into such a harmonious context.

However, all three interpretations avoid going into any detail at all about the three 'misfit' motifs in the window recesses. Norn does not mention Bathsheba or the doves – as the painting was not brought to light until 1962, you could no expect him to – but he only refers briefly to the devil motif.²⁷ Olsen refers to them in passing, but without any supporting documentation for her interpretations. *David and Bathsheba*, she believes, should probably be understood in a Protestant light as referring to the sixth Commandment with its instruction not to commit adultery. The two doves, she writes – actually there are three²⁸ – can be understood "as an old Christian symbol of the spirit's imprisonment in the body and the hope of its release, i.e. its salvation".²⁹ And the "[…] awful devil with a broken lance on a white horse […] can be

Fig. 4. Hesselagergård, wall-painting of David and Bathsheba in the Stag Hall (Photo author).

Fig. 5. Hesselagergård, wall-painting of three doves in the Stag Hall (Photo author).

seen as an image of the defeated grand enemy, maybe with reference to Christ's triumph in the Book of Revelation 19".[30] Taken together, Olsen concludes, "the three images, *without necessarily having a mutual connection* [at least, Olsen does not try to find one], signify that the lord of the house is a good Christian" (my italics).[31] Bøggild Johannsen mentions the doves and the horse-riding devil, but does not suggest any interpretations beyond the most general meaning: a warning against sin and vice.[32] As to the Bathsheba motif, however, she proposes a reading which aims – although in all brevity – to understand the motif in relation to the stags as well as the other images on the walls. According to Bøggild Johannsen, Bathsheba is an example of the *negative* power of women. "The accentuation of the dominating masculine power [as mentioned, Bøggild Johannsen reads the stags as a fertility motif, a symbol of the life-giving procreative force, the quintessence of masculine strength] also occurs through negative counter-images presenting the pernicious influence of the female sex. *David and Bathsheba* was a well-known example

Fig. 6. Hesselagergård, wall-painting of riding devil in the Stag Hall (Photo author).

of a motif pertaining to women's power, in use throughout the Middle Ages and still popular in the 16th century."³³

So, the three scholars do not provide interpretations of the apparently 'misfit' motifs, which are meaningful in relation to one another *as well as* being meaningful in relation to the rest of the decoration. I would argue, however, that if Friis chose to have these motifs painted in the window recesses, they must have had a meaning relevant to the motifs on the walls – and vice versa – as well as a meaning with mutual relevance. Therefore, in the following my ambition will be to suggest an understanding of the decoration *as a unified whole* – including the spectacular round-arched gables of the facades. And to establish such an understanding it would be fruitful, I believe, to look at the images in a Lutheran perspective. I shall begin by examining each of the 'misfit' motifs – which, hopefully, will prove to be quite fitting, after all – and then interpret them in relation to the rest of the decoration.

The Bathsheba Motif

We see Bathsheba sitting in a garden (Fig. 4). She is sitting, with her feet placed in a basin of water and a maid is helping her to wash them. David is standing on a balcony, surveying the scenery and playing the harp. Norn's 1961 study did not mention the Bathsheba motif – as said above, it was not discovered until 1962. In 1965, however, he published a short article dealing exclusively with this painting.³⁴ I shall start by looking at this text.

Norn writes that the Bathsheba motif, since the Late Middle Ages and in the visual arts as well as in literature, has encompassed two principal meanings: it was a so-called *power-of-women* motif warning men against women in general,³⁵ and a motif warning more specifically against adultery.³⁶ This latter significance was topical at the time of the Reformation because the motif illustrated the sixth Commandment ("Thou shalt not commit adultery") in Luther's Large Catechism of 1529.³⁷ Therefore, Norn interprets the scene as *moralising* and writes: "Friis undoubtedly chose the motif because of its moralistic points. […]

The bachelor Friis was warning against the beautiful, but dangerous young women […]".³⁸

Olsen, as already mentioned, also understands the Bathsheba motif as moralising and referring to the sixth Commandment.³⁹ Similarly, Bøggild Johannsen interprets it in this light but, in that Bathsheba gets the blame for the whole wretched business, she sees it as an example of the *negative* power of woman that drives man to such sinful behaviour.⁴⁰

However, I would argue that, after the Reformation, the Bathsheba motif – like many other motifs – acquired a new or, perhaps more likely, an *additional* significance, a particularly Lutheran meaning, which was active and important in the context of the Stag Hall.

Fig. 7. Heinrich Köngsweiser, "King David, an Exemplar of Human Frailty and God's Mercy", c. 1560, Printed in Wittenberg by Peter Corthoys. Rhymes by Paul Eber.

In one of his 1543-1544 lectures on Genesis, Luther interprets the story of David and Bathsheba as a narrative pertaining to one of the central doctrines of Protestantism: the doctrine of 'God's all forgiving mercy'.[41] One of Luther's arguments, however, is to stress that a prerequisite for this mercy is the *acknowledgement* of one's sins. In the lecture, Luther recounts how, at first, David would not acknowledge his adultery, his murder of Uriah and his abuse of power. He denies his guilt. However, David's court prophet, Nathan, makes him understand and *believe* that God would forgive even such serious sins if David would but acknowledge them. In other words, if you acknowledge your sins, as David then did, God will forgive you. Luther contends that because we are human beings we cannot *avoid* sin, but we can learn how to handle sin in the right way: "[…] let us learn [Luther says] to use evils and sins for our good, in order that we may experience how merciful and kind the Lord is."[42]

Thus, the story of David and Bathsheba seen through a Lutheran lens *also* – and even, I believe, *primarily* – becomes a discourse on God's mercy and a story which a powerful man like Friis, with correspondingly powerful sins, would presumably have found important to highlight. That such a Lutheran reading of the David figure was well-known in the period is corroborated by, for example, a woodcut by Heinrich Königswieser (Fig. 7). The sheet has been dated to *c.* 1560 and was printed in Wittenberg by Peter Corthoys. The German title text tells us that it is: "An image of King David, who is an example of human frailty, the wrath of God over sin, and God's mercy to all who turn to him with the *right* faith."[43] In Protestant theology 'the right faith' involves truly believing in God and sincerely confessing your sins because you have faith in His mercy. The rhyme below the image stresses the importance of confession. David's grave sins, i.e. his adultery and his murder of Uriah, were forgiven by God, the text tells us, as God will forgive all who believe in him *and* genuinely repent their sins – "Mit allen den ihr Sünd ist leid, Und glauben fest am geschenckten Son, Dem steht offen der gnaden thron."[44]

The Three Doves

As to the three doves in the birdcage (Fig. 5), the question is, of course, what does this strange and unusual motif signify and why is it placed exactly here, opposite David and Bathsheba? The dove is one of the most meaning-laden images in the Christian culture.[45] Luther also spoke a great deal about doves. In his important lectures on the *Song of Solomon*[46] – delivered during 1530 and 1531, and published in 1539[47] – he set out his 'dove view', as it were, and he refers to these texts when speaking about doves on other occasions.[48] For Luther, the dove is a metaphor for "simplicitas", which is a fundamental notion in his teachings. He celebrates "dovelike simplicity" *both* as a quality of human beings *and* as a quality of things.[49] "Simplicitas" means simplicity, straightforwardness, clarity, non-ambiguity, etc; in other words, *simple-mindedness* in the original and positive sense of the term, connoting "without falseness".[50] The David motif facing the three doves stands in sharp contrast to this *ideal* of a "dovelike simplicity", which none of us can fulfil for the very reason that we are human beings. David is sly and false. The message, however, is that by acknowledging the sins we will inevitably commit because we are *not* dovelike, we can, after all, be sure of God's forgiveness.

But why are there three doves – surely one would suffice to make this point? There is but a single episode in the Bible involving three doves linked to one other, and this is in Genesis when Noah sends out three doves from the Ark.[51] Luther lectured on this text in the years 1535-1536 (the lectures were published in 1544).[52] He interprets Noah's three doves allegorically.[53] Actually, in the Bible text it is the *same* dove Noah sends out three times, but Luther refers to three *different* doves: the first, he says, is *the era of the Law*, when the Law is revealed; the second dove, which came back with an olive leaf and therefore with hope of salvation, is *the era of the Gospel* (the Gospel *is* the hope

of salvation); and the third, which did not come back, is *the era after the end of the world*, when there is nothing more to reveal – except, as Luther writes "the revelation of what we believe and our flight with the third dove into another life, never to return to this wretched and distressed life".[54] If this Lutheran interpretation is accepted, the image is a miniature world history visualised through the three doves; a history which ends happily with salvation and with existence in "another life" – provided, that is, we have acknowledged and confessed our sins and thus qualified for God's mercy.

The Riding Devil

The third 'misfit' image shows a dragon-like devil riding a white horse and carrying, presumably, a flail (Fig. 6). It is placed in such a way that it instantly attracts our attention as we enter the hall. What is really remarkable, however, is the devil's puncturing of the picture frame to the upper left.[55] The devil seems to ride out of the picture – and out of the window (Fig. 8). How are we to understand this? I interpret it as a clear declaration to the visitor that in this house the devil will be turned away, expelled – that here the devil and all his works are renounced. The devil is understood and referred to as a very concrete being that can be physically kicked out – as at Wartburg, when Luther hurled his inkpot at it.

An Interpretation in a Lutheran Perspective

In an endeavour to present a Lutheran interpretation of the Stag Hall decoration as a whole, I would suggest that the wall paintings present the world of humankind, for better or for worse: the vicissitudes of life – pleasures, war, procreation. In other words, we see the *human condition in relation to the world*. In the window recesses, however, other kinds of motif show the *human conditions in relation to God*. We only know three of the, presumably, eight original motifs, which constituted the programme (leaving out of account, for the time being, Friis' four family coats of arms

Fig. 8. Hesselagergård, wall-painting of riding devil, seen from the entrance to the Stag Hall (Photo author).

in the two western recesses, which I shall return to below). These three motifs, however, represent key Protestant themes. *David and Bathsheba* thematises sin and God's all-forgiving mercy – and instructs the viewer in how to achieve this mercy: through consciousness of sin. *The three doves* function, on the one hand, as Protestant role models (the desirable dovelike simplicity) and, on the other, they refer to the three eras in the history of salvation, as interpreted by Luther. *The horse-riding devil* thematises the permanent renunciation of the devil, which for Luther was a pivotal tenet. The old, traditional meanings of the motifs might have been in force as well, but my point is that the *intention* in choosing precisely these motifs was primarily to promote Lutheran teachings.

It is also reasonable, in my opinion, to understand the ancestral heraldry on show in the two western window recesses in a Lutheran perspective and as an integral part of this theologically-informed zone of the decoration – to begin with, because extraction, more precisely ancestry, had become important for the legitimisation of status in a Protestant society; and, furthermore, because this justification of privileges had become rooted in theology. It was *God* who had chosen a particular person to fulfil a particular social rank on the basis of that person's *quality*. And the ancestral line verified this quality.[56] Thus, God's guarantee for Friis' quality was confirmed and displayed by the ancestral heraldry, but at the same time attention was also drawn to Friis' obligation to live up to the Lutheran concept of vocation in a proper Protestant way – for example (and most relevant in this context), by promoting the new faith.

The division of the Stag Hall's images into two zones that supplement one another – the wall paintings displaying the life of humankind (i.e., the *human condition in relation to the world*) and the window recesses displaying the religious guidelines for this life (i.e. the *human condition in relation to God*) – can, in itself, be interpreted in a Lutheran perspective. For Luther it is a central principle to weight "ordinary human life", the day's work *im Beruf und Stand* – here meaning the life, duties and obligations of the *nobility*. But at the same time Luther stresses that this human life must be lived in accordance with the dictates of the Bible, as he understood them, of course!

To reinterpret old motifs – i.e. to give a new, Lutheran meaning to a traditional ('Catholic') motif – was one of Luther's central strategies in his new image concept. And I would argue that the Stag Hall's three religious images are just such a case in point. In the 1520s, Luther had legitimised the 'dangerous', religious image.[57] His tactic was to consider the image solely as an ordinary physical object to which a motif had been added – in contrast to the traditional image concept, which allowed that images *could* be holy and perform divine work.[58] The image, Luther contended, was an object which was neither good nor bad in itself. It was the *use* made of the image that determined whether or not it was acceptable. The viewer's understanding and consequent use of the image thus became a crucial issue. But how was it possible to ensure that the viewer understood and used it in the *right* (Lutheran) way? How was it possible to *control* the meaning of an image, which in principle was uncontrollable and inexhaustible?

Luther's strategy was to try to make the image *un*ambiguous by deactivating the beholder's imagination in the act of perceiving it. And then fixing it (its meaning) by presenting one pre-determined meaning that conformed to his theology. The faithful had to *learn* the authorised meaning of the image. They had to *learn* to read it 'correctly'.

An understanding of meaning as an unstable entity, which is not an integral part of the image itself, but is located in the viewer's intellect and therefore open to manipulation, was one of the most important outcomes of the Lutheran Reformation with regard to images. Luther realised that meaning in images is a changeable feature: it is possible to *choose* a meaning. For example, a picture's 'Catholic' meaning could be changed to one that was in accordance with Lutheran theology. Thus the Lutherans, quite conveniently, were often able to re-use 'Catholic' art.[59] Luther himself exercised this reinterpretation strategy explicitly – for example, in relation to the St Chris-

Fig. 9. Wittenberg, Philipp Melanchthon's House, 1536-1539 (Photo author).

topher motif.⁶⁰ I would argue that it is just such a case of reinterpretation that has been undertaken in the three paintings in the window recesses, where central doctrines of Lutheran theology are highlighted at the expense of the images' traditional content.

Friis as a Well-informed and Dedicated Protestant

It is, however, reasonable to ask if Friis was at all familiar with those of Luther's writings to which I have referred. Or was he perhaps acquainted in other ways with Luther's reflections on the matters relevant here? The answer must be that Friis, politically as well as theologically, was an extremely well-informed man.⁶¹ As the King's chancellor he had been deeply involved in advancing the cause of the Reformation in Denmark during the 1530s. Furthermore, he visited Wittenberg, at least once, namely in the spring of 1535,

with the explicit purpose of becoming better acquainted with Luther's teachings.⁶² He might even have attended some of Luther's lectures on Genesis. He must, in any case, have been familiar with Luther's published works – either by reading them himself or through discussions with Danish theologians – and Denmark and Wittenberg were very closely connected at the time.⁶³ I cannot, of course, *prove* that the intention behind the decoration was as I suggest, but in my view it is evident that Friis, in the reception rooms of his new, spectacular manor house, wanted to proclaim his new faith, his new Protestant worldview.

Against this background, the paintings in the window recesses of the Stag Hall may be defined as Lutheran *Merkbilder* – images of memory. In his seventh sermon on the Deuteronomy, delivered on 31 October 1529,⁶⁴ Luther mentioned the so-called *Groschen-Bilder*, penny images, which were cheap mass-produced woodcuts with roughly cut motifs. He declared that we do not *believe in* these images, they can seduce no one, but they *remind* the observer of something she already knows. In other words, they function as memory, as *Merkbilder*, which was precisely what he believed images should do. The correct and only legitimate function of the image was not actually to *represent* something, but rather, as a sign, to *refer* to something, namely the Word or the dogma, and thereby *to remind* us of this. Luther downgraded the reality effect in images and upgraded the sign effect. The raison d'être of the image was, for Luther, to remind the faithful, as a *Merkbild*,⁶⁵ of central Lutheran doctrines – and this is, I believe, exactly what the paintings in the window recesses are doing.

The Round-Arched Gables

Finally, I shall look at Hesselagergård's extraordinary round-arched gables (Fig. 1). The question is, obviously, why they were built and what they mean? In 1956, Svend Eriksen suggested that they

Fig. 10. Hesselager, church seen from the east (Photo author).

should be understood as a form of "banners of the Lutheran faith".⁶⁶ He argued that Friis must have been familiar with Melanchthon's house in Wittenberg (built 1536-1539) and that he wanted to reproduce its remarkable gables as a memory of the true faith, which Melanchthon incarnated (Fig. 9). Eriksen's idea was later rejected.⁶⁷ In particular, architecture historians did not see much likeness between Melanchthon's gables and those at Hesselagergård; they therefore tried to find gables with a stronger similarity – in this, however, they did not succeed. Eyvind Unnerbäck, who in 1971 wrote a whole book on the subject of round-arched gables, had to acknowledge that the gables of Hesselagergård are completely unique.⁶⁸

Recently, that is in 2006, Bøggild Johannsen also followed this general rejection of the idea and pointed out: "To see the gables as 'banners of the Lutheran faith' on the basis of a *superficial similarity* with Melanchthon's house, hardly matches the patron's intention" (my italics).⁶⁹ I, however, disagree here, and think that an understanding of the gables as banners of the Lutheran faith was indeed intended by the patron. I would argue that the question of *likeness* between the gables at Wittenberg and those at Hesselagergård in respect of their architectural details is of less importance. What matters is that they were intended to be similar as an *effect*, as a *sign* – which, indeed, they are.

But why, in the first place, did Melanchthon choose such gables? Eriksen states that when the round-arched gables spread from their north Italian origins to Germany,⁷⁰ they were here considered to be relics of Antiquity.⁷¹ Or rather, in the North at that time, no sharp distinction was made between what was Antique and what was later Italian.⁷² And to the Lutherans, Antique connoted the Early Church and its purity of faith.⁷³ Thus, when Melanchthon commissioned 'Antique' gables for his house, he was referring to a time when the Roman Church had not yet polluted Christianity – and thus he constructed a parallel between the Early Church and his own Reformed, and therefore pure faith. The round-arched gables may thus be understood as a *sign* communicating (among other things)⁷⁴ that here the pure, original faith prevails, a sign Friis also chose to put on *his* house – as well as on his church, Hesselager Church, situated in the grounds of the estate. And here he even put three (Fig. 10).⁷⁵

To interpret the round-arched gables as a sign referring to particular, chosen meanings (among many possible meanings), and in this case the same meaning as – if I am right – Melanchthon had given to *his* gables, was, as mentioned, a prevalent Lutheran image strategy. These gables, both Friis' and Melanchthon's, also became *Merkbilder*, which reminded the beholder of the true faith. And the followers of this true faith at that time, I believe, were able to read the message 'correctly'.

So, all in all, I would argue that, in the Stag Hall decoration and the round-arched gables, Friis displays central points of Lutheran theology and also, spectacularly, celebrates the Reformation – and in this way he participated in the general Northern European celebration *and visualisation* of the new confession.

Notes

1   For Johan Friis, see Ejvind Slottved, "Johan Friis", in: *Dansk Biografisk Leksikon*³, IV, Copenhagen 1980, 636-640 (includes bibliography). See for example, Anders Sørensen Vedel, *En Predicken som skeede udi* [...] *salige Johan Friisis begraffuelse* [...], Copenhagen 1571; C. T. Engelstoft, "Det første Forsøg paa at oprette et Stamhuus i Danmark", *Samlinger til Fyens Historie og*

Topographie 3 (1865), 117-165; Holger Fr. Rørdam, *Kjøbenhavns Universitets Historie 1537-1621*, 1, Copenhagen 1868-1869, 391-405; Astrid Friis, *Kansler Friis' første Aar*, Copenhagen 1970 (1933-1934); Frede P. Jensen, "Omkring Peder Oxes fald", *Historisk Tidsskrift* 79 (1979), 311-337; Jens William Jensen, "Skifte af adeligt jordegods 1400-1660", in: Per Ingesmann & Jens William Jensen (eds.), *Riget, Magten og Æren. Den danske adel 1350-1660*, Århus 2001, 451-477, on Friis in particular 451-453.

2 For Hesselagergård, see Otto Norn, *Hesselagergaard og Jacob Binck. En Tilskrivning*, Copenhagen 1961 (Meddelelser fra Foreningen til gamle Bygningers Bevaring 8, 4); Hans Henrik Engqvist, "Fire fynske herreborge. Nyt syn på Rygaards, Hesselagergaards, Egeskovs og Ørbæklundes bygningshistorie", *Architectura* 2 (1980), 55-125; Hans Henrik Engqvist, "Hjortesalen på Hesselagergård. Om gårdens bygningshistorie og salens genskabelse", *Architectura* 18 (1996), 7-23; Rikke Agnete Olsen, "Salens udsmykning", *Architectura* 18 (1996), 32-41; Birgitte Bøggild Johannsen, "Johan Friis og Hesselagergård", in: Carsten Bach-Nielsen et al. (eds.), *Danmark og renæssancen 1500-1650*, Copenhagen 2006, 270-279.

3 Norn 1961, 10.

4 Engqvist 1980, 78.

5 Norn 1961, 12.

6 Cf. Norn 1961, 13; Bøggild Johannsen 2006a, 276, 279. The sketches and tracings were made at the beginning of the 20th century, when fragments of the original decoration were still visible. These visual documents are, however, rather simple and rudimentary. Today, they are in Antikvarisk-Topografisk Arkiv, The National Museum of Denmark. See also Helge Bojsen Møller, "Hesselagergaard", *Architekten*, IX (1907), spec. 486.

7 Cf. Engqvist 1996, 14.

8 The images were painted over at an unknown time in the centuries following the execution of the decoration. The rediscovery and restoration of the paintings took place from 1904 onwards. In 1992-1993 the Stag Hall was restored to its original appearance, i.e. the later, interior partition walls were removed. For the first time in the modern era it was possible to get a glimpse of what the Hall had looked like originally. For Hesselagergård's restoration history, see Engqvist 1996, 13-18.

9 Norn 1961, 12.

10 Norn 1961, 17. In 1952, however, a short, well-preserved section of one of the original ceiling beams from the east hall was found during construction work. It is very likely that the decoration of the Stag Hall's beams was similar. Engqvist 1980, 80-81, and Engqvist 1996, 14-15.

11 Norn 1961, 18. However, there is no documentation of the war scene fragment having been part of the east wall decoration in the Stag Hall. The fragment could just as well come from other, now lost, decorations in the manor house – for example, the one in the east hall. The fragment, which was found in connection with construction work, is painted on a board and has a vegetal decoration on the back, which means that it must have been applied somewhere on an interior partition wall. Engqvist 1996, 15.

12 See note 2.

13 Norn 1961.

14 Norn 1961, 10, 21.

15 Norn mentions various sources of inspiration that Binck might have drawn upon; first and foremost, contemporaneous German art, Norn 1961, 26-42. He used, for example, a specific woodcut by Hans Sebald Beham (*The Feast of Herod*, F. W. H. Hollstein, *German Engravings, Etchings, and Woodcuts c. 1400-1700*, III, Amsterdam 1960, 188) as a model for the fashionable outdoor hunting party on the west wall, Norn 1961, 28-32. Likewise, the stags in a woodcut by Lucas Cranach the Elder (Hollstein 1960, IV, 121) are very similar to Binck's stags in the Hall, cf. Norn 1961, 27.

16 Norn 1961, 22.

17 Norn 1961, 17.

18 Olsen 1996, 32-41.

19 Olsen 1996, 35.

20 Olsen 1996, 33-34.

21 Olsen 1996, 38.

22 Olsen 1996, 40.

23 Olsen 1996, 41.

24 Bøggild Johannsen 2006a, 270-79.

25 Bøggild Johannsen 2006a, 277.

26 See note 6.

27 Norn 1961, 17.

28 Two of the doves are seen at the bottom of the birdcage. The third dove is quite difficult to spot due to the rather damaged state of the painting. It is sitting in a ring roughly in the middle of the cage.

29 "[…] som et gammelt kristent symbol på sjælens fængsling i kroppen eller på håbet om befrielsen – frelsen", Olsen 1996, 41.

30 "Den gruelige djævel på hvid hest med brækket lanse […] skal ses som et billede på den overvundne store fjende, måske med tanke på beskrivelsen af Kristi Sejr i

Joh. Åbn. 19", Olsen 1996, 41.

31 "Tilsammen peger de tre billeder *også uden deres videre sammenhæng* på husets beboer som en god kristen", Olsen 1996, 41.

32 Bøggild Johannsen 2006a, 277, 279.

33 "Fremhævelse af den dominerende mandskraft skete også gennem negative modbilleder på kvindekønnets skadelige indflydelse. David og Bathsheba var et velkendt eksempel på "kvindemagt", brugt i middelalderens kunst og stadig populært i samtiden", Bøggild Johannsen 2006, 277. It is a considerable problem that Bøggild Johannsen's text is published in an anthology that does not include annotations. Thus, her interesting interpretations are not substantiated or supported by any documentation

34 Otto Norn, "'Som David saa Bathsheba i det Bad'", *Kulturminder*, 2, V (1965), 51-70.

35 For the Bathsheba motif, see Elisabeth Kunoth-Leifels, Über die Darstellungen der 'Bathsheba im Bade'. Studien zur Geschichte des Bildthemas 4. bis 17. Jahundert, Essen 1962, particularly 34-63. Often the *David and Bathsheba* motif is found as part of a power-of-women series, typically composed of motifs such as Samson and Delilah, Aristotle and Phyllis, and Solomon and the Sibyl – for example, Dürer's sketch from 1521 for the decoration of Nuremberg city hall (Piermont Morgan Library, New York), Kunoth-Leifels, 33 and Fig. 25a-b.

36 The motif had other meanings as well. For example, it was also an illustration of bad government and abuse of power, see Elisabeth Kunoth-Leifels, "Bathsheba", in: Engelbert Kirschbaum (ed.), *Lexikon der christlichen Ikonographie*, 1, Freiburg im Breisgau 1968-1976, 257.

37 Norn 1965, 51.

38 Norn 1965, 60: "Når Friis valgte at afbilde historien, var det utvivlsomt for moralens skyld. […] Pebersvenden ville advare mod de kønne, men farlige piger […]". In 1992 Norn expands this interpretation in a short text, which, however, for the most part repeats his points from the 1965 article. He writes: "It would be only natural to look for the stamp of the grave patron's raised moralistic finger somewhere on the walls of Hesselagergård, and this stamp actually appeared in one of the Stag Hall's deep window recesses, where Johan Friis had ordered a painting of King David watching the beautiful Bathsheba in her bath. Bathsheba, however, shows no daring details and restricts herself to washing her feet. But no observer at the time of the unmarried chancellor could have any doubts about the message of this, for various reasons, very popular motif. It was a warning against the female sex's characteristic wiliness and cunning, inherited from the first ancestress, Eve" ("Det ville være naturligt at lede efter et aftryk af den alvorlige bygherres moralske pegefinger et eller andet sted på Hesselagergårds vægge, og dette dukkede virkelig op i en af Hjortesalens dybe vindueslysninger, hvor Johan Friis har ladet male en fremstilling af, hvorledes Kong David så den yndige Bathsheba i badet. Der findes ingen pikante træk ved Bathsheba-figuren, der nøjes med at vaske fødder. Men ingen betragter har på den ugifte kanslers tid været i tvivl om, hvad dette, af flere grunde så yndede motiv, skulle udtrykke, nemlig en advarsel mod den for kvindekønnet karakteristiske træskhed og list nedarvet fra stammoderen Eva"), Otto Norn, "Hesselagergård", in: Eva Louise Lillie (ed.), *Danske Kalkmalerier. Efter reformationen 1536-1700*, Copenhagen 1992, 96.

39 Cf. Olsen 1996, 41.

40 Cf. Bøggild Johannsen 2006a, 277.

41 Luther's lectures on Genesis were delivered during the years 1535-1545. It was in connection with the story of Joseph and his brothers – and in particular the brothers' bad consciences after selling Joseph to the merchants, Gen. 42:28 – that Luther spoke about David and *his* conscience, Helmut T. Lehmann & Jaroslav Pelikan (eds.): *Luther's Works,* 1-55, Saint Louis 1955-1989 [hereafter: LW], 7, 274-275. Veit Dietrich was the man most responsible for the final transcription of the lectures. They were published in four volumes during 1544-1554. Luther's interpretation of the David and Bathsheba story is found in the final volume.

42 LW, 7, 274.

43 "Bildnis des Königs Davids, welscher ein exempel ist menschlicher schwacheit, zorns Gottes über die Sünd, und Bamhertigkeit, über alle so sich mit rechtem glauben zu Gott bekeren." Walter Strauss, *German Single-Leaf Woodcut 1550-1600*, II, New York 1975, 528.

44 The very didactic, rhymed verse about David's acknowledgement of, and turning away from, sin was written by Paul Eber, who was a pupil of both Luther and Melanchthon at Wittenberg University, and later a professor there himself from 1544 until his death in 1569. "Schaw bei den Konig David an / Welscher war gar ein heilig Man / An welschem Gott gefallen trug / Doch Sicherheit in Niederschlug / Das er Ehbruch und mord begieng / Und als er zu rewen anfieng / Kam er wieder zu gnaden schon / Durch glauben am verheissenen Son / Also thut Gott zu jeder zeit / Mit allen den ihr Sünd ist leid / Und glauben fest am geschenckten Son / Dem steht offen der gnaden thron."

45 As to the meaning of doves in Christianity, see for example Daniel Haag-Wackernagel, *Die Taube. Vom heiligen Vogel der Liebesgöttin zur Strassentaube*, Basel 1988, in particular 106-107.

46 LW, 15, 191f.

47 LW, 15, x. They were edited by Veit Dietrich, who had attended the lectures.

48 For example, LW, 2, 157 (*Lectures on Genesis* – 1535-1536).

49 See, for example, Luther's commentaries on the Song of Solomon, 1:15 (LW, 15, 209), 2:14 (LW, 15, 220), 4:1 (LW, 15, 227). As to Luther's continual praise of "simplicitas", simplicity, in connection with images, see Sergiusz Michalski, *The Reformation and the Visual Arts. The Protestant Image Question in Western and Eastern Europe*, London & New York 1993, 39.

50 For example, when Luther translated Matthew 10.16 (Jesus Sends Out the Twelve Apostles) – "Behold, I am sending you out as sheep in the midst of wolves, so be wise as serpents and *innocent as doves*" – he used the words "ohne falsch" to describe the doves. Haag-Wackernagel 1988, 108, note 572.

51 Genesis 8: 8-12.

52 LW, 2, 161f.

53 In fact, Luther was not very keen on using the allegory as a strategy of communication, but he recognised its effectiveness. "Allegories do not deserve as much time as do the historical accounts and the articles of faith. […] But wherever you want to make use of allegories, do this: follow closely the analogy of the faith, that is, adapt them to Christ, the church, faith, and the ministry of the Word. In this way it will come to pass that even though the allegories may not be altogether fitting, they nevertheless do not depart from the faith." LW, 2, 164.

54 LW 2, 164.

55 According to Mette Kristine Jensen (The National Museum of Denmark), who participated in the latest restoration of the Stag Hall, the devil's puncturing of the picture frame, in all probability, is *not* due to any restoration 'mistake' from the past. At any rate, nothing indicates that it should not be the original image. See also Mette K. Jensen, "Frisens restaurering", *Architectura*, 18 (1996), 26-32.

56 See for example, Kilian Heck & Bernhard Jahn (eds.), *Genealogie als Denkform in Mittelalter und früher Neuzeit*, Tübingen 2000; Kilian Heck, *Genealogie als Monument und Argument: der Beitrag dynastischer Wappen zur politischen Raumbildung der Neuzeit*, Munich & Berlin 2002; Hanne Kolind Poulsen, "Queen Dorothea of Denmark celebrating her dead husband – and herself!", in: Lilian H. Zirpolo (ed.), *Constructions of Death, Mourning, and Memory*. Conference Oct. 27-29, 2006. Proceedings, New Jersey 2006, 121-124.

57 Luther writes about the conditions for his stand in two important texts from the 1520s, in the so-called Lenten Sermons (Invocavitpredigten) from March 1522 (LW, 51, 81-86), and in the tract *Against the Celestial Prophets* (*Wieder die himmlischen Propheten, von den Bildern und Sakrament*) from the turn of the year 1524/1525 (LW, 40, 79-223). Apart from these two longer and more detailed contributions, his remarks on images are scattered throughout his writings.

58 The Roman Catholic Church recognised that images were able to mediate grace; for example, by communicating the divine power that the represented figures were believed to possess. This they could, because in Catholic theology all reality is imbued with the hidden presence of God. God is truly present and *potentially* active everywhere, in all human life and history, and in all objects – including images. The encounter with God is a mediated experience rooted in the historical. Images, like everything else, are actual or *potential* carriers of the divine presence and work. Luther, on the contrary, by way of his concept of the Two Kingdoms, definitively separated the world from the heavens. Where Catholicism saw God as immanent and potentially active in all earthly reality, God was to Luther so 'totally other' that the divine reality could never be identified with anything human or earthly. Richard P. McBrien, *Catholicism*, London 1994, 9f.

59 Luther's thoughts on images is a vast subject. The present account has been extracted mainly from Michalski 1993, chapters 1 & 5 and the introduction in Bonnie-Jeanne Noble, *The Lutheran Paintings of the Cranach Workshop, 1529-1555*, Ann Arbor 1999. See also Elfriede Starke, "Luthers Beziehungen zu Kunst und Künstlern", in: Helmar Junghans (ed.), *Leben und Werk Martin Luthers von 1526 bis 1546*, 1-2. *Festgabe zu seinem 500. Geburtstag*, Göttingen 1983, 1, 531-548; 2, 905-915; Hanne Kolind Poulsen, *Cranach*, Copenhagen 2002 (Exhibition Catalogue), 25-48.

60 For Luther's famous reinterpretation of an image of St. Christopher, see Werner Hofmann (ed.), *Luther und die Folgen für die Kunst*, Munich 1983, 252. See also Kolind Poulsen 2002 (Exhibition catalogue) 38-43.

61 For example, Anders Sørensen Vedel, in his funerary sermon on Friis, describes him as an exceptionally learned humanist who spoke several languages, was thoroughly acquainted with classical literature and the writings of Luther and Melanchthon. Vedel 1571.

62 For Friis' trip to Wittenberg in the spring of 1535, see Rørdam 1868-69, 394.

63 See Martin Schwarz Lausten, *Den Hellige Stad Wittenberg. Danmark og Lutherbyen Wittenberg i reformationstiden*, Copenhagen 2002.

64 *D. Martin Luthers Werke. Kritische Gesamtausgabe*, 28, Weimar 1969, 677.

65 Joseph Leo Koerner, *The Moment of Self-Portraiture in German Renaissance Art*, Chicago & London 1993, 381.

66 Svend Eriksen, *Om vælske gavle og andre problemer i dansk arkitektur i det 16. århundrede*, Copenhagen 1956 (Meddelelser fra Foreningen til gamle Bygningers Bevaring 7,4) 15.

67 For example, Norn wrote that two facts made the hypothesis untenable. Firstly, because round-arched gables are frequently seen also in *Catholic* Poland; and secondly, because Hesselagergård represents "[…] a special solution to the problem of combining round gable arcades with a [pointed] gable" ("en speciel Løsning paa Problemet at kombinere Rundbuearkader og Gavl"), Norn 1961, 64. I would argue, however, that these objections are in themselves untenable. The fact that round-arched gables were used in Protestant areas, and were there imbued with Protestant meaning, by no means excludes the round-arched gable motif from also being used in Catholic areas, and there bearing other meanings – as in, for example, the St. Christopher motif mentioned above (see note 60), which carried both a traditional ('Catholic') meaning as well as the meaning Luther gave to it. Thus, it was the context that activated one meaning of the round-arched gables among many potential meanings. And as to the round-arched gables of Hesselagergård being a special solution to the problem of combining round gable arcades with pointed gables, I could note that this 'technical' solution has nothing to do with the *meaning* of it. This solution to an architectural problem may *mean* different things, and Eriksen, in this case, suggests that the gables mean 'Reformed faith' and refer to Melanchthon's gables. Moreover, also Norn suggests, actually, a meaning of the round-arched gables, namely that they referred to Jacob Binck as a well-informed and cultured artist, Norn 1961, 54-55. And it is very likely that such a meaning was *also* active and, I would add, at the same time indicated that the patron possessed these qualities too. Different meanings do not necessarily exclude one another, but some meanings can play a more prominent role than others.

68 Eyvind Unnerbäck, *Welsche Giebel. Ein italienisches Renaissancemotiv und seine Verbreitung in Mittel- und Nordeuropa*, Stockholm 1971 (Antikvariskt Arkiv 42), 69.

69 Bøggild Johannsen 2006a 275: "At se gavlene som 'faner for den reformerte tro' ud fra en overfladisk lighed med Philipp Melanchthons hus i Wittenberg rammer dog næppe bygherrens hensigt."

70 For the history of the round-arched gables spreading throughout Europe, see particularly Unnerbäck 1971.

71 Eriksen 1956, 17.

72 Eriksen 1956, 17. Eriksen writes that in the contemporary illustrated literature on architecture the round-arched gables can be found registered under two categories: either as "Antique" or as "Italian".

73 See, for example, Mitchell B. Merback, "Torture and Teaching. The Reception of Lucas Cranach the Elder's *Martyrdom of the Twelve Apostles* in the Protestant Era", *Art Journal*, 57, 1, (1998), 14-23. The article addresses the Protestant understanding of the martyrdom of the Disciples and how the Protestants used these histories in their pedagogical project. Merback writes that the Lutherans considered the Apostles as "defenders of the 'True Doctrine'" (14), and that "The Protestant struggle is projected into the past, where the first disciples of Christ also become the first Lutheran martyrs at the hands of a nefarious pagan host. The significance of such a backward projection to the era of the primitive church […] could not have been lost on reformers" (19). For the Reformers' understanding of history (including church history), see, for example, Johannes Schilling, "Die Wiederentdeckung des Evangeliums. Wie die Wittenberger Reformatoren ihre Geschichte rekonstruierten", in: Ludger Grenzmannet et al. (eds.), *Die Präsenz der Antike im Übergang vom Mittelalter zur Frühen Neuzeit. Bericht über Kolloquien der Kommission zur Erforschung der Kultur des Spätmittelalters 1999 bis 2002* (Abhandlungen der Akademie der Wissenschaften zu Göttingen, phil.-hist. Klasse 3, 263), Göttingen 2004, 125-142 (thanks are due to Professor Steffen Kjeldgaard-Pedersen, Department of Church History, Copenhagen University, for bringing this text to my attention).

74 Of course, Melanchthon's round-arched gables may have connoted other things as well. For example – and most likely – they may have referred to Melanchthon as a humanist.

75 For Hesselager Church, see for example Norn 1961, 50-57; Jens Fleischer, "Hesselager kirkes historie", in: *Træk af Hesselager sogns historie*, Hesselager 1983, 56-68. At approximately the same time as Friis built Hesselagergård's round-arched gables, he also built the three round-arched gables on Hesselager Church, i.e., the round-arched gable of the east facade, the one of the sacristy, and the one of the northern transept. His nephew Niels Friis, who inherited the estate, added another round-arched gable on the southern transept in 1597-1598.

Fig. 1. Claus Berg, Altarpiece, c. 1515-1523, Odense Cathedral
(Photo The National Museum of Denmark).

CATALYSTS TO CHANGE

IMPLEMENTING PERSPECTIVE IN DANISH RENAISSANCE SCULPTURE: CLAUS BERG AS A PIONEER

Marianne Marcussen

The implementation of perspective in Danish Renaissance sculpture, *in casu* relief, is demonstrated in the altarpiece of Claus Berg (mid-1470s – 1532), now in the Cathedral of Odense, Funen. The altarpiece (Fig. 1) was ordered by the Danish Queen Christine (1461- 1521) and was in work from c. 1514 to 1523.[1]

The development of perspective in Italy, initiated by Filippo Brunelleschi (1377 – 1446) in the first decades of the 15th century, was taken up by artists in Southern Germany, where it is suggested that Claus Berg took inspiration, especially from Veit Stoss (1447/8 – 1533), besides other Nürnberg artists in the late 1490s.[2] Claus Berg was called to Denmark from Lübeck by Queen Christine c. 1504. She was wife to King Hans of Denmark, daughter of Ernst of Saxony and Elisabeth of Bavaria, and sister to Friedrich the Wise, Elector of Saxony. She represents a learned Maecenas, with an exquisite taste and sense of quality, besides she apparently wanted to use an artist who was acquainted with the latest trends in art. She supported the Franciscan order, too, and the altarpiece was actually intended for their church in Odense.[3]

It is often maintained that influence from the Italian Renaissance spread slowly in Northern Europe, but this idea should as far as perspective is concerned be qualified, since this assessment has often been based on style analysis. It is true of course, that differences in style between Italian art and art north of the Alps were obvious in the 15th and 16th centuries, but this is also true both of earlier and later periods. Hence difference in style cannot indicate that artists north of the Alps either could not understand, or were reluctant to introduce perspective in pictorial practice. Instead it must be argued that artists, when confronted with and inspired by art from other periods and other traditions, not to tell of new ways to convey pictorial space, do not only copy or imitate but investigate the new trend both on a concrete i.e. on a technical level and reflect on its potentials in a philosophical, i.e. scientific and cultural context. Claus Berg is, in my opinion, an example of an artist who absorbed the new trend, albeit the knowledge of his early education is not particularly well documented.

To implement a new method such as perspective, in mathematical terms a central projection, the long term importance of which could not necessarily be understood or accepted at once, *does* take time. The reason for this is that the mathematics of perspective had to be implemented in already given regional traditions in the art education, however, documentation on this point is uneven. Hence documentation must be found in many areas of research such as: trade of books,

CLAUS BERG AS A PIONEER 153

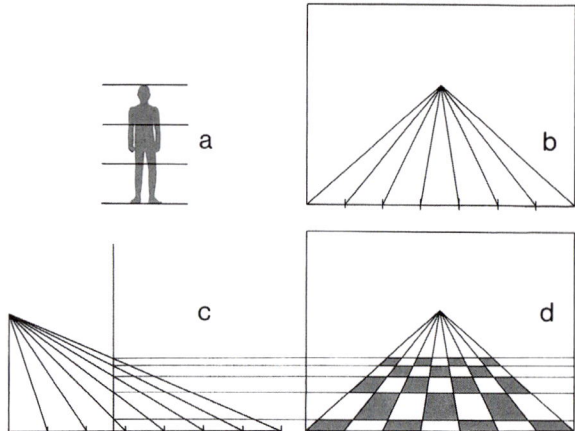

Fig. 2. Leon Battista Alberti, checkerboard floor in perspective i.e. a central projection. Man as measure (a), front-view with vanishing point in height of (theoretically) the eye of man (b), side-view with eye point (e) and perpendicular representing the picture plane (c), finished checkerboard floor (d). Drawing Beth Beyerholm. After Marianne Marcussen, Perspektiv, Copenhagen 1984, 125.

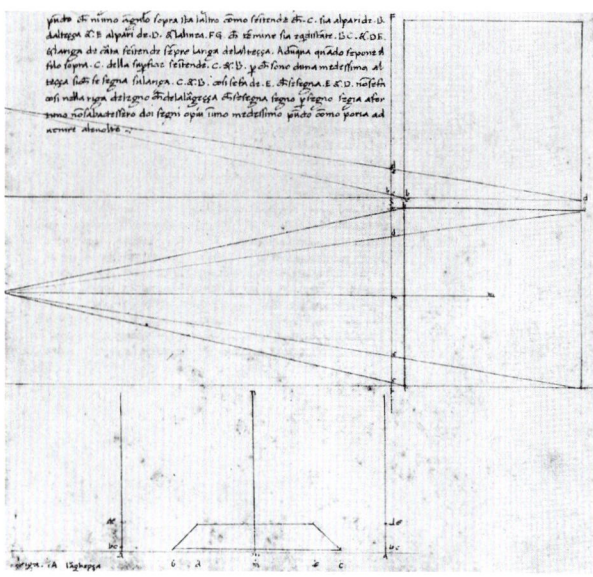

Fig. 3. Piero della Francesca, Plan and elevation as basis for a square in perspective. After Piero della Francesca, De prospettiva pingendi, Nicco Fasola (ed.), Firenze 1942, atlante xxi.

university education, translations of sources from Antiquity and the Middle Ages, private libraries owned by the intellectual upper class, the constitution of libraries in universities, and the role of the artist in society, i.e. access to relevant knowledge such as developments in mathematics, building practises, philosophy and the natural sciences, and not least the art trade and the education of the artist in ateliers or workshops, the best of which also favoured intellectual knowledge, this goes for art both to the south and to the north of the Alps.[4]

In this mass of information the more or less reliable facts of the education and intellectual ambience of Claus Berg seem to support his interest in perspective. To which must be added that a new way to convey space in sculpture might demand a longer period of time to implement in other working procedures than painting, since an altarpiece is a joint work of many hands with different competences such as drawing, cutting, and painting etc.

Claus Berg´s importance for the establishment of perspective in Denmark was evaluated as early as in 1865 by Niels Lauritz Høyen (1798 - 1870), in an article on Claus Berg´s altarpiece. He states: "… the brothers van Eyck…had eventually such impact on the German schools…that perspective in painting (which the van Eyck´s took up, my addition), became the one and only way (of conveying space) especially for sculpture in wood."[5]

Hence he found Claus Berg´s rendering of space related to perspective, a judgement he was indeed competent to make since he had already, in 1821, attended drawing classes, comprising perspective, at the Royal Academy of Fine Arts in Copenhagen. Høyen therefore knew, qua general rules for perspective, what he should look for, i.e. the foreshortening of single figures and how a horizontal vanishing plane can hold a scene, for example qua a chequer board construction as described by Leon Battista Alberti (1404 -1472) in his *De Pictura/Della Pittura* of 1435/36 (Fig. 2) or the plan and elevation method described by Piero della Francesca (1410/20 - 1492) in his *De prospettiva pingendi*, written presumably some decades later (Fig.3).[6]

Høyen judges the figures in the central part and the predella as figures almost in the round hence he does not identify any vanishing lines. However the figures are indeed half circular, with flat backs, which are partially hollowed out, something which cannot be judged from direct sight, since the illusion of space works perfectly well. As we shall see, painting and sculpture differ technically, though not mathematically, in the way in which perspec-

Fig. 4a-e. Claus Berg, reliefs from the side-wings of the altarpiece in Odense Cathedral, cf. fig. 1, showing that the artist used perspective .i.e. central projections and parallel projections. a. Christ washing the feet of the disciples. b. The Resurrection. c. Ecce Homo. d. The Flagellation. e. Christ taken into Captivity (Photo The National Museum of Denmark, Copenhagen).

tive is applied. However Høyen does not discuss this aspect further. Besides, Høyen was not, and we are to a large extent still not, able to describe in a precise manner how the conveying of space was practiced in periods prior to the invention of perspective, in casu in the late Gothic period.

If we look north of the Alps, we can at this point conclude that perspective was used by Jan van Eyck (1380/90 – 1441) and Jean Fouquet (1420 - 1480) in the 1440s and 50s. This development would also reach Claus Berg, but the inspiration from Northern Italy was quite as important, especially Venice, which had strong cultural ties to Southern Germany. Venice was presumably visited by Albrecht Dürer (1471 – 1528) twice, 1494 and 1505/6, where he took up or extended (?) his interest in perspective, already on the first trip, since his woodcut, *Men's Bath-*

House c. 1496 is based on an Albertian chequerboard construction.[7] Piero della Francesca's plan and elevation method might have been learned by Dürer on the second trip to Venice, and both methods were to appear in his *Underweysung der Messung*, Nürnberg 1525 (1538). In any case the drawing of a plan and elevation was necessary to master, especially for preparatory drawings for a large altarpiece, and Claus Berg must have known this method well before he started work on the altarpiece in Odense.[8] Also Hans Holbein the Elder (1460/5 – 1524) in Augsburg introduced perspective in Southern Germany around 1500.[9] Furthermore Queen Christine, who ordered the altarpiece from Claus Berg, could quite easily pick up information about new trends in art qua her family ties to Saxony and Bavaria. I.e. she had access to humanistic circles which collected information both to the north and to the south of the Alps, via travels, personal relations, letters, and by purchasing art works, manuscripts, and printed books. Queen Christine´s brother, Frederick the Wise, the Elector of Saxony who had his portrait painted by Dürer c. 1496, commissioned and owned several other works by him. Besides he erected the University of Wittenberg 1502 with a rapidly growing library, and also invited Italian artists to his court, most important Jacopo de Barbari (1475 – 1516?) in the years 1503-1505.[10]

The construction of perspective, as formulated by Alberti and Piero, would not by itself also supply the artists with a method to convey an appropriate *illusion* of space to be experienced immediately by any onlooker. Alberti and Piero´s methods are handed over to us as text only (Alberti) and as text and diagrams (Piero) without much, if any, pictorial illusion. Consequently older practises could or might be regarded as better to obtain pictorial illusion than the new one, since the way to obtain illusion was already well embedded in the traditions of pictorial practises. This is presumably also why Dürer and other artists at the time switch between older practices and rigorous perspective constructions. Hence the knowledge of how to provide for illusion would be superposed upon i.e. hiding the perspective construction, be it with paints onto a flat surface, or with gesso and paint applied unto three-dimensional surfaces, either sculpture in the round or *in casu* relief, as Claus Berg´s altarpiece.

The mathematics of perspective is the basis of the *experience* of space of course. However an onlooker cannot unveil the mathematics of perspective qua this experience. The pictorial traditions, be it south or north of the Alps, are therefore the correctives - or to put it metaphorically - serve as a cradle to transmit the mathematics of perspective into the already well functioning traditions of pictorial illusion.

Høyen´s statement about Claus Berg´s use of perspective was supported by Hermann Deckert (1927), who states: "There is no doubt that Claus Berg (in the altarpiece in Odense)… is the first in German sculpture…(who) consciously uses perspective in foreshortening in order to enhance the illusion." However Viggo Thorlacius-Ussing, 1922 is of a different opinion, since he holds that Claus Berg´s spaces are mostly "medieval", however he acknowledges that Claus Berg absorbed Renaissance trends.[11]

A short cut to perspective would be to copy prints, where perspective was used, but this idea must be analyzed on more than the copy level, since the artists had to use the prints, qua an understanding of the mathematics of perspective, in order to make them cohere with an overall space construction of many scenes of, for example an altarpiece, such as Claus Berg´s.

The quotes of Høyen, Deckert, and Thorlacius-Ussing must therefore be investigated further, since they basically relate to the illusionary properties of Claus Berg´s works; besides, some stylistic remarks are tied to their descriptions.

However, none of them give a specific technical reason for their assessments. Here we must turn to Birgitte Bøggild Johannsen, who says (I paraphrase): "In the relief showing (the *Last Supper* and *Christ washing the feet of the disciples*) (Fig. 4a) is shown a ceiling with beams, the direction of which converges, as in perspective towards Christ, the centre of composition." (The beams meet in the vanishing point: John's right hand in the *Last supper*, vertical above the left hand of Christ in *Christ washing the feet of the disciples*) (my addition). Such roofs or part of them can also be found in: *Pilate washing his hands*, *Christ before the High Priest Caiphas*, and *Ecce Homo*, where the vanishing points have significant positions, besides, a parallel projection can be seen in one of the much damaged remnants of one of Claus Berg´s (?) paintings on the outer wing of the altarpiece, besides in the reliefs: *Harrowing of Hell*, the *Resurrection*, (Fig. 4b) and the *Pentecost*,[12] Claus Berg had therefore all the sufficient knowledge of the mathematics of perspective to convey space both to sculpture and painting. Indeed, he was in a number of instances (1508, 1510, 1560) called Claus the painter (Claus Maler).[13]

Claus Berg copied prints of for example: Dürer, Lucas Cranach, (1472 - 1553) and Martin Schongauer (c. 1430 - 1491) for single figures,[14] however foreshortening of limbs of figures was common in space constructions prior to perspective. Hence to use prints, in order to paint or sculpt figures in perspective, would entail

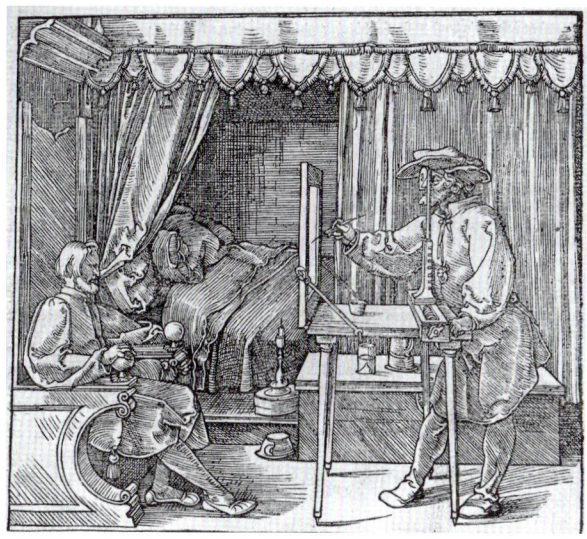

Fig. 5. Albrecht Dürer shows how a velo is used to draw a portrait in correct perspective. The fixed eye point of the artist is kept stable. After Albrecht Dürer, Underweysung der Messung, Nürnberg 1525.

that they should be placed in a vanishing plane, as Alberti´s chequerboard construction, in order to be diminished correctly. A systematic and perspective-like diminishing of figures can be seen in the reliefs: the *Ecce Homo*, (Fig. 4c) the *Crucifixion*, the *Lamentation*, and the *Ascension*, but no chequerboard construction is visible, as would be common practice among painters: Dürer and Holbein the Elder for example. Besides Claus Berg´s use of prints in the altarpiece cannot be taken as proof of his presence in Nürnberg or Augsburg, since books and prints spread rapidly in Europe, and may have been known or in the possession of Queen Christine or her brother Frederick the Wise, Elector of Saxony.[15]

However other methods for correct perspective foreshortening of single figures were known: qua the use of a *velo,* which Alberti stresses he invented,[16] and which Dürer knew well, (Fig. 5), or as useful, though rather cumbersome and time-consuming: Piero della Francesca´s plan and elevation method as basis for drawing figures in perspective.[17]

The difference between perspective on a flat surface (painting) and a surface of some depth (relief) was undoubtedly reasoned in Italy as a result of Brunelleschi´s experiments with perspective, demonstrated in two images which disappeared later in the Renaissance.[18] Of vital importance for the understanding of perspective in relief, is furthermore the art and writings of Lorenzo Ghiberti (1378 – 1455), *I Commentarii*,[19] and the art of Donatello (Donato di Niccolo di Betto Bardi) (c.1386 – 1466), both artistically and socially close to Brunelleschi.[20]

Hence for the documentation of the use of perspective in relief as compared to painting should be a measurement of actual examples. However, since the dimensions of total depths, angle of tilts and sizes of single figures are surprisingly seldom given in publications, the evaluation of the construction of relief perspective is here demonstrated by examples from the Cast Collection, Statens Museum for Kunst, in Copenhagen.[21] There are casts of single figures from Claus Berg´s altarpiece in Güstrow, but not of the reliefs of the altarpiece in Odense. Therefore the way in which to construct a correct perspective in relief is taken from Adolf Stuhlmann, *Lehrbuch der Reliefperspektive*, Hamburg 1914 (Fig. 6).

The reason why it is appropriate to use a much later description of the construction of perspective in Renaissance relief is due to the fact that the earliest printed treatise we have on this matter, Pomponius Gauricus, (c. 1482 – 1528/30), *De Sculptura*, Venice 1504, is not particularly clear as concerns the mathematics of relief perspective.[22] We have therefore also to rely on Alberti and Piero´s treatises on perspective applied to painting, besides what can be gathered from later treatises. The more so since the earliest Renaissance writing on sculpture, Alberti's *De Statua*, dated most likely late in his oeuvre, does not contain an explanation of the construction of perspective in sculpture *in casu* relief, most likely intentionally, since he knew that the mathematical basis for perspective would apply both to painting and sculpture as also Gauricus points to.[23] Stuhlmann's treatise comprises of course a development of the geometry of perspective, which Alberti, Piero, and Gauricus could not foresee, but the starting point for almost any treatise on perspective from the Renaissance to this very day, be it to guide artists in painting or sculpture, would be to con-

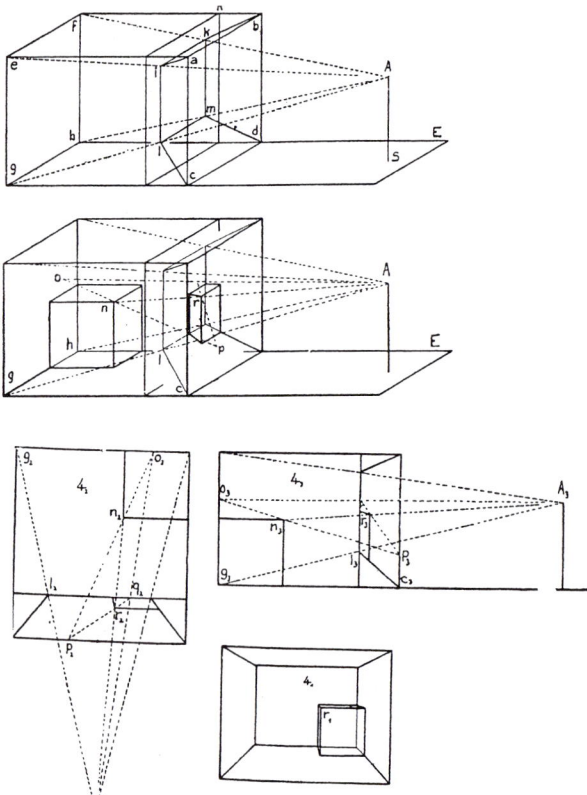

Fig. 6. Two parallel projections show the three dimensional perspective space of a relief. Eye point (A), picture plane (abcd), foreshortened picture plane (iklm), and plan and elevation method to construct a cube in a relief. After Adolf Stuhlman, Lehrbuch der Reliefperspektive, Hamburg 1914, 2-3.

struct a foreshortening of a square or a chequer board floor situated at right angles to the picture plane, often followed by a method to construct a cube in perspective such as in Alberti and Piero's treatises,[24] and this is also the case in the treatise of Gauricus.

Alberti's construction of a chequer board floor (Fig. 2a) is historically behind or taken for granted by Gauricus. Besides, Gauricus of course explains the Italian practice of conveying space since Gauricus *is* an Italian and his treatise *is* on perspective in relief. Hence he explains, in my opinion, how a chequer board floor is tilted upwards at a certain angle, which would entail the illusion of a horizontal floor for an onlooker, followed by a description of how to make a foreshortening of a square tilted inwards at a certain angle to represent a plane ("wall") with the same depth as the floor and (in "reality") at right angles to it, alike to Stuhlmann's construction (Fig. 6).[25]

This interpretation of Gauricus' text is therefore compared to my interpretation of the perspective construction in a cast of the relief of Donatello for the baptismal font for the *Baptistery* in Siena: *The Presentation of the Baptist's Head to Herod*, 1423-1427 (Fig. 7), since – possibly – it can as well be the case that the plane and elevation method to obtain relief perspective, somewhat alike to Stuhlman's (Fig. 6), may have been practiced by artists in the Renaissance, an idea which coheres with what we now know of the mathematical competences of architects, master masons, sculptors, and goldsmiths in Southern Germany. The mathematics of preparatory drawings for architecture, details of architecture, baldachin, and monstrance, is discussed by Hans Huth and Johann Josef Böker.[26]

In our context we must infer that such mathematical drawing traditions were part and parcel of workshop practices, since no huge altarpiece such as Claus Berg's could have come about at all without this kind of competence. Böker characterizes the Gothic preparatory drawings as geometrically constructed, i.e. qua plan and elevation, orthogonal projections, and "perspective-like" drawings and he concludes that: "…(they) served, without exception, as utility drawings".[27] These drawing traditions in Southern Germany were alike to for example Jacopo della Quercia's (c. 1374-1438) drawing for the *Fonte Gaia*, 1409?, besides he did the companion piece, *Zacharias in the Temple*, 1428-1430, to Donatello's relief in Siena (Fig. 7).[28] These drawings were therefore undoubtedly intended to inform the craftsmen, and from which the actual (i.e. proportional) dimensions could be read off in the drawings since "…a precise scale was used …".[29]

Of importance for the artistic ambience of Claus Berg is also the fact that Willibald Pirkheimer, close friend to Dürer, owned a copy of Gauricus' book, where we also find a description of how to construct a figure in perspective, presumably inspired by Piero della Francesca's plan and elevation method.[30]

Besides Gauricus' treatise, many other relevant books related to art and literature, were available in Southern Germany.[31] Hence the artistic ambience of Nürnberg painters, sculptors, and architects, who were observant to Renaissance art theory, was close to Claus Berg if we can trust he worked in the workshop or to put it more cautiously close to Stoss and other Nürnberg artists, for example Tilmann Riemenschneider (c. 1460 – 1531) and Hans Leinberger (- 1511 – 1531/35).

Gauricus´ construction of the depth of a relief to portray a scene in space is followed by a description of how the foremost figures (or elements) must occupy a little more than half the total depth of the relief, the middle ground must occupy (in proportion) less than the foreground and what is shown to be in the background i.e. the portrayal of the most distant figures (or elements) should barely protrude from the surface of (the limit of depth) of the relief, often referred to as being "schiacciato", meaning squashed. In terms of the experience of spatial *illusion* the "schiacciato" conveys the deepest space, most distant from the onlooker, in theory into infinity, the middle ground of the relief represents a nearer space, but not "touchable", and the figures in the foreground can be sculptured almost in the round as in Donatello´s relief (Fig. 7), where the head and foot of the person who presents the head of the *Baptist* are beyond the limit of depth of the relief (in all c. 6 cm) and consequently reach out to the physical space of the viewer. The foreground takes up, in proportion, c. two thirds of the total depth of the relief,[32] hence we can see that, however condensed Gauricus´ text often appears, his description of rules for depth in relief seems to hold water for Donatello´s relief (Fig. 7). Claus Berg used the same technique in the reliefs (depth estimated to around 8 cm) as for example the *Ecce Homo* (Fig. 4c), the *Agony in the Garden*, and *Christ taken into Captivity* (Fig. 4e).[33]

It can therefore with good reason be held that mathematical drawing procedures were necessary for any undertaking of both small and large pieces of sculpture, since the master did, presumably most often, only the utility drawings for the cutters and not the actual cutting. Hence it was important that the cutters could understand the theory of perspective by reading off sizes and forms, both in plan and elevation drawings, i.e. orthogonal projections, parallel projections (Fig. 4b), or in the "perspective-like" drawings. A "perspective-like" drawing might as well serve as the information for the patron, maecenas, or buyer in connection with the *Visierung*, i.e. the showing, which served as basis for contract between master and buyer.[34] In the case of Claus Berg we are close to certain that he did not do the actual cutting of the figures, which may have been due either to his high abilities as a painter or the fact that he was at this point master of workshop and therefore exclusively provided the utility drawings for the cutters. This circumstance is stressed in his grandson's biography of him. Claus Berg therefore presumably also did the drawings, i.e. the model of the altarpiece, for the *Visierung* to Queen Christine. Besides we learn from his grandson's biography that she paid for twelve workmen in the workshop in Odense, a considerable number.[35]

To be modern or trendy would entail the ability to compare and evaluate modern techniques to the ones in Antiquity. In terms of relief one could compare the diminishing of fore-, middle- and background between practises in the Renaissance and in Antiquity. If Donatello´s relief (Fig. 7) is compared for example to the cast of *Bacchus visiting the Poet Ikaros*, c. 100 B.C., which was known in the Renaissance, they resemble each other, i.e. from the protruding in the foreground to the almost "schiacciato " level in the background, but the architecture in the relief is a bit tipped out-wards, and the vanishing lines of the architecture are not congruent with perspective.[36] Brunelleschi and Donatello did therefore not only measure the Roman art works on their joint travel to Rome, they probably also evaluated how space was conveyed in Roman art as compared to their ongoing research in perspective. Besides they surely knew of the Roman architect Vitruvius Pollio´s (1 century A.D.) *De Architectura*, written around 27 A.D. and his notion of "scaenographia", which is:"…the shaded rendering of the front and the receding sides as the latter converge to a point."[37] Regardless of the differences between the mathematics of Renaissance perspective and the (mathematical) rules for foreshortening in Roman art, we can point to a relation as concerns pictorial *illusion* for one

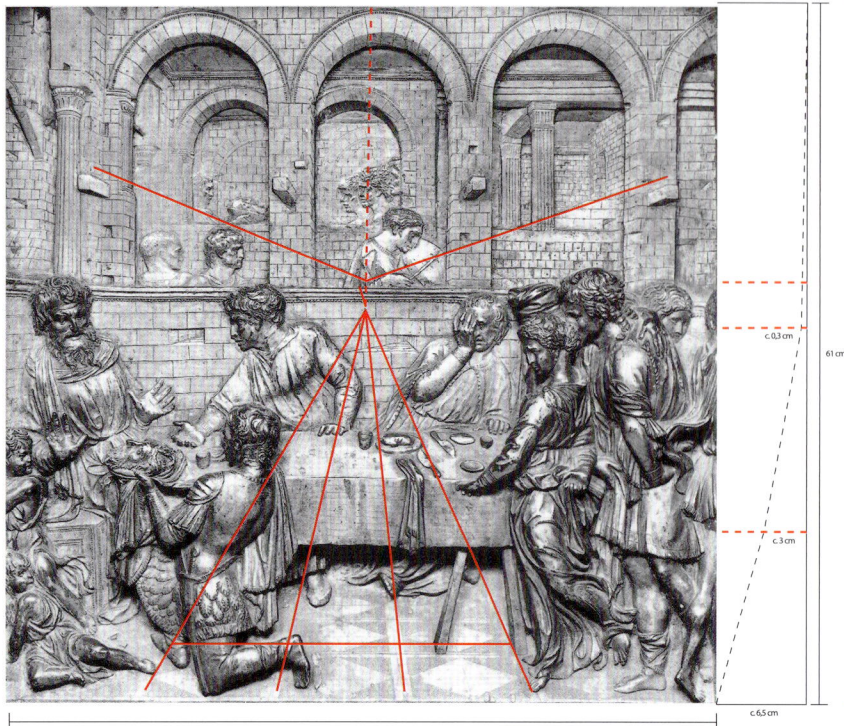

Fig. 7. Donatello, The Presentation of the Baptist´s Head to Herod, 1423-27, Siena, Baptistery. Author's interpretation with indicated vanishing points and depth of relief measured from a cast in The Cast Collection, Copenhagen. Drawing by Merete Rude. The relief after Bonnie A. Bennett & David G. Wilkins, Donatello, Oxford 1984.

thing, but more to the point, the basis (of architecture) was mathematical drawing: plan and elevation, in Vitruvius' terminology "ichnograhia" and "ortographia", i.e. drawings to be used for an actual building construction even to this very day. In addition, this method may also have been the basis for Brunelleschi´s work with the mathematics of perspective and absolutely necessary for any huge altarpiece such as Claus Berg's. Furthermore a printed version of *De Architectura*, Venice, 1511 was available in Southern Germany.[38]

If we focus on the middle section of Claus Berg´s altarpiece, we can see four parallel sections, the three below with rows of saints, and the uppermost with the crowning of Mary. We can experience that some or most of the figures in the lower front row have the same eye height and it is also true for the figures behind, but their heads are smaller and somewhat lower positioned. Translated into perspective it might entail that Claus Berg wanted to make a correct perspective foreshortening of persons in space as seen from a fixed viewing position.

We have one early printed example of such a procedure, namely Jean Pélérin Viator *De artificialis perspectiva*, Toul, 1505 (Fig. 8). This book came in more editions including pirate copies, and was edited by Jørg Glockendohn, *Von der Kunst Perspectiva*, Nürnberg, 1509. Dürer copied from Pélérin and/or vice versa, besides many "Kunstbüchlein" were in circulation.[39] Hence the intellec-

Fig. 8. Persons in perspective on the basis of a checkerboard floor construction with horizon a, b, vanishing lines c, d. After Jean Pélérin Viator, *De artificiali perspectiva*, Toul 1505, 8 recto. Copenhagen, University Library (Photo University Library).

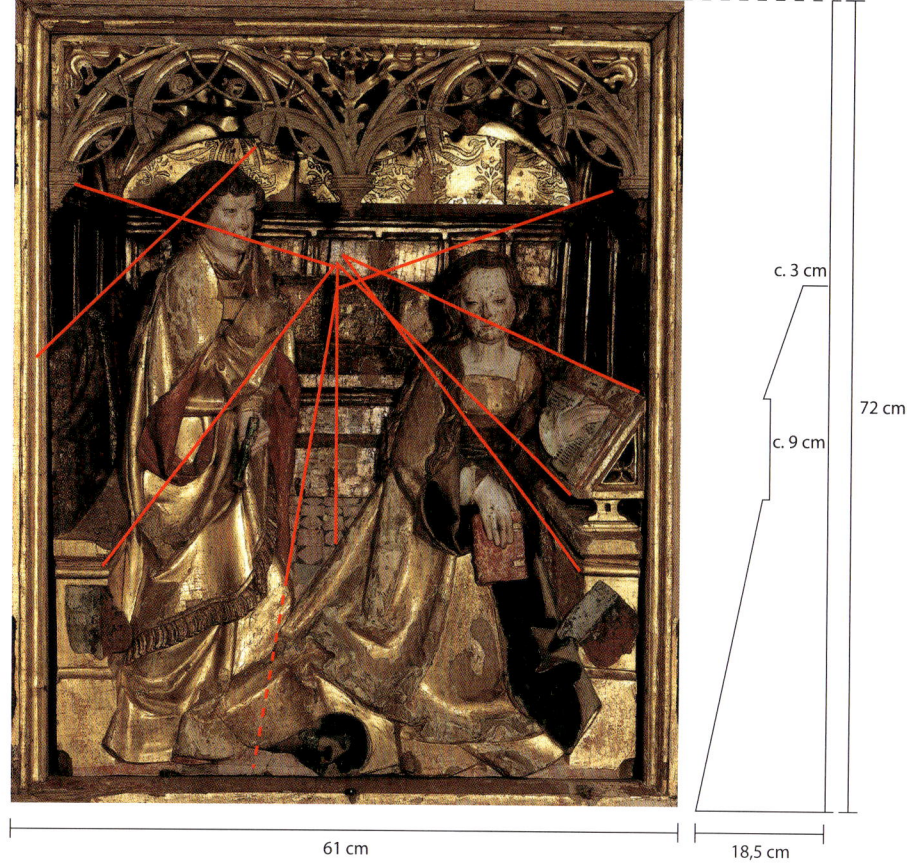

Fig. 9. Altarpiece from Preetz (Schleswig-Holstein), c. 1520, middle section showing The Annunciation with a checkerboard floor construction in perspective. However not all vanishing lines of couch meet in the same vanishing point. Author's interpretation, drawing by Merete Rude. Copenhagen. The National Museum of Denmark (Photo National Museum).

tual distance to Claus Berg is indeed short, albeit we have so far no knowledge of Claus Berg's actual acquaintance with either Viator or Glockendon's books, not to tell of any other publications.[40]

The fixed viewing position is also taken into account in relation to (pondered for) the putti in order to make the overall spatial concept of the middle section cohere: they put their noses out under the feet of the persons in the lowest section, as being viewed somewhat from below, they pop up in the second and are very visible in the third and fourth sections, where they are seen as from below. This coordination of constructed space and viewing position can be a result of an understanding of perspective *de sotto in su* (bottom-up). An especially famous example is Andrea Mantegna's (1431 - 1506) painting in the ceiling in the *Camera degli Sposi* in Mantua, completed 1474, which was undoubtedly heard of in Nürnberg. We do not know if Claus Berg could have seen any works of Donatello or Mantegna, but it is close to impossible that artists north of the Alps,

including Claus Berg, should not have heard of them.[41] As for the "gothic" vaults in Claus Berg's reliefs, for example the *Mocking of Christ*, and the *Flagellation* (Fig. 4d), a similar perspective construction is found in the treatise of Hieronymus Rodler, (fl. 1531 – 1547(?) *Perspectiva*, Frankfurt, 1546, but was known to Dürer already c. 1502 as shown in his drawing, the *Flagellation of Christ* c.1502. In addition we find architecture drawn parallel to the picture plane and foreshortened as in Alberti's chequerboard construction (Fig. 2), in the *Agony in the Garden*, and in *Christ taken into Captivity* (Fig. 4e).

The sculptors and workshops of Southern Germany seem therefore to have been willing, we must conclude, to narrow medieval traditions to convey space down to one, namely perspective, and it goes for Claus Berg, too. If we compare Berg's reliefs to the ones by Tilman Riemenschneider, there are similar "perspective roofs",[42] though this is not typical of the ones of Veit Stoss, which are alike to Claus Berg's in style only.

One problem however of identifying perspective in relief is the fact that we often find more than one (central) vanishing point in the compositions, which is also found in Donatello´s relief (Fig. 7). However we cannot conclude that Donatello was ignorant of the mathematics of perspective, since he belonged to the intellectual and artistic circle which included Brunelleschi and Ghiberti, and he surely was one of the first in art history to implement the mathematics of perspective to relief. Hence rigorous precision is not necessary especially in relief, which also uses shadows to enhance the illusion, besides artists very often manipulated the basic construction in order to obtain maximum illusion of depth.[43]

If we then compare the rendering of space in Claus Berg´s altarpiece to a famous example in Northern Germany, there are significant differences. In Hans Brüggemann´s (1485/90 - 1523-?), *Bordesholm* altarpiece (c. 1514 - 1521), now in Schleswig Cathedral, there is no use of perspective neither in the sense as explained by Gauricus, nor as used by Claus Berg. On the contrary: The figures are placed in rows behind each other as in two of the reliefs on the predella, measured in the cast collection: the *Passahmal* and *Abraham and Melchisedeck*, but are almost not diminished in size. They are placed on steep tilted bases or "steps", which seen from a distance provide for "optical" or "perceptual" diminishing, and the depth of the reliefs are more than three times the depth of Claus Berg´s and five times that of Donatello´s.[44]

However Claus Berg is not alone in the northern part of Germany as concerns perspective in relief, as we can see in the small altarpiece from Preetz, c. 1520 – at that time under Danish rule (Bordesholm and Preetz are both situated in the Duchies (Schleswig-Holstein), belonging to the Danish Realms/the Crown of Denmark) – in the National Museum of Denmark.[45] Here we can identify a relief perspective construction with a chequer board floor, close both to the prescription of Gauricus, and the technique of the Italian sculptors of the 15th century (Fig. 9). Therefore Gert von der Osten and Ingeborg Kähler should have the closing words about the accomplishment of Claus Berg: that he shows "naturalism in perspective" and represents "a new aesthetics".[46]

Notes

1. This paper is related to my project: "The Artist´s Share". Rendering of Space in the Arts from Ancient Egypt to Modernity, kindly supported by the Danish Research Council, Novo Nordisk Fonden, and Beckett-Fonden. On the dating of the altarpiece, see below, note 2.

2. On Claus Berg in general and the Odense altarpiece in particular, cf. Viggo Thorlacius-Ussing, *Billedskæreren Claus Berg*, Copenhagen 1922, 102-122; on the Odense altarpiece, same, *Claus Bergs Altertavle i Sct. Knud i Odense*, Odense 1967; Birgitte Bøggild Johannsen, "Højaltertavlen", in: *Danmarks Kirker. Odense Amt* II, Herning 1995, 459-538; Jan Friedrich Richter, *Claus Berg. Retabelproduktion des Spätmittelalters im Ostseeraum*, Berlin 2007. The last monograph was published after the finishing of the present paper; references, however, have been inserted in the proofs.

3. Thorlacius-Ussing 1967, chapt. II; Bøggild Johannsen 1995, 516-538; further Birgitte Bøggild Johannsen, "Genealogical Representation in Gendered Perspective: on a Lost Royal Mausoleum from Early Sixteenth-Century Denmark", in: Truus van Bueren (ed.) *Care for the Here and the Hereafter: Memoria, Art and Ritual in the Middle Ages*, Turnhout 2005, 79-106; On Queen Christine, cf. Ellen Jørgensen, *Danske Dronninger*, Copenhagen 1910, 76-86; Mikael Venge, in: *Dansk Biografisk Leksikon*[3] 3, Copenhagen 1979, 376; Grethe Jacobsen, in: *Dansk Kvindebiografisk Leksikon* 1, Copenhagen 2000, 324-325.

4. For example the atelier of Verocchio, where Leonardo was an apprentice, or intellectual ambience of Albrect Dürer. See Guilia Bartrum, "Dürer and Humanism", in: Guilia Bartrum (ed.), *Albrecht Dürer and his Legacy*, London 2002, 9-17; Bradin Cormack & Carlo Mazzio, *Book use, book theory: 1500-1700*, Chicago 2005; Ellen Jørgensen, *Studier over danske middelalderlige Bogsamlinger*, Copenhagen 1912; same, *De middelalderlige latinske Manuscripter i Det kgl. Bibliotek*, Copenhagen 1927; S. Birket Smith, *Kjøbenhavns Universitetsbibliotek før 1728*; Copenhagen 1882 (Reprint Copenhagen 1982). Veit Stoss had equally high social status and connection to learned and political circles. Further, Francisco Bethencourt & Florike Egmond (eds.), *Correspondence and Cultural Exhange in Europe 1400-1700* (Robert Muchembled & William Monter (eds.), Cultural Exchange in Early Modern Europe III), Cambridge 2007.

5. Niels Lauritz Høyen, "Claus Berg og hans Altertavle i Odense, 1865", in: J. L.Ussing (ed.), *Niels Laurits Høyens Skrifter* I-III, Copenhagen 1871-76, II, 339-373. "Det store opsving, som Brødrene van Eyck havde givet Malerkonsten i Nederlandene, virkede efterhaanden ogsaa paa de tyske Skoler, men den fik en saa

afgjørende Indflydelse, at den malerisk-perspektiviske Fremstillingsmaade blev den ene gjældende især i Træskulpturen", cf. 345.

6   Leon Battista Alberti, *On Painting and On Sculpture. The Latin Texts of De Pictura and De Statua*, Cecil Grayson (ed.), London 1972, 54-59; see further Cecil Grayson, "Studi su Leon Battista Alberti", esp.: "The text of Alberti´s ´De pictura`" (1968) and "On Painting and On Sculpture (1972)", both in: Paola Claut (ed.), *Ingenium*, Citta di Castello 1998, 1, 245-269, 287-323. Copies of early editions are represented in the following Danish collections: 1540, 1568, (in *Opuscoli morali*), 1651 (The Royal Library), 1547, (Statens Museum for Kunst); Piero della Francesca, *De prospettiva pingendi*, I-II, (text and atlante), G. Nicco Fasola (ed.), Firenze 1942; a Danish translation of De Pictura/Della Pittura have recently been published, cf. Leon Battista Alberti, *Om Billedkunsten*, Lise Bek (ed. and transl.), Copenhagen 2000; selected chapters were also published in translation in: Birgitte Bøggild Johannsen and Marianne Marcussen (eds.), *Rumperception og rumkonstruktion, Kildeskrifter til optikkens og linearperspektivets historie*, Institut for Kunsthistorie, Copenhagen 1978, 100-119; 143-160.

7   Max Steck, *Dürers Gestaltlehre der Mathematik und der bildenden Künste,* Halle 1948, 110-118; (Dürer´s woodcut, Bartsch 128); C.V. Nielsen, *Perspektivens Historie*, I-V, Copenhagen 1895-99.

8   Max Steck, 1948, 114.

9   Checquerboard construction in drawing, 1509, in: Katharina Krause, *Hans Holbein d.Ä*, Munich & Berlin 2002, fig. 73.

10 Ingetraut Ludolphy, *Friedrich der Weise Kurfürst von Sachsen 1463-1512*, Göttingen 1984, 14-22, 101-112, 333-336; Bartrum, 2002, mentions especially Dürer´s paintings *The Adoration of the Magi*, 1504 and *The Martyrdom of The Ten Thousand*, 1508, 216, besides the engraved *Passion* 1509,173; see also Simone Ferrari, *Jacopo de´ Barbari. Un protagonista del Rinascimento tra Venezia e Dürer,* Milano 2006, 61-68, note 17.

11 Hermann Deckert, "Die lübisch-baltische Skulptur im Anfang des 16. Jahrhunderts", *Marburger Jahrbuch für Kunstwissenschaft*, III (1926), 8; "Es ist kein Zweifel, Claus Berg verwendet hier – soviel ich sehe… als erster in der deutschen Skulptur – bewusst die perspektivische Verkürzung zur Steigung der Illusion"; Thorlacius-Ussing 1922, 9,109; Thorlacius-Ussing 1967, II. 3.

12 Bøggild Johannsen 1995, 493: "Scenen er indsat i interiør med bjælkeloft, hvis linjer perspektivisk løber sammen mod Kristus – relieffets indholdsmæssige og kompositoriske midtpunkt." Orthogonal projections are seen in the *Expulsion*, 509 and (by the workshop of Claus Berg) in the remnants of the paintings on the wings of the altarpiece. See: Restoration report and photographic documentation in the National Museum of Denmark.

13 Thorlacius-Ussing 1922, 11, refers to a rather costly (?) painting on a door 1508, he paints a wagon 1510, and is twice referred to as Claus Maler in a case of inheritance, 1560, Richter, 2007, 374-375, albeit we have no secure knowledge in what way or to what extent Claus Berg may have been personally involved in the painting of the wings of the Odense altarpiece, Richter, 2007, 175-179

14 Bøggild Johannsen 1995, note 372, 656; Ulla Haastrup, "Brugen af forlæg i Odense i 1. fjerdedel af 1500-tallet", in: Rudolf Zeitler & Jan O. M. Karlsson (eds.), *Imagines Medievales. Studier i medeltida ikonografi, arkitektur, skulptur, måleri och konsthandverk*, Uppsala 1983 (Ars universitas upsaliensis: ars suetica 7), 113-131; Karl Rapke,"Die Perspektive auf den Dürer'schen Handzeichnungen, Holzschnitten, Kupferstichen und Gemälden", *Studien zur deutschen Kunstgeschichte* 39, (1902), 1-88.

15 (mentioned above: Frederick the Wise Elector of Saxony founded the university in Wittenberg 1502 and can be characterized as a Renaissance humanist). On Frederick the Wise as a Renaissance humanist, see *Handbuch der Bibliothekswissenschaft*, III, Wiesbaden 1956, 566; Ludolphy,1984, 101-112; see also note 10.

16 Alberti (ed. 1972), 70-71.

17 Piero della Francesca (ed. 1942), 174, 180, 182, lxiv, lxv, lxvi.

18 For example Susanne Lang, "Brunelleschi´s panels", in: Marisa Dalai Emiliani (ed.), *La prospettiva rinascimentale. Codificazioni e trasgressioni, I*, Firenze 1980, 63-72; Martin Kemp, *The Science of Art*, New Haven & London, 1990, appendix II.

19 Klaus Bergdolt (ed. and transl.), *Der dritte Kommentar Lorenzo Ghibertis*, Weinheim, 1988.

20 Antonio di Tuccio Manetti, *The Life of Brunelleschi*, Howard Saalman (ed.), London 1970, 52-53.

21 Thanks to curator Britta Tøndborg, Statens Museum for Kunst, Copenhagen, for kindly allowing me to examine the following reliefs (allow gauging qua sighting) in the Cast Collection; Donatello: KAS 971; Güstrow KAS 2055, 2058, Wittstock (Berg?) KAS 2063, 2064; see further, Penelope Curtis, *Depth of Field: the place of relief in the time of Donatello*, Leeds 2004, 18-29.

22 Pomponius Gauricus, "De Sculptura" (1504), in: André Chastel & Robert Klein (eds. and transl.), *Hautes Études médiévales et modernes* 5 (1969). See esp. chapter IV: La perspective (De perspectiva). Though acquired at a later moment, early editions from 1528, 1542 and 1609 exist in Denmark at The Royal Library and Dan-

ish National Art Library. Early editions 1528, 1542 and 1609 (The Royal Library), 1609 (Danish National Art Library). Bøggild Johannsen and Marcussen, 1978, 187-191.

23 Alberti does not explain the mathematics behind the construction, but stresses the fixed position of the eye-point as different from earlier practices, Grayson (ed.) 1972, 54-55; see also Gauricus in Chastel & Klein (eds.) 1969, 182.

24 della Francesca in Fasola (ed.)1942, 76, 100, xiii, xxxi.

25 On an interpretation of Gauricus´ chequerboard floor, see Decio Gioseffi, *Perspectiva Artificialis. Per la storia della prospettiva, spigolature et appunti*, Trieste 1957, 88-95, diagram 90-91. Bøggild Johannsen & Marcussen 1978, 187-191.

26 Hans Huth, *Künstler und Werkstatt der Spätgotik,* Augsburg 1923. Johann Josef Böker, *Die Architektur der Gotik. Gothic Architecture*, Salzburg 2005.

27 Böker 2005, 24, esp. nos. 17.058 c. 1515, 16.829, 1485/1495; 16.838, late 15th century.

28 Jacopo della Quercia, *Study for the Fonte Gaia* 1409?, see James Beck, *Jacopo della Quercia*, I-II, New York 1991, 148-150.

29 Böker 2005, 25.

30 Gauricus in Chastel & Klein (eds.)1969, 190-194; see also Pomponius Gauricus, *De Sculptura*, Heinrich Brockhaus (ed.), Leipzig 1886, 207-213.

31 Lilian Brion Guerry, *Jean Pélerin Viator. Sa place dans l'historie de la perspective*, Paris 1962, 116-150; *Handbuch der Bibliothekswissenschaft*, III, Wiesbaden 1953, 266; Stech 1948, 110-118.

32 Gauricus in Chastel & Klein (eds.)1969, 184.

33 Bøggild Johannsen, 1995, 474, gives dimensions of the altarpiece as : height 490 cm, breadth (open 604 cm), middle section, 372x302x35 cm, predella 100x316x60cm. Depth of figures in middle section max 17 cm. Relief in casing 90x75x16 cm; i.e. actual depth of reliefs approx. 8/10 cm (all in one piece and hollowed out in the back).

34 Beate Knuth Federspiel, *Det gotiske fløjalter: arbejdsgang og teknikker, Teknologihistorie III*, Kunstakademiets Konservatorskole, 1986, 11-16.

35 Thorlacius-Ussing 1922, 4.

36 Phyllis Pray Bober & Ruth Rubinstein, *Renaissance Artists and Antique Sculpture*, Oxford 1986, cat. Nr. 90, 122-124; Cast Collection, KAS 2287. Bøggild Johannsen & Marcussen 1978, 35-37.

37 Vitruvius *Ten Books on Architecture*, Ingrid D. Rowland (transl.), Thomas Noble Have, (ed.) Cambridge 1999, 25.

38 Steck 1948, 111.

39 Guerry 1962, 119–129. Early editions of the relevant treatises exist in Denmark (Dürer 1515, 1528, Glockendohn 1509 (only prints), Reisch 1549, Ryff/Rivius 1558), all in Det Natur- og Sundhedsvidenskabelige Fakultetsbibliotek, Copenhagen.

40 The same Library owns three treatises imperative for perspective: Brawardinus, Viator, and Dürer in one Renaissance binding, albeit the provenance is not known.

41 Queen Christine´s mother-in-law, Queen Dorothea (c. 1430 – 1495) was a sister to Barbara, Duchess of Mantua.

42 On Tilman Riemenschneider, see Julien Chapuis (ed.), Tilman Riemenschneider c. 1460-1531,New Haven & London 2004 (Studies in the History of Art, Symposium Papers XLII), 46; Gottfried Sello, *Veit Stoss,* München 1988, figs. 27-47.

43 Rapke 1902, finds Dürer both unprecise, 49-51, and precise 62-63. A copy of Rodler 1546 is at Det Natur- og Sundhedsvidenskabelige Fakultetsbiliotek, Copenhagen.

44 Brüggemann´s reliefs, KAS 2047 and 2048; Bernd Bünsche, *Das Goschhof-Retabel in Schleswig*, Kiel 2005, 67.

45 Inv. Nr. 2125, depth of middle section (incl. casing) ca. 18 cm, wings ca. 12 cm.

46 Gert von der Osten & Horst Vey, *Painting and Sculpture in Germany and the Netherlands 1500-1600*, Harmondsworth 1969, 53; Ingeborg Kähler, *Der Bordesholmer Altar – Zeichen in einer Krise*, Neumünster 1981 (Studien zur schleswig-holsteinischen Kunstgeschichte 14), 114.

MELCHIOR LORCK'S PORTRAIT OF SULTAN SÜLEYMAN THE MAGNIFICENT (1562): A DOUBLE-CODED VIEW

Mikael Bøgh Rasmussen

Melchior Lorck (1526/27-after 1583) has left an enormous amount of material from his journey to and sojourn at Istanbul or Constantinople in the years 1555 to 1559.

This paper tries to frame Lorck's portrait of Sultan Süleyman the Magnificent, in Turkish called The Lawgiver (Fig. 1), published first time in 1562, and to assess the degree in which Lorck tries to balance the different conceptual frameworks available for a westerner coming to the east and engaging with what is at the time the arch-enemy of Western Europe.[1]

Lorck was member of an embassy sent by the so-called King of the Romans, who in 1558 became German Emperor as Ferdinand I. The embassy was difficult, as most of its kind, and one in a row trying to reach a settlement on the status of the Kingdom of Hungary, particularly Transylvania, which both parties claimed as theirs. It was led by the Netherlandish diplomat and humanist Ogier Ghislain de Busbecq, famous for his *Turkish Letters*, which were published in Antwerp in 1581-1588.[2] The *Turkish Letters* have been classics in diplomatic relations ever since. Even though they were written in the style of letters to a close friend and are dated at different times during the embassy, this was certainly a rhetorical device, as we must assume that they were constructed some time after his return from Constantinople. We know from a number of documents that Melchior Lorck was assigned to the embassy. Particularly clear in this regard is the document set down in 1564 in order to explain the reasons for the elevation of Lorck and his three brothers to noble status.[3] From the works we know and from the position he took at court in Vienna after his return, we must assume that he partly acted as a kind of what we would call an intelligence officer.

A large number of his pictures of the life and customs of the Turks have survived. Here he emerges – as we can see from the 128 woodcuts that he prepared for publication – as especially interested in the structure of the Turkish military and the hierarchy of Turkish society. In order to know one's enemy, these were important things to know. Lorck's pictures seem so perfectly in correspondence with the vast amount of information given by Busbecq in his letters that the one could illustrate or explain the other.

The relationship between Lorck and Busbecq is both very interesting and very difficult to assess.[4] They are two sides of the same phenomenon. Both were sent to Constantinople with an eager eye, trying to learn as much as possible about Turkish matters, and both provide us with an enormous amount of information about Turkish society and military. We also know they lived together for three and a half years at the Elçi Hanı

Fig. 1. Melchior Lorck, Süleyman the Magnificent, 1562. Vienna, Graphische Sammlung Albertina (Photo Albertina).

on the central thoroughfare of the city, where the imperial embassy was installed. According to a letter by one of Busbecq's associate envoys it even seems to emerge that Lorck was sent to the city on Busbecq's request because he was in need of a draughtsman.[5] At the Elçi Hanı they were even confined for long periods due to the ongoing and ever erupting war between Ferdinand and the Sultan. They both tell us about their dwelling and their confinement, Busbecq in lenghty passages in his letters, Lorck on the fabulous 12 meter long prospect of the city that he composed of the city after his return, where he marked the Hanı with an inscription that confirms that he as well was confined there with the embassy.[6] A large number of other correspondences between the author and the artist exist as well, like the keen interest in the antiquities of the city. Both describe the now lost Arcadius-column, for example (Fig. 2).[7]

There exists a drawing in the Printroom in Copenhagen which shows the view from the embassy's lodgings, the Elçi Hanı, across the sea (Fig. 3).[8] The Arcadius Column is seen in the background, the cupolas of a madrasah and a mosque to the right and a small love-making couple on the terrace to the left. We also see a number of parapets facing the viewer. The drawing could be one of the most illuminating examples of the correspondence between Lorck's drawings and Busbecq's letters.

Busbecq tells us the Turks felt that the Christians in the Elçi Hanı were an annoyance, as they disliked being watched by the infidels. In fact they were so annoyed by what they felt as being spied on that they set up parapets to block the view.[9] Lorck's drawing may be the document of some of this spying and certainly forms an illuminating illustration of the situation described by Busbecq – it is unfinished despite its otherwise very thorough rendering, seemingly as a result of an interruption.

After their return to the West, Lorck and Busbecq continued to share the same environment though we cannot tell whether they ever met. Both continued in imperial service and both were connected to one of the hotspots of European humanism, Antwerp, where Busbecq published and Lorck worked with one of the most important publishing houses, that of Christophe Plantin. But despite the fact that they lived together, and that they may well have met or heard of each other later on, Busbecq never even mentions Lorck, which is surprising in the light of the otherwise quite large list of people in the embassy that he names or mentions in passing, and of the fact that Lorck made an engraved portrait of Busbecq in Constantinople. However, because of the many correspondences between Busbecq and Lorck, Busbecq may be used as a framework for the understanding of Lorck's view of the Turks.

Returning to the portrait of Süleyman (Fig.1) it says in the inscription that it was made 15 February 1559. At that time the confinement of the embassy was loosened and we know from Busbecq's letters that he was able to move more freely in Constantinople and the surroundings. He now had the possibility to see a far greater part of

Fig. 2. Melchior Lorck, The upper registers of Arcadius' column, 1559. Copenhagen, The National Gallery of Denmark, Print Room (Photo National Gallery).

Turkish life than at almost any time before and we must assume that the bulk of Lorck's drawings was made from that time on. The date on the print may of course be a conceit in order to provide the portrait with the authenticity of an eyewitness account, but it may – however unlikely – also record an actual session through which Lorck was given a chance to directly portray the sultan, providing a parallel to the way that Gentile Bellini was asked by Mehmet II 80 years earlier despite the picture prohibitions of Islam.

The portrait has two inscriptions, one in Persian, another in Latin. The first lists the official title of the Sultan: "This is Sultan Süleyman Shah, son of Sultan Selim Shah…". The Latin text is different and more elaborate: "The Emperor of the Turks in the East Süleyman, only son of Selim, who ascended in the same year 1520 when in Aachen Charles V, grandson of Emperor Maximilian, was made Christian Emperor of the West; made with greatest exactitude in Constantinople on 15 February 1559 by the most studied in antiquities, the Holsteiner Melchior Lorck from Flensburg."[10]

This inscription is interesting in its parallelisation of Süleyman and Charles V, reinstating the division of empire between east and west and acknowledging the Sultan as *de facto* Eastern emperor and thus as heir to the Byzantine emperors. The Turkish inscription is different, noting the official titles of Süleyman. The inscriptions on the print are thus quite straightforward and, if anything, more affirmative than derogative. The print was first issued in order to be distributed to European princes who had a keen interest in both ruler portraits and the ominous, but fascinating Turk.

The portrait fits well the descriptions by Busbecq of Süleyman's aspect. His sad, melancholy demeanour, but also an air of the stoic, who is never emotionally involved or affected, neither in times of misery nor of victory. Süleyman has thus a very sympathetic and humane aspect about him, and has the complete control over his emotions that was emerging as an ever more essential trait of the ideal superior person during the sixteenth century. The print thus seems to provide the true picture of a good ruler.

Interestingly enough, though, the print was republished in Antwerp in 1574 in a book by Lorck on Süleyman - one of the few things that Lorck ever published - opposite a poem that uses the portrait as a rhetorical starting point for a characterisation of the sitter and thereby provides us with an interpretation of the portrait.

This poem makes a rather different statement than the titles on the print.

"The Turkish emperor had these traits in the last years of his life. […] But can any painter render this mind that was more than barbarically wild, not to speak of its well wrought intrigues. You, Cruel, surpass even Lychaeon in unspeakable massacres, are a wilder creature than the torturer Phalaris. This tells your twisted traits, deep lying eyes, and your skin, wrinkled by overdone love to Mars…"[11]

This very demonizing interpretation of what would emerge as an objective or positively bi-

A DOUBLE-CODED VIEW 167

ased portrait when seen in the light of Busbecq's abovementioned descriptions, is quite puzzling, but also quite typical of the ambivalence inherent in the admiration.

Neither Lorck nor Busbecq are seemingly able to decide whether to admire or despise the Sultan. On the one hand the efficiency, discipline and clean-cut power structure of the Sultan's regime is admired as far superior to those of Western Europe, on the other hand the admired Sultan is the personified arch-enemy of Christendom and as such to be both despised and feared the more the greater he is. In both we find a double-coded view of the Sultan that seems to concentrate in the image of the person.

On the other hand there is the question of market. Lorck needed to publish and wanted to sell. A friendly description of the Sultan would not only be politically incorrect, in modern terms, but would also lack the special quality of supporting common views and prejudices, which even then was essential to success in publishing. Lorck's realization of this dilemma can be seen when his great plans for the publication of Turkish antiquities and modern splendours seem to deteriorate due to lack of funding during the 1560s. He appears to change his strategy from planning elaborate luxury engravings and woodcuts for the elite to produce more popular and exotic motives from his sojourn. In 1568 he apparently tests the market by issuing a poem in the widespread tradition of the *Türckenbüchlein*, called *Ein Liedt vom Türcken und Antichrist* (A song on the Turk and Antichrist),[12] which, it is stated, was written in Constantinople in 1559. Here he elaborates on the danger to all of Christendom that the powerful enemy means, and sees the Turkish expansion as the oncoming end of the world, Judgement Day ahead. The woodcuts for the great book on Turkish matters that he began planning around the same time also display this twist: The mosques are depicted in seemingly objective ways, but small devils in the sky are added to make sure that these are in fact the temples of Antichrist.

We cannot know Lorck's personal position or point of view. The larger amount of drawings and woodcuts from Turkey are clearly descriptive and

Fig. 3. Melchior Lorck, View across the roofs of Constantinople towards the Sea of Marmara, 1555-1559. Copenhagen, The National Gallery of Denmark, Print Room (Photo National Gallery).

seemingly neutral. On the one hand he seems to admire all the new and unknown things that he sees and makes his most impressive portrait by far, that of the Sultan. But on the other, back in the West, where he has to publish his works, he seems to adopt the typical Western framework of thought and view that the subject of his works is in fact the arch-enemy, and that all the splendour, the good rule, the efficiency, control and discipline is all the more terrifying. Especially the Sultan who emerges as almost the epitome of the ideal Christian ruler: just, protective, charitative and orderly, is an ambivalent person in this case, as he is also the ideal enemy. Lorck's Turkish works strike us as on the one hand objective and descriptive; on the other - in its published form - it is framed by a thorough turkophobia typical of the view of the Turk as Antichrist, which is particularly widespread in Protestant interpretations of the sixteenth century.

While Lorck's portrait therefore on the one hand seems to be one of the most psychologically insightful portraits of the second half of the sixteenth century, it changes its message by the framing view that engages it.

As a portrait it is interesting in the sense that it states itself as a direct, uninterested document, on the other it fits the texts that promote a moral superiority, and again it is framed by texts which use it as a picture of evil personified.

Through its historical setting in the midst of closely connected texts by the artist himself and by the most likely congenial Busbecq, it is a splendid example of the ambivalence of the visual and the importance of conceptual frameworks and worldview in the interpretation of art.

Notes

1 The present paper reflects a work in progress, which built on two projects that I was working on at the time of the conference: One on portraiture, which I was engaged in at The Museum of National History at Frederiksborg Castle. The other one assisting Dr. Erik Fischer, who as the world's leading expert on Melchior Lorck has been working on the artist for decades, in finishing his manuscripts for a catalogue raisonnée of Lorck's work and a biography, of which the first four out of five have been published in 2009. I am indebted to Dr. Fischer for a lot of the material that I was able to use because I had been granted access to some partly unpublished material that is not the result of my own research. The interpretations are my own, however. See: Erik Fischer, with Ernst Jonas Bencard & Mikael Bøgh Rasmussen and a contribution by Marco Iuliano, *Melchior Lorck*, 1-4, Copenhagen 2009.

2 Ogier Ghiselin de Busbecq, *Turkish Letters*, Edward S. Forster transl., Oxford 1927.

3 See Fischer et. al. 2009, Document nos. 1564, February 22a-c.

4 See e.g. for an interpretation of the lack of mentioning from Busbecq's side as the result of social rivalry and personal antipathy between them: Barnaby Rogerson, "A double Perspective and a Lost Rivalry: Ogier de Busbecq and Melchior Lorck in Istanbul", in: Gerald MacLean (ed.), *Re-Orienting the Renaissance. Cultural Exchanges with the East*, Houndmills, Basingstoke 2005, 88-95.

5 Zweder R.W.M. von Martels: *Augerius Gislenius Busbequius – Leven en werk van de keyzerlijke gezant an het hof van Süleyman de Grote*, Groningen 1989, 437. Letter fra Willem Quackelbeen (Coturnossius) to Pier Andrea Matthioli.

6 Universiteitsbibliotheek Leiden, inv.no. BPL 1758. See Fischer et al. 2009, Vol. 4.

7 Copenhagen, Statens Museum for Kunst, Den Kongelige Kobberstiksamling, inv.no. 13.188. Fischer et al. 2009, catalogue no. 1559,2.

8 Copenhagen, Statens Museum for Kunst, Den Kongelige Kobberstiksamling, inv.no. KKSgb4625. Fischer et al. (2009), catalogue no. 1555-59, 1.

9 Busbecq (1927 ed.), 3rd letter, 64.

10 IMAGO SVLEYMANNI TVRCORVM IMP.IN ORIENTE, VNICI SELIMY FILII, QVI AN. DO. MDXX IN IMPERIO SVCCESSIT: QVO ETI= / AM ANNO CAROLVS . V . MAXÆMYLIANI CÆSARIS NEPOS AQVISGRANI IN OCCIDENTE CORONATVS EST CHRISTIAN: IMP: A MELCHIO= / RE LORICHS FLENSBVRGENSI, HOLSATIO, ANTIQVITATIS STVDIOSISS^O, CONSTANTINOPOLI, AN. MDLIX, MEN. FEB., DIE XV, VERISSIME EXPRESSA.

11 *Turcicus hos Cæsar vultus, hæc ora gerebat //Cùm tereret*

vitæ lustra suprema suæ.//…//At plus quàm Geticam poterit qui pingere mentem,//Aut vafros astus, pictor an ullus erit?//Cædibus infandis vincit te dire Lycaon,//Quamque ferox Phalaris plus feritatis habet.//Idque volunt torui vultus, oculique reducti,//Contracta & nimio Martis amore cutis.

12 *Ein liedt vom Tür- / cken vnd Antichrist, durch Melchior Lo- / richs zu Constantinopel gedicht, im Jar 1559. / Jtzt im 1568. jar ausgangen. Mag gesungen wer- / den in der Melodey, Erhör mein wordt mein red / vornim, mein König Gott vnd Herre. / Oder im Thon, Auss tieffer nodt schrey ich zu dir, etc. / Jtem der Christlich Glaub, zu singen / im Thon, O mensch bewein die / Sünde gross, etc.,* (s.l., 1568).

DIE KÜNSTLERISCHE AUSSTATTUNG DES DRESDNER RESIDENZSCHLOSSES IN DER ZWEITEN HÄLFTE DES 16. JAHRHUNDERTS ALS AUSDRUCK DER NEU GEWONNENEN KURWÜRDE

Angelica Dülberg

Nach dem Sieg Kaiser Karls V. über den Schmalkaldischen Bund Ende April 1547 in der Schlacht bei Mühlberg an der Elbe, an der sich der Albertiner Herzog Moritz gegen seinen ernestinischen Vetter Kurfürst Johann Friedrich beteiligt hatte, ging die Kurwürde an Moritz über. Gleichzeitig stieg Dresden als Residenz des Kurstaates auf. Der weitgehende Neubau und die Umgestaltungen des Residenzschlosses spiegeln geradezu exemplarisch die neue Stellung des Fürsten wider, gleichwohl auch seine hohen politischen und kulturellen Ansprüche. Es entstand erstmals nördlich der Alpen eine großzügige, fast regelmäßige Vierflügelanlage um den Großen Schlosshof, dessen Hauptschauseite die aufwendig gestaltete nördliche Front darstellte (Fig. 1-3).[1]

Moritz war bestrebt, sein Schloss in jeder Hinsicht zum modernsten auszubauen und auszustatten. Der weitgereiste Festungsbaumeister Voigt von Wierandt setzte, wohl in Zusammenarbeit mit den hochgebildeten kurfürstlichen Räten, wie Dr. Georg von Komerstadt, Christoph von Carlowitz sowie vermutlich auch Philipp Melanchthon und Georgius Agricola, das hochgesteckte Ziel in die Tat um. Moritz selbst hielt sich Anfang 1549 in Trient auf. Von dort unternahm er Ende Januar, Anfang Februar eine dreiwöchige Reise durch Oberitalien an die bedeutenden Höfe von Ferrara, Mantua, Mailand und nach Venedig[2] und hat dort offenbar vielfältige Anregungen für sein Residenzschloss gesammelt. Jedenfalls hat er kurz darauf mit den Brüdern Gabriele und Benedetto Tola aus Brescia die ersten Italiener für die bildnerische Gestaltung seines Schlosses in Dresden, das heißt für die Sgraffiti-Dekorationen und die malerische Ausstattung von Innenräumen, geholt. Wie Ernst Guldan herausstellt, hat der diesseitig orientierte Repräsentationswille des neuzeitlichen Fürsten den Anstoß zur bewussten Aufnahme italienischen Formengutes gegeben.[3]

Mit dem Umbau des Ostflügels und des alten Nordflügels im Großen Schlosshof seit September 1548 wurde offensichtlich gleichzeitig mit der Errichtung des nordöstlichen Wendelsteins begonnen, denn er ist an den beiden mit reichem Kandelaberschmuck versehenen Pilastern über dem zweiten Stock auf je einer skulptierten Inschriftentafel mit der Jahreszahl 1549 datiert (Fig. 4). Ebenso zügig wurde offensichtlich nach der Einwilligung des Kurfürsten Moritz auf den Vorschlag einer neuen, nach Westen erweiterten Baukonzeption im Schreiben des Ernst von Miltitz vom 23. Februar 1549[4] das Pendant in der nordwestlichen Ecke des Großen Schlosshofs gebaut und plastisch geschmückt, wie die Tafeln unmittelbar unterhalb der Kapitelle mit der Jahreszahl 1550 zeigen (Fig. 5).

Fig. 1. Dresden, Residenzschloss, Schlossmodell nach dem Original aus dem letzten Viertel des 16. Jahrhunderts, Ansicht von Südosten, 1998 (Foto Landesamt für Denkmalpflege Sachsen).

Den Nordflügel zur prominenten Schauseite des Schlosshofes zu kreieren, war bereits mit dem aufwendig gestalteten plastischen Dekor der Wendelsteine geplant und verwirklicht, bevor die Fassade mit Sgraffiti geschmückt und die Hofloggia dem nun in die Mitte gerückten Hausmannsturm vorgesetzt wurde. Darüber hinaus spiegeln sie als erste neue Bauelemente bereits die hohen Ansprüche des jungen Kurfürsten wider und können wie andere aufwendig gestaltete Treppentürme in Frankreich und Deutschland als Hoheitszeichen gewertet werden.[5]

Wenngleich sich die beiden Nordtürme in ihrer architektonischen Struktur und in der Anordnung ihrer Bildwerke entsprechen, so unterscheidet sich ihr plastischer Bildschmuck inhaltlich und stilistisch doch wesentlich. Den Bogen des Haupteingangs im Nordosten tragen mit übernatürlichen Kräften ausgestattete männliche Gestalten, Simson mit der Eselskinnbacke und Herkules mit der Keule (Fig. 4). Sie werden vor allem als Bezwinger des Löwen häufig typologisch gegenübergestellt. Weil sie das Böse bekämpfen, verweisen sie auf Christus als Überwinder des Satans und damit auf sein Erlösungswerk. Herkules ist schlechthin ein Sinnbild der Fortitudo.[6] So ist es kein Wunder, dass sich Fürsten gern mit dem Tugendhelden, der als Sieger aus den Kämpfen über das Böse und die Laster hervorgeht, identifizieren. Simson und Herkules gelten gleichzeitig auch als Trabanten der Fama und der Virtú.[7] In mehrfacher Bedeutung werden sie ganz bewusst als flankierende Gestalten des Haupteingangs ausgewählt worden sein und können durchaus auf Moritz als siegreichem Feldherrn und Kämpfer für die gerechte Sache Gottes bezogen werden.

Auf den beiden das Hauptportal flankierenden breiten Pilastern sind die Darstellungen „Adam und Eva unter dem Baum der Erkenntnis" und „Kain und Abel" in die grotesken Kandelaberreliefs einbezogen. Mit dem Sündenfall ist hier ebenfalls der Bezug zu Christi Opfertod gegeben. Der Hirsch selbst ist ein Christussymbol – als Feind der Schlange tötet er sie wie Christus den Teufel.[8] Die Söhne des ersten Menschenpaars stehen neben dem von Gott abgelehnten Ährenopfer Kains, das von einem geflügelten Totenschädel als Hinweis auf den ersten Mord der Menschheit überhöht wird, während unter dem schmalen Podest das Lamm liegt, dessen Opfer Gott gesegnet hat. Es ist Attribut Abels, der den Gerechten verkörpert und als Präfiguration des Kreuztodes Christi gilt.[9] Gleichzeitig ist das Lamm besonders im Protestantismus Sinnbild des Messopfers.[10]

Die beiden anderen Rundbogenportale werden von antithetischen Figuren gestützt, links von zwei Rittern in Rüstung, während rechts ihre Gegenfiguren, ein Paar Wilder Leute im zottigen Fellkleid, erscheinen. Der Ritter ist in der spätmittelalterlichen Zeit nicht nur der tugendhafte Held, sondern auch Vertreter der „hohen Minne", der Wilde Mann derjenige der „niederen" oder

Fig. 2. Dresden, Residenzschloss, Kupferstich aus der Weck'schen Chronik, 1680 (Foto Landesamt für Denkmalpflege Sachsen).

„neuen Minne", weil er sich als Waldmensch frei von seinem Naturtrieb leiten lässt.[11] Als Sinnbild der Fruchtbarkeit tritt der Wilde Mann häufig auch als Wappenhalter auf,[12] hier ist er lediglich mit seinem weiblichen Pendant Stützfigur wie die anderen erwähnten Atlanten. Doch über allen sechs sind in den Zwickeln seitlich der Bögen sechs Wappenschilde der Wettiner angebracht. So werden alle Figuren symbolisch zu Trägern und Stützen des wettinischen Kurfürstentums. Die Gesamtgestaltung des Turmuntergeschosses dient als Glaubensbekenntnis und vor allem als Hoheits- und Herrschaftsanspruch des neuen albertinischen Kurfürsten, wie der aufwendig gestaltete Treppenturm selbst als Hoheitssymbol des Herrschers verstanden werden muss.[13]

Auf der Ebene des Umgangs befinden sich auf den Postamenten unterhalb der Pilaster mit den reichen Kandelaberfriesen zwei große Medaillons mit einer männlichen und einer weiblichen Büste, die beide einen außergewöhnlichen, asiatisch an-

mutenden Kopfschmuck tragen. Die Vermutung Brunhild Werners, es würde sich um Kurfürst Moritz und seine Gemahlin handeln,[14] kann ad absurdum geführt werden, weil beide Köpfe auf phantastische Kopfentwürfe Heinrich Vogtherrs d. Ä. in seinem „Kunstbüchlein" zurückgeführt werden können.[15]

Offenbar beinhalten die sich darüber erhebenden Pilasterreliefs mit grotesken Kandelaberfriesen jeweils vorwiegend männliche und weibliche Aspekte. So erscheinen in der unteren Ebene über dem Männerkopf am Beginn des Kandelabers zwei bärtige Satyrn, während auf dem rechten Pilaster dort offensichtlich Satyrweibchen saßen.

Die beiden Hauptpilaster und auch die einfacheren an den Seiten werden von überaus reich mit figürlichem Schmuck versehenen Kapitellen überhöht. Über einer Reihe Akanthusblättern wachsen zu den Ecken vier Füllhörner, in deren Tröten nackte Putten sitzen, die ihr Hinterteil zum Hof hin strecken. In der Mitte eines jeden Kapitells befinden sich eine nackte weibliche und eine nackte männliche groteskenhafte Büste. Beim rechten Eckkapitell sitzen in den Ecken Sa-

Fig. 3. Dresden, Residenzschloss, Tierhatz im großen Schlosshof unter Georg II., Ansicht von Süden, um 1680 (Foto Sächsische Landesbibliothek, Dresden)

Fig. 4. Dresden, Residenzschloss, Großer Schlosshof, Nordostturm, 1549, Aufnahme Ende des 19. Jahrhunderts (Landesamt für Denkmalpflege Sachsen).

Fig. 5. Dresden, Residenzschloss, Großer Schlosshof, Nordwestturm, 1550, Aufnahme Ende des 19. Jahrhunderts (Bildarchiv Foto Marburg).

tyrn. Sie bliesen ursprünglich ein trötenförmiges Instrument, das sie mit beiden Händen hielten. Vor den Satyrn liegen zwei nackte, behelmte Putten waagerecht über den Akanthusblättern.

Derart plastisch reich gestaltete, groteskenhafte Kapitelle lassen sich kaum in Italien, aber an französischen Schlössern finden, wie zum Beispiel ein Säulenkapitell mit vier Satyrn an den Ecken an der Porte Dorée des Schlosses Fontainebleau.[16]

Den Hauptteil des Treppenturms abschließend, befinden sich zwischen reich profilierten Gesimsen bewegte Kampfszenen. Fast vollplastische, nackte, aber behelmte Kämpfer zu Pferde und zu Fuß agieren vor neutralem Grund in Art antiker Vorbilder, wie sie etwa die Schlachten Alexanders gegen die Perser auf dem berühmten Alexandersarkophag aus Sidon und ihm folgend auf römischen Schlachtensarkophagen, an Triumphbögen und Siegessäulen zeigen. Die italienischen Renaissancekünstler haben die vor Augen stehenden römischen Kampfszenen mit Vorliebe in ihren malerischen und plastischen Werken aufgegriffen und können hier vermittelnd tätig gewesen sein. Möglich wäre aber auch, dass die kleinen Kupferstiche mit Kampffriesen von der Hand deutscher Künstler wie Barthel Beham, Georg Pencz und Heinrich Aldegrever, die als Paraphrase über das Korrespondieren bewegter Körper zu verstehen sind, als Anregung gedient haben.[17] Wie bei diesen Stichen, so können auch beim Fries des nordöstlichen Treppenturms die gegnerischen Parteien nicht unterschieden werden. Plausibel erscheint, dass der siegreiche Kämpfer Moritz gegen die Türken, Franz I. und seinen Vetter Johann Friedrich als krönenden Abschluss des Treppenturms sinnbezogen eine Schlachtendarstellung wählte – inspiriert aus eigener Anschauung während seiner Italienreise oder auf Hinweis seiner humanistisch gebildeten Berater.

Aus dem thematisch freien Schlachtengetümmel fällt in der rechten Ecke eine Szene heraus, denn sie zeigt Krieger in einem Schiff, die eine Frauengestalt entführen. Ihr Kopf war auf alten Fotos noch vorhanden. Nahe liegt, dass es sich hier um die Gemahlin des spartanischen Königs Menelaos, Helena, handelt, die von dem Königssohn Paris nach Troia entführt wurde, denn auf dem gegenüberliegenden Treppenturm wird ebenfalls ein Kampffries gezeigt, auf dem die Folgen der Entführung, der troianische Krieg geschildert wird. Das beweist, dass die plastische Gestaltung der beiden nördlichen Wendelsteine unmittelbar hintereinander geplant war. Die Rüstung tragenden Krieger kämpfen links an den Schiffen, auf dem nächsten Friesstück zu Fuß miteinander, dann erstürmen sie die brennende

174 CATALYSTS TO CHANGE

Stadt und zum Schluss flieht Aeneas mit seinem Vater Anchises aus Troia.

Während sich am Nordostturm durchaus der Einfluss gerade in Dresden angekommener italienischer Künstler widerspiegelt, zeigen die Kampffriese des Nordwestturms die Hand des Dresdner Hofbildhauers Hans Walther II. Die gesamte Gestaltung des Nordwestturms weist eine üppige Steigerung ins Groteske und Manieristische sowie den Einfluss niederländischer Graphik auf (Fig. 5). Den Reliefs und den Trägerfiguren wohnt keine ikonographische Bedeutung inne. Die Dresdner Bildhauer, allen voran der verantwortliche Hofbildhauer Hans Walther II, waren offensichtlich fähig, verschiedenartige Vorbilder und Einflüsse aufzunehmen und sich diesen anzugleichen. Zwei der die Rundbögen im Erdgeschoss tragenden Karyatidhermen gehen auf Vorbilder im „Vitruvius Teutsch" von 1548 zurück, die von Agostino Veneziano 1536 entworfene Terme einer männlichen Rückenfigur mit Schuppenleib und abgebrochenen Armen und eine weibliche doppelgesichtige Figur zeigen. Übernommen wurden beide auch von Cornelis Bos in einer 1538 datierten Kupferstich-Folge.[18] Von ihm stammt auch die Vorlage für einen Putto im Pilasterfries, der von Beschlagwerk eingezwängt ist.[19]

Ein unvergleichliches und nördlich der Alpen erstmaliges Erscheinungsbild erhielt das Dresdner Residenzschloss aufgrund seiner alle Fassaden umfassenden Dekoration mit Sgraffiti (Fig. 1-3). Vermutlich war Moritz während seiner Italienreise von dieser speziellen Fassadengestaltung fasziniert, so dass er die Gebrüder Gabriele und Benedetto Tola aus Brescia nach Dresden holte. Sie waren Musiker am Hofe des Kardinals Christoph Madruzzo und Mitarbeiter des Malers Girolamo Romanino,[20] der weitgehend für die Ausmalung des Trientiner Castello Buonconsiglio verantwortlich war, in dem sich Moritz vor seiner dreiwöchigen Reise an die Fürstenhöfe Oberitaliens aufgehalten hatte.[21]

Ein Holzmodell, das vor 1590 angefertigt wurde und detailliert auch die Fassadenmalereien wiedergab, ist kurioserweise erst 1960 verschollen beziehungsweise wohl zerstört worden. Anlässlich der Ausstellung im Jahre 1998 „Das Dresdner Schloß. Monument sächsischer Geschichte und Kultur" wurde es aufgrund vorhandener Fotos in allen Details von den Künstlern, die auch die bereits im Großen Schlosshof entstandenen Sgraffiti geschaffen haben, rekonstruiert (Fig. 1). In diesem Zusammenhang konnte auch auf Gemälde vom Ende des 16. und 17. Jahrhunderts sowie auf Kupferstiche in Anton Wecks Chronik (Fig. 2) und Gabriel Tzschimmers „Die durchlauchtigste Zusammenkunft ..." von 1680 zurückgegriffen werden.[22]

So ist es gelungen, eine gewisse Vorstellung von dem ursprünglichen ikonographischen Programm zu rekonstruieren. Im Vordergrund stehen römische Historien und Erzählungen aus dem Alten Testament, die allgemein einen Tugendspiegel des Kurfürsten darstellen und gleichwohl verschlüsselt auf aktuelle politische Ereignisse sowie die Rolle des Kurfürsten im Schmalkaldischen Krieg anspielen.[23] Sie sind Vorbilder für den Mut, die Tapferkeit und Gerechtigkeit des Fürsten. In diesem Zusammenhang sei insbesondere auf eine Judith-Darstellung an der südlichen Hoffassade hingewiesen, denn es handelt sich um ein beliebtes und aktuelles Thema der Reformation, das hier speziell als persönliche Allegorie auf das geschickte Taktieren von Moritz gedeutet werden kann.[24] Merkwürdigerweise war die Wand der Schlosskirche zwischen Hausmannsturm mit der vorgelagerten Loggia und dem nordwestlichen Treppenturm wie dieser selbst nur mit Grotesken ornamental gestaltet, dies wohl bewusst, weil sich die Bildinhalte auf die Person des Kurfürsten und nicht auf die kirchliche Lehre bezogen.[25] Die im Fries des Hauptgesims umlaufende Inschrift, die den Bauherrn Moritz mit seinen Herrschaftstiteln nannte, unterstreicht diese Absicht.

Die fünffachsige Loggia unterhalb des Hausmannsturms bildete das beherrschende Architekturelement des Großen Schlosshofs (Fig. 2, 3). Ihre Arkadenöffnungen gaben den Blick frei auf die einzigen farbigen Wandmalereien, die in reizvollem Kontrast zu den grau-weißen Sgraffiti gestanden haben (Fig. 1). Dargestellt war im ersten Obergeschoss die Bekehrung Pauli, darüber die Anbetung der Heiligen Drei Könige, von der eine Entwurfszeichnung Benedetto Tolas mit Maria und Joseph im Stall erhalten ist.[26]

Zwei weitere Zeichnungen des Italieners zei-

gen Entwürfe für die Malereien des dritten Obergeschosses mit der Königin von Saba vor dem Thron Salomos.[27] Für das ikonographische Programm scheint Philipp Melanchthons „Confessio Saxonia" von 1551 herangezogen worden zu sein, in der dieser ein theologisches Programm des protestantischen Fürstenamtes entwickelt.[28] In der Bekehrung des Paulus sah die reformatorische Theologie die Erwählung des sündigen Menschen allein aus der Gnade Gottes. Sie kann ebenso auf die Bekehrung des Kurfürsten Moritz sowie auf sein Bekenntnis zum neuen Glauben bezogen werden. In der Anbetung des Christuskindes unterwerfen sich die weltlichen Fürsten der göttlichen Macht. Der Herrscher wird nicht nur selbst zur Gottesfurcht ermahnt, sondern hat auch die Aufgabe, die christliche Lehre zu fördern und zu beschützen. Auf die Verantwortlichkeit des Fürstenamtes weist auch die Geschichte von Salomo und der Königin von Saba hin.[29]

Auf der Brüstung im ersten Obergeschoss zeigen sieben Reliefplatten Szenen aus dem alttestamentlichen Buch Josua, Kapitel 1-10, die durch inhaltsbezogene Inschriften näher erklärt werden (Fig. 6).[30] Die beim Umbau der Loggia um 1898 teilweise durch Kopien ersetzten Reliefs wurden 1945 bis auf Reste zerstört.[31] Die ebenfalls von Hans Walther II und seiner Werkstatt geschaffenen Reliefs gehen letztlich in ihrer Komposition auf Darstellungen in der Luther-Bibel von 1534 zurück, wenngleich sie frei plastisch umgesetzt wurden.[32] Die Einnahme des gelobten Landes durch Josua kann wie auch die Juditherzählung an der Südwand auf den Konflikt, dem sich Moritz im Dienste des Kaisers und Reiches einerseits und der lutherischen Sache andererseits ausgesetzt sah, bezogen werden, denn bei beiden Geschichten ging es um eine List, die das Volk Gottes vor der Vernichtung durch den gottlosen Feind rettete. In diesem Zusammenhang sei auf die zwiespältige politische Rolle hingewiesen, die Kurfürst Moritz für Zeitgenossen spielte.[33]

Mit der Kurwürde ging auch das Selbstverständnis der bisher ernestinischen Kurfürsten als Schutzherren der Reformation an die Albertiner über. Nach dem Vorbild der von Luther 1544 geweihten Schlosskapelle in Torgau wurde in Dresden ein gleichrangiger Raum im Nordflügel zwischen dem Hausmannsturm und dem nordwestlichen Treppenturm 1551-1553 erbaut, der im Äußeren nur durch das in sie einführende prachtvolle Schlosskapellenportal kenntlich war.[34] Der Kupferstich David Conrads von 1676, der Heinrich Schütz im Kreise seiner Kantorei zeigt, vermittelt einen Eindruck des reichgestalteten Innenraums.[35]

Nachdem 1554 die malerischen und plastischen Ausstattungen am Außenbau und in den Innenräumen weitgehend abgeschlossen waren, galt es als Letztes, im Großen Schlosshof zwischen dem nordwestlichen Treppenturm und dem Hausmannsturm das Schlosskapellenportal fertig zu stellen (Fig. 7).[36]

Wird man das Renaissanceportal zum ersten Mal gewahr, das von 1876-2002 neben dem Johanneum gestanden hat, so ruft es sofort aufgrund seiner architektonischen Gliederung und zahlreicher Details die Assoziation an einen klas-

Fig. 6. Dresden, Residenzschloss, Großer Schlosshof, Brüstungsrelief der Schlosshofloggia, Der Durchzug der Israeliten durch den Jordan, um 1552, Aufnahme 1920 (Landesamt für Denkmalpflege Sachsen).

sischen antiken Triumphbogen hervor.[37] Nachweislich haben sich italienische Künstler mit den vor Augen stehenden römischen Kunstwerken intensiv auseinandergesetzt, sie vermessen, im Großen und im Detail gezeichnet und sie für ihre Architekturentwürfe kompositorisch verwendet. Dies spiegelt insbesondere der um 1522 von Baldassare Peruzzi entworfene Orgelprospekt für die Gonzaga in Mantua wider, bei dem dieser die antiken Hauptelemente aufgreift, jedoch handschriftlich Varianten anbietet. Noch mehr überrascht Giuliano da Sangallos Aufnahme der Elemente im Mittelteil der Fassade von S. Lorenzo in Florenz.[38]

Allgemein wird der Portalentwurf der Schlosskapelle dem quellenmäßig in Dresden bezeugten italienischen Steinmetzen „Johann Maria" zugeschrieben. Er wurde von den meisten Forschern mit dem aus Padua stammenden Architekten, Bildhauer und Medailleur Giovanni Maria da Padova identifiziert, der nach seiner Tätigkeit in Padua von etwa 1520-1529 in Venedig arbeitete. Dort hatte er engen Kontakt mit Jacopo Sansovino, der in Rom von Giuliano da Sangallo am Studium der antiken Bauwerke beteiligt wurde. 1529 folgte er einem Ruf nach Krakau an den Hof des polnischen Königs Sigismund I. und seiner italienischen Frau Bona Sforza.

Seine vor allem mit zahlreichen Grabmälern bis 1571 belegte Tätigkeit in Polen muss jedoch zwangsläufig nicht einem kürzeren, quellenmäßig belegten Aufenthalt von 39 Wochen in Dresden widersprechen. Auf seine besonderen Verdienste in dieser Zeit weist ein Brief des Kurfürsten August vom 28. Oktober 1553 an Hans von Dehn-Rothfelser hin, in dem er diesen anweist, die Abreise „Johann Marias" aufzuhalten, damit er ihn persönlich „mit gnaden abfertigen" kann. Hier liegt nahe, dass der Italiener wesentlich zu einem der Hauptwerke im Zusammenhang der Neugestaltung des Dresdner Schlosses beigetragen hatte, und dabei kann es sich aus zeitlichen Gründen nur um das Schlosskapellenportal handeln.[39]

Aller Wahrscheinlichkeit nach wurde „Johann Maria" noch von Kurfürst Moritz nach Dresden berufen, der auch für die Idee eines klassischen, in die Hofkapelle einführenden Triumphbogens verantwortlich gewesen sein mag und diese mit dem ehemals in Venedig tätigen Künstler zu verwirklichen glaubte.

Genial ist die Idee – möglicherweise von seinen humanistischen Beratern inspiriert – das weltliche Vorbild des Triumphes antiker und zeitgenössischer Herrscher, wie beispielsweise Kaiser Karls V., als Triumphbogen und Ruhmesdenkmal Christi umzufunktionieren.[40]

Kurzfristig nach Dresden berufen, mag „Johann Maria" für den Gesamtentwurf, Detailzeichnungen und eventuell Bozzetti für die Statuen sowie vor allem für Anweisungen an die mit

Fig. 7. Dresden, Schlosskapellenportal, nach der Aufstellung am Jüdenhof, um 1876 (Foto Landesamt für Denkmalpflege Sachsen).

Fig. 8. Dresden, Schlosskapellenportal, Architrav, Akanthusfries im Geison, Ausschnitt, Aufnahme 1968 (Landesamt für Denkmalpflege Sachsen).

ihm zusammen bezeugten sechs welschen Mitarbeiter und die beteiligten Dresdner Bildhauer – wohl wieder unter der Oberleitung des Hans Walther II – verantwortlich gewesen sein. Es steht jedoch fest, dass er ausgezeichnete Mitarbeiter in Dresden zurückgelassen hat, die bis 1555 hervorragende, äußerst feine, venezianisch beeinflusste Reliefs geschaffen haben.

Vermutlich kamen sie aus Prag, wo nach dem Burgbrand von 1541 nach einer Ruhephase das Hauptgeschoss von 1548-1552 von Paolo della Stella und seinen Mitarbeitern vollendet wurde. Da nach seinem Tod im Jahre 1552 zunächst wieder eine Ruhephase eintrat, liegt mit größter Wahrscheinlichkeit nahe, dass sechs der vierzehn italienischen Bildhauer anschließend am Schlosskapellenportal in Dresden tätig waren, zumal die politischen und kulturellen Beziehungen zwischen dem Prager und Dresdner Hof sehr freundschaftlich und eng waren.[41]

Der Akanthusfries des Schlosskapellenportals, in den groteske, meist halbvegetabile Wesen eingebunden sind (Fig. 8), gleicht dem des umlaufenden ionischen Gebälks am Belvedere. Er ist nicht nur sehr ähnlich, sondern auch viele Einzelformen stimmen fast genau überein. Der Akanthusfries über dem Architrav präsentiert sich in der Kombination mit grotesken Figuren, seiner Feinheit im Detail und gleichzeitig seiner Dichte als hochmoderne Variante bekannter antiker und zeitgenössischer Vorbilder.[42]

Ursprünglich habe ich alle anderen plastischen Ausführungen am Schlosskapellenportal eher den Dresdner Bildhauern unter der Oberleitung des Hans Walther II zugewiesen. Nachdem ich jedoch die mit Laser gereinigten Reliefs des Torbogens gesehen habe (Fig. 9), die nun eine außerordentliche Feinheit aufweisen, möchte ich diesen Bereich jetzt ebenfalls italienischen Bildhauern zuschreiben. Die sich auf drei oder vier Ebenen filigran teils mehrfach überlappenden Reliefs stellen eine Höchstleistung bildhauerischer Kunst dar. Fein übereinander liegende Blättchen und Ranken sind hohl herausgearbeitet. Die dünnen Beinchen der Vögelchen stehen frei vor dem Grund und sind erstaunlicherweise noch erhalten

Fig. 9. Dresden, Schlosskapellenportal, Rankenfries des Torbogens, linker Teil innen, nach der Reinigung mit Laser, Aufnahme 2005 (Landesamt für Denkmalpflege Sachsen).

Fig. 10. Dresden, Residenzschloss. Schlosskapellenportal, linker Zwickel mit Viktoria und Rankenfries, nach der Reinigung mit Laser, Aufnahme 2005 (Landesamt für Denkmalpflege Sachsen).

– unglaublich nach 450 Jahren und dem Schicksal des Portals! Die häufigen Anstriche, die die Feinheit der Reliefs verkennen ließen, stellten in gewisser Weise eben auch einen guten „Schutz" dar.

Die in den Zwickeln des Torbogens lagernden Viktorien, die Blumenkränze und Palmwedel wie ihre antiken Vorbilder tragen, jedoch keine Flügel aufweisen, zeigen nun bei der mit Laser gereinigten linken Figur eine außerordentliche Feinheit in der Gestaltung des wie nass anliegenden, fein gefälteten Gewandes und der komplizierten antikischen Frisur (Fig. 10).

Das Besondere und Einzigartige des Dresdner Schlosskapellenportals ist die Idee, mit dem eindeutigen Rückgriff auf einen streng klassischen, römischen Triumphbogen, der Siegeszeichen der zum Gott erhobenen Kaiser war, sinnbildlich protestantische Anliegen zu verwirklichen. Triumphator ist der über der Attika stehende auferstandene Christus mit der Siegesfahne. Sein „Siegeszug" ist auf dem darunter befindlichen Attikarelief dargestellt. Begleitet wurde der Christus triumphator, der Sieger über Tod und Teufel, ursprünglich von den drei christlichen Tugenden, Fides mit dem Kreuz und dem Kelch, Spes und Caritas sowie von der Fortitudo mit der Säule, während in den seitlichen Nischen darunter Vertreter des Alten und Neuen Testaments auf ihn Bezug nehmen und gleichwohl als Kronzeugen seines Sieges auftreten. Die in den Zwickeln lagernden antikischen Viktorien bekräftigen den Sieg des triumphalen Christus und seiner begleitenden Tugenden.[43]

Der protestantische Charakter des ikonographischen Programms wird besonders in der Gegenüberstellung von Sünde und Erlösung deutlich, denn auf der mit reichen Schnitzereien geschmückten Holztür des Portals erscheint

Fig. 11. Dresden, Residenzschloss, Schlosskapellenportal (1555) mit der Holztür (1556), Aufnahme Ende des 19. Jahrhunderts (Staats- und Universitätsbibliothek Dresden).

als zentrales Relief die biblische Geschichte von „Christus und der Ehebrecherin", die hier als Bild der vergebenden Gnade, einem Hauptgedanken der lutherischen Theologie, zu deuten ist (Fig. 11).[44]

Während das Portal auf den Feldern zwischen beiden Seitennischen „MDLV" datiert ist, wurde die Holztür erst ein Jahr später fertig gestellt. Unter den Wappen der Chur und Sachsens erscheint zwischen dem Pilaster und der Säule links und rechts des hier in modifizierter Form aufgegriffenen Triumphbogens die Jahresangabe „ANNO / MDLVI". In der bekrönenden Kartusche, die gleichzeitig Mittelpunkt des gesamten Schlosskapellenportals ist, steht die offensichtlich von den ernestinischen Wettinern übernommene, hier erstmals verwendete, abgekürzte Devise „VDMIE" – „Verbum Domini manet in (a)eternum" – (Das Wort Gottes bleibt in Ewigkeit) für das protestantische Bekenntnis.

Nach Moritz' frühem Tod in der Schlacht bei Sievershausen 1553 führte dessen Bruder, Kurfürst August, der mit der dänischen Prinzessin Anna verheiratet war, im Sinne seines älteren Bruders alle Bau- und Ausstattungsmaßnahmen, von denen ich hier lediglich einen knappen Einblick vermitteln kann, weiter. Unberücksichtigt bleiben mussten unter anderem die Innenraumgestaltungen, die ähnlichen Prämissen folgten.

Notes

*   Forschungsstand Ende 2006.

1   Vgl. u. a. die neuesten Forschungen zum Dresdner Residenzschloss – *Das Dresdner Schloss. Monument sächsischer Geschichte und Kultur*, Dresden 1992³; Heinrich Magirius, "Das Renaissanceschloß der Wettiner als Herrschaftsarchitektur der albertinischen Wettiner", *Dresdner Hefte* 38 (1994), 20-31; Ulrike Heckner, *Im Dienst von Fürsten und Reformation. Fassadenmalerei an den Schlössern in Dresden und Neuburg an der Donau im 16. Jahrhundert*, München 1995; Brunhilde Gonschor, "Die Bilddarstellungen des 16. Jahrhunderts im Großen Hof des Dresdner Schlosses", in: *Denkmalpflege in Sachsen 1894–1994*, II, Halle an der Saale 1998, 333-375; Angelica Dülberg, "'... weitaus die edelste Portalcomposition der ganzen deutschen Renaissance.' Zum Schloßkapellenportal des Dresdner Residenzschlosses", *Wallraf-Richartz-Jahrbuch* 63 (2002), 197-216; Angelica Dülberg, "'... weitaus die edelste Portalcomposition der ganzen deutschen Renaissance.' Geschichte und Ikonographie des Dresdner Schlosskapellenportals", *Denkmalpflege in Sachsen. Jahrbuch 2004* (2005), 52-80; Angelica Dülberg, Norbert Oelsner & Rosemarie Pohlack, *Das Dresdner Residenzschloss*, Berlin & München 2009.

2   Simon Issleib, *Aufsätze und Beiträge zu Kurfürst Moritz von Sachsen (1877–1907)*, Nachdruck, Köln & Wien 1989, I, 231; Friedrich Albert von Langenn, *Moritz, Herzog und Churfürst zu Sachsen*, I, Leipzig 1841, 416-417.

3   Ernst Guldan, "Die Aufnahme italienischer Bau- und Dekorationsformen in Deutschland zu Beginn der Neuzeit", in: *Arte e Artisti dei Laghi Lombardi, I. Architetti e Scultori del Quattrocento*, Como 1959, 381-391, spez. 386.

4   Sächsisches Hauptstaatsarchiv Dresden, Loc. 9125, *Die Bew, Festung, geschütz vnnd munition belangend, 1549–1550*, Bl. 23.

5   Matthias Müller, *Das Schloß als Bild des Fürsten. Herrschaftliche Metaphorik in der Residenzarchitektur des Alten Reiches*, Göttingen 2004, 83-88.

6   Vgl. u. a. Peter Gerlach, "Herkules", in: *Lexikon der christlichen Ikonographie*, II, Rom, Freiburg, Basel & Wien 1990 (Sonderausgabe), 243-246; Wolfger Bulst, "Samson", in: *Lexikon christlichen Ikonograhie*, IV, 1990, 30-38; Hannelore Sachs, Ernst Badstübner & Helga Neumann, *Erklärendes Wörterbuch zur christlichen Kunst*, Hanau s.a., 317- 318; Jutta Seibert, *Lexikon christlicher Kunst. Themen, Gestalten, Symbole*, Freiberg, Basel & Wien 2002, 139, 288-289 ; Sabine Poeschel, *Handbuch der Ikonographie. Sakrale und profane Themen der bildenden Kunst*, Darmstadt 2005, 328-336, spez. 329; ebd. 73f.

7   Bulst 1990, 32.

8   Peter Gerlach, "Hirsch", in: *Lexikon christlichen Ikonographie*, II, 1990, 286-289; Seibert 2002, 144-145; Sachs, Badstübner & Neumann s.a., 181.

9   Leonie Reygers, "Abel und Kain", in: *Reallexikon zur deutschen Kunstgeschichte*, I, Stuttgart 1937, 17-27; George Henderson, "Abel und Kain", in: *Lexikon christlichen Ikonographie*, I, 1990, 5-10; Sachs, Badstübner & Neumann s.a., 204-205; Seibert 2002, 8-9; Poeschel 2005, 41.

10 Seibert 2002, 8-9.

11 Vgl. Ulrich Bischoff, "Wilder Mann mit Keule", in: *Der Mensch um 1500. Werke aus Kirchen und Kunstsammlungen*, Berlin 1977, 161-166; Angelica Dülberg, *Privatporträts. Geschichte und Ikonologie einer Gattung im 15. und 16. Jahrhundert*, Berlin 1990, 114-116.

12 Bischoff 1977, 164; Dülberg 1990, 114-116.

13 Wolfram Prinz & Ronald G. Kecks, *Das französische Schloss der Renaissance. Form und Bedeutung der Architektur, ihre geschichtliche und gesellschaftliche Grundlage,* Berlin 1994, 267-280; Matthias Müller, "Capriccio oder Politikum? Überlegungen zu ungewöhnlichen Treppentürmen an deutschen und französischen Renaissanceschlössern", in: Andreas Beyer, Ulrich Schütte & Lutz Unbehaun (eds.), *Die Künste und das Schloß in der frühen Neuzeit,* München & Berlin 1998, 131-149; Matthias Müller, "Das Schloß als fürstliches Manifest. Zur Architekturmetaphorik in den wettinischen Residenzschlössern von Meißen und Torgau", in: *Hochadelige Herrschaft im mitteldeutschen Raum (1200 bis 1600), Formen – Legitimation – Repräsentation,* Stuttgart 2003, 395-441; Müller 2004, 188-210.

14 Brunhild Werner, *Das Kurfürstliche Schloss in Dresden im 16. Jahrhundert.* Dissertation, Leipzig 1970, 130. Müller übernimmt Werners Vermutungen unkritisch. Müller 2004, 84-85.

15 Das "Kunstbüchlein" wurde erstmals 1538 gedruckt, es folgten Nachdrucke 1539, 1540, 1545, 1559 und 1572. Heinrich Vogtherr, *Ein Frembdes vnd wunderbares Kunstbüchlein,* Straßburg 1559, [4, unten rechts und 5, oben rechts]; *Heinrich Vogtherr's Kunstbüchlein,* Straßburg 1572, Zwickau 1913, [4, unten rechts und 5, oben rechts]; Jutta Funke, *Beiträge zum Werk Heinrich Vogtherrs d. Ä.,* Dissertation, Berlin 1967, 54-66; Frank Muller, *Heinrich Vogtherr l'Ancien. Un artiste entre Renaissance et Réforme,* Wiesbaden 1997, 296-299, Abb. S. 299.

16 Prinz & Kecks 1994, 302-308, Abb. 346 d. Im Jagellonen-Mausoleum an der Südseite der Krakauer Kathedrale erscheinen ebenfalls reich mit Figuren und Grotesken verzierte Kapitele. Vgl. Adam Bochnak, *Das Krakauer Jagellonen-Mausoleum,* Warsaw 1954, Abb. 54, 56-57.

17 Vgl. u. a. Kurt Löcher, *Barthel Beham. Ein Maler aus dem Dürerkreis,* München & Berlin 1999, 47-52.

18 Die männliche Terme kommt auch am Portal des Piastenschlosses in Brieg vor. Albert Brinckmann, *Die praktische Bedeutung der Ornamentstiche für die deutsche Frührenaissance,* Strassburg 1907, 31, Taf. 6; Sune Schéle, *Cornelis Bos. A study of the Origins of the Netherland Grotesque,* Stockholm 1965, 147-148, Pl. 28, No. 82, Pl. 31, No. 96.

19 Schéle 1965, 172, Pl. 39, No. 131.

20 Vgl. Walter Friedensburg, *Die Chronik der Cerbonio Besozzi, 1548-1563,* Wien 1904, 12; *Romanino. Un pittore in rivolta nel Rinascimento italiano.* Ausstellungskatalog, Trient & Mailand 2006, 422, nr. 133, 134.

21 Langenn 1841, 416-417; Issleib 1989, 231.

22 *Das Dresdner Schloss* 1992, Umschlagbild, 16, Abb. 5. Weitere bildliche Quellen für die Sgraffiti-Ausstattung, insbesondere des Großen Schlosshofs, sind: Heinrich Göding d. Ä., Ringstechen im Großen Schlosshof (Nordflügel, Teile des West- und Ostflügels), Öl auf Holz, um 1590, verschollen; Daniel Brettschneider, Das Ringstechen im Großen Schlosshof zur Fastnacht 1609 (Südflügel), Gouache, Sächsische Landesbibliothek – Staats- und Universitätsbibliothek Dresden; Daniel Brettschneider, Aufzug der Zeit und der sieben Planeten am 28. Juni 1613 (Südflügel, kleiner Teil des Ostflügels), Öl auf Leinwand, Dresden, Staatliche Kunstsammlungen, Rüstkammer; Hetzjagd am 19. September 1614 auf der Elbe (Außenansicht des Schlosses von Norden), Ölgemälde, verschollen, ehemals Schloss Moritzburg; Andreas Vogel, Dresdner Schloss aus der Vogelperspektive, a) von Südosten, 1621, b) von Nordwesten, 1623, Öl auf Holz, verschollen; Ringstechen im Großen Schlosshof, Miniaturkopie des Gemäldes von Heinrich Göding d. Ä., Gouache, 1645; Tierhatz im großen Schlosshof unter Johann Georg II., Blick von Süden, Ölgemälde, um 1680, verschollen; Die nördliche, östliche, südliche, westliche Hoffassade des Dresdner Schlosses, Kupferstiche aus Tzschimmer, 1680; Das Dresdner Schloss aus der Vogelperspektive von Süden, Kupferstich aus der Weck'schen Chronik, 1680; Die nördliche Hoffassade des Dresdner Schlosses, Kupferstich aus der Weck'schen Chronik, 1680. George Christian Fritzsche, Aufzug der Wagen und Reiter zum Damenfest am 6. Juni 1709 (Ansicht des Schlosses von Norden), Gouache, Dresden, Staatliche Kunstsammlungen, Kupferstich-Kabinett. Vgl. auch Heckner 1995, Abb. 7a/b, 14-34, 36; Gonschor 1998, 336, Anm. 6, Abb. 3, 5, 10, 10a, 19, 22, 24-32, 38-40.

23 Vgl. Magirius, in: *Das Dresdner Schloss* 1992, 75; Magirius 1994, 26-27; Heckner 1995, 60; Gonschor 1998, 369-375.

24 Vgl. Heckner 1995, 57-60. Bei der Gestalt mit dem aufgespießten Kopf handelt es sich allerdings eindeutig um David mit dem empor gehaltenen Haupt des Goliath. Auch die Vermutung Heckners, dass die Ess- und Trinkgeschirre im darunter befindlichen Metopenfries sich auf die Judith-Geschichte beziehen, die sie fälschlicherweise als Hauptthema der Südfassade annimmt, kann aufgrund des gesamten ähnlichen Metopen-Programms rund um den Hof widerlegt werden. Einzig die sich über zwei Felder im 2. Obergeschoss erstreckende Szene der mit Pfeilen auf den an einem Baum gebundenen Achior zielenden Männer nimmt Beziehung zur Judith-Geschichte auf. In den anderen Feldern zwischen den Fenstern sind fast ausschließlich Einzelfiguren dargestellt, möglicherweise handelt es sich hier um Vertreter der neun Helden und auch neun Heldinnen, wie neben Judith Esther, die auf die hervorragenden Tugenden des Kurfürsten Moritz hinweisen.

Näheres dazu Angelica Dülberg, in: *Das Residenzschloss der Wettiner im historischen Wandel* (in Bearbeitung).

25 Magirius 1994, 26; Heckner 1995, 49; Gonschor 1998, 337.

26 Werner Schade, "Maler am Hofe Moritz' von Sachsen", *Zeitschrift des deutschen Vereins für Kunstwissenschaft* 21 (1968), 29-44, spez. 36-40; Magirius, in: *Das Dresdner Schloss* 1992, 77; Magirius 1994, 26-27; Heckner 1995, 42-43, 50–57, Abb. 37; Gonschor 1998, 342-346.

27 Heckner 1995, Abb. 39-40.

28 Heckner 1995, 53-57.

29 Heckner 1995, 53-57.

30 Magirius, in: *Das Dresdner Schloss* 1992, 77; Heckner 1995, 47; Gonschor 1998, 339-342.

31 Der größte Teil der erhaltenen Fragmente zeigt fein geglättete Rückseiten, was auf Originale des 16. Jahrhunderts hindeutet, während zwei Fragmente der rechten Schmalseite wesentlich dicker sind und sehr grobe, unbearbeitete Rückseiten aufweisen. Auch stilistisch besteht ein großer Unterschied, was darauf hindeutet, dass es sich hier um Kopien des 19. Jahrhunderts handelt. Man kann daraus schlussfolgern, dass die alten Fotos vor dem Zweiten Weltkrieg weitgehend die Originale des 16. Jahrhunderts zeigen.

32 Hermann Degering (ed.), *Faksimile nach der Ausgabe der Bibel von Martin Luther 1545 mit dem Bilderschmuck des in der Preußischen Staatsbibliothek befindlichen Pergamentexemplars der Ausgabe 1541, das von Lucas Cranach für den Fürsten Johann II. von Anhalt illuminiert wurde,* Berlin 1927, Abb. S. 335, 339, 342, 348; Konrad Kratsch (ed.), *Illuminierte Holzschnitte der Luther-Bibel von 1534. Eine Bildauswahl,* Berlin 1982, 30-35.

33 Magirius 1994, 27; Heckner 1995, 19-21; Gonschor 1998, 369-375.

34 Magirius, in: *Das Dresdner Schloss* 1992, 79; Heckner 1995, 45; Gonschor 1998, 351-353; Dülberg 2002; Dülberg 2005; Heinrich Magirius, *Die evangelische Schlosskapelle zu Dresden aus kunstgeschichtlicher Sicht*, Altenburg 2009.

35 Magirius, in: *Das Dresdner Schloss* 1992, 78 (Abb.).

36 Dülberg 2002, 205; Dülberg 2005, 61.

37 Dülberg 2002, 202-203; Dülberg 2005, 58-59.

38 Dülberg 2002, 203-204; Dülberg 2005, 59-60, Abb. 10-12.

39 Dülberg 2002, 204-206; Dülberg 2005, 60-63.

40 Dülberg 2005, 62, 71-74.

41 Dülberg 2002, 205, 207-208; Dülberg 2005, 62, 64-65.

42 Dülberg 2005, 63-64, Abb. 17.

43 Dülberg 2002, 212-213; Dülberg 2005, 71-74.

44 Dülberg 2002, 212-213, Abb. 21; Dülberg 2005, 74, Abb. 49-50.

ANNABURG UND LICHTENBURG.
SCHLOSSBAUTEN DES KURFÜRSTEN AUGUST VON SACHSEN
UND SEINER GEMAHLIN ANNA VON DÄNEMARK

Mario Titze

Die Hochzeit des Herzogs August von Sachsen 1548, ein Jahr nach der Erlangung der Kurwürde durch seinen älteren Bruder Moritz, gehörte zu den ersten Akten der Standesrepräsentation der neuen kurfürstlichen Familie. Die Eheschließung des zweitgeborenen sächsischen Herzogs mit der königlichen Prinzessin Anna von Dänemark war ohne Zweifel eine dynastisch begründete Verbindung, der nicht zuletzt auch religions- und bündnispolitische Überlegungen zugrunde lagen. Daß die Hochzeit auf Schloß Hartenfels in Torgau, der Residenz des von Moritz besiegten früheren ernestinischen Kurfürsten Johann Friedrich, gefeiert wurde, während jener sich zur gleichen Zeit in kaiserlicher Gefangenschaft befand, verlieh der Eheschließung zusätzlich einen symbolhaft-triumphalen Aspekt, denn sie dokumentierte unmißverständlich den Aufstieg der jüngeren Linie des Hauses Wettin in die erste Reihe der europäischen Herrscherfamilien.

Nach dem frühen Tod Moritz' 1553 folgte August ihm im Amt des Kurfürsten. Hatte Moritz die politischen Entscheidungen für die Entstehung des frühneuzeitlichen sächsischen Staates herbeigeführt, so konsolidierte August die albertinische Herrschaft durch den Rückzug aus einer allzu ambitionierten Außenpolitik, durch die konsequente Straffung der inneren Verwaltung und durch die zielgerichtete Modernisierung der Wirtschaft. In einer 33 Jahre währenden, friedlichen Regentschaft wurde er zum eigentlichen Begründer des albertinischen Kurfürstentums Sachsen. Seine Gemahlin Anna spielte dabei eine nicht unwesentliche Rolle.

Viele der unter Kurfürst August errichteten Schloßbauten dienten mit ihrer Repräsentativität und mit zum Teil sehr eindeutiger Symbolik der Etablierung der neuen, nunmehr albertinischen Dynastie. Weithin bekannt ist das ganz und gar denkmalhaft konzipierte Schloß Augustusburg, das den Sieg Augusts über seine ernestinischen Widersacher architektonisch überhöhen sollte.

Unter den ca. 50 kurfürstlichen Bauvorhaben dominierten die Erweiterung des Residenzschlosses in Dresden, Um- und Neubauten an Orten säkularisierten kirchlichen Besitzes und im ehemals ernestinischen Kurkreis.

Im Kurkreis wurde unter August das schon von Moritz begonnene Schloß in Mühlberg, am Ort des Sieges über die Ernestiner, vollendet. August selbst ließ darüber hinaus Schlösser in Glücksburg, Bleesern[1], Annaburg und Lichtenburg erbauen. Sie dienten der demonstrativen Inbesitznahme des neu erworbenen Landes und zeigen Kurfürst August als selbstbewußten, dem äußerlichen Ansehen der Dynastie verpflichteten, modernen Reichsfürsten.

Fig. 1. Annaburg, Schloß, Ansicht vom Vorschloß (Foto Landesamt für Denkmalpflege und Archäologie, Sachsen-Anhalt, Halle).

Der königliche Rang der Kurfürstin war dabei einer der entscheidenden qualitativen Maßstäbe.

Schloß Annaburg

Zwischen 1571 und 1573 wurde Schloß Annaburg (Fig. 1,2) unter der Leitung des kurfürstlichen Baumeisters Christoph Tendler an der Stelle des Schlosses Lochau neu errichtet.[2] Lochau besaß für die Landesgeschichte große Bedeutung. Die Burg befand sich seit 1290 in sächsischem Besitz. 1422 führte eine Brandkatastrophe hier zum Aussterben der askanischen Dynastie und wurde zur Voraussetzung für die Belehnung der Wettiner mit dem Herzogtum Sachsen und der sächsischen Kurwürde. 1525 verstarb in dem von ihm erneuerten spätgotischen Schloß Lochau Kurfürst Friedrich der Weise. Ganz in der Nähe wurden nach der Schlacht von Mühlberg Kurfürst Johann Friedrich und Landgraf Philipp von Hessen am 24. April 1547 gefangen genommen. 1551 handelten die Abgesandten Kurfürst Moritz', Markgraf Georg Friedrichs von Brandenburg-Ansbach, Herzog Johann Albrechts von Mecklenburg, Landgraf Wilhelms von Hessen und des französischen Königs Heinrich II. in Lochau den Vertrag von Chambord aus.

Lochau hatte dem kurfürstlichen Jagdaufenthalt gedient und war von Tiergehegen, Teichen, Gärten und Kanälen umgeben. Diese wurden mit dem Neubau großzügig erweitert und bis 1577 vervollständigt. Unmittelbar am Schloß entstandenen ausgedehnte Gartenanlagen mit einem Lusthaus, dessen toskanische Säulen sich in der Loggia des Amtshauses erhalten haben.[3] Die großen Teiche des Gartens und die Kanäle waren miteinander verbunden; die Kurfürsten und ihre Gäste unternahmen darauf Lustfahrten in Kähnen, für die ein dänischer Schiffer namens Michael Stöhr verantwortlich war.

Trotz der durchgehenden Erneuerung behielten August und Anna die Besonderheiten des schon von Friedrich dem Weisen als persönli-

Fig. 2. Annaburg, Schloß, Gartenseite (Foto Landesamt für Denkmalpflege und Archäologie, Sachsen-Anhalt).

ches Refugium genutzten Ortes bei. Durch die Trennung der unterschiedlichen Funktionen wurde der private Charakter des Anwesens noch verstärkt. Wie Lochau bildet auch Schloß Annaburg einen Komplex aus Vor- und Hinterschloß. Das Hinterschloß diente ausschließlich der Wohnnutzung des kurfürstlichen Paars, während im Vorderschloß Verwaltung, Wirtschaftsräume und Ställe konzentriert waren.

Vor dem Schloß wurden bis 1575 Wohnhäuser für Hofbeamte errichtet, deren Wohnungen sich früher innerhalb des alten Schlosses befunden hatten: für den kurfürstlichen Kammermeister, den Schosser oder Amtmann, den Forstmeister, den Wildmeister, den Fischmeister, den Röhrenmeister und andere. Christoph Tendler ordnete diese auf kurfürstlichen Befehl unmittelbar vor dem Schloß um einen regelmäßigen, langgestreckten Platz an[4] und schuf damit eine auf das Schloß ausgerichtete Planstadt, die frühe Variante einer absolutistischen Residenzstadt.

Seit 1573 gibt es für Lochau die Bezeichnung „Annaburg", wobei in den ersten Jahren auch der Name „Annenfels" auftaucht, der sich angesichts der Lage in der flachen Waldniederung aber nicht durchzusetzen vermochte. Beide Namen beziehen sich jedoch auf die Kurfürstin, als deren geplante Witwenresidenz Annaburg gilt. Das friedvolle Refugium, eingebettet in eine weite Garten- und Teichlandschaft, entspricht ganz der Vorstellung von der Retirade einer verwitweten Königin. Es bildet auch nicht zufällig das typologische Gegenstück zur festungsartig auf einer Bergkuppe thronenden und auftrumpfenden Augustusburg.

Der private Charakter des Hinterschlosses zeigt sich in seiner Geschlossenheit, in dem auf die persönlichen Bedürfnisse zugeschnittenen Raumprogramm, in der Trennung von Hofstube und fürstlichem Tafelgemach, in der stubenartigen Kleinheit der Räume, ebenso in deren Bequemlichkeit und Komfort. Annaburg war für mehr als 10 Jahre ein bevorzugter Aufenthaltsort

Fig.3. Annaburg, Schloß, gußeiserne Ofenplatte mit kursächsischem und dänischem Wappen, Seitenplatte des „Kurfürstlichen Wappen-Ofens", um 1570, Kurfürstliche Gießhütte Königstein, Gießer: Georg Schwarz, Entwurf: Ambrosius Walther (?) (Foto Landesamt für Denkmalpflege und Archäologie, Sachsen-Anhalt).

des kurfürstlichen Paars. Kurfürstin Anna besaß hier eine persönliche Handbibliothek, ein alchimistisches Laboratorium und ein Destillierhaus, wo sie Aquavit brannte, den sie an befreundete Fürstenhöfe schickte. Im Garten wurden dafür Heilpflanzen angebaut. Anna verfaßte 10 Arzneibücher, richtete 1581 die Dresdner Hofapotheke ein und gilt als „erste deutsche Apothekerin".

Kurfürst August verfügte in seinem Appartement über eine Schreibstube und eine Drechselstube. Er unterhielt eine Buchdruckerei, und in Annaburg befand sich auch die kurfürstliche Bibliothek mit einem Bestand von über 2300 Büchern. Als August und Anna älter wurden und ihnen das Treppensteigen schwerer fiel, wurde 1585 ein Turm mit einer Reitertreppe vor dem Großen Haus errichtet, durch den man die kurfürstlichen Wohnräume bequem zu Pferde oder im Tragstuhl erreichen konnte.

Von der Strenge des Schlosses Augustusburg unterscheidet Annaburg sich trotz der deutlichen Tendenz zur Zentralisierung und Regularisierung durch eine gewisse Ungebundenheit des Grundrisses und die Auflockerung des Umrisses. Risalitartige Standerker beleben die Wandflächen. Die turmartig die Fassaden überragenden Zwerchhäuser verleihen dem Bau Distanz und ehrfurchtgebietende Würde. Bezeichnenderweise markieren sie vor allem die Fassade zum vorderen Schloßhof, für die Wahrnehmung durch Ankommende, zum halböffentlichen Ort der Verwaltung und Bewirtschaftung. Zum Garten zeigt das Schloß eine ruhige, glatte Fassade.

Die Eckrisalite dienten ganz dem wohnlichen Komfort, denn als dreiseitig durchfensterte Kabinette gehörten sie zu den lichtesten und schönsten Räumen des Schlosses, die zudem ungehinderte Ausblicke auf die Umgebung ermöglichten. Sie nahmen die privatesten Räume des Kurfürsten auf, seine Schreibstube, die Betstube, die Dreh- oder Drechselstube und seine Kammer. Das Gemach der Kurfürstin befand sich im Risalit über dem Tor.

Das Innere war ganz der Würde eines der ranghöchsten und zugleich wohlhabendsten Reichsfürsten und seiner königlichen Gemahlin verpflichtet.[5] Die Räume besaßen golden und silbern geprägte Ledertapeten, es gab vergoldete und versilberte Betten, Alabastertische, Tische mit Marmorplatten, farblich auf die Wandbespannungen abgestimmte, mit Leder bezogene Stühle, Schmuckfußböden und an den Decken Flasern. Die Ausmalungen der Räume und die Entwürfe für die Flasern schuf der Dresdner Hofmaler Heinrich Göding. Hans Schroer aus Lüttich malte einen Zyklus aus 36 biblischen Darstellungen für die Schloßkapelle[6], das Altarbild lieferte Lucas Cranach d. J.

Trotz aller Privatheit wies Annaburg ein auf die Dynastie bezogenes ikonographisches Dekorationsprogramm auf: Die Schlußsteine der Kapelle zierten die Wappen des Herzogtums Sachsen, der sächsischen Kurwürde und des Königreichs Dänemark; sächsisch-dänische Allianzwappen schmückten die Eisenplatten der Öfen (Fig. 3), und auch die Flaserdecken zeigen Wappendarstellungen, die den hohen Rang des Kurfürstenpaars zur Geltung brachten.

Schloß Lichtenburg

1577 begann ganz in der Nähe Annaburgs der Neubau eines Schlosses am Ort des ehemaligen Antoniter-Generalpräzeptorates Lichtenberg.[7]

In dem nach der Säkularisation leerstehenden Antoniterhaus hatte von 1536 bis 1545 durch die Hilfe Martin Luthers die zum evangelischen Glauben konvertierte brandenburgische Kurfürstin Elisabeth von Dänemark, Tochter König Hans', Zuflucht gefunden. Dem Neubau des Schlosses 1577-1582 ging der Abbruch der Klostergebäude voraus. Noch vor dem Schloßbau begann der Neubau des kurfürstlichen Vorwerkes. Die Antoniter hatten seit dem 14. Jahrhundert den Obst- und Gemüse- sowie den Weinanbau in der Region kultiviert. Der umfangreiche Landbesitz des Klostergutes gehörte schon seit 1540 zum kurfürstlichen Kammergut. August baute das Vorwerk zum landwirtschaftlichen Mustergut aus. Das nunmehr Lichtenburg genannte Schloß wurde zum fürstlichen Gutshaus.

Schloß und Gutshof stellen eine annähernd symmetrisch aufeinander bezogene Gesamtanlage dar, die durch ein gemeinsames Torhaus erschlossen wird. Das Torhaus wird von zwei etwa gleich großen, zweigeschossigen Flügeln flankiert. Dahinter befinden sich im Westen der Schloßhof und im Osten der Gutshof (Fig. 4).

Die für Annaburg charakteristische Trennung zwischen Vorder- und Hinterschloß ist hier zugunsten einer weitgehenden Vereinheitlichung der Gesamtanlage und der Differenzierung von Schloß- und Gutshof aufgehoben. Das Vorderschloß wird zum vorgelagerten, niedrigeren Flügel, der Vorhof zum Binnenhof. Das fürstliche Wohngebäude umschließt keinen Innenhof, sondern öffnet sich in ganzer Breite zur umgebenden Landschaft.[8]

Auch Lichtenburg besteht aus einzelnen Häusern, wie Dresden, Freiberg, Augustusburg oder Annaburg, aber hier sind sie durch gleiche Trauf- und Firstlinien, rhythmisch angeordnete Zwerchhäuser, durchgehende Fluchten und Geschoßebenen, regelmäßige Fensterachsen und glatte Wandflächen in bisher nie gekannter Weise zusammengefaßt. Die separierten Häuser der älteren Schlösser sind hier zu Flügeln einer regularisierten Gesamtanlage zusammengewachsen. Im mittleren Stutzflügel zur Gartenseite wird die Raumwirkung der allseits durchfensterten Kabinette in den Eckerkern von Annaburg auf große, saalartige Räume angewendet, was ein vollkommen neues Wohngefühl ermöglicht. Die leichte Verschiebung des Schlosses aus der Achse des Vorwerks dient der Aufweitung des Hofes, der Belichtung der hofseitigen Räume, und läßt trotz der relativen Enge des Hofes, durch die perspektivische Erweiterung, das kurfürstliche Wohnhaus monumental zur Wirkung kommen.

Die Einheit von Schloß und Gutshof ist Bestandteil einer für den sächsischen Schloßbau bahnbrechend neuen Konzeption. Sie reflektiert auf der einen Seite italienische Vorbilder und steht auf der anderen mit den augusteischen Wirtschaftsreformen in enger Verbindung.

Diese merkantilistischen Reformen beinhalteten die Erprobung und Förderung neuartiger Produktionsmethoden.[9] Dazu gehörte neben der Intensivierung des Bergbaus und der Förderung des Handels auch die Effektivierung der Landwirtschaft, die seit 1567, nach Mißernten und Teuerungen, verstärkt in Augusts Blickfeld trat. Er beschäftigte sich persönlich mit Felderaufteilungen, Fruchtfolgen, verfaßte ein „künstliches Obst- und Gartenbüchlein" und veranlaßte die Herausgabe des Lehrbuches „Haushaltung in Vorwerken". Die kurfürstlichen Kammergüter wurden zu Musterwirtschaften mit beabsichtigter Vorbildwirkung. Dazu gehörten neben anderen das Ostra-Vorwerk bei Dresden, Bleesern bei Wittenberg und Lichtenburg. Kurfürstin Anna hatte daran unmittelbaren Anteil; Ostra galt als Vorwerk der Kurfürstin, wie auch Lichtenburg zu ihrem Leibgedinge gehörte, das heißt, ihren persönlichen Einkünften diente.

Die wissenschaftliche Hinwendung zur Landwirtschaft als Voraussetzung für die Landeskultivierung war in Italien Teil humanistischen Selbstverständnisses. Es fußte auf Überlieferungen antiker Autoren wie Plinius d. J. und fand in zahlreichen Schriften zeitgenössischer Gelehrter von Leone Battista Alberti bis Alvise Cornaro seinen theoretischen und in den aristokratischen Villeggiaturen der venetischen Terraferma seinen architektonischen Ausdruck. Unter dem Einfluß italienischer Berater muß die Idee der Villa suburbana als Ort edler Muße und staatswirtschaftlichen Zielen dienenden Landbaus am Dresdner Hof eingeführt worden sein.

Zu den allgemeinen Merkmalen, die Lichtenburg von den älteren einheimischen Schloßbauten unterscheiden, gehören die Vereinheitlichung der Baukörper, ihre Reduktion auf klare kubische Formen, die regelmäßige Gliederung der glatt geputzten Fassaden, ihre betonte Horizontalität, die Öffnung zur Landschaft und die Verbindung von Innenräumen und freier Natur – Merkmale, die auch die italienischen Villeggiaturen charakterisieren.[10]

Über die Elbe war das Kammergut Lichtenburg mit Dresden verbunden. Es erhob sich abseits der Stadt Prettin, inmitten von Gärten, Feldern und Wiesen. Das fürstliche Haus ist auf den Hof und den Garten gleichermaßen orientiert. Die vielfach durchfensterten Räume der Gartenseite und der Flügel bieten weite Ausblicke auf die umgebende Landschaft.

Von besonderer Bedeutung ist dafür die doppelgeschossige, belvedereartige Loggia (Fig. 5), die sich, im Gegensatz zu vergleichbaren Hofarkaden wie in Wittenberg, Torgau, Dresden, Krakau, Güstrow und auch Annaburg, nicht zum Innenhof öffnet, sondern ins Freie. Kein anderes Schloß dieser Zeit ist architektonisch so unmittelbar mit dem Garten und den umliegenden landwirtschaftlichen Nutzflächen verbunden. Das von der Hofloggia des Dresdner Schlosses inspirierte Arkadenmotiv zitiert gewiß nicht zufällig italienische Vorbilder.

Eine zweite Loggia im Hof betont neben dem Portal den einzigen vor die Fassade tretenden Erkerrisalit, ein architektonisches Würdezeichen vor den herrschaftlichen Gemächern.

Fig. 4. Prettin, Schloß Lichtenburg (Foto Landesamt für Denkmalpflege und Archäologie, Sachsen-Anhalt).

Das Haupthaus ist im Erdgeschoß durchgehend gewölbt, über toskanischen Säulen oder als großzügig-repräsentative Pfeilerhalle. Die fürstlichen Wohnräume weisen bemalte Holzbalkendecken in reicher Variantenvielfalt auf.

Die wenigen bisher freigelegten Wandfassungen zeigen illusionistische Malereien (Fig. 6, 7), die italienische Vorbilder unmittelbar reflektieren. Sie weisen das von dort vertraute Formengut aus Architekturillusion, Landschaftsausblicken, trompe-l-œil-Kunststücken und gemalten Wandnischen mit scheinbar darin aufgestellten vergoldeten Bronzefiguren auf. Die Malereien sind einem internationalen höfischen Stil verpflichtet, der allen hochrangigen kurfürstlichen Bauvorhaben seit dem Beginn der Erweiterung der Dresdner Residenz eigen ist. Vergleichbare Dekorationen schuf Nosseni für das kurfürstliche Lusthaus auf der Dresdner Jungfernbastei. Die kurfürstliche Begräbniskapelle in Freiberg ist – dreidimensional – nach dem gleichen Prinzip ausgestaltet.

Der Verweis auf stilistische Parallelen erklärt jedoch nur einen Aspekt. Kaum weniger wichtig ist die typologische Verwandtschaft mit den aristokratischen Villeggiaturen der venetischen Terraferma, die exakt nach dem gleichen Muster dekoriert sind und für Lichtenburg ohne Zweifel vorbildlich waren.

Innerhalb der Dresdner Hofkunst stehen die Lichtenburger Malereien den Wandbildern der Brüder Gabriele und Benedetto Tola im Residenzschloß am nächsten. Für die Ausführung könnte Heinrich Göding in Frage kommen. *Die nur in einem Rest erhaltenen Schmuckfußböden aus Serpentin und Alabaster wurden von dem seit 1575 am kurfürstlichen Hof angestellten Giovanni Maria Nosseni und seinen italienischen Mitarbeitern geschaffen. Nosseni fertigte für Lichtenburg darüber hinaus kostbare edelsteinbesetzte Prunkmöbel und plante offenbar auch Raumausmalungen.[11] Am 21. November 1580 schrieb er an Kurfürst August, er habe „zu vorfertigung der lichtenbergisch arbeit, etliche erfarne, kunstreiche und wolgeubte wellische gesellen bey der hant: deren gleichen ich nicht alwege haben kann Die ich mit schweren unkost ins Landt ... gebracht".[12] Man geht sicher nicht fehl, ihm einen Hauptanteil an der typologischen Konzeption des Schlosses zuzuschreiben. Nosseni gehörte neben Rocco di Linar zu den einflußreichsten, architektonisch gebildeten italienischen Beratern des Kurfürsten. In der Rolle eines Kunstintendanten italienisierte er durchgreifend die höfische Kultur in Dresden.

Eine schriftliche Urkunde vermeldet die Vollendung des Schloßbaus im Jahr 1580.[13] Sie besagt, daß Kurfürstin Anna alle Gebäude und

Fig. 5. Prettin, Schloß Lichtenburg, ehemalige Loggia zum Garten (Foto Landesamt für Denkmalpflege und Archäologie, Sachsen-Anhalt).

Fig. 6. Johann Fasold (zugeschr.), Wandmalerei ca. 1611/19, Prettin, Schloß Lichtenburg (Foto Landesamt für Denkmalpflege und Archäologie, Sachsen-Anhalt).

Gemächer „angegebenn und ... geordnet" habe. Anna, die selbst nie in Italien war oder Vergleichsbeispiele aus eigener Anschauung kannte, hat sicher keinen Entwurf im wörtlichen Sinn geschaffen. Die Nachricht bestätigt jedoch, daß die Konzeption am Hof, unter unmittelbarer Beteiligung des Herrscherpaares, entstand. Sie findet ihre Parallele im Schloß Augustusburg, das Hieronymus Lotter auf Befehl Kurfürst Augusts nach einem ihm übergebenen, wahrscheinlich von Paul Buchner angefertigten Modell zu bauen hatte.[14]

Für die Bauleitung sind Hans Irmisch und Christoph Tendler überliefert – Maurermeister, denen der Typus der Villa suburbana sicher unbekannt war. Keiner ihrer übrigen Bauten weist vergleichbare italienische Elemente auf, die für sie einen Anteil an der Konzeption des Schlosses Lichtenburg belegen würden. Aus mangelnder Objektkenntnis konnten sie die italienischen Architekturvorbilder nicht kopierend übernehmen. Die theoretischen Vorgaben wurden interpretiert und, wenn nicht anders angewiesen, in der vertrauten Formensprache ausgedrückt.

Fig.7. Johann Fasold (zugeschr.), Merkur, Wandmalerei ca. 1611/19, Prettin, Schloß Lichtenburg (Foto Landesamt für Denkmalpflege und Archäologie, Sachsen-Anhalt).

Zu den wichtigsten Architekturelementen gehören die Schmuckgiebel. In ihrem die augusteische Schloßbaukunst prägenden Aufbau mit Dreieckfrontispiz, seitlichen Voluten und horizontal gliedernden Gurtgesimsen gehen sie auf die Giebel am Dresdner Schloß, nach Entwürfen Caspar Vogts von Wierand, zurück. Sie scheinen in ihrer klassisch gemeinten klaren Form und feinen Profilierung für die Bauvorhaben des Hofes verbindlich gewesen zu sein und wurden von allen kurfürstlichen Baumeistern gleichermaßen angewandt. Die sicher von Tendler projektierten Giebel der Lichtenburg entsprechen daher fast bis ins Detail den Giebeln am Schloß Annaburg, ebenso den Giebeln von Hans Irmisch am Dresdner Kanzleihaus (1565/67), am Entwurf für Schloß Osterstein (1565/69), am Collegium Augusteum der Wittenberger Universität (nach 1569), am Schloß Pretzsch (1571/74)[15], und auch den Giebeln von Paul Buchner am Dresdner Zeughaus (1559/63), am Stallhof (1586/88), an den Schlössern Moritzburg (Modell um 1690/1700) und Zabeltitz (ca. 1590).

In den Akten werden Tendler, Irmisch und Buchner gleichermaßen mit Aufträgen sowohl

Fig. 8. Prettin, Schloß Lichtenburg, Schloßkirche von Süden (Foto Landesamt für Denkmalpflege und Archäologie, Sachsen-Anhalt).

für Annaburg als auch für Lichtenburg genannt.[16] Die Zuständigkeit richtete sich demzufolge nach der jeweiligen Aufgabe und war nicht an das Gesamtprojekt gebunden.

Zu den italienisierenden Motiven, die nicht aus dem vertrauten Formenschatz kamen, gehören in Lichtenburg die Portale zum Schloß sowie zum Gutshof, zum kurfürstlichen Haus und zur Schloßkirche. Während etwa Palladio seinen glatt geputzten Fassaden zur Nobilitierung monumentale antike Architekturmotive in Gänze vorblendete, reichten für die gleiche ikonographische Aussage in Lichtenburg klassische Säulen- oder Pilasterportale. Sie zeichnen sich durch strengen Bezug auf die Säulenordnungen aus, sind als pars pro toto Antiken- und Italienzitat in einem. Sie sind weder in Annaburg noch in Augustusburg zu finden. Ihr unmittelbares Vorbild war, wie auch für die Säulen des Lusthauses im Annaburger Schloßgarten[17], zweifellos das Portal zur Kapelle des Dresdner Schlosses. Die Steinmetzarbeit führte der Torgauer Caspar Reinwald aus. Die künstlerisch anspruchsvollen Skulpturen an den beiden Hauptportalen wie am großen Wappenrelief des Torhauses stehen stilistisch dem Dresdner Bildhauer Christoph Walther II nahe. Die Portale sind, wie die zahlreichen Wappendarstellungen, als Statussymbole zu lesen. Sie demonstrieren in ihrer archäologischen Exaktheit und künstlerischen Qualität – wie die Exklusivität, Modernität und Größe des Schloßbaus – die Magnifizenz des sächsischen Kurfürsten und seiner königlichen Gemahlin.

1581/82 wurde im rechten Winkel an den Ostflügel die Schloßkapelle als nahezu freistehende, gotisierende zweischiffige Hallenkirche angebaut (Fig. 8, 9).[18] Damit unterscheidet sie sich von allen anderen sächsischen Schloßkapellen des 16. Jahrhunderts, die auf den Typus des Emporensaals von Torgau zurückgehen. Die Gründe für diese Abweichung sind nicht bekannt; sie sind vermutlich praktischer Art. Eine nach Torgauer Muster in den Hauptbau integrierte Kapelle hätte die funktional notwendige Kontinuität der Raumkommunikation in den

Fig. 9. Christoph Walther II (zugeschr.), Portal zur Schloßkirche, um 1582, Detail, Prettin, Schloß Lichtenburg (Foto Landesamt für Denkmalpflege und Archäologie, Sachsen-Anhalt).

Fig.10. Wolf Mönch, inneres Hofportal, 1615, Prettin, Schloß Lichtenburg (Foto Landesamt für Denkmalpflege und Archäologie, Sachsen-Anhalt).

herrschaftlichen Gemächern der Obergeschosse unterbrochen. Da Schloß Lichtenburg nicht um einen Binnenhof errichtet ist, wären hinter der Kapelle liegende Räume auf dieser Geschoßebene nicht erreichbar gewesen. Die Kapelle konnte deshalb nur an einem Kopfende angeordnet werden. Traditionell-liturgische Gründe sprachen offenbar für die Orientierung nach Osten. Aus statischer Sicht bot sich für einen in dieser Weise frei stehenden, gewölbten Bau die gotische Wölbtechnik mit Strebepfeilern an, die durch größere Fensterflächen und den dreiseitigen Ostschluß eine im Vergleich zu Augustusburg auch deutlich bessere Belichtung ermöglichte. Typologisch steht der Bau damit zwar nicht in der Nachfolge der Torgauer, sondern der Wittenberger Schloßkirche – im Verständnis des streng lutherischen Kurfürstenpaars dürfte dies jedoch kein Nachteil gewesen sein. Die gotische Formensprache der Architektur hatte dabei keine ikonographische Bedeutung: alle Zeichen herrschaftlicher Würde, das Portal wie auch die Fürstenempore im Inneren, sind demonstrativ im italienisch-antikischen Stil gehalten.

Schloß Lichtenburg unter Kurfürstin Hedwig

Nach dem Tod Kurfürst Christians II. im Jahr 1611 bezog dessen Witwe Hedwig von Dänemark, Tochter Friedrichs II., Schloß Lichtenburg, um dort mit großem Hofstaat bis 1641 wahrhaft königlich zu residieren.[19] Sie ließ mehrere Räume und auch die Kirche durch Johann Fasold neu ausmalen und stiftete der Schloßkirche einen von Nosseni entworfenen, von Sebastian Walther 1612/13 ausgeführten steinernen Altar.[20] Den noch aus der Antoniterkirche erhaltenen spätgotischen Passionsaltar der Schloßkirche schenkte sie 1614 der Stadtkirche in Prettin. In ihrem Auftrag wurden die Gartenanlagen erneuert und darin ein Lusthaus errichtet, 1615 das hofseitige Portal (Fig. 10) des Torhauses dekoriert und 1631 ein italienisierender Ziehbrunnen im Schloßhof aufgestellt, den ein auf Delphinen reitender Neptun ziert.

Der Vergleich zwischen dem Nosseni-Altar und dem Hofportal zeigt nicht nur die stilistischen Unterschiede zwischen der italienisch geprägten Dresdner Hofkunst und der im übrigen Land gepflegten Formensprache, sondern noch deutlicher den Wandel vom klassischen Stilideal der Hochrenaissance zum Manierismus des 17. Jahrhunderts. Das wahrscheinlich von dem Torgauer Bildhauer Wolf Mönch geschaffene Hofportal dokumentiert nicht zuletzt das Vorherrschen des niederländischen Ornamentstils außerhalb Dresdens.

Die von Hedwig initiierten Werke zeigen unübersehbar das Monogramm der verwitweten Kurfürstin: die Schlußsteine der neu dekorierten Schloßkirche wie der Neptunbrunnen, der in die

Prettiner Stadtkirche versetzte Altar ebenso wie der von ihr gestiftete neue Altar der Kirche in Labrun, die Taufsteine der Kirche in Kremitz und aus der Kapelle des von Hedwig als Sommersitz genutzten ehemaligen kurfürstlichen Jagdhauses Glücksburg, heute in Mügeln. Diese Zeichen verweisen auf die Person der Stifterin und die individuelle Donation. Sie unterscheiden sich damit von den sächsisch-dänischen Allianzwappen des Kurfürsten August und seiner Gemahlin Anna an den Schloßbauten, die diese als Objekte der Staatsrepräsentation definieren.

Das Monogramm Hedwigs wirkt dabei wie die Nachahmung des Monogramms ihres Bruders, König Christians IV. von Dänemark. Der offensichtliche Bezug ist zweifellos als Demonstration dynastischer Verbindung und des persönlichen Standesbewußtseins der königlichen Prinzessin zu interpretieren.

Resümee

Die von der bisherigen Forschung als wenig innovativ beurteilte Schloßbaukunst unter Kurfürst August ist angesichts der Hauptwerke Augustusburg, Annaburg, Lichtenburg offensichtlich falsch bewertet. Auch die Charakterisierung Augusts als geizig und schlicht-patriarchalisch, die auf die Interpretation des 19. Jahrhunderts zurückgeht, ist unzutreffend und korrekturbedürftig.

August war durch ein ausgeprägtes dynastisches und Standesbewußtsein geleitet, das sich auch an seinen Schloßbauten ablesen läßt. Alle wichtigen Projekte seiner Regierungszeit haben die sächsisch-mitteldeutsche Schloßbaukunst um Elemente bereichert, die europäische Vorbilder höchsten Anspruchs reflektieren. Zu den wesentlichen Neuerungen gehört die typologische Differenzierung der Schlösser, mit der bereits Grundsätze der Barockbaukunst vorbereitet wurden. Zu den nachweisbaren Typen gehören neben dem Residenzschloß das Jagdschloß, die Villa suburbana, die Retirade, Amtsschlösser und eine Art von „Denkmalarchitektur" wie Schloß Augustusburg.

Der Verweis nicht nur auf die kurfürstliche Würde des Bauherren, sondern auch auf den königlichen Rang der Bauherrin unterstreicht den zeremoniellen Anspruch und begründet die ikonographischen Bezüge.

Notes

1. Mario Titze, "Neue Forschungen zum Vorwerk Bleesern, Ldkr. Wittenberg", *Burgen und Schlösser in Sachsen-Anhalt. Mitteilungen der Landesgruppe Sachsen-Anhalt der Deutschen Burgenvereinigung e. V.* 11 (2002), 368-383.

2. Ernst Gründler, *Schloss Annaburg. Festschrift zur Einhundertfünfzigjährigen Jubelfeier des Militär-Knaben-Erziehungs-Institutes zu Annaburg*, Berlin 1888; Werner Schräpel, *Schloß Annaburg – Ein Beitrag zur Renaissance in Sachsen.* Dissertation, Dresden 1927; W. Donath & D. Schulze (eds.), *Jagdschloß Annaburg. Eine geschichtliche Wanderung*, Horb am Neckar 1994; Georg Dehio, *Handbuch der Deutschen Kunstdenkmäler. Sachsen-Anhalt II. Regierungsbezirke Dessau und Halle*, München & Berlin 1999, 20-26.

3. Harald Kleinschmidt, "Das kursächsische Amtshaus in Annaburg und seine Baugeschichte", in: Reinhard Schmitt, Uwe Steinecke & Mario Titze (eds.) *"ES THUN IHER VIEL FRAGEN..." Kunstgeschichte in Mitteldeutschland. Hans-Joachim Krause gewidmet*, Petersberg 2001 (Beiträge zur Denkmalkunde in Sachsen-Anhalt 2), 187-202.

4. Kleinschmidt 2001, 188.

5. Margitta Çoban-Hensel, "Die archivalisch nachweisbare Verbreitung von Goldledertapeten in den kursächsischen Schlössern vom 16. Jahrhundert bis zum Beginn des 18. Jahrhunderts", in: Staatliche Schlösser, Burgen und Gärten Sachsen (ed.), *Ledertapeten. Bestände, Erhaltung und Restaurierung*, Dresden 2004, 31-43; Margitta Çoban-Hensel, "Kurfürst August von Sachsen als spiritus rector der bildnerischen Schlossausstattungen", in: Barbara Marx (ed.), *Kunst und Repräsentation am Dresdner Hof*, München & Berlin 2005, 108-130.

6. Horst Stierhof, "Hans Schroer d. Ä. aus Lüttich. Hofmaler, Statuarius oder Monumentengießer", *Revue belge d'archéologie et d'histoire de l'art* XLIV (1975), 109-124.

7. Werner Gräbner, *Die Lichtenburg, eine vergessene Schloßanlage der deutschen Renaissance.* Unpubl. Mskr., Landesamt für Denkmalpflege Sachsen, Dresden s. a. (ca. 1953); Christine Nopens, *Die Schloßkirche in Lichtenburg. Ein Zeugnis der Nachgotik am Ende des 16. Jahrhunderts in Sachsen.* Unpubl. Diplomarbeit, Universität Leipzig 1984; Hans-Joachim Krause, "Schloß Lichtenburg und die mitteldeutsche Renaissancear-

chitektur", *Denkmalpflege in Sachsen-Anhalt* 2 (1993), 129-157; Dehio 1999, 673-678.

8   Seit 1812 diente Schloß Lichtenburg als Zuchthaus. 1817 wurde dafür der Westflügel nach Norden verlängert und das Mezzanin wurde eingefügt, 1878/79 entstand der Zellenbau am Kirchenflügel. Der frühere Garten wurde zum Gefängnishof. 1933-1936 befand sich im Schloß eines der ersten nationalsozialistischen Konzentrationslager.

9   Hellmut Kretzschmar, "Staatswirtschaft, konfessionelle Territorialpolitik und materieller Aufschwung im ausgehenden 16. Jahrhundert", in: Rudolf Kötzschke & Hellmut Kretzschmar (eds.), *Sächsische Geschichte*, Würzburg 1965 (Nachdruck: Augsburg 1995), 219-235.

10 Als Beispiele seien genannt: Giangiorgio Trissino(?): Villa Trissino, Cricoli, 1530-1538; Andrea Palladio: Villa Godi, Lonedo di Lugo, ca.1540-1542; Andrea Palladio: Villa Saraceno, Finale di Agugliaro, ab 1548; Andrea Palladio: Villa Poiana, Poiana Maggiore, ca. 1550-1555; Andrea Palladio: Villa Barbaro, Maser, ca. 1560.

11 Monika Meine-Schawe, "Giovanni Maria Nosseni. Ein Hofkünstler in Sachsen", *Jahrbuch des Zentralinstituts für Kunstgeschichte* V/VI (1989/90), 283-325; Krause 1993; Çoban-Hensel 2004; Sächsisches Hauptstaatsarchiv Dresden, Loc. 9126, III. Buch der Churf. Sächs. Artolerey und Bau-Sachsen 1576-1584, fol. 361^r (alt 356^r)-363^v, Vorzeichnis der Decken zu Lichtenbergk.

12 Sächsisches Hauptstaatsarchiv Dresden, Loc. 8524, fol. 353, zitiert nach Monika Meine-Schawe, *Die Grablege der Wettiner im Dom zu Freiberg. Die Umgestaltung des Domchores durch Giovanni Maria Nosseni 1585-1594*, München 1992 (Tuduv-Studien, Reihe Kunstgeschichte, 46), 123, Dok. 3.

13 Krause 1993, 138-140.

14 Lutz Unbehaun, *Hieronymus Lotter. Kurfürstlich-Sächsischer Baumeister und Bürgermeister zu Leipzig*, Leipzig 1989, 114-116.

15 Der Nachweis der Autorschaft Hans Irmischs für Schloß Pretzsch, den Sitz des kursächsischen Erbmarschalls Löser, gelang Andreas Stahl, Landesamt für Denkmalpflege und Archäologie Sachsen-Anhalt, Halle.

16 Sächsisches Hauptstaatsarchiv Dresden, Loc. 9126, III. Buch der Churf. Sächs. Artolerey und Bau-Sachsen 1576-1584.

17 Kleinschmidt 2001, 195, nennt als Meister des Annaburger Gartenhauses "Melcher pertelt", den er, teilweise fehlerhaften älteren Interpretationen folgend, mit einem bislang unbekannten Melchior Berthold identifiziert. Dabei kann es sich jedoch nur um den Dresdner Steinmetz Melchior Barthel handeln, der sich 1554/55 gemeinsam mit Christoph Walther II um die Ausführung des von Kurfürst August in Freiberg geplanten Moritz-Monuments bewarb und von 1579 bis 1584 nach einem Entwurf Hans Walthers II am Turm der Dresdner Kreuzkirche tätig war. Barthel war der Stammvater einer bedeutenden Bildhauerfamilie. Seine Nähe zu Hans Walther II, einem der Bildhauer am Schloßkapellenportal, und Christoph Walther II, dessen Vetter und engstem Mitarbeiter, erklärt auch den Bezug der Annaburger Säulenpostamente auf das Vorbild des Dresdner Schloßkapellenportals und dessen Schulwerke.

18 Nopens 1984.

19 Mara R. Wade, "The Queen's Courts: Anna of Denmark and her Royal Sisters – Cultural Agency at Four Northern European Courts in the Sixteenth and Seventeenth Centuries", in: Clare McManus (ed.), *Women and Culture at the Courts of the Stuart Queens*, New York 2003, 49-80, besonders 66-70.

20 Walter Hentschel, *Dresdner Bildhauer des 16. und 17. Jahrhunderts*, Weimar 1966, 73-76, 143-145.

*   Forschungsstand von 2006. Restauratorische Untersuchungen 2011 haben gezeigt, daß die Malereien die Zweitfassung darstellen. Sie entstanden demnach unter Kurfürstin Hedwig, ca. 1612/1619, und wurden wohl von Johann Fasold gemalt.

DEUTSCHE, FRANZÖSISCHE UND NIEDERLÄNDISCHE EINFLÜSSE ALS WEGBEREITER UND KATALYSATOREN DER DÄNISCHEN RENAISSANCE-ARCHITEKTUR IN DER ZWEITEN HÄLFTE DES 16. JAHRHUNDERTS: DAS BEISPIEL DES HERRENHAUSES

Uwe Albrecht

Seit der Mitte des 16. Jahrhunderts vollzog sich der unaufhaltsame Aufstieg der dänischen Ritterschaft zu einer Wirtschaft, Politik und Kultur prägenden gesellschaftlichen Größe. Rufen wir uns zunächst kurz die Ursachen dieses historisch einschneidenden Prozesses ins Gedächtnis zurück. Bekanntlich waren im Zuge der Reformation die Feldklöster säkularisiert worden und deren Landbesitz dem König und einigen einflussreichen, dem Hof nahe stehenden Familien zugefallen. In dem Bestreben, ihre ohnehin schon umfangreichen Ländereien weiter zu arrondieren, traten letztere insbesondere durch Getreide-, Holz- und Ochsenhandel unternehmerisch hervor, zunehmend aber auch als Kreditgeber im nationalen und internationalen Geldverkehr. Als ökonomische, bald auch politische und vor allem soziale Aufsteiger führten ihre Allianzen mit standesgleichen Geschlechtern im Laufe der Zeit zu einem engmaschigen personellen „Netzwerk", dessen Mitglieder sich zunehmend all jener verarmten kleineren Adligen entledigten, deren Grundbesitz wegen hoher Verschuldung zur Disposition stand und den spekulativ agierenden Gläubigern lukrativen Gewinn versprach. Die Prosperität von Wenigen wurde so der Preis Vieler. Wer hinter seine Standesgenossen zurückfiel, wurde von ihnen rigoros verdrängt und ausgekauft.

Die alten und unbequemen Burgen, zu Beginn des 16. Jahrhunderts noch vielfach kleine Motten mit bescheidenen Wohntürmen, legte man nieder und ersetzte sie durch frühneuzeitliche Gutshöfe, als deren ideeller und struktureller Mittelpunkt das Herrenhaus gelten darf. Umgeben von Wirtschaftsgebäuden, wie Ställen und Scheunen, aber auch von Mühle und Schmiede, und zunehmend erweitert durch Gartenanlagen, die im Laufe der Zeit das Haus immer deutlicher in die Landschaft fortsetzten, bildet das Wohn- und Repräsentationsaufgaben auf sich vereinigende *Corps de logis* den Gegenstand, dem wir uns im folgenden zuwenden wollen. In seinen Mauern entstand eine neuartige Wohnkultur, die nahezu zeitgleich auch den fürstlichen Schlossbau (Gottorf; Malmöhus; Nyborg) erreichte, der hier freilich ausgeklammert bleiben muss.[1]

Anfänge frühneuzeitlicher Wohngewohnheiten

Das bereits vor der Grafenfehde (1534-36) begonnene nördliche Haus der damals noch mitten in einem See gelegenen kleinen Hofinsel von Rygaard (Fünen) zählt zu den wenigen Herrenhäusern, an denen mittelalterliche und neuzeitliche Züge exemplarisch nebeneinander auftreten,

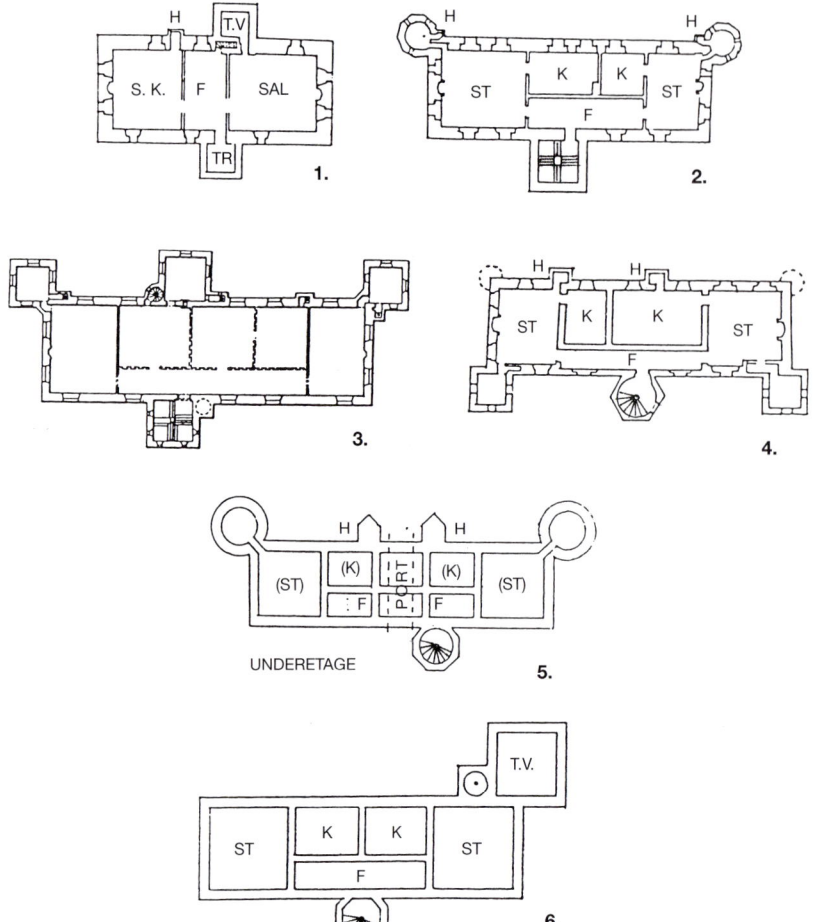

Fig. 1. Schematische Übersicht der Raumaufteilung dänischer *Corps de logis* des 16. Jahrhunderts.
1: Rygaard, 2: Hesselagergaard, 3: Borreby, 4: Hollufgaard, 5: Lindenborg und 6: Skovsbo (F = Forstue/Vorraum, ST = Stue/Stube, K = Kammer, H = Hemmelighed/Latrine). Nach Engqvist, "Fire fynske herreborge", Architectura 2 (1980), 122-123.

so dass es für unsere Betrachtung von besonderer Bedeutung ist und am Anfang stehen soll (Fig. 1.1).[2] Das rechteckige Haus (ca. 24 m x 10 m), das sich im ersten Drittel des 16. Jahrhunderts im Besitz des Ritters und Mitglieds im Reichsrat Johan Urne (gest. 1537) befand, weist über einem zweischiffigen kreuzrippengewölbten Keller zwei Wohngeschosse sowie einen geräumigen Dachboden auf, dessen konstruktive Eigenschaften für eine ganze Reihe von Bauten wegweisend wurden. Um zusätzlichen Platz zu schaffen, sind die Dachgebinde zwischen den mit Speicherluken versehenen blendengeschmückten Treppengiebeln als stehender Stuhl soweit nach innen genommen, dass sich ein rechteckiger Raumquerschnitt ergibt (Fig. 2). Aufschieblinge führen von den Sparren nach außen zu einer etwa mannshohen Drempelmauer hinab, die, mit Schießscharten in regelmäßigen Abständen bestückt, auf großen Steinkonsolen sehr markant aus der Fassadenflucht vorkragt und einem schmalen Wehrgang auf der Mauerkrone der beiden Längsseiten Deckung gibt.

Ein rings umlaufender Rundbogenfries, der das Obergeschoß gegenüber dem Erdgeschoß um eine halbe Ziegellänge vorspringen lässt, ist nicht minder kennzeichnend und erweist sich neben der Dachkonstruktion als ebenso regional- wie zeittypisch (Fig. 3). Das Motiv der schrittweise nach oben hin vorkragenden Fassaden erinnert an die Bauweise mehrgeschossiger Fachwerkhäuser, der vor den Dachansatz tretende Wehrgang an die hölzernen Umgänge, wie sie etwa für den wenig älteren Wohnturm von Glimmingehus (Schonen), zu Beginn des 16. Jahrhunderts entstanden, rekonstruiert werden können. Blendengezierte Treppengiebel sind hingegen ein vor allem im Backsteinbau verbreiteter Bauschmuck, der sowohl Bürgerhäuser, als auch Kirchen, auf Fünen besonders deren Türme (Fig. 4) und Chorgiebel, auszeichnet.

Fig. 2. Raumquerschnitte der *Corps de logis* von Rygaard (links) und Hesselagergaard (rechts). Nach Engqvist, Abb. 4, 13.

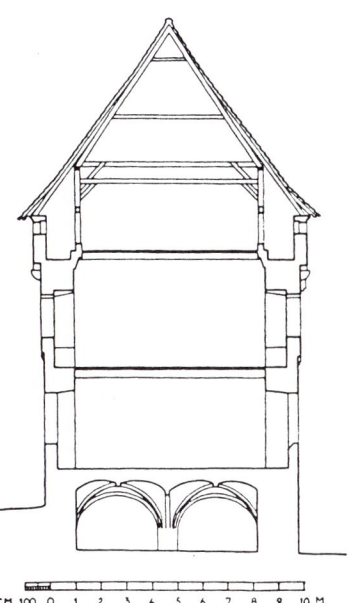
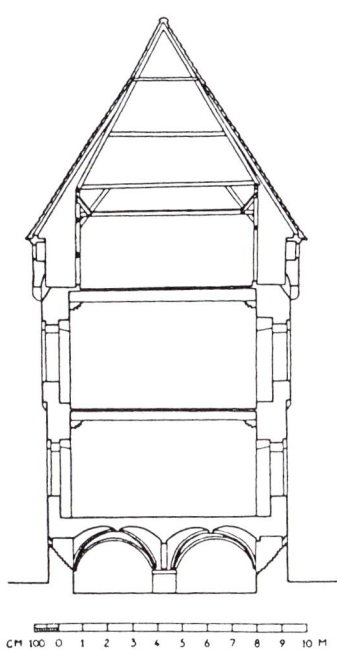

So sehr ältere heimische Bautraditionen das äußere Erscheinungsbild prägten, so deutlich gingen Raumaufteilung und Erschließung des Inneren einen entscheidenden Schritt weiter. Zwar erfolgte der Zugang des Hauses bei seiner Vollendung um 1530 noch über eine geradarmige Außentreppe, doch lief diese frontal auf das Portal im ersten Obergeschoß zu und lehnte sich einem rechtwinklig vorspringenden Bauteil an, in dem wir mit einiger Berechtigung einen ersten Treppenturm vermuten dürfen, den wohl ältesten an einem dänischen Herrenhaus überhaupt. Ihm antwortete auf der Feldseite ein ganz ähnlicher Anbau, der kleine Kabinette enthalten haben wird.[3] Dazwischen entfaltete sich im ersten Obergeschoß eine Raumstruktur, die im Kern bereits alle Züge eines Appartements in sich trug: einen Vorraum, zwei unterschiedlich große Stuben und eine heizbare Kammer. Diesem wohnlichen Bereich folgte im zweiten Obergeschoß die repräsentative Ebene, die neben dem großen Saal mit anhängendem Kabinett ebenfalls einen Vorraum sowie – möglicherweise für Gäste – eine weitere Stube mit Abtritterker umfasste (Fig. 1.1). Das zweite Obergeschoß, wohl von Anfang an allein über die Wendeltreppe in dem hofseitigen Turm erreichbar, enthielt die eigentlichen Prunkräume des Hauses, deren große Fenster in den Leibungen durchweg mit Sitzbänken ausgestattet waren, während Malereien Wände und Kamine schmückten. Kunstsinn und Kommodität gewannen in Rygaard spürbar an Bedeutung, Distribution und Zirkulation traten in ein neues Stadium ihrer Entwicklung ein.

Zu verweisen ist hier auf ältere französische Beispiele kleiner Schlösser, sog. *manoirs*, wie sie exemplarisch, wenngleich heute stark beschädigt und daher nur noch rudimentär, der von Jean

Fig. 3. Rygaard, nordwestliche Giebelseite der *Corps de logis* (Foto Nationalmuseum, Kopenhagen).

DAS BEISPIEL DES HERRENHAUSES

Fig. 4. Revninge, Südgiebel des Westturmes der Kirche (Foto Verfasser).

Bourré, dem *Premier trésorier de France*, in den 1460er Jahren errichtete Landsitz Vaux (Dép. Maine-et-Loire) vor Augen führen kann (Fig. 5).[4] Von Wassergräben rings umzogen, ordnet sich dort die Bebauung in drei Flügeln, eigentlich eigenständigen Häusern unterschiedlicher Firsthöhe, einem mittleren Hofplatz zu. Dem ehemaligen Eingangsportal gegenüber erhebt sich – wie in Rygaard – das *Corps de logis* mit seinem hohen, hier polygonalen Treppenturm, von dem aus sämtliche vier Geschosse des Hauses zugänglich sind. Die Raumaufteilung zeigt im Kernbereich zwei ungleich große Räume, *salle* und *chambre*, die durch zwei Kabinette in den runden Ecktürmen sowie einen zusätzlichen Raum mit Latrine in dem weit ausladenden hinteren Anbau erweitert werden. Als kleiner im Zuschnitt, aber strukturell eng verwandt erweist sich auch das *Corps de logis* von Beauregard (Dép. Loire-et-Cher), das kurz nach 1500 entstand und stellvertretend für zahllose vergleichbare Häuser des niederen Adels in Frankreich stehen kann (Fig. 6). In beiden Beispielen erblicken wir prägnante Vorbilder für die architekturtypologische Herleitung des dänischen Landadelssitzes frühneuzeitlicher Zeitstellung.

Die für dänische Beispiele typische Existenz eines Vorraumes zwischen Treppe und Appartement bzw. Saal kennzeichnet hingegen mitteldeutsche Raumpläne seit dem letzten Drittel des 15. Jahrhunderts, was Stephan Hoppe überzeugend darlegen konnte (Wittenberg, Kurfürstliches Schloß, 1480er Jahre).[5] Auf den Maßstab eines Herrenhauses übertragen, scheint der freistehende Kernbau des zwischen 1542 und 1546 angelegten Jagdschlosses Moritzburg (Fig. 7), eines einflügeligen Gebäudes mit leicht asymmetrisch platziertem schlankem Treppenturm, geradezu idealtypisch auf den Norden gewirkt zu haben.[6] Dieser den Namen seines fürstlichen Bauherrn, Herzog Moritz von Sachsen (reg. 1541-1553, Kurfürst ab 1547), tragende Gründungsbau des im 17. und 18. Jahrhundert einschneidend barock überformten Schlosses unweit von Dresden ist uns vor allem durch ein 1591 von Paul Buchner angefertigtes, maßstabsgetreues Holzmodell überliefert, das zu den wenigen erhaltenen Beispielen seiner Art aus dem 16. Jahrhundert nördlich der Alpen zählt. Wie im Falle der dänischen Herrenhäuser verfügte das „Haupt-Hauß" genannte *Corps de logis* über ein gewölbtes Erdgeschoss und Obergeschosse mit Balkendecken. Während die beiden Dachgeschosse dem Frauenzimmer und dem Gesinde vorbehalten waren, bewohnte im ersten Obergeschoß das Kurfürstenpaar, nach Geschlechtern getrennt, zwei gleichwertige Appartements mit Stube, Kammer und Latrine zu beiden Seiten eines von dem Treppenturm erreichbaren Vorraumes. Die schon seit der Hochzeit 1478 zwischen König Hans und Christine, Tochter der Kurfürsten Ernst von Sachsen, bestehenden engen dynastischen Verbindungen zwischen Sachsen und Dänemark wurden mit der Hochzeit des Prinzen und nachmaligen Kurfürsten August (reg. 1553-1586), Moritz' Bruder, erneuert, der 1548 Anna, die älteste Tochter König Christian III., ehelichte. Einflüsse seitens der hochentwickelten wettinischen Hofkultur, die ihrerseits

Fig. 5a. Vaux, Manoir des Jean Bourré, Ansicht von Süden. Nach Sarrazin, Manoirs et gentilhommes de l'ancienne France, Anjou 1980.

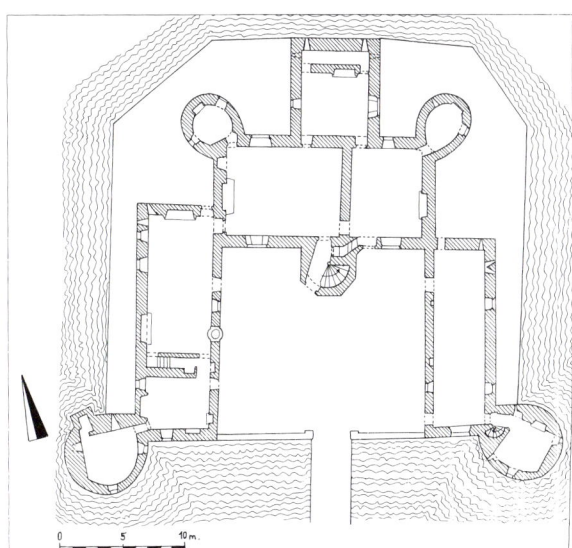

Fig. 5b. Grundriss des Erdgeschosses. Nach Blomme, Anjou gothique, Paris 1988, 221.

nicht ohne französische Voraussetzungen denkbar ist, sind also mehr als wahrscheinlich. Als Reflex sich verändernder Lebensformen und Wohngewohnheiten wurden diese Impulse besonders früh und zugleich sehr nachhaltig im Bereich der dänischen Herrenhausarchitektur aufgenommen, deren emporstrebende Bauherren mit großer Offenheit jeglichen Wegbereitern und Katalysatoren frühneuzeitlicher Planlösungen begegneten.

Die Rezeption von *Corps de logis* und Appartement

In Hesselagergaard (Fünen), wo 1538 noch eine Hofanlage in der Art von Rygaard Gegenstand der Planungen war, verzichtete man schon bald darauf, mehrere Gebäude zu errichten. Stattdessen verlieh man dem einen Flügel, an dem bis gegen 1550 wohl mit Unterbrechungen gearbeitet

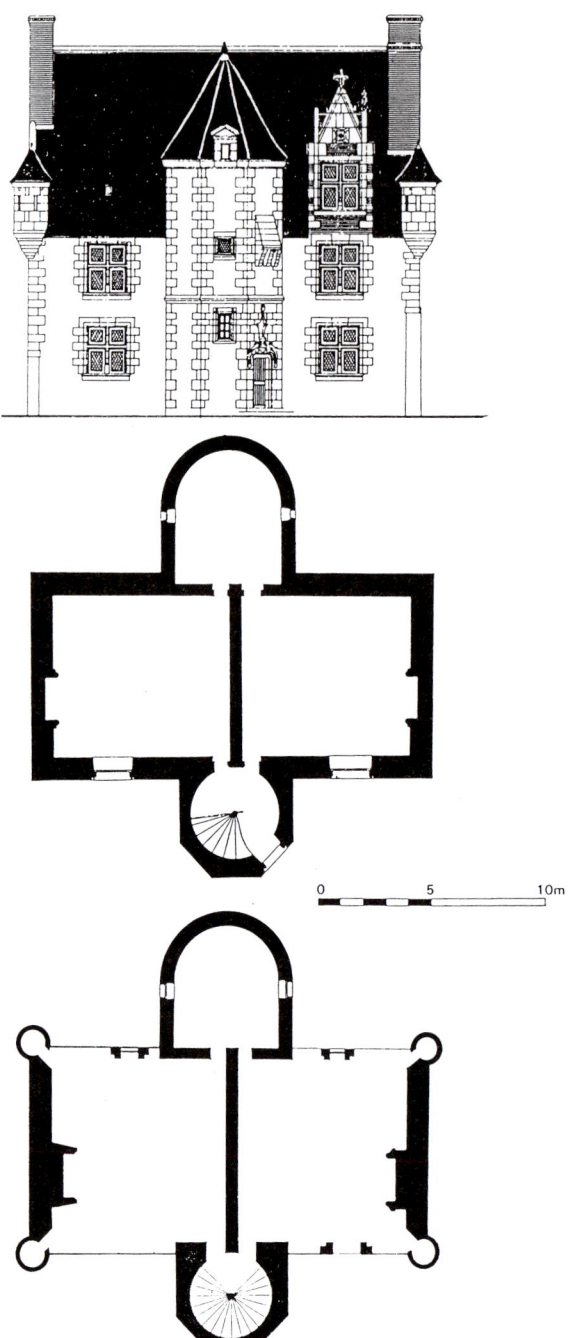

wurde, jenes charakteristische Erscheinungsbild, das in seinen Grundzügen dänische Herrenhäuser von nun an für mehr als ein Jahrhundert bestimmte (Fig. 8).

Das Ergebnis dieser Planänderung war ein *Corps de logis* mit einem Treppenturm vor der Hoffassade und zwei polygonalen Ecktürmen auf der Feldseite, prächtigen Frührenaissance-Schaugiebeln und einer Raumfolge, die, anders als gemeinhin üblich, im ersten Obergeschoss den repräsentativen Bereich aufnahm, während im zweiten Obergeschoß zum ersten Mal ein *appartement double*, ein Doppel-Appartement für den Hausherrn und die -frau, entstand (Fig. 1.2). Drei ungleich große Räume, *chambre*, *cabinet* und *garderobe*, ergänzt um eine Latrine am Ansatz des Eckturmes, bilden in Hesselagergaard jeweils eine abgeschlossene Raumgruppe für sich und stehen nur über einen korridorartigen Vorraum miteinander und mit der Treppe in Verbindung, über die nun vom Keller bis zum Dachboden die gesamte vertikale Zirkulation verläuft. Außentreppen gibt es nicht mehr; allein eine schmale Innentreppe in der Stärke der südlichen Hofmauer, deren Anlage noch aus der ersten Bauphase herrührt, kommuniziert zusätzlich zwischen Keller- und erstem Obergeschoß. Am Fuße des Treppenturmes liegen in einem eigenen kleinen Raum ein Brunnen und ein Ofen; die Küche befindet sich im Keller daneben.

Fig. 6. Beauregard, Manoir, *Corps de logis*, Ansicht der Hoffassade (oben), Grundrisse des Erdgeschosses (Mitte) und des zweiten Obergeschosses (unten). Nach Jeanson, *La maison seigneuriale du Val de Loire. Sa vie, son économie, ses habitants, son architecture*, Paris 1981.

Fig. 7. Moritzburg, Jagdschloss, Grundriss des Erdgeschosses im Zustand um 1585: 1 = Vorraum, 2 = Hofstube (darüber im 1. Obergeschoß das Wohn- und Schlafzimmer des Kurfürsten), 3 = Speisekammer (darüber im 1. Obergeschoß das Wohnzimmer der Kurfürstin), 4 = Silberkammer (darüber im 1. Obergeschoß das Schlafzimmer der Kurfürstin). Nach Kadatz, *Deutsche Renaissancebaukunst von der frühbürgerlichen Revolution bis zum Ausgang des Dreißigjährigen Krieges*, Berlin 1983.

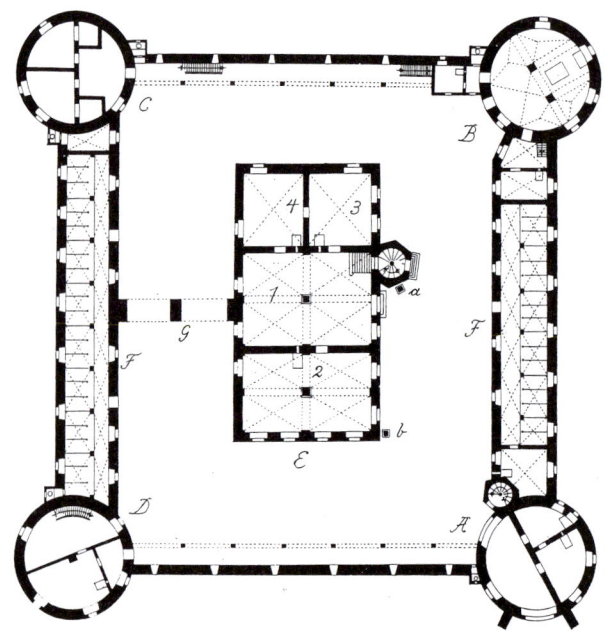

Fig. 8. Hesselagergaard, Ansicht des *Corps de logis* von Südosten (Foto Nationalmuseum, Kopenhagen).

Das Leben und Wohnen hat sich in Hesselagergaard im Laufe eines Jahrzehnts von Grund auf verändert. Die Ursachen dieses ebenso raschen wie tiefgreifenden Wandels liegen nicht allein im allgemeinen Umbruch der Zeit begründet, sondern vor allem in der Bildung, Weitsicht und Weltoffenheit von Auftraggebern wie Johan Friis (1494-1570), dem Bauherrn von Hesselagergaard. Er gehörte jener neuen Generation von Ratgebern des dänischen Königs an, die nach dem Ende der Grafenfehde und der Einführung der Reformation nicht nur im dänischen Reichsgebiet, sondern auch in den nordelbischen Herzogtümern schlagartig an Einfluß gewannen: Was für Fünen und das Königreich die Friis und die Brockenhuus, waren die Rantzaus für Schleswig-Holstein!

Johan Friis, der ein Studium in Kopenhagen und Köln absolvierte, es dort 1519 zum Magister brachte, Frankreich und Italien bereiste und aus persönlicher Begegnung Luther und Melanchthon kannte, war seit 1532 dänischer Kanzler und damit eine der Schlüsselgestalten im politischen Kräftespiel seiner Zeit.[7] Zum ersten Mal in Hesselagergaard, wenig später aber auch in dem ebenfalls von ihm erbauten Borreby (Seeland, 1556; Fig. 9) brach er so weitgehend mit den mittelalterlichen Traditionen, dass beide Bauten als Prototypen neuzeitlicher Herrenhausarchitektur des Nordens schlechthin gelten können.

Bereits in Hesselagergaard besaß besonders die im zweiten Obergeschoß verwirklichte Raumfolge durch ihre geschickte Distribution ein Höchstmaß an Kommodität. Auf je eine große heizbare Stube an den Schmalseiten des Hauses folgten rückwärtig Schlafkammer und *garderobe* (Eckturm). Die beiden letzteren waren so angeordnet, dass weder Luftzug, noch Lärm vom Hofe zu ihnen vordringen konnten, geschweige denn ein störender Kontakt mit den Bediensteten hier möglich gewesen wäre. Von der allgemeinen Zirkulation vollkommen abgeschirmt, bildeten diese Räume den privaten Kernbereich, das Refugium des Hausherren.[8]

Ein Geschoß tiefer hatte das gesellige Leben seinen Schauplatz. Der große Saal, rundum mit Wandmalereien geschmückt, als deren Urheber Otto Norn mit gutem Grund Jacob Binck vermutete[9], war einer der ersten Hirschsäle in Nordeuropa; sein ikonographisches Programm einer beliebten Thematik gewidmet, deren Ideenwelt an deutschen und französischen Höfen zu suchen ist. Ralf Weingart ist diesem Phänomen eingehend nachgegangen und konnte zwischen Güstrow und Grünau bei Neuburg an der Donau zahlreiche Beispiele für das 16. Jahrhundert benennen[10], wobei einmal mehr von französischen Voraussetzungen auszugehen ist, die bis auf das 14. Jahrhundert zurückreichen (Paris, Hôtel de Saint-Pol).

Borreby und das kleinere Nakkebølle (Fünen) sind vortreffliche Beispiele für die rasche und nachhaltige Ausbreitung des neuen Herrenhaustypus'. Sie entwickeln die in Rygaard und Hesselagergaard gefaßte Planlösung folgerichtig weiter, in der äußeren Gestaltung des *Corps de logis* wie auch in der Distribution der Räume (Fig. 1.3). Auffälligstes Kennzeichen am Außenbau ist im Unterschied zu Hesselagergaard der Wechsel von der polygonalen zur quadratischen Grundform der Ecktürme, die in Borreby und Nakkebølle

DAS BEISPIEL DES HERRENHAUSES

Fig. 9. Borreby, Aufriß der westlichen Giebelseite des Corps de logis. Nach einer Bauaufnahme der Kgl. Kunstakademie, Kopenhagen.

voll und ganz in die Gliederung der Fassaden mit eingebunden werden. Wie bei zahlreichen französischen Schlössern des späten 15. und frühen 16. Jahrhunderts hat sich auch bei ihnen der ehemalige Wehrgang am Dachansatz in ein baukünstlerisches Motiv mit Symbolwert verwandelt, das um der Einheitlichkeit willen sogar an den Giebelseiten und im Bereich der Turmobergeschosse auftritt, wo in Borreby links und rechts großer Fenster Schießscharten vollkommen funktionslos als rein dekorative Zierblenden wiederkehren. Profilierte Formziegel schmücken nicht nur die umlaufenden Rundbogenfriese, über denen in gewohnter Weise die Fassade vorkragt, sondern auch die korbbogigen Traufleisten über sämtlichen Fensteröffnungen sowie nicht zuletzt die horizontalen Gesimse, die nun anstelle gotischer Hochblenden die zahlreichen großen und kleinen Giebel in bestimmten Abständen durchziehen. Erste Ansätze zur Vereinheitlichung der Fassaden werden spürbar, doch bleiben Mittel und Motive weitgehend die alten. Auf der eher noch tastenden Suche nach den Regeln von Symmetrie und Ordnung, von Harmonie und Proportion kommt es zu Lösungen, für die Vilhelm Lorenzen den Begriff der »gotischen Renaissance« prägte.[11]

Das Augenmerk der Hofseite gilt wiederum dem Treppenturm, der auch in Borreby und Nakkebølle — wie schon in Hesselagergaard — über annähernd quadratischem Grundriß jenen eigentümlichen Lauf einer geradarmig-gewendelten Treppe enthält, bei dem bekanntlich um ein gemauertes Kernstück herum kurze Stufenfolgen und Absätze einander abwechseln. Treppen dieser Art waren sowohl in Frankreich (Lille, Palais Rihour; Blois, Schloß, Flügel Ludwigs XII.; Les Bories, Dép. Dordogne), als auch in den Niederlanden im späten 15. und zu Beginn des 16. Jahrhunderts verbreitet. In ihnen verbinden sich Merkmale mittelalterlicher Wendeltreppen mit den Vorzügen geradarmiger Lösungen, wie sie zuerst in Italien geläufig waren.[12]

Auch wenn die Portale noch nicht frontal in das Innere führen, sondern in traditioneller Weise auf einer dem Haus zugewandten Seite des Turmes liegen, so werden sie doch immer mehr zur »Visitenkarte« des Herrensitzes. Statt Zugbrücke (Hesselagergaard), Fallgitter und Pechnase findet sich in Nakkebølle zu ebener Erde eine inschriftlich 1559 datierte Sandsteineinfassung deren Formensprache mit den kurzen seitlichen Pilastern, dem kleinteilig ornamentalen Fries und der hohen Dreiecksverdachung bereits ganz im Geiste der Frührenaissance steht. In dem etwas älteren Borreby, wo am Portal noch keinerlei klassische Architekturzitate vorkommen, müssen hingegen Rahmen und Wortlaut der von Johan Friis 1556 gesetzten Haustafel, deren Text — wie schon in Hesselagergaard — nicht mehr auf dänisch, sondern in Latein abgefaßt ist, dem humanistischen Anspruch Genüge tun.

An der Spitze der Treppentürme waren in Hesselagergaard, Borreby und Nakkebølle kleine heizbare Stuben eingerichtet; sowohl in Nakkebølle, wo zu Beginn des 18. Jahrhunderts die Dachzone

Fig. 10. Hollufgaard, Ansicht des Corps de logis von der Hofseite (Foto Verfasser).

leider verändert wurde, als auch in Borreby soll sich dort oben jeweils ein Bad befunden haben,[13] ganz wie wir es ausnahmsweise auch von den *chambres hautes* französischer Beispiele (Saint-Ouen bei Chemazé, Dép. Mayenne) her kennen.[14]

Hinsichtlich der Distribution der Räume setzt sich seit der Mitte des 16. Jahrhunderts mehr und mehr das Anlageschema des eigenständigen und in sich abgeschlossenen Appartements durch. Wie im zweiten Obergeschoß von Hesselagergaard scheint ursprünglich auch in Borreby die horizontale Erschließung von einem hofseitig verlaufenden *stengang*, einem Korridor, aus möglich gewesen zu sein (Fig. 1.3). Neben zwei heizbaren größeren Räumen an den beiden Enden des Hauses, denen die Ecktürme zugeordnet waren, umfasste der Wohnbereich eine Reihe kleinerer Räume in der Hausmitte, die paarweise miteinander in Verbindung standen und jeweils eine eigene Latrine besaßen. Vier nachweisbare Latrinen lassen im ersten Obergeschoß von Borreby auf ebenso viele Wohneinheiten schließen. Den mittleren Kabinetturm begleitet zusätzlich eine kleine Wendeltreppe, die im Gegensatz zum großen Treppenturm bis in den Keller hinabführte. Wie in Rygaard ist auch hier, im Kernbereich herrschaftlicher Wohnnutzung, die *brevkammer*, das Hausarchiv, vielleicht auch das private Studierzimmer des Johan Friis zu erwarten. Das besonders aufwendige kuppelige Gewölbe mit seinen applizierten Netzrippen könnte ein entsprechender Hinweis darauf sein.

Die in Hesselagergaard und Borreby verwirklichte Raumstruktur kennzeichnet auch eine ganze Reihe jüngerer Herrenhäuser. Hollufgaard bei Odense (1576-79; Fig. 1.4), Skovsbo nordwestlich von Nyborg (1572-79; Fig. 1.6) und Lindenborg in Nordjütland (1583; Fig. 1.5) stehen exemplarisch für drei unterschiedliche Lösungen ein und derselben Problemstellung. Allen gemeinsam sind die einflügelige Grundgestalt des *Corps de logis* sowie die Forderung, möglichst viele vollständige Wohneinheiten unter einem Dach zu vereinigen. Das Doppelappartement, von einem Gang an der Hofseite erschlossen, erfüllt in ihnen auf vorbildliche Weise den Anspruch auf Wohnlichkeit. Die Eigenart, dass die Haupträume jeweils an den Hausenden, die kleineren Kammern dafür in der Hausmitte zu liegen kommen, bewirkt bisweilen eine ungewöhnliche Streckung des Baukörpers. Vierzig und mehr laufende Meter Fassadenlänge sind daher bei dänischen Herrenhäusern während des letzten Drittels des 16. Jahrhunderts durchaus keine Seltenheit.

Der Durchbruch der Renaissance

Erneut erfasst die Bauten um 1570 ein tiefgreifender Wandel, der nun auch ihr Äußeres von letzten Zügen mittelalterlicher Gestaltung befreit. In dem für Jørgen Marswin erbauten Hollufgaard (Fig. 10) ist von wehrhaften Elementen keine Rede mehr.[15] Kein Wehrgang markiert mehr den Dachansatz, keine Befestigung sichert mehr das reichgeschmückte Portal, das nun auch in seinen Proportionen gegenüber demjenigen von Nakkebølle ungleich stimmiger ist. Große Fenster sitzen stattdessen in nahezu regelmäßigen Abständen. Sandsteinverdachungen sind an die Stelle der profilierten Traufleisten getreten, geschweifte Hauben ersetzen einfache Satteldächer als Abschluß der Türme, die hier sogar zu dritt die Hoffassade bestimmen. Nach der Distribution verrät nun auch der Stil die Nähe zu westlichen, genauer: niederländischen Vorbildern.

Niederländisch ist die Formensprache der Fassaden: das koloristische Spiel mit verschiedenen Materialien, aber auch der ornamentale Reichtum des Florisstils, der ab 1570 im Norden voll wirksam wird. Stichvorlagen und der jetzt immer häufiger werdende Zustrom niederländischer Künstler und Handwerker, die an den Höfen von Kopenhagen und Gottorf ein breites Betätigungsfeld finden, bilden die Grundlage für diese Rezeption.

Das Badstubengebäude im Park von Schloß Frederiksborg (1580 von Johan Floris) und das Herrenhaus Lystrup (Seeland, 1579; Fig. 11) gehören neben zahlreichen anderen zu denjenigen Bauten, die auf charakteristische Weise den neuen niederländischen Einfluß verdeutlichen (vgl. etwa Mechelen, Stadtpalast der Margarethe von Österreich, um 1510-30; Fig. 12). Kennzeichnend für die Gestalt ihrer Fassaden sind neben den sogenannten »speklagen«, horizontal verlaufenden Sandsteinbändern, die Sohlbank, Querteilung und Sturz der Kreuzstockfenster hervorheben, Staffel-, wenig später auch Schweifgiebel und Lukarnen mit dekorativen Aufsätzen in Form

Fig. 11. Lystrup, Ansicht des *Corps de logis* von der Hofseite (Foto Nationalmuseum, Kopenhagen).

Fig. 12. Mechelen, Stadtpalast der Margarethe von Österreich, Teilansicht der Hoffassade (Foto Verfasser).

Fig. 13. Lystrup, *Corps de logis*, Grundriß des Erdgeschosses. Nach Christensen, Lystrup (Ældre Nordisk Architektur IX), Kopenhagen 1936, Taf. 1.

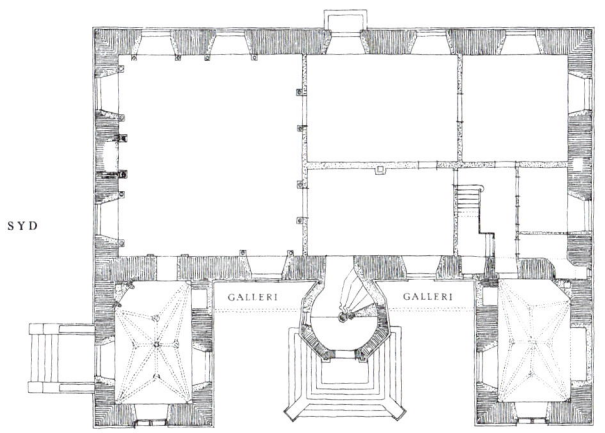

von Kugelknäufen oder Zierobelisken. Vielfältig gebildete Turmhauben und durchbrochene Laternen, die bisweilen auch als Schornsteinköpfe in Erscheinung treten, bestimmen die abwechslungsreiche Silhouette dieser Häuser.

Der Bauherr von Lystrup, Ejler Grubbe, wie sein Vorgänger Johan Friis dänischer Reichskanzler und enger Vertrauter des Königs, lässt sich ein Haus errichten, das ähnlich wie einst Hesselagergaard Maßstäbe für die weitere Entwicklung setzt.[16] Erstmals unterliegt der Baukörper vollständig den Regeln der Symmetrie und Axialität. Standen in dem unmittelbar zuvor fertiggestellten Hollufgaard noch Ecktürme links und rechts des mittleren Treppenturms, so nehmen hier kurze Flügel diese Stelle ein. Die Fenster sind in Achsen angeordnet; das Portal wendet sich nun als Abschluss einer kurzen Freitreppe frontal dem Besucher zu. Sein dekorativer Reichtum und die für ein Herrenhaus ungewöhnliche Qualität der Ausführung weisen auf Verbindungen zu den königlichen Baustellen der Zeit um 1580 hin. In der Tat findet auch die koloristische Effekte auskostende Fassadentextur ihre nächste Parallele in dem für Friedrich II. 1580 errichteten Badstubengebäude im Schlossgarten von Frederiksborg.

Eine Besonderheit der Distribution waren in Lystrup die vor der Fassade verlaufenden Erschließungsgänge, die ursprünglich die beiden kurzen Flügel mit dem mittleren Treppenturm verbanden (Fig. 13). Aus Holz gezimmert, gehörten auch sie — wie andernorts die inneren Korridore — zu den wichtigen Neuerungen einer sich mit der Veränderung der Wohngewohnheiten stärker differenzierenden Zirkulation. In den im letzten Viertel des 16. Jahrhunderts vermehrt entstehenden Dreiflügelanlagen gewährleisteten sie einen vom Kopfbau des *Corps de logis* unabhängigen Zugang zu den seitlichen Flügeln, deren Räume mit wachsender Präferenz dem Wohnen gewidmet wurden, während der Repräsentation die Hausmitte vorbehalten blieb. In Stein umgesetzt, kommen sie als gedeckter Bogengang in

Fig. 14. Skaføgaard, Hofansicht des Herrenhauses mit gedecktem Verbindungsgang vor dem Umbau von 1811. Nach Burman Becker (Nationalmuseum, Kopenhagen).

DAS BEISPIEL DES HERRENHAUSES 207

Skaføgaard (Jütland, um 1580; Fig. 14), als offener Arkadengang in Nørlund (Jütland, 1580er Jahre) vor.

Wiederum sind es mitteldeutsche Schlösser, deren Außenlaufgänge, offen oder geschlossen, sich zum Vergleich und zur Herleitung dieser Schaubedürfnis und Kommunikation befriedigenden Einrichtungen anbieten. In Hartenfels/Torgau (ab 1533) und am Berliner Stadtschloß (ab 1538), in Detmold, Bückeburg und Celle etwa kann bzw. konnte man unterschiedliche Ausprägungen solcher Gänge, bald auf Konsolen schwebend, bald von Stützen getragen, studieren.[17]

Portal und Treppe als Bereiche zeremonieller Bestimmung

In Brejninggaard und Lindenborg, in Visborggaard und Voergaard, sämtlich im hohen Norden Jütlands gelegen, aber auch in Svenstorp in Schonen, haben wir es mit einem Sondertypus frühneuzeitlicher Herrensitze zu tun, bei dem Torhaus und *Corps de logis* eine untrennbare Einheit bilden: eine Disposition, deren typologische Vorbilder wiederum im französischen Schlossbau zu suchen sind, wo es schon seit dem 15. Jahrhundert keineswegs an entsprechenden Beispielen mangelte.[18]

Im Falle des langgestreckten Einflügelbaues von Lindenborg (Fig. 15) durchquerte ein gewölbter Torweg, der heute auf beiden Seiten vermauert ist, ursprünglich das Haus auf seiner Mittelachse. Hauptansicht ist hier nicht wie gewöhnlich die Hofseite mit dem Treppenturm, sondern — gerade umgekehrt — die Feldseite mit den zwei stattlichen runden Ecktürmen und dem von Latrinenvorbauten flankierten Portal. Wie an dem unter Ludwig XII. entstandenen Eingangsflügel (ca. 1498-1510) des Schlosses von Blois, deutlicher aber noch bei einer Anzahl normannischer *manoirs* des frühen 16. Jahrhunderts (Martainville und Auffay-le-Mallet, beide: Seine-Maritime; Tilly, Eure; Fervaques, Calvados)[19] sind Tor und Treppe, die beiden vornehmsten Bereiche eines mittelalterlichen Herrensitzes, zu einer architektonischen Wegmeile zusammengerückt, die ganz im Sinne von repräsentativer Wirkung und zeremonieller Absicht steht.

Der Fassadenprospekt des *Corps de logis*, von den Türmen seitlich gerahmt und von einer Vielzahl von Fensterachsen streng symmetrisch gegliedert, bildet den würdigen Hintergrund für den Empfang hoher Gäste. Das Durchschreiten des Hauses, das dem Betreten vorausgeht, wird zum Ereignis. Hier spielt der erste Akt zeremonieller Begrüßung. Auf dem Hof angekommen, gewährt der Treppenturm in gewohnter Weise den Zugang zu den Geschossen. Aus der schlichten Pforte früherer Zeiten ist in Lindenborg ein weites Portal geworden, in dem nur wenig späteren Voergaard (1586-91; Fig. 16) gar ein üppig geschmückter Triumphbogen. Dort, aber auch schon in dem älteren Visborggaard (um 1575), in Brejninggaard (um 1580; Fig. 17) und um 1600 noch einmal in Svenstorp (Fig. 18), setzt bauplastischer Schmuck neue Akzente. Aufgewertet durch Figurennischen und Masken, umgeben von Rollwerkkartuschen und Schweifwerk, gipfelt in Voergaard der Aufbau in dem großen Wappenaufsatz — eine selbstgefällige Demonstration eines gefestigten Standesbewußtseins und zugleich ein überdeutliches Zeichen einer neuen Epoche: der Renaissance. Die *Entrée solennelle* ist in diesen Häusern unversehens zur *Entrée triomphale* geworden. Was Zugbrücke und Fallgitter einst verschlossen hielten, öffnet sich jetzt, empfängt den Eintretenden in großer Parade.

Atavismus oder Originalität?

Wie traditionsgebunden, ja geradezu mittelalterlich erscheint trotz aller äußerlichen Schmuckfreude und Ausgewogenheit der Gliederung bei näherer Betrachtung hingegen das 1580-83 für Hans Blome, den streitbaren Widersacher Heinrich Rantzaus, in Holstein erbaute Seedorfer Herrenhaus (Fig. 19). Gemeinhin als »Torhaus« bezeichnet, unterliegt seine wirkliche Bestimmung bis heute einem Mißverständnis. Der drei Geschosse hoch aufragende stämmige Backsteinbau, den zwei seitliche schlanke Treppentürme elegant überragen, besitzt in der Mitte des Erdgeschosses eine korbbogige Durchfahrt. Von ihr aus war das Haus ursprünglich allein zugänglich.

Fig. 15. Lindenborg, Eingangsseite des Corps de logis von Süden (oben) und Hofseite von Norden (unten). Vorschlag für eine Rekonstruktion des Torweges von 1925. Nach Hother Paludan (Nationalmuseum, Kopenhagen).

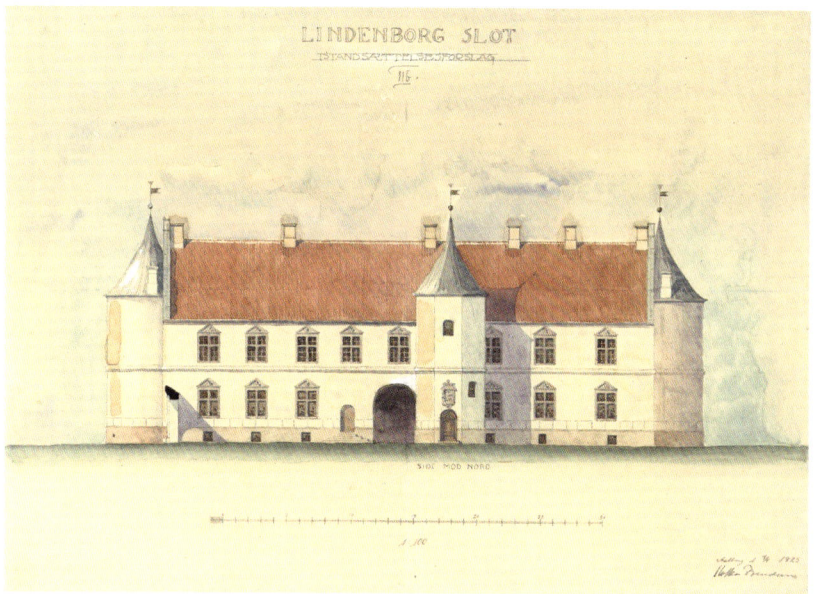

Hier erschlossen auf jeder Seite zwei Türen insgesamt vier gleich große Räume (Fig. 20). Über einen Nebenraum erreicht man noch heute den westlichen Treppenturm, der alle Ebenen einschließlich des hohen Dachgeschosses erschließt. Die Disposition der gegenüberliegenden Seite ist jüngst in ihrer spiegelbildlichen Entsprechung nach Befund rekonstruiert worden.

Enthielt das Erdgeschoß neben Vorräumen die Burgstube und wohl auch die Küche, so dienten die beiden Obergeschosse Wohnzwecken. Eine starke mittlere Trennmauer, die der Firstlinie folgt, zerlegt in Seedorf die Geschoßfläche in zwei gleiche Hälften. Die eine wird im Norden von je einem großen Saal eingenommen, während auf der anderen Seite zwei kleinere Räume bestehen, die beide durch gemauerte Kamine beheizt werden konnten. Alle Räume besitzen mächtige Deckenbalken, die von Sattelhölzern mit geschnitzten Voluten unterfangen werden, wie sie wenige Jahre zuvor schon im herzoglichen Reinbeker Schloss (1571-78) Verwendung fanden. Latrinen waren ursprünglich als altertümliche konsolengetragene Abtritterker an der West- und Ostseite des Hauses unmittelbar neben den Treppentürmen den beiden Wohnstuben zugeordnet. Bis in

DAS BEISPIEL DES HERRENHAUSES

Fig. 16. Voergaard, Eingangsseite des Corps de logis von Südosten (Foto Nationalmuseum, Kopenhagen).

Fig. 17. Brejninggaard, Eingangsflügel, Feldseite (Foto Verfasser).

Fig. 18. Svenstorp, Corps de logis, Eingangsseite des Corps de logis von Westen (Foto A. Henning).

Fig. 19. Seedorf, Hans Blomes Herrenhaus von 1583, Ansicht der Hofseite (Foto Verfasser).

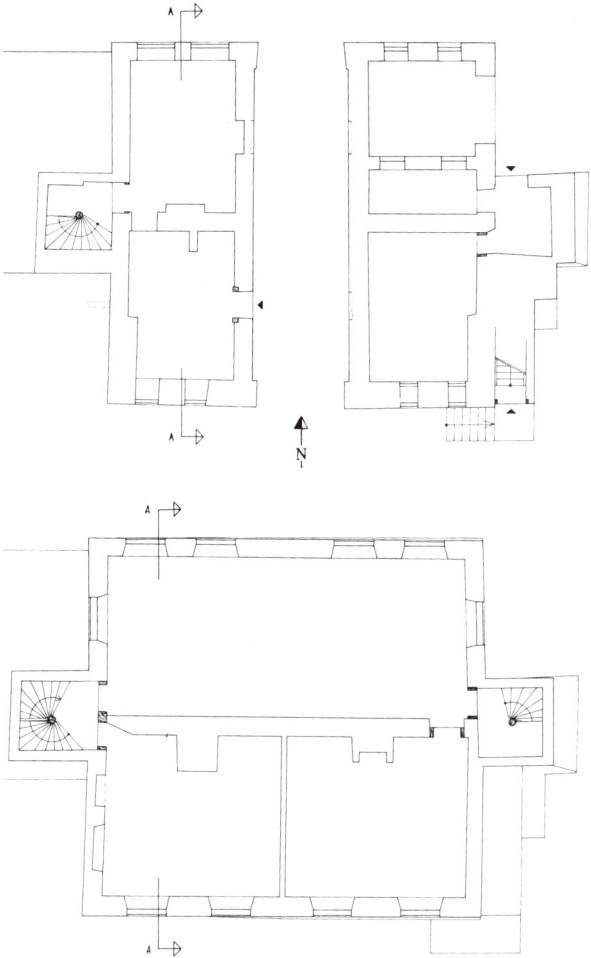

Fig. 20. Seedorf, Herrenhaus, Grundrisse des Erdgeschosses (oben) und des zweiten Obergeschosses (unten). Nach Baehr, Levin und Schnedler (Landesamt für Denkmalpflege Schleswig-Holstein, Kiel).

diesen Bereich muss einst ein Wassergraben die Anlage umgeben haben, wofür auch die Reste einer hölzernen Brücke sprechen, die vor Jahren bei Straßenbauarbeiten feldseitig vor der Durchfahrt entdeckt wurden.

Es kann kein Zweifel bestehen: Hans Blomes Seedorfer „Torhaus" war ein vollwertiges Herrenhaus. Wie Lystrup streng symmetrisch angelegt und von niederländischen Elementen nicht nur in der Gestaltung der Fassaden geprägt, vereint es den auf französische Vorbilder zurückgreifenden Typus des von einem Torweg erschlossenen *Corps de logis* mit dem altertümlich anmutenden Umriss eines Turmes. Das Ergebnis ist singulär, denn die Betonung liegt weder auf einer ausgeklügelten Distribution, noch in dem Bemühen um Kommodität. Hans Blomes Seedorfer Haus »übersetzt« als wahrzeichenhaft hoch aufragender Kompaktbau vielmehr die Erinnerung an mittelalterliche Wohntürme in die architektonische Sprache des späten 16. Jahrhunderts, eine letztlich atavistische Idee, die die Nachwelt schon bald zu der irrigen Überzeugung verleitete, es handele sich hier um nicht mehr als ein Torhaus.[20]

Holsteinische und dänische Doppelhäuser

Einem zweiten Sondertypus begegnen wir in Gestalt des vor allem in den Herzogtümern verbreiteten Doppelhauses. An ein einräumiges Vorderhaus, das in der Regel über einem flachen Keller in zwei Geschossen je einen großen Saal

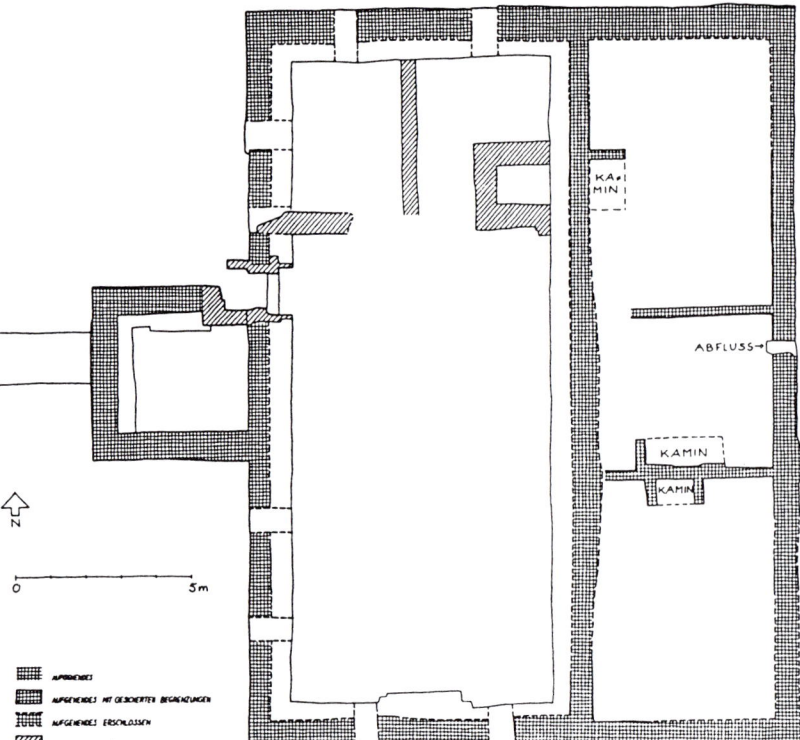

Fig. 21. Alt-Wensin, Archäologisch nachgewiesenes Doppelhaus des 16. Jahrhunderts.Interpretation des Ausgrabungsbefundes. Nach Struve, "Die Ausgrabung eines spätmittelalterlichen Herrenhauses auf der "Schierau" bei Grabek, Kreis Segeberg, in: Die Heimat 84 (1977), 159-167.

aufnimmt, schließt sich rückwärtig eine zweite, meist etwas schmalere Hausparzelle an, die unter einem eigenen Satteldach über kleinere heizbare Stuben, oftmals auch über Latrinen verfügt. Auf der Hofseite kann ein Treppenturm hinzutreten, der das Haus erschließt und die Geschosse miteinander verbindet.

Herrenhäuser dieser Art, deren Hauptverbreitungsgebiet sich im wesentlichen auf das östliche Holstein, die Gegend zwischen Lübeck und Kiel, beschränkt (Fig. 21), kommen oder kamen sonst nur sehr vereinzelt vor, in Jütland einzig und allein in Fussingø und auch auf den dänischen Inseln nur hin und wieder: In Hillerødsholm, dem späteren Frederiksborg, und in Tølløse auf Seeland, zwei Häusern, die sich nicht mehr oder nur stark verändert erhalten haben, in Østerholm auf Alsen, dessen Fundamente ergraben sind,[21] in Fraugdegaard auf Fünen, einem schlichten Fachwerkbau, und in Egeskov, dem größten und wohl auch schönsten Doppelhaus, das, 1554 für Frants Brockenhuus[22] errichtet, allerdings gleichzeitig nicht wenige Elemente spezifisch fünischer Herrenhausarchitektur in sich vereinigt.[23]

Bis auf den heutigen Tag wohlerhalten, kommen in Egeskov (Fig. 22) auch die Vorzüge des kurz zuvor schon in Hesselagergaard verwirklichten Doppelappartements zum Tragen. So formieren sich im Erdgeschoß links und rechts eines mittleren Vorraumes, beide Häuser sowie die runden Ecktürme einnehmend, jeweils drei unterschiedlich große Räume – Stube, Kammer und Kabinett – zu einem vollständigen Appartement. Der hintere Hausteil, der – wie üblich – schmaler ist, enthält darüber hinaus eine Reihe weiterer Räume, die jeweils mit eigenen Latrinen versehen, möglicherweise auch Gästen zur Verfügung standen. Der Vorraum übernimmt in Egeskov anstelle des Korridors die Aufgaben der horizontalen Erschließung. Er ist jedoch mehr als nur ein Vestibül, er ist der kommunikative Mittelpunkt des Hauses: ein Raum, der, im 17. und 18. Jahrhundert als „Halle" oder „Diele" wohlbekannt, der Rezeption der Gäste dient.

Im ersten Obergeschoß von Egeskov liegt der Fest- oder Rittersaal, dessen Zuschnitt bei weitem das Maß vergleichbarer Bauten übertrifft. Hier zeigt sich ein Vorteil des Doppelhauses, denn normalerweise wäre zu seiner Unterbringung ein eigener Flügel vonnöten, wie es in Holckenhavn (Fünen) etwa der Fall ist. Weitere Wohnräume schließen sich an. Wie in Hesselagergaard

Fig. 22. Egeskov, Doppelhaus von 1556, Grundrisse des ersten Obergeschosses (oben) und des Erdgeschosses (unten). Nach Engqvist, Abb. 29.

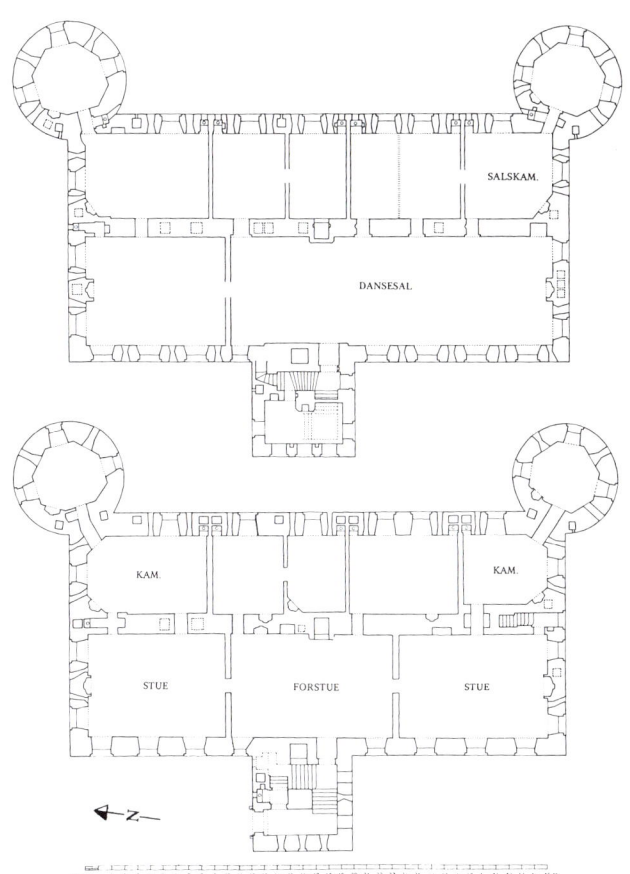

„bekrönt" eine *chambre haute* auch in Egeskov den Treppenturm, verläuft ein Wächtergang am Dachansatz, von dem äußeren Erscheinungsbild der Fassaden im Einzelnen ganz zu schweigen.

Zentralisierende Grundrisse

Blicken wir zum Abschluss noch auf das idealtypische Anlageprinzip des axialsymmetrischen, mittenerschlossenen Baukörpers mit Ecktürmen. Dem südholsteinischen Herrenhaus Ahrensburg, das sich Peter Rantzau, ein Vetter des bekannten Staatsmanns und Humanisten Heinrich Rantzau, errichten ließ, steht von der Zeitstellung her der erste Platz zu, seitdem man die dendrochronologisch ermittelten Fälldaten des Bauholzes für die Grabenaussteifung (1571-77) und den Dachstuhl (Ostturm um 1585) kennt.[24] In Ahrensburg (Fig. 23) darf man sich die ursprüngliche Aufteilung des Inneren so vorstellen, dass in allen drei Geschossen der etwas breiteren Hausmitte große Säle übereinander gelegen haben, die von einer Fensterwand zur anderen durchgingen. In der Mitte der Südwand saßen zwischen den Fenstern Kamine. Links und rechts waren diesen zentralen Sälen — wie im etwa zeitgleichen herzoglichen Schloss Glücksburg — die Wohnräume zugeordnet, die mit den vier schlanken Ecktürmen in Verbindung standen. Da nur von diesen Ecktürmen aus die Abtritte benutzbar waren, deren Fallschächte jeweils in der Mauerstärke der inneren Polygonseiten im Winkel zum Hauptbau verliefen, dürfte sich eine durchgehende Treppenführung, wie sie heute an dieser Stelle besteht, ursprünglich von selbst verbieten. Eine Wendeltreppe mit einem lichten Durch-

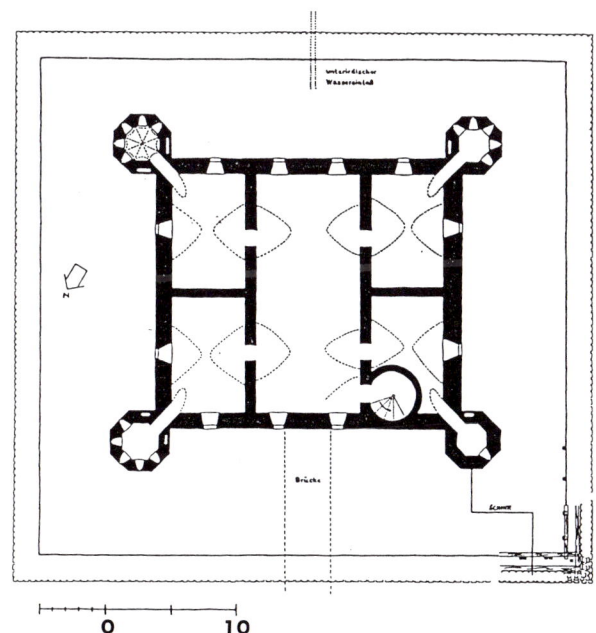

Fig. 23. Ahrensburg, Grundriss des Kellergeschosses und archäologisch nachgewiesene Grabenaussteifung. Nach Teuchert, "Bericht über neue Ergebnisse der Bauforschung des Landesamtes für Denkmalpflege Schleswig-Holstein 1969-1984", in: *Nordelbingen* 54 (1983), 249-258.

messer von immerhin 3,56 Metern befand sich vielmehr im nordwestlichen Bereich rechts neben dem Haupteingang.

Rechteckige Pavillons mit Schweifhauben sind wenige Jahre später in dem mitteljütischen Engelsholm, das 1592 von Knud Brahe, dem Bruder Tycho Brahes, zu bauen begonnen wurde, an die Stelle polygonaler Ecktürme getreten (Fig. 24). Bescheidener, doch strukturell ähnlich präsentiert sich auch das nur wenig jüngere Herrenhaus Damp, das 1595-97 für Melchior von der Wisch und seine Familie in der Landschaft Schwansen nördlich von Kiel unweit der Ostsee entstand (Fig. 25).[25] Ein Jahrzehnt nach Fertigstellung des Tönninger (1580-84) wie des Glücksburger Schlosses (1582-87), hielt der idealtypische Zentralbaugedanke, der im italienischen Villen- und französischen Schlossbau seit dem späten 15. Jahrhundert entwickelt worden war und durch druckgraphische Wiedergaben in der zeitgenössischen Traktat- und Musterbuchliteratur bald weite Verbreitung erfahren hatte, sichtlich Einzug in die Kreise des bodenständigen niederen Adels. Unklar ist in Damp bis heute, ob der Mitteltrakt schon vor der barocken Umgestaltung der Jahre um und nach 1700 eine durch beide Geschosse reichende Halle mit umlaufender Empore gewesen ist oder ob hier einst – wie in Engelsholm – zwei Säle übereinander folgten. Eindeutige Spuren einer früheren Treppenanlage fehlen am Bau, Reste einer älteren Empore sind hingegen vor einiger Zeit zum Vorschein gekommen.[26]

Fazit

Dänische und schleswig-holsteinische Herrenhäuser erweisen sich im 16. Jahrhundert als sensible Gradmesser humanistischer Bildung und als effiziente Rezeptoren höfischer Zivilisation. In Abhängigkeit von ihrem Bauherren, dessen Kultiviertheit und der Nähe oder Ferne zur Fürstenresidenz, differieren sie bisweilen beträchtlich.

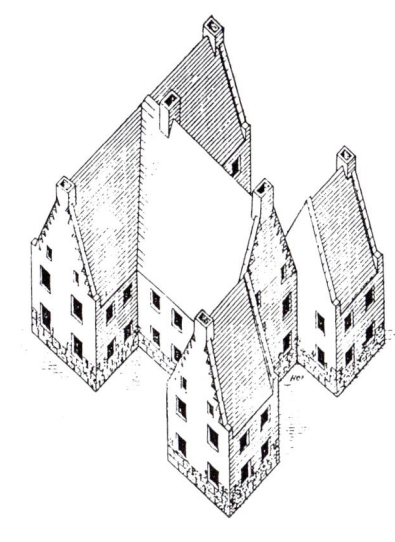

Fig. 25. Damp, perspektivischer Rekonstruktionsversuch des *Corps de logis* im Zustand von ca. 1600 (oben) und Grundriss des Erdgeschosses. Der Bau von 1595-97 ist schraffiert eingetragen. Nach einem Rekonstruktionsversuch von Höppner, in: Schütz, *Adeliges Gut Damp* (Kleine Kunstführer, 1066), München-Berlin 1976.

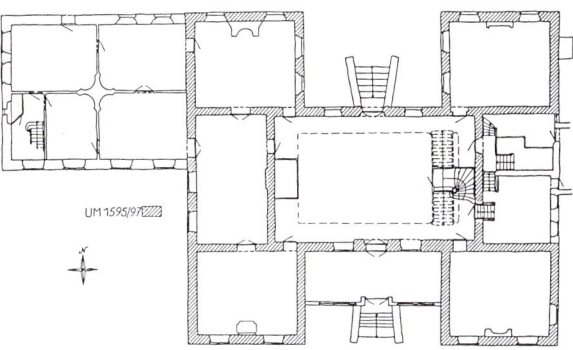

Analog dazu vereinigen sie in ihrer architektonischen Erscheinung einheimische Traditionen, wie das landestypische Baumaterial Backstein oder die besonders für die Insel Fünen charakteristische Fassadengliederung mit umlaufenden, die Geschoßteilung hervorhebenden Rundbogenfriesen und von Konsolen getragenen „Wächtergängen", mit fremden Einflüssen. Letztere verweisen auf unterschiedliche „Quellgebiete", die im wesentlichen mit dem mitteldeutschen Raum des im 15. Jahrhundert zum Kurfürstentum rangerhöhten wettinischen Sachsen, mit den konjunkturstarken städtischen Zentren der südlichen Niederlande und dem für die europäische Hofkultur wegweisenden französischen Kronland, besonders den tonangebenden Territorien entlang der Loire sowie in der Normandie und der Ile-de-France, umrissen werden können. Die 1548 erfolgte Eheschließung der ältesten Tochter König Christian III., Anna, mit dem sächsischen Prinzen und nachmaligen Kurfürsten August, ist für diese Zusammenhänge symptomatisch.

Trotz vielfältiger Fremdeinflüsse bleibt allerdings festzuhalten, dass die dänischen Herrenhäuser der zweiten Hälfte des 16. Jahrhunderts keineswegs nur kompilieren und kopieren, sondern durchaus eigenständig und innovativ mit den befruchtenden Impulsen umgehen. Nach dem Ende der Grafenfehde (1536) entwickelte sich in nur zwei Generationen im Umkreis der führenden Vertreter des Reichsrates, zu denen gebildete und einflussreiche Persönlichkeiten in hohen diplomatischen oder militärischen Ämtern, wie die Kanzler Johan Friis und Ejler Grubbe oder der Reichsmarschall Frants Brockenhuus gehörten, eine frühneuzeitliche Architektur, die im europäischen Kontext bestehen kann. Auf der Suche nach dem Anschluss an die Wohnkultur und die Lebenswelten der führenden Höfe des Südens und Westens kam es zu Berührungen mit mitteldeutschen Planlösungen, wie dem von Treppenturm, Vorraum und Korridor erschlossenen Doppelappartement, das seinerseits auf genuin französische Vorbilder zurückgreift, in denen eine besondere Kommodität hinsichtlich Kaminheizung und Latrinenanordnung, aber auch bei der Etablierung diskreter Rückzugsräume, wie den Turmkabinetten oder den *chambres hautes*, zu verspüren war. Neben diesen eher typologischen und funktionalen Aspekten bestimmte der niederländische Fassadenschmuck mit seinem koloristischen Wechselspiel von Backstein und Haustein sowie der opulenten Verwendung von ornamentalem oder figürlichem Zierrat an Portalen, Fenstern, Giebeln und nicht zuletzt als Bekrönung der immer abwechslungsreicher werdenden Turmdächer den ästhetischen Charakter der dänischen Herrenhausarchitektur, die im Ostseeraum der zweiten Hälfte des 16. Jahrhunderts

Fig. 24. Engelsholm, *Corps de logis*, Hofseite (Foto Hugo Johannsen).

DAS BEISPIEL DES HERRENHAUSES 215

qualitativ und quantitativ konkurrenzlos dasteht und dem Norden Europas ihren unverwechselbaren Stempel aufdrückte.

Wie die Villen Italiens oder die englischen *manor houses* der elisabethanischen Epoche verstehen sich die Herrenhäuser des südlichen Skandinaviens als spezifischer Beitrag der Frühneuzeit zur architektonischen Identitätsstiftung einer in wenigen Jahren zu Ansehen, Reichtum und Machtfülle gelangten gesellschaftlichen Schicht von Aufsteigern. Die glückliche Verbindung von Haus und Hof, Bauwerk und Landschaft, die in den dänischen Herrenhäusern ihren sichtbaren, ja das Land prägenden Ausdruck findet, gehört zu den gelungensten Schöpfungen profaner Bau- und Raumkunst am Beginn der Neuzeit und hat, von der Nachwelt bewundert, frühzeitig das Forschungsinteresse geweckt, dem wir an dieser Stelle nur eine Facette hinzufügen wollen.

Notes

1 Die folgenden Ausführungen geben Gedankengänge wieder, die ausführlicher Darstellung gefunden haben in: Uwe Albrecht, *Der Adelssitz im Mittelalter. Studien zum Verhältnis von Architektur und Lebensform in Nord- und Westeuropa*, München & Berlin 1995.

2 Zu Rygaard und den anderen hier erwähnten fünischen Herrensitzen des mittleren 16. Jahrhunderts vgl. Hans Henrik Engqvist, "Fire fynske herreborge", *Architectura* 2 (1980), 55-125.

3 Beide Bauteile sind seit langem verschwunden. ihre einstige Stellung ist jedoch aus dem Baubefund ablesbar. H.H. Engqvist bezeichnet den rückwärtigen Anbau als *brevkammertårn*, da sich neben seinem Zugang im ersten Obergeschoß eine feuersichere kleine Abseite in der Mauer des Haupthauses erhalten hat, die am ehesten als Archiv oder Tresor zu deuten ist.

4 Albrecht 1995, 96-100. Uwe Albrecht, "Le petit château en France et dans l'Europe du Nord aux XVe et XVIe siècles", in: Jean Guillaume (ed.), *Architecture et vie sociale. L'organisation intérieure des grandes demeures à la fin du Moyen Age et à la Renaissance*, Paris 1994, 193-205. Darüberhinaus: Uwe Albrecht, "Maison forte et maison de plaisance: Le château français à l'époque de Louis XI", in: Bernard Chevalier & Philippe Contamine (eds.), *La France de la fin du XVe siècle. Renouveau et apogée*, Paris 1985, 215-220.

5 Stephan Hoppe, *Die funktionale und räumliche Struktur des frühen Schlossbaus in Mitteldeutschland. Untersucht an Beispielen landesherrlicher Bauten zwischen 1470 und 1570*, Köln 1996 (Veröffentlichungen der Abteilung Architekturgeschichte des Kunsthistorischen Institutes der Universität Köln, 62).

6 Hans-Günther Hartmann, *Moritzburg. Schloß und Umgebung in Geschichte und Gegenwart*, Weimar 1990.

7 Zur Biographie von Johan Friis: *Dansk Biografisk Leksikon*[3], 4, Kopenhagen 1980, 636-640.

8 Zum Stand Hesselagergaard als Stammsitz seiner Erben, siehe auch Birgitte Bøggild Johannsen, "Johan Friis og Hesselagergård", in Carsten Bach-Nielsen et al. (eds.), *Danmark og renæssancen 1500-1650,* Kopenhagen 2006, 270-79.

9 Otto Norn, *Hesselagergaard og Johan Binck*, (*Foreningen til gamle Bygningers Bevarings årsskrift)*, Kopenhagen 1961.

10 Ralf Weingart, "Der Rotwildfries im Güstrower Schloß. Voraussetzungen und Nachfolge", *Mecklenburgische Jahrbücher* 115 (2000), 119-152.

11 Vilh. Lorenzen, *Studier i dansk Herregaardsarkitektur i 16. og 17. Aarhundrede*, Kopenhagen 1921, 135.

12 Vertiefend zur Typologie der frühneuzeitlichen Treppen: André Chastel & Jean Guillaume (eds.), *L'escalier dans l'architecture de la Renaissance*, Paris 1985.

13 Hans Berner Schilden Holsten, "Nakkebølle", in: Louis Bobé (ed.), *Danske Herregaarde ved 1920*, 2.1 (Fyn), Kopenhagen 1923, 125.

14 Albrecht 1995, 107. Henri Chanteux, "Le château de Saint-Ouen en Chemazé", *Congrès Archéologique* (1964), 289-300. Wolfram Prinz & Ronald G. Kecks, *Das französische Schloß der Renaissance. Form und Bedeutung der Architektur, ihre geschichtlichen und gesellschaftlichen Grundlagen*, Berlin 1985, 497-502.

15 Flemming Oluf Jerk, *Herregårde i Danmark, 2: Fyn*, Kopenhagen 1980, 122-125.

16 Chr. Axel Jensen & Charles Christensen, *Lystrup,* (Ældre Nordisk Arkitektur IX), Kopenhagen 1936.

17 Uwe Albrecht, *Der Renaissancebau des Celler Schlosses. Zur Genese des Zwerchhauses und zum Bildprogramm der Fassaden des 16. Jahrhunderts*, Celle 2003. Darüber hinaus: Uwe Albrecht, "Gänge [Umgänge]", in: Werner Paravicini (ed.), *Höfe und Residenzen im spätmittelalterlichen Reich. Bilder und Begriffe*, Ostfildern 2005 (Residenzenforschung, 15.II), 395-397.

18 Uwe Albrecht und Matthias Landt, "Torhaus oder Herrenhaus? Überlegungen zu einem Sondertypus frühneuzeitlicher Schlossbaukunst am Beispiel von Seedorf und Dollrott", *Kunstsplitter. Beiträge zur nordeuropäischen Kunstgeschichte (Festschrift für Wolfgang J. Müller zum 70. Geburtstag)*, Husum 1984, 42-65.

19 Albrecht 1995.

20 Zur weiteren Wirkung vgl. das Quarnbeker Torhaus von 1671. Dazu: Uwe Albrecht & Matthias Landt, "Die erste barocke Gutsanlage im Lande. Neue Ergebnisse der Bauforschung auf Quarnbek", *Nordelbingen* 56 (1987), 27-46.

21 Otto Norn, "Østerholms Slotsruin på Als", *Nationalmuseets Arbejdsmark* 1956, 103-114.

22 Frants Brockenhuus hielt sich von 1540-42 in diplomatischer Mission am französischen Hofe auf, wurde nach seiner Rückkehr Schloßhauptmann von Nyborg, 1562 Mitglied im Reichsrat und 1567 Reichsmarschall. Er fiel 1569 bei der Belagerung von Varberg im Dänisch-Schwedischen Krieg. Vgl. *Dansk Biografisk Leksikon*[3], 2, Kopenhagen 1979, 551-552.

23 Engqvist 1980, 87-112; Jerk 1980, 44-51.

24 Wolfgang Teuchert, "Bericht über neue Ergebnisse der Bauforschung des Landesamtes für Denkmalpflege Schleswig-Holstein 1969-1984", *Nordelbingen* 54 (1985), 249-258.

25 Bernhard Schütz & Christian Stocks, *Adeliges Gut Damp,* München/Berlin 1976 (Kleine Kunstführer 1066). Bernhard Schütz, "Das Herrenhaus Damp", in: *Kunstsplitter. Beiträge zur nordeuropäischen Kunstgeschichte (Festschrift für Wolfgang J. Müller zum 70. Geburtstag)*, Husum 1984, 66-71; Teuchert 1985, 259-264.

26 Teuchert 1985, 263-264.

A NETHERLANDISH MODEL? REFRAMING THE DANISH ROYAL RESIDENCES IN A EUROPEAN PERSPECTIVE

Krista De Jonge

The architecture of the Danish court of the sixteenth and early seventeenth centuries must be considered a uniquely Danish phenomenon, not in the sense of being purely home-grown, but as a characteristic assimilation of "local" manners of building with elements consciously taken from elsewhere. It is the latter choices I would like to examine here. This paper means to address a phenomenon of the *longue durée*, with the intention of broadening the perspective in which the Danish royal residences of the Renaissance can be interpreted. The presence of Netherlandish architects, engineers, masons and sculptors has long been noted on the royal building sites, especially on Kronborg (1574-1586), Frederiksborg (earliest the Bathhouse, 1580 and in particular the rebuilding after the Calmar War 1611-13) and Rosenborg (from 1606). Consequently the high "Netherlandish content" of the so-called Danish Renaissance constitutes an axiom in the historiography of the phenomenon.[1] Nevertheless, a new attempt should be made to identify possible Netherlandish models for the most characteristic features of this royal architecture. These past ten years, research on the lost court architecture of Charles V, Mary of Hungary and Philip II, and on its specific Netherlandish roots, not only has "resurrected" lost buildings once considered the vanguard of architecture, but has also led to new insights in the way this architecture was perceived, first, in the periphery of the Low Countries, and secondly, outside its borders, particularly in Spain.[2]

Bricks and Stones

One of these choices is the use of a very particular type of brick-and-sandstone masonry, as can be seen in manor houses belonging to high officials and noblemen, such as Rosenholm (1559-1562/67), built for royal counsel Jørgen Rosenkrantz, and Lystrup, begun in 1579 for Chancellor Eiler Grubbe, as well as in princely buildings such as Reinbek in Schleswig-Holstein (1571-1573), built for Adolf of Schleswig-Holstein-Gottorf, and the bath house at Frederiksborg (Hans Floris, 1580/81).[3] A most decorative variant is still visible in the courtyard façades of Frederiksborg, although in a damaged state because of later repairs: here the red brick wall masonry is adorned with a lozenge pattern in blue (sintered) brick (Fig. 1).[4]

Although considered as generically 'Netherlandish' with a nebulous medieval origin, in the Low Countries this masonry type arose only as a valid alternative to stone cladding at the close of the fifteenth century.[5] Philip the Good, duke

Fig. 1. Hillerød, Frederiksborg Castle, chapel wing, masonry (Photo author).

Fig. 2. Lille, Palais Rihour, chapel complex, masonry (Photo author).

Fig. 3. Heverlee, Arenberg castle, formerly in possession of the Croÿ family, west tower, before 1519/20 (Photo author).

of Burgundy, indeed took care to specify that his new hall in the Brussels palace (1451-1461) should be entirely covered in the whitish sandy limestone of Brabant, on the pain of heavy fines and demolition of the offending parts. The city of Brussels paid for this extravagance.[6] In 1462, Philip tried to force this technique upon the magistrates of the city of Lille, who had agreed to build him – at equally vast expense – a new residence, now known as the Palais Rihour. The town fathers would have none of it, complaining that the stone did not resist frost and humidity very well (not altogether untrue); they probably feared the high cost of transport.[7] The surviving chapel complex offers ample evidence that the Duke did not altogether succeed: red brick masonry patterned with Burgundian crosses and lozenge motifs in blue bricks rises above the stone-clad ground floor (Fig. 2). By the last decades of the century, brick-and-sandstone masonry had widely gained acceptance with the Burgundian-Habsburg elite, as it had with the French royal entourage during the reign of Louis XII[8] (in the Loire valley and in Northern France).

Four to six layers of brick, alternating with stone bands, constituted the pattern in fashion

Fig. 4. Adrien de Montigny, Boussu Castle, interior view of the courtyard, south façade, early seventeenth century (Albums of Croÿ). Vienna, Österreichische Nationalbibliothek (Photo Nationalbibliothek).

around 1500; some ten to fifteen years later, the use of stone was reduced to the structuring elements of the façade composition. Henceforth, a properly built *logis* would be made of brick above a stone plinth, judiciously strengthened by cut stone at the corners only; stone was also used for window surrounds, door frames, cornices, and coping stones on the stepped gables. For particular applications, stone of a better quality was needed: from the fifteenth century at least, arcades, for instance, were executed in the dark, carboniferous limestone of Ecaussines (*escarsyns* in Flemish sources). This colourful combination, enhanced by a thin layer of red plaster on the bricks (as reported by Albrecht Dürer on his Antwerp visit in 1520),[9] was called *the manner of Brabant* in sixteenth-century sources,[10] most probably after the "nationality" of its principal masters, Anthonis I and Rombout II Keldermans from the duchy of Brabant, who created the main court residences of the time.

Other particular features include, at the start of the 16th century, increasingly regular plans ordered around a courtyard, courtyard elevations consisting of an open arcade on the ground floor and closely serried ranks of cross-mullioned windows above, prominently placed turning staircases and square tower pavilions at the corners, crowned by pyramidal slate roofs with bulbous spires (Fig. 3).[11] The latter invention may be dated as early as 1510-1520, and shows up both in the civil and the religious domain at the same time. By the early 1530s, perfectly symmetrical plans may be found, with four wings arranged around a square or rectangular central courtyard, and a grand staircase on the central axis.

The antique formal repertory (*anticse wercken*), which we call Renaissance today, was easily assimilated into this model, as can be shown in the (lost) palaces built by Mary of Hungary's architect, Jacques Du Broeucq, at Boussu and at Binche in the 1540s and early 1550s,[12] and the residence of Henry III of Nassau at Breda, which was begun in 1536.[13] It should be stressed here that brick-and-stone masonry and square towers

with fanciful spires are in no way indigenous to the county of Hainaut, which is where Boussu, the residence of the Emperor's Master of Horse Jean de Hennin-Liétard, is situated (Fig. 4). In that sense, Boussu's architecture can also be called an import. The imperial court and especially, its prominent foreign members and visitors, had ample occasion to appreciate this architecture when Mary of Hungary received her nephew, Philip of Spain, in 1549, then on his first visit to the lands he was to inherit.[14]

Importing Know-How

This manner of building indeed turned out to be most influential in Spain in the early 1550s, where it was expressly introduced by Philip II even before he left the Low Countries for good (1559).[15] Philip sent his master architect Gaspar de Vega on a study trip (1556) which included the famed Boussu. On May 16, the latter dutifully reported that the castle, while unfinished, is the "best designed and worked" piece of architecture he has seen on his travels.[16] At Valsaín near Segovia, at the Pardo near Madrid (Fig. 5) and at the old Alcázar in Madrid (Torre Dorada II), Philip imported Flemish bricklayers, carpenters, glazers and slate roofers, thus leaving an indelible stamp on Spanish royal architecture well into the seventeenth century.[17] Misleadingly called *estilo austríaco* or "Austrian style" after the origin of the Habsburg dynasty, it was considered explicitly royal even when absorbed in the urban context (e.g. Madrid's and Valladolid's Plaza Mayor).[18]

Frederik II's and Christian IV's showpieces (Fig. 6) thus seem to refer to a well-established model from the Habsburg context, even if taking into account that stone cladding was progressively introduced at Kronborg in the 1580s. In any case, the use of brick in Habsburg royal architecture elevated this humble ersatz material to a new level, and thus also validated a rich, local Danish and Northern German tradition.[19] Of particular interest must have been the lively silhouette with towers and gables, which is characteristic of this architecture from the earliest decades of the sixteenth century. Vredeman de Vries, the only Northern theorist to evoke this construction mode as something specifically Netherlandish,[20] offered the latest version of brick-and-stone masonry, modernized with the most advanced repertory of forms.

Like Philip II, the Danish Kings and noblemen imported specialists whose knowledge of this manner of building was assured. Reinbek's mason and carpenter remain unknown, some mention

Fig. 5. Giuseppe Leonardi (attr.), View of the Pardo, early seventeenth century (Photo © Madrid, Patrimonio Nacional, 10014337).

of a Joris de Vries and Hermen of Ghent (van Genten) in the documents excepted, but the type of masonry, windows and even roof trusses indicate a (Southern) Netherlandish origin (Fig. 7).[21] At Kronborg, the choice of Hans van Paesschen as master mason by Frederik II in 1574 may be explained by referring to Hendrik van Paesschen, a well-known master mason from Antwerp, possibly a relative. Together with Jan Daems, Hendrik van Paesschen had been able to translate Cornelis Floris' design for the new town hall (1561-1565) into workable execution drawings. In particular, the foundations and the staircase – a true master builder's test – were ascribed to these experts in later court documents (1595).[22] The building was known throughout Europe by numerous engravings,[23] and some of its many different kinds of stone had come from Northern Germany (e.g. Bremen).[24] Sir Thomas Gresham called upon Van Paesschen and upon a team of Flemish masons and carpenters for the new Royal Exchange of London, built from 1566 to 1569.[25] Gresham also imported bricks, wainscoting, ironwork, slates, columns and other prefabricated elements wholesale from the Low Countries, including the statue of Queen Elizabeth placed above the entrance. The King, but also the upper strata of Danish society – such as Herluf Trolle and Birgitte Goye – had impeccable connections with the Antwerp milieu, as shown by the history of the tombs they ordered in the 1550s and 1560s from the sculptor Cornelis Floris.[26] Antwerp may very well have served as the hub between the Danish court and the artistic milieu of the court of Mary of Hungary. One of the jury members judging the competition entries for the Antwerp town hall in 1560 had been her architect Jacques Du Broeucq, whom she had left behind when retiring to Spain in 1556.[27] He obviously became well-known to the Antwerp elite, as suggested by the explicit way Lodovico Guicciardini mentions his work at Boussu and Mariemont in his *Descrittione di tutti i Paesi Bassi* of 1567.[28] Although of Florentine origin, Guicciardini had made his home in Antwerp, and the city and its artists have pride of place in his text; as a result, he can be called a well-informed witness.[29]

Architectural Fantasies and Prodigy Houses

Aside from the Antwerp connection, many written reports, in French, Italian, Spanish and German, have survived of the festivities at Binche

Fig. 6. Hillerød, Frederiksborg Castle, general view of the main complex (Photo author).

Fig. 7. Reinbek, residential wing (Photo author).

in 1549 and of the Prince's Progress in general through the Low Countries at the time.[30] They are illustrative of a far broader phenomenon, which is of interest in this context. The European courts, most of which were, after all, linked by ties of blood, however inimical their politics, looked to one another also in the matter of architecture.[31] Cases of explicit rivalry are difficult to find in this field, contrary to, for instance, the collecting of antique statues. Nevertheless, there are examples, such as Mary of Hungary wanting a copy of the drawing of Chambord, Francis I's prodigy house *par excellence*, in the possession of Cardinal Antoine Perrenot de Granvelle in 1554-1555.[32] Francisco de Morães, secretary to the Portuguese ambassador to France, provided a detailed description in Portuguese, no doubt read at the court in Lisbon.[33] The English ambassadors carefully described Francis I's royal gallery at Fontainebleau, with its stuccoed décor created by Primaticcio and Rosso, not forgetting to stress how a great privilege was shown to them, since the King carried its key on his own person.[34] It seems more than a coincidence that Francis' gallery, built from 1529, got a counterpart at the English court (the Queen's gallery at Hampton Court), and at the Habsburg court (Mary of Hungary's gallery at Brussels), at the same time (1533-1537).[35] The gallery, however, is not particularly French in itself. It is characteristic of both the English and the Netherlandish-Burgundian court architecture already before 1500. But it obviously carries great prestige, and can be used in the game of one-upmanship linking these courts. The decorative system of Francis' gallery duly inspired that of Mary's great hall at Binche – one step up from the private to the public, in fact.[36]

It is only prodigy architecture, and the sense of wonder it evokes, which can count on such a jealous reception, and indeed on instant transmission. One way has not received much attention so far. Some of the more extravagant features of the Netherlandish court architecture, which came from the oeuvre of Jacques Du Broeucq, were sublimated into Hans Vredeman de Vries' earliest architectural fantasies, e.g. the terraced roof adorned with a banqueting house, the compact, turreted pavilion placed in a pond, the sunken courtyard with water basin and fountains, the roof garden, and travelled around Europe in this way (Fig. 8).[37] Mary of Hungary's hunting pavilion at Mariemont (built mainly 1547-1549),[38] thus constitutes the prototype for the new garden residence at Clausen (built from the late 1560s).[39] It is the generic type which can also be recognized in the tower-like *Lusthäuser* of the late sixteenth-century German courts, such as the one at Saarbrücken, built for Philip of Nassau-Saarbrücken from 1575.[40] It must be counted among the sources of Christian IV's prodigy house Rosenborg.[41] Raised on its bastionated platform – a new feature possibly inspired by Jacques Androuet Du Cerceau the Elder's paper architecture[42] – and surrounded by water, Rosenborg indeed conforms to the characteristics of the fairy-tale castle, such as described in the popular romance *Amadis de Gaule* (the palace of Apolidon on the Isle Ferme) (Fig. 9).[43] This tale of Spanish origin was available to the northern European courts in the French version of Nicolas Herberay, baron des Essars, who added a lengthy (and fantastical) description of the palace of Apolidon to the Fourth Book (1543).[44] As such, it was immediately recognized for what it was by cultivated visitors from other courts. As luck would have it, the compact noble residence as a type was not without precedents in pre-Renaissance Denmark, and as in France and in the Low Countries, the modernized version fit in with a long-standing tradition.[45] At the time

Fig. 8. Jan and Lucas van Duetecum after Hans Vredeman de Vries, Small perspective view dedicated to Antoine Perrenot de Granvelle, Antwerp 1562, pl. 28. After Peter Fuhring & Ger Luijten, The New Hollstein. Dutch & Flemish Etchings, Engravings and Woodcuts 1450-1700. Vol. XLVII. Vredeman de Vries, Part I, 1555-1571, Rotterdam 1997, Fig. 100.

of its building, in the early decades of the seventeenth century, the type remained in fashion in the Low Countries, as shown by various examples, such as the castle of Lembeek near Brussels, built in 1618 for Guillaume Richardot and Anne de Rye.[46]

Ceremony and Decorum

Visitors' tongues clacked the busiest when discussing the mores of the court, as shown both by the private correspondence of foreign ambassadors and their official reports.[47] The whole of Europe – as it had at the apogee of Burgundian splendour in the middle of the fifteenth century – reacted to the elaborate Spanish-Burgundian court ceremonial, the *Etiquetas de la Casa de Austria*.[48] We should not forget that the court residences offered the framework for this "ceremonial" (understood as the set of regulations which govern daily life and all special events at court), and existed in a dialectic relationship with this code. The disposition and evolution of the Spanish royal residences, and that of the main Netherlandish court residence, the palace at Brussels, can only be understood through this process of continuous exchange, as we have shown elsewhere.[49] There were sometimes surprisingly direct consequences. The innovations in plan, developed in the Netherlandish context in the first half of the sixteenth century, had a direct impact, for instance, on the disposition of the hunting castle of the Pardo near Madrid (see Fig. 5).[50] As shown by his own sketch in his *Rasguños*, the King had the party walls broken out in the north and south wing, thus creating two closed courtside galleries on the first floor, which were doubled by open loggias on the external façades (from 1559): thus an absolutely essential component was added to the residence. This remodelling was further completed in a distinctly Flemish style, by adding square towers with a bulbous spire to the corners; here smaller private spaces were concentrated, to replace the ones lost when the interior walls were demolished. In addition, high slate roofs in the Flemish mode were erected to cover the wings. In 1556, as we have mentioned, Philip's architect Gaspar de Vega had indeed been sent to look at the most important work of Jacques Du Broeucq at Boussu, where a similar double-pile disposition with courtside galleries, abutted by square pavilions, existed since 1540 on the first floor.[51] One of these new state galleries, decorated with dynastic portraits, in its turn must have served as the model for the new long gallery at Clausen, home to one of Philip's most seasoned generals in the Low Countries.[52]

Even more than his Burgundian ancestors, whose ceremonial he basically used, Philip cultivated the distance between his person and his visitors. From the 1560s he systematically extended the sequence of rooms they had to cross before being received in his august presence.[53] The Spanish *antecámaras* duly made their appearance at the Brussels court, which was remodelled from 1598, but *antichambres* also showed up in the apartments of the French King at the time of Henry III and Charles IX, equally noted for their love of ceremony.[54] This new buffer zone between the more public rooms (*salle, sallette*) and the private chamber (*chambre*) with its annexes (*garderobe, cabinet*) served to sort out visitors according to even finer distinctions in rank. A thorough study of the Danish royal apartment related to the Danish ceremonial is still being eagerly awaited, but even the most cursory glance at the disposition of Frederiksborg's north wing with the king's and queen's apartments suggests that a comparative study with other European courts could be very fruitful.[55] Did the spatial organisation of the Danish royal residences show the same tendency towards more complex arrangements? There remains, in particular, the question of the use of ceremonial rooms of a particular type – and of great prestige – at the Danish court. For example, did a true long gallery exist at Kronborg; i.e. as an integral part of the public, state apartments, such as the *Salón de Batallas* of the Escorial, for instance, which closes off the sequence of ceremonial spaces on the main floor?[56] The state galleries of the Habsburg world are not primarily connecting spaces,[57] while the superimposed galleries of the east wing at Kronborg, built by Anthonis van Obbergen in the 1580s, seem to function mainly as corridors between the main apartments and the great hall and chapel respectively (Fig. 10).

Fig. 9. Copenhagen, Rosenborg Castle, general view from the south-east (Photo author).

To Speculate

Why did Danish Kings choose Netherlandish artists such as Van Obbergen to realize their architectural ambitions? It has been surmised that they were appreciated as much for their technical expertise and familiarity with a particular brand of masonry, as with their familiarity with the latest repertory of forms.[58] If technical know-how were not relevant, why not after all limit oneself to paper models, such as offered by Vredeman de Vries, and use the local workforce only? Or was it a mark of sophistication in patronage to have some Netherlandish artists – such as having an Italian cook – at your beck and call? Netherlanders could evidently be counted on for the necessary ability to realize one of the latest models of court architecture, neither French nor Italian but still equipped with the latest vocabulary of forms (into which French and Italian sources were also assimilated). If a "Habsburg" court architecture truly existed, in the middle of the sixteenth century it wore Netherlandish dress, at least in the Low Countries and in Spain. The Habsburg connections of the hated predecessor, Christian II, were surely never forgotten, and even if political enmity precluded any overt reference to him in the royal iconography of Frederik II and Christian IV. It should be noted that the official image of the deposed King, as created by Netherlandish court artist Jan Gossaert, conforms to a Habsburg imperial model; it was known throughout Europe thanks to the mass medium of the time, the engraving.[59]

To understand the Netherlandish component in the Danish Renaissance fully, at least in the royal context, the particular mentality of European court society needs to be taken into account, across the boundaries of religion. The greatest prestige lay, I would like to suggest here, in having foreign specialists in military architecture at one's disposal, war being, after all, the primary raison d'être for the nobility. Hans van Paesschen came in as a military engineer in 1564. It may be recalled here that at the time, Antwerp's bastioned fortifications were amongst the most modern in Northern Europe; Anthonis van Obbergen's study trip of 1577-1578 is also readily explained by the fact that by that time, they had been augmented by one of the most modern citadels, designed by Francesco Paciotto (1567).[60] Hans van Steenwinckel the Elder's tombstone in

Fig. 10. Elsinore, Kronborg Castle, south wing and gallery wing seen from south-east (Photo author).

A NETHERLANDISH MODEL? 227

the Nicolaikirke at Halmstad (d. 1601) specifically mentions his activities in this field, amongst others at Christianopel/Auskær and Halmstad, as the high point of his career.[61] The *palazzo in fortezza*, created at Kronborg by the addition of a bastioned outer defence works, is a specifically imperial type. The well-known surviving example at Jülich, built for William V the Rich of Jülich-Kleve-Berg from 1549, was most probably modelled after Charles V's most personal creation in the Low Countries; i.e. Ghent citadel (1540), but the designs of Jan Mijnsheeren and Jacques Du Broeucq for the imperial palace on the latter site were never realized.[62] The continuing Habsburg-Valois conflict created a laboratory for avant-garde fortifications along the southern border of the Low Countries, in which many specialists from Italy and the Low Countries were active.[63] Traffic in specialists occasionally went the other way, as shown by the following Danish example from the early seventeenth century. Frederiq Kierurt, one of the engineers who built the famed heptagonal city and pilgrimage church of Scherpenheuvel/Montaigu for Albrecht of Austria and Isabella of Spain, was a Dane. Christian IV stressed that this expert in "all manner of fortifications" had to come back after a specified time: Kierurt was lent to the Archdukes, not given.[64] Such specialists, especially when they had military expertise, could constitute valuable "gifts", and thus play an essential role in court life.

Notes

1. For instance, see D. F. Slothouwer, *Bouwkunst der Nederlandsche Renaissance in Denemarken*, Amsterdam 1924, and the contribution of Dirk Van de Vijver to this volume. On a more general level, see Thomas DaCosta Kaufmann, "Ways of Transfer of Netherlandish Art", in: Małgorzata Ruszkowska-Macur (ed.), *Netherlandish artists in Gdańsk in the Time of Hans Vredeman de Vries. Material from the conference organized by Museum of the History of the City of Gdańsk and Weserrenaissance-Museum Schloß Brake Lemgo*, Gdańsk & Lemgo 2006, 13-21.

2. Parts of the following are discussed more extensively in Krista De Jonge, "Antiquity Assimilated: Court Architecture 1530-1560", in: Krista De Jonge & Konrad Ottenheym (eds.), *Unity and Discontinuity. Architectural Relations between the Southern and Northern Low Countries (1530-1700)*, Turnhout 2007 (Architectura Moderna 5), 55-78.

3. Recent synthesis (with older bibliography) in Birgitte Bøggild Johannsen & Hugo Johannsen, "Adelsvælde og renæssance", in: John Erichsen & Mikkel Venborg Pedersen (eds.), *Herregården. Menneske – landskab – samfund - bygninger* 2, Copenhagen 2005, 21-94, and in Birgitte Bøggild Johannsen & Hugo Johannsen, "Architektur og billedkunst", in: Carsten Bach-Nielsen et al. (eds.), *Danmark og renæssancen 1500-1650*, Copenhagen 2006, 112-129.

4. Overview of Frederiksborg's chronology and architects in Steffen Heiberg, "Et kongeligt triumftog", in: Steffen Heiberg (ed.), *Christian 4. og Frederiksborg*, Copenhagen 2006, 28-41 (with older bibliography). See also Slothouwer 1924, 89-119, Joakim A. Skovgaard, *A King's Architecture. Christian IV and His Buildings*, London 1973, 41-66, and Juliette Roding, *Christiaan IV van Denemarken (1588-1648). Architectuur en stedebouw van een Luthers vorst*, Alkmaar 1991, 63-81 (all based on older source publications).

5. The following is discussed more at length in Krista De Jonge, "'Up die maniere van Brabant'. Brabant en de adelsarchitectuur van de Lage Landen (1450-1530)", in: Raymond Van Uytven (ed.), *Gotiek in Brabant. De Brabantse stad. Dertiende colloquium, Leuven 18-19 oktober 2002*, s. l. 2003 (*Bijdragen tot de geschiedenis* 86, no. 3-4), 409-423.

6. Alfonsine Maesschalck & Jos Viaene, "Het Leuvense stadhuis en de Brusselse *Aula Magna*, Brabantse gotiek of niet?", in: Van Uytven 2003, 294.

7. See in general Max Bruchet, "Notice sur la construction du palais Rihour à Lille", *Bulletin de la Commission historique du Département du Nord* 31 (1922), 209-299.

8. Josiane Sartre, *Châteaux "brique et pierre" en France. Essai d'architecture*, Paris 1981, 39-40; Uwe Albrecht, *Der Adelssitz im Mittelalter. Studien zum Verhältnis von Architektur und Lebensform in Nord- und Westeuropa*, Munich & Berlin 1995, 103.

9. Henri Plard, "Anvers dans le 'Journal de voyage aux Pays-Bas' de Dürer (1520-1521)", in: Pierre Jodogne (ed.), *Lodovico Guicciardini (1521-1589),* Leuven 1990 (Travaux de l'Institut Interuniversitaire pour l'étude de la Renaissance et de l'Humanisme X), 247.

10. Averbode, Archive of the Norbertine Abbey, *Register van Herkenrode* VI, 112, *Verdincknisse Clooster van Herckenrode 1512-1550*: contract of Master Lauwerys Ballen with Abbess Mechtildis de Léchy for the refuge of the Cistercian abbey of Herkenrode at Hasselt (Limburg, Belgium), 14 January 1542; Edouard Van Even,

Renseignements inédits sur la construction du refuge de l'abbaye de Herkenrode, à Hasselt (1542-1545), s. l. 1874.

11 De Jonge 2003, 414-415; Krista De Jonge, "Hofordnungen als Quelle der Residenzenforschung? Adlige und herzogliche Residenzen in den südlichen Niederlanden in der Burgunderzeit", in: Werner Paravicini & Holger Kruse (eds.), *Höfe und Hofordnungen 1200-1600. 5. Symposium der Residenzen-Kommission der Akademie der Wissenschaften in Göttingen veranstaltet gemeinsam mit dem Deutschen Historischen Institut Paris und dem Staatsarchiv Sigmaringen, Sigmaringen 5. bis 8. Oktober 1996,* Sigmaringen 1999 (Residenzenforschung, 10), 190-217.

12 Krista De Jonge & Marcel Capouillez (eds.), *Le château de Boussu*, Namur 1998 (Etudes et Documents, Monuments et Sites 8).

13 Gerard W. C. van Wezel, *Het paleis van Hendrik III graaf van Nassau te Breda,* Zeist & Zwolle 1999 (De Nederlandse Monumenten van Geschiedenis en Kunst 100).

14 See the following chronicle: Juan Cristoval Calvete de Estrella & Jules Petit (transl.), *Le très-heureux voyage fait par très-haut et très-puissant prince don Philippe, fils du grand empereur Charles-Quint, depuis l'Espagne jusqu'à ses domaines de la Basse-Allemagne, avec la description de tous les Etats de Brabant et de Flandre*, I-V, Brussels 1873-1884 (Société des Bibliophiles de Belgique 7, 10, 11, 15, 16), reprint Brussels 2000 (Algemeen Rijksarchief en Rijksarchief in de provinciën, reprints 161).

15 The following is discussed at length in Krista De Jonge, "Triunfos flamencos: Felipe II y la arquitectura del Renacimiento en Flandes", in: José Martínez Millán (ed.), *Felipe II (1527-1598). Europa y la Monarquía Católica*, IV. *Literatura, Cultura y Arte*, Madrid 1998, 347-369.

16 "un pedaço de edificio el mejor labrado y tratado que yo aca ni alla hasta agora he visto" (Archivo General de Simancas, Obras y Bosques: Segovia, legajo 1); Francisco Iñiguez Almech, *Casas reales y jardines de Felipe II*, Rome 1952 (Consejo superior de investigaciones científicas, delegación de Roma), 156.

17 On these residences, see José J. Martín González, "El palacio de 'El Pardo' en el siglo XVI", *Boletín del seminario de estudios de arte y arqueología* 36 (1970), 5-41; Javier Rivera Blanco, "El Palacio de El Pardo entre Carlos V y Felipe II", *Reales sitios* 37, 145 (2000), 2-15; Véronique Gérard, *De castillo a palacio. El Alcázar de Madrid en el siglo XVI*, Madrid 1984, 81-83; María Angeles Martín González, *El Real Sitio de Valsaín*, Madrid 1992; José Manuel Barbeito, *El Alcázar de Madrid*, Madrid 1992, 37-38; José Manuel Barbeito, "Felipe II y la arquitectura. Los años de juventud", in: Fernando Checa Cremades (ed.), *Felipe II un monarca y su época. Un príncipe del Renacimiento*, Madrid 1998 (Sociedad Estatal para la Conmemoración de los Centenarios de Felipe II y Carlos V), 83-103. The Escorial also had "Flemish" roofs; Georg Kubler, *Building the Escorial*, Princeton 1982, 103-105; Agustín Bustamante García, *La octava maravilla del mundo. Estudio histórico sobre el Escorial de Felipe II*, Madrid 1994, 495.

18 See also Fernando Chueca Goitia, "La influencia de los Países Bajos en la arquitectura española", in: Fernando Chueca Goitia, *El Escorial, piedra profética,* Madrid 1986, 195-215.

19 Albrecht 1995, 174-226. See also the contribution of this author to the present volume.

20 In his ARCHITECTURA *Oder Bauung der Antiquen auss dem Vitruvius*, Antwerp 1577, introduction to the Doric order. Krista De Jonge, "'Anticse wercken': la découverte de l'architecture antique dans la pratique architecturale des anciens Pays-Bas Livres de modèles et traités 1517-1599", in: Marie-Christine Heck, Frédérique Lemerle & Yves Pauwels (eds.), *Théorie des arts et création artistique dans l'Europe du Nord du XVIe au début du XVIIIe siècle. Actes du colloque international organisé les 14 et 16 décembre 2000 à Lille*, Lille 2002 (Travaux et recherches), 65-68.

21 Antje Wendt, *Das Schloß zu Reinbek. Untersuchungen zur Ausstattung, Anlage und Architektur eines landesherrlichen Schlosses*, Ph.D. dissertation, Kiel 1991, 163-167.

22 Floris Prims, *Het stadhuis te Antwerpen. Geschiedenis en beschrijving*, Antwerp 1930; August Corbet, "Cornelis Floris en de bouw van het stadhuis van Antwerpen", *Belgisch tijdschrift voor oudheidkunde en kunstgeschiedenis/Revue belge d'archéologie et d'histoire de l'art* 6 (1936), 223-264; Jozef Duverger, "Cornelis Floris II en het stadhuis te Antwerpen", *Gentse bijdragen tot de kunstgeschiedenis* 7 (1941), 37-72; Holm Bevers, *Das Rathaus von Antwerpen (1561-1565). Architektur und Figurenprogramm*, Hildesheim, Zürich & New York 1985 (Studien zur Kunstgeschichte 28). For the court documents, see J. Rylant & Marguerite Casteels, "De metsers van Antwerpen tegen Paludanus, Floris, de Nole's en andere beeldhouwers", *Bijdragen tot de geschiedenis* 31 (1940), 185-203; Jozef Duverger & M. J. Onghena, "Beeldhouwer Willem van den Broecke alias Guilielmus Paludanus (1530 tot 1579 of 1580)", *Gentse bijdragen tot de kunstgeschiedenis* 5 (1938), 75-140, especially 102; Marguerite Casteels, *De beeldhouwers De Nole te Kamerijk, te Utrecht en te Antwerpen*, Brussels 1961 (Verhandelingen van de Koninklijke Vlaamse Academie voor Wetenschappen, Letteren en Schone Kunsten van België, Klasse der Schone Kunsten 16), 51-52.

23 The oldest known of which dates from the year of the

building's completion, 1565 (by Melchisedech van Hooren). Exemplar in Vienna, Graphische Sammlung Albertina. Jan Van der Stock (ed.), *Antwerpen, verhaal van een metropool 16*^{de}*-17*^{de} *eeuw*, Antwerp 1993, 244, cat. 92. The (augmented) Plantin editions of Lodovico Guicciardini's popular text on the Low Countries (from 1581) also comprised a double-page illustration, see for instance Lodovico Guicciardini, *Description de touts les Pais-Bas, autrement appellés la Germanie inférieure, ou Basse Allemagne…*, Antwerp 1582, between pages 26 and 27.

24 On this topic, see Roger Adriaenssens, "Sur l'hôtel de ville d'Anvers et les apports des carrières wallonnes dans son édification", *Bulletin de la commission royale des monuments et des sites*, N. S. 9 (1980), 125-141.

25 John F. Murray, *Vlaanderen en Engeland. De invloed van de Lage Landen op Engeland ten tijde van de Tudors en de Stuarts*, Antwerp 1985, 298; Jean Imray, "The Origins of the Royal Exchange", in: Ann Saunders (ed.), *The Royal Exchange*, London 1997, 26-35; Ann Saunders, "The Building of the Exchange", in: Saunders 1997, 36-49.

26 Antoinette Huysmans, "De sculptuur", in: Antoinette Huysmans et al. (eds.), *Cornelis Floris 1514-1575 beeldhouwer architect ontwerper*, Brussels 1996, 81-83, 86-92, 103.

27 Corbet 1936, 232-233; Duverger 1941, 40-41, 52-53; Domien Roggen & J. Withof, "Cornelis Floris", *Gentse bijdragen tot de kunstgeschiedenis* 8 (1942), 132; Adriaenssens 1980, 125.

28 Lodovico Guicciardini, *Descrittione… di tutti i Paesi Bassi, altrimenti detti Germania inferiore…*, Antwerp 1567, 101.

29 Lodovico Guicciardini, *De idyllische Nederlanden. Antwerpen en de Nederlanden in de 16*^{de} *eeuw*, Monique Jacqmain (ed.), Antwerp & Amsterdam 1987, 5-13; Dina Aristodemo, "La figura e l'opera di Lodovico Guicciardini", in: Pierre Jodogne (ed.), *Lodovico Guicciardini (1521-1589)*, Leuven 1990 (Travaux de l'Institut Interuniversitaire pour l'étude de la Renaissance et de l'Humanisme X), 19-35.

30 See, amongst others, Calvete de Estrella & Petit 1873-1884, III, 81-152; Jean de Vandenesse, "Sommaire des voyaiges faictz par Charles, cinquiesme de ce nom (…) depuis l'an mil cincq cens et quatorze jusques le xxve de may de l'an mil cincq cens cinquante-ung inclusivement (…)", in Louis-Prosper Gachard (ed.), *Collection des voyages des souverains des Pays-Bas*, II, Brussels 1874, 384-389; Charles Ruelens, *Le siège et les fêtes de Binche, 1543 et 1549. Deux documents publiés avec traduction, liminaires et notes*, Mons 1878 (Publication de la Société des bibliophiles belges, séant à Mons 25); Hieronymo Cabanillas, *Relacion muy verdadera de las grandes fiestas que la Serenissima Reyna doña Maria ha hecho al Príncipe nuestro señor en Flandes ….*, Medina del Campo 1549, republished in: Cristóbal Pérez Pastor (ed.), *La imprenda en Medina del Campo*, Madrid 1895, 57-67; Vicente Álvarez, *Relación del camino y buen viaje que hizo el Príncipe de España D. Phelipe (…)*, Marie-Thérèse Dovillée (ed.), Brussels 1964, 90-110; Léon Marquet & Samuel Glotz, *Une relation allemande méconnue (1550) des fêtes données par Marie de Hongrie, à Binche et à Mariemont, en août 1549*, Binche 1991 (*Les cahiers binchois*, special issue); Samuel Glotz, *De Marie de Hongrie aux Gilles de Binche. Introduction critique aux Triomphes de Binche célébrés du 22 au 31 août 1549*, Binche 1995 (*Les cahiers binchois* 13); Samuel Glotz, *Lettre-harangue adressée à Charles Quint, par les chevaliers errants de la Gaule Belgique. Bruxelles et Binche, 1549. Un document viennois inédit*, Binche 2000 (*Les cahiers binchois*, 17).

31 In general, see David Thomson, *Renaissance architecture. Critics, Patrons, Luxury*, Manchester & New York 1993, 143-151.

32 Between 23 November 1554 and 9 December 1555, Du Broeucq made a copy of the "platte-fourme de Chambourch appartenant à Monsieur d'Arras" (Antoine Perrenot de Granvelle, Bishop of Arras), for the Emperor. Document quoted by Robert Hedicke, *Jacques Dubroeucq de Mons*, Brussels 1912 (*Annales du cercle archéologique de Mons* 40), 431-432.

33 Thomson 1993, 88.

34 William McAllister Johnson, "On some neglected usages of Renaissance diplomatic correspondence", *Gazette des Beaux-Arts*, 6, 79 (1972), 51-54; Monique Chatenet, *La cour de France au XVI*^{e} *siècle. Vie sociale et architecture*, Paris 2002 (De Architectura), 252-253.

35 Sylvie Béguin et al., "La galerie François Ier à Fontainebleau", *Revue de l'art* 16-17 (1972); Simon Thurley, *The Royal Palaces of Tudor England. Architecture and Court Life 1460-1547*, Yale 1993, 141-143; Krista De Jonge, "Le palais de Charles Quint à Bruxelles. Ses dispositions intérieures aux XVe et XVIe siècles et le cérémonial de Bourgogne", in: Jean Guillaume (ed.), *Architecture et vie sociale. L'organisation intérieure des grandes demeures à la fin du moyen age et à la Renaissance*, Paris 1994 (De Architectura 6), 116-121.

36 Krista De Jonge, "Le langage architectural de Jacques Du Broeucq", in: De Jonge & Capouillez (eds.) 1998, 180-185; De Jonge 2007a, 72-75; Krista de Jonge, "Marie de Hongrie, maître d'ouvrage (1531-1555), et la Renaissance dans les anciens Pays-Bas", in: Bertrand Federinov & Gilles Docquier (eds.), *Marie de Hongrie. Politique et culture sous la Renaissance aux Pays-Bas* (Monographies du Musée royal de Mariemont 17), Morlanwelz 2008, 124-139.

37 Krista De Jonge, "Vredeman de Vries as a Disseminator of Architectural Novelties", in: Heiner Borggrefe & Vera Lüpkes (eds.), *Hans Vredeman de Vries und die Folgen*, Marburg 2005 (Studien zur Kultur der Renaissance 3), 83-90.

38 Krista De Jonge, "Mariemont, 'Château de chasse' de Marie de Hongrie", *Revue de l'art*, 149 (2005), 45-57.

39 Krista De Jonge, "Le château et le jardin de 'La Fontaine' à Clausen dans leur contexte européen", in: Jean-Luc Mousset & Krista De Jonge (eds.), *Un prince de la Renaissance. Pierre-Ernest de Mansfeld (1517-1604). II. Essais et catalogue*, Luxembourg 2007, 239-262, in particular 254-256.

40 Ulrike Kiby, "Der Pavillon auf Säulen. Kunst zwischen Tradition und Religion", in: Ursula Härting & Ellen Schwinzer (eds.), *Gärten und Höfe der Rubenszeit. Internationales Symposium im Gustav-Lübcke-Museum der Stadt Hamm vom 12.01.2001 bis 14.01.2001*, Worms 2002 (*Die Gartenkunst* 14,1, special issue), 56-64; Ulrike Weber-Karge, '… einem irdischen Paradieß zu vergleichen…'. *Das Neue Lusthaus in Stuttgart. Untersuchungen zu einer Bauaufgabe der deutschen Renaissance*, Sigmaringen 1989, 102-108.

41 Recently discussed in Peter Kristiansen, "Christian 4. og det store lysthus i haven", in: Jørgen Hein et al., *Christian 4. og Rosenborg 1606-2006*, Rosenborg 2006, 7-24 (with older literature); Slothouwer 1924, 120-132; Skovgaard 1973, 67-73; Roding 1991, 41-61.

42 See the models in the *Livre d'architecture* of 1582, or the Verneuil pavilion designed in the 1560s and illustrated in *Les plus excellents bastimens de France* (1576-1579). The bastionated platform can be seen in the French context starting with Chambord and Ecouen. With thanks to Jean Guillaume.

43 André Chastel, *The Palace of Apolidon*, The Zaharoff Lecture for 1984-5, Oxford 1986; Thomson 1993, 85-89.

44 The original Spanish romance was translated by Herberay in twelve volumes, published by Denys Janot in Paris between 1540 and 1546. Stephen Ph. J. Rawles, "The earliest editions of Nicolas de Herberay's translations of Amadis de Gaule", *The Library*, 6, 3, no. 2 (1981), 91-108; Jean-Marc Chatelain, "L'illustration d'Amadis de Gaule dans les éditions françaises du XVIe siècle", in: *Les Amadis en France au XVIe siècle*, Paris 2000 (Cahiers V. L. Saulnier, 17), 41-52. On fictional architecture of the time, see Thomson 1993, 51-96.

45 See note 19 and also Krista De Jonge, "Images inédites de la villégiature dans la périphérie de Bruxelles, XVIe-XVIIIe siècles. Maisons des champs et maisons de plaisance", in: Monique Chatenet (ed.), *Maisons des champs dans l'Europe de la Renaissance, Actes des premières Rencontres d'architecture européenne, Château de Maisons, 10-13 juin 2003*, Paris 2006 (De Architectura 11), 276-277.

46 Chris De Maegd, "Een einde en een nieuw begin: de creatie van een Hof van Plaisantie", *Monumenten & Landschappen* 17 (1998) 1, 6-44; Krista De Jonge & Konrad Ottenheym, "The Production Process for Architecture within the Context of the Courts (1580-1700)", in: De Jonge & Ottenheym 2007, 175-178.

47 On the French court, see Chatenet 2002, 106-141.

48 Antonio Rodríguez Villa, *Etiquetas de la Casa de Austria*, Madrid 1913; Ludwig Pfandl, "Philipp II und die Einführung des Burgundischen Hofzeremoniells in Spanien", *Historisches Jahrbuch* 58 (1938), 1-38; Ottavio Cartellieri, *La Cour des Ducs de Bourgogne*, Paris 1946; Cristina Hoffmann, *Das Spanische Hofzeremoniell von 1500 to 1700*, Frankfurt 1985 (Erlanger Historische Studien 8); Rafael Domínguez Casas, *Arte y etiqueta de los reyes católicos. Artistas, residencias, jardines y bosques*, Valladolid 1993, 557-564; Werner Paravicini, "The Court of the Dukes of Burgundy: A Model for Europe?", in: Ronald G. Asch & Adolf M. Birke (eds.), *Princes, Patronage, and the Nobility. The Court at the Beginning of the Modern Age c. 1450-1650*, Oxford 1991 (Studies of the German Historical Institute London), 69-102; Cristina Hoffmann-Randall, "Die Herkunft und Tradierung des Burgundischen Hofzeremoniells", in: Jörg Jochen Berns & Thomas Rahn (eds.), *Zeremoniell als höfische Ästhetik in Spätmittelalter und Früher Neuzeit*, Tübingen 1995 (Frühe Neuzeit. Studien und Dokumente zur deutschen Literatur und Kultur im europäischen Kontext 25), 150-156; Jacques Paviot, "Ordonnances de l'hôtel et ceremonial de cour aux XVe et XVIe siècles, d'après l'exemple bourguignon", in: Kruse & Paravicini 1999, 167-174; G. Redworth & Fernando Checa, "The Courts of the Spanish Habsburgs, 1500-1700", in: John Adamson (ed.), *The Princely Courts of Europe: Ritual, Politics and Culture Under the Ancien Régime, 1500-1700*, London 1999, 47-50.

49 De Jonge 1994; Krista De Jonge, "'t Hof van Brabant als symbool van de Spaanse hofhouding in de Lage Landen", *Bulletin van de Koninklijke Nederlandse Oudheidkundige Bond* 98 (1999), 183-198.

50 See note 17, in particular Barbeito 1998, 96-99. Reconstruction of the décor of the galleries in María Kusche, "La antigua galería de retratos del Pardo: su reconstrucción arquitectónica y el órden de colocación de los cuadros", *Archivo Español de Arte* 64, 253 (1991), 1-28; María Kusche, "La antigua galería de retratos del Pardo: su reconstrucción pictórica", *Archivo Español de Arte* 64, 255 (1991), 261-283; and María Kusche, "La antigua galería de retratos del Pardo: su importancia para la obra de Tiziano, Moro, Sánchez Coello y Sofonisba Anguissola y su significado para Felipe II, su

fundador", *Archivo Español de Arte* 65, 257 (1992), 1-36.

51 De Jonge & Capouillez 1998, 69-158.

52 De Jonge 2007b, 246-250.

53 As shown by the transformation of the Alcázar of Madrid, see Gérard 1984², 81-89.

54 Chatenet 2002, 135-140, 179-184, 250-253 points to Italian and English precedents for the earliest examples, which appear in Henry II's time. See also Monique Chatenet, "Architecture et cérémonial à la cour de Henri II: l'apparition de l'antichambre", in: Hervé Oursel & Julia Fritsch (eds.), *Henri II et les arts. Actes du colloque international Ecole du Louvre et musée national de la Renaissance-Ecouen*, Paris 2003 (XVes Rencontres de l'Ecole du Louvre), 355-380.

55 Also with the Northern German courts, especially related ones. See Stephan Hoppe, *Die funktionale und räumliche Struktur des frühen Schlossbaus in Mitteldeutschland 1470-1570*, Cologne 1996 (62. Veröffentlichung der Abteilung Architekturgeschichte des Kunsthistorischen Instituts der Universität zu Köln); Stephan Hoppe, "Die ursprüngliche Raumorganisation des Güstrower Schlosses und ihr Verhältnis zum mitteldeutschen Schloßbau. Zugleich Beobachtungen zum 'Historismus' und zur 'Erinnerungskultur' im 16. Jahrhundert", in: *Burgen und frühe Schlösser in Thüringen und seinen Nachbarländern*, Munich 2000 (Forschungen zu Burgen und Schlössern, 5), 129-148. We thank Uwe Albrecht and Jens Martin Neumann for having made their research notes on Frederiksborg available to us.

56 Cornelia von der Osten-Sacken, *El Escorial. Estudio iconológico*, Madrid 1984 (Libros de Arquitectura y Arte), 115-116; Bustamante García 1994, 672-673.

57 Argued in De Jonge 1994, 116-121 and De Jonge 2007b, 246-250. One splendid exception, the gallery in Mary of Hungary's palace at Binche (built 1547-1549), served as entrance corridor and "vestibule" for the great hall; however, the imperial theme of its decoration points to a similar representative function. Walter Cupperi, "Arredi statuari italiani nelle regge dei Paesi Bassi asburgici meridionali (1549-56). I. Maria d'Ungheria, Leone Leoni e la galleria di Binche", *Prospettiva. Rivista di storia dell'arte antica e moderna*, nos. 113-114 (2004), 98-116.

58 On the latter topic, see Konrad Ottenheym, "Architectura Moderna. The Systemization of Architectural Ornament around 1600", in: De Jonge & Ottenheym 2007, 111-136 and the contribution of this author to the present volume.

59 Ariane Mensger, *Jan Gossaert. Die niederländische Kunst zu Beginn der Neuzeit*, Berlin 2002, 99-104.

60 Clearly shown in the many maps of the city which circulated at the time, and extensively described by Guicciardini, Antwerp's fortifications must have been well known to the whole of Europe. Guicciardini 1582, 104-107, 156-157. See Anne-Marie Adriaenssens, *Het iconografisch stadsbeeld van Antwerpen in de 16[de] eeuw*, Master's Thesis, Katholieke Universiteit Leuven, 1982 and Jan Grieten & Paul Huvenne, "Antwerpen geportretteerd", in: Jan Van der Stock (ed.), *Antwerpen, verhaal van een metropool 16de-17de eeuw*, Antwerp 1993, 69-77.

61 Roding 1991, 31-36.

62 Hedicke 1911, 296-297, 430-432; Victor Fris, *La citadelle de Charles-Quint et le château des Espagnols à Gand*, Antwerp 1922; Charles van den Heuvel & Bernhard Roosens, "Los Países Bajos. Las fortificaciones y la coronación de la defensa del imperio de Carlos V", in: Carlos J. Hernando Sánchez (ed.), *Las fortificaciones de Carlos V*, (Sociedad Estatal para la Conmemoración de los Centenarios de Felipe II y Carlos V), Madrid 2000, 578-605, especially 593-599. On Jülich, see amongst others Hartwig Neumann, *Zitadelle Jülich. Grosser Kunst- und Bauführer*, Jülich 1986 and Jürgen Eberhardt, *Die Zitadelle von Jülich – Wehranlagen, Residenzschloß und Schloßkapelle – Forschungen zur Planungs- und Baugeschichte*, Jülich 1993.

63 Charles van den Heuvel, 'Papiere Bolwercken'. De introductie van de Italiaanse stede- en vestingbouw in de Nederlanden (1540-1609) en het gebruik van tekeningen, Alphen aan den Rijn 1991. Krista De Jonge, "Architekturpraxis in den Niederlanden in der frühen Neuzeit: Die Rolle des italienischen Militärarchitekten; der *status quæstionis*", in: Günter Bers & Conrad Doose (eds.), *Der italienische Architekt Alessandro Pasqualini (1493-1559) und die Renaissance am Niederrhein: Kenntnisstand und Forschungsperspektiven,* Jülich 1994, 363-383; Bernhard Roosens, "Die Modernisierung älterer Festungen im niederländischen Grenzgebiet zu Frankreich und die italienischen Ingenieure (1534-1560)", in: Günter Bers & Conrad Doose (eds.), 'Italienische' Renaissancebaukunst an Schelde, Maas und Niederrhein. Stadtanlagen – Zivilbauten – Wehranlagen, Jülich 1999, 155-165; Van den Heuvel & Roosens 2000; Bernhard Roosens, *Habsburgse defensiepolitiek en vestingbouw in de Nederlanden (1520-1560)*, Ph.D. Thesis, University of Leiden 2005; Pieter Martens, "Pierre Ernest de Mansfeld et les ingénieurs militaires: la défense du territoire", in: Jean-Luc Mousset & Krista De Jonge (eds.), *Un prince de la Renaissance. Pierre-Ernest de Mansfeld (1517-1604). II. Essais et catalogue*, Luxembourg 2007, 97-112.

64 This reference was communicated to me by Luc Duerloo, to whom I am most indebted. Brussels, Algemeen Rijksarchief, *Duitse Staatssecretarie* 475, fol. 34, Letter

from Christian IV to Archduke Albrecht, November 14, 1606. On Scherpenheuvel/Montaigu, see J. H. Plantenga, *L'architecture religieuse dans l'ancien duché de Brabant depuis le règne des archiducs jusqu'au gouvernement autrichien (1598-1713)*, The Hague 1926, 33-43; Piet Lombaerde, "Dominating Space and Landscape: Ostend and Scherpenheuvel", in: Werner Thomas & Luc Duerloo (eds.), *Albert & Isabella 1598-1621. Essays*, Turnhout 1998, 173-183; Tine Meganck, *De kerkelijke architectuur van Wensel Cobergher (1557/61-1634) in het licht van zijn verblijf te Rome*, Brussels 1998 (Verhandelingen van de Koninklijke Academie voor Wetenschappen, Letteren en Schone Kunsten van België, Klasse der Schone Kunsten 60, no. 64), 52-94; Pieter Martens & Joris Snaet, "De Mariale bedevaartskerk van Scherpenheuvel. Een onderzoek naar dynastieke relaties en de verspreiding van ontwerpen en denkbeelden over architectuur", *Bulletin van de Koninklijke Nederlandse Oudheidkundige Bond* 98 (1999), 214-225; Luc Duerloo & Marc Wingens, *Scherpenheuvel, Het Jeruzalem van de Lage Landen,* Leuven 2002.

KING SOLOMON AND THE IMPERIAL PARADIGM OF CHRISTIAN IV (1588-1648)

Juliette Roding

When Christian IV was seven years old, in 1584, his father Frederik II organized an official homage to his son throughout Denmark at the regional courts ('landsting') in the nation's provincial capitals. For this occasion in Viborg, a play was performed that was written by Hieronymus Justesen Ranch, the rector of the town's cathedral school. This play was entitled: *Kong Salomons Hyldning* (The Paying of Homage to King Solomon).[1] In one of the play's most important scenes twelve angels form a circle around seven planets while singing praise to the young Christian who – as Solomon – is dressed in a white robe and kneeling down in the centre. This poignant scene clearly portrays the little prince as the centre of the universe. In another act of the play the dying king David expresses his joy in knowing that his son Solomon has been paid homage to by his people. These parallels between David-Solomon and Frederik-Christian are very important as they clearly reveal King Frederik's intention of making the Danish kingship hereditary instead of elected, though this would not become a historical reality until the year 1660. With respect to David, the Book of Samuel reveals that it was God himself who made David's dynasty heritable.[2]

Hieronymus Justesen Ranch's play stresses the fact that the biblical King Solomon is the model for the world's new Solomon: Christian IV. Just like the biblical king, he too is destined to become the master builder in God's service and build a temple, a new royal castle, fortifications, warehouses for corn and other 'useful' buildings. And extending the parallel between the two, it was also believed that these buildings would be amongst the most beautiful and well-built on earth. Jens Skafbo, in his 'Mirror of Princes' from 1590, advises the young Christian IV to follow the example of King Solomon.[3] In 1603 the town of Hamburg paid homage to the Danish king, an event which was considered of high political importance. Christian IV showed his thankfulness by presenting the town with a splendid triumphal procession of five carriages, each of which displayed various 'inventions'. Christian IV rode in the last carriage, presenting himself as the Sun King in full Roman costume, surrounded by sunbeams, and sitting on the throne of Solomon.[4]

In 1606 Christian IV visited his brother-in-law King James I, the husband of his sister Anna, most probably to gain his support for his endeavour to become German-Roman emperor. Among the many festivities which were held during his

Fig. 1. Poul Rumler (attr.), Copenhagen, Rosenborg Castle, Ceiling from the first castle, 1607 (Photo Rosenborg).

stay in England, the ones at the Castle of Theobalds were unsurpassed and also incorporated the Solomon motif. In a masque written and designed by Ben Jonson, Christian IV appeared and presented himself as King Solomon, receiving gifts from the Queen of Sheba.[5] Further testament to the link with the Solomon figure is the fact that in 1608 Jonas Charisius, who was in charge of purchasing musical instruments and works of art for Christian IV in the Netherlands, bought a huge painting with a *Judicium Salomonis* by the painter Cornelis van der Voort in Amsterdam.[6]

Around 1600 there was a strong belief throughout Europe that there would soon be a new and wealthy world empire headed by a wise spiritual leader.[7] Ezekiel's visions of the Temple of Solomon were an important source for this belief, while Solomon himself served as the role model for the wise ruler, the temple builder, who possessed magical powers and who stimulated colonization, trade, industry, mining, as well as the arts and sciences. Between 1596 and 1604 Juan Bautista Villalpando published his reconstructions of the Temple of Solomon in a treatise which was dedicated to Philip II of Spain, a ruler who, just like Christian IV, saw himself as the new Solomon, in the line of the emperors Justinianus and Charles the Great.[8] Philip II's own temple was the Escorial, built by Juan de Herrera and finished in 1584. Villalpando's ideas achieved widespread popularity all over Europe and were translated and taken up by scholars and writers in northern Europe, particularly those in England and the Netherlands.

Until now the centrality of Solomon – and the Queen of Sheba – in European court culture in the Early Modern Period has not been recognized and therefore also not sufficiently studied. It is interesting to see that an overwhelming number of rulers identified themselves with Solomon and tried to make the Solomon figure operational, both interpretatively and actively, in the hope to acquire and have at their disposal, just like the Biblical king, a universal wisdom ordained by God. If attained, this wisdom would presumably place them, as an *alter deus*, at the forefront of a new empire, in a new age which would find itself on the eve of the New Jerusalem. Solomon thus plays a crucial role in the development of Absolutism. Central to this search for a divine ruling principle was the investigation of the natural world in all its diversity.

A vast array of mystical-religious, utopian-political, alchemistic and cabbalistic literature was available to these rulers and to their chief scholars and artists. The Wisdom of Solomon and the brilliant expertise for which he was famous were comprehensively described by Joannes de Pineda in his *De Re Salomonis* of 1609: this book encompasses philology and the art of writing, poetry, music, astronomy, cosmography, geography, medicine, architecture, mathematics, hydraulics, but also agriculture and livestock breeding, fruit farming and mining.[9]

Some of the rulers who – as far as my research has thus far indicated – identified themselves, or at least allowed themselves to be openly identified with Solomon, include the Emperor Rudolph II, who was addressed by his courtiers as the 'Solomon of Bohemia',[10] Ferdinand I of Tirol, Henri IV and later on Louis XIV of France, James I of England and a number of important German ruler princes: of Braunschweig-Wolfenbüttel, the Palatinate, Saxony, Gottorp, Hessen-Kassel and Bavaria.

Moritz of Hessen-Kassel, for example, described the visit by a Persian legation to the Kassel court in 1600 while on its way to Prague stating that representatives from the East had stopped at Kassel to marvel at the wisdom and learning of the German Solomon.[11] The Biblical King was also a role model for the 16th century Turkish Sultan, Suleiman the Magnificent, as his name indicates.

The various dynastic ties and aspirations, specific geographical circumstances, the presence of mineral resources, internal jealousies and the desire for *aemulatio*, inspiration from Italy, as well as personal interests, must have led to very diverse interpretations of the Solomon-theme amongst the different courts. An in-depth comparative study of the way in which each of the above-mentioned royals demonstrated his Solomonic wisdom could shed much light on the diversity regarding the Solomon-motif. Architecture, both permanent and semi-permanent, decoration programmes and individual artworks, together with literary expression in the form of odes, inaugural and marital sermons, as well as libretti for court ballets, joyous entrees and scientific experiments, were important means for this expression. These rulers' spouses often profiled themselves as the queen of Sheba. The popularity of the theme is further reflected in the many paintings on this subject. Perspective painters in particular have often chosen this theme and have portrayed the Biblical love couple within the architectural framework of an ideal palace.[12]

As I have demonstrated before, the meaning behind some of Christian IV's most important building enterprises and his plans for the Stock Exchange in Copenhagen can, in my opinion, only be properly understood in relation to the specific claims to the Lutheran world empire made by the Danish king, an empire over which he hoped to preside as a new Solomon. Let us therefore take a closer look at some of these projects, beginning with the Castle of Rosenborg whose construction began in 1606.[13]

According to the alchemist tradition, the pleasure-castle or Castle of Love with its *hortus conclusus* was the place where the Philosopher's Stone, the Stone of Wisdom, was to be found.[14] This Stone of Wisdom was said to be the result of the happy union of king and queen. The architecture and interior decoration of the castles and the therein contained objects and collections were naturally important spearheads for showcasing the couple's Solomonic wisdom. Alchemist laboratories, workshops for the 'divine lathwork', water mills and grinderies all belonged to the sphere of the pleasure-castle, as did objects springing from an interest in the subterranean world, the heavenly, the workings of light, sound and smell and sensory perception, the breeding of animals and cultivation of new crops, as well as the development of medicines. All of these interests were pursued and cultivated in the context of the Castle of Love.

The painted ceiling of the first Rosenborg (Fig. 1) clearly shows that Christian IV was familiar with this alchemist tradition.[15] The ceiling reveals a celestial *hortus conclusus* marked by obelisks and surrounded by birds. The middle of this arrangement portrays a seated royal couple. Furthermore there are the depictions of the four seasons, goddesses of fertility and the Muses playing on instruments. Also of great significance are the two birds, one flying, one not flying, keeping each other in balance. Within the alchemist tradition they represent the 'white union' between king and queen, the chemical wedding, which leads to the creation of the Stone of Wisdom.[16] We know from a treatise written in 1615 by the Paracelsist Peder Payngk, a court alchemist who had a small house and a laboratory within the gardens of Rosenborg, and from a written account of the years 1648 and 1649, that within the Rosenborg *hortus conclusus* all kinds of experiments were conducted in an attempt to find the Stone of Wisdom.[17]

Rosenborg, like many other pleasure castles (cf. also the paper by Krista de Jonge, p. 223-225) in Europe, therefore served in a complex manner as a laboratory for new expressions of culture and scientific knowledge where symbolism and both artistic and scientific practice went hand in hand. One can only wonder what texts from classical times may have existed and been referred to in order to make possible the 'invisible music' of Rosenborg and the automatic bridge in the garden which Christian IV could operate from a distance. Were these texts sufficient to make manifest these triumphs or had these new discoveries really been arrived at en passant?

It is also of great importance to consider the roles of the various scholars and artists present at court, both those who remained there by invitation and those who offered their services to rulers during their travels. One of the most notable of these travelling artists was the architect-sculptor-philosopher Giovanni Maria Nosseni (1544-1620) from Lugano, who created the inventions for the crowning ceremonies of Christian IV in 1596 and afterwards received commissions for the pleasure house Sparepenge ('Saving Money') and the castle of Frederiksborg. According to Nosseni, a new world order would soon come into existence following the Babylonian, Persian, Greek, Roman, Papal and Turkish empires.[18]

In addition to all the allusions made to the Solomon figure during his lifetime, even Christian IV's death sermon spoke to the idea that Frederiksborg was Solomon's temple and Christian IV the excellent architect who had been very much inspired by David[19] (although it was de facto Frederik II who started the huge enterprise of rebuilding the castle). The Christian IV – Solomon link was also reflected within the intimate atmosphere of the king's private study. Two huge paintings by the Dutch artist Jan van Wijck hung in this room, one representing the Anointment of Solomon and the other the Meeting of Solomon and the Queen of Sheba.[20] As Hugo Johannsen has demonstrated, the complex programme of the church interior from about 1608 can be read as a glorification of the Danish king who would protect and propagate True Christianity throughout the four continents, to eventually lead to a New Golden Age.[21]

The ceiling of the more worldly Dance Hall above the church (which is now a reconstruction following the fire of 1859) shows an elaborate depiction of seven mechanical arts ranging from the building of watermills, instruments for navigation, book printing, distillation, clock making, and the production of gunpowder and fortification. The surrounding texts make clear that these mechanical arts could only flourish if based on piety. In the Lutheran way of thinking, religion had to be the basis of science, and science itself had to be first and foremost a useful and pragmatic pursuit. It is precisely this philosophy which was espoused in Rosecrucian circles around 1600 and which was written about by Johann Valentin Andreae in his *Christianopolis* of 1619, constituting the first specifically Lutheran vision of a utopian town and world.[22]

The Round Tower

The first stone of Trinity Church, church of the University, was laid in 1637.[23] The architects were Hans van Steenwinckel the Younger, and after his death in 1639, Leonard Blasius from Amsterdam. This building too expressed the close relationship between religion and science. Situated above the church itself was the university library, next to which the Round Tower was erected with its indoor riding ramp and on top, the university's observatory (Fig. 2). Both library and tower are clearly distinct from the church in their architectonical expression. In these areas, which constitute the 'scientific' part of the building, we find rather heavy Romanesque-like windows. A painting representing 'Christian IV and David in one body'[24] once hung in the Trinitatis Church. At the time depicted in the painting, Christian IV has grown older and his son Christian has been elected to become the next Solomon. The tower bears a rebus which, according to Thomas Bang, a professor of Hebrew who dedicated a small treatise to it, imploringly states the following: "Jehova, please send true knowledge to the heart of the crowned king Christian IV".[25] According to Bang, Christian IV as the new King David, with his tower, recreated the *Turris Davidica*, the tower of wisdom that was situated on Mount Sion in Jerusalem where astrological observations were carried out and interpreted by prophets. Johannes de Pineda also mentions this Tower of David, which according to him was "aedificata con propugnaculis": built with buttresses.[26] I think it is exactly this motif that we find back in the Round Tower.[27] The idea to include a spiral tower in the cylindrical corpus of the tower – which as we know is typical of the Tower of Babylon – was perhaps a way of underscoring the fact that during Christian IV's reign there was no longer a contradiction between the old 'Eastern' knowledge and the Christian knowledge based on the Bible and its teachings.

According to the astronomer Christian Longomontanus, the tower was so wide and strong that it would have been possible for Christian IV, who is said to have personally drawn the plan for the installation of its celestial globes and other scientific instruments, to reach the observatory in a horse-drawn carriage by riding up the ramp. This ramp circled the Round Tower's middle pier seven times: "ut curru ascensus in sublimitatem Turris pro R. M. fiat, amplitudem suam, firmitudinemq. Justam nascisceretur".[28] The last part of this 'route to heaven' consisted of a small staircase. In this way the king could symbolically ascend through the various stages of knowledge to reach the stars, the light and eternal wisdom. The Round Tower of David signifies and bears testimony to the fact that, at

Fig. 2. Johan Andreas Greyss, The Round Tower of Trinity Church. Title page, 1646, of Thomas Bang, Phosphorus Inscriptionis Hierosymbolicae… Copenhagen 1648. Copenhagen, The Danish Royal Library (Photo Royal Library).

the time, Copenhagen was considered to be the New Jerusalem, with Trinity Church as its spiritual centre.

Most interesting about Denmark is the fact that the Solomon metaphor seems to have persisted as part of Danish court culture until well into the eighteenth century. Between 1663 and 1671 Frederik III ordered a throne of Solomon made of Narwhale tusk ('unicorn horn'), adorned with eight-sided amethyst and surrounded by silver lions. This throne was placed at the south side of the Long Hall of Rosenborg Castle. The painting *Salomon's Judgement* by Rubens, now in the Statens Museum for Kunst, which was a present given to Frederik III in the late 1640s by Josias Rantzau, was hung on the wall near this throne. The throne of Frederik III can thus be seen – as Jørgen Hein has recently argued – as a northern version of the throne which belonged to the east-Roman emperor in Constantinople.[29]

Fig. 3. King Solomon, emblem in W. Westhovius, Cimbri emblemata...Christiano IV...dedicata, Copenhagen 1640. Copenhagen, The Danish Royal Library (Photo Royal Library).

In her 1999 article published in *Architectura*: 'The King's Temple: Frederik's Church as a religious and political symbol',[30] Birgitte Bøggild Johannsen points out that in 1740 the Solomon-metaphor was used in the inaugural sermon of the new church at Christiansborg. This metaphor was also referred to in 1749 in not less than three sermons in praise of the 300-year anniversary of the Oldenburg dynasty and the laying of the foundation stone of the new Frederik's Church (Frederikskirken). The allusion to Solomon was again made on King Frederik V's birthday in 1757 when the Danish king was compared with Solomon as *Rex Edificator Optimus*, the highest king-architect. At that time, as Bøggild Johannsen demonstrates, the image of Copenhagen as a Nova Roma and as a New Jerusalem in literary sources was still very much alive as well.[31]

With this in mind it is interesting to turn to the hypothesis put forward by the Danish architect Nis Nissen in 1989. In his book on the town planning of Copenhagen he explains that it seems that there had been a certain continuity in the town planning of Copenhagen from Christian IV's time onwards, until about 1760, with the aim of turning the Danish capital into an ideal city, with a perfect circular ground plan.[32]

Now that we know how important the Solomon metaphor was for the Danish kings, it seems reasonable to conclude that Nissen was right in his observations. There must have been a kind of master plan for Copenhagen, though this may have existed more as an idea rather than as a fixed drawn plan. One Danish king after the other tried to emulate and become a Solomon figure, tried to obtain eternal wisdom, and tried to build the new eternal city. It is interesting that in Heinrich Khunrath's *Rosarium Philosophalis* of 1609, the Stone of Wisdom is symbolized by a representation of the Heavenly Jerusalem as an 'ideal city' from which the new world leader would send out his ships throughout the world.[33]

In 1642 the Jewish scholar Beniamin Musaphia, who for some years was the personal doctor of medicine and advisor of Christian IV, dedicated a treatise to him, the *Epistola regia*, written in Amsterdam, in which he praises Christian IV for his great wisdom and knowledge of the Jewish cabbala. The dedication pays honourable tribute to the notion of Christian IV's divine rulership stating that, just like the great King Solomon, he was able to control the tides of the sea: "… Ad regim clementissimi, daniae …, veram, a sapientissimo hominum Rege Salomoh, fluxus et refluxus maris causam, olim assignatam.[34]

Notes

1   A. Karker (ed.), Hieronymus Justesen Ranch *Kong Salomons hyldning… (1584)*, Copenhagen 1973.

2   H. Johannsen, "Regna firmat Pietas. Eine Deutung der Baudekoration der Schloßkirche Christian IV zu Frederiksborg", *Hafnia. Copenhagen Papers in the History of Art* 3 (1974), 67-140.

3   The Royal Library, Copenhagen, Gl. Kgl. Saml. 386, 2⁰, 80-89. See Karker 1973; further on Jens Skafbo's work, see Sebastian Olden-Jørgensen, "Johann Damgaards Alithia (1597): Genrehistorie, tekstshistorie og idehistorie: Omkring et dansk fyrstespejl til Christian 4", *Fund og Forskning* 45 (2006), 35-55.

4   M. R. Wade, "The Politics of Splendor. Christian IV of Denmark's Hamburg Pageant", *Chloë* 23 (1995), 25-39.

5   H. Glarbo, "Om den dansk-engelske Forbindelse i Christian IV's og Jacob I's tid", *Fra Arkiv og Museum*, 2, 2 (1943), 49-80.

6   E. Nyström, "Jonas Charisius' Indkøb af Malerier og Musikinstrumenter i Nederlandene 1607-08", *Danske Magazin*, 5, 6 (1909), 225-236. See also the contribution by Badeloch Noldus.

7   C. Hinrichs, "Die Idee des geistigen Mittelpunktes Europas im 17. und 18. Jahrhundert", in: *Das Hauptstadtproblem in der Geschichte. Festgabe zum 90. Geburtstag Friedrich Meineckes*, Tübingen 1952 (Jahrbuch für die Geschichte Mittel- und Ostdeutschland, 1), 85-109; F. Schalk, 'Das goldene Zeitalter als Epoche', *Archiv für das Studium der neueren Sprache und Literatur*, 199 (1962), 85-98; H. Levin, *The Myth of the Golden Age in the Renaissance*, London 1970.

8   J. Rykwert, *On Adam's House in Paradise. The Idea of the Primitive Hut in Architectural History*, New York 1972, 120-129.

9   Joannes de Pineda, *De Re Salomonis…*, Mainz 1613 (1609).

10 Mentioned in H. Carrington Bolton, *The Follies of Science at the Court of Rudolph II 1567-1612*, Milwaukee 1904, 14.

11 B. T. Moran, *The Alchemical World of the German Court. Occult Philosophy and Chemical Medicine in the Circle of Moritz of Hessen (1572-1632)*, Stuttgart 1991 (Sudhoffs Archiv, Zeitschrift für Wissenschaftsgeschichte, 29), 16, note 12.

12 See e.g. the many examples in H. Borggrefe & V. Lüpkes (eds.), *Hans Vredeman de Vries und die Renaissance im Norden*, Munich 2002.

13 J. Hein et al. (eds.), *Christian 4. og Rosenborg 1606-2006*, Copenhagen 2006.

14 H. M. E. de Jong, *Michael Maier's Atalanta fugiens. Bronnen van een alchemistisch emblemenboek.* Dissertation, Utrecht 1965, 94-96, 119-123.

15 J. Roding, *Christiaan IV van Denemarken (1588-1648). Architectuur en stedebouw van een Luthers vorst.* Dissertation, Alkmaar 1991, 41-61.

16 As for example shown in an illustration in Myllus (1632).

17 A. Fjelstrup, *Guldmagere i Danmark i det XVII aarhundrede*, Copenhagen 1906; *Das hochste Geheimbnus der gebenedeiten Steins der Weisen nach dem Process und Meinung Theophrasti Paracelsi…Von dem aller durchleuchtigsten Könning Christian den 4'…mitgetheillt worden im Iahr 1615*; Roding 1991, 56-58; *Ephemerides Laboratorii Regii*, The Royal Library, Copenhagen, Gl. Kgl. Saml. 272, 2^0 [1648-49].

18 W. Mackowsky, *Giovanni Maria Nosseni und die Renaissance in Sachsen*, Dissertation, Berlin 1904, 106-107.

19 H. Bramsen, "Frederiksborg som emblem og arkitektur", in: Axel Thygesen (ed.), *Tilegnet Mogens Koch*, Copenhagen 1968, 63.

20 S. Heiberg, "Art and the Staging of Images of Power – Christian IV and Pictorial Art", in: B. Noldus & J. Roding (eds.), *Pieter Isaacsz (1568-1628), Court Painter, Art Dealer and Spy*, Turnhout 2007, 231-243, especially 233, note 11.

21 Johannsen 1974.

22 Roding 1991, 72-81; Johann Valentin Andreae, *Reipublicae Christianopolitanae Descriptio …*, Strassbourg 1619; Th. Topfstedt, "Die 'Christianopolis' des Johann Valentin Andreae. Städtebaugeschichtliche Aspekte einer protestantischen Utopie", *Blätter für Württembergische Kirchengeschichte* 83-84 (1984), 20-33.

23 J. Steenberg, *Rundetaarn og sneglegang*, Copenhagen 1952; H. Bramsen, *Symbolik i Christian den Fjerdes arkitektur med særligt hensyn til Trinitatis-komplekset i København*, Copenhagen 1982; J.- Chr. Klamt, "Die Runde Turm in Kopenhagen als Kirchturm und Sternwarte", *Zeitschrift für Kunstgeschichte* 38 (1975) 153-170; J.- Chr. Klamt, "The Round Tower in its Relation to Architecture of the 16th Century", *Hafnia, Copenhagen Papers in the History of Art*, 4 (1976), 55-70.

24 Bramsen 1982, 36.

25 Thomas Bang, *Phosphorus Inscritionis Hierosymbolicae …*, Copenhagen 1648 (1646).

26 De Pineda 1613, 200-201.

27 Roding 1991, 101-112.

28 Christian S. Longomontanus, *Introductio in Theatrum astronomicum …*, Copenhagen 1639, 10.

29 J. Hein, "En trone af enhjørninghorn og løver af sølv", *Siden Saxo* 23 (2006), 2, 38-45.

30 B. Bøggild Johannsen, "Kongens tempel, Frederikskirken som religiøst og politisk symbol", *Architectura, Arkitekturhistorisk Årsskrift* 21 (1999), 131-157.

31 Bøggild Johannsen 1999, 157.

32 N. Nissen, *Københavns bybygning 1500-1856, visioner, planer, forfald*, Copenhagen 1989.

33 Heinrich Khunrath, *Rosarium Philosophalis (Amphiteatrum Sapientiae Aeternae)*, Hannover 1609; Roding 1991, 60.

34 B. Musaphia (Dionysius), *Epistola regia, de maris reciprocatione ad potentissim. Daniae regim …*, Amsterdam 1642, dedication.

DUKE ULRIK (1578-1624) AS AGENT, PATRON, ARTIST: REFRAMING DANISH COURT CULTURE IN THE INTERNATIONAL PERSPECTIVE C. 1600

Mara R. Wade

National cultures of the Renaissance are frequently measured in terms of the achievements of the courts, usually focusing on the towering figures of the rulers – Cosimo Medici, Queen Elizabeth, and Louis XIV, for example. In Denmark the Renaissance was initiated by a flowering of the arts and learning under Frederik II (1559-1588) and culminated in the long and productive reign of Christian IV (1588-1648). Maintaining a focus on the years around 1600, this investigation shifts the emphasis from the monarch himself to another key figure at court, the monarch's brother, thereby providing a new lens for examining elite cultural activity. This highly focused study of a single figure at the Danish court, Duke Ulrik (1578-1624), examines his role as an agent, a mediator, and a patron of Renaissance culture among Northern European courts in the decades around 1600 (Fig. 1).[1] Ulrik, Duke of Holstein and brother of King Christian IV (1577-1648) of Denmark, is a virtually unknown figure whose career suggests that he played a pivotal role in the personal transfer of cultural knowledge among Northern European courts around 1600.[2]

Court spectacles – tournament pageants and theatrical performances – during the decade from approximately 1596 to 1606 offer a framework for analyzing Duke Ulrik's central role in the transfer of culture among Northern European courts. The sisters of Ulrik and Christian – Elisabeth (1573-1626), Anna (1574-1619), Augusta (1580-1639), and Hedevig (1581-1641) – became leading cultural figures at courts known for meteoric advancements in theatre and performance at Wolfenbüttel, Edinburgh and London, Gottorf, and Dresden, respectively[3] while Christian IV himself presided over a splendid court known for the increasing theatricality of its tournaments and fireworks and where Danish, German, and Latin theater flourished.[4] The research below documents that Ulrik rivaled his siblings in his patronage of, and participation in, theatrical events and performances of all kinds.

Duke Ulrik is – even to many Danes – a shadowy figure about whom little is known,[5] and his crucial role as an important cultural mediator has often been underestimated in Danish Renaissance culture: "Ulrik was not a prominent personage, but he was a useful pawn in Christian IV's North German policy."[6] This statement accompanies the catalogue description of his portrait from ca. 1620 now at Frederiksborg. The Danish museum bought the picture from a Dresden art dealer, and its provenience can be traced to the Saxon collections, confirming a further link between Ulrik and his sister Hedevig (1581-1641) and underscoring in general the strong dynastic links between Saxony and Denmark.

Fig.1. Anonymous artist, Duke Ulrik, c. 1620. Hillerød, The Museum of National History, Frederiksborg Castle (Photo Frederiksborg).

Owing to the fact that Ulrik never reigned, never presided over a splendid court, and never married to a prominent court, he has been consistently overlooked as a significant agent of culture exchange. As the younger son who did not succeed to the Danish throne, Ulrik, however, moved easily among the courts of Copenhagen, Edinburgh, London, Dresden, Wolfenbüttel, Gottorf, and Mecklenburg, and the network of his dynastic connections and personal travels suggests an important model of cultural transfer among Northern European Protestant courts around 1600.

Ulrik's Early Years in Mecklenburg and Denmark

In Denmark Ulrik received the education of a future king, which in an age of high infant mortality was a practical necessity, although in the end his elder brother Christian outlived all of his siblings and even two of his own sons. After spending his earliest childhood at his grandparents' court in Mecklenburg, Ulrik returned to Denmark in 1583 where he was then educated with his brother, the future king, at Sorø cloister and at various royal residences.[7] From 1584-1586 the prince's teachers were Hans Mikkelsen (1538-1601), the rector first of the elite school at Herlufsholm and then at Sorø,[8] and Poul Pedersen (1550-1616) of Roskilde.[9] This same Poul Pedersen matriculated with Ulrik at Helmstedt in 1590. Anders Sørensen Vedel's funeral sermon for Frederik II states that all the princes and princesses received an excellent education,[10] while Ulrik's own funeral sermon emphasizes the duke's accomplishments in mathematics, history, and languages.[11] The sermon notes his study of literature with an emphasis on his quick intellect and good memory, underscoring the duke's education and perhaps indicative of his later interests in the arts and sciences.[12] The work makes special mention of Ulrik's horsemanship,[13] and states that he was called a new Alexander the Great and traveled to foreign kingdoms.[14] It also describes how he loved to study and engage in military matters, having served in Belgium and the Spanish Netherlands,[15] and how he fought against the Turks while in the service of Rudolph II.[16] His military career included service for Denmark in the Kalmar War against Sweden in 1611-1613. While there is much uncertainty about when Ulrik might have fought against the Turks, my research strongly suggests that Ulrik served between March 1605 when he left England and May 1606 when he is documented in Dresden. Johann Simon, author of another funeral sermon writes explicitly that Ulrik was in Croatia and Hungary. Simon also states that Ulrik returned from the Turkish wars and was with his sister Hedevig in Saxony in 1606, confirming that his imperial service must have been after his stay in London in March 1605 and before his visit to Dresden.[17] Other sources document that the entire Saxon court was with Ulrik at the burial place of the Wettins at Freiberg in Meissen on 3 May 1606.[18]

Ulrik was deeply interested in letters and was literate in Danish, Latin, German, French, and presumably English and Scottish, having enjoying extensive stays at his sister Anna's courts.[19] He was an excellent horseman as well as soldier. At his death his collection of mathematical instruments included a magnificent globe, which had been purchased for him in Holland.[20] A certain Joachim Liperman of Rostock matriculated at that university in Easter term 1615 (entry no.1), where it was noted that he was Duke Ulrik's mathematician at Bützow.[21] Mathematical and optical instruments were often part of the *Kunstkammer*, although there is no indication that Ulrik himself established a cabinet. His interest in these instruments illustrates his fascination with new technologies, maps and globes, geography, and accurate measurement. Owing to his military experience and education (Christian IV, for example, is reputed to have been an expert at fortifications), Ulrik may also have acquired these instruments for military and political purposes. There also appears to be a compelling connection between Ulrik's collecting instruments and the collection of his grandfather Duke Ulrich (1527-1603) of Mecklenburg.[22]

The Foreign Education of the Prince

There are two distinct aspects of Ulrik's education which were to prepare him for a future role in the life of the Danish crown: his study at German universities after completing his education in Denmark and his travel abroad, especially to dynastically related courts. In this respect Ulrik enjoyed significantly more privileges than his brother King Christian IV. While the heir to the crown did not travel extensively abroad in his youth, his princely brother could do so. While Christian IV later traveled more than any other monarch since the Habsburg emperor Charles V, he did not have the benefit of studies at the important North German Protestant universities and extended tours outside of Denmark as part of his education. Christian's travels in 1595 through the duchies and to the courts at Wolfenbüttel, Brandenburg and Mecklenburg can therefore be seen as his cavalier's tour.[23] In contrast, Duke Ulrik lived and traveled in Denmark, North Germany, France, the Low Countries, Scotland, and England, served the emperor in the Turkish wars, and spent most of his later years in Mecklenburg, after having succeeded his grandfather in 1603 as archbishop in Schwerin. He also traveled with Christian IV in times of peace as well as of war.

The wedding of his sister Elisabeth and Duke Heinrich Julius of Braunschweig-Lüneburg (1564-1613) at Wolfenbüttel seems to have provided the impetus for his having been sent to the court at Wolfenbüttel, thereby inaugurating Ulrik's foreign education at its nearby university at Helmstedt (1590). The Danish duke (entry no. 163) matriculated at Helmstedt on 12 October 1590 together with Henningus Belde (164), Georgius Schongardus (165), and Magnus Pachs [Mogens Pax] (166), all called "nobiles Dani," while on 6 October Bartram Gadendorph, Nobiles Holsatus (167); his teacher Paulus Petrejus [Poul Pedersen], Roschildensis Danus (168); and Petrus Thomæ [Peder Thomsen], Rechingensis Danus (169) and on October 14 M. Laurentius Andreæ, Roschildensis Danus (173) were entered into the matriculation records.[24] According to Vello Helk, Mogens Pax til Torup (1577-1642), son of Christian IV's master of the stall Christopher Pax, was educated at court with Ulrik from 1584-1590 and spent four years traveling with him abroad in Heidelberg, Jena, Wittenberg, and Helmstedt from 1590-1594.[25]

Ulrik's further academic sojourns can be documented at the universities of Rostock (1592)[26] and Leipzig (1593-1594 and again 1595).[27] As the future bishop of Schwerin, Ulrik had a special connection to the University of Rostock and the matriculation records provide valuable evidence for his activities. He is first mentioned as "Vlricus princeps Holsatiæ, etc." as entry 66 under the month of October for Michelmas term 1592. A further entry on the same page states he matriculated on 10 October and was elected rector on 18 October 1592. The entry for April 1603 notes the death of Duke Ulrich of Mecklenburg, stating that his daughter Dowager Queen Sophie of Denmark and his granddaughter Duchess Elisabeth of Braunschweig-Lüneburg, wife of Duke Heinich Julius from Wolfenbüttel, were present. The entry notes further that Duke Ulrich was succeeded by his brother Carl as Duke of Mecklenburg and by Duke Ulrik as administrator of the diocese Schwerin. David Lobechius held Duke Ulrich's Latin sermon and Lucas Bacmeister the German one.[28] His Danish successor Ulrik was a maecenus, making many gifts, both of food and drink as well as of money, to the university.[29] There is a note, presumably added at a much later date, next to the entry from Easter term 1577 (no. 24) for Heinrich Gerlach of Hamburg, stating he was Ulrik's praeceptor, and later professor of poetry at Rostock.[30] As prince bishop of Schwerin Ulrik continued his affiliation with the university and served as rector again in Michelmas term 1614.[31] Ulrik made further gifts to the university for an important anniversary in 1619, where also the two dukes of Mecklenburg, Johann Albrecht and Adolph Friedrich were present.[32] The matriculation registries record Ulrik's death on 27 March 1624.[33] Both at Rostock, the *Landesuniversität* for his grandfather's territories of Mecklenburg and later of his own bishopric of Schwerin, and at Leipzig, Ulrik was created *rector magnificus* of the university.

The influential pastor and emblematist Daniel Cramer (1568-1637) from Reetz in Neumarkt, who knew Holger Rosenkrantz the Learned (1574-1642), collected his impressions of Denmark in a series of "fabula" which he reworked in dramatic form and dedicated to Duke Ulrik. Cramer's *stambog* locates him in Denmark in May 1592.[34] The "fabula" must refer to Cramer's Latin comedy which was translated into German verse, *Areteugenia: De Aretino Et Eugenia...*, a play about a young nobleman who undertakes a trip to bring his sister from a cloister to her wedding, a robber's attack on them, and their adventures, admonishing the viewer to pursue virtue in all things.[35] The title page clearly states that the published version of 1602 postdates the play by a decade, that is, the comedy was written ca. 1592, when Ulrik studied at German protestant universities. *Areteugenia*, the "fabula, ficta et comice" referred to on the title page, was dedicated, in addition to Duke Ulrik, to Christophorus Radzivil and Philip Julius of Pomerania. The five imprints of the play are all from the North German areas where Ulrik studied and traveled, although only the Leipzig edition is dedicated to him.[36]

Together with his grandfather, the renowned Duke Ulrich of Mecklenburg, the Danish Duke Ulrik was in the retinue that greeted Christian IV at the castle at Güstrow on 8 November 1595 during the minor king's tour of the Duchies and North Germany.[37] After a royal welcome that included a splendid fireworks display, Ulrik accompanied Christian IV to Rostock where they visited the churches and the university, taking

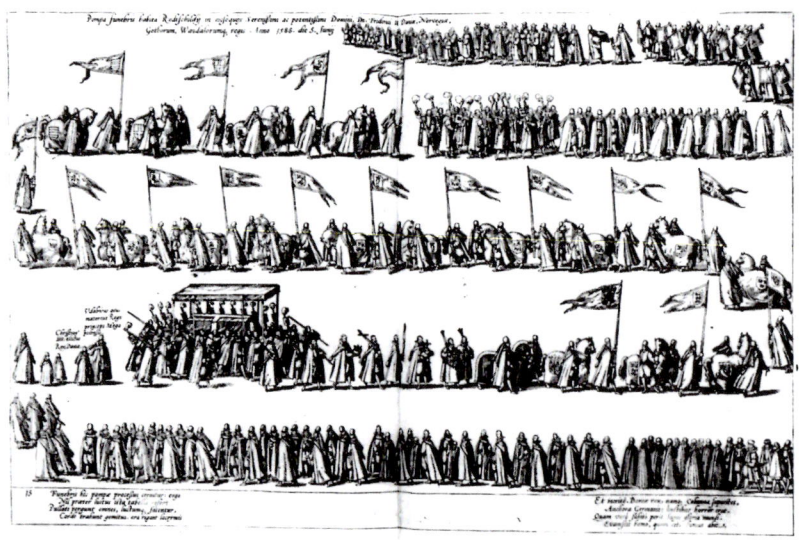

Fig. 2. Frederik II's funeral procession in Roskilde 1588, after Franz Hogenberg and Simon Novellanus, Res Gestae... Friderici II, 1589. Copenhagen, The Danish Royal Library (Photo Royal Library).

Fig. 3. Philip Uffenbach, Pageants for the coronation of Christian IV, Copenhagen, August 1596, engravings 1597. Copenhagen, The Danish Royal Library (Photo Royal Library).

leave of his brother at Warnemünde on 14 November. Ulrik was in Denmark for his brother's coronation in 1596, and at the request of his new brother-in-law Johann Adolph, accompanied the bride, his sister Augusta, from Denmark to her new home in Gottorf.[38]

Ulrik and Danish Court Festivals 1588-1596

Beginning with the splendid exequies for his father King Frederik II in 1588, Duke Ulrik was in attendance at all major dynastic events for the Danish court in his lifetime (Fig. 2). The royal funeral marks a decisive new turn in Danish court ritual and must have made a lasting impression on young Ulrik, shaping his sense of ceremony and theater, impressing upon him the essential nature of the creation of dynastic memory. Of particular interest is the role of his mother, the young widow Queen Sophie, in determining the funeral ceremony in the context of its international precedents.[39] Ulrik was in Denmark for the weddings of his sister Anna (1574-1619) to James VI (1566-1625) of Scotland, later James I of England, in 1589 and that of his sister Elisabeth (1573-1626) to Duke Heinrich Julius of Braunschweig-Lüneburg at Wolfenbüttel in the spring of 1590.[40]

After his foreign studies, outlined above, Ulrik returned to Copenhagen for the coronation of King Christian IV in August 1596 (Fig. 3).[41] This was the politically most significant event at the Danish court in decades and ushered in the new century, setting high artistic standards for Northern European festivals for the first half of the seventeenth century.[42] The spectacles lasting two weeks included entries, allegorical fireworks, masked tournament pageants, dancing, and mummings. Of particular importance to the present discussion is Christian IV's mumming in which court noblemen appeared in black face. Christian's "masque of blackness" thereby predated the famous masque of his sister Anna in England by nearly a decade.[43] While I am not suggesting that Ben Jonson (1572-1637) and Inigo Jones (1573-1652) derived their *Masque of Blackness* from the Danish court, I am proposing that Ulrik directly transmitted the conceit of blackness in a court entertainment to Scotland and England from the Danish court.[44] The festivities celebrating the coronation of Christian IV – at which occasion his sister Augusta married Duke Johann Adolf (1575-1616) of Schleswig-Holstein at Gottorf – featured many other noteworthy innovations as well. Most prominent among them was the splendid pageant invention on the theme of the Mountain of Virtue, or *Tugendberg*, which was commissioned by the Brandenburg court from the Dresden master of court spectacles, the Italian Giovanni Maria Nosseni (1544-1620), and brought to Denmark.[45]

Another first in the development of Northern European court festivals, the themes of the coronation pageants focused on the revival of Classical Rome, its heroes, and its virtues with strongly anti-Catholic tones,[46] prefiguring by a decade and more the Stuttgart court festivals which Helen Watanabe-O'Kelly has called the "Festivals of Protestant Union."[47] Ulrik can also be linked to these festivals, if only peripherally, as he also signed the *stambog* of Barbara Sophie of Brandenburg in 1602.[48] Barbara Sophie (1584-1636), sister of Queen Anna Catharina (Ulrik's sister-in-law, 1575-1612) of Denmark, was a key figure in the Stuttgart court festivals which were initiated with her wedding and several of which were held for the christening of her children.[49] Christian IV sent Jens Sparr to her wedding to Duke Johann Friedrich (1582-1628) of Württemberg in November 1609.[50] The importance of this event to the Danish court is illustrated by the fact that Prince-Elect Christian (1603-1647) had a copy of this festival book in his personal library.[51]

Ulrik's Travels Abroad

Looking at the septentrionic world through the lens of Ulrik's experiences helps to reframe Danish culture during the Renaissance, by opening up new perspectives and avenues of inquiry. After Christian IV's coronation Ulrik, accompanied by his preceptor Albert Skeel, embarked on a study, or cavalier's, tour, from 1597-1598, to finish his education in languages, politics, comportment, and courtly accomplishments.[52] Traveling first to France and then to England, he then visited his sister Queen Anna and King James in Scotland. Ulrik arrived in Scotland 14 March 1598 and left for Denmark around 1 June 1598. He stayed at Holyrood Palace, traveled from there over the Forth to Ravenscraig, Balcomie, Pittenweem, St. Andrews, Dundee, Perth, Stirling and back to Edinburgh, among other places.[53] In spring 1598 Henry, later Prince of Wales, was four years old and Elisabeth, later Queen of Bohemia, was two. Margaret, who did not survive earliest infancy, was born that year. Ulrik signed the *stambog* of the Scottish nobleman Michael Balfour in Copenhagen in the summer (late June?) of 1598 as did Christian IV, Anna Catharina, and Hedevig.[54] It is a sign of Ulrik and Anna's close relations that he visited her in Scotland and then also later in England. In spite of the long distances separating them, Anna and Ulrik maintained close ties, and Ulrik can be seen as a direct cultural link to the court of her birth. In a striking attestation of their close relationship, Ulriks's funeral sermon contends that Anna, who had died five years earlier in 1619, and Ulrik were now enjoying themselves in heaven.[55] Ulrik provided a crucial link between Scotland and England and Denmark, as Anna never returned to Denmark after her marriage. As can be seen below, familial networks were essential to cultural transfer as Christian IV also visited England in 1606 and 1614.[56]

Ulrik in Dresden and Copenhagen

A dense cluster of dynastic and cultural events occurring in Dresden, Hamburg, London, and Copenhagen from 1602 until 1606 illuminates the political and festival life of the Danish court and demonstrates the importance of studying events geographically removed from, yet culturally central to, the court. These occasions showcase the international profile and cosmopolitan nature of Danish court culture as well as Ulrik's role as a personal agent of, and active participant in, Northern Renaissance culture.

In 1602 Ulrik escorted his sister Hedevig and his mother, the dowager Queen Sophie, to Dresden, where Hedevig married the Saxon Elector Christian II (1583-1611). For the entry of the

Fig. 4. Christian IV's tournament pageant, Hamburg, October 1603. After Georg Engelhard von Loehneyss, *Della Cavalleria…* 1610. Wolfenbüttel, Herzog August Bibliothek (Photo Herzog August Bibliothek).

bridal entourage into Dresden the Saxons held a pageant on the Elbe consisting of the mythical sea god Glaucus with whales, sea horses, and sirens. There were magnificent, thematic pageants for the running at the ring as well as other tournaments on foot and horseback. The spectacles also included allegorical fireworks, banquets, and dancing, confirming the increasing theatricality of Dresden wedding festivities as programmatic events.[57] As the highest ranking Danish male representative at the nuptials, Ulrik was a key figure at the royal wedding in Dresden. Owing to his positions in German territories as the titulary bishop of Schleswig (1602) and since 1591 as co-administrator ("Ko-adjutor") of the bishopric of Schwerin, where he succeeded his revered grandfather Duke Ulrich in 1603, Ulrik was a young man of influence, especially in German-speaking Protestant lands. In Dresden he fulfilled significant ceremonial roles at this important dynastic event renewing the union of Denmark and Electoral Saxony. The wedding of Hedevig and Christian II was seen very much in the light of the long marriage of the Elector August (1526-1586) and Anna of Denmark (1532-1585) and the prosperous development of Saxony in the third quarter of the sixteenth century.[58] As a direct participant in the Dresden spectacles, Ulrik necessarily figured as an agent of cultural exchange among Scotland, Denmark, and Saxony.

In July and August of 1603 Christian IV celebrated the birth and baptism of an heir, Prince-Elect Christian, in Copenhagen. This occasion was extremely significant to the Danish crown as Prince Frederik, the first child born to Christian IV and Queen Anna Catharina, had died in 1599, the year of his birth. For the royal baptism, Duke Ulrik; the Brandenburg Elector Joachim Friedrich (1546-1608), the child's grandfather; and King James stood as godfathers to the young prince. The English embassy sent by James and Anna is particularly noteworthy, as James had succeeded Elizabeth I of England only a few months earlier in March 1603. Christian and Ulrik's sister Anna was now Queen of England and Scotland. James dispatched the embassy of Roger Manners, Earl of Rutland, to the baptism, bearing the Order of the Garter for his brother-in-law Christian

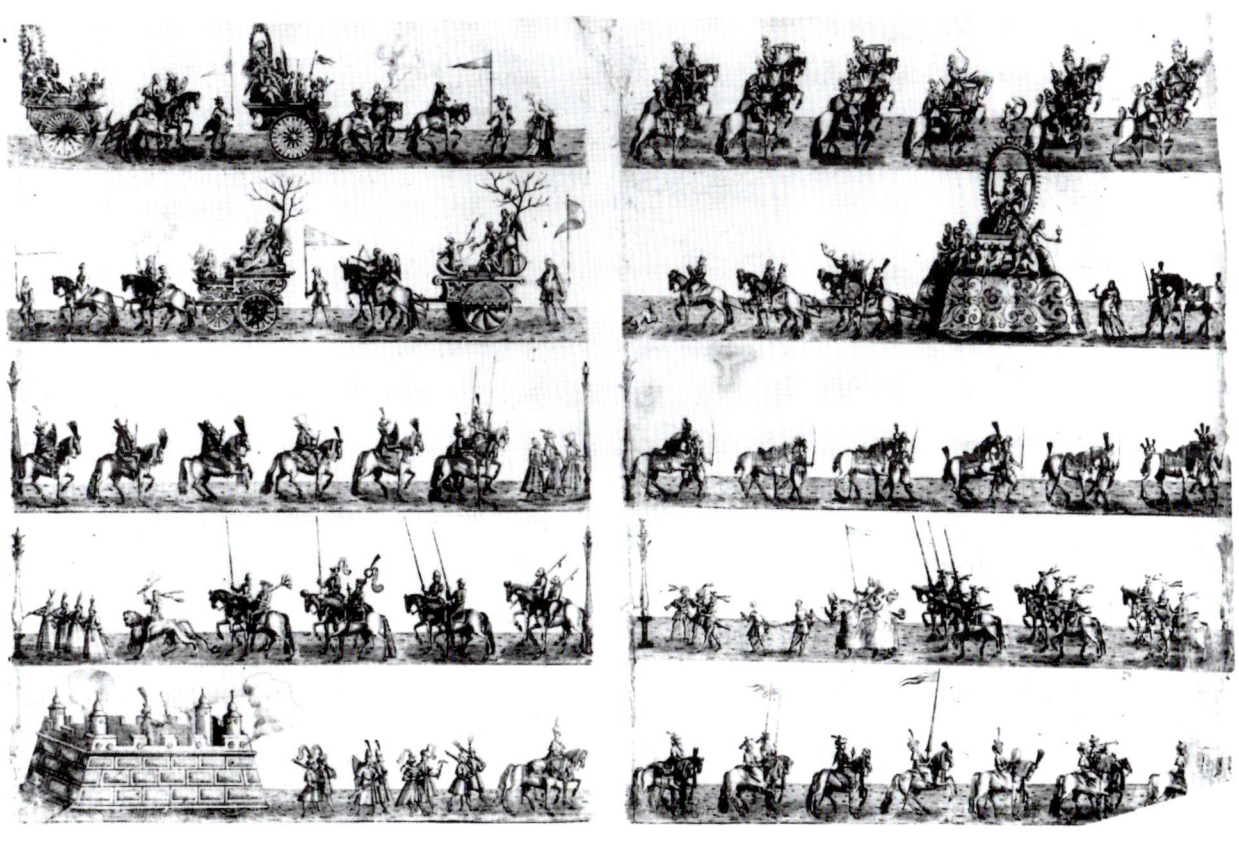

IV. (Christian received the Order of the Garter in person when he visited England in 1606). It is extremely noteworthy and has largely escaped scholarly attention that the diary of the Danish nobleman Sivert Grubbe (1566-1636) locates Inigo Jones in Manners's embassy in Denmark in the summer of 1603.[59] Also present in Denmark at this time was the famous lutenist John Dowland (1563-1626), who received his last payment from the Danish court on 15 July 1603.[60] Dowland was in England by September 1603 where he had an audience with Queen Anna.[61] I suggest here that Inigo Jones and John Dowland returned to England simultaneously, if not together, probably with the ambassadors, for the royal baptism. Critical to the present investigation is the fact that immediately upon his return to England, Inigo Jones entered the service of Anna of Denmark, and his first commission for her was to produce the designs for her *Masque of Blackness* which entertained the court the following year at Twelfth Night 1604-1605.[62]

Ulrik in Hamburg

In October 1603 the city of Hamburg swore an oath of allegiance to the Danish King Christian IV and his brother-in-law Johann Adolf, Duke of Schleswig-Holstein, a monumental event in the life of the Danish crown (fig.4).[63] After the ceremonies, splendid spectacles celebrated the event with much pomp. This was especially noteworthy as the Emperor had banned the event that Christian IV nonetheless eagerly pursued. The list of attendees reads like a who's who of North Germany. While many of the male rulers, not wishing to offend the Emperor, did not attend, their female consorts did. Thus, for example, Christian IV's sister, Augusta attended with her husband who was also honored on this occasion. Their sisters, Elisabeth, Duchess of Braunschweig-Lüneburg at Wolfenbüttel, and Hedevig, Electress of Saxony, traveled to Hamburg for this important dynastic event, although Duke Heinrich Julius and Elector Christian II were absent. The women's presence underscores the role of female participation in the highly charged political sphere. The nexus of familial cultural transfer is confirmed by Georg Engelhard von Loehneyss's splendid presentation manuscript of the occasion made as a New Year's gift 1604 for Christian II, Elector of Saxony.[64]

Von Loehneyss's splendid pageant for Christian IV was the first emblematic pageant in Northern Europe (Fig. 5). Consisting of 55 knights and their attendants, the allegorical pageant on the four ages of humankind, each represented by allegorical figures in pageant wagons, culminated in a striking triumphal chariot in which Christian IV appeared seated in a ring of flames as the sun king, with the motto, "Agnitionis tandem post nubila Phoebus" (after the clouds at last the sun of knowledge). At least seven different publications were published concerning this event, confirming

Fig. 5. Emblem of the Sun King, detail from Christian IV's pageant tournament, Hamburg, October 1603. After Loehneyss. Wolfenbüttel, Herzog August Bibliothek (Photo Herzog August Bibliothek).

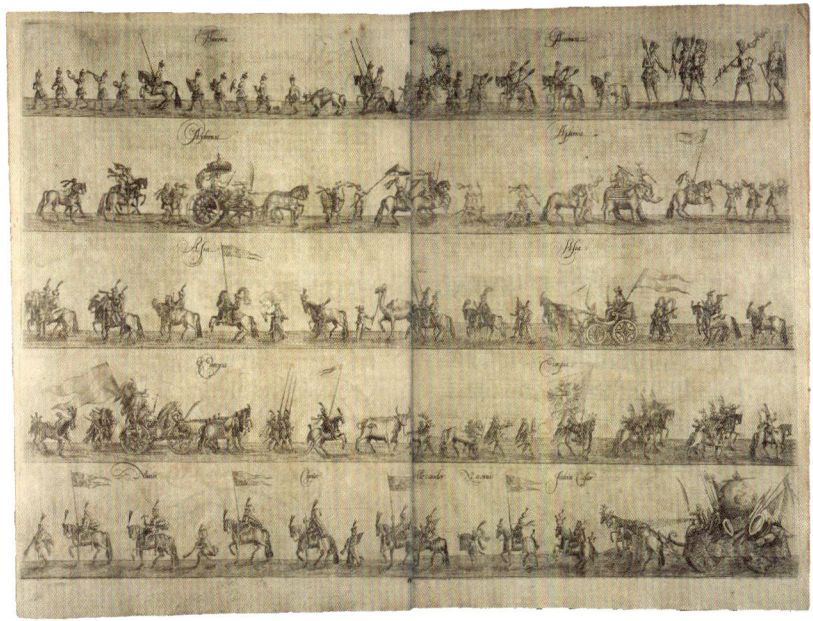

Fig. 6. Duke Ulrich's tournament pageant, Hamburg, October 1603. After Loehneyss. Wolfenbüttel, Herzog August Bibliothek (Photo Herzog August Bibliothek).

its great political significance for North Germany on the eve of the Thirty Years' War. A description of Christian IV's emblematic pageant was even used as an allegorical moralizing example in a funeral sermon from 1699.[65] The allegorical tournament pageants for this event are well documented by their inventor, Georg Engelhard von Loehneyss, the master of the stall, previously in the employ of the Saxon electors and then that of Duke Heinrich Julius at Wolfenbüttel.[66] The web of familial connections as conduits for cultural exchange becomes quite clear in the Hamburg pageant. Dresden, Wolfenbüttel, and Copenhagen, among many other courts, were personally represented in Hamburg. The single figure that circulated among all these courts was Ulrik, who had accompanied Hedevig to Dresden for her wedding and now appeared in Hamburg, and, as we shall see below, spent several months the following year at the English court.

For Hamburg's homage to the Danish crown, the Wolfenbüttel master of the stall von Loehneyss also designed Ulrik's pageant on the theme of the four monarchies of the world (Fig. 6). Ulrik's personal appearance in Hamburg lent crucial political support to his brother King Christian and brother-in-law Duke Johann Adolph. As an influential figure in North German politics, his presence helped legitimate the occasion in face of the imperial prohibition. His allegorical pageant allowed for colorful national attire with the costumed knights of Nimrod, Cyrus, Alexander the Great, and Julius Caesar with their lance bearers and hand-led horses.[67] In what might be perhaps considered excessive praise, we recall here that Ulrik's funeral sermon states that he was called a new Alexander the Great and traveled to foreign kingdoms.[68] The juxtaposition of this pageant theme with a personal attribute of the Danish duke is noteworthy. The concluding pageant wagon for Ulrik's display was a triumphal chariot heaped with weapons and the attributes of battle surrounding a globe of the world. The theme of the four monarchies recurred in Saxon pageants from the late sixteenth through the seventeenth centuries, and it is noteworthy that Ulrik sponsored this pageant, designed by the former Saxon pageant inventor von Loehneyss, in Hamburg.[69]

In March 1603 Ulrik had succeeded his illustrious grandfather Duke Ulrich of Mecklenburg as Prince Bishop of Schwerin, confirming the duke's political interests in North German territories and the Baltic region. That their sister, the Electress Hedevig, attended the Hamburg event with a group of singers of Saxon mining songs also underscores the vitality of court festival traditions and practices, especially their political dimensions. The importance of Hedevig contributing to the festivities with the performances of the singers, whom Christian IV rewarded well, must be stressed here. Saxon wealth depended on its mines and the good husbanding and exploitation of the territory's mineral wealth.[70] Pageants about mining and singers of mining songs (*Bergsänger*) were traditional features of Saxon festivals, emphasizing the wealth and resources of the Electorship. The two pageants by Christian and Ulrik with their respective focus on allegories of the sun king and the four monarchies can be read together as a very clear statement about empire, expansion of the realms, and kingship. The Danish brothers – with the support of their Saxon, Gottorf, Wolfenbüttel, and other North German relatives – themselves performed in these very public theatrical presentations in German territories, thereby confirming Danish intentions for North Germany and the Baltic and expressing their stance *vis à vis* the Holy Roman Empire of the German Nation. That this event occurred in Hamburg is most significant.

Ulrik in England

Just a year later, Duke Ulrik can be documented in England, where he was present from November of 1604 until late May 1605.[71] Ulrik, who apparently enjoyed excellent relations with his brother-in-law James, shared his passion for the hunt and spent two weeks in mid-November with him hunting at Royston. On December 27, 1604 Ulrik escorted Lady Susan de Vere (1587-1629), bride of Sir Philipp Herbert (1584-1650), to the church for their wedding. James I played a prominent part in the elaborate ceremony, and gave the bridal couple substantial gifts of land.[72] Ulrik clearly circulated among the highest nobles at court and was accorded all respects and honors due the brother of reigning monarchs. His funeral sermon states that the English crown granted Ulrik a substantial annual pension and that the English respected the duke's many virtues.[73] As one of the highest ranking guests of honor, we can assume that Ulrik was present for the performance of the masque celebrating this wedding that appropriately focused on the theme of Juno and Hymenaeus.

Even more interesting is the remark by a contemporary letter writer stating: "They say the Duke of Holst[ein] will come upon us with an after-reckoning, and that we shall see him on Candlemas Night in a Mask, as he hath shewed himself a lusty reveler all this Christmas."[74] Unfortunately, we know nearly nothing about the theatrical aspects – theme, actors, designer, music – of Ulrik's English masque. However, we do know that James rewarded Ulrik handsomely and suggest that extraordinary payments to Ulrik are related to the successful performance of the otherwise unknown masque. Among the "Free Gifts in the second year of the King's Reign, 1604-1605," there is a payment to the "Duke of Holst" for "£ 4,000."[75] The accounts for the following year indicate he also received an additional £1,000. Since James was already supporting Ulrik at the sum of £100 per week while the duke was in England, we can only assume that the New Year's gifts totaling £5,000 were highly extraordinary and can be seen as compensation, at least in part, for his apparently very successful masque. To place the payments to Ulrik in context, Anna's splendid masque during the same season, *The Masque of Blackness*, cost about £3,000.

Theater at the English court thrived during Ulrik's sojourn, and he was present at Twelfth Night (January 6, 1604-1605) for the performance of *The Masque of Blackness*, the first of Queen Anna's masques by Ben Jonson and Inigo Jones. Her stunning entertainment with the radical conceit of blackness established Jonson and Jones with a single stroke as the poet and architect respectively for subsequent court masques. There has been much theoretical speculation in English Renaissance scholarship about the appearance of Anna and her circle of noblewomen as blackamoors.[76] Given the cultural contexts outlined above, I suggest that the conceit of blackness originated at the Danish court almost ten years earlier in the mummings for Christian IV's coronation. While Anna may have been informed by court reports, published festival accounts, and emissaries about Christian IV's performance, I have also conclusively shown that personal connections among the courts were extremely active and provided viable, direct pathways for the transmission of court culture. Ulrik had visited Anna in Scotland the year after the coronation and certainly also functioned as an informant about the splendid festivities in Denmark. The fact cannot be without significance that Anna appeared as a Moor in the first masque of her English reign, in her coronation mumming, so to speak, when Ulrik was at the English court.

Court records clearly demonstrate the Ulrik was not a passive visitor, but an active player, appearing in entertainments himself and offering a masque of his own. In addition to escorting the bride to the church and staging his own masque, Ulrik performed in many other theatrical and ritual events at the English court, including the accession day tilts on 24 March marking James' accession to the throne, his own investiture with the Order of the Garter on St. George's day 23 April, and the baptism of his niece Princess Mary (1605-1607) on 5 May, for whom he stood as godfather, and the churching of Queen Anna. His highly visible role as patron, agent, and perhaps artist in England is further supported by his participation in the Dresden wedding spectacles and his own masked pageant in Hamburg in the year immediately preceding his visit to London. I suggest here that the processes of cultural transfer were reciprocal and bi-directional and that Ulrik transferred a startling innovation of Anna's masque – the use of perspective stage scenery – immediately to Denmark and North Germany.[77]

A further link between Ulrik and the cultural life of the Jacobean courts is Tobias Hume's composition number forty-three from his *Musicall Humors* (London 1605) entitled the "Duke of Holstone's Almaine."[78] This collection of over 100 compositions for the bass viol is critical to the understanding of the instrument's repertoire when it was evolving in competition with the lute as the most preferred instrument for the expression of human emotion. A pioneer of the "lyra viol," Hume is noteworthy because he was the first to produce solo music for the viol, using innovative techniques such as "col legno" and pizzicato.[79] *The First Part of Ayres or Musicall Humors* have a strong autobiographical component,[80] suggesting a close association of his piece dedicated to Ulrik, Duke of Holstein ("Holstone"), and the duke's visit to England in 1605. While sources vary, giving Hume's birthdate as either ca. 1569 or ca. 1579, the latter date would make Hume an exact contemporary of Ulrik, who was born in 1578.[81] As a Scot, Hume may even possibly have become acquainted with Ulrik when the queen's brother visited the court of James and Anna in Scotland during the last decade of the sixteenth century. Apparently, Hume played before Queen Anna in England in 1606, the year in which Christian IV visited her there, a constellation of persons and events which lends credibility to Hume's claim in his petition of 1642 that his hunting song had been performed "before two Kings, to the admiring of all braue huntsmen." Queen Anna is the dedicatee of Hume's *Poeticall Musicke* (London 1607) for which she rewarded him with one hundred schillings.[82] Hume was a professional soldier and thus shared this pursuit with Ulrik as well. In later life Hume served both Sweden and Russia,[83] and he is documented at the court of Wolfenbüttel in January 1623, at Gottorf in April 1624, and in Hamburg on 4 September 1624.[84] Thus, Tobias Hume would have been in North Germany at the time of Ulrik's death and funeral in the spring of 1624. The Scottish solider and musician Hume can be favorably compared with the English violist, William Brade, whose career as a professional soldier and musician was spent largely in Germany and Denmark.[85] A number of Hume's works are dedicated to the Danish siblings Ulrik, Anna, and Christian: "Cease leaden slumber, The Queenes New-yeares gift, " "A Mery Conceit, The Q delight" (to Anna), "The King of Denmarkes delight," and "The King of Denmarkes health."[86]

Deeply connected to the splendid performativity and political importance of Jacobean court festivities during Ulrik's sojourn is the pageantry surrounding Ulrik's receipt of the Order of the Garter (Fig. 7). It is noteworthy that in 1603 James awarded, at the same time as Henry Prince of Wales, Christian IV the Garter in absentia in one of the earliest acts of his reign. Before Ulrik left England in 1605, he was awarded the Garter together with James's favorite, Henry Howard (1540-1614), Earl of Northhampton. Innovative recent research demonstrates that the Lesser George preserved today at Rosenborg belonged to

Fig. 7. Duke Ulrich's Lesser George. Copenhagen, Rosenborg Castle (Photo Rosenborg).

Ulrik.[87] When Christian IV himself visited England in 1606, Ulrik was in attendance when James personally endowed the Danish king with the Order of the Garter. Ulrik's high profile is confirmed here: he is the third man mentioned after James and Christian.[88] After the decade of intense travel and multiple court festivals commemorating dynastic events around 1600, Ulrik continued his ceremonial duties, traveling to Holstein in 1616 to represent Denmark at the investiture of Duke Friedrich III (1597-1659) at Gottorf.

Ulrik's funeral sermon confirms the symbolic power of the Garter insignia, explaining that his insignia figured prominently in his exequies. Ulrik, whose motto was "In dextera Jehovæ sortes meæ" ("I cast my lot in God's right hand"), died in March and was buried with great ceremony in May 1624. Caspar Brochmand's funeral oration is dedicated to Ulrik's nephew Prince-Elect Christian of Denmark, who represented the crown at Ulrik's exequies in Mecklenburg. While Christian IV did not attend Ulrik's funeral, his son and presumed heir Prince-Elect Christian traveled there with an entourage of 100 noblemen.[89] (Duke Ulrik was the prince-elect's godfather).

Ulrik's mother Sophie was there, as were his sisters, Elisabeth and Augusta, then both widows, who had traveled to Bützow for their brother's burial. In 1642, Christian IV had Ulrik's coffin removed to Roskilde for reburial in the royal chapel he built there. There has been important research investigating the coffin, clothing, and ceremonial sword buried with Ulrik.[90]

Ulrik, His Siblings, and Their Correspondence: Further Models of Dynastic Cultural Transfer

Not only did Ulrik maintain intimate contacts with his siblings through personal visits, but they all regularly corresponded with one another. A preliminary sample from correspondence preserved today in the Danish National Archives (*Rigsarkivet*), Copenhagen, confirms the life-long reciprocal communication and close relations among these royal offspring, demonstrating the need for more research on their lives and patronage.

They had a younger brother Hans (1583-1602), who was to marry the daughter of the Russian Tsar Boris Gudonov, but, having traveled to Moscow in September 1602 to marry Xenia, died before the wedding. Much like Ulrik, he was being prepared for a dynastic and political role for the crown, and in the year before, that is 1601, he had gone to France, and he fought against the Spanish in the siege of Ostende.[91] Christian IV and Ulrik both were present at his departure from Denmark on 1 August 1602. Shortly thereafter Ulrik then accompanied Hedevig and Queen Sophie to Dresden.[92]

In a letter to Christian IV dated 27 March 1603, the newly wed Hedevig reports the death of their grandfather Ulrich of Mecklenburg, also writing about the death of their brother Hans in Moscow. In a letter dated the same day to Christian's wife Queen Anna Catharina, Hedevig does not mention these deaths.[93] She is clearly deeply troubled by the loss of both their grandfather and youngest brother, yet she reserves these topics for her brother alone. On 30 August 1603 Christian II of Saxony writes that Ulrik had reported to him in person about the forthcoming "family gathering" in Hamburg and that he gives Hedevig permission to travel there and wishes them all a pleasant time together. He writes: [Herzog Ulrik hat] mündtlich vermeldet vnd angezeiget, daß I[hre] Kön[igliche] W[ürde] sich mit derselben geliebten geschwistern einer zusammenkunfft auf den 28. Octobris [1603] negst künfftig nach hamburg … gesucht… ." The Elector's comments seem to go beyond mere compliment and indicate his awareness of the sibling's closeness: "Wünschen wir darneben, das E[uere] Kön[igliche] W[ürde] sambt dero geliebten geschwister in guter Leibesgesundheit zusammen kommen, sich freundltich miteinander … ergotzen, auch durch göttliche beschirmung in dergleichen wolfärigen zustandt zu mehrmaln einander besuchen mögen."[94] The Saxon Elector illuminates the cordial relations among the adult Danish siblings, all of whom with the exception of Anna, Queen of England, and the recently deceased Hans, were in Hamburg for this occasion. Moreover, that Ulrik traveled to Dresden to make this request on behalf of Christian IV demonstrates that he was entrusted with highly sensitive political issues, especially in view of the imperial prohibition concerning Christian IV and Johann Adolph of Schleswig-Holstein at Gottorf receiving Hamburg's homage on this occasion.[95]

The correspondence in this generation between Denmark and Saxony began well before Hedevig's wedding, however. Christian IV and Christian II exchanged letters during the 1590's,[96] and the regent Friedrich Wilhelm II of Saxony wrote Ulrik while he was studying at Rostock concerning placing a boy at the prestigious academy Schulpforta.[97] Naturally, there is ample archival evidence documenting the wedding of Elector Christian II and Hedevig that more logically falls in the realm of political correspondence.[98] Such archives exist for all of the Danish-Saxon royal weddings.

A series of letters documents Christian and Hedevig's correspondence about sending personnel (a cook, a law student, a Danish boy for the school at Meissen, soldiers, and other servants) between Dresden and Saxony. These letters also concern the courts of the siblings, such as mediating a gardener to England and involving persons at the court in Wolfenbüttel. For example, Hedevig sent Christian a dog and a master of the hounds in 1623. This very limited sample preserved in Denmark confirms that regular correspondence as well as the exchange of personnel and gifts supplemented Ulrik's many visits among the courts during these years.

From her widow's residence at Lichtenburg Hedevig writes on 24 April 1624 poignantly of Ulrik's death: "Es ist zwar leid, daß gott unser bruder so zeitlich von hir gefordert, weill es gott so gefallen, so ist im nicht zu widerstreben …" She writes again on 30 April 1624, responding to Queen Sophie's arrangements that the funeral is to be 24 May and her desire for Hedevig to attend. Owing to the long distance and short time to prepare such a journey, Hedevig is unable to travel to Mecklenburg and sends a representative.[99] Ulrik's funeral sermon stresses that he and Hedevig delighted in each other's company and how her husband Elector Christian II of Saxony honored Ulrik.[100] That Christian and Hedevig maintained their close relationship after Hans's, Anna's, Ulrik's, and Elisabeth's deaths is confirmed by Christian's gift of a lion, a lioness, and a tiger to Hedevig in November 1629.[101] While Hedevig had traveled to Denmark and spent several weeks at their mother's bedside in 1631, the elderly queen had urged her daughter to return to Dresden. Hedevig's letter from Mölln on 21 October 1631 informs Christian that, having learned of their mother's death, she will return to Nyköbing and accompany their mother from there to her final resting place at Roskilde.[102] When the Thirty Years' War struck Saxony particularly hard, there was a stream of letters between the siblings with requests from Hedevig to accept various persons into Danish service. Most poignant is her request on behalf of the widow Regina Gilbert, whose husband Dr. Christian Gilbert, was a pastor in Magdeburg during the sack of that city.[103] Hedevig often had to delay in sending Christian letters owing to the war and pestilence.[104] While Hedevig's biographers state that she went to Denmark for the so-called "great wedding" (Det Store Bilager) of 1634, a letter in the present file indicates she did not attend.[105]

Owing to the general lack of knowledge about Ulrik, these letters, in which he is often a subject, serve to indicate his centrality among the siblings.[106] He was the glue that held them together during these central years of marriages away from the Danish court, international events, and dynastic occasions outside of Copenhagen. Even the early letters documenting his efforts to secure a position for himself and the resultant problems between Ulrik, his brother, and their mother suggest Ulrik's significance to the family.[107] It is also noteworthy that Christian IV named his youngest son Ulrik (1611-1633).[108] The small sample of letters presented here demonstrate that the siblings visited one another, wrote one another, and circulated family information in a closely woven web of familial, dynastic connections.

During the decade around 1600 Ulrik served as a personal link among his far-flung family, while twenty years later they mourned his death in 1624 together. Hedevig writes at Ulrik's death that they will all enjoy each other's company in heaven.[109] That Ulrik was important and shared in the creation of dynastic memory is clearly evidenced by his visit with Hedevig in 1606 to the Church of St. Mary's in Freiberg in Meissen, the burial place of the Wettins. Their aunt Anna Electress of Saxony is buried there, together with her husband Elector August, who commissioned the monument for his fallen brother Elector Moritz (1521-1553), who had won the electorship for the Albertine line.[110] Their visit with the entire Saxon court to the burial place of the Albertine electors emphasizes the role of family in the creation of memory and stresses this site's importance for both familial and political memory, where Danish-Saxon alliances and shared history are made visible. Ulrik himself commissioned a magnificent pulpit for his local church at Bützow where he was first buried and which he had chosen for his own burial place. This so-called Danish chapel included a lengthy inscription about the royal donor, his coat of arms, and his portrait, demonstrating the importance of constructing dynastic memoria.[111] It is a poignant confirmation of the crucial significance of sites of dynastic memory that Christian IV moved Ulrik from his resting place in Mecklenburg to Roskilde in 1642. Similarly, he returned his prematurely deceased son Prince-Elect Christian from Saxony for burial at Roskilde. In the royal monuments at the cathedral at Roskilde, Christian IV's efforts in the few years before his own death in 1648 make visible the continuity of Danish monarchy and its dynastic connections. These forms of posthumous creation and nurturing of memory strongly parallel the cultivation of living personal connections during Ulrik's lifetime.

Duke Ulrik and the Danish Renaissance

Duke Ulrik was the centre of a complex web of interconnections among the courts of Copenhagen, Dresden, Edinburgh, London, Wolfenbüttel, Mecklenburg, and Gottorf. The fact that he personally embodied these dynastic relationships is noteworthy and emphasizes the significant role of both education and travel in cultural exchange in early modern Europe. Ulrik's linguistic and equestrian accomplishments, his passion for the life of the mind as well as that of the courtier mark him as a true Renaissance man. Owing to the attention that heretofore has focused on the splendor of the courts of his siblings, Ulrik, who ended his life at the manor Rühn near Bützow by Schwerin, has escaped scholarly study. This highly focused investigation of his role as an agent of cultural transfer points to the benefit of approaching Renaissance culture from a number of perspectives other than solely the vantage point of the monarch. By questioning a critical decade around 1600 when a cluster of important dynastic events occurred both in Denmark and, more importantly, outside of Denmark that directly involved the Danish crown, significant avenues for cultural agency and transfer come to light. Most important among these is the role of personal contact and family networks. This study also confirms the critical role of the well educated younger son, who, in fact, is often more mobile and flexible than the monarch himself. The figure of Duke Ulrik demonstrates the social, political, institutional, personal, and cultural contexts that motivated the processes of transfer among the Northern courts and confirms a powerful network of multidirectional exchange among the Protestant elites. Focusing scholarly attention on Ulrik provides a powerful new frame for investigating the Danish Renaissance and its European contexts.

Notes

1 In this study "Ulrik" refers to the second born son of King Frederik II and Queen Sophie of Denmark, while "Ulrich" is applied to his grandfather, Duke Ulrich of Mecklenburg.

2 Hans H. Fussing, "Ulrik", *Dansk Biografisk Leksikon*[3] [hereafter *DBL*], 15, Copenhagen 1984, 168-169; and [L. Laursen], "Ulrik", *Salmonsens Konversationsleksikon*, 24, Copenhagen 1928, 227. See the poem celebrating his birth by Paul Lutrifonius, *Regio infanti …*, Copenhagen 1579.

3 Mara R. Wade, "The Queen's Courts: Anna of Denmark and her Royal Sisters – Cultural Agency at Four Northern European Courts in the 16th and 17th Century", in: Clare McManus (ed.), *Women and Culture at the Courts of the Stuart Queens,* London 2003, 49-80. Anna also engaged players as Queen of Scotland. See Thomas Riis, *Should Auld Acquaintance Be Forgot… Scottish-Danish Relations c. 1450-1701*, Odense 1988, I, 281.

4 Mara R. Wade, "German Theater in Denmark during the Age of King Christian IV (1577-1648)", *Thalia Germanica* (forthcoming).

5 Riis 1988, II, 296.

6 Steffen Heiberg (ed.), *Christian IV and Europa: The 19th Art Exhibition of the Council of Europe*, Copenhagen 1988, no. 108, 44, the artist is unknown. See also Hans H. Fussing, "Ulrik", *DBL*[2], 24, Copenhagen 1943, 517-519: Ulrik "synes ellers ret ubetydelig, godmodig og livsglad" [Otherwise Ulrik appears very insignificant, good natured, and he enjoys life] (518).

7 On Ulrik's and Christian's education, see Chr. Molbech, "Historiske Bidrag til Kundskab om K. Christian den Fierdes Opdragelse og Ungdomsundervisning", *Historisk Tidsskrift* 2, 3 (1850), 245-306. See also Holger Fr. Rørdam, "Bidrag til Sønderjyllands Kirkehistorie i 16de Aarhundrede", *Kirkehistoriske Samlinger* 2, 4 (1868), 626-732, on Ulrik's education, see 729, and note 2 with further references.

8 C. O. Bøggild-Andersen, "Mikkelsen, Hans", *DBL*[3], 9, Copenhagen 1981, 584.

9 E. C. Werlauff, "Sophia von Mecklenburg, Königin von Dänemark …", *Jahrbücher des Vereins für Mecklenburgische Geschichte* 9 (1844), 111-165, in translation from the Danish states that Pedersen was Ulrik's teacher (149). See J. A. Fridericia, "Ulrik", *DBL*[1], 18, Copenhagen 1904, 73-75; on Pedersen see Holger Fr. Rørdam, "Pedersen, Poul", *DBL*[1], 12, Copenhagen 1898, 637. According to Vello Helk, Pedersen studied in Copenhagen and Wittenberg, receiving the master's degree 16 April 1579. From 1584 he was Ulrik's teacher. The *stambog* of Christian Holck (377) places him in Copenhagen on 14 October 1589 (Anna's wedding by proxy?) and that of Anders Schwendi (228) at Frederiksborg 15 May 1590 (Elisabeth and Heinrich Julius's wedding?). He then traveled with Duke Ulrik and was at Helmstedt on 6 October 1590, while the *stambog* of Peder Mikkelsen Arboe locates him at Roskilde on 21 July 1592 and that of Laurentius Quenslovius records him for 25 October 1600. See Vello Helk, *Dansk-Norske Studierejser*, Odense 1987, 344-345.

10 See Werlauff 1844, 146.

11 Casp. Erasmio [Caspar Jesper] Brochmand, *Oratio Funebris… Uldarici… dicta Esuggestu Bytzoviano [Bützow], 24. Maij, Anni M.DC. XXIV,* Copenhagen 1624. Copy used from the Herzog August Bibliothek, Wolfenbüttel, call number Xb 509 with provenance marks "ex Bibliotheca Academiæ Rostochiensis." See also the funeral sermon by Johann Simon, *Justa funebria… Udalrico…*, Rostock 1624, which provides overlapping information about Ulrik. Simon's funeral sermon is dedicated to Queen Sophie, who outlived her children Hans, Anna, Ulrik, and Elizabeth.

12 See also Simon 1624, CivB.

13 Brochmand 1624, AivB.

14 Brochmand 1624, BiA.

15 Brochmand 1624, BiiB.

16 Brochmand 1624, BiiiA.

17 See Simon 1624, DivA-EiA for Croatia and Hungary and EiiB for Saxony.

18 Reinhard Kade, "Der Freiberger Domglöckner Johann Kröner und die kurf[ürstliche] Sächs[ische] Begräbniskapelle 1585-1625", in: *Mitteilungen des Freiberger Altertumsvereins* 25 (1888), 19-26, here 25. My thanks to Hugo Johannsen for alerting me to this information and for kindly sending me a copy of this article. See Hugo Johannsen, "The Saxon Connection. On the Architectural Genesis of Christian IV's Palace Chapel (1606-1617) at Frederiksborg Castle", in: Jan Harasimowicz, Piotr Oszczanowski & Marcin Wisłocki (eds.), *On Opposite Sides of the Baltic Sea. Relations*

between Scandinavian and Central European Countries, Wrocław 2006, 369-379.

19 Werlauff 1844, 695 cites Lyschander's *Slægtebog* in saying Ulrik "taler fine adskillige Tungemaal" [spoke several languages well].

20 Anette Kruse & Karen Stemann-Petersen, "Hertug Ulrik den Ældres kiste i Roskilde Domkirke", *Nationalmuseets Arbejdsmark* 2006, 149-165, esp. 151. I would like to thank Anette Kruse for kindly sending me a copy of their article.

21 Adolph Hofmeister, *Die Matrikel der Universität Rostock*, 3, Rostock 1895, 17.

22 Carsten Neumann, "Herzog Ulrich als Förderer der Künste und Wissenschaften. Gelehrte und Künstler am Güstrower Hof", in: Kornelia von Berswordt-Wallrabe (ed.), *Schloss Güstrow. Prestige und Kunst 1556 bis 1636*, Güstrow 2006, 30-37, 181-193.

23 See *Verzeichnus der Reise / welche die Kön. May. zu Dennemarken Norwegen Anno 1595. zu etlichen ihren Anverwandten Chur vnd Fürsten in Teutschland angestellet*, Copenhagen 1595.

24 Paul Zimmermann (ed.), *Album Academiæ Helmstadiensis*, I, Hannover 1926, 85.

25 Helk 1987, 338.

26 Fussing 1943; Hofmeister 1891, 2, 241.

27 Georg Erler, *Die jüngere Matrikel der Universität Leipzig 1559-1809*, 1, Leipzig 1909, 73, which places Ulrik at Leipzig in 1593. I would like to thank Dr. Volker Bauer, Herzog August Bibliothek, Wolfenbüttel, for kindly providing me with a copy of this entry. Helk 1987, 413 locates Ulrik in Leipzig in 1593 and 1594 (the latter in the *stambog* of Jeremias Gundlach) and states that Ulrik was *rector magnificus* of Leipzig in 1595, returning to Denmark in 1596.

28 See Hofmeister 1891, 2, 275.

29 See Hofmeister 1891, 2, 287, in October 1606, for example: "Illustrissimo principi Uldarico, espiscopo Suerinus, duci Holsati etc., academia cancellario, missae sunt 2 librae confecti, 5 pottae Malvatici et unus Ioachimus episcopi cancellario, qui tum erat D. Erasmus Reutzius."

30 See Hofmeister 1891, 2, 193. Since Ulrik was born in December the following year, this note can only be a much later addition.

31 See Hofmeister 1895, 3, 15-16.

32 See Hofmeister 1895, 3, 36: "Reverendissimo episcopatus Suerinensis administratori, domino Uldarico, academio cancellario, usitate missa fuerunt ab academia munuscula, quattor canthari clareti Hippocrati, duae librae confectionis saccaratae, eiusque cancellario D. Henrico Stalmestero Ioachimicus in specie."

33 See Hofmeister 1895, 3, 56.

34 See Vello Helk, *Stambogsskikken i det danske Monarki indtil 1800*, Odense 2001, 235, with reference (note 203) to J. Oskar Andersen, *Holger Rosenkrantz den Lærde*, Copenhagen 1896, 38-40.

35 Daniel Cramer, *Areteugenia: De Aretino Et Eugenia,... Fabula/ Ficta & Comice descripta a M. Daniele Cramero. Ante decennium fere ab ipso Autore: iam, vero exemplarium penuria denuo edita, adiectis ad singulos actus rythmis Germanicis*, [Leipzig]: Rosa/Lantzenberger 1602. This is record VD17 39:140110K at http://www.vd17.de. I would like to thank Professor Sabine Moedersheim, University of Wisconsin, for her kind help in identifying Cramer's work.

36 One imprint from 1604 was anonymous; the others listed in VD17 are from Magdeburg, Alt Stettin, Stettin, and Leipzig 1602.

37 Mara R. Wade, *Triumphus Nuptialis Danicus. German Court Culture and Denmark – The Great Wedding of 1634*, Wiesbaden 1996 (Wolfenbütteler Arbeiten zur Barockforschung, 27), 41. See also *Verzeichnus der Reyse … 1595*, BiA.

38 Rigsarkivet [The Danish National Archives, Copenhagen, hereafter RA], Kongehuset. Frederik 2.s døtre og sønnen Ulrik, 1573-1642. Diverse korrespondance, 1589-1617, no. 2, 3 October 1596, Gottorf, where Duke Johann Adolph wants to have the "Heimführung."

39 For a well documented critical assessment of Frederik II's funeral in an international context, see Birgitte Bøggild Johannsen, "The Polish Paradigm. On the Heraldic Funeral of King Frederik II of Denmark and its European Context", in: Harasimowicz, Oszczanowski & Wisłocki 2006, 2, 555-568. I would like to thank Birgitte Bøggild Johannsen for kindly sending me a copy of her article.

40 The *stambog* of Christian Holck illuminates the constellations of persons at court during 1589-1590. That of Anders Schwendi also has entries by Christian IV and Ulrik from 1590. Helk 2001, 138-140.

41 Ulrik signed Morten Bornholm's *stambog* on this occasion. Helk 2001, 142.

42 Mara R. Wade, "Drama in Denmark and Norway", in: Helen Watanabe-O'Kelly & Pierre Béhar (eds.), *Spectacvlvm Evropævm. Theatre and Spectacle in Europe 1580-1750*, Wiesbaden 1999 (Wolfenbütteler Arbeiten zur Barockforschung 31), 289-297; Mara R. Wade, "Opera in Denmark and Norway", in: Watanabe-O'Kelly & Béhar 1999, 465-470; Mara R. Wade, "Ballet in Denmark and Norway", in: Watanabe-O'Kelly & Béhar 1999, 571-575; Mara R. Wade, "Fireworks and Entries in Denmark and Norway", in:

Watanabe-O'Kelly & Béhar 1999, 743-749. See also Mara R. Wade (ed.), *Pomp, Power, and Politics: Essays on German and Scandinavian Court Culture and their Contexts*, New York & Amsterdam 2004 (Daphnis. Zeitschrift für Mittlere Deutsche Literatur und Kultur der Frühen Neuzeit (1400-1750) 32, 1-2 (2003)).

43 For an account of the mumming, see Wade 1996, 42-47. For an extract of the original festival account and English translation, see Mara R. Wade, "The Coronation of King Christian IV 1596", in: J. R. Mulryne, Helen Watanabe-O'Kelly & Margaret Shewring (eds.), *Europa Triumphans. Court and Civic Festivals in Early Modern Europe,* Basingstoke 2004, 2, 245-267.

44 There is both a German and Danish copy of the coronation description in the British Library, see Helen Watanabe-O'Kelly & Anne Simon (eds.), *Festivals and Ceremonies. A Bibliography of Works Relating to Court, Civic and Religious Festivals in Europe, 1500-1800*, London & New York 2000, nos. 2759-2760.

45 See Wade 1996, 45.

46 See Mara R. Wade, "Pax Danica und die frühneuzeitliche Idee der klassischen Monarchie", in: Ulrich Heinen et al. (eds.), *Welche Antike? Konkurrierende Rezeptionen des Altertums im Barock*, Wiesbaden 2011, 373-396 (Wolfenbütteler Arbeiten zur Barockforschung 47).

47 Helen Watanabe-O'Kelly, "Festivals of the Protestant Union", in: Mulryne, Watanabe-O'Kelly & Shewring (eds.) 2004, 2, 3-118.

48 Helk 1987, 413.

49 For digital editions of the most important Stuttgart court festivals, see http://www.hab.de/bibliothek/wdb/festkultur/dig-inha.htm

50 Johann Oettinger, *Wahrhaffte Historische Beschreibung …*, Stuttgart 1610, 43. In the entourage were also "Jörg Breda", "Moritz Gala", and "Dottag Trotta." See the digital copy at: http://diglib.hab.de/wdb.php?dir=drucke/126-quod-2-1

51 See Wade 1996, 249-250. See the inventory of his library made at his death: RA, *Lensregnskaber*. Nykøbing (Falster). Kvittantiarumbilag 1647-1661 (Bog 20, No. 4), "Nÿekiöbing Slodtz Inventarium" (signed by Magdalena Sibylla on 17 December 1647), f. 7B.

52 For Albert Skeel's til Fussingø (1572-1639) travels, see Helk 1987, 379. Skeel, who became the admiral of the navy under Christian IV, traveled widely, including for two years with Duke Ulrik, and can be located through *stambog* entries in Orleans and Paris in 1597.

53 Riis 1988, 2, 296.

54 Helk 2001, 237, who also writes that in 1622 the Englishman Thomaas Seghetus was recommended to Holger Rosenkrantz by Ulrik's advisor Thomas Busch (242).

55 See Brochmand 1624, BiB.

56 See Wade 1996, 73-74.

57 *Kurtze und doch außführliche Relation … von gehaltenem Beylager … Des … Herrn Christiani II. …*, Jena 1603, Biii B.

58 See Mara R. Wade, "Widowhood and Patronage: Hedevig, Princess of Denmark and Electress of Saxony (1581-1641)", *Renæssanceforum* (http://www.renaessanceforum.dk) 4 (2008), 1-28. See also the German version, "Witwenschaft und Mäzenatentum: Hedwig, Prinzessin von Dänemark und Kurfürstin von Sachsen (1581-1641)", in: Susanne Rode-Breymann (ed.), *Orte der Musik. Kulturelles Handeln von Frauen in der Stadt,* Cologne 2007, 219-231. My studies of Ulrik and Hedevig are results from research for the book in progress on Danish-Saxon court festivals with working title "Splendid Ceremonies: The Great Spectacles of the Early Modern Period in Electoral Saxony and Denmark, 1548-1709." A preliminary survey is: Mara R. Wade, "Dänisch-Sächsische Hoffeste der frühen Neuzeit", in: Jutta Kappel & Claudia Brink (eds.), *Mit Fortuna übers Meer. Sachsen und Dänemark – Ehen ind Allianzen im Spiegel der Kunst (1548-1709)*, Berlin & Munich 2009, 62-69.

59 The Royal Library, Copenhagen, Ms. Uldall 449 4°, f. 147, "M[r]. Johns." The entry for the baptism lists all persons present at the dinner, including George Manners, the ambassador's brother. Grubbe also describes the ceremony for Christian IV's receipt of the Order of the Garter, Wade 1996, 50; See also John Harris & Gordon Higgot, *Inigo Jones. The Complete Architectural Drawings*, New York 1989, 13.

60 Diana Poulton, *John Dowland*, Berkeley 1982², 59.

61 Poulton 1982, 60-61. An outstanding study of the musical culture of this time is Arne Spohr, *'How chances it they travel?' Englische Musiker in Dänemark und Norddeutschland, 1579-1630*, Wiesbaden 2009 (Wolfenbütteler Arbeiten zur Barockforschung 45).

62 Riis 1988, 1, 296.

63 While negotiations with Hamburg were vigorously pursued under Frederik II, that king never received Hamburg's homage and the oath to Christian IV was the last time the city paid this respect to a Danish monarch. While the ceremony was reduced to a handshake, the fact remains that Hamburg paid its homage to the Danish king.

64 Sächsische Landes- und Universitätsbibliothek Dresden, Hs H3.

65 Mara R. Wade, "Publication, Pageantry, Patronage: Georg Engelhard von Loehneyss' *Della Cavalleria*

(1609-1610; 1624) and His Hamburg Tournament Pageant for King Christian IV of Denmark (1603)", in: Wade (ed.) 2004, 166-197.

66 For correct biographical information about Loehneyss, his connections to the Dresden and Wolfenbüttel courts, and further confirmation of the web of cultural connections between these courts and Denmark, see Jill Bepler, "Practical Perspectives on the Court and the Role of Princes: Georg Engelhard von Loehneyss's *Aulico Politica* and Christian IV of Denmark's *Königlicher Wecker* (1620)", in: Wade (ed.) 2004, 137-164. See also Jesper Düring Jørgensen, "Introduktion til Georg Engelhard Löhneyssens ridebøger i Det Kongelige Bibliotek", *Fund og Forskning* 34 (1995), 35-60 and Jesper Düring Jørgensen, "Georg Engelhard Löhneysen fra den skrevne Bidbog til den trykte Ridebog", *Fund og Forskning* 36 (1997), 11-43. See also Spohr, 2009, 250-266.

67 There is a full description of all the pageants in Hamburg in the Sächsische Landes- und Universitätsbibliothek Dresden, Hs H3. The description of Ulrik's allegorical pageant is on ff. 6B-7A. The scoring for the tournament indicates that Ulrik won "50 Thaler" for his direct hits at running at the ring, thereby placing him second in his group (f. 11A). Ulrik ran several times in a variety of masquerades and also participated in the barriers (ff. 13B, 14A, 16B, 21A, 22B, 24B).

68 See Brochmand 1624, BiA.

69 Georg Engelhard von Loehneyss, *Della Cavalleria …*, Remlingen 1609-1610, 383-387. For the digital edition, see http://diglib.hab.de/wdb.php?dir=drucke/1-bell-2f-1

70 See Helen Watanabe-O'Kelly, *Court Culture in Dresden. From Renaissance to Baroque,* Basingstoke 2002, 100-129.

71 This discussion is based on Wade 1996, 74-78.

72 David Smith, "Herbert, Philipp", *Oxford Dictionary of National Biography*, 26, Oxford 2004, 714-720. Herbert also shared the king's passion for hunting and figured as James's court favorite from 1603.

73 See Brochmand 1624, BiB.

74 John Nichols, *The Progresses … of James I*, 1, London 1828, 473-474.

75 Perhaps this payment also confirms the pension mentioned in his funeral sermon, see Brochmand 1624, BiB.

76 Clare McManus, *Women on the Renaissance Stage: Anna of Denmark and Female Masquing in the Stuart Court, 1590-1619*, Manchester 2002, 11. See also, for example, the discussion about "averse disguises: the drama of feminine blackness" (194-199) by Sophie Tomlinson, "Theatrical Vibrancy on the Caroline Stage: *Tempe Restored* and *The Shepherd's Paradise*", in: McManus (ed.) 2003, 186-203.

77 Apparently, the perspective stage was then unknown in Denmark, and the first evidence for it is in the ballet for the Great Wedding of 1634. On its importance for the court masque, see Stephen Orgel, *The Illusion of Power*, Berkeley 1991.

78 See Jordi Savall, *Tobias Hume: Musicall Humors,* track 13, Alia Vox CD B0002K6ZPC. Spain 2004.

79 From the CD notes to Emma Kirkby, Labyrinto, Paolo Pandoolfo, Tobias Hume: The Spirit of Gambo. Glosso CD C80402. Switzerland 1996/2008 and from Michael Morrow, Colette Harris/Frank Traficante, "Hume, Tobias," *Oxford Music Online*. 26 September 2009.

80 Jordi Savall, Prague, 28 May 2004. http://www.alia-vox.com/cataleg.php?id=36 (consulted 26 September 2009).

81 *Oxford Music Online*. 26 September 2009. His birth is listed as "?c 1579" and his death as 16 April 1645.

82 My argument contradicts David Pinto's CD notes to Tobias Hume: The Spirit of Gambo. Glosso CD C80402, where he disparages Hume's claims as braggadocio and completely without credibility.

83 Morrow, *Oxford Music Online*. 26 September 2009.

84 Spohr, 55 and 241. Hume is listed as a communicant in the Anglican church established in Hamburg for the Merchant Adventurers.

85 Spohr, 83.

86 Tobias Hume, *Captain Humes Poeticall Musicke*, Vol. 1-2, CD Naxos 8.5541276 and 8.554127. This two-volume set also contains the music dedicated to Ulrik as well as the hunting song.

87 Jørgen Hein, "An unknown cameo of James I and the Order of the Garter", *The Burlington Magazine* CXLVIII (2006), 400-405. See also Elias Ashmole, *The Institution, Laws, Ceremonies of the Most Noble Order of the Garter,* London 1715, 275 (CW3302217999), 298 (CW3302218022), and 301 (CW3302218025). This text is available on-line at: *Eighteenth Century Collections Online*; the numbers in parentheses after the page numbers refer to the document number in the database.

88 Ashmole 1715, 300 (CW3302218024).

89 Ulrik married a Mecklenburg woman, Katharina Hahn. See G. C. Friedrich Lisch, "Katharina Hahn, Gemahlin des Herzogs Ulrik, Prinzen von Dänemark, Administrators des Bisthums Schwerin", *Jahrbücher des Vereins fur Mecklenburgische Geschichte* 23 (1858), 33-40. His article is based primarily on her inheritance of the manor at Ziebühl, which Ulrik had purchased before his death and left to her.

90 Kruse & Stemann-Petersen 2006, 149-165.

91 *Wahrhafftige vnd kurtze Relation der Reussischen … Reise … deß … Hertzog Johann deß jüngeren …*, Hamburg 1603.

92 The correspondence between Christian IV and Christian II of Saxony also mentions Ulrik, for example, soon after Hedevig's and Christian's wedding. RA, Tyske Kancelli, Udenrigske Afdeling [hereafter: TKUA]. Speciel del, Sachsen A I, 12. Brevveksling mellem fyrstehusene. Breve, til dels med bilag fra kurfyrst Christian II og gemalinde Hedvig til kong Christian IV og dronning Anna Cathrine, 1596-1639. Breve fra kurfyrst Christian II, 1596-1611, nr. 22, 25 September 1602 with thanks for sending Ulrik to Dresden.

93 RA, TKUA Speciel del, Sachsen A I, 12. Breve fra kurfyrstinde Hedvig, 1603-39, 40-12.Nr. 5-6.

94 RA, TKUA. Speciel del, Sachsen A I, 12 Breve fra kurfyrst Christian II, 1596-1611, nr. 27.

95 Wade 2003, 165-197. See also Jørgensen 1995 and 1997; Spohr, 2009.

96 See the letters in RA, TKUA, Speciel del, Sachsen A I, 12. Breve fra kurfyrst Christian II, 1596-1611.

97 RA, Kongehuset. Frederik 2.s døtre og sønnen Ulrik, 1573-1642. Diverse korrespondance, 1589-1617, nr 1, 19 October 1593, Torgau.

98 RA, TKUA, Speciel del, Sachsen A II, 22. Akter og dokumenter vedr. det politiske forhold til Sachsen. Akter og dokumenter vedr. ægteskabet mellem kurfyrst Christian II af Sachsen og prinsesse Hedvig af Danmark …, 1602-51, i.a. treating the time of her death and her inheritance 1641-1651.

99 RA, TKUA, Speciel del, Sachsen A I, 12. Breve fra kurfyrstinde Hedvig, 1603-39, 40-12. Nr. 46-47.

100 Brochmand 1624, BiiA.

101 RA, TKUA, Speciel del, Sachsen A I, 12. Breve fra kurfyrstinde Hedvig, 1603-39, 40-12. Nr. 52

102 RA, TKUA, Speciel del, Sachsen A I, 12. Breve fra kurfyrstinde Hedvig, 1603-39, 40-12. Nr. 54.

103 RA, TKUA, Speciel del, Sachsen A I, 12. Breve fra kurfyrstinde Hedvig, 1603-39, 40-12. Nr. 57.

104 RA, TKUA, Speciel del, Sachsen A I, 12. Breve fra kurfyrstinde Hedvig, 1603-39, 40-12. Nr. 58.

105 RA, TKUA, Speciel del, Sachsen A I, 12. Breve fra kurfyrstinde Hedvig, 1603-39, 40-12. Nr. 59.

106 For an exciting study of the correspondence of a Danish royal woman, see Pernille Arenfeldt, *The Political Role of the Female Consort in Protestant Germany, 1550-1585. Anna of Saxony as 'Mater Patriae'*. Dissertation. European University Institute, Florence 2005.

107 RA, Kongehuset. Frederik 2.s døtre og sønnen Ulrik, 1573-1642. Diverse korrespondance, 1589-1617, letters from King Christian IV, the Queen Dowager Sophia and the Chancellor Christian Friis to Prince Ulrik, administrator of the bishopric of Schwerin 1609-10 and further letters. This reference to two collections of letters apparently belongs to the same source, the abovementioned one.

108 See Holger Fr. Rørdam, "Hertug Ulrik, Christian IV's Søn", *Historiske Samlinger og Studier* 8 (1896), 1-141, esp. 2-3.

109 RA, TKUA, Speciel del, Sachsen A I, 12. Breve fra kurfyrstinde Hedvig, 1603-39, 40-12. Nr. 46.

110 Kade 1888, 25.

111 Kruse & Stemann-Petersen 2006, 151.

WOLFENBÜTTEL AND COPENHAGEN: THE EXCHANGE OF ARCHITECTURAL IDEAS IN THE TIME OF CHRISTIAN IV

Barbara Uppenkamp

This essay focuses on the architectural activities of Christian IV (1577-1648) in the area of city planning and church building. Taking up a reference made by Juliette Roding in her book on Christian IV, I will compare Christian's foundation of Christiansstad (1614) to the ideal plan of Wolfenbüttel (c. 1570), which may have played a pivotal role in its conception.[1] I will first of all examine the links that connect Christian IV to Wolfenbüttel, and then discuss the ideal plans of both cities against the background of Lutheran Protestant politics around 1600. This also involves a discussion of the Protestant churches of Christiansstad and Wolfenbüttel within the context of the city foundations. In order to understand the political meaning of these foundations, it is also useful to look at the architectural theory and political writings of the time.

Dynastic links

The dynastic links between the Danish court and the courts of Saxony and Lower Saxony were traditionally strong in the 16th and 17th centuries.[2] Anna of Denmark (1532-1585), sister of Frederik II (1534-1588) and aunt to Christian IV, married elector August I of Saxony (1526-1586) in 1548. In 1585, Heinrich Julius of Brunswick-Wolfenbüttel (1564-1613) married their daughter Dorothea (1563-1587).[3] When Dorothea died in childbirth in 1587, Heinrich Julius married Elisabeth of Denmark (1573-1626), the eldest sister of Christian IV. Heinrich Julius's father, Duke Julius of Brunswick-Wolfenbüttel (1528-1589), had started the wedding negotiations with the Danish court immediately after Dorothea's death.[4] In the initial stages of the negotiations it seems that it was not completely clear whether Heinrich Julius should marry Elisabeth or her younger sister Anna (1574-1619), who instead became the wife of King James VI of Scotland – subsequently James I of England (1566-1625) – in 1589.[5] The wedding of Heinrich Julius and Elisabeth took place at Kronborg Castle on 19 April 1590 in the presence of the Danish and the Scottish kings.[6] Shortly after the wedding, Duke Heinrich Julius welcomed Elisabeth in Wolfenbüttel with a ceremonial entry.[7] Two woodcuts by Elias Holwein from 1603 (Figs. 1-2) show the couple in an architectural setting.[8] The Duke is shown standing in front of the castle of Wolfenbüttel, while the Duchess is presented against the backdrop of a landscape that is not easily identifiable. It may be a fantasy landscape, but it is equally possible that it is a view of Wolfenbüttel with the church of St Mary's, which was demolished to make way

Fig. 1. Elias Holwein, Duke Heinrich Julius of Brunswick-Wolfenbüttel, 1603. Herzog Anton-Ulrich-Museum Braunschweig. After Jochen Luckhardt (ed.), *Hofkunst der Spätrenaissance: Braunschweig-Wolfenbüttel und das kaiserliche Prag um 1600*, Brunswick 1998.

for the new church of Beatae Mariae Virginis in 1608.

Heinrich Julius was one of the best-educated princes of his age, and also a distinguished lawyer. From 1607 onwards he spent most of his time at the Imperial court in Prague. He was an eminent diplomat and became the director of the Imperial Privy Council at the court of Rudolf II (1552-1612) in 1611.[9] During the last years of his reign until his death in Prague in 1613, Duchess Elisabeth took charge of affairs in Wolfenbüttel, and after Heinrich Julius's death it was Christian IV who became an important political figure in Lower Saxony and Brunswick.

Christian had been in Wolfenbüttel several times on different occasions, first of all during his trip to the north German courts from September to November 1595.[10] In 1605, Christian joined Heinrich Julius in the siege of Brunswick, which may have been one of his first serious military engagements.[11] The city of Brunswick and the Dukes of Brunswick-Wolfenbüttel had been engaged in a power struggle since the times of Heinrich Julius's grandfather, Heinrich the Younger (1489-1568).[12] The city council of Brunswick had not sworn the oath of allegiance to the Dukes for three generations, and the city council acted as if the city were subject only to the emperor ("reichsunmittelbar"). This was in fact not the case, although Brunswick was a rich and powerful member of the Hanse. When Heinrich Julius's siege did not succeed, he went to Prague to plead his cause and achieve a banishment of the city by Emperor Rudolf II.[13]

When Heinrich Julius, who had died on 20 July 1613 in Prague, was buried in Wolfenbüttel in October of that year, Christian IV attended the funeral.[14] From 1613 on, the Danish king spent more time in Wolfenbüttel and frequently took the opportunity to influence the politics of the duchy, since his nephew, the young Duke Friedrich Ulrich (1591-1634), was regarded as a weak character.[15] In 1615, Christian IV joined Friedrich Ulrich in another siege of Brunswick, which ended when the Dutch united provinces sent troops to relieve the besieged city.[16] In the same year – 1615 – Elisabeth and Christian advised Friedrich Ulrich to hand over the regency to a group of noblemen from lower ranks, the so-called "Landdrostenregiment". Led by Anton von der Streithorst (1562 or 1563-1625), this group immediately started to line their own pockets, cheat the population and debase the coinage.[17] In 1620, the situation had become so bad that Christian IV wrote a letter to Friedrich Ulrich, the "Königlicher Wecker" (Royal Alarm), expressing his concern about the young Duke's naivety.[18] The "Landdrostenregiment" was stopped in 1622, and Friedrich Ulrich was reinstalled as a regent in 1623, but he did not really come to power again. Instead it was his brother, Christian the Younger (1599-1626), administrator of Halberstadt, and

Fig. 2. Elias Holwein, Duchess Elisabeth of Brunswick-Wolfenbüttel, 1603. Herzog Anton-Ulrich-Museum Braunschweig. After Luckhardt.

Christian IV who influenced Brunswick politics in the following years. Christian IV had a strong interest in extending his power in Lower Saxony. As Duke of Holstein, he held a seat on the Imperial Council of Lower Saxony, and he successfully installed his two younger sons as administrators of the Protestant north German episcopates. When Christian the Younger withdrew from the administration of the episcopate Halberstadt in 1624, Christian IV's second son, Duke Frederik, later King Frederik III (1609-1670), who was already Archbishop of Bremen and Verden, succeeded him as administrator.[19] In March 1625, Christian IV was appointed captain of the troops of Lower Saxony, with Wolfenbüttel as his headquarters. In alliance with his nephew Christian the Younger, Christian IV sought to play a major part in the early stages of the Thirty Years' War as a leader of the Protestant forces. Christian IV's military engagement was not very successful, however, and ended with his defeat in the battle near Lutter am Barenberge on 27 August 1626 against the Imperial troops, led by Count Tilly (1559-1632). With the peace of Lübeck (May/June 1629), the Danish claim for hegemony in the north-western part of the Empire came to an end. The Danish princes, however, did not sign the contract and thus kept their claim for the episcopates of Bremen and Verden alive.[20]

Christian IV's city foundations

During his sixty-year reign, Christian IV founded or rebuilt and extended no less than ten cities. His city foundations can be divided into three periods.[21] The first, from 1588 to 1611, is marked by Christian's accession to the Danish throne and by the outbreak of the Kalmar War. During this period, the city of Christianopel was founded (1599).[22] The second period, from 1613 to 1625, is marked by the peace pact with Sweden, the so-called "Peace of Knærød", and by Christian's engagement in the Thirty Years' War as a captain of the troops of Lower Saxony. This period of twelve years was characterised by an exceptionally good financial situation and thriving building activity.[23] During this period, Christiansstad (1614), Glückstadt (1616), a new city near Bredstedt (1616), Christianshavn (1617) and Christiania (later Oslo) (1624) were founded. The third period, from 1629 to 1648, is marked by the peace of Lübeck (1629) and by Christian's death on 28 February 1648. This period was similarly characterised by intense building activity, although the financial situation was more difficult than in the earlier years. The most important city project carried out during the third period was Christiansand in Norway (1641), while projects for two new fortified cities north of Kolding had to be abandoned for the time being (one of these was established after 1648, i.e. Frederiksodde (later Fredericia)).

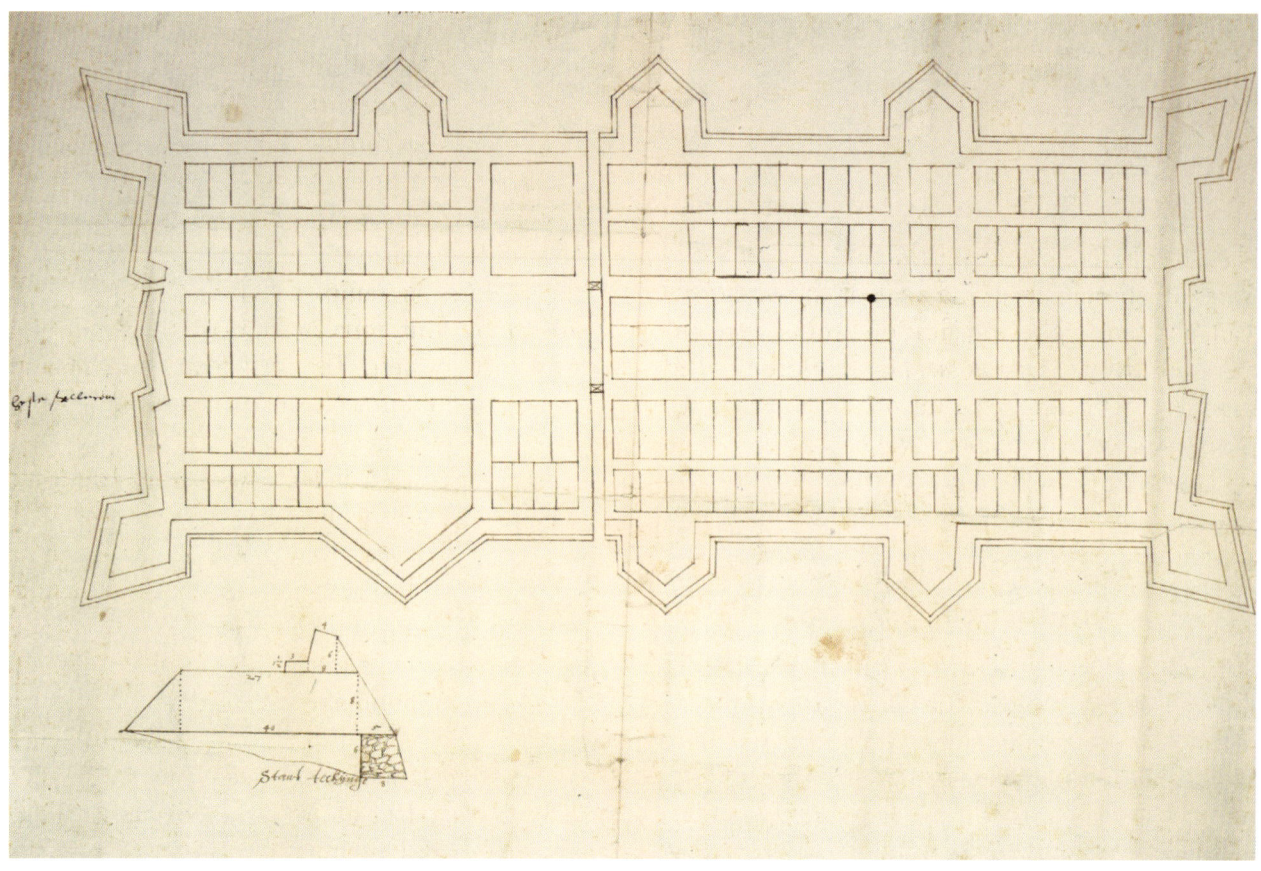

The foundation of Christiansstad

Among all of Christian's city foundations, Christiansstad in north-east Scania has the most regular ground plan.²⁴ The city was founded in 1614 and subsequently built during the period when Christian's engagement in Wolfenbüttel was at its peak. The city was founded for military reasons: during the Kalmar War, Swedish troops had devastated the region of Scania, and in February 1612 the city of Vä was burned down. This had happened several times before in history, but instead of rebuilding Vä, Christian now decided to build a completely new, fortified city, which was also to become an administrative centre in the region. The first inhabitants of Christiansstad were people who had left the destroyed city of Vä and who were offered a plot in the new city.²⁵

The site for the city foundation was chosen by Gert Rantzau (1558-1627), who led the Danish troops in the Kalmar War.²⁶ This becomes clear from a letter Rantzau wrote to the King on 13 March 1612. There is, however, another legendary story of the foundation of Christiansstad, according to which the Danish king had fallen asleep during an excursion and dreamed that he should build a new city and a church on the place where he was lying. Juliette Roding has pointed out the political meaning of this myth, which links Christian IV with the Emperor Constantine and Pope Liberius, who founded a city and a church respectively on the spot where they had fallen asleep. In this myth, the order for the new city foundation seems to come directly from God, and the king is acting according to His will.²⁷

The city boundaries and the fortifications of Christiansstad were laid out on 19 May 1614.²⁸ Shaped like a regular rectangle, the city was situated on the Allø peninsula close to the Baltic Sea, and was surrounded by a lake and the river Helgeå. A canal was built along the river to make

Fig. 4. Simon Stevin, Project of an Ideal City, c.1605-1610, published in *Materiae Politicae*, Leyden 1649. Wolfenbüttel, Herzog August Bibliothek (Photo Herzog August Bibliothek).

Fig. 3. Johan Sems (attr.), map of Christiansstad, c. 1629. Copenhagen, The Danish Royal Library (Photo author?).

it possible to sail from the Baltic to Christiansstad. Christiansstad is the first Danish city foundation where a "clear distinction between the work of the engineer and that of the architect" can be seen.[29] The fortification works were supervised by Poulus Buysser, Jacob Borbeck and Christian van der Sluys, all presumably Dutchmen, whereas architectural works were entrusted to David Nyborg from Køge, who probably had the status of a master builder and mason, not an autonomous architect).[30] On account of the two inspection trips he undertook in 1617 and 1618, Johan Sems (1572-1635), an engineer from Groningen who had studied in Leiden and worked on several city projects for Christian IV, namely the layout of Christianshavn, is presumed to have designed the city plan (Fig 3).[31]

The city consisted of ten streets along with a larger and a smaller market square. There was no central axis running through the city; instead, Christian IV stipulated that a visitor should cross the large market square when coming from the north and going south and this route was paved with stones, as were the market squares.[32] Two main streets ran through the city, connecting the north and south gates and the two squares. Two subordinated streets ran parallel in the east and west, and two narrow lanes separated the building blocks from the ramparts. These six streets were crossed by four equally straight streets running from east to west. The streets were completely subject to the form of the fortifications. A canal ran along the larger square and the second street from east to west; it divided the city into two unequal parts, of which the smaller part can be regarded as the more prestigious one, as this was where the royal palace was planned and the monumental building of the Trinity Church erected.[33]

The function of the canal was more to drain the swampy ground on which the city was erected than to provide a transportation route for materials or goods. It was not part of the first planning phase, but it had an aesthetic quality and was reminiscent of Dutch trading cities. It is also important to note that the canal is a standard feature in all of Christian's city foundations.

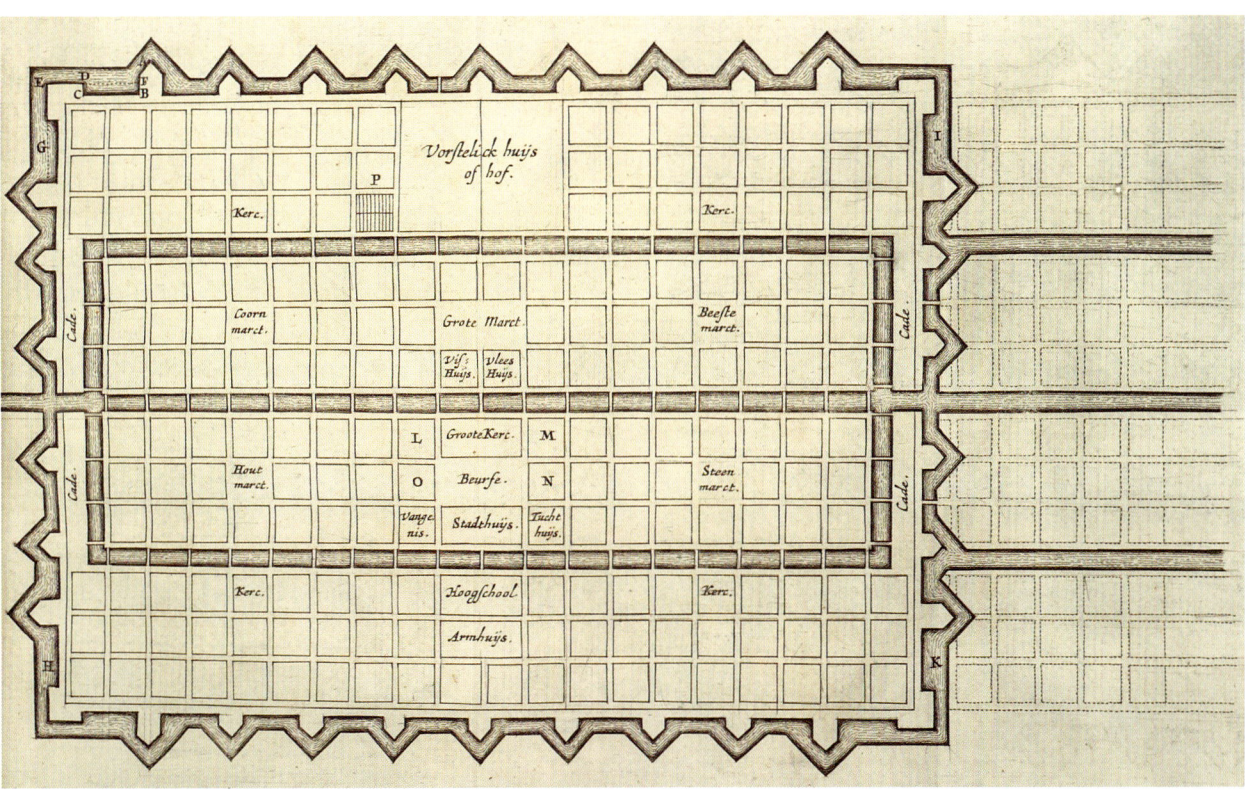

WOLFENBÜTTEL AND COPENHAGEN   267

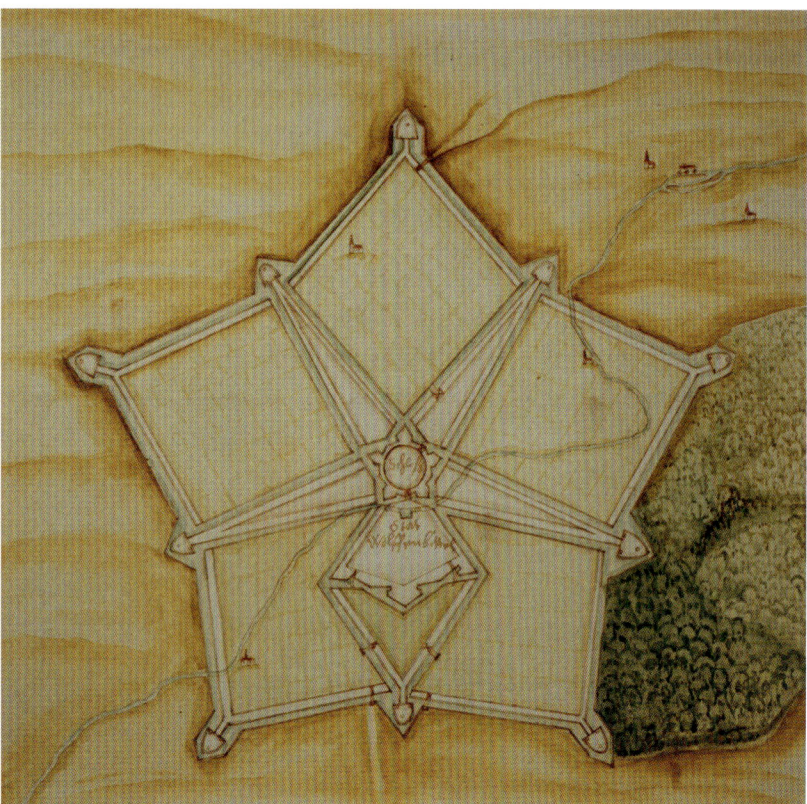

Fig. 5. Daniel Specklin, Ideal Project of Wolfenbüttel, in *Architectura von Festungen*, ms 1583. Musées de Strasbourg, Cabinet des Estampes (Photo Musées de Strasbourg).

The city was surrounded by an almost symmetrical system of ten bastions: one at each of the four corners and three on each longitudinal side. The bastions at the corners were more pointed than those of the long city ramparts, and there was a larger, triangular bastion in the northern part of the west wall to support the building of the Trinity Church. As the plan attributed to Johan Sems shows, the building blocks were plotted out according to a regular pattern. The plots could be subdivided into smaller construction sites, a principle that Sems also adopted in the layout of Christianshavn.[34] The houses varied in size according to the location of the construction site within the city, and the lots reflected the social rank of the owner or the inhabitants. This meant that wealthy noblemen lived along the main streets and on the market squares in the city centre, while craftsmen lived in the less important streets and workmen in the lanes. One plot close to the northern square was foreseen for the erection of a royal palace, but this was never implemented.

With its rectangular form, its rigid grid of streets and squares and its canal, the city seems to be directly inspired by Simon Stevin's (1548-1620) ideal city project, as described in his book "Vande oirdeningh der steden" (c. 1600/1649) (Fig. 4).[35] Similar to Stevin's plan, the streets are laid out in a subtle way to conform with the bastions of the fortifications. Stevin, too, planned the modulation of the building blocks to correspond with the place of people in society. Like Stevin, Sems planned a royal palace and schools, administrational buildings and a hospital. But unlike Stevin's ideal plan, the canal in Christiansstad did not run through the city as a central axis, and it has no side arms. Another difference is that the church was not placed centrally or according to the grid pattern of the plots. It must also be noted that Stevin's book was only known in manuscript versions at that time, which may have circulated among the members of the Leiden Academy and thus may have been known to Johan Sems.[36] Although it cannot be excluded that a transfer of knowledge took place between the Leiden academy and the Danish court with regard to city foundations, this essay sets out to explore the possible influence of the court of Wolfenbüttel on Christian IV.

Wolfenbüttel as a model of an ideal city

Duke Julius of Brunswick-Wolfenbüttel planned and partly executed his residence according to an ideal plan from 1570 onwards. According to his own words, the Duke was most impressed by the extension of Antwerp, which he witnessed during his stay in Leuven as a student in the early 1550s. It was therefore no wonder that he tried to attract artists from the Netherlands for his own projects. Among the engineers who worked in Wolfenbüttel were Willem de Raet (c. 1537-1583) and Hans Vredeman de Vries (1526-1609) from Antwerp, but also German architects like Philipp Müller (died 1609) and Paul Francke (1537 or 1538-1615).[37] The project comprised the ducal castle of Wolfenbüttel as a heavily fortified citadel in the centre. East of the citadel, a residential city, called Heinrichstadt after Duke Julius's father, was to serve as an administrative and trading centre in the region. According to the Duke's plans, Heinrichstadt was to be extended with the addition of the "Gotteslager", a suburb containing 36,000 houses. The whole complex was shaped like a huge, regular pentagon (Fig. 5).[38] Duke Julius planned to transfer the Academia Julia University from Helmstedt and the episcopal sea from Halberstadt to Wolfenbüttel. He also planned to connect the city with the trading centres on the rivers Weser and Elbe via canals. In 1571 Duke Julius issued building regulations containing stipulations on future constructions, which were to be erected according to a specific plan. The Duke's concept was radical in the sense that the buildings of pre-existent settlements had to be torn down and replaced by new buildings of equal height and width along straight streets. Rebuilding the city meant that the new houses were to be arranged in different quarters according to a plan that reflected the social rank of the inhabitants. There were three types of houses – varying in size and decoration – for the nobility, for the burghers and merchants, and for the workers and soldiers.[39] Duke Heinrich Julius continued with the project on a much smaller scale. He abandoned the pentagonal plan and the Gotteslager, and changed some of the fortification works. During his reign he concentrated on the completion of Heinrichstadt and its buildings. Most of the houses that are still intact in Wolfenbüttel today date back to the early years of Heinrich Julius's reign from 1591 to 1605, although many of them have been altered and rebuilt over the centuries. When Heinrich Julius died in 1613, the Beatae Mariae Virginis Church, the arsenal and some fortification works were still underway. After Heinrich Julius's death, Elisabeth assumed an important role in directing the building projects, especially the completion of the church.

On the eve of the Thirty Years' War, under the reign of Duke Friedrich Ulrich, it became clear that the city could not be extended beyond a tenth of the original plan. Most of the construction work stopped in 1626, but what had been completed by then was already quite impressive. Although the extensive plans for Wolfenbüttel were never fully realised, it can be said that the city and its inner structure were built according to a strictly rational, early modern pattern. All the core elements that were later to become important components of Christian IV's city foundations can already be found in Wolfenbüttel: a plan that comprised the fortifications and the inner structure of the city, as well as a grid pattern of streets, canals and type houses. However the foundation of the ideal city of Wolfenbüttel was only one step in a series of important reforms introduced by Duke Julius. Other aspects of a dynamic process of modernisation included the centralisation of power, professional administration, the introduction of Roman law, the foundation of the Academia Julia University in Helmstedt, and the introduction of the Reformation. Duke Julius planned to erect a mercantile, Lutheran state, and for him and his followers, architecture was an appropriate means of achieving this aim. In a Protestant country of the early modern period, it was the ruler who felt directly responsible for the welfare and salvation of his people – a notion of power that can also be traced in the foundation of churches.

The Holy Trinity Church

The Holy Trinity Church in Christiansstad was placed at an angle to the large market square, with the choir facing east (Fig. 6).[40] There are several

possible interpretations for this position. There may be a traditional element in the positioning of the choir and altar which prevented the church building from being integrated into the grid pattern of the city. Ed Taverne suspects that the unusual placing of the church may have had something to do with the perspective view from the market square, and Holmér also refers to the theatrical element of the perspective.[41] If the royal palace had been erected according to the plans, it would have been the second largest building after the church, and an axis of view would have connected these two eminent buildings via the market square. Roding correctly remarks that Dürer's book on fortification may have played a role in the positioning of the church.[42] Dürer's proposals were carried out by the Saxon Dukes in the foundation of the mining cities Annaberg and Marienberg.[43] It is worth noting that Daniel Specklin, too, shows an ideal plan of a city with the church placed at an angle to a polygonal market square in his treatise on fortification, and that this situation was put into practice in Christian IV's foundation of Glückstadt in Schleswig-Holstein (1616).[44] Specklin was asked to give his advice on the ideal plan of Wolfenbüttel in 1575, and he dedicated his treatise to Duke Heinrich Julius's father, Duke Julius of Brunswick-Wolfenbüttel.[45]

The architects of the Trinity Church in Christiansstad were presumably the Steenwinckel brothers and David Nyborg, the last-mentioned as an entrepreneur and mason.[46] Building work on the church began in 1617, and it was consecrated in 1628. The tower was not completed at that time; the spire was not added until 1865/66. In the 17th century the tower only had a pyramid-shaped roof. The church is by far the largest building in the city, and this huge structure must have made an even stronger impact in Christian's day than it does today.[47]

Fig. 6. Christiansstad (Scania), Holy Trinity Church, exterior facing South (Photo author).

The church has the ground plan of a Greek cross, but it could also be described as a longitudinal building with two short, broad transepts (Fig. 7). Roding describes the ground plan as an attempt to combine the traditional late Gothic type of a hall church with the Greek cross on the basis of a grid.[48] Other more traditional elements are the tower on a quadrangular base on the west side and a choir consisting of two bays on the east. The hall is divided into three equal naves by ten tall granite columns supporting a simple rib vaulting. The impression of a unity of space that one might expect from a centrally organised ground plan like the Greek cross is eliminated in the cross-axis by two columns that are set in the openings of the transepts towards the church, and by the balconies. The columns are octagonal and have Romanesque capitals (Fig. 8). While the ground plan gives the impression of a central church, the actual impression of the space is that of a late Gothic hall, with strong emphasis placed on the longitudinal axis.

Due to the large windows, the space is filled with light. The church is said to have been inspired by the churches of Hendrik de Keyser in Amsterdam, especially the Westerkerk, but the Westerkerk was only begun in 1620 and finished in 1631.[49] It is therefore hard to imagine that the Westerkerk could have served as a direct model. There were, however, some connections with Hendrik de Keyser, and the altar is said to be from his workshop. It was ordered from Amsterdam in 1620 and installed in the choir in 1630.

The model of the Beatae Mariae Virginis Church

With regard to the octagonal shape of the columns of the Trinity Church, Juliette Roding has made reference to the Beatae Mariae Virginis Church in Wolfenbüttel (Figs. 9-10).[50] Here, the late Gothic hall is divided into three naves by six octagonal columns. The Wolfenbüttel church combined the functions of a parish church, a funeral church of the House of Brunswick-Wolfenbüttel and a major church of the Protestant episcopate of Halberstadt. It can justifiably be called one of the earliest and most prominent Protestant churches in Germany. It is, however, not unique. As Hermann Hipp established with his survey on church building in the Holy Roman Empire between c. 1570 and c. 1650, the vast majority of those built were late Gothic hall churches with simple rib vaulting, octagonal columns and large windows featuring a simplified form of tracery.[51] These

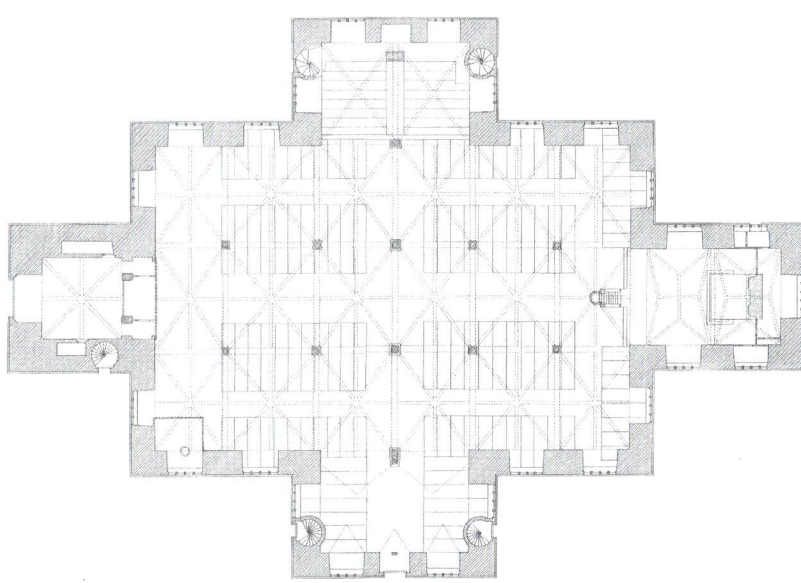

Fig. 7. Christiansstad, Holy Trinity Church, ground plan, 1889. After Hans J. Holm (ed.), *Studiereiser af Kunstakademiets Elever*, Copenhagen 1897.

WOLFENBÜTTEL AND COPENHAGEN 271

Fig. 8. Christiansstad, Holy Trinity Church, interior facing East (Photo Ole Akhøj).

late Gothic churches are frequently decorated with ornaments derived from the Italian Renaissance, images that were disseminated via pattern books.[52] On the other hand, it is obvious that the church in Wolfenbüttel was the modern church building that Christian IV knew best. Work on the church began in 1608, and in 1613 the choir was vaulted for the funeral of Duke Heinrich Julius. Apart from the spire of the tower, which was never erected, the church was completed in 1620, and it was Duchess Elisabeth who took charge of the completion of the building after Heinrich Julius's death. If we consider the similarities of both churches, their first common feature is their dimensions: the Beatae Mariae Virginis Church in Wolfenbüttel is approx. 70 m long and approx. 36.5 m wide, while the Trinity Church in Christiansstad is approximately 64.5 m long and approximately 44 m wide.

The ground plan reveals another principle that both churches have in common: both are conceived according to a strictly rational design. They are composed of sections – simple geometrical forms that are combined in a very straightforward way. Of course there are also differences: the tower of the Wolfenbüttel church is integrated into the ground plan and protrudes only slightly from the west wall, whereas the tower of the Trinity Church is attached to the west wall. The choir of the Wolfenbüttel church has a polygonal apse, whereas the choir of the Christiansstad church is a rectangle composed of two squares. Again, it must be noted that most churches of that time had a choir.[53] Both churches have portals adorned with

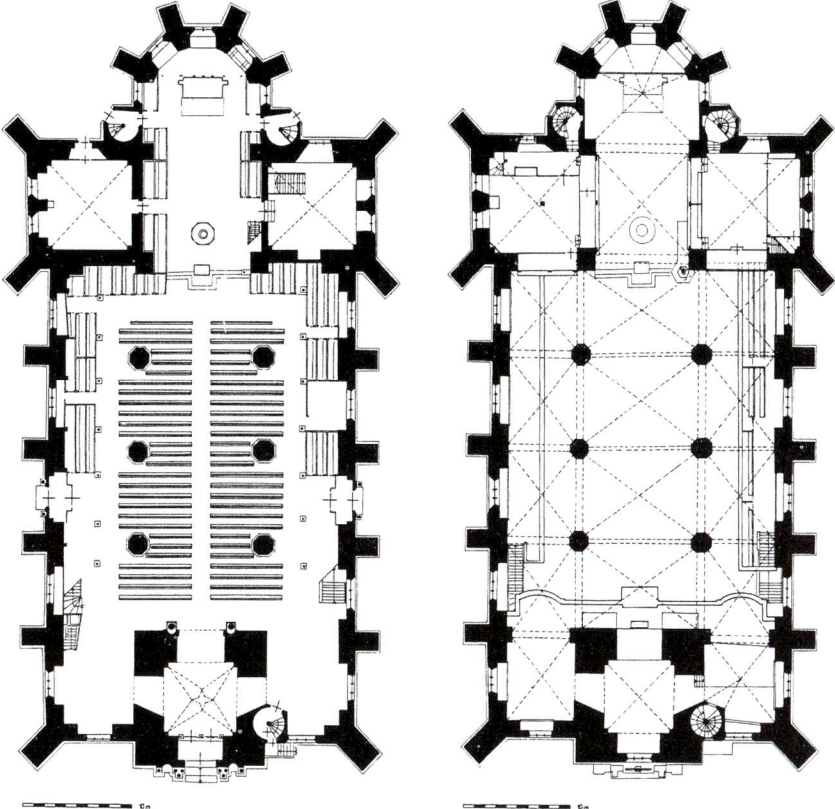

Fig. 9. Wolfenbüttel, Beatae Mariae Virginis Church, ground plan and vaulting. After Hans-Herbert Möller (ed.), *Die Hauptkirche Beatae Mariea Virginis in Wolfenbüttel*, Hameln 1987 (Forschungen der Denkmalpflege in Niedersachsen 4).

columns and strapwork ornamentation, as well as the coats of arms of their patrons. In Christiansstad, it is the monogram of Christian IV that is placed most prominently above the west entrance, but also at various other places inside and outside the church. In Wolfenbüttel, it is the coat of arms of the House of Brunswick and the life-size figures of Duke Heinrich Julius and Duke Friedrich Ulrich on the west portal that leave no doubt as to the patronage of the church. The dukes are literally standing next to Christ, who is represented on the top of the portal.[54] Both churches feature scrolled gables, which are crowned with sculptures. In Wolfenbüttel, the figurative programme comprises prophets, the four evangelists, the apostles, virtues, and female saints.[55] The Trinity Church in Christiansstad features personifications of virtues and evangelists, while Christ, St. Peter and St. Paul are depicted on the gable of the choir. Both churches contain large organs, and from the outset they also have benches for the citizens to sit on, which are arranged according to their rank in society. Both churches also have special seats on the balconies for the Duke and the King respectively. It can indeed be said that the place where the people were seated in the church corresponded to the place where they lived in the city, and that this was a typical feature of Protestant churches of the 17th and 18th centuries.[56]

Political Theory and Building Practice

With regard to the question of the interaction of political theory and architectural practice, it is important to look at the newly founded Academia Julia University in Helmstedt. It was here that political theory became part of the academic curriculum for the first time. Christian IV may have been well acquainted with the university since his younger brother Duke Ulrik of Holsatia (1578-1624) took up his studies in Helmstedt in October 1590.[57] During the early 17th century, the university attracted eminent political theorists, including Henning Arnisaeus (c. 1575-1636), who in 1620 became Christian IV's private physician.[58] Arnisaeus wrote a two-volume book on politics as an architectural science, which was published in

Fig. 10. Wolfenbüttel, Beatae Mariae Virginis Church, exterior facing South (Bildarchiv Foto Marburg).

1615. The book is based on the Aristotelian idea that politics is a kind of building activity, that it is in fact architecture.[59] This theory can easily be linked to the ideal city, and even more so to the Protestant ideal city of the early absolutist period, since it was equally rooted in Lutheran theology and in Jean Bodin's theory of sovereignty.[60] It was Friedrich Engelhard von Löhneyss (1552-1622) who criticised Arnisaeus for his rather scholastic method of political theory, while he himself put forward a more pragmatic approach in his treatise "Aulico Politica".[61] But if we examine the content of both theories, there are also clear similarities. Both were concerned with a theory of sovereignty and absolutist monarchy, and it was Löhneyss who staged triumphant entries for Christian IV, where the Danish king himself appeared as a sun king.[62] It is, therefore, perhaps no surprise to discover that another Helmstedt 'politician', Hermann Conring (1606-1681), was the private physician of Queen Christina of Sweden (1626-1689) and later became a counsellor of Louis XIV of France (1643-1715).[63]

It is important to note that for the Aristotelian philosophers at the Helmstedt University politics represented a kind of building activity. This can be directly linked to Christian IV's understanding of city planning as part of stately organisation. The city is a model of the state, and it is a Protestant state that is being erected, a social organism where every man has his place, and where the ruler is the representative of God on earth. Apart from the model character of the ideal plan of Heinrichstadt and of the church Beatae Mariae Virginis, it is the idea of architecture as political practice that informed Christian IV's building activities.

Notes

1. Juliette Roding, *Christiaan IV van Denemarken (1588-1648). Architectuur en stedebouw van een Lutherse vorst*, Alkmaar 1991, 131-132.

2. On the dynastic links between the courts of Copenhagen, Dresden and Wolfenbüttel see Roding 1991, 19; Mara R. Wade, *Triumphus Nuptialis Danicus. German Court Culture and Denmark. The Great Wedding 1634*, Wiesbaden 1996, 35-47; Mara R. Wade, "The Queen's Courts: Anna of Denmark and her Royal Sisters – Cultural Agency at Four Northern European Courts in the Sixteenth and Seventeenth Centuries", in: Clare McManus (ed.), *Women and Culture at the Courts of the Stuart Queens*, Basingstoke & New York 2003, 49-80.

3. Johannes Caselius, *Domino Henrico Iulio Guelpho et Dominae Dorotheae Saxonicae Sponsis illustrissimis*, Rostock 1585. Two pageants were performed during the wedding celebrations: a triumph of Henry the Lion and a triumph of Diana, in which Heinrich Julius himself featured as the goddess of hunting (Niedersächsisches Landesarchiv-Staatsarchiv Wolfenbüttel 1 Alt 23 Nr. 147).

4. Niedersächsisches Landesarchiv-Staatsarchiv Wolfenbüttel 1 Alt 23 Nr. 157-162. See Barton W. Browning, "Heinrich Julius von Braunschweig's 1590 Welcoming Celebration for Princess Elisabeth of Denmark", in: Mara R. Wade (ed.), *Pomp, Power, and Politics: Essays on German and Scandinavian Court Culture and their Contexts* (Daphnis. Zeitschrift für Mittlere Deutsche Literatur und Kultur der Frühen Neuzeit (1400-1750) 32 (2003)), New York & Amsterdam 2003, 73-82, esp. 75-76.

5. See the entries by C. O. Bøggild-Andersen on "Anna" and on "Elisabeth" in: *Dansk Biografisk Lexikon*³, I, Copenhagen 1979, 252-253 and VI, Copenhagen 1980, 155-156. Wade 2003, 55-58.

6. Johannes Caselius, *Nuptijs Herois Henricii Iulii Guelfii et Heroinae Elisabethae Cimbricae Trikopeion*, Helmstedt 1590. For a short account of the wedding see Hilda Lietzmann, *Herzog Heinrich Julius zu Braunschweig und Lüneburg (1564-1613). Persönlichkeit und Wirken für Kaiser und Reich*, Langenhagen 1993 (Quellen und Forschungen zur Braunschweigischen Geschichte 30), 12; Karl Koppmann, "Zur Einholung der Prinzessin Elisabeth von Dänemark durch ihren Gemahl Herzog Heinrich Julius i. J. 1590. Auszüge aus den Rostocker Ratsprotokollen", *Jahrbuch des Geschichtsvereins für das Herzogtum Braunschweig* 3 (1904), 58-68.

7. Browning 2003, 78-80.

8. Elias Holwein, Portraits of Duke Heinrich Julius and Duchess Elisabeth, woodcuts, 52.5 x 34.0 and 52.6 x 31.2 cm, 1603, Herzog Anton-Ulrich-Museum Braunschweig, inv. E. Holwein AB 2.8003 and AB 2.8004. See Jochen Luckhardt (ed.), *Hofkunst der Spätrenaissance: Braunschweig-Wolfenbüttel und das kaiserliche Prag um 1600*, Brunswick 1998, 48-51.

9. Lietzmann 1993, 65-66.

10. *Verzeichnus der Reise / welche die Kön. May. zu Dennemarken Norwegen Anno 1595. zu etlichen ihren Anverwandten Chur vnd Fürsten in Teutschland angestellet*, Copenhagen 1595, Aii^B-Aiiii^B; Svend Ellehøj, *Christian IVs Verden*, Copenhagen 1988, 438; Steffen Heiberg, *Christian 4. Monarken, Mennesket og Myten*, Copenhagen 1988, 47-48; Jill Bepler, "Practical Perspectives on the Court and Role of Princes. Georg Engelhard von Loehneyss' *Aulico Politica* 1622-24 and Christian IV of Denmark's *Königlicher Wecker* 1620", in: Wade (ed.) 2003, 137-163, esp. 139-140; Wade 1996, 40; Wade 2003, 174.

11. Gustav Hassebrauk, "Der Sturm auf Braunschweig 16.-17. October 1605", *Braunschweigisches Magazin* 7 (1901), 81-83, 93-96, 179-182.

12. On the conflict between the city of Brunswick and the dukes of Brunswick-Wolfenbüttel see Gustav Hassebrauk, "Herzog Heinrich und die Stadt Braunschweig 1514-1568", *Jahrbuch des Geschichtsvereins für das Herzogtum Braunschweig* 5 (1906), 1-61; Gustav Hassebrauk, "Herzog Julius und die Stadt Braunschweig 1568-1589", *Jahrbuch des Geschichtsvereins für das Herzogtum Braunschweig* 6 (1907), 1-78; Gustav Hassebrauk, "Herzog Heinrich Julius und die Stadt Braunschweig 1589-1613", *Jahrbuch des Geschichtsvereins für das Herzogtum Braunschweig* 9 (1910), 62-108.

13. Lietzmann 1993, 38. For a contemporary description of the conflict from the Duke's point of view see: [Heinrich Meibom], *Außführlicher Wahrhaffter Historischer Bericht/ die Fürstliche Land= und Erbstadt Braunschweig/ Auch den Hertzogen zu Braunschweig und Lüneburg Wolfenbüttelschen Theils darüber habende Landesfürstliche Hoch= Obrig= und Gerechtigkeit/ auch ihre der Stadt unmittelbare angeborne schüldige Subjection und Unterthenigkeit etc. betreffend*, I-III, Helmstedt 1607-1609, so-called "Braunschweigische Historische Händel".

14. For a description of the funeral with a woodcut illustration see Georg Engelhard von Löhneyss, *Aulico Politica*, Remlingen 1622.

15. On Friedrich Ulrich see Friedrich Wagnitz, "Herzog Friedrich Ulrich, Ein glückloser Fürst in schwerer Zeit", *Jahrbuch der Gesellschaft für niedersächsische Kirchengeschichte* 87 (1989), 51-70; Friedrich Wagnitz, "Ein Wolfenbütteler Fürstenschicksal im Dreißigjährigen Krieg. Würdigung von Herzog Friedrich Ulrich anläßlich des 400. Geburtstages", *Braunschweigische Heimat* 77 (1991), 5-34.

16 Marten Jan Bok, "Christian von Braunschweig in den Niederlanden", in: Jochen Luckhardt & Nils Büttner (eds.), *Der Krieg als Person. Herzog Christian d. J. von Braunschweig-Lüneburg im Bildnis von Paulus Moreelse*, Brunswick 2000, 14-39, esp.19.

17 Paul Zimmerman, "Anton von der Streithorst", in: *Allgemeine Deutsche Biographie*, 36, Leipzig 1893, 569-572; Bepler 2003, 145.

18 For a reprint see Bepler 2003, 149-163.

19 Erling Ladewig Petersen, "Defence, War, and Finance: Christian IV and the Council of the Realm 1596-1629", *Scandinavian Journal of History* 7 (1982), 280-297, esp. 298; Wade 1996, 204.

20 On Lower Saxony in the Thirty Years' War and Christian IV's engagement see Christine van den Heuvel & Manfred von Boetticher (eds.), *Geschichte Niedersachsens. 3,1. Politik, Wirtschaft und Gesellschaft von der Reformation bis zum Beginn des 19. Jahrhunderts*, Hannover 1998 (Veröffentlichungen der Historischen Kommission für Niedersachsen und Bremen 34), 121-130. For the Danish engagement in Lower Saxony see Julius Otto Opel, *Der niedersächsisch-dänische Krieg*, I-III, Halle 1872-1894; Jørgen Hein, "Der 'Dänische Krieg' und die weitere Rolle Dänemarks", in: Klaus Bußmann & Heinz Schilling (eds.): *1648. Krieg und Frieden in Europa. I. Politik, Religion, Recht und Gesellschaft, Europaratsausstellung 350 Jahre Westfälischer Friede Münster und Osnabrück 1998/99*, Munich 1998, 103-110; Erling Ladewig Petersen, "Danish Intermezzo", in: Geoffrey Parker (ed.), *The Thirty Years War*, London 1987, 71-81; Heiberg 1988, 266-293; Ellehøj 1988, 104-108.

21 On Christian IV's city foundations in general see Vilhelm Lorenzen (ed.), *Christian IVs Byanlæg og andre Bybygningsarbejder*, Copenhagen 1937; Gerhard Eimer, *Die Stadtplanung im schwedischen Ostseereich 1600-1715*, Stockholm 1961, 153-160; Lars Bisgaard, "Cities and fortresses", in: Steffen Heiberg (ed.), *Christian IV and Europe: the 19th Art Exhibition of the Council of Europe, Denmark 1988*, Herning 1988, 483-489; Roding 1991.

22 Bisgaard 1988, 485; Roding 1991, 33-36.

23 Bisgaard 1988, 484-485; Roding 1991, 83.

24 On Christiansstad see Folke Holmér, "Christianstad", in Lorenzen (ed.) 1937, 160-177; Thorsten Andersson, "De byggde staden", in: Axel Kroon, Nils Gustaf Hagander & Anders B. Andersson (eds.), *Staden ved Helgeå. En bok i anledning af Kristianstads 350-årsjubileum*, Kristianstad 1964, 95-244; Bisgaard 1988, 485; Roding 1991, 83-99.

25 Juliette Roding, "Myten om den hollandske renæssance. Christian IV's byanlæg i Skandinavien", *B. Arkitekturtidsskrift* 47/48 (1990/91), 25-31, esp. 28; Roding 1991, 83.

26 Gottfried Heinrich Handelmann, "Gerhard Rantzau", in: *Allgemeine Deutsche Biographie*, 27, Leipzig 1888, 287; Andersson 1964, 107; Roding 1991, 83.

27 Roding 1991, 83-84; Roding 1990/91, 28-29.

28 See "Kong Christian IVdes Skrivecalendee for Aarene 1614 og 16", in: P. F. Suhm (ed.), *Nye Samlinger til den danske Historie* 2, II (1793), 97; Holmér 1937, 160.

29 Roding 1990/91, 29.

30 Roding 1991, 85-86.

31 Map of Christiansstad, c. 1629, paper and pen, c. 41,0 x 52,5 cm, Det Kongelige Bibliotek (The Royal Library, Copenhagen), Collection of Maps, 1113, 111, 213-0-1620/1. Eduard Robert Marie Taverne, *In 't land van belofte: in de nieue stadt. Ideaal en werkelijkheid van de stadsuitleg in de Republiek 1580-1680*, Maarssen 1978, 84; Holmér 1937, 163; Andersson 1964, 141-143; Heiberg (ed.) 1988, 498-499; Roding 1990/91, 30; Roding 1991, 85.

32 Holmér 1937, 163; Eimer 1961, 154; Roding 1990/91, 29; Roding 1991, 88.

33 Taverne 1978, 82-85; Roding 1990/91, 29-30; Roding 1991, 87-88.

34 See for instance Johan Sems, Project of Christianshavn, c. 1636, paper and pen, c. 30,5 x 40,5 cm, The Royal Library, Copenhagen, Collection of Maps, A 1636, 57513. Vilhelm Lorenzen, *Haandtegnede Kort over København 1600-1660*, Copenhagen 1930, VI, 2; Heiberg (ed.) 1988, 502; Roding 1991, 117-120.

35 Taverne 1978, 84-85.

36 Simon Stevin wrote this book c. 1600 in Leiden, but it was only published by his son in 1649 as part of his political writings. See Simon Stevin, "Vande oirdeningh der steden. Byvough: vande oirdeningh der deelen eens huys met 't gheene daer ancleeft", in: Hendrick Stevin (ed.), *Materiae politicae: burgherlicke stoffen*, Leiden 1649. A copy of the book is preserved in The Royal Library in Copenhagen, Sfv. I 266,4°. On Simon Stevin see Charles van den Heuvel, *De 'huysbou': a reconstruction of an unfinished treatise on architecture, town planning and civil engineering by Simon Stevin*, Amsterdam 2005, esp. 47-49, 252-257 on the ideal city plan.

37 On the ideal city plan of Wolfenbüttel see Barbara Uppenkamp, *Das Pentagon von Wolfenbüttel. Der Ausbau der welfischen Residenz 1568-1626 zwischen Ideal und Wirklichkeit*, Hannover 2005 (Veröffentlichungen der Historischen Kommission für Niedersachsen und Bremen 229).

38 Musées de Strasbourg, Cabinet des Estampes, Daniel Specklin *Architectura von Festungen* (ms. 1583, fol.

38 ... 70r). A second copy of the ideal plan of Wolfenbüttel by Specklin is in the private collection of Rodolphe Peters. See Albert Fischer, *Daniel Specklin 1536-1589. Festungsbaumeister, Ingenieur und Kartograph*, Stuttgart 1996, 97; Uppenkamp 2005, 163-168.

39 Klaus-Walther Ohnesorge, *Wolfenbüttel. Geographie einer ehemaligen Residenzstadt*, Brunswick 1974 (Braunschweiger Geographische Studien 5); Uppenkamp 2005, 111-119, 239-241.

40 On the Trinitatis church see Matheus Lundborg, *Heliga Trefaldighetskyrkan i Kristianstad. Beskrivning och Historia*, Kristianstad 1928; Holmér 1937, 173-174; Mette Smed, "The Architecture of Christian IV", in: Heiberg (ed.) 1988, 463-483, esp. 481-482; Roding 1991, 92-98.

41 Taverne 1978, 85; Holmér 1937, 174.

42 Albrecht Dürer, *Etliche underricht zu befestigung der Stett, Schloß und flecken*, Nuremberg 1527; Roding 1991, 91-92.

43 On the Saxon mining cities see Klaus Kratzsch, *Bergstädte des Erzgebirges. Städtebau und Kunst zur Zeit der Reformation*, Munich & Zurich 1972 (Münchner Kunsthistorische Abhandlungen IV); Heinrich Douffet, "Erzgebirgische Bergstädte. Historische und städtebauliche Kennzeichnung", in: Dieter Dolgner & Irene Roch (eds.), *Stadtbaukunst im Mittelalter. Festschrift für Hans-Joachim Mrusek*, Berlin 1990, 182-186; Eva-Maria Seng, *Stadt – Idee und Planung. Neue Ansätze im Städtebau des 16. und 17. Jahrhunderts*, Munich 2003, 185-192.

44 Daniel Specklin, *Architectura Von Vestungen*, Strasbourg 1589. On Glückstadt see Evi Jung-Köhler, "'Ungebautes Imperium – Dänemarks und Schwedens Traum vom Ostseereich'", in Michael Maass (ed.), *"Klar und lichtvoll wie eine Regel". Planstädte der Neuzeit vom 16. bis zum 18. Jahrhundert*, Karlsruhe 1990, 169-179, esp. 176-177; Lorenzen 1937, 329-353; Roding 1991, 133-140.

45 See Uppenkamp 2005, 149-150, 163-168.

46 Holmér 1937, 173-174; Roding 1991, 94-96; on the Steenwinckels, see Hugo Johannsen, "Hans II van Steenwinckel" and "Lorenz van Steenwinckel", in: *Weilbachs Kunstnerleksikon*[4], 8, Copenhagen 1998, 43-44, 45-46; on David Nyborg, see Ebbe Hædersdal, "David Nyborg", in: *Weilbachs Kunstnerleksikon*[4], 6, Copenhagen 1997, 197.

47 Holmér 1937, 174-175.

48 Roding 1991, 94-95.

49 This supposition goes back to Vermeulen and is taken up by Taverne. See F. A. J. Vermeulen, *Handboek tot de geschiedenis der Nederlandsche bouwkunst*, I-III, 's-Gravenhage 1928-1941, esp. II, 494-496; Taverne 1978, 85.

50 On the church Beatae Mariae Virginis see Hans-Herbert Möller (ed.), *Die Hauptkirche Beatae Mariae Virginis in Wolfenbüttel*, Hameln 1987 (Forschungen der Denkmalpflege in Niedersachsen 4); Harmen Thies, "Die Wolfenbütteler Hauptkirche Beatae Mariae Virginis von Paul Francke", in: Georg Ulrich Großmann, *Renaissance in Nord-Mitteleuropa*, I, Munich & Berlin 1990 (Schriften des Weserrenaissance-Museums Schloß Brake 4), 171-188; Harmen Thies, "Die Baugeschichte der Hauptkirche Beatae Mariae Virginis", in: Rainer Bürgel, Helmut A. Müller & Rainer Volp (eds.), *Kirche im Abseits? Zum Verhältnis von Religion und Kultur*, Stuttgart 1991, 203-221; Hermann Hipp, "Die Hauptkirche Beatae Mariae Virginis in Wolfenbüttel und der protestantische Kirchenbau um 1600", in: Bürgel, Müller & Volp (eds.) 1991, 181-202; Uppenkamp 2005, 81-88.

51 Hermann Hipp, *Studien zur "Nachgotik" des 16. und 17. Jahrhunderts in Deutschland, Böhmen, Österreich und der Schweiz*, I-III. Diss. phil., Tübingen 1979.

52 As the most popular examples of such pattern books one may look at Hans Vredeman de Vries "Dorica-Ionica" and "Corinthia-Composita", both of which were published in Antwerp by Hieronymus Cock in 1565. See Peter Fuhring & Ger Luijten (eds.), *Hollstein's Dutch & Flemish Etchings, Engravings and Woodcuts 1450-1700*, XLVII-XLVIII, *Hans Vredeman de Vries*, Rotterdam 1997, esp. XLVII, 183-222; Heiner Borggrefe et al. (eds.), *Hans Vredeman de Vries und die Renaissance im Norden*, Munich 2002, 192-194.

53 Hermann Hipp, "Die Bückeburger "structura". Aspekte der Nachgotik im Zusammenhang mit der deutschen Renaissance", in: Großmann (ed.) 1990, 159-170, esp. 163.

54 The coat of arms was replaced by a shield with the inscription "Soli Deo Gloria" in 1657. The figures of the dukes still exist. Uppenkamp 2005, 83-85.

55 On the iconographic programme see Eberhard Grunsky, "Die ev. Hauptkirche Beatae Mariae Virginis in Wolfenbüttel. Bemerkungen zum ikonographischen Programm", *Niederdeutsche Beiträge zur Kunstgeschichte* 12 (1973), 204-228.

56 On this topic see Reinhold Wex, *Ordnung und Unfriede. Raumprobleme des protestantischen Kirchenbaus im 17. und 18. Jahrhundert in Deutschland*, Marburg 1984; Hipp 1991, 197-199.

57 Johann Heinrich Schlegel, *Geschichte der Könige von Dänemark aus dem oldenburgischen Stamme. 2. Geschichte Christians des Vierten von 1588 bis 1629*, Copenhagen 1777, 4-5; Paul Zimmermann, *Album Academiae Helmstediensis. I. Studenten, Professoren etc. der Universität Helmstedt von 1574 bis 1636*, Hannover 1926 (Veröffentlichungen der Historischen Kom-

58 mission für Hannover 9), 85, no. 163; Bepler 2003, 139.

58 Horst Dreitzel, *Protestantischer Aristotelismus und absoluter Staat. Die "Politica" des Henning Arnisäus,* Wiesbaden 1970 (Veröffentlichungen des Instituts für europäische Geschichte Mainz 55, Abteilung für Universalgeschichte); Barbara Uppenkamp, "Politische Macht – Architektonische Imagination?", in: Christian Hochmuth & Susanne Rau (eds.), *Machträume der frühneuzeitlichen Stadt*, Konstanz 2006, 59-74, esp. 65-67; Uppenkamp 2005, 227-230; Bepler 2003, 143.

59 Henning Arnisaeus, *De republica seu relectionis politicae libri duo*, Frankfurt 1615.

60 Jean Bodin, *Six livres de la République*, Paris 1572.

61 Georg Engelhard von Löhneyss, *Aulico Politica*, Remlingen 1624. The book was published by the sons of Löhneyss two years after their father's death.

62 See Mara R. Wade, "Publication, Pageantry, Patronage: Georg Engelhard von Loehneyss' *Della Cavalleria* (1609; 1624) and His Hamburg Tournament Pageant for King Christian IV of Denmark (1603)", in Wade (ed.) 2003, 165-197.

63 Uppenkamp 2006, 65-66.

ART AND MUSIC ON DEMAND
– A PORTRAIT OF THE DANISH DIPLOMAT JONAS CHARISIUS AND HIS MISSION TO THE DUTCH REPUBLIC

Badeloch Vera Noldus

Introduction

At first glance, Denmark and the Dutch Republic made an odd couple in early modern Europe: the esteemed kingdom and the young rebel. Denmark was then the largest country in Northern Europe and could boast a century-old lineage while the small Republic had announced her independency only in 1579 and had to await full international recognition until 1648. Still, around 1600, the two were engaged in intense relations that were valuable for both partners – political, diplomatic, economic, and not least, cultural. The Netherlands were a cultural marketplace for Denmark, used by an intricate network of patrons, middlemen, artists, and suppliers in general, and by Danish diplomat Jonas Charisius in particular.

In recent years we have witnessed an increasing interest in the dissemination of Netherlandish art and architecture in Northern Europe, as reflected in several publications.[1] Yet, as an independent subject of study, the topic is still young and significant players like Jonas Charisius (1571-1619) have been left mostly unattended. Except short mentions in biographical lexica, no research on Charisius alone has been conducted, leaving him in the shadow of other learned diplomats like Jakob Ulfeldt, with whom Charisius attended the peace negotiations in The Hague 1607-1608. This essay's intention is to show how the commoner Charisius, climbing his way up in the hierarchy of the Danish Chancellery, became both an influential diplomat and a middleman of importance in Danish cultural affairs. Since his significance as a royal 'taste maker' has been overlooked hitherto, this aspect is of major interest here. For this purpose, primary sources not published before are used, such as the highly-detailed travel journal from Charisius's mission to the Dutch Republic in 1607-1608. Also, a new light is cast on other archivals, including the account of paintings and musical instruments Charisius acquired in the Republic, as I will explore the mechanisms behind Denmark's interest in the Dutch cultural market. An interest that is apparent in Charisius's strong involvement in the development of Frederiksborg Castle as King Christian IV's preferred stage. Charisius's own epitaph in Roskilde Cathedral (Fig. 1), an important piece of art on itself, is the subject of a new attribution, making the epitaph a key to understanding his role at Frederiksborg. All in all, Jonas Charisius is revealed as a man occupying a key position in the cultural traffic between the Netherlands and Denmark, who knew how to cross-fertilize networks from both worlds and let them profit from one another.[2]

Fig.1. Aris Claeszn (attr.), epitaph of Jonas Charisius, c. 1620. Roskilde Cathedral (Photo Henrik Wichmann).

The mother of all trades

The *gold* from the Dutch Golden Age stemmed largely from the Baltic area and consisted of little appealing products such as grain, salt, timber and rope. Each year, hundreds of vessels sailed between Amsterdam and trading cities around the Baltic Sea, earning great sums of money. With good reason, Dutch statesman Johan van Oldenbarnevelt (1547-1619) even labelled the Baltic grain trade 'the mother of all trades' as it was the Dutch Republic's largest source of income.[3] Although the East Indian Company's trade on Asian destinations occupies a more prominent place in the collective memory, the Baltic trade yielded a greater surplus. In the wake of these strong economic ties, relations in the arts followed.

Through the sixteenth century, Danish kings had still relied heavily on German contacts but from around 1600 commissioners, royal and noble, purchased and ordered their luxury goods to a greater extent in the Netherlands, first at the Antwerp art market, then in Amsterdam, which came to play an important role in visualising their status and position.[4] Danish-Dutch cultural relations reached their zenith in the first quarter of the seventeenth century when the Dutch Republic held Europe's largest staple market, where a wide variety of commodities was available, and also housed a flourishing art market. These relations resulted in a presence of Netherlandish culture in Northern Europe comparable to that of Anglo-Saxon culture in our times, a presence in a way even more prominent due to the great number of Flemish and Dutch artists, draughtsmen et cetera living and working in Denmark in the era c.1570-1630. Amongst them we find sculptors Johan Gregor van der Schardt and Gert van Egen, draughtsmen Willem van den Blocke, Hans Floris, Anthonis van Opbergen, Hans van Paeschen, and the Steenwinckel family, painters Hans Knieper and Pieter Isaacsz., and engravers Albert Haelwegh and Simon de Passe.

Jonas Charisius in the Dutch Republic 1607-1608

Within the framework of these cultural relations, the diplomat Jonas Charisius came to play a significant role. As a commoner, Charisius was no exception in the state's office. At the lower administrative levels, commoners dominated. Yet, how he developed into King Christian IV's chief advisor in economic and mercantile affairs, of great influence on the king's economical initiatives, was extraordinary though, and underlines his capacities. Born in Nykøbing at the Danish island Falster as the son of a rural dean, Charisius was sent to the University of Padua at the age of 18. After six years in Padua, followed by studies in Heidelberg, Charisius returned to Denmark with a doctorate in medicine, which he supplemented with a doctorate in law from Copenhagen University in 1603. In the meantime, his international experience and versatile capacities had gained him a position as secretary in the German Chancellery in 1598. From then on, he climbed the career ladder in the state's office and participated in numerous embassies, bringing him to England, Spain, Germany and the Dutch Republic.[5] Between 1606 and 1619, Charisius visited the Republic four times on diplomatic and trade missions. The mission of 1607, which lasted almost a year, belonged to his life's major assignments. As the representative of a major protestant ally, Charisius was, together with the much-respected member of the Council of the Realm Jacob Ulfeldt (1567-1630), dispatched to partake in the peace negotiations between the Republic and Spain, which had been in conflict since 1568. Shortly upon their arrival, the Dutch engraver Hendrick Hondius I (1573-c.1649), who regularly worked for Stadholder Maurits, portrayed the entire delegation, all of them *cum privilegio*. Due to this series of engravings *Portraits of the pacificators of the Netherlands* (1608), we know that besides Charisius (Fig. 2) and Ulfeldt, the 45 pacificators included Spanish representatives Ambrogio Spinola and Jean de Mancicidor, Dutch statesmen like Maurits van Nassau, Frederik Hendrik van Nassau, and Johan van Oldenbarnevelt, the French diplomat Pierre Jeannin, and the English diplomats Robert Spencer and Ralph Winwood.[6] The negotiations did not lead to peace but eventually to the Twelve Year Truce, lasting from 1609 to 1621 when the war was continued.[7] Charisius had died by then; Ulfeldt however – promoted to Chancellor of the Realm in 1609 – was present again in 1621.

Of Jonas Charisius's stay in the Dutch Republic a journal exists, not previously published, written by the embassy's secretary Keld Krabbe (1583-1612) who kept secure account of the envoys' expenses.[8] Accounts, such as a journal like this or diaries, notebooks, or maybe an *album amicorum*, are indispensable sources to early

Fig. 2. Hendrick Hondius the Elder, Jonas Charisius, 1608. Hillerød, The Museum of National History, Frederiksborg Castle (Photo Frederiksborg).

modern travelling. Although often conventional in their selection of sites and routes, journals are nevertheless valuable because they show the relevant *must-sees* of the time and give an insight into the traveller's daily life.[9] In Krabbe's account we read that the party, consisting of Charisius, Ulfeldt, Krabbe, and young nobleman Peder Hundermarck, arrived in Amsterdam by boat on 19 November 1607. Upon a welcome by mayor and city council with performances by musicians, they were shown the city and visited the East Indian House and a hospital. The next day, the envoys continued to Haarlem by track boat. Here too, the mayor treated them to a recital. From Haarlem they continued to The Hague, their final destination, by carriage, lent to them by the Haarlem council. The servants had left a day earlier with the luggage in order to prepare the envoys' arrival at *De Eenhoorn* where the company lodged during the entire stay.[10] The next day early in the morning, trumpeters, drummers and horn players from Dutch, Scottish, English and French regiments came to salute them – "as is customary" as Krabbe noted. Then 6 December, the delegates made their official entrée at the States General, to offer their Letters of Credence and instructions, where they were received by the Land's Advocate Johan van Oldenbarnevelt, Abel Coenders van Helpen, States General deputy of the province of Groningen, Tinco Oenema, Frisian deputy, and not least Stadholder Maurits van Nassau and his cousin Willem Lodewijk van Nassau, married to Maurits's sister Anna.[11] Jonas Charisius had met the stadholder before when Maurits had been present at King Christian IV's coronation in 1596. Besides, Charisius knew of Maurits's endeavours as a renewing military strategist, about which he could have read in *Mes chroniques toutes illuminées, avec les chartes inferees de toutes les victoires de Monseigneur le Prince Maurice*, sent to him by the author Jean Francois le Petit, notary in service of the States General, in 1603.[12] Soon the envoys were invited to private parties in The Hague's inner circle, such as at the residence of Christiaan Huygens, the stadholder's secretary, where they were entertained with the musical performances of the young Maurits and Constantijn Huygens.[13] In a letter to his father from May 1610, the young Constantijn Huygens referred to the event.[14] Quite an experience was the day they were invited to Scheveningen at the seaside with the stadholder's carriage to see a large sailing wagon ["Wind Wogenn"], invented by Maurits's engineer Simon Stevin. The vehicle, equipped with a sail and driven by the wind, could carry 28 persons. It took the guests from Scheveningen to Petten (a distance of app. 80 km) in well over two hours. The wagon's fame had reached Denmark already years earlier when Duke Ulrik, King Christian's brother, had also tried a ride during a visit to the Republic in 1602. Obviously, Stevin's invention had made quite an impression and was later immortalized on a linen damask cloth (Fig. 5), designed by Dutchman Passchier Lammertijn, who worked for Christian IV in the 1620s.[15] Besides their Dutch acquaintances, Charisius and Ulfeldt were also in contact with other Danes residing in the Republic, including Otto Brahe, who served in Maurits's army, Anders Bille and Christen Friis. The young noblemen Bille and Friis had travelled with Ulfeldt and Charisius to the Republic, not to participate in the negotiations but as an educational journey, and spent their time on their own.[16]

In January, the negotiations commenced, as can be understood from Krabbe's account who noted the purchase of large quantities of writing paper for Charisius and the receiving and sending of letters, always from Amsterdam that was to remain the Republic's postal hub throughout the century. But there was still, and would be throughout the entire stay, time for leisure as well. Especially Jakob Ulfeldt spent much time exploring the Province of Holland, studying cities, industries, inventions relevant to Denmark. In a carriage, put at his disposal by Maurits, he went to see – sometimes being kept company by Charisius – seaside villages Loosduinen, Katwijk and Ter Heide, the port cities Dordrecht and Rotterdam, and various gardens and estates, including Honselaarsdijk (Fig. 6), owned by Maurits until 1609. In Delft, he visited the collection of Antwerp-born Abraham Gorlaeus, where he saw "antiquities and Indian things". And only days before the embassy returned to Denmark, on 23 July 1608, he travelled to Enkhuizen to visit the even more illustrious museum of Berent Broecke, or Bernardus Paludan, who exhibited curiosities from all over the world. As Krabbe's journal testifies, land reclamation projects, water works and mills were also of great interest to the Danes. In June 1608, they went to Alkmaar, Petten, Schagen and Avenhoorn, all located north of Amsterdam, in an area with several reclamation projects. A man who showed them "a dam at a water called Beemster" received 47 *stuivers* from them. Beemster was a large lake, which was being reclaimed just around that time.[17]

Besides supporting the Republic in their claim for independence and viewing Dutch places of interest, the Danish representatives were also to find craftsmen and merchants interested in a new career in Denmark, "with most discretion, and in great secrecy" as it said in their instruction.[18] Yet, nothing points in the direction of success in this perspective; neither in Krabbe's journal nor in Charisius's papers. In 1621, the Dutch agent Theodoor Rodenburg had more success; he sent Christian IV a proposal, including the names of merchants, brewers, founders, casters, tapestry makers, weavers and painters who were all ready to move to Denmark. Rodenburg's harvest of potential Danish immigrants was due to "the aggravating situation in this country", as he wrote: in 1621, the Republic was at war again whilst in 1608, the future had looked bright and nobody had been interested in leaving.[19] Apparently, in this perspective Ulfeldt and Charisius did not make great achievements. But while Ulfeldt went out exploring, Charisius had received one more assignment. He was supposed to act as a middleman and purchase musical instruments and paintings for the royal collection on the king's behalf. An order he executed most effectively.

Buying art

Charisius set to work at full tilt, and the results are clear: upon the embassy's return he was able to hand in an overview of 141 paintings and seven keyboard instruments he had bought. The complete account, including names of painters, subject descriptions, and prices, written in Charisius' own hand, was published by Eiler Nyström in 1909.[20] Among the paintings, we find works of masters like Gilles van Coninxcloo, Aert Pietersz, Pieter Isaacsz., Otto van Veen, Frans Francken, Frans Pietersz de Grebber, and Frans Badens. Nyström did not think much of Charisius' selection: "Considering the pure artistic value, they [the paintings] will not have been particularly appealing, since they all belonged to that unfortunate transferral era in Dutch painting before the blossoming in the seventeenth century."[21] An opinion he shared with his contemporary, art historian Francis Beckett, who wrote of Christian IV's art acquisitions: "Besides, it was an unfortunate period in which to attempt to establish a collection of contemporary painting. Italy's sun had gone down, and the art of the Netherlands had not yet risen to meet the day".[22] Today, we hold quite a different view on these art works and have a greater understanding of early Dutch painting, which arose with a number of publications in the late 1980s and 90s.[23] Therefore, we know that the works Charisius shipped to Denmark belonged to the top of the market; well-paid then and much-appreciated today. Charisius bought the majority of the paintings in Amsterdam, which was no coincidence.[24] In the 1610s, the city developed into the commercial heart and the artistic centre of the Netherlands, once described as *"le Marché du Monde, & la Boutique des Raretez de tout l'Univers"*.[25] The availability of luxury products from the Americas and Asia, brought in for the first time after the establishment of the Dutch East India Company in 1602, contributed to this development. A virtuous spiral of supply and demand saw the output of Dutch artists rise to an unparalleled level – more than five million paintings in all genres in the seventeenth century.[26] Immigrants from the Southern Netherlands were responsible for the introduction of new genres, such as the still life and landscapes, while portrait and history painting, typical Northern Netherlandish genres, were refined. Although Jonas Charisius resided in The Hague, he ordered primarily in Amsterdam, whether it was furniture, fabrics, books, paper, and wine, or paintings.[27] Amsterdam was, however, never a metropolis like London was to become later that century; it was,

rather, part of a large city network. Even though Amsterdam stood out in the quantity and the range of commodities on offer, other cities in this network, Utrecht, Gouda, Leiden, Haarlem and Delft, housing the famous tapestry workshops of François Spiering and Karel van Mander, were artistic centres in their own right. Besides the variety of products available here, the Danes also had other reasons for buying their goods in the Republic: the countries were close, sharing the protestant faith and standing on the same side in the Thirty Years War, it was convenient as a trade network already existed, and finally, there were personal ties; Christian IV's father, Frederik II, was Stadholder Frederik Hendrik's godfather.

Art commodities were sold at local workshops, auctions, and markets. The Delft annual art market was exceptional in so far that here artists and dealers from outside the city could sell their work, not bothered by the guild regulations.[28] In Krabbe's journal, we read that Jonas Charisius "went to Delft to see some paintwork" on 20 June.[29] In Charisius's account, we can see he bought, among many other pieces, "History of Herodes, large, on canvas" and "Judith and Holofernes" by Pieter Isaacsz., "Adonis and Venus" and "David and Goliath" by Frans Badens, "A monk with a nun" by Cornelis Cornelisz van Haarlem, "Mercury, naked, on canvas" by Cornelis van der Voort, and a "Lucretia" by Frans de Grebber. Although mythological scenes and motives from the Old Testament dominated, he also acquired a few landscapes and genre pieces. In total, he spent 1150 *dalers* at the Delft fair, including packaging and shipment to The Hague. Paintwork was also purchased in Antwerp and for a great deal in Amsterdam, where Pieter Isaacsz. (1568-1625) was among the painters whose workshop Charisius

Fig. 3. Cornelis van Haarlem, Fall of the Titans, 1588-1590. Copenhagen, The National Gallery of Denmark (Photo National Gallery). Christian IV purchased the painting in 1621 from the Dutch art trader Franz Bastiaensz.

paid a visit. Isaacsz., who appears several times in his papers, seems to have introduced the Danish diplomat to the Dutch art market. As a painter and an art dealer, he knew the art world inside out, and Isaacsz. even spoke Danish since he was born and raised in Denmark, making him the perfect 'guide'. Most of the painters Charisius acquired paintings from were members of Isaacsz' personal network; Gilles van Conincxloo and Frans Badens for example lived in the same quarter in Amsterdam as Isaacsz.'s did and had even used the same workshop.[30]

... and music

When Jonas Charisius went out for musical instruments in July, again Isaacsz.'s wide network proved useful. The painter himself was a connoisseur, advising the Amsterdam city council on the purchase of an instrument late 1608, and he was a close friend of city organist Jan Pietersz Sweelinck (1562-1621) (Fig. 7). In 1606, the council had desired a harpsichord whereupon Sweelinck had ordered it from the Antwerp-based harpsichord builders Ionannes and Andreas Ruckers, and Isaacsz. had decorated it.[31] Isaacsz. has either advised Charisius himself, or directed him to Sweelinck. With their help, Charisius was able to lay his hands on seven instruments; five appeared with a double manual, two with a single manual. Nyström presumed that the instruments were keyboard instruments, either organs or clavichords. Indeed, they were keyboard instruments, but probably not organs and certainly not clavichords.[32] Organs were usually not acquired from the Netherlands but rather from Germany that excelled in organ building. Various organs in Denmark originate from Germany, including the outstanding organ by Esaias Compenius from 1610 at Frederiksborg Castle. The Netherlands, in particular the Southern provinces, were famous for its harpsichord and virginal industry

and, as can be understood from his account, it was such instruments Charisius took home to Denmark. In all six harpsichords, wing-shaped with the strings in line with the keyboard, were obtained in Haarlem, The Hague, and from the collector Abraham Gorlaeus in Delft. Charisius also bought a so-called mother and child virginal, in a rectangular case with the strings transverse to the keyboard and with a double manual, one large and one small next to one another, hence the name (Fig. 8). The instruments varied in sizes, material and decorations, and prices ranged from 27,5 to 125 *dalers* for a large, double instrument of cypress wood from Antwerp, which must have been constructed at the celebrated Ruckers workshop.[33] Prior to the purchase, Charisius had the instruments tested by "Jan organist", who can be identified as Jan Sweelinck. Although based in Amsterdam, Sweelinck earned an extra income travelling around, dealing in instruments and testing them for others. All approved, they were shipped to Denmark. Harpsichords and virginals are highly sensitive instruments, very receptive to climate and humidity changes. Once at their destination, King Christian will not have taken the instruments with him when moving between residences. As a true lover of music, he will have desired to have at least one at each of his main castles; Copenhagen, Frederiksborg, Kolding, and later Rosenborg. The mother and child virginal was a curiosity item; rather to please the eye than the ear.[34] Possibly it was exhibited at Frederiksborg, where the king often received foreign guests. Yet, as goes for the other instruments, both its history and possible whereabouts are unknown.[35]

When August came, it was time to leave. Charisius and Ulfeldt had accomplished their mission, their belongings had been packed, and provisions were stocked up. Before they left for Amsterdam, from where they would depart, the diplomats were once more lionized by the States General at an official farewell ceremony on 3 August. Each of them received a necklace crafted by local goldsmiths Marcus Dubout and Jacques Mirou. Charisius's memento consisted of a 5 pound gold necklace with gems for 600 *guilders*, a precious gift expressing his hosts' gratitude for his efforts and underlining the strong ties between Denmark and the Dutch Republic.[36]

Going international: Danes in the Republic

Charisius's purchases and the mission as a whole should be held against the background of the shifting relations between Denmark and the Dutch Republic through the seventeenth century. In the second half of the century, Denmark was not considered of much significance in the Republic, according to some newsagents.[37] However, around 1600 the roles were still reversed and the Dutch-Danish relations considerably stronger. Not without reason, the Dutch had greatly desired Denmark's participation at the negotiation table in 1607 and had fêted the Danish delegates during the months they resided in The Hague with musical performances, parties, excursions, and gifts. At that time, Amsterdam was developing into a migrant city where thousands of foreigners took their refuge for different reasons. The number of immigrants that settled in the Republic as a whole even counted hundreds of thousands. Late in the sixteenth century, the newcomers chiefly originated from the Southern Netherlands where they left cities like Ghent and Antwerp in great numbers after the Spanish troops had bashed the reformation and the revolt against their regime. If the emigrants had not left for religious reasons, then it was on economic grounds; the fall of Antwerp was wrought by blocking the river Schelde, causing a drastic spin of trade in the once so lively port city. Initially, the Flemish did not choose the Dutch provinces but established themselves in England and especially in the German cities Frankfurt, Cologne and Bremen. In the 1590s, many of them came to live in the Republic, and mostly in Amsterdam. Here the future looked extraordinarily bright now that Amsterdam had taken over Antwerp's role as major trading city of the North. The southerners, amongst them great numbers of merchants, artists and intellectuals, largely contributed to this development.[38] Soon, the city became highly attractive for foreigners other than Flemish. They came from far and near, yet primarily from the German states closely followed by immigrants from Denmark and Sweden. In the first half of the century around 16.500 immigrants in the city originated from Scandinavia.[39] As Philip von Zesen wrote in his description of the city of Amsterdam, "It swarms and teems with Danish, Norse and eastern people as ship masters, boatswains, carpenters, porters and others ..."[40] Whilst the Netherlandish artists and entrepreneurs moving to Sweden and Denmark have been the subject of several studies, the Scandinavian immigration to the Netherlands has hardly been dealt with, despite the fact that great numbers of Swedes, Norsemen and Danes settled in the Republic from where they imported new commodities and ideas. The ambitious two-volume book *Holland Danmark. Forbindelserne mellem de to Lande gennem Tiderne* (1945) intended to involve this side of the story, but never got round to it due to the war, as the editors wrote in their introduction.[41]

The Scandinavian immigrants were mainly attracted by the economic boom the Dutch Republic underwent. Except for holding a public office, newcomers could basically practise any profession, which made it easy to participate in society. In addition to the economic aspects, there was freedom of worship; the Republic favored the Calvinist faith but membership was not obligatory, which implied that everybody could practise his own faith.[42] The Danes and other Lutherans in Amsterdam met in the still-standing Lutheran church at Spui. Finally, the fact that people were able to understand each other was an obvious plus; Low German was spoken from Middelburg to Danzig. The Danes in Amsterdam were employed in shipping, chiefly in the East Indian trade, in ship building, as soldiers in the armies of stadholder Maurits of Orange and of his brother and successor Frederik Hendrik, as tailor, shoemaker, or maid.

Parallel to this low-class immigration, growing numbers of northerners from higher social classes came to the Republic. During a sojourn of varying length, they gained trading experiences, became acquainted with the cultural market, or enrolled at university, as Godofredo Lindenow (Godtfred Lindenov) did, who published his dissertation *Plea for the best way of life to be*

Fig. 6. Balthazar Florisz van Berckerode, view of Honselaarsdijk, c. 1638. The Hague, Municipal Archives (Photo Municipal Archives).

Charisius and Frederiksborg

The majority of the works Charisius brought from the Republic were intended for the grand Frederiksborg Castle in Hillerød, 30 kilometres outside Copenhagen. The medieval castle in Copenhagen was considered old-fashioned and was not used as the king's residence while Rosenborg Castle was commenced in 1606-1607 and not ready for use yet. Christian IV had started rebuilding Frederiksborg in 1602. The Chapel Wing was begun 1606, the Princess Wing in 1608, the Oratory was installed at the end of the second decade. Now, the magnificent structure had to be decorated with furniture, tapestries, and paintings. If Christian IV had put the origin of the art works in the inventory of Frederiksborg Castle, the name of Jonas Charisius would have occurred many times.[57] Identifying the paintings is, however, an almost insurmountable task. The castle burnt in 1859 and most of the interior was lost in the fire, other paintings were taken as war booty by Swedish troops as early as in 1658, or were transferred to the Royal Kunstkammer (cf. below). The inventory of the collection, made up in 1650, is very brief; describing the paintings' subject but rarely naming the artist. Several unspecified works by Valckenborch appear in the inventory, and Charisius acquired two paintings by Valckenborch from a "mester Luis" in Antwerp.[58] From Pieter Isaacsz., he bought a "peasant's dance" by Valckenborch, which could be one of the two Peasant Weddings by Lucas van Valckenborch (c.15?-1597), now in the Statens Museum for Kunst in Copenhagen, evolved out of the Royal Kunstkammer's collection. Charisius also purchased a "Judith and Holofernes". There were two pictures with this title at Frederiksborg Castle in 1650.[59] Yet, Judith was a very popular subject, painted by numerous artists. It seems obvious that relating Charisius' purchases to the Frederiksborg inventory can only be based upon assumptions.

Jonas Charisius had not only selected paintings, and musical instruments, for Frederiksborg, he must have been involved in other aspects of the castle's interior and exterior as well. In the years following the completion of the castle's main construction, work commenced on the sculptural decoration programme, foremost the lavish Marble Gallery (Fig. 4).[60] Draughtsman was Hans van Steenwinckel the Younger, architect of Netherlandish descent in royal service, while the gallery, with its lavish sculptural decoration, was executed at the workshop of Hendrick de Keyser, Amsterdam's city architect. No coincidence as van Steenwinckel and his brother Laurens had worked as apprentices at de Keyser's, somewhere between 1602 and '10. Presumably, the contact and the assignment for the gallery came about due to Charisius, who in his turn had leaned once again on Pieter Isaacsz.'s network. He and de Keyser moved in the same circles and when Isaacsz. bought a property and built a house in

Fig.7. Gerrit Pietersz. Sweelinck, Jan Pietersz. Sweelinck. Amsterdam Museum (Photo Amsterdam Museum).

ART AND MUSIC ON DEMAND 291

1603-04, de Keyser stood guarantor.⁶¹ Therefore it has been tempting to attribute Charisius's epitaph in Roskilde cathedral to Hendrick de Keyser. The epitaph, centrally placed on the north wall in the church's middle aisle, is executed in white, black and red Belgian marble. The material was not a novelty in Denmark, where the funerary momuments for the Danish kings Christian III and Frederik II, also in Roskilde, by Cornelis Floris and Gert van Egen respectively form an early example. The use of Italian marble, introduced in the Netherlands by Hendrick de Keyser, was still in its infancy then and would reach its heights in the second half of the seventeenth century. Charisius's epitaph is built around a central text, flanked by double columns and herms.⁶² In the top, we see a broken frontispiece with lying putti, at the bottom a time glass, a skull, and Charisius's coat-of-arms. A white marble bust of Charisius in an oval frame tops the epitaph. The bust portrait is more refined than the rest of the piece, and possibly by another hand. Except the bust,

neither the sculpural elements nor the motives are typical for Hendrick de Keyser. He did apply the broken fronton, but only in gates, never in burial monuments. Also the central text panel is not a typical de Keyser element. The presumption that the epitaph can be attributed to de Keyser should therefore be left aside. But the piece is positively Northern-Netherlandish, considering the material that was applied: Belgian marble was chiefly traded and processed in Amsterdam by stone traders like the Neurenberg family.⁶³ An argument of greater significance is, however, the stylistic relation of Charisius's epitaph to the epitaph of Johan Füchting and his wife in the Marienkirche in Lübeck, where Füchting was a councillor.⁶⁴ Füchting's monument was executed by Pieter Adriaensz. van Delft and Aris Claesz. from Haarlem, and dates from 1633.⁶⁵ Charisius's epitaph may be described as a toned-down variety of the larger and more elaborate Füchting memorial. The marble colour scheme is identical, and several elements – columns supported by

Fig. 4. F. C. Lund, The Marble Gallery of Frederiksborg Castle, 1854. Designed by Hans II van Steenwinckel, executed at Hendrick de Keyser's workshop, 1618-1620. Hillerød, The Museum of National History, Frederiksborg Castle (Photo Frederiksborg).

chosen by the young nobleman at the University of Franeker in Friesland in 1602.[43] Leiden University counted most Danish enrolments and was in general the chief destination for Danish students in the seventeenth century.[44] Henrik Fuiren from Copenhagen was one of them. He had left Copenhagen in 1631 to study in Leiden and Amsterdam with philologist Gerard Jan Vossius, who inscribed his motto in Fuiren's *stambog* on 9 August 1634. Other inscriptions testify to Fuiren's scientific and literary interests and include Adolp Vorstius, Claude de Saumaise, Johannes Pontanus, and fellow countrymen Poul Moth and Rasmus Bartholin.[45] A great name among the Leiden professors was historian Johannes Meursius, who took several young Danish noblemen under his guidance. Meursius' good Danish contacts, among them member of the Council of the Realm Holger Rosenkrantz, were formalised in 1624 when he was appointed Danish historiographer. The following year he moved to Denmark where he became professor at the new academy in Sorø.[46]

The growing number of Danes studying abroad – from 89 in the 1540s to 415 in the 1590s[47] – was related to the changing of educational ideals. One of the arguments Lindenow put forward in his *Plea* was that king and fatherland could no longer make do with a gentry that excelled as strategists at the battlefield alone. Instead, they were in demand of noblemen who were at least as strategic in a diplomatic context. The nobility of the sword was to be converted into, or rather supplemented by, a nobility of the study, where 'study' should be understood both literally and metaphorically as a universe of new knowledge. The way to get there was, apart from books, travelling. The Danish crown actively followed this strategy when it financially supported noblemen like Sivert Grubbe and Christian Barnekow with enfeoffments during their travels. The royal aid came on one condition: upon return, the experiences gained abroad were to be put in the fatherland's service. For members of Christian IV's Council of the Realm, international experience was part of their career; apart from a few exceptions all members had studied outside Denmark, for example Anders Bille and Christen Friis, who had accompanied Ulfeldt and Charisius.[48] Following their return, Bille became member of the council and Friis eventually became Chancellor. Hence the fact that considerably more Danes went abroad from the end of the sixteenth century was not related to a romantic idea of widening one's horizon but to a need of higher educated, versatile government officials. Jonas Charisius was one of those 'new' diplomats and belonged to the first generation educated abroad. His studies in Padua and Heidelberg in the 1590s had supplied him with excellent language and political skills, giving access to a splendid career in government service.

Representation

Against the background of this increasing internationalisation, a system of national representation abroad developed. Sending a letter to mark one's position in a certain case was time-consuming and little reliable while sending off an envoy was not always sufficient either.[49] It had become necessary to be represented on a permanent basis if one really wanted to keep acquainted. Permanent personal representation was new to the Northern courts, contrary to Southern Europe where dispatching envoys between states and courts had been customary since the fifteenth century, in imitation of the Papacy that had been the model for the early modern court's working.

With the traffic to and from the Baltic increasing and the interfering in various conflicts, the Danish crown too had to keep itself informed of the latest international diplomatic, political and economic news on a continuous basis. Dutch newspapers were only available in Copenhagen from around 1630, when publishers Elsevier from Leiden and Janssonius from Amsterdam opened a local division in the stock market and Vor Frue Kirke respectively.[50] International newspapers had their breakthrough around 1650 so information gathering was left to envoys even representing their state in a diplomatic context. In the Republic, they lived in The Hague, as Jonas Charisius did, or in Amsterdam, depending on whether their mission was concerned with diplomatic or trade matters. In the years 1600-1650, Denmark had at its disposal of 11 residents, agents and other representatives in The Hague and Amsterdam, after 1650 they even counted 17 while after 1685 there were only five left.[51] This fluctuating number was related to the rise and fall of Amsterdam as a centre of world trade. The hegemony achieved at the beginning of the seventeenth century – chiefly based upon the Baltic trade in

Fig. 5 Passchier Lammertijn (attr.), details of table cloth in linen damask, picturing Maurits of Orange's wind wagon, invented by Simon Stevin, 1621. Copenhagen, Rosenborg Castle (Photo Rosenborg).

grain and copper – was transferred to London at the end of the century. Besides, the Dutch Republic was a young nation – considered valiant by some, rebellious by others – whose status was only made official with the Peace of Westphalia in 1648. For many years diplomatic ties with the Republic were therefore complicated and before 1587, when the Republic was declared independent at the Union of Utrecht, there simply was no such thing as Dutch foreign politics. Although trading relations with the Baltic region existed, diplomatic contacts were not yet formalised. In 1596, the year of Christian IV's coronation, the first Dutch government official, Isaac Pietersz., was established in Denmark. The first permanent Danish representative in the Republic was Adriaan Strick, appointed in 1619, two years before the Truce with Spain came to an end. Amongst Strick's successors we find residents Paul de Willem and Josias van Vosbergen, both in Amsterdam in the late 1620s, Martin Tancke, resident in the 1640s in The Hague, and Jonas Charisius's son Peder Charisius, also in The Hague, in the 1660s.

A minority of these representatives occupied themselves with more than writing newsletters and political despatches.[52] These men also supplied their commissioners with what we may call 'cultural intelligence', keeping them informed with news from the Dutch art market. Now that high quality paintings, tapestries, sculptures et cetera were available in abundance, it was only natural that the Danish king and aristocrats became interested in these products, alongside their involvement in political and trade news. Purchasing or ordering these commodities for them could be a good sideline for a diplomat who knew how to let his diplomatic network take advantage of his cultural activities, and vice versa. Jonas Charisius was such a diplomat. As a representative of the Danish king, known as a lover of the arts and music, he made a highly valued customer of the painters he visited, while his collected expertise in

Fig. 8. Hans Ruckers the Elder, double virginal 'Mother and child', 1581. New York, Metropolitan Museum of Art (Photo Metropolitan Museum).

corbels, herms, putti, and the broken fronton – reappear.

Pieter van Delft descended from a family of stone masons and stone traders, but we know him primarily as a trader.[66] Van Delft and his three brothers, all in the stone business as well, cooperated with Hendrick de Keyser on several occassions: his eldest brother Claes had worked with de Keyser at the Lebuïnus tower in Deventer in 1612-13 while his younger brother Herman held a position as de Keyser's assistant at that time. Pieter's marriages, first to Mayke van Steenwinckel, a member of the famous master masons Steenwinckel family, and later to Anna van Neurenberg, whose family belonged to the most significant stone traders in the Netherlands, were of great importance to his career. Due to his family network and marriages, van Delft became a succesful trader, involved in major building activities in Amsterdam and Nijmegen, and supplying Lübeck, Copenhagen, and Kalmar. Stone mason Aris Claesz. from Haarlem had Scandinavian connections as well; from 1622 we find him in Sweden where he worked at the Stockholm palace Tre Kronor under the guidance of royal architect Caspar Panten from Amsterdam. In 1628, he made the first, yet not accepted, design for the House of Nobles (Riddarhuset), also in Stockholm, and the following year, Claesz. executed Gustav Banér and his wife Kristina Sture's funerary monument in Uppsala cathedral.[67]

Jonas Charisius's earlier contacts with Hendrick de Keyser and his workshop must have made de Keyser and his circle an evident choice when his heirs were finding the executor of his memorial. The master himself died in 1621, whereupon his son Pieter continued the business. Pieter and other Amsterdam masons operated in a small circle, where everybody knew each other, using the same suppliers and sawmills, and often cooperating on assignments. Both Claesz. and van Delft belonged to this circle, the first as stone mason and sculptor, the latter chiefly as stone trader. Considering their Scandinavian liasons and the stylistic relation to the Füchting memorial, Jonas Charisius's epitaph can be atrributed to Aris Claesz., who executed the work shortly before he left for Sweden in 1622, possibly in cooperation with Pieter de Keyser to whom Charisius's white marble bust portrait may be attributed. Perhaps Claesz. assembled the entire piece on location on his way north. The red, white and black marbles might very well have been delivered by Pieter van Delft. Claesz., de Keyser, and van Delft later all three maintained Scandinavian contacts.[68] The Roskilde epitaph might have been an entrée on

Fig. 9. Reinhold Timm, Musicians from Christian IV's chapel, c. 1622. Copenhagen, Danish Music Museum- Musikhistorisk Museum & The Carl Claudius Collection (Photo Ole Woldbye).

this market. Also, the work underlines the connections between Jonas Charisius and the de Keyser workshop.

Netherlandish artists were also hired for Frederiksborg's interior decoration, including tapestry designer Karel van Mander, son of Isaacsz.'s close friend, the painter and writer Karel van Mander I. Van Mander initially worked for François Spiering in Delft but in the year he set up his own business, he received a commission from Christian IV to do a series of tapestries commemorating the Kalmar War (1611-1613), which was to decorate the Great Hall.[69] In January 1614, Charisius received a letter from Spiering; although the letter itself is lost we may assume that he has tried to persuade Charisius to give the assignment to him, and not to his former employee.[70] The same year, Pieter Isaacsz. himself came into the service of Christian IV as royal portrait painter, a position he owed to Jonas Charisius and for which the seeds were sown during Charisius's visit to Amsterdam seven years earlier.

painting gained him respect as a learned man in diplomatic circles.

Art in politics

The combination of arts and politics was highly relevant in early modern Europe, and so it was in Northern Europe. Some art was produced on commission, while another share was produced for the free market. The market was only relatively free since artists geared their pieces to the prevailing taste and to the wishes of potential buyers. With his purchase, the buyer could make an easy-to-read statement, as subject choice, selected artist and style showed his inclinations, both religious and political. The works Charisius acquired on Christian IV's behalf were chiefly history pieces; picturing either mythological or biblical scenes. In the hierarchy of genres, historical scenes were considered the most esteemed, preceding genre paintings, portraits, landscapes, and still lifes. On a larger scale, rulers exploited art works for propaganda purposes, as an expression of power, and as an instrument to ventilate their political intentions. For this aim, they did not limit themselves to painting but used architecture, sculpture, music, and ceremonies as well. Moreover, they could illustrate their status by means of an art work, immortalizing a specific glorious event. Not only possessing art, even the act of buying art was in itself a significant social activity with which one could join in with the affluent elite. It visualised the status of the owner as it was a means to express individuality and position in society. As such, art objects became instruments in one's personal political program, building a powerful decorum.

For the sovereigns of Northern Europe buying art works was a natural sideline, while for their noblemen and patricians it was a relatively new pastime. Collecting art increased in the highest circles, on equal terms with mastering several languages and possessing books. Yet, Danish nobility would always cherish science over art, they preferred to establish themselves as men of letters rather than of the arts, and collections such as Ole Worm's cabinet contained primarily objects of scientific value rather than solely art works. In that perspective, Danish 20th-century historiography is comparable to the early modern Danish nobleman, more interested in learning than art. A scholar like the historiographer Johannes Pontanus has been the subject of several studies, whilst his brother the portraitist Pieter Isaacsz. only recently came into the picture.[53]

Purchased art works did not necessarily stay in the owner's possession but were also bought as gifts. Presented in a diplomatically charged con-

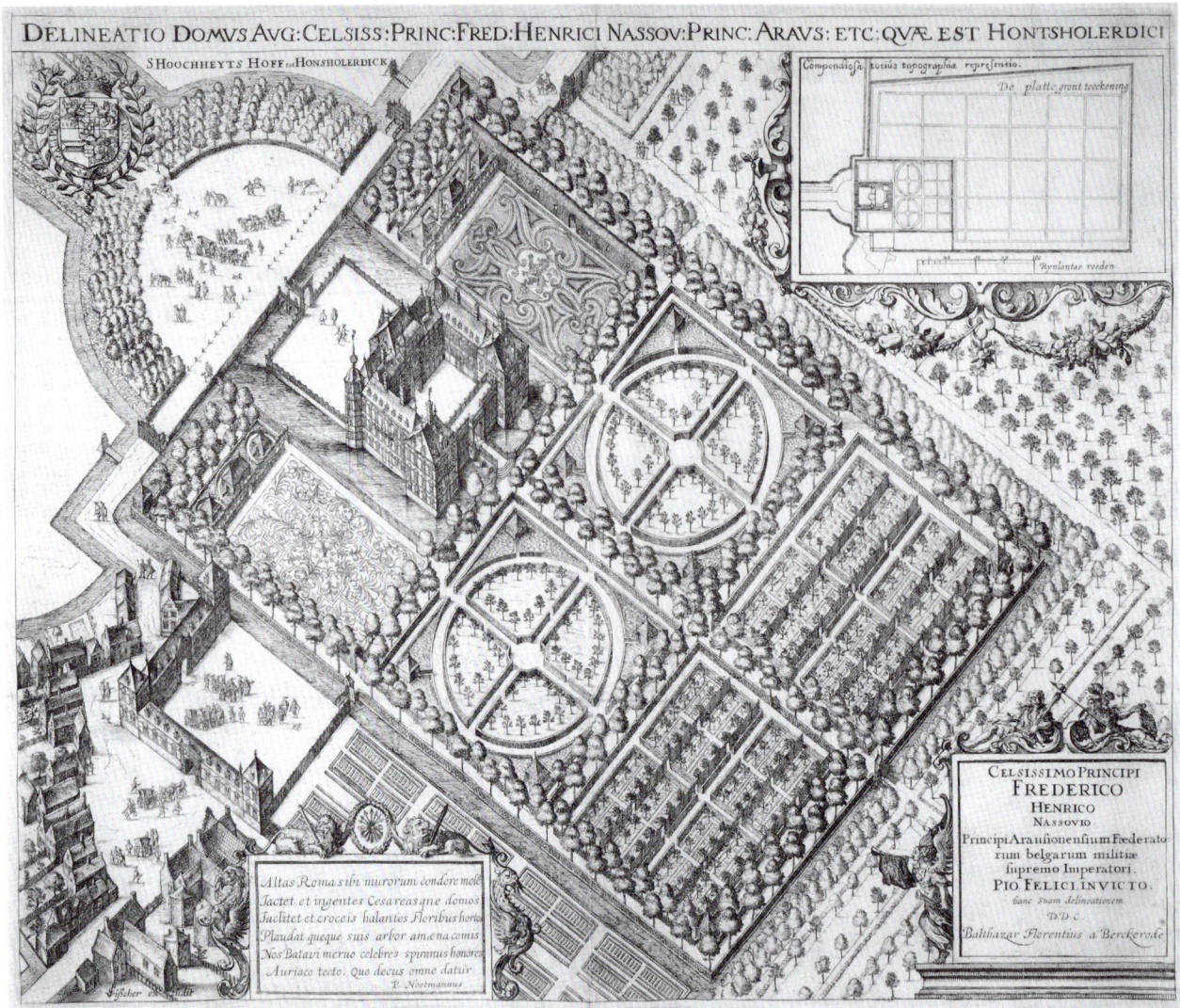

text, a piece of art could be a very effective means to manipulate an important relation, because of "its ability to say that which the envoy is not permitted to say, without uttering a single word", as Anthony Colantuono has put it, describing paintings as the mute diplomats of early modern times.[54] Whether art was obtained for royal or noble collections or as diplomatic gifts, it was rarely bought personally by the patron but mostly by a representative, such as Jonas Charisius. These middlemen played an important role in the development of collections and courtly art politics, negotiating contracts or actually purchasing art works, which gave a man like Charisius decisive influence on the collection. Sometimes the *art agent* had an artistic background, as was the case with painter Jacob Binck, who worked for King Christian III, and Pieter Isaacsz, and poet-playwright Theodoor Rodenburg, in the service of Christian IV.[55] Although connoisseurship was a pro, being an artist was not a requirement. King Christian IV's father, Frederik II, had a factor in his service, Philip Gardin, who resided in Antwerp. Besides being the king's trade contact, Gardin also acted as middleman in ordering sculpture works from Antwerp to Denmark.[56] Diplomat and part-time art agent Jonas Charisius did not have a background as an artist either. Jonas Charisius was active in both politics and the world of the arts, combining his main diplomatic career with his dealings as a middleman in international art transactions. Most benefit gained his patron Christian IV, who due to Charisius' efforts and good taste built a high-quality collection.

Fig. 10. Dirck de Bray, Interior of an Amsterdam shop, offering paintings, globes, and books. Amsterdam, Rijksmuseum (Photo Rijksmuseum).

Collecting

In these years, Netherlandish art found its way to Denmark, more than it had before. A development due to increased mobility and improved possibilities for travelling, but another factor played a role as well: collecting. The desire to surround oneself with precious objects is of all times but private collecting expanded enormously in the sixteenth century.[71] These compilations of curiosa, art works, and *bizarrie* of dynastical and historical importance, and not at least of esthetical value, were accommodated in a so-called *Kunstkammer*. The term emerged for the first time in 1550 when Emperor Ferdinand I as the first ruler in Central Europe brought the art works and curiosities, standing and hanging across his palaces, together in an especially designed room. Art was herewith given a new value as object in itself. An essential aspect of the *Kunstkammer*, or *Wunderkammer*, was its private character. The collections were not supposed to be for the public but meant for the owner and his guests (and any court painters, who used the objects for study purposes). The collections' exclusive character enhanced the esthetical experience of the object giving art objects a value next to their political value. The importance of art works as a lead in diplomatic contexts did not diminish since the solitary appreciation of the objects raised the value of art and enlarged its role in diplomatic traffic.

A visit to a king's private collection could very well be a lead in diplomatic negotiations. Envoys would regard it as a privilege, a personal favour, when they were allowed to visit the royal *Kunstkammer*. As it had been a privilege for Jakob Ulfeldt and Jonas Charisius to be taken for a ride in the 'wind wagon'. In the *Kunstkammer*, the diplomat could expect to see both wonders of nature and art works made by human hand, diverging from drawings, paintings, sculptures to coins, sea shells, butterflies, and instruments. Exactly the *Kunstkammer*'s eclectical character was typical for the well-educated ideal of the *homo universalis* at the time. Ferdinand's *Kunstkammer* heralded a time in which art cabinets were created throughout Europe, such as in Vienna, Munich, Ambras, and Prague where Rudolf II kept the most magnificent collection of all. Internationally renowned in its time, his princely cabinet soon became famous for its large selection of high quality works by celebrated artists, including sculptor Adriaen de Vries and painter Hans von Aachen.[72] The Prague art chamber was no less famous for its size; Rudolf built separate structures to house the extensive quantities of art works and rarities. The inventory counted almost 400 folios.[73] In the Dutch Republic, Bernardus Paludanus's cabinet was the first example of an encyclopaedic collection, attracting scholars and sovereigns from far and away. When Ulfeldt had visited Paludan, it had certainly been at Stadholder Maurits van Nassau's intercession.

The *Kunstkammer* first of its kind north of Hamburg was located in Schleswig, in Gottorf castle, the seat of the Duchy of Schleswig-Holstein, which was united with Denmark from 1460 to 1864.[74] Like elsewhere in Europe, it was established to glorify the incumbent ruler and the collected items were the means to express his magnificence.[75] Yet, collecting art and curiosities in itself had found its way to Denmark long before that. As early as in the 1540s, King Christian III sent his court painter Jacob Binck to Antwerp to buy art works on his behalf. For 35 *dalers*, he purchased five paintings, including a portrait of the Spanish prince Philip II and of Prince Edward VI of England.[76]

His son and successor Frederik II was well aware of the power of art and knew how to use art and architecture as the physical expression of power. He employed a wide range of artists, amongst them the Netherlandish painters Gerrit Cornelisz. van Haarlem and Hans Knieper and the architect Antonis van Opbergen, and ordered works from famous artists such as Cornelis Floris from Antwerp who designed Christian III's burial monument in Roskilde. Frederik was excelled by his son Christian IV, who collected on a larger scale than previous kings. It has been suggested that King Christian only had a minor interest in art, a suggestion based on the fact that he bought paintings by the dozen. Hence, quantity prevailed over quality at the king's court.77 More than that, the numerous letters and notes from Christian's hand that have survived do not hold any passages wherein he divulged either a profound knowledge of or a fascination for art. There is no reason, however, to understand this as a lack of interest in the arts. At the time, it was not unusual for rulers to purchase art in great quantities. Other sovereigns, who have gone down in history for their good taste, such as Duke August of Wolffenbuttel, famous for his book collection, and Queen Christina, had a similar policy when it came to collecting. Christina acquired art in huge quantities, a great deal of it as the spoils of war. Her above-mentioned *Inventaire des Raretez* reveals that the number of paintings and other works of art she succeeded in amassing in her ten-year reign ran into the thousands.78 For a seventeenth-century monarch this was not necessarily a sign of a lack of taste, but rather an awareness of the power of collecting and owning art. By the late sixteenth century, an art collection had become part of royal protocol; an intellectual interest that a modern ruler was expected to have.

There has never been mentioned an actual *Kunstkammer* at Frederiksborg Castle, Christian IV's most significant residence, nor at *Sparepenge*, the pavilion in Frederiksborg's garden.79 Yet, some rooms in the castle come close to what is defined as a *Kunstkammer*. The inventory made up by the castle's keeper Johan Adam Berg in 1646 describes the queen's *Smykkekammeret* as a room where precious objects were kept, including paintings, goldleather wall tapestries, fine textiles, ebony furniture decorated with silver, a large silver-gilt chandelier as well as the supposed horn of a unicorn.80 Also the king's exclusive private oratory was richly decorated; all walls covered with Dutch masters and furnished with ebony and silver furniture. Considering the rather extraordinary contents of these rooms, we could regard them as an early Danish *Kunstkammer*.81

Epilogue

In the years following Jonas Charisius's mission to the Dutch Republic, he revisited the country in 1611, 1618, and again prior to his death in 1619. The correspondence with tapestry weaver François Spiering in 1614 and composer Jan Pietersz. Sweelinck in 1617 underlines that Charisius still was an authority at court when it concerned cultural affairs. Another expert was Pieter Isaacsz., who due to Charisius came to Denmark in 1614 where he soon became the king's favoured portraitist and history painter. More than that, he was put in charge of the decoration of the king's private oratory in Frederiksborg for which he was sent to Amsterdam in 1618. Here he recruited friends and former pupils to execute the paintwork. Charisius was in the Republic at that time as well, for diplomatic reasons but surely also to see how the Marble Gallery was getting along at Hendrik de Keyser's workshop, and it is only natural that Isaacsz. and Charisius worked on the Frederiksborg decoration in a *joint venture*. Upon Charisius's death, Isaacsz. continued his work, made responsible for a monumental series of history paintings in Rosenborg. Christian left the choice of painters for the twenty canvases entirely to him. Isaacsz. died in 1625, and only in the 1630s his role as art agent was taken over. Again, a Dutch artist was found for the job; Simon de Passe, engraver from Utrecht and brother of the eminent Crispijn de Passe. Besides his duties as a court artist, Christian appointed de Passe artistic leader of his last grand project; a series of 80 paintings on the history of the nation to decorate the rebuilt Kronborg Castle. As Isaacsz. had done previously, de Passe used his personal network and hired the renowned Gerrit Honthorst and other artists from his Utrecht circle.82

Christian IV's artistic policies, including a key role for his art agents, are evidence of his understanding of the multifaceted significance of art and were instrumental in the creation of Frederiksborg, Rosenborg, and Kronborg. Moreover, the fact that Christian largely left the responsibilities to his art agents – among them the diplomat Jonas Charisius and later Isaacsz. and de Passe –

and trusted their knowledge, network, and taste, testifies to the king's ability to put the right men to the task.

Notes

1. Including J. Roding & L. Heerma van Vos (eds.), *The North Sea and Culture (1550-1800)*, Hilversum 1996; S. Turk Christensen & B. Noldus (eds.), "Cultural Traffic and Cultural Transformation around the Baltic Sea, 1450-1720", in: *Scandinavian Journal of History* 28, 3-4 (2003); J. Kreslins, S. A. Mansbach & R. Schweitzer (eds.), *Gränsländer. Östersjön i ny gestalt*, Stockholm 2003; M. Krieger & M. North (eds.), *Land und Meer: Kultureller Austausch zwischen Westeuropa und dem Ostseeraum in der Frühen Neuzeit*, Cologne, Weimar & Vienna 2004; B. Noldus, *Trade in Good Taste. Relations in Architecture and Culture between the Dutch Republic and the Baltic in the 17th Century*, Turnhout 2004.

2. On cultural and political agency, see H. Cools, M. Keblusek & B. Noldus (eds.), *Your Humble Servant. Agents in Early Modern Europe*, Hilversum 2006.

3. As thoroughly documented by M. Tielhof, *The 'Mother of All Trades': The Baltic Grain Trade in Amsterdam from the Late Sixteenth to the Early Nineteenth Century*, Leiden 2002.

4. Although German contacts dominated the sixteenth century, the Danish court had many Netherlandish relations as well. See Birgitte Bøggild Johannsen's publications, "Til Kongens og Rigets behov. Nogle betragtninger om kunstforbruget ved Frederik II's hof", www.renæssanceforum.dk 2 (2006); "Promising Enterprises and Broken Dreams. Netherlandish Architectural Influences in Denmark during the Early 16th Century" in: Krista de Jonge & Konrad Ottenheym (eds.), *The Low Countries at the Crossroads* (forthcoming).

5. C. O. Bøggild-Andersen, "Jonas Charisius", in: *Dansk Biografisk Leksikon*[2] 4, Copenhagen 1934, 603-606; Steffen Heiberg (C. O. Bøggild-Andersen), "Jonas Charisius", in: *Dansk Biografisk Leksikon*[3] 3, Copenhagen 1979, 216-217.

6. Not all the men Hondius portrayed were actually present though, as was the case with King Christian IV of Denmark. On Hendrick Hondius see N. Orenstein, *Hendrick Hondius*, Roosendal & Amsterdam 1994 (G. Luijten (ed.), *The New Hollstein. Dutch & Flemish Etchings, Engravings and Woodcuts 1450-1700*), 106-122.

7. A. Th. Deursen, *De last van veel geluk. De geschiedenis van Nederland 1555-1702*, Amsterdam 2004, 167-169.

8. Rigsarkivet [The Danish National Archives, Copenhagen, hereafter: RA], Tyske Kancelli, Udenrigske Afdeling [hereafter: TKUA], Gesandtskabsregnskaber 1551-1776, vol. 83-13, 1607-1630. On Keld Krabbe, son of Niels Krabbe of Østergård see Louis Bobé (ed.), *Danmarks Adels Aarbog*, XLV, Copenhagen 1928, II, 118.

9. The Royal Library (Det Kongelige Bibliotek) in Copenhagen holds an impressive collection of such albums, called *stambøger*. Originally family record books, in the sixteenth century they were taken on travels and used to let others write their autograph, turning it into an *album amicorum*. Hieronymus Pleninger's is a fine example, holding illustrations by those he met during his journey. Painter Isaac Isaacsz. drew a water colour in Pleninger's book in 1618, picturing a drinking-bout. Det Kongelige Bibliotek, Center for Manuskripter & Boghistorie [hereafter: CMB], Ny Kongelig Samling [hereafter: NKS] 802 8º. On Isaac Isaacsz see Hannemarie Ragn Jensen, "Isaac Isaacz" in: Noldus & Roding 2007, 205-217.

10. O. Schutte, *Repertorium der buitenlandse vertegenwoordigers, residerende in Nederland 1584-1810*, The Hague 1983, 412.

11. Nationaal Archief, The Hague, Rijks Geschiedkundige Publicatiën [hereafter: RGP], Res. S-G 1607-1609, no. 131, inv.no. 3158. Lias Denemarken, inv. no. 7238.

12. Det Kongelige Bibliotek, CMB, NKS 1305 b, fol. The book's genuine title is *La Grande Chronique Ancienne et Moderne, de Hollande, Zelande, West-Frise, Utrecht, Frise, Overyssel & Groeningen, jusques à la fin de l'An 1600*. The fact that le Petit had been present at many of the events he described enhances the book's value. It includes engravings by Christoffel van Sichem. Le Petit also tried to catch Charisius's interest for a work "la grande histoire de Danemark en Francois".

13. Constantijn Huygens (1596-1687), then only 11 years old, also performed for James I of England. He became a diplomat, Stadholder Frederik Hendrik's secretary, and a celebrated poet.

14. Huygens' letters have been published by J. A. Worp (ed.), *De Briefwisseling van Constantijn Huygens, 1608-1687*, 1-6, The Hague 1911-1917 (see also: http://www.inghist.nl/Onderzoek/Projecten/Huygens).

15. Picturing such earthly goods on a fine cloth was highly unusual. Rosenborg Castle, inv. no. N.a. 3 D, 31 Rulle 26 a-b-c. K. Zandvliet, *Maurits Prins van Oranje*, Amsterdam & Zwolle 2000, 324.

16. Otto Brahe, who had previously served the Spanish troops, "lent" the envoys his vicar to preach for them. Brahe's, Bille's and Friis's biographies can be found in: *Dansk Biografisk Leksikon*[3].

17. "en demning wed it Wand kaldiß Bemster". Other

Danes too held an interest in reclamation; Christen Jørgensen Skeel visited more or less the same places during his Dutch journey in 1642 (Det Kongelige Bibliotek, CBM, NKS 141 f 8º). His destinations were standard, yet not his speed: 1 May, he entered the country at "Nimmege" [Nijmegen], continued by track boat to "Bommel" [Zaltbommel], arrived next day. Following day, proceeded to Gorinchem, same day to Rotterdam, next day to Delft, further to The Hague, passing Rijswijk. Followings days, visited Leiden, Haarlem, Alkmaar, Petten, Hoorn, Purmerend and "Vatterlandene" [Broek in Waterland], then all situated at or in the vicinity of land reclamation projects. Only in Amsterdam he resided two weeks, including a trip to Enkhuizen, presumably to see Paludanus' cabinet.

18 "mit grosser bescheidenheit, auch in höchster stille und heimbligkeit", quoted in E. Nystrøm, "Jonas Charisius' Indkøb af Malerier og Musikinstrumenter i Nederlandene 1607-8", *Danske Magazin* 5, VI (1905-1909), 225. See also Schutte 1983, 414.

19 G. W. Kernkamp, "Memoriën van ridder Theodorus Rodenburg betreffende het verplaatsen van verschillende industrieën uit Nederland naar Denemarken, met daarop genomen resolutiën van koning Christiaan IV (1621)", *Bijdragen en Mededelingen betreffende de geschiedenis der Nederlanden* 23 (1902), 189-256.

20 Nystrøm 1905-1909, 225-236. Charisius' account is kept at RA, TKUA, Holland C Regnskaber 1607-27.

21 Nystrøm 1905-1909, 226. "… ved deres rent kunstneriske Værdi vilde de næppe have været synderlig tiltrækkende, fordi de alle tilhørte den uheldige Overgangstid i nederlandsk Malerkunst før Blomstringen i det 17. Aarhundrede."

22 Fr. Beckett, *Frederiksborg II: Slottets Historie*, Copenhagen 1914, 88. "Det var for øvrigt et uheldigt Tidspunkt, naar man vilde grundlægge en Samling af samtidig Malerkunst. Italiens Sol var gaaet ned, den nederlandske Malerkunst endnu ikke staaet op."

23 In particular, the exhibition catalogue. G. Luijten et al. (eds.), *Dawn of the Golden Age. Northern Netherlandish Art 1580-1620*, Amsterdam 1993-94.

24 Due to John M. Montias, research on the early modern Dutch art market has reached a high level. His socio-economic approach effected a different view on the arts's position in seventeenth-century society. In his *Art at Auction in 17th-Century Amsterdam*, Amsterdam 2002, Montias analyses the auction system, and therewith an essential aspect of the Amsterdam art market. However, when he claims that auctions at the beginning of the seventeenth century were a local phenomenon, without outside buyers, he surpasses the fact that amongst the bidders were art agents purchasing pieces for foreign patrons, including King Christian's portraitist and art agent Pieter Isaacsz.. Other relevant publications include Michael North (ed.), *Economic History of the Arts*, Cologne 1996; F. Vermeylen, *Painting for the Market. Commercialization of Art in Antwerp's Golden Age*, Turnhout 2003; N. De Marchi & H. J. Miegroet (eds.), *Mapping Markets for Paintings in Europe, 1450-1750*, Turnhout 2006.

25 J. le Laboureur, *Histoire et relation de la Royne de Pologne*, Paris 1648, 67-73.

26 M. J. Bok, "The rise of Amsterdam as a cultural centre: the market for paintings, 1580-1680", in: P. O'Brien et al. (eds.), *Urban Achievement in Early Modern Europe. Golden Ages in Antwerp, Amsterdam and London*, Cambridge 2001, 186-209.

27 Montias 2002, 120, mentions the sale of six works of the painter Lucas Luce to an agent of the Danish king in 1607; this must have been Jonas Charisius.

28 J. van der Veen, "De Delftse kunstmarkt in de tijd van Vermeer", in: D. Haks & M. C. van der Sman (eds.), *De Hollandse samenleving in de tijd van Vermeer*, Zwolle 1996, 128.

29 "drog til delfft at besie nogit maelwerck". Keld Krabbe's journal in RA, TKUA, Gesandtskabsregnskaber 1551-1776, vol. 83-13, 1607-1630.

30 S. A. C. Dudok van Heel, "The Birth of an Artists' Quarter – Pieter Isaacsz's Amsterdam Years", in: Noldus & Roding (eds.) 2007, 76.

31 Dudok van Heel 2007, 76; H. Miedema, "Cover of the Amsterdam City Harpsichord", in: Noldus & Roding 2007, 270.

32 A clavichord has a rectangular case and a single manual; an instrument not appearing in Charisius's account: "2 dobblllt och 5 einfachtige instrumenter, kiøbtt udj Holland: 1firekandt dobbelt, kiøbtt till Harlem for 15 ½ lib. / 1 enfachtigt instrument, kiøbt sammestedts for 11 lib. / 1 aflangt instrument, giortt till Brysell och kiøbt udj Hagen aff Jan organiste for 26 lib. / 1 anditt Brysels instrument, lige stortt, kiøbtt sammestedts for 28 lib. / 1 stortt dobbelt instrument med cipres bonde, giortt till Antwerpen, kiøbt for 50 lib. / 1 anditt stortt med gule sandell clauere, kiøbt for 45 lib. / 1 nogid mindre, huor paa er affmalid thett Bryselske slott, kiøbtt for 30 lib."

33 G. Grant O'Brien, "Ioannes and Andreas Ruckers. A quatercentenary celebration", *Early Music* 7 (1979), 453-466.

34 I wish to express my gratitude to Dr. Peter Hauge, senior researcher at the Royal Library in Copenhagen, for his help interpreting Charisius's description.

35 Years later, Charisius is again in touch with Sweelinck when he receives a letter from "Jan P. Sweelnick [sic]. In Amsterdam desen 10. April 1617." The letter itself is

lost. Det Kongelige Bibliotek, CBM, NKS, 1305, 2., a.

36 For unknown reasons, Charisius was not present. The States General sent representatives after him to Amsterdam, in order to hand him the gift there, but he had left. Schutte 1983, 414-415. Nationaal Archief, The Hague, Resolutiën Staten-Generaal, inv.no. 1360 fol., 3 August 1608.

37 Swedish resident Harald Appelboom wrote to his government in 1663: "In Holland, Denmark is considered powerless and poor, and they hold the opinion that a friendly attitude and an alliance with that country is more troublesome than useful to the States, since it can only accept help, and without that, or on its one foot, it cannot stand. This is how Holland thinks of Denmark now." Uppsala Universitetsbibliotek, vol. E 437, 2 June 1663. Quoted in G. W. Kernkamp, "Memoriën van den Zweedschen resident Harald Appelboom", *Bijdragen en Mededelingen van het Historisch Genootschap* 26 (1905), 306-343.

38 See O. Gelderblom, *Zuid-Nederlandse kooplieden en de opkomst van de Amsterdamse stapelmarkt (1578-1630)*, Hilversum 2000.

39 E. Kuijpers, *Migrantenstad. Immigranten en sociale verhoudingen in 17de-eeuws Amsterdam*, Hilversum 2005, 373, 379.

40 Ph. von Zesen, *Beschreibung von der Stadt Amsterdam etc*, Amsterdam 1664, 413. Quoted in Kuijpers 2005, 139. With "eastern", Zesen meant German immigrants.

41 K. Fabricius, L. L. Hammerich & Vilh. Lorenzen (eds.), *Holland Danmark. Forbindelserne mellem de to Lande gennem Tiderne*, I-II, Copenhagen 1945; Kuijpers 2005 is the most recent work dealing with Scandinavian 17th-century migration to the Netherlands, mostly Amsterdam.

42 Holding a catholic service in a public building was prohibited, but the city turned a blind eye to services in private chapels. Synagogues existed, and in Amsterdam, as the only city in the Republic, a Jew could become burgher.

43 *Oratio de optimo vitæ genere nobili adolescenti deligendo*.

44 Vello Helk, "Den danske adels dannelsesrejser i Europa 1536-1660", in: Per Ingesman & J. V. Jensen (eds.), *Riget, magten og æren: Den danske adel 1350-1660*, Århus 2001, 545.

45 Det Kongelige Bibliotek, CBM, NKS 373 8º (Cf. ovf.). Helk 2001, 554.

46 On Meursius, see Karen Skovgaard-Petersen, *Historiography at the Court of Christian IV. Studies in the Latin Histories of Denmark by Johannes Pontanus and Johannes Meursius*, Copenhagen 2002 (Renæssancestudier, 11).

47 Helk 2001, 527.

48 L. Jespersen, "Rekrutteringen til rigsrådet i Christian 4.s tid", in: Knud J. V. Jespersen (ed.), *Rigsråd, adel og administration 1570-1648*, Odense 1980, 53.

49 Sending a letter from Stockholm to for example Wolfenbuttel took seldom less than three months around 1600, even in summer, see Heiko Droste, *Im Dienst der Krone. Schwedische Diplomaten im 17. Jahrhundert*, Berlin 2006, 66.

50 B. Bennich-Björkman, „De Leidse en Amsterdamse Elzeviers in Skandinavië, 1630-1680", in: B. P. M. Dongelmans, P. G. Hoftijzer & O. S. Lankhorst (eds.), *Boekverkopers van Europa. Het 17de-eeuwse Nederlandse uitgevershuis Elzevier*, Zutphen 2000, 148.

51 Cf. Schutte 1983, however, not including embassies.

52 H. Ilsøe, "Gesandtskaber som kulturformidlende faktor. Forbindelser mellem Danmark og England-Skotland o. 1580-1607", *Historisk Tidsskrift* 6 (1960-62), 574-600.

53 On Pontanus see Skovgaard-Petersen 2002, on Isaacsz see Noldus & Roding (eds.) 2007.

54 A. Colantuono, "The Mute Diplomat: Theorizing the Role of Images in Seventeenth Century political Negotiations", in: E. Cropper (ed.), *The Diplomacy of Art. Artistic Creation and Politics in Seicento Italy*. Florence 1998 (Villa Spelman Colloquia 7), 53.

55 A. Bolvig, *Altertavlen i Roskilde Domkirke. Et u-almindeligt kunstværk*, Copenhagen 1997, 33-34; B. Noldus, "Pieter Isaacsz's Other Life – Legal and Illegal", in: Noldus and Roding (eds.) 2007, 156-157.

56 Bøggild Johannsen 2006c, 18.

57 Frederiksborg's 1650 inventory is published by A. Petersen, "Frederiksborg Slots Inventarium af 1650", *Danske Samlinger* 2 (1866-67), 118-234.

58 Nystrøm 1905- 09, 229. "ii stuck De bello Amazonum, von Valkenburg gemacht". Which member of the Valckenborch family he meant, is unknown.

59 Petersen 1866, 65, 67. See also Beckett 1914, 89.

60 On the gallery, see P. Kragelund, "Olympens guder", in S. Heiberg (ed.), *Christian 4. og Frederiksborg*, Copenhagen 2006, 43-61. Laurens Pietersz. Sweys erected the gallery in 1620-21 while de Keyers's master pupil Gerrit Lambertsz executed the sculptures. Lambertsz, and probably Sweys, had been contacted in Amsterdam by Theodoor Rodenburg. See also Konrad Ottenheym's contribution in this volume.

61 T. Schulting, "Pieter Isaacsz, Pupil of the 'Artistic, sensible Mr Cornelis Ketel' ", in: Noldus & Roding (eds.) 2007, 36.

62 I express my gratitude to Dr. Gabri van Tussenbroek

(Bureau Monumenten & Archeologie Amsterdam) and Dr. Frits Scholten (Rijksmuseum Amsterdam) for discussing Charisius's epitaph and sharing their knowledge with me.

63 On the Van Neurenberg family and their network, see G. van Tussenbroek, *The Architectural Network of the Van Neurenberg Family in the Low Countries*, Turnhout 2006.

64 For an illustration of the Füchting epitaph see F. Scholten, *Sumptuous Memories. Studies in seventeenth-century Dutch tomb sculpture*, Zwolle 2003, 43 and Tussenbroek 2006, 182.

65 Scholten 2003, 43, 105,

66 Tussenbroek 2006, 181-183.

67 In Noldus 2004, I erroneously wrote that Claesz stayed in Sweden until 1650. However, he already returned to Amsterdam in 1631; see also Scholten 2003, 253.

68 In 1637, Pieter de Keyser executed the funeral monument for Erik Soop and Anna Posse in Skara Cathedral, Sweden.

69 Noldus 2004, 102-104. On Spiering see further B. Noldus, „An "unvergleichbarer Liebhaber" - Peter Spierinck, the art-dealing diplomat", *Scandinavian Journal of History* 31, 2 (2006), 173-185.

70 Det Kongelige Bibliotek, CMB, NKS 1305, 2, a (cf. ovf.) , "Franchoys Spierinx In Delft desen 8 Januarij 1614."

71 Thomas DaCosta Kaufmann, *Court, Cloister, and City. The Art and Culture of Central Europe 1450-1800*, Chicago 1995, in particular Chapter 7.

72 E. Fučíková (ed.), *Rudolf II and Prague. The Court and the City*, Prague 1997.

73 DaCosta Kaufmann 1995, 181.

74 Established by Duke Frederik III at Gottorf Castle, cousin of King Frederik III (reigned 1648-70). Gottorf was an eminent cultural centre where he "*eine kostbare Kunst-Cammereen [hat] angeordnet / und in zweyen Gemächern verlegt*", J.Drees, „Die ‚Gottorfische Kunst-Kammer. Anmerkungen zu ihrer Geschichte nach historischen Textzeugnissen", in: J. Drees & H. Spielmann (eds.), *Gottorf im Glanz des Barock. Kunst und Kultur am Schleswiger Hof 1544-1713*, II: *Die Gottorfer Kunstkammer* , Schleswig, 1997, 12. The basis of the Gottorf collection originated from Paludanus's cabinet. Upon Paludanus's death in 1651, a major part of his collection was bought by Duke Frederik III. The Gottorf cabinet was enriched with treasures every now and again. Amsterdam dealer Gerrit Uylenburgh travelled to Gottorf in 1655 to deliver paintings for 250 *rijksdaler*. Ten years later he delivered engravings and "3 rare Bücher für Jahren", or almanacs (Schmidt 1922, 93). Jürgen Ovens, the Schleswig dukes's portraitist and former Rembrandt pupil, was sent to the city to purchase sculptures and paintings including pieces by Peter Paul Rubens and Pieter Lastman (Lammertse & van der Veen 2006, 260-263). The Gottorf Kunstkammer was transferred to Copenhagen to be incorporated in the Royal Danish Kunstkammer from 1750-51. See B. Gundestrup, *Det Kongelige danske Kunstkammer 1737 / The Royal Danish Kunstkammer 1737*, Copenhagen 1991 and J. Hein, *The treasure collection at Rosenborg Castle, the inventories of 1696 and 1718. Royal heritage and collecting in Denmark-Norway 1500-1900*, Copenhagen 2009.

75 Skougaard 2002; Drees 1997.

76 Besides, Binck made drawings of buildings that could be of his king's interest and ordered an epitaph from Cornelis Floris for Duke Albrecht of Prussia's deceased wife, Princess Dorothea of Denmark and the tomb monument for Frederik I, to be erected in Schleswig Cathedral 1555. On Binck, cf. Steffen Heiberg, "Jacob Binck", in: *Weilbachs Kunstnerleksikon* , 1, Copenhagen 1994, 253-254..

77 Koester 1988, 302 in S. Heiberg (ed.), *Christian IV and Europe: The 19th Art Exhibition of the Council of Europe, Denmark 1988*, Herning 1988.

78 *Inventaire des Raretez qui sont dans le cabinet des antiquitez de la serenissime Reine de Suede. Fait l'an 1652.* KBS, Håndskriftsamlingen, vol. S 4 (cf. above).

79 See Hein 2009 on royal collecting in Denmark.

80 M. Skougaard, "Interiører", in: Heiberg (ed.) 2006, 74.

81 Berg did not have access to the Audience Chamber, which is therefore not described in the 1646 inventory.

82 On the private oratory see H. Johannsen, "Christian IV's Private Oratory in Frederiksborg Castle Chapel", in: Noldus & Roding (eds.) 2007, 165-179; on Honthorst see H. Ragn Jensen, "Christian 4.s malerier", in: Heiberg (ed.) 2006, 81-97.

PIETER ISAACSZ., JACOB VAN DER DOORDT, HANS ROTTENHAMMER AND THEIR ARTISTIC NETWORKS

Heiner Borggrefe, Thomas Fusenig

The present paper deals with some observations on works which have hitherto arisen little attention in the context of Danish art. It is our aim to illustrate the contacts between different artistic milieus which influenced the arts around 1600 in Central Europe, Northern Germany and Denmark.[1] The Danish court painter Pieter Isaacsz. had contacts with different artistic centres, various European courts and was well informed about political events.[2] To know more about this background helps us to understand the close artistic correspondence between the royal Danish court in the time of Christian IV and the much smaller court of Count Ernest of Holstein-Schaumburg (1564 - 1622) at Bückeburg, to the West of Hannover in Northern Germany.[3]

Shortly after his accession to the government in 1601 Count Ernest started to rebuild the castle and made the small town his princely seat. Today the general lay-out of the city, the magnificent main church and some parts of the castle remain in their original state. Its chapel and the doorway in the so-called Golden Chamber give a good overall impression of Ernest's artistic predilections. The count engaged artists of European acclaim.[4] After 1612, when the castle at Bückeburg was full of sculptures, paintings and all types of decorative arts, it became the destination for international travellers like the poet John Taylor from London, whose enthusiastic description of his visit in 1616 includes a euphoric portrayal of the Bückeburg prince.[5]

Among others the count ordered works by Adrian de Vries, Joseph Heintz the Elder and Hans Rottenhammer, who are well known from their outstanding works for Emperor Rudolf II. Shortly after 1620 De Vries sold to count Ernest his marvellous copy of the *Toro Farnese*, which is today at Gotha.[6] The count's funeral monument at Stadthagen is a breathtaking ensemble of sculptures by De Vries.[7] Of course his works are well known in the context of the Danish Renaissance, so that we do not broaden this theme.

Less well known until now is Count Ernest's intent to order a fountain by Adriaen de Vries, which should be placed at the forecourt of Bückeburg castle, in a very similar way to the situation later realized at Frederiksborg castle.[8] In 1615 the Count asked the artist for a design. He wished the fountain adorned with wild or exotic animals, but in general De Vries was free in finding the shape. Two columns in front of the inner bridge of the castle stood close to the fountain. The statues of Hercules and Samson by the sculptor Hans Wulff were put on top of the columns in 1604.[9]

Some years ago the princely family at Bückeburg acquired a hitherto unknown portrait of Ernest of Holstein-Schaumburg that shows the

Fig.1. Jacob van Doordt (attributed), Prince Ernest of Holstein-Schaumburg. Bückeburg castle (Photo Lemgo, Weserrenaissance Museum Schloß Brake).

prince in splendid attire (Fig. 1).[10] The painting resembles Pieter Isaacsz.'s famous portrait of King Christian IV at Frederiksborg, which was painted in 1614 after the victorious Kalmar war (Fig. 2).[11] The prominent hat (*Fürstenhut*) worn by Ernest in the Bückeburg portrait is the symbol of his elevation to the position of Prince of the Holy Roman Empire (*Reichsfürst*) and so documents his closeness to the emperor himself. The portrait can therefore be dated after 1619 and before 1622, when Ernest died. His new title as Prince and Count (*Fürst und Graf*) of Holstein and Schaumburg was a decisive factor in his conflict of 1621 with Christian IV, since the Danish king and his relatives from Gottorf also claimed the exclusive right to the title of Duke of Holstein.[12]

To be frank, at first we considered it possible to attribute the beautiful Bückeburg portrait to Pieter Isaacsz, because of its seemingly close connection to his Christian IV at Frederiksborg. However, on closer inspection differences with Isaacsz.'s style are evident. Although the Bückeburg picture is finely executed, it does not have the sculptural vitality that is a feature of portraits by Isaacsz.. An attribution to the painter Jacob van der Doordt (active 1606-1629) is much more plausible.

Van der Doordt was based in Hamburg, but from 1606 travelled for to stay in Copenhagen, London, Gottorf and Brunswick.[13] He was son of the Hamburg engraver Peter van der Doordt, who engraved some views of the city and made a print after an alchemistical painting by Hans Vredeman de Vries.[14] Jacob van der Doordt was obviously trained in the same tradition of elegant, late-mannerist portraiture as the Amsterdam painter Cornelis Ketel, who was the first teacher of Pieter Isaacsz..[15] Van der Doordt's style suggests that he might have been trained in Am-

Fig.2. Pieter Isaacsz., Christian IV, c. 1614. Hillerød, The Museum of National History, Frederiksborg Castle (Photo Frederiksborg).

sterdam. That may have taken place in the workshop of Ketel, but at the present state it is also allowed to air the speculation, that he was an apprentice to Pieter Isaacsz. around 1600. During a sojourn in England some years later, where his brother Abraham van der Door(d)t became surveyor of king Charles' pictures,[16] Jacob van der Doordt learnt the English manner of miniature portraiture.

Jacob van der Doordt was active about 1612 at the court of Wolfenbüttel, and 1620-21 for the Holstein dukes. Wolfenbüttel was a neighbouring state of Bückeburg, and Duke Heinrich Julius of Braunschweig-Wolfenbüttel was a brother-in-law of King Christian IV.[17] But count Ernest probably knew Van der Doordt from Hamburg, from where Ernest purchased many of his luxury goods. Ernest owned Pinneberg, a small territory near Hamburg, today a part of the modern city.[18]

With regard to the similarities between Bückeburg and Copenhagen, another aspect caught our attention. In 1619 Pieter Isaacsz. painted the ceiling of the Audience Room in Rosenborg castle for King Christian IV. Nowadays the ceiling is to be seen at a different location in the Winter Room, which originally had a stucco ceiling (Fig. 3).[19]

The ceiling has two rhombic-shaped central scenes depicting *The Fall of the Giants* and *The Feast of the Gods*. The latter is inspired by Hendrick Goltzius's famous engraving.[20] The centre pieces are surrounded by eight smaller scenes showing subjects typical of European court painting around 1600 such as, for example, Jupiter and Mercury, Neptune and Minerva.

The design of the former Audience Room ceiling is dependent on European models. In the early 16th century most of the prestigious ceilings followed the ancient Roman coffered type. However, in the second half of the century the Venetian type became widespread throughout courts in Europe. Venetian coffered ceilings have a centrepiece surrounded by smaller paintings that are, for the most part, extravagantly framed.[21]

The most famous examples in Venice are to be seen in the Doge's palace and in the Scuola di San Rocco. Such Venetian-type ceilings also became fashionable north of the Alps, as the "Goldener Saal" in the town hall at Augsburg proves. Around 1610, the council of Gdansk sent a delegation to Venice before deciding to install such a ceiling in their own town hall.[22]

The Rosenborg ceiling follows largely the Venetian type, though the shape of its two centrepieces is somewhat unusual. The rhombic shape is not common for Venetian ceilings, which almost always have rectangular, circular or oval frames. It seems to be a northern invention, of which we hitherto know only one clear forerunner, the *Golden Chamber* in the castle of Bückeburg (Fig. 4).[23]

Unlike Adrian de Vries and Joseph Heintz, who worked for Prince Ernest in their studios at Prague and Augsburg, Hans Rottenhammer travelled twice to Bückeburg. In the summer 1609 and 1612 he stayed at Bückeburg.[24] He worked on diverse pictures for the princely rooms.[25]

Ernest probably came into contact with Rottenhammer during a journey, since the young count stayed repeatedly in Italy. As a young man with only few political responsibilities he travelled for almost a year via Florence and Rome to Malta (September 1589 - August 1590). In 1593 he started a second trip to Italy in order to study at Bologna and Florence, from which he returned in 1594.[26] On both occasions he may have met with members of the circle of Northern painters at Rome and Venice. At this time Hans Rottenhammer, Joseph Heintz and also Pieter Isaacsz. were living in Rome and/or Venice.[27]

Rottenhammer worked on two ceilings for Bückeburg castle. Only one is known today. 1732 a fire destroyed the east wing of the castle, where the most prestigious rooms were located, except the chapel of the castle. The only room, which gives an impression of the splendour of its original interior today, is called the Golden Chamber (described in older inventories as the White Chamber, probably because of the white walls).[28]

The ceiling today contains four paintings by Rottenhammer depicting the *Four Elements*.[29] Unfortunately, the centrepiece was removed in the late 19th century and inserted into a newly built neo-Renaissance ceiling in the nearby castle of Stadthagen. The painting was dismantled again in the early 1920s, when the family of Schaumburg-Lippe removed furnishings and works of art from the castle. Today Rottenhammer's Bückeburg centrepiece is lost, and its former presence at Stadthagen known only from an old photograph from the late 19th century (Fig. 5).[30]

The subject of the picture in the centre was probably some sort of gathering of the Olympian gods. Count Ernest's old guardian, Simon VI zur Lippe owned an early masterpiece by Abraham Bloemaert, the wedding of Peleus and Thetis.[31]

Fig.4. Hans Rottenhammer, Ceiling of the Golden chamber. Bückeburg castle (Photo Lemgo, Weserrenaissance Museum Schloß Brake).

Fig.3. Pieter Isaacsz., Ceiling of the Winter room. Copenhagen, Rosenborg castle (Photo Rosenborg).

This or a similar subject with ample occasion to show female beauty would have been a good occasion to show Rottenhammer's talents.

You will certainly have noticed that Rottenhammer's Bückeburg centrepiece had a rhombic shape like that of the Audience Room in Rosenborg castle. The Bückeburg ceiling was laid out in 1606 (or shortly after 1612 at latest). So it is fair to assume it influenced the Rosenborg ceiling, which was constructed in 1619.

Both the Bavarian-Italian artist Rottenhammer and the Danish-Dutch painter Pieter Isaacsz. moved in culturally similar environments. Probably they knew each other personally from the very beginning of their careers at the court of Munich. Pieter Isaacsz. was Von Aachen's young collaborator ca. 1585 – 1592, when Von Aachen worked in Cologne, Munich, Augsburg, Venice and Rome, before he later became court artist of the emperor at Prague.[32] Rottenhammer finished 1588 his apprenticeship in the workshop of the Bavarian court painter Hans Donauer. His formal education as painter ended thus with Von Aachen's and Isaacsz.' stay in Munich.[33] Rottenhammer subsequently went to Venice, where he arrived 1591 and was 1594/95 at Rome.[34]

In his early works Isaacsz. was clearly influenced by Hans von Aachen. This is not surprising, because the latter was a strong artistic personality, who rendered his Italian impressions with an original and formative power. But it seems that Isaacsz. was also influenced by other painters. The *Baptism of Christ* in Houston is without any doubt by Isaacsz, because the preparatory drawing in Paris gives clear evidence of his authorship (Fig. 6).[35] In the *Baptism* we can detect the influence of the Venetian tradition. The group of angels in heaven refers indirectly to Titian's *Baptism* for Giovanni Ram in about 1520.[36] The subject was rendered repeatedly by Veronese and Tintoretto. Hans Rottenhammer came to a analogous solution in a successful composition, which is known in different versions.[37] Hans Rottenhammer transformed the theme in a manner typical of his many compositions on copper that are characterised by the inclusion of numerous small figures (Fig. 7). Schlichtenmaier dates the composition with reference on a drawing by Rottenhammer around 1595/96, almost the time when Isaacsz. probably painted his Houston picture.[38]

The motif of a cloud of hovering angels was used repeatedly by Rottenhammer. A picture in the Ambrosiana shows a winter landscape with a view of Antwerp, which was painted by Brueghel, and hovering angels, who are by Rottenhammer.[39] Since Brueghel started to paint Flemish landscapes only in the first years of the 17th century, this cooperation with Rottenhammer would be from a later date.

We do not know much about Isaacsz's travels in Europe and Italy but the similarity of his Houston-painting to Rottenhammer's *Baptism of Christ* may indicate he saw the latter around 1600

Fig.5. Stadthagen castle, former ballroom with Rottenhammer's centrepiece of the Golden chamber (Photo Lemgo, Weserrenaissance Museum Schloß Brake).

Fig. 6. Pieter Isaacsz., Baptism of Christ, c. 1590. Houston, The Museum of Fine Arts. From Badeloch Noldus & Juliette Roding (eds.), *Pieter Isaacsz. (1568-1625) Court Painter, Art Dealer and Spy*, Turnhout 2007, p. 62.

in Venice or Prague. The reason why Isaacsz. might have been interested in Rottenhammer's invention probably has little to do with the iconography or the composition. Rottenhammer enjoyed some fame as a painter of extremely fine works on copper. Together with Paul Bril and Jan Brueghel the Elder he established this new type of cabinet painting on copper. This happened about 1595 in Rome, where curial collectors discovered the charm of his vivid and colourful small copper paintings.[40] Pieter Isaacsz. may have been attracted by Rottenhammer's pretty and fashionable manner of painting on copper and was inspired to follow him.

The Houston *Baptism of Christ* seems to be not the only artistic contact between Pieter Isaacsz and Hans Rottenhammer. Isaacsz's *Vanitas* at Basel is another connection (Fig. 8).[41] The painting was strongly inspired by Titian's *Venus with a lute player* in the Fitzwilliam Museum in Cambridge (Fig. 9).[42] Isaacsz. gives a free interpretation of the reclining female figure and quotes the lute player exactly. Titian's marvellous canvas once belonged to the collection of Rudolf II. It is unclear when it came to Prague. But it seems probable that Rottenhammer bought it for the imperial collection about 1600. We know from contemporary sources that Rottenhammer purchased a number of Venetian paintings in order to sell them to Rudolf II.[43] A clue for the assumption that he sold Titian's Fitzwilliam-Venus to Prague is that he himself painted a reclining Venus on copper after it (Fig. 10).[44]

It seems that Rottenhammer was himself never at Prague, but had some contact with Rudolf II. In 1600 he painted the *Wedding of Neptune and*

Fig. 7. Hans Rottenhammer, Baptism of Christ. Augsburg, Deutsche Barockgalerie. From Heiner Borggrefe, Lubomír Konecný, Vera Lübkes and Vít Vlas (eds.), *Hans Rottenhammer, begehrt – vergessen – neu entdeckt*, Munich 2008, p. 124.

Amphitrite for the emperor.⁴⁵ In the foreground we see three children collecting the fruits of the sea. They could have inspired Isaacsz., who also shows a group of three homo-bulla children in the foreground of his *Vanitas* in the manner of Rottenhammer. Both paintings, Rottenhammer's *Feast of Gods* and Isaacsz *Vanitas*, are dated 1600. Isaacsz could have seen Rottenhammer's *Feast of the Gods* and Titian's *Fitzwilliam Venus* either in Venice, in Rottenhammer's workshop, or in Prague. The fact that his *Vanitas* was painted the same year as Rottenhammer's *Wedding* may indicate that Isaacsz saw both paintings while they were in Venice or Prague in 1600.

Isaacsz could also have seen Rottenhammer's *Baptism of Christ* at this time. In any case Isaacsz.'s Houston *Baptism* cannot have been painted before Rottenhammer invented his composition around 1596. Isaacsz could have seen the Bückeburg ceiling in Bückeburg itself or in Augsburg where Rottenhammer worked from 1605/06.

That Isaacsz. actually was in Bückeburg is not totally out of the question, since King Christian IV and count Ernest had some political dealings with each other. Both princes knew each other quite well, but one can hardly say that they were close friends. Christian once called Ernest an *"Italian and Spanish count"*, which was meant as a major insult to a protestant German prince.⁴⁶

The political situation was complex - as was so often the case in the Holy Roman Empire. The king and the count were both Lutherans, but concurred on economic resources and political renommé. As mentioned before, Christian and Ernest were neighbours. The small territory of Pinneberg in the direct vicinity of Hamburg bordered on Danish territory. Ernest tried to bring merchants to Pinneberg from Hamburg who felt uncomfortable with the strict Lutheran regiment

Fig. 8. Pieter Isaacsz., Allegory of Vanity, 1600. Kunstmuseum Basel. From Noldus & Roding, p. 51.

in the growing port. Nominally, Hamburg belonged to the dukes of Holstein. In 1616 Christian IV founded a new city, Glückstadt, some kilometres down the river Elbe.[47] Both princes wanted their share of the growing economic trade on the river. For this reason Christian IV was interested in buying Pinneberg but Ernest was not willing to sell. In 1621 Christian invaded Pinneberg, and only withdrew his troops after Ernest paid a high ransom of 50.000 thalers.

The conflict had some underlying causes. Count Ernest was eager to acquire the title of *Reichsfürst*, prince of the Holy Roman Empire, in order to satisfy his desire for dynastic advancement. In 1618 King Christian informed emperor Matthias that he was interested in acquiring the domain of Pinneberg if Count Ernest were to remain without a lineal heir. On the 28th of September 1618 Christian visited Pinneberg castle. Ernest however persisted in his quest to have his personal ownership of Pinneberg recognised and after some legal wrangling dispatched the famous lawyer Melchior Goldast von Haiminsfeld to the coronation of emperor Ferdinand II in 1619. Goldast was successful (with the help of 100.000 Goldthaler), so that from then on Ernest was allowed to call himself Prince and Count of Holstein and Schaumburg.

Ironically the emperor asked Ernest to act on his behalf as an envoy to England and to Denmark in order to dissuade the kings from supporting the election of the palatinate count Frederick as King of Bohemia. The Bohemian conflict quickly escalated. For Christian it was quite out of the question to support the emperor. In 1620 he raised an army in support of the Dutch project of a protestant alliance. When this undertaking failed, King Christian occupied Pinneberg with his troops and extorted from Ernest of Holstein-Schaumburg the above-mentioned ransom.

It is possible that Van der Doordt's picture served as a representative portrait at the castle of Pinneberg. The similarity with that of Christian IV by Isaacsz. may be an expression of a competition of power. In any case it was commissioned in order to visualize Ernest's claim to the controversial title.

On the occasion of this conflict various delegations moved between Bückeburg, Copenhagen and Vienna from 1618 on. In view of the parallels in the structure of the ceilings in Copenhagen and Bückeburg it is tempting to assume that Pieter Isaacsz. may have learnt about the Rottenhammer ceiling from some envoy. But it is also possible that he himself visited Bückeburg earlier. Isaacsz. may have visited Bückeburg during one of

Fig. 9. Titian, Venus and Cupid with a lute-player. Cambridge, Fitzwilliam Museum. From Noldus & Roding, p. 51.

his travels to the Netherlands.[48] Another former pupil of Hans von Aachen, Christoph Gertner, was probably working in Bückeburg at about the same time as Rottenhammer painted the ceiling for the so-called *White Chamber*.[49]

To conclude: The great similarity between the artistic patronage at the small court of Ernst von Holstein and Schaumburg and his much more powerful neighbour Christian IV has various reasons. A decisive factor may have been, that both were rivals in the field of politics. The common artistic taste was based on Italian art as practised in the late 16th century at Rome and Venice and brought to the North mainly by artists from the Netherlands. A large number of the court artists spent some time in Italy and moved in the same circle of foreign painters. Therefore we should reconstruct the system of contacts which existed between individuals who may be separated by long distances and political borders and to establish the social network of artistic and personal relationships in order to learn more about the many ways in which contacts may be realized.

For these reasons we certainly need to pay more attention to archival material. On the other hand, we should always bear in mind that not all contacts are documented in the scattered heritage of our archives and the few artistic biographies of the time. In this regard, simple biographical positivism is too timid an approach to cover all cultural dimensions.

A second reason for the congruence of artistic means that art historians usually call style may be associated, in the case of Bückeburg and Copenhagen, with the common function of art as the bearer of a symbolic message denoting social

Fig. 10. Hans Rottenhammer, Reclining Venus, private property. From Borggrefe, Konecný, Lübkes and Vlnas, p. 40.

standing and political ambition. To understand this function of art better, our second task is to reconstruct the patron's own perspective, with their underlying interests. In this way we can hope to deconstruct the prevailing history of styles into a story of art as part of our past. This view of style as a socio-symbolic language will help us to reframe the Northern European Renaissance in general and the place of Denmark in it.

Notes

1. For an overview of the scattered literature in the field of Central Europe see Thomas DaCosta Kaufmann, *Art and Architecture in Central Europe, 1550-1620. An annotated bibliography*, Marburg 2002².

2. On Pieter Isaacsz see H. C. Bering Liisberg, "Peter Isacksen", in: *Kunstmuseets Aarsskrift* XI-XII (1926), 196-218; N. de Roever, "Drie Amsterdamse schilders (Pieter Isaaksz, Abraham Vinck, Cornelis van der Voort)", *Oud Holland* 3 (1885), 171-208; Eliška Fučíková, "Towards a reconstruction of Pieter Isaacsz.' earlier career", in: G. Cavalli Björkman (ed.), *Netherlandish Mannerism, Papers given at a symposium in the Nationalmuseum Stockholm, 1984*, Stockholm 1985, 165-175; Juliette Roding & Marja Stompé, *Pieter Isaacsz (1569-1625) - een Nederlandse schilder, kunsthandelaar en diplomat aan het Deense hof*, Hilversum 1997; Heiner Borggrefe, "Pieter Isaacsz in the Company of Hans von Aachen", in: Badeloch Noldus & Juliette Roding (eds.), *Pieter Isaacsz – Court Painter, Art Trader and Spy*, Turnhout 2007, 42-57. For the importance of courtly agents and envoys see Badeloch Noldus, *Trade in good taste - relations in architecture and culture between the Dutch Republic and the Baltic world in the seventeenth century*, Turnhout 2004; Hans Cools, Marika Keblusek & Badeloch Noldus (eds.), *Your humble servant - agents in early modern Europe*, Hilversum 2006.

3. For the Danish court see Steffen Heiberg (ed.), *Christian IV and Europa: the 19th Art Exhibition of the Council of Europe, Denmark 1988*, Herning 1988. For Bückeburg see Heiner Borggrefe, *Die Residenz Bückeburg – Architekturgestaltung im frühneuzeitlichen Fürstenstaat*, Marburg 1994; Helge Bei der Wieden, *Ein norddeutscher Renaissancefürst. Ernst zu Holstein-Schaumburg 1569-1622*, Bielefeld 1994 (with further literature); Heiner Borggrefe, *Schloss Bückeburg. Höfischer Glanz – fürstliche Repräsentation*, Hannover 2008.

4. A documented overview on local and international artists at Bückeburg gives Johannes Habich, *Die künstlerische Gestaltung der Residenz Bückeburg durch Fürst Ernst (1601-1622)*, Bückeburg 1969, and Borggrefe 2008.

5. Borggrefe 1994, 249: "*and in a word, [count Ernest] is one of the best accomplished gentlemen in Europe for his person, port, and princely magnificence*".

6. Frits Scholten (ed.), *Adriaen de Vries 1556 – 1626*. Exhibition catalogue, Amsterdam, Stockholm, Los Angeles, Zwolle l998, cat. 33, 206 – 209; José Kastler & Vera Lüpkes (eds.), *Die Weser - EinFluß in Europa: Aufbruch in die Neuzeit*. Exhibition catalogue, Weserrenaissance-Museum Schloß Brake, Lemgo 2000, 304-311. An inventory of the castle from 1635 mentions in the rooms of the count "*1 Marmelsteinen tisch, worauf der gegoßene ochße steht*" (a marble table, on which the cast of the ox stands).

7. Scholten (ed.) 1998, 29; Lars Olof Larsson, *Adrian de Vries in Schaumburg. Die Werke für Fürst Ernst zu Holstein-Schaumburg 1613-1621*, Ostfildern 1998, 46-71.

8. Lars Olof Larsson, *Adriaen de Vries*, Wien, Munich 1967, 80; Habich 1969, 58. For Frederiksborg see Steffen Heiberg (ed.), *Christian 4. og Frederiksborg*, Copenhagen 2006, 46-47.

9. Borggrefe 1994, 95.

10. First published in Bei der Wieden 1994, 49.

11. Heiberg (ed.) 1988, cat. 185, fig. 14.

12. Helge Bei der Wieden, *Fürst Ernst Graf von Holstein-Schaumburg und seine Wirtschaftspolitik*, Bückeburg 1961, 58.

13. Roding & Stompé 1997, 37. – Steffen Heiberg, "Jakob van Doordt", in: *Weilbachs Kunstnerleksikon²*, 2, Copenhagen 1994, 155-156 (with further literature).

14. Heiner Borggrefe, Paul Huvenne & Vera Lüpkes (eds.), *Hans Vredeman de Vries und die Renaissance im Norden*. Exhibition catalogue, Munich 2002, cat. 185, 345-347.

15. Roding & Stompé 1997, 11. For Ketel see Nicolas Galley, "Cornelis Ketel - a painter without a brush", *Artibus et historiae*, 25, 49 (2004), 87-100 (with further literature).

16. Stefanie Kollmann, *Niederländische Künstler und Kunst im London des 17. Jahrhunderts*, Hildesheim, Zürich & New York 2000, 183.

17. Silke Gartenbröecker (ed.), *Hofkunst der Spätrenaissance. Braunschweig-Wolfenbüttel und das kaiserliche Prag um 1600*. Exhibition catalogue, Braunschweig 1998 (unfortunately with only passing references to Danish connections).

18. Bei der Wieden 1961, 187-192. - The importance of Pinneberg for the self-image of the counts of Schaumburg illustrates a big painted map, which is today in

the castle at Bückeburg; Lorenz Petersen, "Daniel Freses 'Landtafel' der Grafschaft Hollstein (Pinneberg) aus dem Jahre 1588", *Zeitschrift der Gesellschaft für Schleswig-Holsteinische Geschichte*, 70-71 (1943), 224-246.

19 The ceiling pictures have been moved to this room in 1705, cf. Roding & Stompé 1997, 52-54; Jørgen Hein, "Christian 4. og Rosenborgs billedverden", in: Jørgen Hein et al. (eds.), *Christian 4. og Rosenborg*, Copenhagen 2006, 25-50, especially 35.

20 Meir Stein, "Da muserne kom til Valby bakke…", in: same, *Christian den Fjerdes Billedverden*, Copenhagen 1987, 9-19; see also Hugo Johannsen, "The Graphic Art of Hendrick Goltzius as Prototype for Danish Art during the Reign of Christian IV", *Art in Denmark 1600-1650, Leids Kunsthistorisch Jaarboek* 2 (1983), 85-110.

21 Wolfgang Wolters, *Plastische Deckendekorationen des Cinquecento in Venedig und im Veneto*, Berlin 1968.

22 Susan Tipton, *RES PUBLICA BENE ORDINATA. Regentenspiegel und Bilder vom guten Regiment. Rathausdekorationen in der Frühen Neuzeit*, Hildesheim, Zürich & New York 1996, 201-218 (Augsburg), 239-292 (Gdansk). - For Gdansk see Borggrefe, Huvenne & Lüpkes 2002, cat. 168-170, 323-333.

23 Habich 1969, 147-148.

24 Habich 1969, 22-24, 152.; Kastler & Lüpkes 2000, 300-303.

25 Harry Schlichtenmaier, *Studien zum Werk Hans Rottenhammers des Älteren (1564-1625). Maler und Zeichner mit Werkkatalog*. Dissertation, Tübingen 1988, 146-147, 256-257, G I63-66. Heiner Borggrefe, Lubomir Konecný, Vera Lüpkes, Vit Vinas (ed.), *Hans Rottenhammer – begehrt, vergessen, ney entdeckt*, München 2008. – Heiner Borggrefe, Lubomir Konecný, V. Lüpkes, Michael Bischoff (ed.) *Hans Rottenhammer (1564-1625) – Ergebnisse des in Kooperation mit dem Institut für Kunstgeschichte der Tschechischen Akademie der Wissenschaften durchgeführten internationalen Symposions (17.-18. Februar 2007)*, Marburg 2007. – Heiner Borggrefe, Hans Rottenhammer and his influence on the Imperial Collection of Prague, in: *Studia Rudolphina* 7, Prag 2007, 7-21.

26 Bei der Wieden 1961, 30.

27 Rottenhammer stayed only 1594-1595 in Rome, see Michel Hochmann, "Hans Rottenhammer and Pietro Mera: Two northern artists in Rome and Venice", *Burlington Magazine* 145 (2003), 641-645. - In 1593 Isaacsz was in Rome, where he received a visit of his younger brother; Roding & Stompé 1997, 15. - Heintz was 1584-1587 in Rome and then till 1589 in Venice; on a second stay in Rome 1592-1595, see Nicole Dacos (ed.), *Fiamminghi a Roma 1508 – 1608. Kunstenaars uit de nederlanden en het prinsbisdom Luik te Rome tijdens de Renaissance*. Exhibition catalogue, Brussels, Rome 1999, 229.

28 Borggrefe 1994, 32.

29 Schlichtenmaier 1988, cat. G I 63-66; Rudolf Peltzer, "Hans Rottenhammer", *Jahrbuch der Kunsthistorischen Sammlungen des Allerhöchsten Kaiserhauses* 33 (1916), 293-365, 308, 338, 344, Verz. I, Nr. 14 a, Tf. 35.

30 See Heiner Borggrefe & Guido von Büren, *Schloß Stadthagen – eine Residenz der Renaissance*, Hannover 2008.

31 Marcel G. Roethlisberger, *Abraham Bloemaert and his sons. Paintings and prints*, Doornspijk 1993, 1, 62-65. Kastler & Lüpkes 2000, 284-287.

32 Thomas Fusenig e.a. (ed.), *Hans von Aachen (1552-1615). Hofkünstler in Europa*, München 2010. Roding & Stompé 1997, 11-14.

33 For the many commissions which Von Aachen received in Munich in these years, see Joachim Jacoby, *Hans von Aachen 1552 – 1615*, Munich 2000, 21-23; Borggrefe 2007, 46-47.

34 Hochmann 2003. Harry Schlichtenmaier speculated if Rottenhammer went together with Van Aachen to Venice, when Van Aachen closed down his workshop there. See Schlichtenmaier 1988, 26. In this case he must have also travelled together with Isaacsz, see Borggrefe 2007, 46.

35 Roding & Stompé 1997, 13, ill. 3; Fucikova 1985, 165-175, 172, ill. 15 and 16. Emmanuelle Brugerolles, *Renaissance et Manierisme dans les Ecoles du Nord. Dessins des collections de l'Ecole des Beaux Arts*, Paris 1985, 222-223.

36 Filippo Pedrocco, *Tiziano*, Milan 2000, 90.

37 Schlichtenmaier 1988, G I 12.

38 Schlichtenmaier 1988, Z I 8.

39 Bert W. Meijer, *Fiammingi e Olandesi, dipinti dalle collezioni lombarde*, Milan 2002, 127-128, no. 72.

40 A general introduction to this theme is *Copper as canvas - two centuries of masterpiece paintings on copper, 1575 – 1775*. Exhibition catalogue, Phoenix Art Museum, New York 1999. - See for Rome: Francesca Cappelletti, "Enticement of the North: Landscape, Myth and Gleaming Metal supports", in: Beverly Louise Brown (ed.), *Genius of Rome. 1592-1623*. Exhibition catalogue, London, Rome 2001, 174-205.

41 Roding & Stompé 1997, 34, ill. 13.

42 Harold Wethey, *The Paintings of Titian,* III, London 1975, 196. - Heiner Borggrefe, "Tizians ruhende Göttinnen und Dienerinnen der Liebe", in: Andreas

Tacke (ed.), *"…wir wollen der Liebe Raum geben" – Konkubinate geistlicher und weltlicher Fürsten um 1500*, Göttingen 2006, 393-421; Borggrefe 2007.

43 Schlichtenmaier 1988, D 25.6: "*vnd wolle er mir (Hainhofer) dises vnd die andere altern stück wol auß bessern vnd frisch machen alß wie er dem Kaiser vil der gleichn stück in venedig haufft habe*".

44 Rüdiger Klessmann, "Eine unbekannte venezianische Venus von Hans Rottenhammer", *Niederdeutsche Beiträge zur Kunstgeschichte* 28 (1989), 131-142.

45 Schlichtenmaier 1988, G I 37. The identification of this picture with one which was mentioned by Ridolfi as painted for the emperor for 500 scudi, was proposed by Peltzer 1916, 266. - See Schlichtenmaier 1988, Q 3, 458.

46 For the following see Bei der Wieden 1961, 54-60; Hans-Dieter Loose, *Hamburg und Christian IV. Von Dänemark während des Dreissigjährigen Krieges. Ein Beitrag zur Geschichte der hamburgischen Reichsunmittelbarkeit*, Hamburg 1963, 18.

47 For Glückstadt see Juliette G. Roding, *Christiaan IV van Denemarken (1588 – 1648). Architectuur en stedebouw van een luthers vorst*, Alkmaar 1991.

48 In the years between 1609 and his final move to Denmark 1614 only little is known about Isaacsz.'s activities. In 1618 and 1620 trips to the Netherlands are documented; Roding & Stompé 1997, 31, 45, 62.

49 Isaacsz. may have been also at Wolfenbüttel in order to meet with Christoph Gertner. It was Heinrich Geissler who first pointed out that the Wolfenbüttel court painter Christoph Gertner must have been another pupil of Hans von Aachen; see Heinrich Geissler, *Zeichnung in Deutschland. Deutsche Zeichner 1540-1640*, 2 vols., Stuttgart 1979-80, 2, 118-121; see furthermore Jürgen Zimmer, "Christoph Gertner, Hofmaler in Wolfenbüttel – Eine neu entdeckte Danaë und ein vorläufiges Werkverzeichnis", *Niederdeutsche Beiträge zur Kunstgeschichte* 23 (1984), 117-138.

HENDRICK DE KEYSER AND DENMARK

Konrad Ottenheym

Introduction

In many publications 'Netherlandish' influence on Danish Renaissance architecture is simply limited to scrolled gables. Too often, any strap-work scroll on a Danish façade is immediately said to have been inspired by Vredeman de Vries or one of the other artists who had emigrated from the Low Countries into the Baltic region.[1] Also the influence of Hendrick de Keyser, sculptor and architect in Amsterdam during the first two decades of the 17th century, is often indiscriminately related to the same type of scrolled gables. Recently a more realistic view of Vredeman de Vries' influence in Northern Europe has been introduced.[2] This paper focuses on de Keyser's contribution to the Danish Renaissance. Comparing the architecture of de Vries and de Keyser, one should be aware that the latter is of a younger generation (de Vries lived 1526-1609, de Keyser 1565-1621). De Keyser's work really can and must be distinguished from that of his predecessors. Those among us today, who seek to detect contemporary Dutch influences in the magnificent building programme of Christian IV in the first decades of the 17th century, have to look closely at the modern features of de Keyser's architectural design that had not existed before in the so-called Vredeman de Vries repertoire.

The Marble Gallery of Frederiksborg, 1619-1622

The crowning witness of de Keyser's contribution to the Danish renaissance is the famous Marble Gallery of Frederiksborg Castle (Fig. 1). The historical facts have been well known for over half a century, especially from Elisabeth Neurdenburg's publication of 1943.[3] To summarise that history briefly:

In December 1619 Hans van Steenwinckel was appointed royal architect by Christian IV to succeed his brother Lourens, who had died the same year.[4] Earlier in the same year, in February, Hans van Steenwinckel received the commission to construct the new gallery of Frederiksborg according to designs that were delivered to him.[5] Thus, most probably, his brother Lourens was the original designer of it. The gallery consists of two superimposed arcades of seven bays, Doric below, Ionic above. The upper arches were crowned by seven sandstone sculptures of Antique gods and goddesses, representing the planetary system.[6] The balustrade of the first-floor arcade was filled in with various sea creatures, sculptured in relief. It is not certain whether the statues within the niches belonged to the original plan.

The seven statues on top, as well as the sandstone reliefs, were sculpted in Amsterdam, in the

workshop of Hendrick de Keyser. He was personally responsible for the design, while the actual execution in his workshop was under the control of his foreman, Geraert Lambertsz. In 1619 Theodorus Rodenburg visited de Keyser's workshop to look for some able sculptors who might be interested in coming to Denmark to work for Christian IV. In his letter to the Danish king, written after this visit, Rodenburg said he had seen the statues and reliefs for Christian IV under execution in de Keyser's workshop:

> "'t'Amsterdam zijnde heb ick wesen besichtigen het werkhuys van Mr. Hendrick, die besondere beelden en figuuren voor u Kon. Ma.t gemaeckt heeft en noch onderhanden heeft, so hy seyden, Welcke beelden en figuuren alle ghehouden zijn door een van zyn princepaelste kneghts, ghenaemt Geraert Lambertsen".[7]

(Translation:)
"In Amsterdam I visited Master Hendrick's workshop that has made some exceptional statues and sculptures for Your Maj. and he is still working on them. These statues and sculptures are wrought by one of his principal assistants, called Geraert Lambertsen".

The *trait-d'union* between the project of the Frederiksborg gallery and de Keyser in Amsterdam was the Dutch building constructor and stone merchant, Lorenz Pietersz. Sweys. In 1619 he had shipped sandstone from Gotland for the original

Fig. 2. Frederiksborg Castle, Marble Gallery, designed by Hans II van Steenwinckel. After Salomon de Bray and Cornelis Danckerts, Architectura Moderna, ofte Bouwinge van onsen tyt, Amsterdam 1631, plate XLII.

Fig.1. Hillerød, Frederiksborg Castle, Marble Gallery, designed by Hans II van Steenwinckel, executed in Hendrick de Keyser's workshop, 1618-1620 (Photo Hugo Johannsen).

statues and reliefs for the gallery to de Keyser in Amsterdam.[8] In 1620, Sweys was sent by Christian IV to Archduke Albrecht of Habsburg in Brussels, asking permission for the exportation of blue freestone and red and black marble from the Southern Low Countries for the gallery of Frederiksborg and the altar in the Trinity Church of Christiansstad.[9]

Designs of the Frederiksborg gallery must have been handed over to de Keyser, with some raw sketches by Steenwinckel, indicating where and in what scale sculpture was demanded. The sculptor had a free hand for the exact appearance of these statues and sculptures as was usual in such cases.[10] In 1631, ten years after de Keyser's death, a series of engravings was published, using various drawings left in the latter's office. The book was called Architectura Moderna.[11] It contained 44 engravings of the most important buildings erected by de Keyser in Amsterdam and elsewhere in the previous decades; churches, towers, gates, and a number of façades of private buildings. At the end of the volume, some designs of others are added, among them an illustration of two bays of the gallery of Frederiksborg (Fig. 2) and some details of the orders. This engraving was presumably based on Steenwinckel's drawing that had been sent to Amsterdam in 1619 – the architecture is clearly depicted while the sculptures are only vaguely indicated. The text to the illustration, plate XLII, explains clearly that the architecture is the design of Hans van Steenwinckel. Hendrick de Keyser is not even mentioned here:

"Galderije des Konighs van Denemercken tot Frederickx-burgh, gedaen by Hans Steenwinckel.

De Konstvoedende vruchtbaerheyd, van onse tijdtsche Eeuw en Landt is sodanigh, dat de Koningen selfs van uyt den Noorden die by ons komen soecken, en bearbeyden de selve van alhier by hen te trecken, en onses konstens dienst aldaer te gebruycken, 't welck met dese tegenwoordige Galderije, waer te zijn bewesen werdt, die gedaen is by den vindigen en seer verzierlijcken Hans Steenwinckel, den welcken wy hier met desen Koninghlijken wercke wel billijck hebben te gedencken. Seker dese Galderije (welcke is gemaeckt voor, en ten dienste van zyne Koningl: Majesteyt van Denemercken, in zijn Koninglijcke Hof tot *Frederickx-burgh*) is een werck van grooter kostelijckheydt, met overvloet van gesneden, verheven, en uyt-gehouwen wercken, en is by near in zijn geheel of immer ten meerdeele, van Marbre en andere kostelijcke steen ghebout; hy begrijpt in de lengde seven alsulcke boghen als hier vertoont werden, en houdt in de hooghde twee stadien, zijnde de onderste van *Dorische*, en d'ander van *Ionischen* wercke; yder deser vacken of twee boven-een-staende bogen, zijn toe-ge-eyghent aen eene der seven Planeet-Goden, 't welcke in yder boghe met beeldnisse, en alle soorten van wercken daer op passende werdt uyt-gebeeldt, en bovendien komt het beeldt van yder der Planeten, selve boven op het opperste van zijn toe-ghewyde boge te staen, gelijck uyt dit stucks-wyse vertoon der tegenwoordighe Bouw-form van de gheseyde Galderije XLII te sien is: Wy vertoonen van dies so weynigh, om dattet genoegh is voor de verstandige, omme hier voorts de hoedanigheydt van 't geheel uyt te begrypen ende te verstaan, also het doch alle, uytgenomen de beelden en beeldenisse, een selvige wreck is".

(Translation:)
"Gallery of the King of Denmark at Frederiksborg, by Hans Steenwinckel.

In our time the art of our country is flourishing in such a way that it attracts even kings from the north who persuade artists to come and work in their countries. Such is the case with this gallery, made by Hans Steenwinckel, an innovative master and inventor of elegant details, whom we want to praise with the publication of this royal work. This gallery (made for His Majesty the King of Denmark in his royal residence of Frederiksborg) is a precious work, with an abundance of sculptured details in high relief, constructed almost completely in marble and other precious stones. It is seven arches wide; all like those shown in print, and it has two levels: the lower arcade is of the *Doric* order and the upper one is *Ionic*. Each bay of two superimposed arches is dedicated to one of the seven Planet-Gods, with accordingly sculptured decorations in the niches and elsewhere. Moreover, statues of the Gods are placed on the top of the upper arches, as shown in the illustration of the actual situation of the gallery aforementioned, XLII. We show

Fig. 3. Hendrick de Keyser, Marine Gods and Godesses. After Cornelis Danckerts, *Nouveau livre des Dieux et Déesses de la Marine del'invention de Henri de Caiser*, Amsterdam, s.a., plate 1.

only a small part of the gallery since this will be enough for the educated reader to understand its complete appearance. All seven bays are equal except the statues and sculptured plaquettes".

There is a second printed source from Amsterdam informing us that Hendrick de Keyser was the designer of the sculptured parts of this gallery. At an unknown date, the publisher of the Architectura Moderna, Cornelis Danckerts, published a series of twelve small engravings designed by Hendrick de Keyser, showing various sea creatures and gods from the Frederiksborg gallery (Fig. 3, 4), titled, *Nouveau livre des Dieux et Déesses de la Marine del inventio de Henri de Caiser / Bouckje van zeegoden en godinnen geinveteert door Hendrik d'Caiser*.[12]

The twelve engravings show six gods and goddesses in sea chariots as well as six sea creatures, half man half sea horse, copied from the designs of the reliefs of the first-floor balustrade of the Frederiksborg gallery. The elongated models with the gods on chariots are used for the reliefs under the open arches of the gallery; the smaller ones with sea creatures are placed in between, under the niches.

Hendrick de Keyser and Hans van Steenwinckel the Younger

The workshop of Hendrick de Keyser had a wealth of international relations. In 1595 Hendrick Jansz., son of Jan Hendricx, master bricklayer of the city of Embden, came to Amsterdam as an apprentice of de Keyser.[13] Nicholas Stone came from London in 1607 to stay for six years in de Keyser's workshop. He even became Hendrick de Keyser's son-in-law.[14] Later, back in England, Nicholas Stone became one of the most important master masons of his time, cooperating for example, with Inigo Jones at the Banqueting House in Whitehall. In 1611 Hans Schut from Gdansk was accepted as an apprentice in de Keyser's workshop.[15] Presumably de Keyser had also been in contact with the Steenwinckel brothers from Denmark long before the gallery project at Frederiksborg. Seventeen years earlier, in 1602, Lourens and Hans Steenwinckel were sent to Amsterdam to finish their training after the death of their father.[16] Some scholars suggest they may have stayed some time in de Keyser's workshop during the following years (their return to Denmark is proved in archival sources after 1610 only). Unfortunately the apprentice register of the Amsterdam Guild of St Barbara, the guild of stonemasons and sculptors as well as bricklayers, is preserved only from 1610 onwards. Nevertheless the hypothesis that both the van Steenwinckel brothers stayed with de Keyser for some time is still quite reasonable regarding the international connections of the latter's workshop. According to the guild regulations, the regular period of apprenticeship was two to four years, in which time an apprentice was trained in stone-cutting, as well as sculpting portraits and architectural ornamentations (het steenhouwen, contrefeyten ende alle cyraet te maecken).[17]

Since the case of the Frederiksborg gallery evidently illustrates the cooperation between de Keyser and Steenwinckel at that time, one may wonder whether these contacts also had some

Fig. 4. Hendrick de Keyser, Marine Gods and Godesses. After Danckerts, plate 2,3,8 and 9.

influence on van Steenwinckel's architecture. In other words, can we find some typical 'de Keyser' elements in the Danish royal works of the first decades of the 17th century? To answer this question some characteristics of de Keyser's architectural work must be analysed first.

Hendrick de Keyser and late 16th century 'modern' architecture

In 1595 Hendrick de Keyser was appointed a "master sculptor and stonecutter of the works of this town" (Mr. Beeltsnijder ende steenhouwer over deser stede wercken).[18] Together with Hendrick Staets and Cornelis Danckertsz. he led the Amsterdam building yard at a time of enormous expansion and numerous building projects, such as the construction of the new ring of canals, three new city churches in the new suburban areas, the new Exchange building and various trade halls as well as various private houses. De Keyser in his role as town stonemason and sculptor carried out the part of the building activities that was creative. He was the artistic force within the building company and, as such, was responsible for sculptural ornamentation, and in all likelihood was also largely responsible for the entire architectural design of various new public buildings. The quality of contemporary representative architecture depended on the quality of the sculpture on the façade.

In a document from 1613, de Keyser was described as the "town's master of antique decorations" (stads antyc meester).[19] Apparently he was also considered a specialist in "antique works" (antiekse werken) and to have expert knowledge of the repertoire of classical forms. However, purely ancient forms are not to be found in his work; rather, he repeatedly devised new 'finds' that had never been seen before. In the Architectura Moderna of 1631, de Keyser does not receive praise for his successful imitation of ancient architecture; on the contrary, the comments accompanying the illustrations express great awe for his 'original' and 'modern' inventions. The texts to the engravings praise the novelty of the ornament and the designer's ingenuity. "Decorative and rare finds full of unusual interruptions" were a pleasure to "the eye that is ever keen on new things".[20] A broken pediment is praised as "an absolute delight",[21] as are the "rare, decorative interruptions",[22] the "decorative changes" and the "excellent rarity of inventions by our Master".[23] The descriptions of the illustrations mark a direct appeal to the high ideals of innovation and invention, the ability to enrich the repertoire of classical orders with new, authentic inventions.

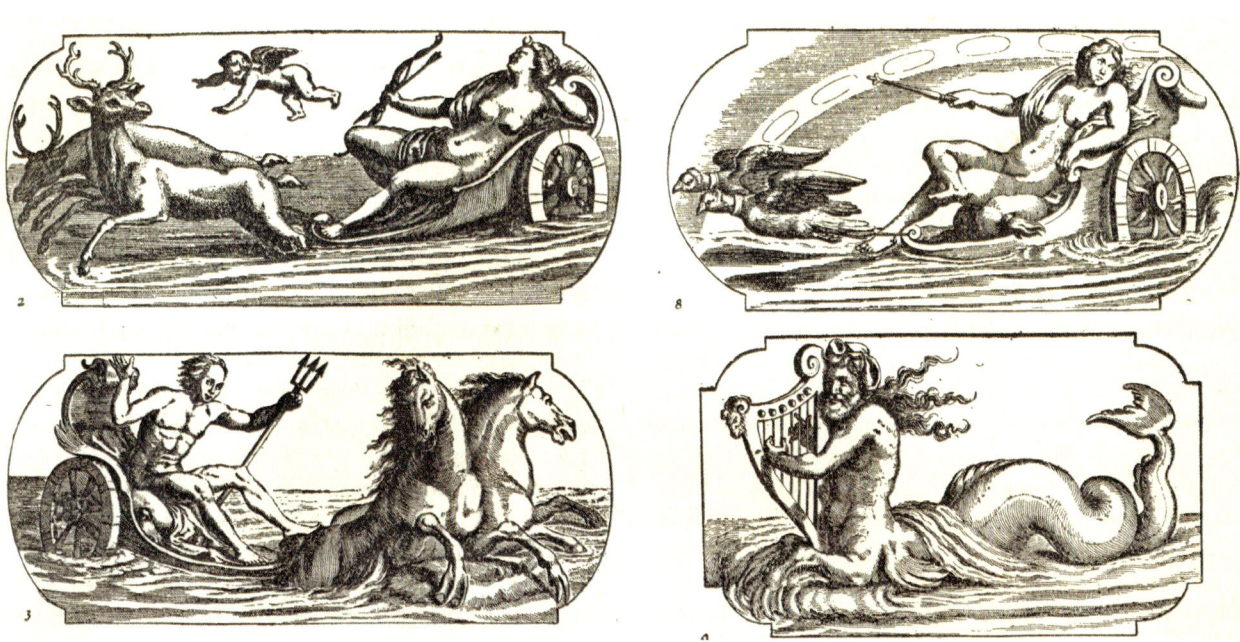

Fig. 5. Amsterdam, Herengracht 170, the Bartolotti House, 1618 (Photo author).

The five orders and their ornament

The inventiveness of Hendrick de Keyser and his contemporaries in architectural sculpture around 1600 was part of a tradition that had begun earlier in the Low Countries during the second half of the 16th century, especially in Antwerp, in the circles of Cornelis Floris and Hans Vredeman de Vries. Within the rich gamut of the imaginative architectural ideas that prevailed from the final decades of the 16th century in the Netherlands, there existed a clear architectonic system based on the five classical orders. But this subtle system was not understood well by every stone mason or architect.

The differences in character between the various columns, varying from the robust Doric to the refined Corinthian, were first set forth by Sebastiano Serlio in 1537. The distinct nature of each of these five types of columns is expressed in its proportions, but in the same book Serlio also explained how to create differences in character when there were no columns. In the *Libro Quarto* from 1537, Serlio also presents a matching fireplace for every order; a Doric fireplace for a Doric hall, an Ionic fireplace for an Ionic hall, and so forth. There are no columns or pilasters on these fireplaces; the specific Doric or Ionic characteristics are contained within the architectural ornament. Serlio devised a specific and distinctive type of ornamentation derived from the column, capital or entablature of each of the orders.[24]

The Doric ornament is recognisable by its triglyphs and the guttae of the Doric frieze. The striking grooves of the triglyphs appear on other parts as well, such as on the consoles supporting the chimney-breast. The most characteristic feature of the Ionic order is its capital volutes. Serlio uses a stretched Ionic capital as a cornice over the fireplace. The Corinthian fireplace is given herms in the shape of water nymphs, and the Composite fireplace is literally a composition of decorative elements taken from various orders, among them the abundant acanthus leaf of the Corinthian capital.

Fig. 6. Newly invented detail in the Ionic order, from the Bartolotti House, 1618 (Photo author).

Fig. 7. Rome, Porta Pia, designed by Michelangelo. After Vignola, Regola delle cinque ordini, 1602, Amsterdam 1617.

Vredeman de Vries follows Serlio's lead. His *Dorica-Ionica* and *Corinthia-Composita* from 1565 and his *Architectura* from 1577 both contain a wide range of new 'order-related' ornamentation. Again, like Serlio before him, he derives his new ornaments from typical features of the five orders, such as Tuscan rustic, Doric triglyphs, the Ionic volutes and the Corinthian acanthus. These elements are detached, as it were, from their original position and function within the order, and remodelled as new and independent plastic forms for pedestals, consoles, friezes, profiles, door and window cornices *et cetera*.

De Keyser did not copy from Vredeman de Vries but continued to design according to the same principle, creating new ornaments within the system of the five classical orders. The façade of the house of the Bartolotti on the Herengracht 170 in Amsterdam (Fig. 5), built in 1618, may serve as an example of this decoration system.[25] It is a splendid showpiece of de Keyser's 'modern' architecture with a full range of new inventions of architectural ornaments never seen before, but nevertheless in some way related to the classic orders. The ground floor has Doric pilasters and some reminiscences of the Doric triglyph, the three *guttae*, can be found on the scrolls below the windows of the first floor. The first floor shows a kind of 'phase of transition', it has Ionic pilasters, with some free-style scrolled Ionic capitals as well as references to the Doric triglyphs (not concave but convex wise) in its frieze. The decoration of the second floor and the adjacent balustrades is utterly Ionic, with various variations of the Ionic capital (Fig. 6). The gable top is once more a free style Doric-Ionic composition, with Ionic scrolled ornaments as well as solid, freestanding Doric columns.

Inspiration of Michelangelo's Porta Pia

Although Hendrick de Keyser was rightly considered one of the most 'inventive' and creative architects of his time, not all of his inventions were original. He updated the existing design repertoire that Vredeman de Vries in particular had compiled, with a number of remarkable new features that came straight from Italy. The prime example had been set by Michelangelo, whom Vasari had praised for freeing contemporary art from the tight strictures of Antiquity, and demonstrating how these new inventions could even surpass classical art.[26] Examples of some new details were the geniculated arch, the broken pediment with curving ends, heavy blocks or triglyphs used as consoles, and heavy keystones extended upwards. It is the application of these new Michelangelo-style designs in particular that distinguish de Keyser's work from that of the generation before, as well as from other architects in the Northern Netherlands during the first two decades of the 17th century. These rich new decorations reinforced architecture's power of expression.

One of the most remarkable new forms within this new repertoire is the polygonal or 'geniculated' arch. The origin of this three-sided span is Michelangelo's Porta Pia in Rome (Fig. 7), de-

Fig. 8. Amsterdam, gate of the Zuiderkerk cemetery, designed by Hendrick de Keyser. After de Bray and Danckerts, plate VI.

monumental entrance of the municipal arsenal.[29] In Antwerp it was used at the monumental gate on the interior courtyard of Rubens' new house ca.1616 as well as in various variations in Francart's model book for entrance gates, his *Livre d'Architecture* from 1617.[30] Even Inigo Jones, who always claimed to prefer 'solid' architecture instead of whimsical novelties, used it once, in a gate design for Arundel House, London.[31]

New inventions by Van Steenwinckel at Frederiksborg

Returning to the question of whether Hendrick de Keyser influenced the architecture of the Danish royal works in the first decades of the 17th century, especially in the circles of Lourens and Hans van Steenwinckel, the answer seems to be negative.

The façades of Frederiksborg and of Rosenborg, just to mention the most prominent build-

signed in 1563 as a gate to the new Strada Pia, the road crossing the Quirinal Hill. An engraving of this design was made as early as 1567. The most important source for the distribution of the Porta Pia's various unusual motifs in the 17th century was its reproduction in the supplement of the 1602 Vignola edition, which was subsequently included in the five-language Amsterdam edition of 1617.[27] Hendrick de Keyser in Amsterdam used various motifs from the Porta Pia, most notably at the cemetery gates of the Zuiderkerk and the Westerkerk (Fig. 8).[28]

The Porta Pia really became a hit tune all over Europe in the early 17th century. It was used, for example, in 1603 in Augsburg, Germany, at the

Fig. 9. Frederiksborg Castle, Marble Gallery, detail (Photo author).

Fig. 10. Wendel Dietterlin, *Architectura*, Nuremberg 1598, plate 130, detail.

Fig. 11. Frederiksborg Castle, Audience House, 1612-1616, detail (Photo Hugo Johannsen).

Fig. 12. Dietterlin, *Architectura*, plate 160, detail.

ing activities of that period, are designed according to a system of pure strap-work and scrolled gables, without the specific order-related new inventions, so typical of de Keyser, nor any of his michelangelesque novelties.

The same can be said about Lourens van Steenwinckel's Stock Exchange of Copenhagen, although the composition of the entrance facade is enriched by herms, a motif never used by de Keyser. Apparently the international fashion of Porta Pia variations seems to have bypassed Denmark. But here too existing solutions were not merely copied. In fact, both the van Steenwinckel brothers elaborated the late 16th century vocabulary their own way. They, too, invented new possibilities for strap-work and scrolls but, notably, almost without introducing new, contemporary European fashionable details.

The only exceptions can be found in Frederiksborg, in the gallery, most prominently, as well as the gateway in the tower of the second court-yard of the castle, and the triumphal gate in the reception house of Frederiksborg. Here indeed, a display of modern, contemporary inventions has been introduced; arches surmounted by scrolls, niches with scrolls, and, in the gate, a broken pediment.

These are obvious modern ornamentations but they cannot be convincingly related to de Keyser's work. Not Dutch but German models were used as a starting point for these new inventions, especially Wenzel Dietterlin's *Architectura* from 1598.[32] Dietterlin's world of seemingly endless variations on combinations of the classical orders, strap-work, scrolls and rustic blocks was well known to the van Steenwinckel brothers. The Royal Library of Copenhagen still possesses their own copy of Dietterlin's volume.[33]

To illustrate this point, the idea of putting scrolls on top of the upper arches of the gallery resembles only vaguely the inner doorway of the Noorderkerk by de Keyser,[34] while a closer relationship can be found with inventions from Dietterlin's *Architectura* of 1598, as, for example, the decoration on top of an entrance gate shown on folio 77. The ground-floor arches of the Frederiksborg gallery have very particular impost scrolls that cannot be found in Holland at that time. Again the source presumably was Dietterlin's *Architectura*, folio 130 - the niches between the columns of an epitaph. Other specific new, modern inventions were introduced in Frederiksborg, at the gateway of the tower that stands in front of the gallery, where the outer parts of the pediment are turned inside-out. This motif was introduced in 1577 by Buontalenti at the Porta delle Suppliche of the Uffizi in Florence. Dietterlin uses it only once, as the decoration of a window, on folio 55. Also the Audience House of Frederiksborg is enhanced by some exquisite novelties. The entrance gate is modelled after a triumphal arch with a rich sculptural programme.[35] Here also some specific novelties can be related to Dietterlin's inventions. The arched frieze and its cornice above the Corinthian columns, and the scrolled volutes on top of the pilasters of the first floor supporting a lute and a harp are very close to Dietterlin's model on folio160.

Conclusion

If we agree that the development of architecture in the North had its own dynamic, more or less independent from Italy, what kind of relation existed between the Low Countries and the Scandinavian and Baltic regions?[36] Should we see the Low Countries as the centre of this architectural movement (Antwerp in the 16th century and Amsterdam in the 17th), spreading their influence to various peripheral regions in the North, or should we think of parallel centres, all using the same models and to some degree even the same artists?[37]

The influence of Hendrick de Keyser and his workshop on the dissemination of the new repertoire cannot be denied, but it would be a simplification to call ornate buildings in Scandinavia and around the Baltic Sea merely 'Dutch' or 'Flemish'.[38] The Steenwinckel family had their roots in the Low Countries, but their father Hans the Elder had already left that region as a young man in the 1560s. Once abroad, he and his fellows from the Low Countries worked independently of their former home land, creating new artistic centres of their own, as was the case in Gdansk or at the royal court of Denmark.

Hans van Steenwinckel the Younger was even born in Copenhagen, it is incorrect to call him merely a 'Flemish' architect. He and other first- and second-generation *émigrés* did not reproduce works or details from Holland and Flanders. Rather they created their own inventions using, on the one hand, the same sources and principles as their contemporaries in the Low Countries, but on the other hand, also adapting other influences from surrounding regions, especially the rich repertoire of various German publications from the late 16th and early 17th centuries, as demonstrated with the examples from Dietterlin.

The development of the *modern antique* of the early 17th century was an international movement with an important Dutch contribution, but the invention of new forms at that time was not restricted to the Low Countries. It was a European phenomenon.

Notes

1 D. F. Slothouwer, *Bouwkunst der Nederlandse Renaissance in Denemarken*, Amsterdam 1924; H. R. Hitchcock, *Netherlandish scrolled gables of the sixteenth and early seventeenth centuries*, New York 1978.

2 J. G. Roding, "The North Sea coasts, an architectural unity?", in: J. Roding & L. Heerma van Voss (eds.), *The North Sea and Culture (1550-1800)*, Hilversum 1996, 96-106; H. Johannsen, "On the Significance of Hans Vredeman de Vries for Architecture, Arts and Crafts in Denmark during the Reigns of Frederick II and Christian IV", in: H. Borggrefe & V. Lüpkes (eds.), *Hans Vredeman de Vries und die Folgen,* Marburg 2005 (Studien zur Kultur der Renaissance 3), 42-49; A. Bartetzky, "Hans Vredeman de Vries' geschweifte Beschlagwerkgiebel. Zu ihrer Herkunft, Aneignung und Verbreitung in der Architektur Mittel- und Nordeuropas", in: Borggrefe & Lüpkes (eds.) 2005, 75-82; K. De Jonge, "Vredeman de Vries as a Disseminator of Architectural Novelties", in: Borggrefe & Lüpkes (eds.) 2005, 83-90. For a general introduction on Danish-Dutch artistic relations, see Steffen Heiberg, "Art and politics. Christian IV's Dutch and Flemish painters", in: *Art in Denmark 1600-1750*, Delft 1984 (Leids Kunsthistorisch Jaarboek 2 (1983)) (1983), 7-24.

3 E. Neurdenburg, "Hendrick de Keyser en het beeld-

houwwerk aan de galerij van Frederiksborg in Denemarken", *Oudheidkundig Jaarboek* 12 (1943), 33-41; L. O. Larsson, "Bildhaukunst und Plastik in Dänemark in der Regierungszeit Christian IV", in: *Art in Denmark 1600-1650* 1983, 69-84.

4   Cf. L. Laursen (ed.), *Kancelliets Brevbøger vedrørende Danmarks indre Forhold, 1616-1620*, Copenhagen 1919, 741 (10 December 1619); J. Roding, *Christiaan IV van Denemarken. Architectuur en stedebouw van een Luthers vorst.* Dissertation KU Nijmegen, Alkmaar 1991, 148-149.

5   Cf. *Kancelliets Brevbøger 1616-1620*, 535; Roding 1991, 147.

6   Patrick Kragelund, "Olympens Guder", in: Steffen Heiberg (ed.), *Christian 4. og Frederiksborg*, Copenhagen 2006, 44-61.

7   See Rigsarkivet [The Danish National Archives, Copenhagen, hereafter: RA]. *Danske Kancelli.* Indkomne Breve til Danske Kancelli, 13 February 1621. Published at length by G.W. Kernkamp, "Memoriën van Ridder Theodorus Rodenburg betreffende het verplaatsen van verschillende industrieën uit Nederland naar Denemarken met daarop genomen resolutiën van koning Christiaan IV (1621)", *Bijdragen en Mededeelingen van het Historisch Genootschap* 23 (1902), 189-257 (231, no.19: "Geraert Lambertsen, beeldthouwer").

8   Royal permission for Sweys to buy Gotland stone and to ship it free of toll to Holland from 16 September 1619, cf. *Kancelliets Brevbøger 1616-1620*, 685 (with reference to: RA. *Danske Kancelli.* Skånske Registre 1615-1630, 4, 143b (B. 48D)). Beckett, *Frederiksborg. II. Slottets Historie*, Copenhagen 1914, 129, 263.

9   Royal commission from 17 May 1620. Beckett 1914, 126-127.

10 Well documented cases some decades later clearly illustrate this way of cooperation: The architect Pieter Post made the designs of the weighing houses in Leiden (1658) and Gouda (1668). In both cases he gave drawings with very strict instructions to all craftsmen, including stone carvers, but for the sculptured reliefs in the centre of the façades, he only handed rough sketches to the sculptors (Rombout Verhulst in Leiden, Bartholomeus Eggers in Gouda). These artists were free to give their own interpretation of the subject demanded. J. J. Terwen & K.A. Ottenheym, *Pieter Post (1608-1669), architect*, Zutphen 1993, 185-193.

11 S. De Bray & C. Danckerts, *Architectura Moderna, ofte Bouwinge van onsen tyt*, Amsterdam 1631. K. De Jonge & K. A. Ottenheym, *Unity and Discontinuity. Architectural Relationships between the Southern and Northern Low Countries (1530-1700)*, Turnhout 2007, 111-136.

12 Neurdenburg 1943. When Neurdenburg published her article, this rather unique series was in the collection of J. C. J. Bierens de Haan, Amsterdam. Since 1952 it has been in the print collection of Museum Boymans-van Beuningen, Rotterdam.

13 Amsterdam Gemeentearchief, NA 47, nots. Lieven Heylinck (ditto), fol.128, 13 April 1595.

14 A.W. Weissman, "De schoonzoon van Hendrik de Keyser", *Oud Holland* 38 (1920), 155-164.

15 Amsterdam Gemeentearchief, apprentice register of the St Barbara guild. See E. Neurdenburg, "Pieter de Keyser als beeldhouwer", *Oudheidkundig Jaarboek* 9 (1940), 62-72.

16 Beckett 1914, 65.

17 "het steenhouwen, contrefeyten ende alle cyraet te maecken, gelyck een steenhouwer tot synder neeringhe noodich ende van doen heeft", Amsterdam Gemeentearchief, NA 47, nots. Lieven Heylinck fol.128, 13 April 1595: contract between de Keyser and his apprentice Hendrick Jansz. A. W. Weissman, "Het geslacht De Keyser", *Oud Holland* 22 (1904), 65-91 (for the contract and the guild regulations of 1498, see 70-71).

18 E. Neurdenburg, *Hendrick de Keyser. Beeldhouwer en bouwmeester van Amsterdam*, Amsterdam 1930. He was officially appointed on 19 July 1595 (Amsterdam Gemeentearchief, 2ᵉ Groot Memoriaal. fol. 170v.).

19 This is what he was called at the wedding of his daughter Maria to Nicholas Stone on 25 April 1613. (Amsterdam Gemeentearchief, *Puiboek*). Weissman 1920.

20 "Verzierlicke en seltsame vindinghe vol van onghemeene breeckinghe … het veranderingh-begheerighoogh" (ills. XVIII-XXIII).

21 "seer aenghename heerlijckheydt" (ill. XXV).

22 "seltsame verzierlijcke breeckingen" (ill. XXIX).

23 "verzierlijcken veranderingh (…) uytnemende seltsaemheydt van vindinghen van onsen Bouw-meester" (ill. XVI).

24 Serlio provides no fireplace design for the simplest of all orders, the Tuscan, as it would never have been allowed in any interior. He identified the rugged, earthy character of the Tuscan order as best suited to rustic stone.

25 G. Leonhardt, *Het huis Bartolotti en zijn bewoners*, Amsterdam 1979; R. Meischke, P. Rosenberg & H. Zantkuijl, *Huizen in Nederland*, Zwolle & Amsterdam 1995, 245-260.

26 In particular, see his remarks on Michelangelo's designs for the Medici chapel and for the Biblioteca Laurenziana in Florence. G. Vasari, *Le vite …*, ed. G. Milanesi, III, Florence 1886, 83

27 Twelve prints with designs by Vignola and Michelange-

lo, *Nuova e ultima aggiunta delle porte d'architetura di Michelangelo Buonarotti*, added as a supplement to G. Barozzi da Vignola, *Regole Generali*, Rome 1602, published by Giovanni Orlandi. This edition was the source for the five-language edition of Vignola's *Regole de'cinque ordini d'architettura*, Amsterdam 1617.

28 *Architectura Moderna,* ills. VI- VII, XX-XXI.

29 Façade design 1603 attributed to Elias Holl and Joseph Heintz Sr.; B. Roeck, *Elias Holl. Architekt einer europäischen Stadt*, Regensburg 1985, 97-104. For problems of this attribution, see Th. Fichtner & K. Wezel, „Elias Holl", in: A. Bartetzky (ed.), *Die Baumeister der "Deutschen Renaissance". Ein Mythos der Kunstgeschichte?*, Beucha 2004, 213-236.

30 Jacques Francart, *Premier Livre d'Architecture de Jacques Francart. Contenant diverses inventions de portes serviables à tous coeux qui desirent bastir & pour sculpteurs, tailleurs de pieres, esoriniers, maesons et autres*, Brussels1617; A. De Vos, *Jacques Francart. Premier Livre d'Architecture (1617). Studie van een Zuid-Nederlands modelboek met poortgebouwen*, Brussels 1998 (Verhandelingen van de Koninklijke Academie voor Wetenschappen, Letteren en Schone Kunsten van België, Klasse der Schone Kunsten 65).

31 J. Harris & G. Higgott, *Inigo Jones. Complete Architectural Drawings*, London 1989, see the 'Italian' gate at Arundel House, London, 126-127, cat. 40, see also the design for a gateway at New Hall, Boreham, Essex, 132, cat. 42. For Jones' preference for 'solid' inventions, see C. Anderson, "Masculine and Unaffected. Inigo Jones and the Classical Ideal", *Art Journal* 2, 56 (1997), 48-54.

32 W. Dietterlin, *Architectura. Von Ausstheilung / Symmetria und Proportion der Fünff Seulen*, Nuremberg 1598.

33 Steenwinckel's own copy of W. Dietterlin, *Architectura*, Strassbourg 1598, is preserved in The Royal Library, Copenhagen.

34 *Architectura Moderna* 1631, ill. X.

35 M. Bligaard, "The Privy Passage and the Audience House at Frederiksborg Palace", in: *Art in Denmark 1600-1650*, Delft 1984 (Leids Kunsthistorisch Jaarboek 2 (1983)), 55-68; S. Heiberg, "Et kongeligt triumftog", in: Heiberg (ed.) 2006, 28-41.

36 For these problems in general, see Th. DaCosta Kaufmann, *Towards a Geography of Art*, Chicago & London 2004; Th. DaCosta Kaufmann & E. Pilliod (eds.), *Time and Place. The Geohistory of Art*, Aldershot & Burlington 2005.

37 Białostocki's famous tripartite scheme of 'centre-depending region-periphery' does not seem to fit at all in the relation between Denmark and the Low Countries.

38 For this problem, see J. Roding, "The Myth of the 'Dutch Renaissance' in Denmark. Dutch Influence on Danish Architecture in the 17th Century", in: J. Ph. S. Lemmink & J. S. A. M. van Koningsbrugge (eds.), *Baltic Affairs. Relations between the Netherlands and North-Eastern Europe 1500-1800*, Nijmegen 1990 (Baltic Studies I), 343-353.

EBONY AND SILVER FURNITURE AT FREDERIKSBORG CASTLE

Mogens Bencard

Christian IV (1577-1648) became king of the twinkingdom of Denmark-Norway on his father's untimely death in 1588. He was not, however, crowned until 1596, when he came of age. Before that he was carefully educated for his future role, while a regency of trusted noblemen ruled the countries.

It was an ambitious young man who came into power, and it did not last long before he started to create new frames for himself as well as for his realm. He began in 1598 at Frederiksborg, where he had a small *maison-de-plaisance*, built by his farther, torn down and a new Italian-styled villa, Sparepenge, erected in its place.[1]

His ambition became even more apparent, when he had his father's main house at Frederiksborg demolished. Perhaps it looked too much like a manor, fit for a nobleman, not a residence for a king. There is, no doubt, a great difference between Christian's three-winged, many-towered palace and Frederik II's compact double-house.

In 1602, when the command was given to tear down the older house, the erection of the new palace was begun with the King's Wing to the north. Erection of the western wing containing chapel and long hall started in 1606, the eastern, so-called Princesses' Wing in 1608. Finally a low gallery with a gate-house, begun in 1609, connected the western and eastern wings. Later on several extensions were made to the main house, but they do not concern us here, where the topic is the furnishing of the main house.

The castle disastrously burnt down in 1859, and only part of the Royal chapel was spared. There are, however, three documents which can give us some idea of how the other interiors looked at the time of Christian IV. The oldest one is a journal of a young prince, Christian of Anhalt, who visited Denmark in 1623;[2] in 1646 the castle steward Adam Berg on the king's initiative and expense published a description of Frederiksborg. Comparing the castle to the most elaborate collections and residences of Europe, Berg states the purpose of the book, namely to spread the knowledge of this, his king's most magnificent creation.[3] Written as it is, after the defeat against Sweden in the war of 1643-45, and thus prone to exaggerations, Berg's book should be treated with a certain reservation. An inventory, dated 1650, but referring to an older inventory of 1636, must be considered more trustworthy.[4] Inventories may be compared to accounts, where all movements were carefully recorded. They were kept by the various castle stewards, and if anything was missing at the time of their death, the family would be held responsible for the loss. It is mainly this source I have used to illustrate one specific feature of the furnishings of Frederiksborg, namely

Fig. 1. Silver altar, c. 1606, Chapel of Frederiksborg Castle, delivered by Hamburg goldsmith Hans Mores (Photo Hillerød, Museum of National History, Frederiksborg Castle).

the ebony and silver furniture, which adorned the most important rooms.

All three descriptions begin in the chapel with the major item, the tall, magnificent altarpiece (Fig. 1), which is preserved to this day.

With its silver-clad columns and architraves, the altarpiece takes up classical architectural motives. Parcel-gilt, chased reliefs, and richly embellished cast full-length figures in the round are set in silver-inlaid ebony frames. Some of the reliefs are stamped with Hamburg marks and with those of the goldsmiths Jacob Mores I and Hinrich Lambrecht I.[5] Hans Mores was paid for the altar in 1606 and 1608.[6] Even though the marks are not complete, there can be little doubt that the altar in its entirety was made in Hamburg.

No less magnificent is the pulpit (Fig. 2), also made of ebony. At the corners are double, silver-clad columns with composite capitals, and in the niches between them are placed Christ and the four apostles, all cast in the round. It was erected before 1623, when Christian of Anhalt saw it. It bears no marks, so there is no certain information on its provenance, though it is reasonable to assume that it was also made in Hamburg, possibly by Hinrich Lambrecht I.[7] It is curious that it is not marked, but a reason might be that the king commissioned it directly from the silversmith, making guarantees from the town as well as from the silversmith superfluous.

On the gallery stood a smaller organ, made of ebony, and richly decorated on all sides with silver. In 1610 it was mentioned as having been ordered by the king in Hamburg, and in 1613 it was sent from Copenhagen to Frederiksborg. In 1659, when the Swedes had occupied the castle, it was brought to Sweden and has since disappeared.[8]

At the opposite end of the colourful and richly decorated chapel stood the equally splendid organ, and beneath that, at the gallery-level, were the king's oratory and the queen's chamber.[9] Both had large-paned windows towards the church, but the queen's chamber was far more modest than the king's. This latter room had a ceiling of ebony, from which was hung all sorts of fruits in cast silver, richly gilt. In the middle of the room a chandelier of silver, at the top of which was the royal globe with a ruby, and below a ball, in which a clockwork.

On a table was an altar of ebony (Fig. 3) with ornaments of silver. All this was seen by Christian of Anhalt in 1623. The room, with its walls covered by biblical paintings (by Dutch artists), was totally destroyed in 1859. The splendid altar in ebony and silver has survived, because it was taken to the Kunstkammer in 1816 and did not come back until 1937-38. It is stamped with Augsburg's mark around 1600, and the mark of the silversmith Mathäus Wallbaum.[10] Somewhat surprising in a Lutheran royal oratory the theme

Fig. 2. Silver pulpit, before 1623, Chapel of Frederiksborg Castle (Photo Hugo Johannsen).

EBONY AND SILVER FURNITURE AT FREDERIKSBORG CASTLE

Fig. 3. Mathäus Wallbaum, silver altar, c. 1600, the King's Oratory in the Chapel of Frederiksborg Castle (Photo Copenhagen, the National Museum of Denmark).

of the altar is Mary's history as the mother of Christ. Perhaps it is a chance acquisition. The silver chandelier has perhaps partly survived, but since several chandeliers appear in various later inventories, it is uncertain.[11]

Moving upstairs from the oratory, one comes to the Long Hall, built for festive purposes. One entered originally on the transverse axis of the long side under the Musicians' Gallery, made of ebony. This was supported by five columns with pediments embellished with musical instruments of chased silver. The bays were framed by silver-embellished herms, while ten panels showed engraved plates with landscapes and 'allerhandt Geschichten'. The cornice, decorated with pierced silver panels, had cranks with silver cherub heads in foliation.

The southern end of the hall was embellished with a magnificent chimney-piece of polished black marble (cf. Fig. 4). Its cornice, with pierced silver reliefs, was supported by four marble columns with Ionic capitals of silver. On the corners of the cornice stood large silver candlesticks with grapes and foliation; besides them were silver-embellished pediments supporting Phoebus and Luna cast in silver and almost full-sized. Behind the two figures stood two pyramids with rosettes and foliation and between them a marble panel flanked by composite columns with bases and capitals of silver. In the panel was a cast silver relief of the Parcae, 'nach dem Leben'. The whole thing was crowned by a silver eagle with outstretched wings. In 1618, the king in his calendar wrote that Hans Mores was to have 500 thaler, when he presented proper accounts for the 'chimney', which should perhaps be identified with this. Christian of Anhalt noted that by the chimney-piece stood a parcel-gilt silver fire screen, two andirons and a bellows of silver. This is a very early example of silver fire sets, and the only one at Frederiksborg, which otherwise had many andirons of brass. In 1607 the king paid Jacob Mores for two silver andirons.

The opposite end of the hall boasted an ebony buffet intended to display the large decorative silver cups that were a part of the period's symbolism of royal power.[12] The lower part of the buffet, whose horizontal elements were decorated with silver and had cranks with silver masks, seems to have been divided into twelve bays framed by silver-clad, Ionic double herms. A canopy ('die Decke'), divided into twelve panels with perforated foliation and gilded fruit, was supported by two silver-clad ebony Ionic columns.

The king's and the queen's apartments, which were also graced with silver furniture, were located on the first floor of the King's Wing. Berg's description and the inventory of 1650 do not quite agree as to the lay-out and the contents of these rooms. The apartments, however, seem to have been laid-out on a symmetric plan, with a larger room at each end, a connecting corridor towards the courtyard, and two smaller rooms for each

Fig. 4., Cross-section of the west wing of Frederiksborg Castle, viewed towards the south, showing the lost chimney-piece, c. 1618, of the Great Hall above the altar, c. 1606, of the Chapel. After Laurids de Thurah, *Den Danske Vitruvius*, vol. 2, Copenhagen 1749 (Photo Copenhagen, the National Museum of Denmark).

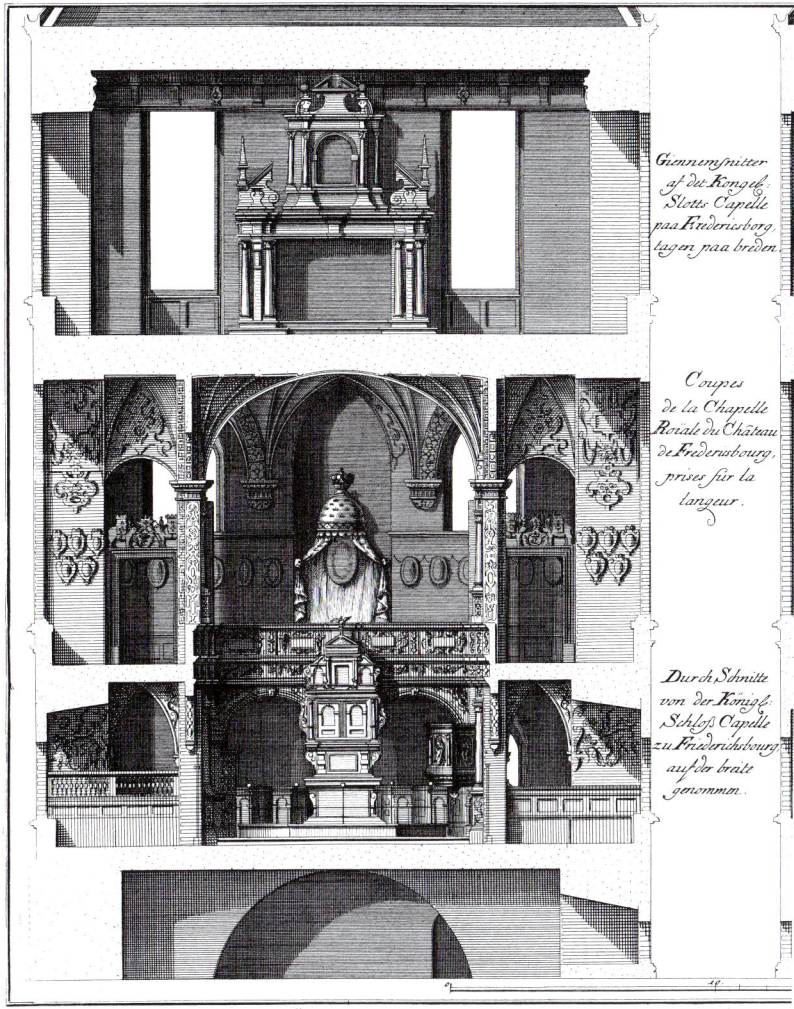

apartment towards the lake. In the central axis in a tower towards the lake was the queen's jewel room.[13] In the inventory the names of the rooms differ from Berg's description, perhaps due to the fact that the registrar referred to an inventory prior to the one of 1636, because to him it was important that there should be no possible mistakes. Consequently one finds the rooms named after persons long dead. Berg, on the other hand, could – and did – act more freely.

The king's large room, called the 'Summer Room', contained three mirrors, of which one had a frame of black marble and alabaster columns with gilt capitals, and another a frame of ebony. According to the inventory of 1650, the latter, which was inlaid with gilt silver, was purchased from Hans Mores of Hamburg. The third was a more complicated structure. It had a frame of embossed silver, which – if the two sources can be interpreted correctly – could be opened to reveal nine silver-embellished drawers. These contained the king's writing implements in silver. Underneath the frame, as a part of it, it seems, a silver clock was hanging.

In a tower in a cabinet adjacent to the Summer Room stood a parcel-gilt silver fountain upon an ebony pediment. It was decorated with shells and conches spouting water. Four large figures, "die auff Lampetten stehen", surrounded the crowned figure of Hercules and the Hydra. According to the description this fountain, the most splendid of the silver-ebony furnishings of the apartments, seems like a version of Adriaen de Vries's Hercules fountain in Augsburg.[14]

The King's Chamber, probably his study, situated between the Summer Room and the Bed

EBONY AND SILVER FURNITURE AT FREDERIKSBORG CASTLE 329

Room, contained another fountain with a large figure of silver in the middle. This fountain is only mentioned by Berg. Furthermore two large cabinets, of which one was made of ebony and had a drawer front inlaid with ivory and silver lions' heads. In the middle of the front was set a mirror, protected by a curtain of white taffeta.

No ebony and silver furniture stood in the king's bedroom. Perhaps it is because of his habit of getting up in the very early morning to go on a tour of inspection, which would prevent any ceremonial use. Between 1636 and 1650, however, a silver clock striking the hour as well the quarter was added.

The room connecting the gallery with the jewel room, however, contained a cabinet ('ein grosses Kuntor') of ebony inlaid with silver and ivory, and an ebony table inlaid with silver and mother-of-pearl and with inlaid, engraved plates. A table with engraved silver plates after Bartholomæus Spranger, today at The National Museum of Denmark (Fig. 5), has a newer stand but no mother-of-pearl inlays. It was added to the Kunstkammer in 1704 with no information as

Fig. 6. Table top of black marble with silver engravings after Simon de Pas, after 1623, formerly at Frederiksborg Castle(?). Now in Copenhagen, Rosenborg Castle (Photo Rosenborg).

Fig. 5. Table top of black marble with silver engravings after Bartholomeus Spranger, c. 1609, formerly at Frederiksborg Castle(?). Copenhagen, the National Museum of Denmark (Photo National Museum).

to the provenance, and if it is identical with the Frederiksborg table, the inlay must have been on the stand.[15] In 1609 Jacob Mores was paid for an ebony table inlaid with silver.[16]

The Jewel Room is not mentioned in the inventory, but is to be found in Berg. The reason for this must be that this room belongs to the category where the registrar was not responsible for its contents. It represented a parallel to the Regalia Room at Rosenborg, or the 'Grünes Gewölbe' in Dresden, to which 'only the king has the key'. Berg informs us that a silver-gilt chandelier is hanging from the ceiling. In the ball at the bottom is a clock striking the hour as well as the quarter.[17] In the room an ebony table, inlaid with silver and mother-of-pearl, was also to be found. On the top in the middle was a large silver plate engraved with a landscape, surrounded by smaller plates engraved with virtues. Next to the table was a splendid mirror, framed in ebony, and inlaid with chased silver. These two pieces of furniture may be identical with two, found today at Rosenborg, where they have been since they were first mentioned in the eldest complete inventory dated 1718 (Fig. 6 and 7).

The engravings on the table are ascribed to Simon de Pas,[18] who came to Denmark in 1623. If the table is Danish, though Dutch of type, it must be dated after 1623. The mirror is closely related to furniture of this type from Augsburg, thus to be dated around 1600.

Made of a different sort of silver, and for that reason most probably additions are two reliefs, depicting Christian IV and his queen Anne Catharine, and the queen's initials below the mirror. Queen Anne Catharine died in 1611, so the mirror must be dated earlier than that year.[19] Furthermore Berg lists two cabinets of ebony ('Schranken von gleichem Holtz') likewise inlaid ('ebenmässig eingeleget'), in which is kept what belongs to the royal treasures ('was zum königl. Schmuck gehöret'). This may be the reason why the jewel room was not included in the inventory.

The queen's apartment was more modestly furnished, although it was not completely without ebony pieces. The large room, which was called the Winter Room, contained three cabinets ('Tresorer') of which one was of ebony, delicately inlaid. On the top stood two nautilus-cups, with stands of silver, and set with large diamonds.

The floor above had contained the apartment of the Dowager Queen Sophia. It was also richly furnished, but the only piece of ebony and silver was the magnificent bed. The pillars as well as the top were once again embellished with chased and cast figures and ornaments, and with engraved plates. The bed was bought in 1621 from Hans Mores for 8,000 thaler in specie, and it was thus fairly new, when Christian of Anhalt admired it.

In the Princesses's Wing only one piece was mentioned. It was a large mirror with an ebony frame inlaid with silver and mother-of-pearl, found in the Blue Room, the major room in the apartment of Christian, the Prince Elect. As heir to the throne (he died in 1647 a year before his farther), he was thus to be invested with the status conveyed by silver.

All this can be supplemented with yet another source from King Christian's prosperous years. The Swedish heir to the throne, Karl Filip, duke of Södermanland, visited Frederiksborg in 1617. His doctor, Johan Richter, wrote that all the rooms were furnished with imposing tapestries and shone and glowed from the glitter of the many silver and gold objects displayed. The Duke was installed in a room furnished with a fairly large silver table, a silver chair, a small, low silver chair, a warming pan, a chamber pot, a bellows, a poker, and other bedchamber accessories, all of silver and parcel-gilt.[20] Nothing of this can be identified with the objects mentioned so far. Perhaps the king had them brought in from other residences to impress the visitor.

The inventory and not least Berg's description give us an impression of the castle's multicoloured rooms: the marbled floors, the coloured stucco on the ceilings, the textiles on the walls, covered with tapestries and paintings, and the carved, painted and inlaid furniture, all of which can still be seen in the Chapel, and to a certain extent in the reconstructed rooms of the 19th century. Against

Fig. 7. Silver mirror with initials of Queen Anne Catherine, †1612, formerly at Frederiksborg Castle(?). Copenhagen, Rosenborg Castle (Photo Rosenborg).

this backdrop of colour the accents of black and silver had an especially powerful effect, placed as one can see in the rooms, where the king might be admired in all his glory.

I have not been able to locate a similar collection of ebony and silver furniture anywhere else in contemporary Europe – at least not prior to the silver furniture of Louis XIV. Both are costly materials, and it is not clear where Christian might have obtained it – if he had to supply the various makers with raw material, that is. A silver mine, Kongsberg, was discovered in Norway in 1623, but before that, there was no local silver in his realm. Ebony is of course an imported type of wood.[21] One seems to be left with the open question: did Christian IV introduce this conscious use of such particular furniture as a personal idea, or – if not – where did he get the inspiration from?

The Netherlands might be a natural place to look, since this country had so much influence on artistic development in Denmark. Lunsingh Scheurleer, who published the Dutch silver furniture, could only list a single cabinet of this type.[22] Another inspiration might have come from England, since Christian visited his sister Anne and her husband James I several times. Simon Jervis, who published the dethroned royal couple's possessions, collected in 1649, listed only few pieces of silver furniture, and noted that this type of furniture was generally little known in England before 1649.[23]

Examples are known from Paris (before Louis XIV) and Prague, but not mentioned in a way that would be illuminating in this connection.[24]

There is, however, one place where one can find an identical use of silver and ebony, namely in "Die Reiche Kapelle" in the Residence at Munich (Fig. 8). It was built for Maximilian I of Bavaria in 1607, and first used in 1615, but did have a forerunner before that time.[25] The main altar, side altars, the organ, and a great deal of the other furnishings in this resplendent chapel are made of ebony and silver. The Bavarian and the Danish chapels were more or less contemporary, but they differ not only in size, but also in the fact that one is made for a Roman Catholic, the other for a Lutheran prince. The Munich altar has a larger, central panel with surrounding, smaller panels, giving it a certain likeness to the front of cabinets with drawers, which is enhanced by the two carrying handles on each side. This brings to mind the cabinet-like reredos of the Frederiksborg altar where one furthermore finds the many 'secular' drawers on the back. There is no evidence to show whether this similarity is intentional. Maximilian was the leading political figure among the Roman Catholic German princes, so perhaps Christian – always competitive – wanted to demonstrate an equal position. In general one can say, however, that there is no proof of any connection between the two chapels. The idea would seem more probable, if it could be demonstrated that other rooms in the Residence had been fitted out like those of

Fig. 8. Main altar, c. 1607, in the so-called 'Reiche Kapelle'. Munich Residence (Photo Marburg Bildarchiv).

Frederiksborg, but that is not possible, because no sources that may provide information have survived.[26]

This may, of course, be possible for many other princely residences in Europe, but as the case stands I should like to venture the assertion that the idea of stressing his princely magnificence and wealth by introducing particularly costly and demonstrative furniture in the main rooms of his residence was introduced by Christian IV.

Notes

1. The classical monograph on Frederiksborg Castle is F. Beckett, *Frederiksborg II. Slottets Historie*, Copenhagen 1914. See also S. Heiberg (ed.), *Christian 4. og Frederiksborg*, Copenhagen 2006 (with references to more recent literature).

2. G. Krause (ed.), *Tagebuch Christian des Jüngeren Fürst zu Anhalt*, Leipzig 1858.

3. Johan Adam Berg, *Kurtze und eigentliche Beschreibung Des fürtrefflichen und weitberühmten Königlichen Hauses Friederichsburg in Seeland gelegen* (…), Copenhagen 1646.

4. A. Petersen, "Frederiksborg Slots Inventarium af 1650", *Danske Samlinger* 2 (1866-67), 118-234.

5. *Danmarks Kirker, Frederiksborg amt (Frederiksborg*

Slotkirke), Copenhagen 1973, 1796-1816; Bernhard Heitmann & Renate Scholz, "Die Ebenholz-Silber-Arbeiten in der Schlosskapelle von Frederiksborg bei Hillerød auf Seeland (Altar und Kanzel)", in: Ernst Schliemann (ed.), *Die Goldschmiede Hamburgs*, Hamburg 1985, I, 78-92, in particular 78-89; II, 54 (no. 115, 4); 70 (no. 127, 7).

6 H. Bering Liisberg, *Christian den Fjerde og Guldsmedene*, Copenhagen 1929, 158.

7 Heitmann & Scholz in: Schliemann (ed.), I, 89-92; II, 70 (no. 127, 8). Though referring to Bering Liisberg's mention (Bering Liisberg 1929, 159) of the large payments in 1622 to Hans Mores, implying that it was certain that he had received money for the pulpit, the authors, as well as Liisberg, and later research agree that the pulpit was the work of Hans Lambrecht I, cf. Heitmann & Scholz in: Schliemann (ed.) 1985, I, 89.

8 *Danmarks Kirker. Frederiksborg amt (Frederiksborg Slotskirke)* 1973, 1858-1859.

9 Hugo Johannsen, "Christian IV's Private Oratory in Frederiksborg Castle Chapel – Reconstruction and Interpretation", in: Badeloch Noldus and Juliette Roding (eds.), *Pieter Isaacsz (1568-1625) Court Painter, Art Dealer and Spy*, Turnhout 2007, 164-179.

10 *Danmarks Kirker. Frederiksborg amt (Frederiksborg Slotskirke)* 1973, 1889-1892.

11 One is presently preserved in the Church of the Holy Ghost, Copenhagen, while a ball with a built-in clock is extant at The National Museum of Denmark, see *Danmarks Kirker. Frederiksborg amt (Frederiksborg Slotskirke)* 1973, 1925, note 229.

12 M. Bencard and G. A. Markova, *Christian IV's Royal Plate and his Relations with Russia*, Copenhagen 1988.

13 M. Skougaard, "Interiører", in: Heiberg 2006, 64-79.

14 Beckett 1914, 107, fig. 101.

15 S. Heiberg (ed.), *Christian IV and Europe: the 19th Art Exhibition of the Council of Europe, Denmark 1988*, Herning 1988, cat. 724; B. Gundestrup, *The Royal Danish Kunstkammer 1737*, II, Copenhagen 1991, 367.

16 Bering Liisberg 1929, 158.

17 As mentioned (note 9) this may still exist, but it cannot be proven.

18 Heiberg (ed.) 1988, cat. 726; M. Bencard, *Silver Furniture*, Copenhagen 1992, cat. 2.

19 Heiberg (ed.) 1988, cat. 726; Bencard 1992, cat. 1.

20 Bencard 1992, 15.

21 The most costly ebony is Mauritius-ebony (*Diospyros ebenum Koenig*), which grows in Ceylon and South India. It is a small tree, a little over ½ metre in diameter and very difficult to dry. The bark is usually ringed two years before it is felled. In India there are also two less costly species, D. melanoxylon and D. tomentosa, the centres of which are black with brown stripes. In Burma and the Moluccas grows another species, D. ebenaster, which is also traded. (All the above are known in England under the term East Indian Ebony, the last is also called Omander wood). In Africa, in Ghana and Angola, there are several species, of which the most important one is D. Crassiflora Hiern, (African Ebony). The quality varies, however, dependent upon the place of growth. Although the wood is very difficult to dry (it becomes pierced by small cracks on drying), it is hard and difficult to work up, and some species even provoke allergy, it is nonetheless much sought-after due to its black colour and its surface, beautiful when polished. It is fortunate, that the wood is easy to colour, because lighter areas often appears. Tradesmen as well as carpenters often use this method. Already the Egyptians used ebony, imported from Ethiopia. It was known by the Greeks and in the Middle East. It appeared in Europe in the 16th century. All the Trading Companies in North Europe, the Dutch, the British, as well as the Danish, were in contact with the places mentioned. The most probable company, however, must be the Dutch, who may have sold it to Augsburg as well as to Hamburg. I owe thanks to my learned friend Peter Wagner, who has advised me on this question.

22 T. H. Lunsingh Scheurleer, "Silver Furniture in Holland", in: *Opuscula in honorem C. Hernmarck*, Stockholm 1966 (Nationalmusei skriftserie 15), 142.

23 S. Jervis, "'Shadows, not substantial things'. Furniture in the Commonwealth Sale Inventories", in: A. MacGregor (ed.), *The Late King's Goods,* London & Oxford 1989, 284, 287.

24 H. d'Orleans, *Inventaire de tous les Meubles de Cardinal Mazarin 1653*, London 1861; J. Guiffrey, *Inventaire Général du Mobilier de la Couronne sous Louis XIV*, I-II, Paris 1884-1886; R. Bauer and H. Haupt (eds.), *Das Kunstkammerinventar Kaiser Rudolfs II 1607-1611*, Vienna 1976 (Jahrbuch der Kunsthistorische Sammlungen in Wien, n.s. 72).

25 H. Brunner, G. Hoyer & L. Seelig, *Residence Munich*, Munich 1987.

26 I am indebted to Dr. Lorenz Seelig, Munich, for useful discussions and valuable information in this connection. In March this year I had the opportunity to present this problem to the Furniture History Society. None among the listeners seemed to be able to come up with any suggestions as to earlier or contemporary examples.

CHRISTIAN IV'S ITALIANATES. SCULPTURE AT THE DANISH COURT

Kristoffer Neville

The literature on the arts in Denmark under Frederik II and Christian IV is largely in two languages: Danish, as we might expect, and also Dutch. With the exception of the limited bibliography in English and German, this literature is thus primarily in a pair of languages that are not particularly accessible; even specialists in northern European art, who could easily take a deeper interest in the high-quality works made in and for the Danish court, are unlikely to feel comfortable in both Dutch and Danish.[1] This characteristic of the literature is not accidental, but arose from the interpretation of the works. A very broad description of the historiography on Christian IV's patronage would put it in two basic camps. One of these sees the works of the Danish court as an outpost of Netherlandish art. This view was particularly popular with earlier writers in the Low Countries, who were drawn to the material largely through the perceived Netherlandish character of the buildings and paintings. The other long-standing interpretation describes them largely as a distinctly local product, in one formulation that of a king with a remarkably developed aesthetic sense – which would evidently make the works only minimally related to artistic trends elsewhere.[2] Both of these are basically isolationist positions of an earlier generation that, at most, admit a Netherlandish influence in the kingdom. Both interpretations present significant problems and limitations.

These approaches make it difficult to derive a nuanced view of what the Danish kings, and particularly Christian IV, looked for in the artists supported by the court, and how they perceived the works they commissioned. One often speaks of Netherlanders offering generically 'modern' work. But this does not permit much insight into the kinds of works and talent that Christian might have sought if he had been unconstrained by the financial and geographical realities of his position as king of Denmark – a land relatively far from the Mediterranean, but close to the Netherlands and bound to them by water and trade routes. This essay will thus explore the degree to which we can determine what Christian would have wished for in a perfect world, how he pursued this ideal, and how he may have regarded at least some of his commissions in a somewhat different manner than we generally recognize today.

The interpretation of the Danish royal commissions as essentially Netherlandish, ("a transplanted crop" in Johan Huizinga's memorable formulation),[3] arose through two basic observations: there were many skilled Netherlanders at work in Denmark in the sixteenth and seventeenth centuries, and many of the monuments in the kingdom seem to reflect a Netherlandish style quite closely. Following this approach, we might assume that in cultural matters Christian IV was in some ways comparable to his younger peer, Friedrich Wilhelm, the "Great Elector" of Brandenburg. Friedrich Wilhelm studied in Leiden in the 1630s, and was acquainted with the Stadholder, Frederik Hendrik. In 1646 he married Henriette Louise of Orange, but by this time he was already deeply taken with many aspects of Netherlandish culture. He imported both ideas and people from the Low Countries, and their influence on Brandenburg was profound.[4] The elector was evidently deeply interested in architecture, and was personally involved in the development of the project for the Potsdam city palace. The basis for his contribution may have been his purchase of a group of drawings by Jacob van Campen, who had built the Mauritshuis in The Hague and the Amsterdam town hall.[5] These sheets have never been found, making it is difficult to parse the origins of the various aspects of the design, but this episode seems emblematic of the elector's desire to recreate in Brandenburg what he had seen in the Netherlands.

Friedrich Wilhelm was unable to bring van Campen, Pieter Post, or any of the other leading Dutch architects to Berlin. Paintings and sculptures could more easily be imported, however. He commissioned a number of canvases from Gerrit van Honthorst, and, apparently unable to persuade him to accept a court position, appointed his younger brother and assistant, Willem van Honthorst, court painter.[6] Neither of the Honthorst brothers spent much time in Berlin, but other outstanding figures, such as the sculptor Bartholomäus Eggers, visited for longer periods and produced excellent works in Brandenburg.

In all of these endeavors, Friedrich Wilhelm's Netherlandish orientation came out of a deep and self-conscious appreciation of the cultural and technological achievements of the Low Countries, as well as through his own dynastic ties to the region. The same cannot be said of Christian IV. The Danish king traveled in England and parts of the Holy Roman Empire – the regions to which he was bound by marriage – but never visited the Netherlands. So far as we can tell, he had no particular interest in Netherlandish culture *per se,* and he harbored a deep disdain for the nascent United Provinces (the northern Netherlands, to become the independent Dutch Republic in 1648, the year of Christian's death). He considered their struggle for independence from Spain illegitimate, the result of a group of rebellious burgers overstepping their place in society, and he is supposed to have told a group of envoys that "I recognize no States General, only the king of Spain."[7]

If Christian did not share Friedrich Wilhelm's appreciation of the Netherlands, we must explain the perceived Netherlandish character of his commissions in other ways. Unfortunately, his correspondence provides little help in this. It has long been recognized that it is nearly impossible to distill a coherent view of the arts from his letters.[8] There are other approaches to the problem, however. Christian seems not to have been equally interested in all of the arts. He generally devoted more resources and attention to sculpture and music than to painting.[9] The Kronborg series, the oratory at Frederiksborg, and some other outstanding works stand as exceptions to this generalization, but many other paintings entered his collections as wholesale purchases from traveling dealers or agents, some of dubious quality. These mass purchases can hardly be accepted as indicative of the king's particular interests in the arts, except perhaps that he was not always as discriminating as we might expect.

The sculptors and musicians who worked for the court were more consistently of the highest quality. This had also been largely true of Christian's grandfather and father, Christian III and Frederik II, who had both commissioned major works from Cornelis Floris and (in the case of the latter) from Johann Gregor van der Schardt. Christian continued this pattern with commissions from Hendrik de Keyser, Adriaen de Vries and François Dieussart. He also brought John Dowland and Heinrich Schütz to the court. Because of this apparent preference for sculpture

Fig.1. Adriaen de Vries, Neptune Fountain, Frederiksborg Castle, 1615-1618. (Copies; the original bronzes taken to Sweden 1659 and installed in the gardens at Drottningholm Palace) (Photo author).

and music, it is in this core group that we are most likely to distill a core group representative of Christian's interests in the arts.

Hans Reichle, Adriaen de Vries, and Christian IV

Floris, van der Schardt, de Vries and Dieussart all had roots in the Netherlands, and might superficially be grouped with the other Netherlanders who worked in or for the Danish court. It seems that Christian viewed them rather differently, however. The commission for the Neptune fountain at Frederiksborg in 1613 was loaded with political symbolism, as the king made much of his position as master of the sound leading to the Baltic Sea (Fig. 1).[10] It was to a large degree this position, and the tolls that he charged merchant ships passing between the trade centers of the Baltic and the Netherlands and elsewhere, that filled the Danish treasury and facilitated artistic commissions at the court. Although Christian evidently had a clear idea of the allegorical conception of the fountain, he was hardly determined that de Vries should receive the contract. Rather, he sent his mintmaster, Nicolaus Schwabe, to southern Germany to settle the commission, but did not indicate a particular sculptor.

Three figures stand out for the kind of commission that Christian had in mind: de Vries, Hubert Gerhard, and Hans Reichle. It seems that he initially leaned towards the latter. Schwabe was given a sum for a "Posserer" (sculptor or modeler) that he would find in Innsbruck or Augsburg. Soon thereafter we find Schwabe looking for Reichle by name in Brixen (Bressanone) and Bozen (Bolzano) in Tyrol, and, not finding him there, continuing to Verona and Venice.[11] He found the sculptor and signed an agreement that he would come to Copenhagen to make the fountain and "other artful things," but, for whatever reason, Reichle never went to Denmark. One of the stipulations of the contract was that the sculptor should travel to Copenhagen; even after the commission for the fountain was transferred to de

Fig.2. François Dieussart, Henrietta Maria, 1640. Copenhagen, Rosenborg Castle (Photo Rosenborg).

Vries in 1615, Schwabe was to convince Reichle to keep his word and move to the Danish court. Evidently the king had other projects in mind and wanted to appoint one of these men as a longer-term or permanent court sculptor. It may be because he thought that de Vries and Gerhard could not be dislodged from Prague and Munich that he pursued Reichle from the beginning.[12]

The common feature among de Vries, Reichle, and Gerhard is their background: all had Italian training. All studied in Florence, where de Vries and Reichle are documented as assistants to Giambologna, and all were influential in bringing the courtly style of the later sixteenth century into northern Europe. The supposition that all three men were in some way representative of the Florentine master, himself with Netherlandish roots, would seem to be further supported by Schwabe's purchase in Dresden of wax *bozzetti* by him at the same time that he bought several small bronzes by de Vries.[13] Christian visited Dresden in 1595, where he would have seen the *bozzetti* and small bronzes by Giambologna, and he may have had these in mind when he sent Schwabe abroad.[14] If these older Italianate works were the true objects of the king's interest, the particular sculptor would have been less important than his training in the Giambologna's workshop or his having a similar background.

François Dieussart in Copenhagen

Working for the Danish court three decades after de Vries, François Dieussart (c. 1600-1661) can be considered in a similar framework as the older master: a Netherlander trained in Italy. He worked primarily in Rome (rather than Florence, as de Vries did), where we find him working for the papal Borghese family around in 1618-1619.[15] In the summer of 1630 he was still in the city, working under Gianlorenzo Bernini on the catafalque of Carlo Barberini. He seems to have established himself in Roman artistic circles by this point, as he regularly attended the meetings of the *Accademia di San Luca,* and in 1633 he was nominated to the *Accademia dei virtuosi al Pantheon.* It was in Rome that he caught the attention of Thomas Howard, Lord Arundel, in whose service we find him by 1635.

It may well have been Dieussart's work in London that brought him to Christian's attention. There is a bust of the English queen, Henrietta Maria, in Rosenborg Palace that can be traced back to the Danish royal collections, and very likely to Christian's reign (fig. 2). Charles I was Christian's nephew, and the courts had always enjoyed cordial relations, which occasionally facilitated cultural or artistic contacts. Inigo Jones, later famous as an architect, possibly worked as a painter for Christian from about 1603-1605. Likewise, the Copenhagen court painter Franz Cleyn was recruited for the court of James I after a visit to England in 1623. These sorts of ties

Fig. 3. François Dieussart, Christian IV, c. 1644. Copenhagen, Rosenborg Castle (Photo Rosenborg).

alone could explain the movement of the bust to Denmark as a royal or diplomatic gift. It has also been suggested that the bust came to Copenhagen more specifically in connection with the disruptions of the English civil war in the early 1640s, with the accompanying need to rally support for the Stuart cause abroad.[16] If the transfer of the bust to Copenhagen was an overtly political act, it may have had the more purely cultural effect of bringing Dieussart to Christian's attention. Certainly the disruptions in England would have forced Dieussart to look for a new, more stable, center of patronage. After a period in The Hague, he arrived in Copenhagen in 1643.

It is possible that Dieussart returned to Italy at some point in the earlier 1640s, for Christian paid his expenses for travel "from Italy." This may have been a useful fiction for the sculptor, but it seems also to have reflected what the king wished to see in him. Documents regularly refer to Dieussart as "Francesco" or some similarly Italianate version of his name. More significantly, his most important project for Christian, a bronze bust, is an all' antica portrait, showing the king in a breastplate with a pallium and a laurel wreath (Fig. 3), referring unmistakably to the Roman sculptural tradition. The bust was most likely cast after Dieussart left Denmark, but another commission for a similar portrait bust of Prince Frederik (III) demonstrates that it was not an afterthought or a variant of the somewhat less refined marble bust in the same format.[17]

Christian's and Dieussart's ambitions in bronze are even more apparent in a commission for a bronze equestrian monument.[18] The project seems never to have progressed very far, and we cannot discuss it in any detail. We know only that Dieussart was paid a great deal over a number of months for a "metal horse," and a document from January 1644 mentions a drawing for a "statuam equestrem."[19] Although it is not explicit, these suggest that it was to be a large work. In the 1640s, before François Girardon's equestrian statues of Louis XIV and various similar works either planned or executed for Berlin, Munich, Stockholm and elsewhere, equestrian monuments were not only the greatest technical challenge for the sculptor, they were also unmistakably bound to the Italian sculptural tradition. The imperial statue of Marcus Aurelius on the Campidoglio in Rome was the ultimate source for this format (as it would later be for Girardon's works), and it found numerous variants in the Renaissance, from Donatello's *Gattamelata* in Padua and Andrea del Verrocchio's *Bartolomeo Colleoni* in Venice in the fifteenth century, to Giambologna's Medici statues in Florence (Fig. 4), to Francesco Mochi's statue of Alessandro Farnese in Piacenza (1620-1625) and, later, Bernini's statues of Constantine in the Vatican and Louis XIV. The equestrian monuments to Henri IV on the Pont-Neuf in Paris (1604-1614), and to Philip III (1606-1617) and Philip IV (1634-1640) in Madrid were major examples of this tradition outside of Italy, and all

were by Giambologna's assistant and heir, Pietro Tacca.

Tacca's statues in Paris and Madrid reflect a larger desire in the European courts for equestrian monuments. Already as crown prince, Charles (I) tried to bring Tacca to London to make a comparable statue of James I, but Tacca refused to leave Tuscany. Charles finally attained his wish a decade later, when in 1630 Hubert Le Sueur began such a monument, now depicting Charles himself. Le Sueur was not a student or even a particularly close follower of Giambologna. He may not even have been to Italy at this point,[20] though he must certainly have been familiar with Tacca's statue of Henri IV in Paris. Nonetheless, the inspiration for the statue was immediately obvious to those with an interest in the arts. The English writer, Henry Peacham, wrote of Le Sueur's project: "... the great horse with his Majesty upon it, twice as great as life, and now well nigh finished, will compare with that of the New Bridge [the Pont-Neuf] at Paris, or those others at Florence, and Madrid, though made by Sueur his John de Bolonia [Giambologna], that rare workman, who not long since lived at Florence."[21]

De Vries, who had already made a major fountain for Christian, is comparable to Tacca in that both trained in Giambologna's workshop and carried on and developed the tradition in Italy (he is documented working in Milan and Turin) and farther afield. Indeed, their work was still sufficiently similar that Tacca's son, Ferdinando, would later cast smaller works designed by de Vries.[22] De Vries never produced a monumental equestrian statue, but he showed his facility in the format with several smaller bronzes of horses, and a small equestrian statue of Duke Heinrich Julius of Braunschweig-Wolfenbüttel, which the duke may have been contemplating around the time that Christian visited him in 1605.[23] The Neptune fountain was commissioned before the vogue for equestrian statues had taken hold outside of Italy. But by the 1630s, equestrian monuments were underway in some form for many of Christian's peers. He may have realized that he had missed a chance to have de Vries take on such

Fig. 4. Giambologna, Cosimo I de' Medici, 1587-1593. Florence, (Photo author).

a project, and instead set Dieussart to work on an equestrian statue. His idea would come to completion in c. 1685 with the equestrian statue of Abraham-César Lamoureux at the King's New Square (Kongens Nytorv), to be followed 1752-70 with the monument of Frederik V by Jacques-François-Joseph Saly on Amalienborg Square, both in Copenhagen.

Christian IV had a strong interest in music, and accounts for the purchase of various instruments for the king's "own use" suggest that he considered himself something of a musician as well.[24] His most prominent composers are in many ways comparable to de Vries and Dieussart. John Dowland came to Copenhagen as one of the best-paid courtiers in 1598, shortly after studying in Italy. Heinrich Schütz, who came to Copenhagen from Dresden for two extended periods in the 1630s, never admitted any teacher other than Giovanni Gabrieli in Venice.[25]

If we take this small group of figures as representing Christian's tastes and desires more closely than many of the other artists active at the Danish court, we can make some basic generalizations. All would have considered themselves Italianates to a greater or lesser extent, and all worked in a number of centers on a circuit of northern European courts. With the possible exception of Dieussart, for whom Christian paid travel expenses from Italy, all came to Copenhagen from elsewhere in northern Europe. Although Netherlanders might be heavily represented in this group, it seems to have been their reputations based on successes at other courts that made them most appealing to Christian.

Indeed, the tacit and explicit process of acceptance and recommendation by other courts may have been as important a consideration as any other. Just as Christian never visited the Netherlands, so was Italy foreign to him. His awareness of international courtly taste was thus based largely on the general reputation of Italy and what he had seen at peer courts.[26] His nephew, Charles I, was certainly an important part of this process. This was particularly true in later years – we have already seen that Dieussart's success in London very likely set up his move to Copenhagen – a but even when Christian visited London in 1614 he almost certainly encountered works by Giambologna, precisely during the prolonged commission process for the Neptune fountain.[27] Other courts were no less important, however. It has been pointed out that the Saxon court chapels were essential for the conception of the magnificent chapel in Frederiksborg Palace, near Copenhagen,[28] and we have seen that Christian could well have remembered the small bronzes and wax figurines by Giambologna in Dresden that he was unable to experience in Florence. Prague was less familiar, but the king was certainly well aware of its fame. Quite apart from de Vries's significant abilities, his position as imperial sculptor (as well as a successor of Giambologna) would have made him a major figure in Christian's view.

With these observations in mind, we can consider some of Christian's commissions for paintings in a somewhat different light. Gerrit van Honthorst has been proposed as a figure exactly comparable to François Dieussart.[29] Both trained in Rome, and both worked in The Hague, London, Copenhagen, and Berlin. Honthorst was very successful in Rome in the 1610s, and returned to the Netherlands as a leading figure among the Utrecht "Caravaggists" in the following decade. His work for the court of Charles I in London in 1628 helped to establish him in The Hague, and he may well have come to Christian's attention through his work at one or the other of these courts. It is true that other painters – Isaac Isaacz, Claes Moeyaert, and others – contributed to Christian's series of paintings for Kronborg castle, but Honthorst received a significantly larger share of the commission than did the others.[30]

Gerrit van Honthorst also worked for Friedrich Wilhelm, the Great Elector, and this brings us back to the problem of the cultural and artistic interests of the Margrave-Elector of Brandenburg and the King of Denmark. Like Honthorst, Dieussart worked for Friedrich Wilhelm in the years after he worked for Christian, and was based in Berlin from 1650 to 1655. If, as seems likely, their Italianate qualities appealed to Christian –

Fig.5. François Dieussart, Friedrich Wilhelm of Brandenburg, 1651-1652, Potsdam (Photo courtesy Stiftung Preussische Schlösser und Gärten Berlin-Brandenburg).

at least in principle – we would seem to have a conflict with the avowedly Netherlandish tastes and interests of the elector.

There are several ways to address this problem, which is entangled in the larger problem of what early-modern observers meant when they spoke of styles in geographical or national terms. But even if we put these questions aside for the moment and take Italianate and Netherlandish styles and traditions largely at face value, several possibilities stand out. One explanation is that the artists could adjust their work to the perceived wishes of their patrons. Thus we may compare Dieussart's all' antica bust of Christian IV to a full-length marble statue of Friedrich Wilhelm made in 1651-1652, about seven years after the sculptor left Copenhagen (Fig. 5; cf. Fig. 3). The later statue is less animated than the bust of Christian, and very clearly contained within the block of marble from which it was carved. Charles Avery considered the work *retarditaire*, and could not explain its perceived conservatism in light of the works Dieussart had produced in Denmark.[31] The relevant question is not of progressive versus regressive style so much as it is of local taste, however. The statue of Friedrich Wilhelm is fully comparable to other Netherlandish works from the mid-seventeenth century, including a series of four works that Dieussart himself made of the princes of Orange in the early 1650s.[32]

A second explanation, simpler and more generally applicable, might be that these stylistic categories were much more flexible than we tend to suppose, and that both Christian and Friedrich Wilhelm could find a great deal to appreciate in all of the artists who worked in both of their courts. Certainly Christian was never dogmatic about Italianate work, however he might have understood the notion. Two Copenhagen painters who stand out from the others as fixtures of the court and closely involved in the king's projects are Pieter Isaacsz and Karel van Mander III. Both studied in Italy, but both also came from Netherlandish backgrounds. Christian evidently saw no contradiction in this blending of backgrounds. In this he was much like his contemporaries in both northern and southern Europe. "Utrecht Caravaggism," "Italian Landscape," and "Dutch Classicism" (both in painting and architecture) are all recognized aspects of seventeenth-century art in the Low Countries, just as Rubens, van Dyck, Adam Elsheimer and other northern painters were highly regarded by Italian patrons and collectors.

Yet, the legacy of de Vries and Dieussart in Copenhagen, like that of Schütz, suggests that Christian, like many of his peers in the northern-European courts, valued studies in Italy, and most likely was discerning enough to recognize the tradition that informed the work of these men. Certainly Dieussart's work in Copenhagen is recognizably distinct from his work in Berlin, and we must accept the probability that this reflected the king's interests.

Dieussart's work in Copenhagen is much closer to what he produced in London than in Brandenburg. With Honthorst and others considered in this way, the Copenhagen court in general begins to look less like Antwerp or Utrecht, and more like the English capital in the later 1620s and 1630s, where Charles I very clearly wanted an Italianate artistic milieu. Although he commissioned a bust from Bernini and persuaded Orazio Gentileschi and Francesco Fanelli to come to London, Charles was unable to bring Pietro Tacca, Guercino or Francesco Albani north. Although outstanding artists, his Italianates were stand-ins, and primarily from the Netherlands: van Dyck, Inigo Jones, Dieussart, and Honthorst, among others.

Except for Peder Griffel, it is not clear whether Christian tried to bring any Italians to Copenhagen, nor did he have anyone comparable to Inigo Jones to take on his building projects.[33] Painters travel most easily, but since painting seems not to have been a high priority among the arts for him, as it may have been for Charles, the absence of Italian painters in Copenhagen may not be significant on this point. For sculptural commissions, however, he may have secured in Adriaen de Vries the finest Italianate on the continent active after the death of Giambologna in 1608. Dieussart's quality and significance have yet to be established, but he produced some of his best works for Christian. But while Charles's Italianates came almost exclusively from the Netherlands, Christian had a much broader view. He looked not only to the Netherlands, but also to London and the major courts in the Holy Roman Empire for his most prized artists. With de Vries, Schütz, and others, he may have come even closer than Charles to his mark.

Notes

1 Many of those who have mastered the literature have been based at the Christian-Albrecht-Universität in Kiel, in the duchy of Holstein, which was subject to the Danish crown until 1864, and have thus found themselves, quite literally, between the two traditions.

2 A good overview of the historiography is available in Juliette Roding, "The Myth of the 'Dutch Renaissance' in Denmark. Dutch Influence on Danish Architecture in the Seventeenth Century", in: J.Ph.S. Lemmink & J.S.A.M. van Koningsbrugge (eds.), *Baltic Affairs. Relations Between the Netherlands and North-Eastern Europe, 1500-1800,* Nijmegen 1990, 343-353, and in Dirk van de Vijver's contribution to this book.

3 Johan Huizinga, *Nederland's beschaving in de zeventiende eeuw,* Haarlem 1956 (1941), 144-145: "Met uitzondering van de schaarse gebouwen van groteren omvang vond de Nederlandse architectuur haar kracht niet in het monumentale. Het blijft uiterst merkwaardig, en een van de sterkste bewijzen voor de expansieve energie van onze nationaliteit, dat deze bouwkunst tot de opgave van het monumentale geroepen werd buiten de grenzen van het vaderland. In Denemarken vroeg men van haar koninklijke sloten, en de Hollandse bouwmeesters voldeden aan dien eis en bouwden het ene slot na het andere, in de afmeting van koninklijke majesteit, maar met de stijl- en versieringselementen, die eigenlijk bij de voorname burgerwoning thuishoorden. Men ziet dien Deensen sloten mijns inziens toch een weinig het hybridische aan. De decoratie van die trotse gevels mist tenslotte een element van fantazie. Men heeft hier te klaarblijkelijk te doen met een overgeplant gewas." For an English translation, cf. "Dutch Civilisation in the Seventeenth Century", in: Johan Huizinga, *Dutch Civilisation in the Seventeenth Century and other essays,* transl. Arnold J. Pomerans, London & Glasgow 1968, 94-95

4 For the Netherlandish influence in Brandenburg, see Horst Lademacher (ed.), *Onder den Oranje boom. Niederländische Kunst und Kultur im 17. und 18. Jahrhundert an deutschen Fürstenhöfen,* Munich 1999.

5 Konrad Ottenheym, "Fürsten, Architekten und Lehrbucher. Wege der holländischer Baukunst nach Brandenburg im 17. Jahrhundert", in: Lademacher (ed.) 1999, 287-298.

6 J. Richard Judson & Rudolf E.O. Ekkart, *Gerrit van Honthorst 1592-1656,* Doornspijk 1999, 42-46.

7 Cited in J. Römelingh, "Christian IV and the Dutch Republic. An Introduction", *Leids kunsthistorisch Jaarboek* 2 (1983), 1-6.

8 Many of Christian IV's letters are published in C.F. Bricka & J.A. Fridericia (eds.), *Kong Christian den Fjerdes egenhændige Breve,* I-VIII, Copenhagen 1887-1947.

9 This was observed by Ulla Houkjær, "Dutch Artists in the Service of Danish History – the Kronborg Series", *Apollo (London)* 128 (1988), 99-103, and by Thomas DaCosta Kaufmann, review of *Christian IV and Eu-*

rope, Konsthistorisk tidskrift 58 (1989), 19-22. Christian was also clearly interested in architecture, but this raises a somewhat different set of problems, and will not be discussed here.

10 Lars Olof Larsson, "Die Brunnen auf Schloss Frederiksborg", *Art in Denmark 1600-1650. Leids Kunsthistorisch Jaarboek* 2 (1983), 69-84; Frits Scholten (ed.), *Adriaen de Vries 1556-1626.* Exhibition catalogue, Amsterdam, Stockholm, Los Angeles, Zwolle 1998, cat. 37; Charlotte Christensen, "Adriaen de Vries' Neptunspringvand", in: Steffen Heiberg (ed.) *Christian 4. og Frederiksborg*, Copenhagen 2006, 153-172.

11 The documents related to Schwabe's trip are published in F. R. Friis, *Bidrag til dansk Kunsthistorie*, Copenhagen 1890-1901, 206-215. The parts related to Reichle are excerpted in Friedrich Kriegsbaum, "Hans Reichle", *Jahrbuch der Kunsthistorischen Sammlungen in Wien* N.F. 5 (1931), 199-200. For Reichle generally, see Kriegsbaum 1931; Thomas Paul Bruhn, *Hans Reichle (1565/70-1642). A Reassessment of his Sculpture,* Dissertation: Pennsylvania State University 1981.

12 Although Reichle did not travel to Denmark, a certain Peter Griffel did, and may have been sent or recommended by Reichle. Griffel (Peder Italien, Petro (Pietro) Crivelli/ Gravile/ Greffueldt or Creffuille) was apparently a native Italian, who probably came to Denmark (from Prague?) at the agency of Nicolaus Schwabe. He got his official commission in Denmark in December 1615 as a "stucco worker and sculptor of Italy" with the considerable yearly wage of 300 rix-dollars and stayed at the Danish court till 1622, when he acquired a travel passport for Italy. No works can be securely attributed to him, but according to the documentary sources he was involved i.a. in the production of small bronzes after antique models. Among his commissions was the deliverance of a model in gesso for an image of a sitting (person), holding his foot with both hands, apparently a version of the *Spinario*. On Griffel, see Birgitte Bøggild Johannsen, "Peder Griffel", in: *Dansk Biografisk Leksikon*[3] 5, Copenhagen 1980, 291; Hanne Honnens de Lichtenberg, "Christian IV and the Art of Sculpture", *Apollo* 128 (1988), 107; Karin Kryger, "Pietro Crivelli", in: *Weilbachs Kunstnerleksikon*[4] 2, Copenhagen 1994, 86.

13 The Giambologna *bozzetti* and the de Vries bronzes were listed more or less interchangeably in Schwabe's list of acquisitions, published in Friis 1890, 211-212.

14 For the works by Giambologna in Germany, see Dorothea Diemer, "Giambologna in Germania", in: Beatrice Paolozzi Strozzi & Dimitrios Zikos (eds.), *Giambologna. Gli dei, gli eroi,* Florence 2006, 106-125. For Giambologna in Dresden, see Dirk Syndram et al. (eds.), *Giambologna in Dresden. Die Geschenke der Medici*, Munich 2006.

15 For Dieussart, see Charles Avery, "François Dieussart (c. 1600-1661), Portrait Sculptor to the Courts of Northern Europe", *Victoria and Albert Museum Yearbook* 4 (1974), 63-99; Frits Scholten, "Sir Constantijn Huygens and François Dieussart, Constantine Huygens, and the Classical Ideal in Funerary Sculpture", *Simiolus* 25 (1997), 303-328; Marion Boudon Machuel, "François Dieussart in Rome: Two Newly Identified Works", *The Burlington Magazine* 145 (2003), 833-840.

16 Avery 1974, 69.

17 Both of Dieussart's busts of Christian are now in Rosenborg Palace in Copenhagen. The portrait of Frederik III, cast 1661-1664, is in the citadel in Copenhagen. A contract between Crown Prince Christian and Dieussart for the purchase of "some copper [i.e., bronze] and other works of art" further shows the sculptor's more frequent work in bronze in Denmark. See Avery 1974, 79.

18 It seems that Christian IV had planned an equestrian monument in bronze already before 1623. During a stay in Copenhagen in March of that year, Prince Christian the Younger of Anhalt visited a modeler in wax to admire *inter alia* "a horse in wax in life size" ("ein entworfenes Pferd von Wachs in Lebensgröße"), cf G. Krause (ed.), *Tagebuch Christians des Jüngeren, Fürst zu Anhalt*, Leipzig 1858, 97. See also Birgitte Bøggild Johannsen & Hugo Johannsen, *Kongens kunst*, Copenhagen 1993 (Ny dansk kunsthistorie, 2) 112.

19 Avery 1974, 78.

20 Le Sueur's first trip to Italy may have been his commission to make casts of famous antique statues in 1631. See Charles Avery, "Hubert Le Sueur, the 'Unworthy Praxiteles' of King Charles I", in: Charles Avery, *Studies in European Sculpture*, II, London 1988, 173.

21 Quoted in Avery 1988, 172. Peacham wrote about 1633, the year that the statue was finished.

22 See e.g. the *Rape of a Sabine,* cast by Ferdinando Tacca in Florence c. 1640-1650 after a model by de Vries. Scholten (ed.) 1998, 102-105.

23 The dating of the statue of Heinrich Julius is uncertain. Scholten 1998, 26, dates it c. 1610. Lars Olof Larsson, *Adriaen de Vries. Adrianus Fries Hagiensis Batavvs 1545-1626,* Vienna 1967, 118, dates it c. 1607-1611. If the commission were placed in the earlier part of this period, the duke may already have had it in mind during Christian's visit.

24 For a short overview of the music at Christian's court, see Mette Müller & Ole Kongsted, "Christian IV and Music", in: Steffen Heiberg (ed.), *Christian IV and Europe: The 19th Art Exhibition of the Council of Europe, Denmark 1988*, Herning 1988, 119-141; Bjarke Moe,

"Italian Music at the Danish Court during the Reign of Christian IV. Presenting a Picture of Cultural Transformation", *Danish Yearbook of Musicology* 38 (2010-2011), 15-32. For a more thorough treatment, see Angul Hammerich, *Musiken ved Christian de Fjerdes Hof*, Copenhagen 1892.

25 For Dowland see Diana Poulton, *John Dowland*, Berkeley 1982; for Schütz, see Basil Smallman, *Schütz*, Oxford 2000.

26 Christian's large collection of prints could also have been an informative resource.

27 Cosimo II de' Medici sent a shipment of twelve small bronzes cast by Tacca after models by Giambologna to Henry, Prince of Wales, in 1611-1612, in the hope of facilitating a marriage between the prince and Caterina de' Medici. Henry died soon after receiving the works, which were inherited by Charles. Christian would almost certainly have seen these when he visited London in 1614. For the bronzes, see Katherine Watson & Charles Avery, "Medici and Stuart: A Grand Ducal Gift of 'Giovanni Bologna' Bronzes for Henry, Prince of Wales (1612)", *The Burlington Magazine* 115 (1973), 493-507. It has been argued that Christian was also an enormous influence for the young Prince Charles, and that Christian's interests in patronage, particularly of sculpture, were formative for the young prince's own artistic interests. See David Howarth, "Charles I, Sculpture and Sculptors", in: Arthur MacGregor (ed.), *The Late King's Goods. Collections, Possessions and Patronage of Charles I in Light of the Commonwealth Sale Inventories*, London 1989, 75.

28 Hugo Johannsen, "The Saxon Connection. On the Architectural Genesis of Christian IV's Palace Chapel (1606-1617) at Frederiksborg Castle", in: Jan Harasimowicz, Piotr Oszczanowski & Marcin Wisłocki (eds.), *On Opposite Sides of the Baltic Sea. Relations between Scandinavian and Central European Countries/Po obu stronach Bałtyku. Wzajemne relacje między Skandynawią a Europą Środkową* II, Wrocław 2006, 369-379.

29 This was proposed by Avery 1974, 63, and seconded by Judson & Ekkart 1999, 46.

30 For the Kronborg series, see Houkjær 1988, and H.D. Schepelern & Ulla Houkjær, *The Kronborg Series. King Christian IV and his Pictures of Early Danish History*, Copenhagen 1988.

31 Avery 1974, 90.

32 The statues of Frederik Hendrik and Willem II are illustrated in Elisabeth Neurdenburg, *De zeventiende eeuwsche beeldhouwkunst in de noordelijke Nederlanden*, Amsterdam 1948, 122; those of Willem the Silent and Maurits are illustrated in Avery 1974, 83. Johannes Bloemendael's statue of Prince Willem III, made in The Hague in 1676 (illustrated Neurdenburg 1948, 229), shows the conventions that Dieussart had used a quarter-century earlier.

33 Though never actually being attested in Denmark, Giovanni Maria Nosseni of Lugano, active at the court of Saxony 1575-1620, delivered architectural works for Sparepenge (1600) and Frederiksborg Castle (1615-1616).

CLAIMING DANISH RENAISSANCE. THE HISTORIOGRAPHY OF THE ARCHITECTURAL RELATIONS BETWEEN THE LOW COUNTRIES AND THE BALTICUM/DENMARK

Dirk Van de Vijver

Since the rise of architectural history in the 19th century, architectural historians of Belgium and the Netherlands have noticed the resemblances between 'their' 16th- and 17th-century architecture and the Danish one. In this lecture we want to study some important 'moments' in the Belgian and Dutch historiography on the architectural relations between the Low Countries and the Baltic/Denmark. Through a close reading of these key texts, we want to bring to the surface the mechanisms and politics that are at stake in the construction and the conceptualization of the Netherlandish-Baltic/Danish architectural relationships.

Auguste Schoy and the definition of the phenomenon

The Paris World Exhibition of 1878 invited the participating countries to propose a pavilion in their national architectural style for the so-called *Rue des Nations*.[1] The Belgian architect and architectural historian Auguste Schoy (1838-1885)[2] noticed the close relationship between the Belgian pavilion (Fig. 1), based on the prints by Cornelis Floris (1514-1575) and Hans Vredeman de Vries (1527-1607), the Dutch pavilion (Fig. 2), based on the town halls of The Hague and Leiden, the pavilion of the prince of Wales (Fig. 3) in a 'pure Elizabethan style', and the Danish pavilion (Fig. 4), inspired by the Stock Exchange of Copenhagen at the *Rue des Nations*.[3] In an article on the Belgian façade by the architect Charles-Emile Janlet (1839-1919),[4] Schoy reflects upon the 'influence of the Antwerp School' in the Northern Netherlands, England, and especially in Sweden, Norway and Denmark, a subject which intrigued him already for more than a decade. It's a pity he stated that Germany and Austria preferred a 'false Italian disguise' and didn't build in their national manner, that of the Nurnberg School. Then he enumerated a number of examples of the influence of the Antwerp school in the Palatinate: Alexandre Colyn in Heidelberg, Innsbruck and Prague, Pierre de Witte (or Candido) and Hubert Gerhard (c. 1540-1620) in Munich, Guillaume Vernickel (Wilhelm Vernuken) in Köln, and again Gerhard in Augsburg.[5] He also stressed the importance of prints such as those of Floris and Vredeman for the diffusion of Netherlandish architecture. It is also relevant that although he observed the relations between the Flemish Renaissance, the Dutch variant, the so-called 'style Christian IV' – Schoy was very critical about the role of Christian IV[6] - and the 'Elizabethan style', he did not consider them identical nor interchangeable; he was convinced that a well-informed person could distinguish the peculiarities

Fig. 1. Charles-Emile Janlet, Belgian pavilion at the Rue des Nations, World Exhibition in Paris of 1878. After S. De Vandières, L'exposition universelle de 1878, Paris 1879, p. 71 (Stadsbibliotheek Antwerpen).

of each idiom. Being such a 'connoisseur' (and purist) himself, he strongly protested for instance against the use in the Belgian pavilion of a porch inspired by Hendrick de Keyser (1565-1621), a northern architect who worked a generation later than the golden age of the Flemish Renaissance. In fact, the context of all these reflections was his search for a new national Belgian style, the "style néo-flamand" or "style Léopold II', rationally developed upon the basis of both the products of the 'Antwerp Renaissance circle' (Floris, Vredeman)' and the heritage of Rubens.[7]

Schoy's case for an influence of the Netherlands in Scandinavian Renaissance architecture was based on a series of observations which was the fruit of his meetings with Scandinavian scholars and architects, whom he had met as a leading Belgian architect and architectural historian in the international forum.[8] Some represented monuments on the coloured drawings by Mandelgreen of old interiors of Norway, presented at the world exhibition of 1867, and destined to be published in the *monumenta scandinaviae* (Groupe I, Classe II n°2), seemed for Schoy to belong to the 'Flemish Renaissance'. He observed a similar phenomenon when he consulted *Den Danske Vitruvius* by Lauritz de Thurah (1746-1749). In 1870, Stockholm's correspondent member of the Belgian Academy for Archeology, the attorney Herman Odelberg, published an article in the society's journal, the *Annales de l'Académie d'archéologie de la Belgique*, on the wooden retable of Strängnäs in Sweden, which was imported from Brussels in the late 15th century (Fig. 5).[9] Two years later, the latter published together with the librarian of the Royal Library at Stockholm, E. Eichhorn, in the same journal a monograph on the painter, sculptor and architect Wilhelm Boy (c. 1520-1592) (fig. 6), a man, "who by the diversity of his tal-

Fig. 2. Van den Brinck, Dutch pavillion at the Rue des Nations, World Exhibition in Paris of 1878. After De Vandières, p. 81 (Stadsbibliotheek Antwerpen).

Fig. 3. Pavillion of the Prince of Wales at the Rue des Nations, World Exhibition in Paris of 1878. After De Vandières, p. 27 (Stadsbibliotheek Antwerpen).

ent and the thoroughness of his knowledge merits without doubt a distinguished place amongst the Belgian artists of the 16th century".[10] In 1870 and 1880, the Belgian scholars M. A. Galesloot (Fig. 7), a Brussels archeologist, and Pierre Génard (1830-1899), city librarian of Antwerp, wrote on a Danish work by Cornelis Floris: the monumental tomb (1569-1575) for King Christian III of Denmark in Roskilde Cathedral.[11] In 1877, at last, Schoy saw at the industrial art exposition at the Volksvlijt Palais in Amsterdam (groupe XII, 24) an unpublished study by Vilhelm Klein (1835-1913)[12] on the "flat ornament (ornamentation lisse) in Denmark from the XVIth to the XVIIIth century", which obtained the first prize there. As an important collector of architectural treatises, Schoy knew of course also the print of the Marble Gallery at Frederiksborg Castle, published by Danckers in the *Architectura moderna*.[13] All these elements established for Schoy clear evidence of Flemish influence on Scandinavian architecture. He demanded if it was not the role of the government to send out some scholars, artists and archeologists "to add these far away flowers to our splendid artistic crown and to inform the learned public of those Flemish masterpieces".[14]

In Belgium, we find no public or private reaction to this open research invitation. Only Paul Saintenoy (1862-1952),[15] a very productive author of artist's biographies for the *Biographie nationale*,[16] published in 1906 an article in the *Annales de l'Académie royale d'Archéologie de Belgique* on Flemish architects in 16th-century northern Germany. However, this was no original work, but based on an article by the German scholar Georg Cuny, published in the *Deutsche Bauzeitung* a year before.[17] Moreover, the mentioned monumental series of biographical articles of important 'Belgians', the *Biographie nationale*, a project of the Royal Belgian Academy started in 1966, did not include these so-called 'Flemish' artists working abroad. In fact, Cornelis Floris and Vredeman de Vries were almost the only artists with an important 'German and Scandinavian architectural oeuvre' which obtained an entry in it. They were also almost the only ones who, from time to time, continued to be the object of study by 'Belgian' scholars.[18] The van den Blocke, van Steenwinckel or van Obbergen, to name only some, did not receive an entry in the Belgian national biography.[19] Also Belgian architectural historiography, strongly interwoven within the practice of conservation and restoration of the national heritage, concentrated heavily and almost exclusively on the productions on Belgian soil (be it within their new national borders or within those of the historic Southern Netherlands) and forgot almost the masterpieces created or present abroad by 'Belgian' artists.

Dutch architects and translated scholarship

Although it is not certain that the formulation of the problem by Auguste Schoy in the 1870s was known to Dutch architects and architectural

Fig. 4. Vilhelm Dahlerup, Danish pavillion at the Rue des Nations (second from the left), World Exhibition in Paris of 1878. After De Vandières 1879, p. 73, centre (Stadsbibliotheek Antwerpen).

historians, the latter seem to have taken up the challenge and did treat the phenomenon. It is not clear however to which extent those studies in architectural history benefited from the governmental programme to map the archival sources for the Low Countries in Scandinavia and the Balticum.[20] In the summer of 1900, from 7 July till 12 September, the professor at the University of Amsterdam Gerhard Wilhelm Kernkamp (1864-1943)[21] made, by order of the government of the Netherlands, an archive trip to Lund, Linköping, Stockholm and Uppsala in Sweden, to Kristiania (Oslo) in Norway and to Copenhagen in Denmark.[22] The emphasis was put on the diplomatic and economic relations between the Scandinavian countries and the Netherlands; the elements on art and architecture remained limited.[23] In fact, regarding architecture, he only mentioned the manuscripts after Goldmann and by Post on the Mauritshuis in the Royal Library of Copenhagen.[24] A second mission at the end of 1906, from 12 November 1906 till 11 January 1907, which started in Copenhagen and ended in Königsberg, with stops in Kiel, Lübeck, Wismar, Rostock, Stralsund, Greifswald, Stettin and Gdańsk, revealed especially the importance of the archives of Gdańsk for the relations between the Low Countries and the Balticum in general, and for architecture in particular.[25] His 1909 publication even contained a separate section on Netherlandish artists, art agents, architects and engineers in Gdańsk.[26]

Around 1920, two Dutch architects produced a book on the subject. In the year 1917, the architect of public works of the city of Amsterdam, A. A. Kok (1881-1951), published some articles on "Netherlandish architecture abroad" (*Nederlandsche bouwkunst in den Vreemde*) in the journal *Het Zoeklicht*, founded in 1913 as a publication of the Polytechnical Bureau of the Netherlands (*Politechnisch Bureau Nederland*). These articles were reworked into a book, published in 1918 as *Nederlandsche bouwkunst langs de Oostzee* (Netherlandish architecture along the East Sea/ the Baltic Sea) (Fig. 8).[27] The actual content of the book – seven small chapters on Denmark and one on

Fig. 5. Herman Odelberg, "Les retables de Strengnas (Suède)", Annales de l'Académie d'Archéologie de Belgique 26 (1870), 475-480.

Gdańsk[28] – did not contain much new art historical data. In fact, almost all the elements could be found in a publication of thirty years earlier by the Danish architects Ferdinand Meldahl (1827-1908) and Frederik Skjold Neckelmann (1853-1903), the 1888 *Denkmäler der Renaissance in Dänemark*,[29] from which it also borrowed the illustrations. The part on Gdańsk did not contain more information than one could find at the time in German manuals on Renaissance architecture.[30] In short, he synthesized and translated German texts for a Dutch audience with particular emphasis on the Flemish and Dutch artists involved. More interesting is his discourse in the introduction and conclusion of his book: scholars of 'old national brick buildings' have to look also outside the Netherlands, especially to the 'pure' Netherlandish architecture of the 16th and the beginning of the 17th century" in Denmark. His point is that one finds in Denmark more important buildings than in the Netherlands, because the Danish kings addressed themselves to Flemish or Dutch artists and artisans, and because once established, this architecture was more free of the foreign (Italian) influences they underwent in the Netherlands. For Kok, these artists contributed to the spread and fame of the Low Countries, just as much as did Holland's military fame and sea trade. It is this architecture of the Baltic, "here and there mingled with foreign elements", that he wanted to present to his audience.[31]

D. F. Slothouwer's *Bouwkunst der Nederlandsche renaissance in Denemarken* of 1924[32] is a more substantial publication (Fig. 9). This architect, fascinated by Danish Renaissance architecture – he drew the Kronborg palace in an 'envoi de Rome'-like manner (a drawing by his hand, dated 1910, appears as frontispiece of his book) (Fig. 10), married a Danish woman and continued to spend some weeks every year in Denmark. This book, which was also his PhD at Delft University, made use of the available Danish scholarship – he was in close contact with Emil Hannover (1864-1923) and especially with Francis Beckett (1868-1943) – and he added an architectural analysis of the monuments to it. After an historical introduction, he treated the Van Steenwinckel and Van Obbergen family, and then studied more closely their works: Kronborg, Frederiksborg, Rosenborg and other buildings. He stressed not only the Flemish and Dutch origin of those architects, but he was also interested in the use of prints (we observe here the influence of Robert Hedicke's book on Floris[33]) and the possession of architectural books; he mentioned for instance the Wendel Dietterlin's (c. 1550-1599) *Architectura* treatise which belonged to three brothers of the second generation of the Van Steenwinckels.[34] The book is carefully illustrated with photographs

Fig. 6. E. Eichhorn and Herman Odelberg, "Guillaume Boyen (Wilhelm Boy), peintre, sculpteur et architecte belge. Etude biographique", *Annales de l'Académie d'Archéologie de Belgique* 28 (1872), 94-132.

taken by Kristian Hude of Roskilde, and with drawings, plans and elevations. In short, it makes this 'Dutch Renaissance architecture on Danish soil' (and the Danish scholarship on it) available to a Dutch public.

With Slothouwer in mind, one is not astonished by the presence of a chapter of twenty pages on "Netherlandish Renaissance in Denmark and in the Balticum" in the second volume, dating from 1931, of Frans André Jozef Vermeulen's (1883-1961) manual on Dutch architectural history, the *Handboek tot de geschiedenis van de Nederlandse Bouwkunst*.[35] However, one must stress that even without Slothouwer, this chapter would not be quite different from the 1880's German architectural manuals' systematic mention the Netherlandishness of Danish Renaissance architecture. It is therefore not surprising that in the American post-war reconstruction of Belgium, these huge Danish Renaissance buildings formed the inspiration of new large-scale university buildings, such as the Leuven University library designed and built from 1921 onwards by the American architect Whitney Warren (1864-1943).[36]

Around 1930, the cultural contacts between Denmark and the Netherlands articulated interestingly. In 1930, the *Bibliothec. Danic.* was created as a loan given by the society *Dansk Samfund i Holland* to the University Library of Amsterdam.[37] Four years later, on the occasion of an exhibition on Danish art in Amsterdam in 1934, the Danish art historian Vilhelm Lorenzen (1877-1961) gave a lecture for the society *Arti et Amicitiae* on the life and work of Netherlandish architects and city planners in Denmark in the 17th century.[38] He enumerated the architects Hans van Steenwinkel, Willem Cornelissen, "lands-bouwmeester" Leonard Blasius, and the engineers Eggert Speerfork, Johan Sems, Abraham de la Haye, Isaac van Geelkerk (Norway), Henrik Ruse (fortification engineer of Amsterdam) and Joost van Scholten. Also here, the message was that "several of the best Netherlandish architecture was produced in Denmark" and that the influence of these Dutch artists on Danish architecture, especially in the 17th century, was crucial.[39] The 'Netherlandish architecture abroad' stayed a *topos* in the cultural and economic history of the Netherlands.[40]

In Ed Taverne's PhD on the history of Dutch Urbanism at the end of the 16th and the beginning of the 17th century *In 't Land van belofte: in de nieue stadt. Ideaal en werkelijkheid van de stadsuitleg in de Republiek 1580-1680*,[41] the work of two Dutch engineers in Denmark, Johan Sems [Semp] (1572-c. 1656) and Isaac van Geelkerk, was incorporated.

Fig. 7. M.A. Galesloot, "Le tombeau de Christian III, roi de Danemark, dans la cathédrale de Roeskilde, et celui de Gustave Wasa, à Upsala", Annales de l'Académie d'Archéologie de Belgique 26 (1870), 470-474.

It was for the first time that the urbanism aspect of the phenomenon was treated in more detail in Dutch historiography. However, extensive Danish monographs were already available for both engineers.[42] Hence, also here the essence of Dutch historiography was the 'translation' and contextualization of foreign contributions.

Dutch scholars on Scandinavian architecture

Till now, we did not see Netherlandish scholars do real archive research on the topic of the influence of Netherlandish architecture in Scandinavia or the Baltic. This situation, however, changed with the research by Juliette G. Roding - inspired by Taverne's book. Started in 1979 and presented in 1991 as a PhD on 'Christian IV of Denmark: architecture and urbanism of a Lutheran sovereign',[43] this work is based on archive work in Denmark and gives a new iconological reading of the material. This is serious Danish scholarship, written in Dutch. Her synthetic view of the period makes her refuse to identify Danish architecture with Netherlandish architecture,[44] stressing both the role and presence of architects of other nationalities, as well as the role of the king.[45] In another work, she emphasizes the continuing importance of Netherlandish architects for Danish architecture, centuries after the famous work by the van Obbergens and the Steenwinckels.[46] In this period, the 1983 *Leids Kunsthistorisch Jaarboek* even gave Danish research a forum in the special issue *Art in Denmark 1600-1650*;[47] although focused more upon painting and sculpture than on architecture, the message again was that "artists from the Netherlands played a prominent role [in 17th-century Denmark]".)

The PhD of Badeloch Noldus for Sweden must also be mentioned here.[48] Like the work of Juliette Roding, it is based on archive work, and it has a strong methodological basis, distinguishing four mechanisms of Netherlandish influence: the activity of Netherlandish artists, the use of prints (and their attested presence at the time), the role of Netherlandish patrons, and the role of cultural agents. In doing so, she broadens the horizon of the phenomenon. Recently, with reference to the role of Vredeman the Vries, as exemplified in the book by Anthony Wells-Cole, *Art and Decoration in Elizabethan and Jacobean England. The Influence of Continental Prints*, 1558-1625 (New Haven/London 1997), prints are in the centre of attention again, at a moment when some basic working instruments were published.[49]

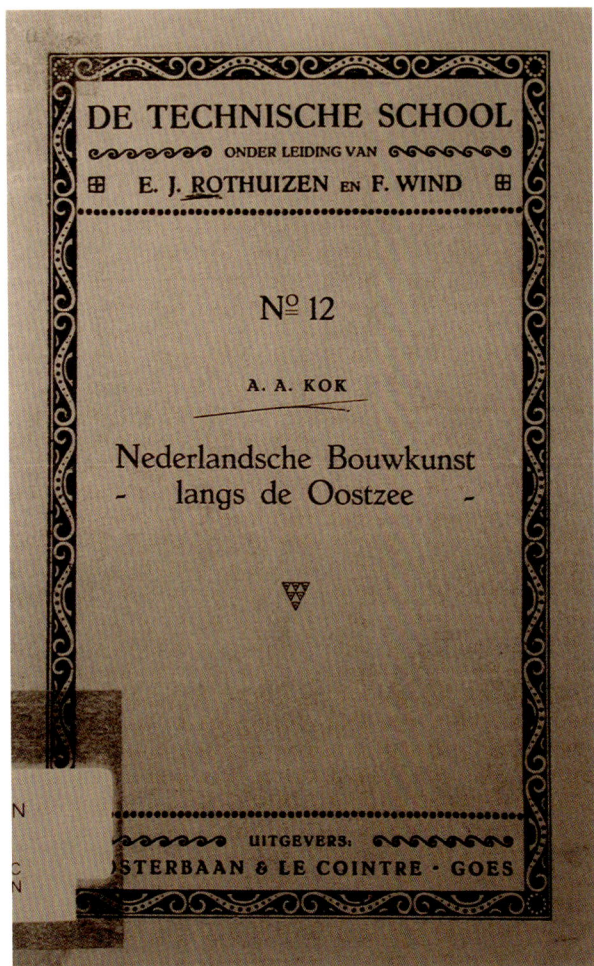

Fig. 8. A.A. Kok, Nederlandsche bouwkunst langs de Oostzee, (De Technische School, 12), Goes 1918 (Universiteit Utrecht).

The international research project *The Low Countries at the Crossroads. Netherlandish Architecture as an Export Product in Early Modern Europe (1480-1680)* on the influence of Netherlandish architecture in Europe, directed by prof. dr. Koen Ottenheym (Utrecht University) and prof. dr. Krista De Jonge (Catholic University, Louvain), financed by the Dutch and Flemish government is the last event in this field, started in January 2006.[50] Although some older rhetoric nationalist formulae were used successfully to convince the financing parties, the participation of international experts guarantees a counter balance for the treats of 'nationalistic recuperations' inherent to this sort of project. More than proving the 'importance' of Netherlandish architecture, its real ambition is to contribute to the (further) development of a 'pluricentral or multipolar' view on the art and architectural history of the 16th and 17th century. Still at the beginning of the 18th century, Peter the Great judged the Netherlands (Brabant and Holland) complementary to Italy and France for the architectural development of Russia.[51]

Conclusion

The research question of the influence of Netherlandish architects in Europe in the 16th and second half of the 17th century can be traced back to the pioneering phase of Belgian architectural historiography. With a remarkable inside knowledge and intuition, Schoy formulated it in the 1870s as the question of the 'expansion of the Antwerp school', including both the works abroad of Netherlandish architects and the influence of prints. One can not but regret that Schoy's idea was not taken up in the research of others and that it took 130 years for the government to fi-

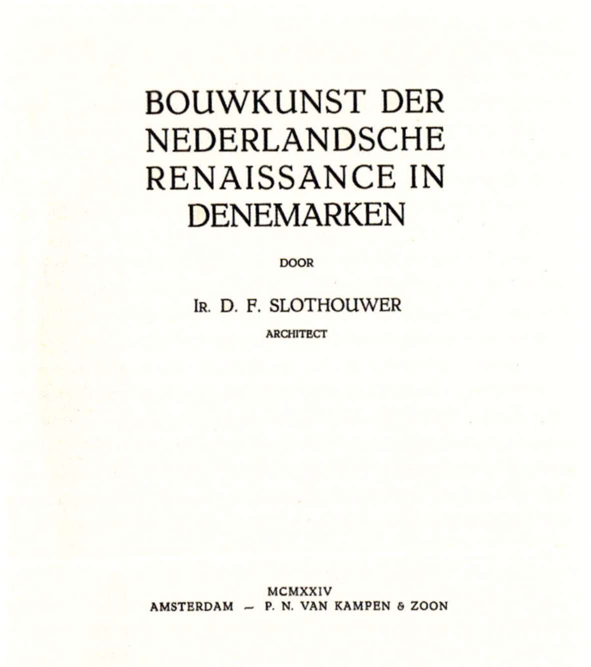

Fig. 9. D. F. Slothouwer, Bouwkunst der Nederlandsche renaissance in Denemarken, Amsterdam 1924.

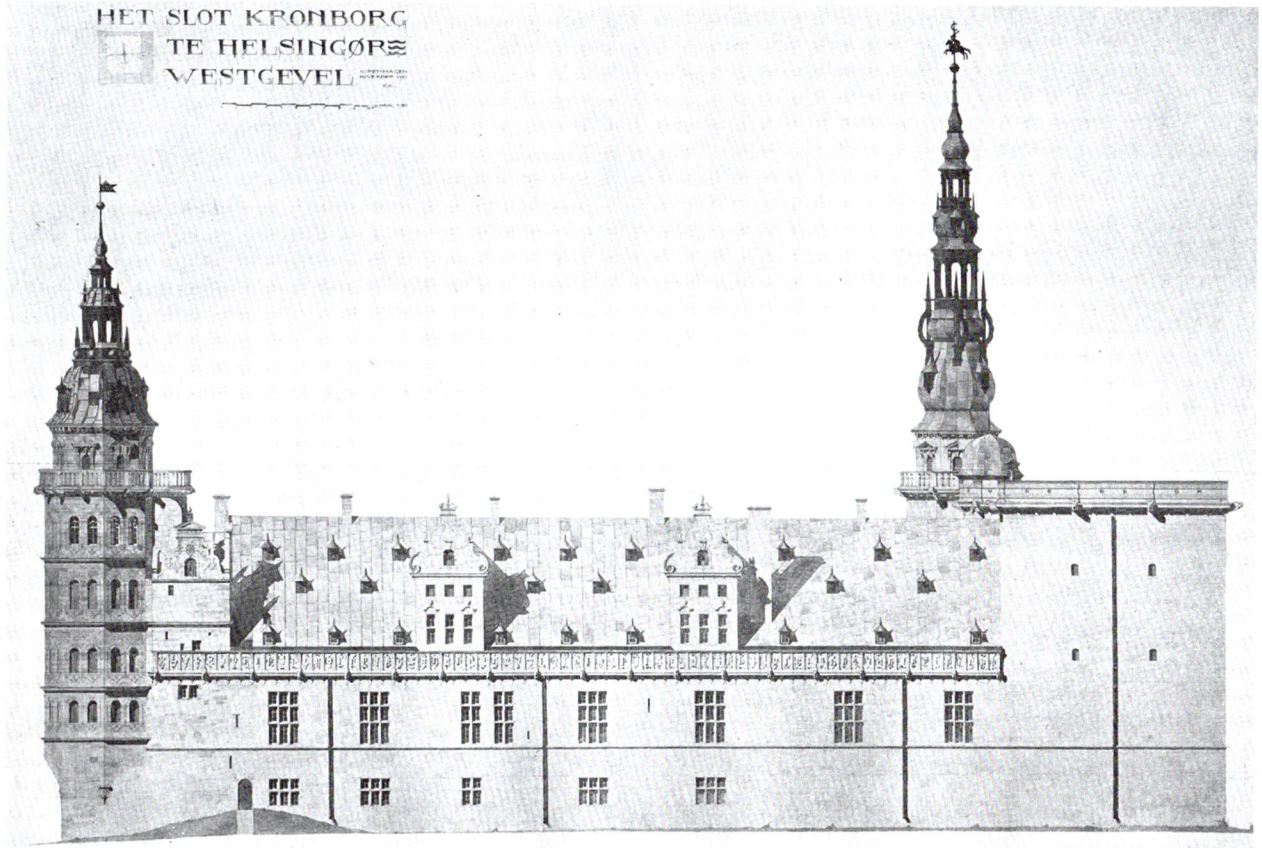

Fig. 10. D. F. Slothouwer, West façade of Kronborg castle. Frontispiece of D. F. Slothouwer, Bouwkunst der Nederlandsche renaissance in Denemarken, Amsterdam 1924.

nance such a research project. In the meantime, Danish research was made available to a Dutch-speaking audience in publications which added a Dutch nationalistic interpretation to it, identifying it as ('pure') Netherlandish architecture, only differing by the fact that it was realized abroad. Recent scholarship by Roding and Noldus contrasts with those old works in new and thorough archive research, in the introduction of a more elaborated methodological frame of mechanisms of influence – taking into account not only architects and prints, but also patrons and agents, and in taking in full credit for the local context.

Notes

1   S. De Vandières, *L'exposition universelle de 1878 illustrée. Quatre-vingt-sept belles gravures sur bois*, Paris 1879; Hippolyte Gautier & Adrien Desprez, *Les curiosités de l'exposition de 1878. Guide du visiteur*, Paris 1878, 33-45; Auguste Schoy, "Architecture – matériaux de construction. Façade nationale belge", in: Edmond Frederix (ed.), *La Belgique à l'exposition universelle de 1878*, Brussels, Paris, London & Leipzig 1878, 237-268; E. Allard, "L'Exposition universelle de Paris", *L'Emulation* 4 (1878), 49-52, 55-57, 61-63 and 73-77, esp. 62-64 ("Faits divers"); *Façade nationale belge. Catalogue*, Brussels 1878; Anna Morris, *Het tijdschrift l'Emulation en de architektuurtentoonstellingen in de periode 1874-1890*. Unpubl. Master thesis, Leuven 1989, 46-50; Gabriëlle Ingang, *Klein en toch te pronk voor de wereld. De Belgische deelneming aan de grote wereldtentoonstellingen in de negentiende eeuw*, unpubl. master thesis, Leuven 1986, 191-215; Martin Wörner, *Vergnügung und Belehrung. Volkskultur auf den Weltausstellungen 1851-1900*, Münster 1999, 28-33.

2 Paul Saintenoy, "Schoy, Auguste", in: *Biographie nationale*, Brussels 1914-1920, XXII, 26-32; Eric Hennaut, "Auguste Schoy (1838-1885)", in: Jean-Paul Midant (ed.), *Académie de Bruxelles. Deux siècles d'architecture*, Brussels 1989, 240-244; Marcel Celis, "Schoy, Auguste", in: Anne Van Loo (ed.), *Repertorium van de Architectuur in België van 1830 tot heden*, Antwerp 2003, 500-501.

3 Schoy 1878, 241: "Nous avons déjà fait remarquer les liens de parenté étroits qui unissent la façade Danoise, exécutée d'après des motifs de la Bourse de Copenhague, bâtie sous Christian IV (1619-23); la façade Néerlandaise rappelant le charmant Hôtel-de-Ville de La Haye (1564-65) ou celui de Leijden (1599); non moins que le Pavillon de S.A.R. le prince de Galles en pur style Elisabeth. L'Allemagne et l'Autriche auraient pu s'y joindre si elles n'eussent préféré mettre un faux masque italien à leur art national de l'Ecole de Nürnberg."

4 *Poelaert en zijn tijd*, Gemeentekrediet van België, Brussels 1980, 231-237; Herman Stynen, *De onvoltooid verleden tijd. Een geschiedenis van de monumenten- en landschapszorg in België 1835-1940*, Brussels 1998, 238-241; Marcel Celis, "Janlet, Emile", in: Van Loo (ed.) 2003, 367.

5 Schoy 1878, 241.

6 Schoy did not believe in Christian IV as "veritable architecte" of his Frederiksborg residence, a position defended in the Danish catalogue of the 1878 World Exhibition. Schoy stated: "nous croyons qu'il n'y a là qu'une tradition populaire dont l'origine remonte à l'époque où tout était considéré uniquement comme moyen de rehausser la majesté royale et où l'on rapportait sans partage au monarque la gloire des monuments élevés sous son règne." Schoy 1878, 249.

7 Schoy 1878, 268. On the neo-Flemish Renaissance see for instance: Alfred Edward Willis, *Flemish Renaissance Revival in Belgian Architecture (1830-1930)*, Ann Arbor (Mich.), PhD-dissertation, Columbia University 1984, 106-109, 138-145.

8 Already in his 1870 study, which received a price of the Royal Belgian Academy in 1873 and which was published in 1879: Auguste Schoy, *Histoire de l'influence italienne sur l'architecture dans les Pays-Bas*, Brussels 1879, 284-285.

9 Herman Odelberg, "Les retables de Strengnas (Suède)", *Annales de l'Académie d'Archéologie de Belgique* 26 (1870), 475-480.

10 "par la diversité de son talent et la solidité de ses connaissances, il [Boy] mérite sans doute une place distinguée parmi les artistes belges du XVIe siècle." E. Eichhorn & Herman Odelberg, "Guillaume Boyen (Wilhelm Boy), peintre, sculpteur et architecte belge. Etude biographique", *Annales de l'Académie d'Archéologie de Belgique* 28 (1872), 94-132, esp. 132.

11 M. A. Galesloot, "Le tombeau de Christian III, roi de Danemark, dans la cathédrale de Roeskilde, et celui de Gustave Wasa, à Upsala", *Annales de l'Académie d'Archéologie de Belgique* 26 (1870), 470-474; Pierre Génard, *Le tombeau de Christian III, roi de Danemark, dans la cathédrale de Roeskilde*, Antwerp 1880 (overprint of *Bulletin de l'Académie d'archéologie de Belgique*). For the work of Cornelis Floris (1514-1575), see recently: Antoinette Huysmans et al., *Cornelis Floris 1514-1575. Beeldhouwer, architect ontwerper*, Brussels 1996. Review by Zsuzsanna Van Ruyven-Zeman, *Oud Holland* 112/4 (1998), 259-271; Hugo Johannsen, "Floris (F. de Vriendt), Cornelis (II)", in: *Saur Allgemeines Künstlerlexikon*, 41, Munich & Leipzig 2004, 358-359.

12 Knud Millech, "Klein Vilhelm", in: *Weilbachs Kunstnerleksikon³*, II, Copenhagen 1949, 131-133; Bente Holst, "Klein, Vilhelm", in: *Weilbach Dansk Kunstnerleksikon⁴*, IV, Copenhagen 1995, 301-303.

13 Auguste Schoy, "Cérémonies publiques célébrées aux Pays-Bas du XVIe au XVIIIe siècle", *Journal des Beaux-Arts et de la littérature. Peinture, Sculpture, Gravure, Architecture, Musique, Archéologie, Bibliographie, Belles-Lettres, etc.* 14 (1872), 104-105, esp. 105. See also the contribution by Konrad Ottenheym in these proceedings.

14 "Au point de vue artistique, l'influence flamande dans les contrées scandinaves est aujourd'hui positivement établie [...] Les faits indiscutables [...] ne devraient-ils pas déterminer notre gouvernement à députer quelques chercheurs, artistes et archéologues, pour rattacher ces fleurons lointains à notre splendide diadème artistique et apprendre au public lettré ce que recèlent encore de chefs-d'oeuvres flamands, le Danemark, la Suède et cette vieille Norwège *Gamle Norge*, contrées aux *Sunds* profonds, aux iles verdoyantes, où, sous les rutilants rayons des auroras boréales, les eaux paisibles des *fjords* semblent de lave ou d'airain liquide." Schoy 1872, 105; quoted in: Schoy 1878, 250.

15 Henri Lacoste, "Notice sur Paul Saintenoy", *Annuaire de l'Académie royale de Belgique*, Brussels 1962, 79-100; Eric Hennaut, "Saintenoy, Paul", in: Van Loo (ed.) 2003, 493-494.

16 Paul Saintenoy, "Les architectes flamands dans le Nord de l'Allemagne au XVIe siècle", *Académie royale d'archéologie de Belgique, Bulletin* 5 (1907), 161-172; also: G. van Doorslaer, "Antoine van Oberghen, grand architecte Malinois", *Mechlinia* 2 (1923), 164-167.

17 Georg Cuny, "Hieronimus und Antonius von Obbergen", *Mitteilungen des Westpreussischen Geschichtsverein* 3 (1904), 51-57; republished as: Georg Cuny, "Antonius von Obbergen", *Zeitschrift für Bauwesen* LVI (1906),

419-442. On the same topic see also: Georg Cuny, *Danzigs Kunst und Kultur im 16. und 17. Jahrhundert*, Frankfurt am Main 1910.

18 Pierre Génard, "Floris de Vriendt", *Biographie nationale*, VII, Brussels 1880-83, 118-138. For further Belgian research on these topics (with attention to ther 'foreign work' of the artists), see for instance: R. Roggen & J. Withof, "Cornelis Floris", *Gentsche Bijdragen tot de Kunstgeschiedenis* VIII (1942), 79-171 and IX (1943), 133-136. For a long time major studies were foreign, cf. Robert Hedicke, *Cornelis Floris und die Florisdekoration, Studien zur niederländischen und deutschen Kunst im XVI. Jahrhundert*, Berlin 1913; H. Mielke, *Hans Vredeman de Vries. Verzeichnis der Stichwerke und Beschreibung seines Stiles sowie Beiträge zum Werk Gerard Groennings*. Dissertation, Berlin 1967. An analysis of the old and new Weilbach's Danish art biographical dictionaries (third and fourth editions) gave the names of numerous artists which originated from the actual territory of Belgium and the Netherlands active in Denmark: at least 65 painters, 3 textile artists, 14 engravers, 28 sculptors, 12 military engineers, 41 architects and numerous other building professions, such as *nagelsmed* (1), *stenhugger* (20), *snedker* (5), *tømrer* (3), *murermester* (3), or *blydækker* (1).

19 The major studies on these artists are foreign, cf. Eugeniusz Gasiorowski, "Antonis van Obbergen", *Hafnia, Copenhagen Papers in the History of Art – Comité international d'histoire de l'art VIIe colloque international. Les Pays du Nord et l'Europe. Art et Architecture au XVIe siècle. Copenhague 1-6 septembre 1975* (1976), 71-90; Arnold Bartetzky, *Das Grosse Zeughaus in Danzig. Baugeschichte - Architekturgeschichtliche Stellung - Repräsentative Funktion*, 2 vols., Stuttgart 2000 (Forschungen zur Geschichte und Kultur des Östlichen Mitteleuropa).

20 This work was a part of a vast short inventory research project on foreign archival sources for the history of the Netherlands. Other historians involved in this series of publications were P. J. Blok (1897), G. Busken Huet (1900) and J. S. van Veen for Paris, P. J. Blok for Italy (1901) and Germany (1886, 1887 and 1888), C. C. Uhlenbeck for Russia (1891), and P. J. Blok and H. Brugmans for England (1891, 1895). Gerhard Wilhelm Kernkamp, *Verslag van een onderzoek in Zweden, Noorwegen en Denemarken naar archivalia, belangrijk voor de geschiedenis van Nederland op last der regeering ingesteld*, 's-Gravenhage 1903.

21 P. B. M. Blaas, *Historicus tussen wetenschap en journalistiek: G.W. Kernkamp*, Rotterdam 1983; L. J. Dorsman, *G.W. Kernkamp. Historicus en democrat 1864-1943*, Groningen 1990.

22 Kernkamp 1903.

23 Kernkamp 1903, 371. See also his publication of Swedish archive sources in: Gerhard Wilhelm Kernkamp, "Memoriën van Ridder Theodorus Rodenburg betreffende het verplaatsen van verschillende industriën uit Nederland naar Denemarken, met daarop genomen resolution van koning Christian IV (1621)", *Bijdragen en Mededelingen van het Historisch Genootschap te Utrecht*, 23 (1902), 216-236 (with attention to brick production and lime kilns).

24 For a short description of these Goldmann's manuscripts in The Royal Library in Copenhagen see: Jeroen Goudeau, *Nicolaus Goldmann (1611-1665) en de wiskundige architectuurwetenschap*, Groningen 2005, 532-537 (Ms. 7-9).

25 "Voor de Duitsche Oostzeesteden levert juist Danzig het belangrijkste material voor onze geschiedenis", Gerhard Wilhelm Kernkamp, *Baltische archivalia: onderzoek naar archivalia, belangrijk voor de geschiedenis van Nederland, in Stockholm, Kopenhagen en de Duitse Oostzeesteden*, 's-Gravenhage 1909 (Rijks geschiedkundige publication, Kleine ser., 4), XII. He continued his work with a research stay in Stockholm. Gerhard Wilhelm Kernkamp, *Zweedsche archivalia*, Utrecht 1908 (Bijdragen en Mededelingen, Historisch Genootschap te Utrecht XXIX).

26 Kernkamp 1909, 354-355, "XI. Nederlandse kunstenaars, kunstkoopers, bouwmeesters en ingenieurs te Danzig" mentioning Regnier of Amsterdam, Johan van Wensbeeck, Cornelis Boch and Joris Standart.

27 A. A. Kok, *Nederlandsche bouwkunst langs de Oostzee*, Goes 1918 (E. J. Rothuizen & F. Wind (eds.), De Technische School, 12). On Kok, see for instance: Marijke Beek, *Drie eeuwen Amsterdamse Bouwkunst. Catalogus van architectuurtekeningen in de verzameling A.A. Kok*, Amsterdam 1984.

28 Table of content: I. Introduction; II. Kronborg in Helsingør; III. Frederiksborg in Hillerød; IV. Rosenborg in Copenhagen; V. Less important castles; VI. The Stock Exchange of Copenhagen; VII. Churches of Danish Renaissance; VIII. Buildings in Gdansk.

29 Ferdinand Meldahl & Frederik Skjold Neckelmann, *Denkmäler der Renaissance in Dänemark*, Berlin 1888.

30 Georg Galland, *Geschichte der holländischen Baukunst und Bildnerei im Zeitalter der Renaissance, der nationalen Blute und des Klassicismus*, Frankfurt a. M. 1890.

31 "[…] onzer zuiver Nederlandsche zestiende- en vroegzeventiende eeuwsche bouwkunst in de Skandinavische landen. De bouwkunst der Hollandsche renaissance, uit de periode van voor de overwegend Italiaanschen invloed heeft – merkwaardig genoeg – in den vreemde belangrijker werkstukken voortgebracht dan in de Nederlanden zelf." (Kok 1918, 5). "[er] aandacht op te vestigen dat zij, die studie wenschen te maken van

de oud-vaderlandse baksteenbouw, hun material niet uitsluitend moeten zoeken in Nederland's oude steden en stadjes. Verde rook om te doen weten dat in de zestiende en zeventiende eeuw niet alleen Holland's krijgsroem en handelsgeest over de zeeën ging, doch ook de kunstenaren en belangrijk aan hebben meegewerkt den Hollandschen en Vlaamschen naam in alle werelddeelen een goede klank te geven." (Kok 1918, 71).

32 D. F. Slothouwer, *Bouwkunst der Nederlandsche renaissance in Denemarken*, Amsterdam 1924.

33 Hedicke 1913.

34 Slothouwer 1924, 42. Copenhagen, Royal Danish Library, inscription in the book: "Lourens v. Stenwinckel/ Hans v. Stenwinckel/ ende nu(n)/ M v Stenwinckel 1629/ Otto de Willarts Anno 1700".

35 Frans André Jozef Vermeulen, *Handboek tot de Geschiedenis der Nederlandsche Bouwkunst*, 3 vols., 's-Gravenhage 1928-41, II, 1931, 458-499 ("De Nederlandsche Renaissance in Denemarken en in de Landen aan de Oostzee") and pl. 691-719.

36 Chris Coppens, Marc Derez & Jan Roegiers (eds.), *Sapientia Aedificavit sibi domum. Universiteitsbibliotheek Leuven 1425-2000*, Leuven 2005.

37 Caroline Godfried, *Nederland en Denemarken – Danmark og Holland. Een expositie over de wederzijdse relaties sinds de zestiende eeuw. Een keuze uit de zestigjarige Bibliothec. Danic. en een selectie uit de collecties van de Algemene Bibliotheek Universiteit van Amsterdam. Catalogus*, Amsterdam 1990; *Bibliotheek der Universiteit van Amsterdam, Catalogus van de Bibliothec. Danic. en van de overige Deensche en IJslandsche werken aanwezig in de Universiteitsbibliotheek van Amsterdam*, Amsterdam 1939, 468-471 ("Bouwkunst"). See also: *Bibliotheek der Universiteit van Amsterdam, Catalogus van de Bibliothec. Svecic. en van de overige Zweedse werken aanwezig in de Universiteitsbibliotheek van Amsterdam*, Amsterdam 1948, 549-550 ("Bouwkunst en bouwmateriaal").

38 Vilhelm Lorenzen, "Nederlandse bouwmeesters en stedebouwers in Denemarken in de 17de eeuw en hun werken", *Roomsch-Katholiek Bouwblad. Veertiendaagsch tijdschrift voor bouw- en sierkunsten. Officieel orgaan der algem. Katholieke kunstenaarsvereeniging* 5 (1933-34), 287-288.

39 "[dat] verschillende van de beste Nederlandsche architektuur in Denemarken liggen"; "Het feit dat de Nederlanders zooveel invloed hebben uitgeoefend op de Deensche architectuur, in het bijzonder in de 17de eeuw, is toch wel van zooveel belang, dat het in de herinnering moet worden gebracht van de tegenwoordige landgenooten".

40 The 'architectural' topos of Dutch architects in Denmark is also found in studies on Dutch-Danish literary relations: P. M. Den Hoed, *Iets over de cultuuraanraking van Nederland met Denemarken en Zweden. Openbare les gehouden bij de aanvaarding van het lectoraat in Zweedsche en Deensche taal- en letterkunde aan de universiteit van Amsterdam op vrijdag 27 september 1929*, Haarlem 1929, 6-7; or in studies of cultural history: J. Huizinga, *Nederland's beschaving in de 17de eeuw. Een schets*, Haarlem 1963 (1941), 144; Remmelt Daalder et al. (eds.), *Goud uit Graan. Nederland en het Oostzeegebied 1600-1850*, Zwolle 1998, 121-123.

41 Ed Taverne, *In 't Land van belofte: in de nieue stadt. Ideaal en werkelijkheid van de stadsuitleg in de Republiek 1580-1680*, Maarssen 1978, 81-109, 81-82, 82-90, 90-94. He also treated Sweden, Mühlheim am Rhein and Friedrichstadt: Taverne 1978, 94-109.

42 C. S. Widerberg, *Norges første militæringeniør Isaac van Geelkerck og hans virke 1644-1656: et bidrag til de norske befæstningers historie*, Oslo 1924; Vilh. Lorenzen (ed.), *Christian IV's Byanlæg og andre Bybygningsarbejder*, Copenhagen 1937. Recently see also Nils Ahlberg, *Stadsgrundningar och planförändringar. Svensk stadsplanering 1521-1721*. PhD-dissertation, Uppsala 2005 (Acta Universitatis Agriculturae Sueciae, Agraria 2005:94).

43 Juliette G. Roding, *Christiaan IV van Denemarken (1588-1648). Architectuur en stedebouw van een Luthers vorst*, PhD-dissertation, Alkmaar 1991. Chapter 6 was also published as: Juliette G. Roding, "Voorstellingen van vermaak in de plafonddecoratie van de grote zaal in het lustslot Rosenborg (circ. 1620)", in: J. de Jongste, J. Roding & B. Thijs (eds.), *Vermaak van de elite in de vroegmoderne tijd*, Hilversum 1999, 262-287.

44 Juliette G. Roding, "The Myth of the 'Dutch Renaissance' in Denmark. Dutch Influence on Danish Architecture in the 17th century", in: J. Ph. S. Lemmink & J. S. A. M. van Koningsbrugge (eds.), *Baltic Affairs. Relations between the Netherlands and North-Eastern Europe 1500-1800*, Nijmegen 1990, 343-353.

45 "Christian IV used Flemish and Dutch architects, as well as Danish, German and Swiss ones, to give shape to his own political and dynastic ideals. The same is true for the engineers, whom he needed because of their specific technical knowledge. Out of this an architecture arose which fully deserves the name 'Christian IV style'". Roding 1990a, 353.

46 On the 18th-century architect Philip de Lange see Juliette G. Roding, "Philip de Lange (ca.1744-1766). Het indrukwekkende oeuvre van een onbekende architect uit de Republiek in dienst van de Deense Marine", in: Leo Akveld et al. (eds.), *In het kielzog. Maritiemhistorische studies aangeboden aan Jaap R. Bruijn bij zijn vertrek als hoogleraar zeegeschiedenis aan de Universiteit Leiden*, Amsterdam 2003, 494-504), in which

she also asks attention for Evert Janssen, architect of the navy. See also H. E. Nørregård-Nielsen, "Omkring Evert Janssen. Af Charlottenborgs bygningshistorie", *Architectura; Arkitekturhistorisk Årsskrift* 6 (1984), 140-160. On De Lange, see also Christian Elling, "Philip de Lange som Søetatens Bygmester", *Historiske Meddelelser om København* 2, III (1928), 375-403; Christian Elling, *Philip de Lange. En Studie i Dansk Barokarkitektur*, Copenhagen 1931; Rikke Tønnes, *Stephen Hansens Palæ: bygherren: arkitekten Philip de Lange: Livet i og omkring et helsingørsk handelshus*, Copenhagen 1997.

47 *Art in Denmark, 1600-1650*, in: *Leids Kunsthistorisch Jaarboek* 2 (1983) with contributions by J. Römelingh, Lars Olof Larsson, Hanne Honnens de Lichtenberg, Mette Bligaard, Lars Olof Larsson, Hugo Johannsen, Meir Stein, Karen Holst, and Otto Norn.

48 Badeloch Noldus, *Trade in Good Taste. Relations in Architecture and Culture between the Dutch Republic and the Baltic World in the Seventeenth Century*, Turnhout 2004 (Architectura moderna 2).

49 See the catalogues of Vredeman-prints and of 17th-century prints in the Amsterdam Rijksmuseum by the Dutch scholar working in Paris, Peter Fuhring: Peter Fuhring, *Vredeman de Vries,* Rotterdam & Amsterdam 1997 (Hollstein's Dutch & Flemish Etchings, Engravings and Woodcuts 1450-1700, XLVII); Peter Fuhring, *Ornament prints in the Rijksmuseum, II, The seventeenth century,* Amsterdam & Rotterdam 2004, 3.

50 *The Low Countries at the Crossroads. Netherlandish Architecture as an Export Product in Early Modern Europe (1480-1680)*. Prof. Thomas DaCosta Kaufmann (Princeton University), Ethan Matt Kavaler (University of Toronto), Hugo Johannsen (The National Museum of Denmark), Heiner Borggrefe (Weserrenaissance-Museum, Schloss Brake), Juliette Roding (Universiteit Leiden), Luc Duerloo (Universiteit Antwerpen), Bernardo J. García García (U. Complutense de Madrid).

51 Dirk Van de Vijver, "L'étude de la science architecturale. Formation d'un gentilhomme architecte russe en Brabant et en Hollande (1718-1727)", *Cahiers du monde russe* 47/3 (2006), 515-550.

Participants in the conference *'Reframing the Danish Renaissance'* in front of Kronborg Castle on the 29th September 2006 (Photo Jens Vellev).

LIST OF AUTHORS

Uwe Albrecht, Studium an den Universitäten Kiel, Poitiers und Frankfurt/Main (1982 Promotion, 1989 Habilitation), seit 1995 apl. Professor für Mittlere und Neuere Kunstgeschichte am Kunsthistorischen Institut der Christian-Albrechts-Universität zu Kiel. Arbeits- und Forschungsschwerpunkte: Geschichte des europäischen Adelssitzes in Spätmittelalter und Früher Neuzeit, Kunstgeschichte des Ostseeraumes, insbesondere der mittelalterlichen Holzskulptur und Tafelmalerei Norddeutschlands und der Lübecker Wandmalerei. Mitglied der Residenzen-Kommission der Göttinger Akademie der Wissenschaften und des „Steering Committee" des von der European Science Foundation geförderten internationalen Forschungsprojektes „Palatium". Erster Vorsitzender der Arthur-Haseloff-Gesellschaft e.V. – email: albrecht@kunstgeschichte.uni-kiel.de

Mogens Bencard, studied History of Art at the University of Copenhagen, 1961 head of The Antiquarian Collection, Ribe, 1980 Director (retired) of the Royal Danish Collections at Rosenborg and Amalienborg. As an archaeologist he carried out important excavations in Ribe, fundamentally revising its history. After his appointment as Director of the Royal Collections at Rosenborg he has increasingly focused on topics like Kunstkammer/Wunderkammer, 17th century interiors and their furnishings. Among his publications in this field are *Christian 4.s Pragtsølv* (1988) and *Silver Furniture* (1992). For a bibliography, see Niels-Knud Liebgott (ed.), *Rosenborg Studier* (2000). – email: mogens@bencard.dk.

Heiner Borggrefe, PhD, Dr. Studied History of Art, Philosophy and Architecture. Until 2001 Head of the "Institute für Architektur-, Kunst- und Kulturgeschichte" at the Weserrenaissance-Museum Schloss Brake in Lemgo, Germany. Since 2002 academic curator. Co-editor of a number of academic series. Numerous published writings on subjects including Titian, Lucas Cranach the Elder, Palma il Giovane, Hans Vredeman de Vries, Hans Rottenhammer, Moritz von Hessen and on courtly pictorial programmes. –email: wrm.borggrefe@t-online.de

Birgitte Bøggild Johannsen. Since 1980 Editor of *Danmarks Kirker*, The National Museum of Denmark. Co-organizer of the conferences "Reframing the Danish Renaissance" (2006) and "Beyond Scylla and Charybdis. European Courts and Court Residences outside Habsburg and Valois/Bourbon Territories, 1500-1700" (PALATIUM, 2012). Member of the steering or working committees of "Mémoire Monarchique" (Versailles), "Medieval Memoria Online. The Functions of Art, Ritual and Texts in Medieval Memoria"(Utrecht) and "PALATIUM. Court Residences as Places of Exchange in Late Medieval and Early Modern Europe 1400-1700" (www.courtresidences.eu). Her research and publications focus upon Late Medieval and Early Modern church and court art and culture, including the re-forming of Early Lutheran churches, royal funerals, memorial strategies of the Danish elite and visual constructions of political and gender identities. – email: birgitte.b.johannsen@natmus.dk

Angelica Dülberg, Since 1992 Principal of academic publications and expert for all questions of history of art in Saxony with the main emphasis on the Royal Castle in Dresden at the regional authorities of preservation of historical monuments. Honorary Professor for History of Art at the College of Fine Arts in Dresden. Member of the Commission for the History of Art in East Germany at the Academy of Science in Leipzig. Several publications about the iconography and iconology of painting and sculpture from the middle ages to the baroque. – email: gelidueli@t-online.de.

Claire Farago is Professor of Renaissance art at the University of Colorado at Boulder. Her publications include *Reframing the Renaissance: Visual Culture in Europe and Latin America 1450 to 1650* (1995); *Transforming Images: New Mexican Santos in-between Worlds*, co-authored with Donna Pierce (2006); *Re-Reading Leonardo: The Treatise on Painting across Europe 1550-1900* (2009); and *Art Is Not What You Think it Is*, co-authored with Donald Preziosi (2012). In 2011-12, she is Fulbright-York Scholar at the University of York, England, completing a critical edition of Leonardo da Vinci's Treatise on Painting originally published in 1651. – email: farago@colorado.edu

Thomas Fusenig, art historian, Essen (Germany), with main interest in Renaissance and Baroque painting in Northern Europe and Italy; besides connoisseurship he is mostly interested in the social rôle of the arts, iconography and the transfer of artistic ideas; finished his study at RWTH Aachen with a ph.d. thesis on Venetian painting of the 16th century (1993); worked for the RWTH Aachen (1992-1993), Suemondt-Ludwig-Museum, Aachen (1994-1996), and Weserrenaissance-Museum Schloß Brake, Lemgo (1997-2002). From 2002 on he is a freelance art historian, realizing projects for different German museums (Aachen, Zwickau) and private collectors. – email: falkfusenig@aol.com

Krista De Jonge is full Professor of History of Architecture at the Katholieke Universiteit Leuven, Belgium. Her work concerns late medieval and early modern architecture in the Southern Low Countries in its relation to France, Italy and Spain, and especially the architecture of the Burgundian and Habsburg Court. She currently directs a research programme on early modern Netherlandish architectural drawings as design tools, and chairs the European Science Foundation Research Networking programme "PALATIUM. Court Residences as Places of Exchange in Late Medieval and Early Modern Europe 1400-1700". – email: krista.dejonge@asro.kuleuven.be

Maria Fabricius Hansen, Dr. phil, Associate Professor, Department of Art History, Aarhus University, member of the direction of the Ny Carlsberg Foundation. Has previously worked on the reception of Antiquity in medieval and fifteenth-century Italy and is now engaged in research in the relation between art and nature in the sixteenth century (e.g. grotesques, gardens, curiosity cabinets). Her publications include *The Eloquence of Appropriation. Prolegomena to an Understanding of Spolia in Early Christian Rome* (Analecta Romana Instituti Danici, Supplementum XXXIII)(2003). – email: kunmfh@hum.au.dk

Jan Harasimowicz, Studium der Kunstgeschichte und Theologie an den Universitäten Breslau und Zürich, Promotion 1985, Habilitation 1991. 1997-2001 Professor für Kunstgeschichte an der Universität Thorn, seit 2003 Inhaber des Lehrstuhls für Kunstgeschichte der Renaissance und Reformation an der Universität Breslau. Seit 1996 Mitglied der Kommission für Kulturgeschichte der Polnischen Akademie der Wissenschaften, seit 2000 Korrespondenz-Mitglied der Historischen Kommission für Schlesien, seit 2002 Präsident des Polnischen Vereins für Reformationsforschung, seit 2008 Korrespondenz-Mitglied von Comité International d'Histoire de l'Art. Träger des Kulturpreises Schlesien des Landes Niedersachsen (2004), Ehrendoktor der Martin-Luther-Universität Halle-Wittenberg (2010). Wichtigste Bücher: *Kunst als Glaubensbekenntnis. Beiträge zur Kunst- und Kulturgeschichte der Reformationszeit* (1996); *Atlas architektury Wrocławia [Architekturdenkmäler der Stadt Breslau]*, 2 Bde (1997-98); *Sztuka i dialog wyznań w XVI i XVII wieku [Kunst und Konfessionalisierung im 16. und 17. Jh.]*(2000); *Po obu stronach Bałtyku [An beiden Seiten der Ostsee]*, 2 Bde.(2006); *Dolny Śląsk [Niederschlesien]* (2007); *Adel in Schlesien*, Bd.1: *Herrschaft – Kultur – Selbstdarstellung* (2010); *Schwärmergeist und Freiheitsdenken. Beiträge zur Kunst- und Kulturgeschichte Schlesiens in der Frühen Neuzeit* (2010). – email: jharasim@uniwroc.pl.

Thomas DaCosta Kaufmann is Frederick Marquand Professor of Art and Archaeology at Princeton University, where he teaches courses on art and architecture of the sixteenth to the eighteenth century in Europe and its relations with other parts of the world. The author of many books and 200 articles and reviews, including *Court, Cloister and*

City. The Art and Culture of Central Europe 1450-1800 (1995); *Toward a Geography of Art* (2004); *The Eloquent Artist. Essays on Art, Art Theory and Architecture. Sixteenth to Nineteenth Century* (2004) and *Archimboldo: Visual Jokes, Natural History and Still-Life Painting* (2009). He is a member of the Polish, Royal Swedish, Royal Flemish Academies of Science, as well as of the American Academy in Rome. He has received many fellowships, most recently to the Netherlands Institute for Advanced Study. In 2011 he was awarded an honorary doctorate by the Technical University, Dresden, which along with his scholarship cited "his services for international collaboration and mutual understanding among nations". – email: kaufmann@princeton.edu.

Krista Kodres, Professor at the Institute of Art History of the Estonian Academy of Arts in Tallinn, researches at the University of Tallinn, Institute of History. Head of doctoral studies of Institute of Art History. Member of the board of Doctoral school of Estonian universities. Fields of research: history and theory of art and architecture of the Baltic region in Early Modern period; history of Estonian architecture and design of the Soviet period; history and theory of art history writing. Her publications include *Short History of Estonian Art* (2000, co-author), *Beautiful House and Room* (2001) and *History of Estonian Arts, vol. 2, 1520-1770* (2005, editor and author). Forthcoming *Social Life of Architecture, Art and Things. Tallinn in 16th to 18th century*. Also: editor-in-chief of the new *History of Estonian Art* (6 volumes) and board member of Estonian academic journal *Studies in Art and Architecture*. – email: krista@artun.ee.

Marianne Marcussen, MA in Art History, University of Copenhagen 1967. Assistant curator at the National Gallery of Denmark (Dep. of painting and sculpture) 1968; Curator at Thorvaldsens Museum and Assistant Professor in Art History, University of Copenhagen 1969; Associated Professor 1974- 2004 (retired). She has published on: French art, especially 19th-20th century painting; Perspective, i.e. space in the pictorial arts from Antiquity to Modernism; Aesthetics, with emphasis on description, interpretation and the notion of Beauty, related to the Laocòen, Fuseli, Sergel, Thorvaldsen, Marcel Duchamp, and the historiography of Art History, and Danish art (especially 19th century painting). Co-founder of the Nordic Aesthetic Society. – email: marianne.marcussen@email.dk.

Keith Moxey is Barbara Novak Professor and Chair of Art History at Barnard College, Colombia University, New York City. He is author of books on the historiography and philosophy of art history, as well as on sixteenth century painting and prints in Northern Europe. His publications include: *The Practice of Persuasion: Paradox and Power in Art History* (2001); *The Practice of Theory: Poststructuralism, Cultural Politics, and Art History* 1994); *Peasants, Warriors, and Wives: Popular Imagery in the Reformation* (1989). He is also the co-editor of several anthologies: *Art History, Aesthetics, Visual Culture* (2002); *The Subjects of Art History: Historical Objects in Contemporary Perspective* (1998); *Visual Culture: Images and Interpretations* (1994); and *Visual Theory: Painting and Interpretation* (1991). – email: pm154@columbia.edu.

Kristoffer Neville is Assistant Professor of Art History at the University of California, Riverside. His publications include *Nicodemus Tessin the Elder. Architecture in Sweden in the Age of Greatness* (2009), as well as articles on architecture and culture in the Germanic world from Stockholm to Vienna in the sixteenth to the eighteenth centuries in *Journal of the Society of Architectural Historians, Journal of the History of Ideas,* and the *Wiener Jahrbuch für Kunstgeschichte*. – email: kneville@ucr.edu.

Badeloch Vera Noldus, Ph.D. (2002) in Architectural History, Utrecht University, has published widely on cultural exchange and art history, including *Trade in Good Taste* (2004), *Pieter Isaacsz* (2007) and *Double Agents* (2011). At present, she prepares a publication on the 18th-century architect Philip de Lange. She owns a consulting practice in Copenhagen, with expertise in the re-use and transformation of historic buildings and sites. – email: b.v.noldus@badeloch.com.

Konrad Ottenheym is Professor of Architectural History at Utrecht University, The Netherlands, and member of The Royal Dutch Academy of Sciences. He is a specialist on Dutch 17th century architecture, its sources in the Italian renaissance and its influence in Europe. He is author of various monographs on Dutch architects of the Golden Age, Philips Vingboons, Pieter Post and Jacob van Campen, as well as on the influence of Italian architectural treatises in seventeenth-century Dutch architecture. He has cooperated in the recent English editions (Architectura et Natura Publishers, 2004 and 2007) of Vincenzo Scamozzi's treatise *L'Idea della architettura universale*, the main handbook on classical design theories in 17th century Holland. He is coauthor with Krista De Jonge (Belgium) of *Unity and Dis-*

continuity, Architectural Relationships between the Southern and Northern Low Countries 1530-1700 (2007). Currently he is working on The Low Countries at the Cross Roads, a book on the contributions of Netherlandish architects to the architecture elsewhere in Europe in the 16th and 17th centuries. – email: k.a.ottenheym@uu.nl

Hanne Kolind Poulsen, 1994-96 scholarship from the Carlsberg Foundation, 1999-2002 Research Curator at The National Gallery of Denmark, Copenhagen, 2002-03 research fellow at The Danish Institute for Advanced Studies in the Humanities, 2004-05 Associate Research Professor at The Department of Art History, Copenhagen University, since 2006 Senior Researcher and Curator in the Royal Collection of Graphic Art, National Gallery of Denmark, Copenhagen. Her main research interests are the visual arts of Europe of the 16th century, focusing on the impact of Luther's Reformation. Her publications include *Cranach* (exhibition catalogue, Copenhagen 2002) and a number of articles on related topics. For a bibliography, see www.smk.dk. – email: hanne.kolind@smk.dk.

Mikael Bøgh Rasmussen, PhD in Art History, ass. curator at The Department of Prints and Drawings at The National Gallery of Denmark, Copenhagen, The Museum of National History at Frederiksborg Castle and at The Danish National Art Library, Copenhagen. He is an External Lecturer in Art History and Renaissance Studies at the University of Copenhagen. The primary research interests are renaissance graphic arts, the interactions between audience expectations, the practice surrounding images and their reception, particularly in relation to renaissance art, and early modern "orientalism". Among the publications are *German Drawings before ca.1540* (2001) and as co-author, *Melchior Lorck*, 5 Vols., Copenhagen, Vols.1-4: 2009, Vol. 5 forthcoming. – email: mikael.boegh@gmail.com

Juliette Roding is Lecturer in Art and Architectural History at Universiteit Leiden. Her research focuses on the cultural interaction between the Netherlands and the North and Baltic Sea areas in the period 1550-1800. Her publications include *Christian IV van Denemarken (1588-1648). Architectuur en stedebouw van een Luthers vorst* (1991) and *Pieter Isaacsz (1568-1625). Court Painter, Art Dealer and Spy* (co-editor, 2007). At present she prepares – with an international group of researchers – an exhibition and catalogue raisonné on the Dutch-Danish court painter Karel van Mander III (1609-1670) and his networks (Frederiksborg Museum, Hillerød, 2015). – email: j.roding@hum.leidenuniv.nl.

Margit Thøfner, the Danish born art historian was educated in Great Britain and is presently senior lecturer at the University of East Anglia, Norwich. Her research interests focuses on civic ritual in the Netherlands in the early modern period, the arts of the Reformation and early modern print culture. Her books include *A Common Art: Urban Ceremonials in Antwerp and Brussels During and After the Dutch Revolt* (2007). – email: m.thofner@uea.ac.uk.

Mario Titze, 1983-1988 studies on art history at Leipzig University and Georgian Academy of Sciences in Tbilisi;1992 PhD; since 1991 State Dept. for Conservation of Hist. Heritage of Saxony-Anhalt, Halle, Germany; since 2006 Commission for Central German art history at Saxon Academy of Sciences, Leipzig; numerous articles about Renaissance and Baroque art history. – email: mtitze@lda.mk.sachsen-anhalt.de

Barbara Uppenkamp studied Art History, Philosophy, and Languages at the University of Hamburg. She worked as a researcher at the Weserrenaissance-Museum Schloss Brake, Lemgo, and as a lecturer at the universities of Hamburg, Lüneburg and Reading. Currently, she works as a Research Associate at the University of Hamburg's Department of Art History and as a Lecturer at the Department of Lifelong Learning. Research interests include Northern Renaissance and Baroque art and architecture, with an emphasis on German and Netherlandish art and art theory; religious and political iconography; modern architecture. Her publications include *Kunst und Repräsentation. Beiträge zur europäischen Hofkultur im 16. Jahrhundert* (co-editor, 2002); *Das Pentagon von Wolfenbüttel* (2005) and several articles on related topics. – email: barbara.uppenkamp@web.de.

Mara R. Wade is Professor of Germanic Languages and Literatures at the University of Illinois. Together with Dr. Thomas Stäcker, Herzog August Bibliothek, Wolfenbüttel, she directs the bilateral digital humanities project, "Emblematica On-line." Her research explores the interstices between literature and the other arts, and she publishes on literature and music, theater, and the visual arts. Her research reflects her strong orientation to gender studies. She held a named professorship at the Hochschule für Musik, Theater und Medien in Hannover, Germany, and was a Visiting Professor at the University of Göttingen. She has taught consortium seminars at the Newberry Library, Chicago and also the Wolfenbüttel Summer Course, "Communication and the Culture of the Body in Early Modern Europe," in August 2011. She is currently the Chair of the International Society for Emblem Studies. Her publications include *Triumphus Nuptialis Danicus. German Court Culture and Denmark* (1996) and numerous articles inside her research field. – email: mwade@illinois.edu.

Jacob Wamberg, Dr. Phil., Professor of Art History at the University of Aarhus, Denmark.

He works on evolutionistic theories of the history of the visual arts, especially in relation to nature and technology. His publications include *Art & Alchemy* (editor, 2006), *Landscape as World Picture: Tracing Cultural Evolution in Images* (2009) and *Totalitarian Art and Modernity* (co-editor, 2010). – email: kunjw@hum.au.dk.

Dirk van de Vijver, Art historian, since 2006 attached, as a post-doctoral researcher, to the research group Architectural History of the University of Utrecht and is working on the project "The Low Countries at the Crossroads. Netherlandish Architecture as an Export Product in Early Modern Europe (1480-1680). His research field is history of architecture and engineering, engineers and contractors in Belgium in the 18th and 19th centuries, involving the interactions between art and science (French-Belgian) with their international relations. –email: d.r.e.vandevijver@uu.nl.

BIBLIOGRAPHY

Abrahamsen, Søren, "Hjortesalen på Hesselagergård. Stabilisering af bjælkeloftet over hjortesalen", *Architectura. Arkitekturhistorisk Årsskrift* 18 (1996), 24-25.

Adriaenssens, Anne-Marie, *Het iconografisch stadsbeeld van Antwerpen in de 16de eeuw*, Katholieke Universiteit Leuven 1982 (Master's Thesis).

Adriaenssens, Roger, "Sur l'hôtel de ville d'Anvers et les apports des carrières wallonnes dans son édification", *Bulletin de la commission royale des monuments et des sites* (1980), 125-141.

Agerbæk, Kirsten, "Børsen og Sparepenge. Eksempler på manieristisk arkitektur i Danmark?", in: Hakon Lund (ed.), *En bog om kunst til Else Kai Sass*, Copenhagen 1978, 174-185.

Agerbæk, Kirsten, *Høyen mellem klassicisme og romantik. Om idegrundlaget for N. L. Høyens virke for kunsten i fortid og samtid*, Esbjerg 1984.

Ahlberg, Nils, *Stadsgrundningar och planförändringar. Svensk stadsplanering 1521-1721*, Uppsala 2005 (Agraria 94. Acta Universitatis Agriculturae Sueciae (PhD-Dissertation)).

Alberti, Leon Battista, *On Painting and On Sculpture, The Latin Texts of De Pictura and De Statua*, Cecil Grayson (ed. and transl.), London 1972.

Alberti, Leon Battista, *Om Billedkunsten*, Lise Bek (ed. and transl.), Copenhagen 2000.

Albrecht, Uwe, "Maison forte et maison de plaisance: Le château français à l'époque de Louis XI", in: Bernard Chevalier & Philippe Contamine (eds.), *La France de la fin du XVe siécle. Renouveau et apogée*, Paris 1985, 215-220.

Albrecht, Uwe, "Le petit château en France et dans l'Europe du Nord aux XVe et XVIe siècles", in: Jean Guillaume (ed.), *Architecture et vie sociale. L'organisation intérieure des grandes demeures à la fin du Moyen Age et à la Renaissance*, Paris 1994 (De Architectura 6), 193-205.

Albrecht, Uwe, *Der Adelssitz im Mittelalter. Studien zum Verhältnis von Architektur und Lebensform in Nord- und Westeuropa*, Munich & Berlin 1995.

Albrecht, Uwe, "Frührenaissance-Architektur in Norddeutschland und Dänemark (1530-1570)", *Nordelbingen* 66 (1997) 25-47.

Albrecht, Uwe, *Der Renaissancebau des Celler Schlosses. Zur Genese des Zwerchhauses und zum Bildprogramm der Fassaden des 16. Jahrhunderts*, Celle 2003.

Albrecht, Uwe, "Gänge (Umgänge)", in: Werner Paravicini (ed.), *Höfe und Residenzen im spätmittelalterlichen Reich. Bilder und Begriffe*, Ostfildern 2005 (Residenzenforschung 15, II), 395-397.

Albrecht, Uwe & Matthias Landt, "Torhaus oder Herrenhaus? Überlegungen zu einem Sondertypus frühneuzeitlicher Schloßbaukunst am Beispiel von Seedorf und Dollrott", in: *Kunstsplitter. Beiträge zur nordeuropäischen Kunstgeschichte. Festschrift für Wolfgang J. Müller zum 70. Geburtstag*, Husum 1984, 42-65.

Albrecht, Uwe & Matthias Landt, "Die erste barocke Gutsanlage im Lande. Neue Ergebnisse der Bauforschung auf Quarnbek", *Nordelbingen* 56 (1987), 27-46.

Albrectsen, Esben, Karl-Erik Frandsen & Gunner Lind, *Konger og Krige 700-1648* (Carsten Due-Nielsen, Ole Feldbæk & Nikolaj Petersen (eds.), *Dansk udenrigspolitiks historie* 1), Copenhagen 2001.

Allard, E., "L'Exposition universelle de Paris", *L'Emulation* 4 (1878), 49-52, 55-57, 61-63, 73-77.

Alpers, Svetlana, *The Art of Describing: Dutch Art in the Seventeenth Century*, Chicago 1983.

Álvarez, Vicente, *Relación del camino y buen viaje que hizo el Príncipe de España D. Phelipe …*, Marie-Thérèse Dovillée (ed.), Brussels 1964.

Andersen, Michael, Ebbe Nyborg & Mogens Vedsø (eds.), *Masters, Meanings & Models. Studies in the Art and Architecture of the Renaissance in Denmark. Essays published in Honour of Hugo Johannsen*, Copenhagen 2010.

Anderson, C., "Masculine and Unaffected. Inigo Jones and the Classical Ideal", *Art Journal* 56, 2 (1997), 48-54.

Anderson, Jaynie (ed.), *Crossing Cultures: Conflict, Migration and Convergence*, Melbourne 2009.

Andersson, Thorsten, "De byggde staden", in: Axel Kroon, Nils Gustaf Hagander & Anders B. Andersson (eds.), *Staden ved Helgeå. En bok i anledning af Kristianstads 350-årsjubileum*, Kristianstad 1964, 95-244.

Andreae, Johann Valentin, *Reipublicae Christianopolitanae Descriptio…*, Strassbourg 1619.

Arenfeldt, Pernille, "The Political Role of the Female Consort in Protestant Germany, 1550-1585. Anna of Saxony as 'Mater Patriae'", European University Institute, Florence 2005 (PhD-Dissertation).

Aristodemo, Dina, "La figura e l'opera di Lodovico Guicciardini", in: Pierre Jodogne (ed.), *Lodovico Guicciardini (1521-1589)*, Leuven 1990 (Travaux de l'Institut Interuniversitaire pour l'étude de la Renaissance et de l'Humanisme X), 19-35.

Arnisaeus, Henning, *De republica seu relectionis politicae libri duo*, Frankfurt 1615.

Art in Denmark, 1600-1650, Delft 1984 (Leids Kunsthistorisch Jaarboek 2, 1983).

Arvidsson, Bengt, *Bildstrid Bildbruk Bildlära: En idéhistorisk undersökning av bildfrågan inom den begynnande lutherska traditionen under 1500-talet*, Lund 1987 (Studia Theologica Lundensia 41).

Ashmole, Elias, *The Institution, Laws, Ceremonies of the Most Noble Order of the Garter*, London 1715.

Assmann, Aleida, "Gedächtnis als Leitbegriff der Kulturwissenschaften", in: Lutz Musner & Gotthart Wunberg (eds.), *Kulturwissenschaften: Forschung – Praxis – Positionen*, Vienna 2002, 27-45.

Avery, Charles, "François Dieussart (c. 1600-1661), Portrait Sculptor to the Courts of Northern Europe", *Victoria and Albert Museum Yearbook* 4 (1974), 63-99.

Avery, Charles, "Hubert Le Sueur, the 'Unworthy Praxiteles' of King Charles I", in: Charles Avery, *Studies in European Sculpture*, London 1988, 145-235.

Bach, Friedrich Teja, "Albrecht Dürer – Figuren des Marginalen", in: Isabelle Frank & Freia Hartung (eds.), *Die Rhetorik des Ornaments*, Munich 2001, 121-145.

Bach-Nielsen, Carsten, "The Runes: Hieroglyphs of the North", in: Gerhard F. Strasser & Mara R. Wade (eds.), *Die Domänen des Emblems: Ausserliterarische Anwendungen der Emblematik*, Wiesbaden 2004, 157-172.

Bach-Nielsen, Carsten et al. (eds.), *Danmark og renæssancen 1500-1650*, Copenhagen 2006.

Bang, Thomas, *Phosphorus Inscriptionis Hierosymbolicae…*, Copenhagen 1648^2 (1646).

Bann, Stephen, *Romanticism and the Rise of History*, New York 1995.

Barbeito, José Manuel, *El Alcázar de Madrid*, Madrid 1992.

Barbeito, José Manuel, "Felipe II y la arquitectura. Los años de juventud", in: Fernando Checa Cremades (ed.), *Felipe II un monarca y su época. Un príncipe del Renacimiento*, Madrid 1998 (Sociedad Estatal para la Conmemoración de los Centenarios de Felipe II y Carlos V), 83-103.

Baron, Hans, *The Crisis of the Early Italian Renaissance: Civic Humanism and Republican Liberty in an Age of Classicism and Tyranny*, Princeton 1955.

Bartetzky, Arnold, "Hans Vredeman de Vries' geschwifte Beschlagwerkgiebel. Zu ihrer Herkunft, Aneignung und Verbreitung in der Architektur Mittel- und Nordeuropas", in: Heiner Borggrefe & Vera Lüpkes (eds.), *Hans Vredeman de Vries und die Folgen*, Marburg 2005 (Studien zur Kultur der Renaissance 3), 73-82.

Bartetzky, Arnold, *Das Grosse Zeüghaus in Danzig. Baugeschichte - Architekturgeschichtliche Stellung - Repräsentative Funktion*, Stuttgart 2000 (Forschungen zur Geschichte und Kultur des Östlichen Mitteleuropa).

Bartrum, Guila, "Dürer and Humanism", in: Guila Bartrum (ed.), *Albrecht Dürer and his Legacy*, London 2002, 9-17.

Barüske, Heinz, *Erich von Pommern. Ein nordischer König aus dem Greifengeschlecht*, Rostock 1997.

Bauer, R. & H. Haupt (eds.), "Das Kunstkammerinventar Kaiser Rudolphs II", *Jahrbuch der Kunsthistorischen Sammlungen in Wien* 72 (1976), XI-XXXVIII, XLV, 1-185.

Baxandall, Michael, *The Limewood Sculptors of Renaissance Germany*, New Haven & London 1980.

Beck, James, *Jacopo della Quercia*, New York 1991.

Beckett, Francis, *Renaissancen og Kunstens Historie i Danmark*, Copenhagen 1897.

Beckett, Francis, *Frederiksborg, II, Slottets Historie*, Copenhagen 1914.

Beek, Marijke, *Drie eeuwen Amsterdamse Bouwkunst. Catalogus van architectuurtekeningen in de verzameling A.A. Kok*, Amsterdam 1984.

Beer, E. S. de, "Gothic: Origin and Diffusion of the Term: The Idea of Style in Architecture", *Journal of the Warburg and Courtauld Institutes* 11 (1948), 143-162.

Béguin, Sylvie, "La galerie François Ier à Fontainebleau", *Revue de l'art* 16-17 (1972).

Behling, Holger, *Hans Gudewerdt. Bildschnitzer zu Eckernförde*, Neumünster 1990.

Belozerskaya, Marina, *Rethinking the Renaissance. Burgundian Arts across Europe*, Cambridge 2002.

Bencard, Mogens, *Silver Furniture*, Copenhagen 1992.

Bencard, Mogens & G. A. Markova, *Christian IV's Royal Plate and his Relations with Russia*, Rosenborg 1988.

Bencard, Mogens et al., *Die Gottorfer Kunstkammer* (Heinz Spielmann & Jan Drees (eds.), *Gottorf im Glanz des Barock. Kunst und Kultur am Schleswiger Hof 1544-1713*, II), Schleswig 1997.

Bendixen, Kirsten, "Medailleportrætter af de ældste oldenborgske konger", *Nationalmuseets Arbejdsmark* (1979), 68-79.

Benjamin, Lloyd, *The Empathetic Relation of Observer to Image in Fifteenth Century Northern Art*, University of North Carolina 1973, Ann Arbor 1975 (PhD-dissertation).

Bennich-Björkman, B., "De Leidse en Amsterdamse Elzeviers in Skandinavië, 1630-1680", in: B. P. M. Dongelmans, P. G. Hoftijzer & O. S. Lankhorst, (eds.), *Boekverkopers van Europa. Het 17de-eeuwse Nederlandse uitgevershuis Elzevier*, Zutphen 2000, 145-163.

Bepler, Jill, "Practical Perspectives on the Court and the Role of Princes: Georg Engelhard von Loehneyss's *Aulico Politica* and Christian IV of Denmark's *Königlicher Wecker* (1620)", in: Mara R. Wade (ed.), *Pomp, Power, and Politics: Essays Commemorating the 400th Anniversary of the Coronation of King Christian IV of Denmark (1596),* Amsterdam 2003 (Daphnis. Zeitschrift für Mittlere Deutsche Literatur und Kultur der Frühen Neuzeit (1400-1750) 32), 137-164.

Berg, Johan Adam, *Kurtze und eigentliche Beschreibung Des fürtrefflichen und weitberühmten Königlichen Hauses Friedrichsburg in Seeland gelegen*, Copenhagen 1646.

Berge-Gerbaud, Mària van, "Some "Background" Information", in: Villads Villadsen et al. (eds.), *Festschrift to Erik Fischer. European Drawings from six Centuries*, Copenhagen 1990, 279-294.

Bethencourt, Francisco & Florike Egmond (eds.), *Correspondence and Cultural Exchange in Europe 1400-1700*, Cambridge 2007 ((Robert Muchembled & William Monter (eds.), *Cultural Exchange in Early Modern Europe*, III).

Bevers, Holm, *Das Rathaus von Antwerpen (1561-1565). Architektur und Figurenprogramm*, Hildesheim, Zürich & New York 1985 (Studien zur Kunstgeschichte 28).

Bezold, Gustav von, *Baukunst der Renaissance in Deutschland, Holland, Belgien und Dänemark*, Stuttgart 1900 (Handbuch der Architektur 2,VII).

Białostocki, Jan, *The Art of the Renaissance in Eastern Europe*, Oxford & Ithaca 1976.

Białostocki, Jan, "Some Values of Artistic Periphery", in: Irving Lavin et al. (eds.), *World Art: Themes of Unity in Diversity* 1, Pennsylvania 1989, 49-58.

Białostocki, Jan, "Langsames und schnelles Geschehen in der Geschichte der Kunst", in: Friedrich Möbius & Helga Sciurie (eds.), *Stil und Epoche. Periodisierungsfragen*, Dresden 1989, 210-216.

Bibliotheek der Universiteit van Amsterdam, *Catalogus van de Bibliotheca Danica en van de overige Deensche en Ijslandsche werken aanwezig in de Universiteitsbibliotheek van Amsterdam*, Amsterdam 1939.

Bibliotheek der Universiteit van Amsterdam, *Catalogus van de Bibliotheca Svecica en van de overige Zweedse werken aanwezig in de Universiteitsbibliotheek van Amsterdam*, Amsterdam 1948.

Bidsted, Kirsten Lading, "Holger Danske i Skævinge", *ICO* 1 (1989), 21-31.

Bieber, Dietrich, "Die Kapelle von Schloß Gottorf – ein Sakralraum des Frühabsolutismus", in: Heinz Spielmann & Jan Drees (eds.), *Gottorf im Glanz des Barock: Kunst und Kultur am Schleswiger Hof 1544-1713. Kataloge der Ausstellung zum 50-jährigen Bestehen des Schleswig-Holsteinischen Landesmuseum auf Schloß Gottorf und zum 400. Geburtstag Herzog Friedrichs III.*, Schleswig 1997, I: Die Herzöge und ihre Sammlungen, 157-177.

Bischoff, Ulrich, "Wilder Mann mit Keule", in: Hanna Gagel (ed.), *Der Mensch um 1500. Werke aus Kirchen und Kunstkammern,* Berlin 1977, 161-166 (Exhibition Catalogue).

Bisgaard, Lars, "Cities and fortresses", in: Steffen Heiberg (ed.), *Christian IV and Europe: the 19th Art Exhibition of the Council of Europe, Denmark 1988*, Herning 1988, 483-489.

Bisgaard, Lars, "Kampen om enhjørningen. Christian IIs planlagte Grønlandstogt 1514-22 i danske kalkmalerier", in: Lars Bisgaard, Jacob Isager & Janus Møller Jensen (eds.), *Renæssancen i svøb. Dansk renæssance i europæisk belysning 1450-1550*, Odense 2008, 245-278.

Bisgaard, Lars, Jacob Isager & Janus Møller Jensen (eds.), *Renæssancen i svøb. Dansk renæssance i europæisk belysning 1450-1550*, Odense 2008.

Bjørnbo, Axel, "Adam af Bremens Nordensopfattelse", *Aarbøger for nordisk Oldkyndighed og Historie* 2, XXIV (1909), 120-244.

Blaas, P. B. M., *Historicus tussen wetenschap en journalistiek: G.W. Kernkamp*, Rotterdam 1983.

Bligaard, Mette, "The Privy Passage and the Audience House at Frederiksborg Palace", in: *Art in Denmark 1600-1650,* Delft 1984 (Leids Kunsthistorisch Jaarboek 2, 1983), 55-68.

Bligaard, Mette, *Frederiksborgs genrejsning. Historicisme i teori og praksis*, 1-2, Copenhagen 2008.

Bober, Phylis Pray & Ruth Rubinstein, *A Handbook of Sources*, Oxford 1986.

Bochnak, Adam, *Das Krakauer Jagellonen-Mausoleum,* Warsaw 1954.

Bock, Nicolas, "Patronage, Standards and *Transfert culturel*: Naples between Art History and Social Science Theory", *Art History* 31 (2008), 574-597 (special issue, Cordelia Warr & Janis Elliott (eds.), *Import/Export: Painting, Sculpture and Architecture in Naples, 1266-1713*).

Bodin, Jean, *Six livres des la Republique*, Paris 1572.

Böker, Johann Josef, *Architektur der Gothic. Gothic Architecture,* Salzburg & Munich 2005.

Bok, Marten Jan, "Christian von Braunschweig in den Niederlanden", in: Jochen Luckhardt & Nils Büttner (eds.), *Der Krieg als Person. Herzog Christian d. J. von Braunschweig-Lüneburg im Bildnis von Paulus Moreelse*, Brunswick 2000, 14-39.

Bok, Marten Jan, "The rise of Amsterdam as a cultural centre: the market for paintings, 1580-1680", in: P. O'Brien et al. (eds.), *Urban Achievement in Early Modern Europe. Golden Ages in Antwerp, Amsterdam and London*, Cambridge 2001, 186-209.

Bolton, H. Carrington, *The Follies of Science at the Court of Rudolph II 1567-1612*, Milwaukee 1904.

Bolvig, Axel, *Altertavlen i Roskilde Domkirke. Et u-almindeligt kunstværk*, Copenhagen 1997.

Bonsdorff, Jan von, "The Inertia of the Canon: Nationalist projections onto the Works of Hans Brüggemann and Bernt Notke", in: James Elkins & Robert Williams (eds.), *Renaissance Theory*, New York & London, 2008 (The Art Seminar 5), 278-286.

Boogert, Bob van den, "Macht en pracht. Het mecenaat van Maria van Hongarije", in: Bob van den Boogert & Jacqueline Kerhoff (eds.), *Maria van Hongarije, koningin tussen keizers en kunstenaars, 1505-1558,* 's-Hertogenbosch & Utrecht 1993 (Exhibition Catalogue), 269-301.

Borggrefe, Heiner, *Die Residenz Bückeburg – Architekturgestaltung im frühneuzeitlichen Fürstenstaat*, Marburg 1994.

Borggrefe, Heiner, "Tizians ruhende Göttinnen und Dienerinnen der Liebe", in: Andreas Tacke (ed.), *"…wir wollen der Liebe Raum geben" – Konkubinate geistlicher und weltlicher Fürsten um 1500*, Göttingen 2006, 393-421.

Borggrefe, Heiner, "Pieter Isaacsz in the Company of Hans von Aachen", in: Badeloch Noldus & Juliette Roding (eds.), *Pieter Isaacsz – Court Painter, Art Trader and Spy,* Copenhagen 2007 (Exhibition Catalogue), 42-57.

Borggrefe, Heiner, *Schloss Bückeburg. Höfischer Glanz – fürstliche Repräsentation*, Hannover 2008.

Borggrefe, Heiner, "Kitchen windows, Italian gables and court ceremonial – ornamentation in early Renaissance castles", in: Michael Bischoff & Hillert Ibbeken (eds.), *Castles of the Weser Renaissance/Schlösser der Weserrenaissance*, Stuttgart & London 2008, 29-35.

Borggrefe, Heiner et al. (ed.), *Hans Vredeman de Vries und die Renaissance in Norden*, Munich 2002 (Exhibition Catalogue).

Borggrefe, Heiner & Guido von Büren, *Schloß Stadthagen – eine Residenz der Renaissance*, Hannover 2008.

Boym, Svetlana, *The Future of Nostalgia,* New York 2001.

Bramsen, H., "Frederiksborg som emblem og arkitektur", in: Axel Thygesen (ed.), *Tilegnet Mogens Koch*, Copenhagen 1968.

Bramsen, H., *Symbolik i Christian den Fjerdes arkitektur med særligt hensyn til Trinitatis-komplekset i København*, Copenhagen 1982.

Brinckmann, Albert, *Die praktische Bedeutung der Ornamentstiche für die deutsche Frührenaissance,* Strasbourg 1907.

Brion-Guerry, Liliane, *Jean Pélerin Viator. Sa place dans l'historie de la perspective*, Paris 1962.

Brochmand, Casp. Erasmio [Caspar Jesper], *Oratio Funebris… Uldarici… dicta Esuggestu Bytzoviano [Bützow], 24. Maij, Anni M.DC. XXIV*, Copenhagen 1624.

Brotton, Jerry, *The Renaissance Bazaar: From the Silk Road to Michelangelo,* Oxford 2002.

Brown, Christopher, "British Painting and the Low Countries", in: Karen Hearn (ed.), *Dynasties. Painting in Tudor and Jacobean England 1530-1630*, London 1995, 27-31.

Brown, Christopher, "Artistic Relations between Britain and the Low Countries (1532-1632)", in: Juliette Roding & Lex Heerma van Voss (eds.), *The North Sea and Culture (1550-1800)*, Verloren 1996, 340-354.

Browning, Barton W., "Heinrich Julius von Braunschweig's 1590 Welcoming Celebration for Princess Elisabeth of Denmark", in: Wade, Mara R. (ed.), *Pomp, Power and Politics Pomp, Power, and Politics: Essays on German and Scandinavian Court Culture and their Contexts*, New York & Amsterdam 2004 (Daphnis. Zeitschrift für Mittlere Deutsche Literatur und Kultur der Frühen Neuzeit (1400-1750) 32, 2003), 73-82.

Bruchet, Max, "Notice sur la construction du palais Rihour à Lille", *Bulletin de la Commission historique du Département du Nord* 31 (1922), 209-299.

Brugerolles, Emmanuelle, *Renaissance et Manierisme dans les Ecoles du Nord. Dessins des collections de l'Ecole des Beaux Arts*, Paris 1985.

Bruhn, Thomas Paul, *Hans Reichle (1565/70-1642). A Reassessment of his Sculpture,* Pennsylvania State University 1981 (Dissertation).

Brunner, H., G. Hoyer & L. Seelig, *Residence Munich*, Munich 1987.

Bryson, Norman, "Art in Context", in: Ralph Cohen (ed.), *Studies in Historical Change,* Charlottesville 1992, 18-42.

Buchloh, Benjamin, *Neo-Avant-Garde and Culture Industry: Essays on European and American Art from 1955-1975*, Cambridge (Mass.) 2000.

Budick, Sanford, "Crises of Alterity. Cultural Untranslatability and the Experience of Secondary Otherness", in: Sanford Budick & Wolfgang Iser (eds.), *The Translatability of Cultures. Figurations of the Space Between*, Stanford 1996, 1-22.

Bugge, Ragne, "Tekstaltertavlene i Danmark-Norge omkring 1600", in: Ingmar Brohed (ed.), *Reformationens konsolidering i de nordiska länderna 1540-1610*, Oslo 1990, 306-325.

Bullen, J. B., *The Myth of the Renaissance in Nineteenth Century Writing*, Oxford 1994.

Burke, Peter, *The Renaissance*, New Jersey 1987.

Burke, Peter, "State-Making, King-Making and Image-Making from Renaissance to Baroque: Scandinavia in a European Context", *Scandinavian Journal of History* 22 (1997), 1-8.

Burke, Peter, *The European Renaissance: Centres and Peripheries*, Oxford 1998.

Burke, Peter, *What is Cultural History?*, Cambridge 2004.

Burke, Peter, "Decentering the Italian Renaissance: The Challenge of Postmodernism", in: Stephen J. Milner (ed.), *At the Margins. Minority Groups in Premodern Italy*, Minneapolis 2005, 36-49.

Burke, Peter, "Cultures of Translation in Early Modern Europe", in: Peter Burke & R. Po-Chia Hsia (eds.), *Cultural Translation in Early Modern Europe*, Cambridge 2007, 7-38.

Burke, Peter, "Translating histories", in: Peter Burke & R. Po-Chia Hsia (eds.), *Cultural Translation in Early Modern Europe*, Cambridge 2007, 125-141.

Burke, Peter, *Cultural Hybridity*, Cambridge 2009.

Busbecq, Ogier Ghiselin de, *Turkish Letters*, Edward S. Forster (transl.), Oxford 1927.

Bustamante García, Agustín, *La octava maravilla del mundo. Estudio histórico sobre el Escorial de Felipe II*, Madrid 1994.

Bøggild Johannsen, Birgitte, "Odense Domkirke. Højaltertavlen", in: *Danmarks Kirker. Odense Amt* 2, Herning 1995, 459-538.

Bøggild Johannsen, Birgitte, "Odense Domkirke. Gravminder", in: *Danmarks Kirker. Odense Amt*, 2, Herning 1997, 733-740.

Bøggild Johannsen, Birgitte, "Kongens tempel, Frederikskirken som religiøst og politisk symbol", *Architectura, Arkitekturhistorisk Årsskrift* 21 (1999), 131-157.

Bøggild Johannsen, Birgitte, "Genealogical Representation in Gendered Perspective: on a Lost Royal Mausoleum from Early Sixteenth-Century Denmark", in: Truus van Bueren & Andrea van Leerdam (eds.), *Care for the Here and the Thereafter: Memoria, Art and Ritual in the Middle Ages*, Turnhout 2005, 79-106.

Bøggild Johannsen, Birgitte, "Johan Friis og Hesselagergård", in: Carsten Bach-Nielsen et al. (eds.), *Danmark og renæssancen 1500-1650*, Copenhagen 2006, 270-279 (Bøggild Johannsen 2006a).

Bøggild Johannsen, Birgitte, "The Polish Paradigm. On the Heraldic Funeral of King Frederik II of Denmark and its European Context", in: Jan Harasimowicz, Piotr Oszczanowski & Marcin Wislocki (eds.), *On the Opposite Sides of the Baltic Sea. Relations between Scandinavian and Central European Countries*, 2, Wroclaw 2006, 555-568 (Bøggild Johannsen 2006b).

Bøggild Johannsen, Birgitte, "Til Kongens og Rigets behov. Nogle betragtninger om kunstforbruget ved Frederik II's hof", *Renæssanceforum* 2 (2006), 1-28 (http://www.renaessanceforum.dk.) (Bøggild Johannsen 2006c).

Bøggild Johannsen, Birgitte, "Køn, magt og minde. Omkring den rituelle og monumentale iscenesættelse af senmiddelalderens dronningebegravelser", in: Agnes S. Arnórsdottir, Per Ingesman & Bjørn Poulsen (eds.), *Konge, kirke og samfund. De to øvrighedsmagter i dansk senmiddelalder*, Aarhus 2007, 179-218.

Bøggild Johannsen, Birgitte, "Epigraphik im dänischen Inventar *Danmarks Kirker* – Paradigmen, Potentiale und Perspektiven – Mit einem Exkurs über das frühe neulateinische epitaph in Dänemark", in: Christine Magin et al. (eds.), *Traditionen, Zäsuren, Umbrüche. Inschriften des späten Mittelalters und der frühen Neuzeit im historischen Kontext*, Wiesbaden 2008, 349-367.

Bøggild Johannsen, Birgitte, "Promising Enterprises and Broken Dreams: Netherlandish Architectural Influences in Denmark during the Early 16th Century", in: Krista de Jonge & Konrad Ottenheym (eds.), *The Low Countries at the Crossroads. Netherlandish Architecture as an Export Product in Early Modern Europe (1480-1680). Papers from an international symposium at Heverlee, 2008* (forthcoming, a).

Bøggild Johannsen, Birgitte, "Conflit, Concurrence et Coévolution. Pratiques autour de la mort des rois et reines danois et suèdois à l'epoque moderne", in: Mark Hengerer & Gérard Sabatier (eds.), *Mémoire monarchique et la construction de l'Europe aux XVI-XVIII siècles. Papers from two international conferences at Cracow and Madrid 2007-08* (forthcoming, b).

Bøggild Johannsen, Birgitte & Hugo Johannsen, *Kongens kunst*, Copenhagen 1993 (*Ny dansk kunsthistorie*, 2).

Bøggild Johannsen, Birgitte & Hugo Johannsen, "Adelsvælde og renæssance", in: John Erichsen & Mikkel Venborg Pedersen (eds.), *Herregården. Menneske-samfund-landskab-bygninger*, I-IV, Copenhagen 2004-2006, II, 21-94.

Bøggild Johannsen, Birgitte & Hugo Johannsen, "Arkitektur og billedkunst", in: Carsten Bach-Nielsen et al. (eds.), *Danmark og renæssancen 1500-1650*, Copenhagen 2006, 112-129.

Bøggild Johannsen, Birgitte & Hugo Johannsen, "Re-forming the Confessional Space: Early Lutheran Churches in Denmark c. 1536-1600", in: Andrew Spicer & Margit Thøfner (eds.), *Lutheran Churches in Early Modern Europe*, Oxford (forthcoming).

Bøggild Johannsen, Birgitte & Marianne Marcussen, *Rumperception og rumkonstruktion, Kildeskrifter til optikkens og linearperspektivets historie i Vesteuropa fra antikken til renæssancen*, Copenhagen 1978.

Bricka, C. F., J. Skovgaard & J. A. Fridericia (eds.), *Kong Christian den Fjerdes egenhændige Breve*, 1-8, Copenhagen 1887-1947.

Cabanillas, Hieronymo, *Relación muy verdadera de las grandes fiestas que la Serenissima Reyna doña Maria ha hecho al*

Príncipe nuestro señor en Flandes ..., Medina del Campo 1549, republished in: Cristóbal Pérez Pastor (ed.), *La imprenda en Medina del Campo,* Madrid 1895, 57-67.

Calvete de Estrella, Juan Cristoval & Jules Petit (transl.), *Le très-heureux voyage fait par très-haut et très-puissant prince don Philippe, fils du grand empereur Charles-Quint, depuis l'Espagne jusqu'à ses domaines de la Basse-Allemagne, avec la description de tous les Etats de Brabant et de Flandre*, I-V, Brussels 1873-1884 (Société des Bibliophiles de Belgique 7, 10, 11, 15, 16), reprint Brussels 2000 (Algemeen Rijksarchief en Rijksarchief in de provinciën, reprints 161).

Campbell, Gordon (ed.), *The Grove Encyclopedia of Northern Renaissance Art*, I-III, Oxford 2009.

Campbell, Stephen, *The Cabinet of Eros: Renaissance Mythological Painting and the Studiolo of Isabella d'Este*, New Haven & London 2006.

Campbell, Stephen J. & Stephen J. Milner (eds.), *Artistic Exchange and Cultural Translation in the Italian Renaissance City*, Cambridge 2004.

Cappelletti, Francesca, "Enticement of the North: Landscape, Myth and Gleaming Metal supports", in: Beverly Louise Brown (ed.), *Genius of Rome. 1592-1623*, London & Rome 2001, 174-205.

Capra, Dominick La, "History and Psychoanalysis", in: Dominick La Capra, *Soundings in Critical Theory*, Ithaca 1989, 30-66.

Cartellieri, Ottavio, *La Cour des Ducs de Bourgogne,* Paris 1946.

Caselius, Johannes, *Domino Henrico Iulio Guelpho et Dominae Dorotheae Saxonicae Sponsis illustrissimis*, Rostock 1585.

Caselius, Johannes, *Nuptijs Herois Henricii Iulii Guelfi et Heroinae Elisabethae Cimbricae Trikopeion*, Helmstedt 1590.

Casteels, Marguerite, *De beeldhouwers De Nole te Kamerijk, te Utrecht en te Antwerpen*, Brussels 1961 (Verhandelingen van de Koninklijke Vlaamse Academie voor Wetenschappen, Letteren en Schone Kunsten van België, Klasse der Schone Kunsten 16).

Castelnuovo, Enrico, "La frontiera nella storia dell'arte", and "Le Alpi, crocevia e punto d'incontro delle tendenze artistiche nel XV secolo", in: Enrico Castelnuovo, *La cattedrale tascabile. Scritti di storia dell'arte*, Livorno 2000, 15-45.

Celis, Marcel, "Janlet, Emile", in: Anne Van Loo (ed.), *Repertorium van de Architectuur in België van 1830 tot heden*, Antwerp 2003, 367.

Celis, Marcel, "Schoy, Auguste", in: Anne Van Loo (ed.), *Repertorium van de Architectuur in België van 1830 tot heden*, Antwerp 2003, 500-501.

Chakrabarty, Dipesh, *Provincializing Europe: Postcolonial Thought and Historical Difference*, Princeton 2000.

Chanteux, Henri, "Le château de Saint-Ouen en Chemazé", *Congrès Archéologique* (1964), 289-300.

Chastel, André, *The Palace of Apolidon*, Oxford 1986 (The Zaharoff Lecture for 1984-1985).

Chastel, André & Jean Guillaume (eds.), *L'escalier dans l'architecture de la Renaissance*, Paris 1985.

Chatelain, Jean-Marc, "L'illustration d'Amadis de Gaule dans les éditions françaises du XVIe siècle", in: *Les Amadis en France au XVIe siècle*, Paris 2000, 41-52.

Chatenet, Monique, *La cour de France au XVIe siècle. Vie sociale et architecture*, Paris 2002 (De Architectura).

Chatenet, Monique, "Architecture et ceremonial à la cour de Henri II: l'apparition de l'antichambre", in: Hervé Oursel & Julia Fritsch (eds.), *Henri II et les arts. Actes du colloque international Ecole du Louvre et musée national de la Renaissance-Ecouen*, Paris 2003 (XVes Rencontres de l'Ecole du Louvre), 355-380.

Chatenet, Monique, Ethan Matt Kavaler, Krista de Jonge & Norbert Nussbaum, "Architecture européenne du XVIe siècle: un "gothique de la Renaissance"?", *Perspective* 2 (2006), 290-299.

Chatterjee, Partha, *Nationalist Thought and the Colonial World: A Derivative Discourse,* Minneapolis 1993.

Christensen, Carl C., *Princes and propaganda: Electoral Saxon Art of the Reformation,* Ann Arbor 1992 (Sixteenth Century Essays and Studies XX).

Christensen, Charlotte, "Adriaen de Vries' Neptunspringvand", in: Steffen Heiberg (ed.) *Christian 4. og Frederiksborg*, Copenhagen 2006, 153-172.

Christensen, Hans Dam & Louise C. Larsen (eds.), *Det kunsthistoriske studieapparat. Hånd- og debatbog fra den videnskabelige hverdag*, Copenhagen 2004.

Christensen, Hans Dam, "Billedkunsten. Om kunsthistorien, N. L. Høyen og folkets billedkunst", in: Palle Ove Christiansen (ed.), *Veje til danskheden. Bidrag til den moderne nationale selvforståelse*, Copenhagen 2005, 66-94.

Christensen, Stephen Turk, "Christian I's promovering af Rom som pilgrimsby", in: Per Ingesman & Bjørn Poulsen (eds.), *Danmark og Europa i senmiddelalderen*, Aarhus 2000, 134-159.

Christensen, Stephen Turk & Badeloch Noldus (eds.), "Cultural Traffic and Cultural Transformation around the Baltic Sea, 1450-1720", *Scandinavian Journal of History* 28, 3-4 (2003).

Christensen, Stephen Turk, "Introduction", in: Stephen Turk Christensen & Badeloch Noldus (eds.), "Cultural Traffic and Cultural Transformation around the Baltic Sea, 1450-1720", *Scandinavian Journal of History* 28, 3-4 (2003), 151-164.

Chueca Goitia, Fernando, "La influencia de los Países Bajos en la arquitectura española", in: Fernando Chueca Goitia (ed.), *El Escorial, piedra profética,* Madrid 1986, 195-215.

Clark, T. J., *Image of the People: Gustave Courbet and the 1848 Revolution*, London 1973.

Çoban-Hensel, Margitta, "Die archivalisch nachweisbare Verbreitung von Goldledertapeten in den kursächsischen

Schlössern vom 16. Jahrhundert bis zum Beginn des 18. Jahrhunderts", in: Staatliche Schlösser, Burgen und Gärten Sachsen (ed.), *Ledertapeten. Bestände, Erhaltung und Restaurierung*, Dresden 2004, 31-43.

Çoban-Hensel, Margitta, "Kurfürst August von Sachsen als spiritus rector der bildnerischen Schlossausstattungen", in: Barbara Marx (ed.), *Kunst und Repräsentation am Dresdner Hof*, Munich & Berlin 2005, 108-130.

Colantuono, A., "The Mute Diplomat: Theorizing the Role of Images in Seventeenth Century political Negotiations", in: E. Cropper (ed.), *The Diplomacy of Art. Artistic Creation and Politics in Seicento Italy*, Florence 1998 (Villa Spelman Colloquia 7), 51-76.

Cole, Michael, "*Nihil sub Sole Novum*", *The Art Bulletin* 87 (2005), 421-424.

Connerton, Paul, "Seven Types of Forgetting", *Memory Studies*, 1, 1 (2008), 59-71.

Cools, Hans, Marika Keblusek & Badeloch Noldus (eds.), *Your humble servant - agents in early modern Europe*, Hilversum 2006.

Coppens, Chris, Marc Derez & Jan Roegiers (eds.), *Sapientia Aedificavit sibi domum. Universiteitsbibliotheek Leuven 1425-2000*, Leuven 2005.

Corbet, August, "Cornelis Floris en de bouw van het stadhuis van Antwerpen", *Belgisch tijdschrift voor oudheidkunde en kunstgeschiedenis/Revue belge d'archéologie et d'histoire de l'art* 6 (1936), 223-264.

Cormack, Bradin & Carlo Manzo, *Book use, book theory: 1500-1700*, Chicago 2005.

Cotta-Schønberg, Michael von, "De Daniae regno aliqua non indigna cognitu: Danmarksbilledet hos en italiensk renæsssancehumanist, Æneas Silvius Piccolomini (Pius II)", in: Lars Bisgaard, Jacob Isager & Janus Møller Jensen (eds.), *Renæssancen i svøb. Dansk renæssance i europæisk belysning 1450-1550*, Odense 2008, 83-110.

Cramer, Daniel, *Areteugenia: De Aretino Et Eugenia,… Fabula/Ficta & Comice descripta a M. Daniele Cramero. Ante decennium fere ab ipso Autore: iam, vero exemplarium penuria denuo edita, adiectis ad singulos actus rythmis Germanicis*, [Leipzig] 1602.

Crow, Thomas, "The Practice of Art History in America", *Daedalus* 135, 2 (2006), 70-90.

Culler, Jonathan, *The Pursuit of Signs: Semiotics, Literature, Deconstruction*, Ithaca 1981.

Cuny, Georg, "Hieronymus und Antonius von Obbergen", *Mitteilungen des Westpreussischen Geschichtsvereins* 3 (1904), 51-57.

Cuny, Georg, "Antonius von Obbergen", *Zeitschrift für Bauwesen* LVI (1906), 419-442.

Cuny, Georg, *Danzigs Kunst und Kultur im 16. und 17. Jahrhundert*, Frankfurt am Main 1910.

Cupperi, Walter, "Arredi statuari italiani nelle regge dei Paesi Bassi asburgici meridionali (1549-56). I. Maria d'Ungheria, Leone Leoni e la galleria di Binche", *Prospettiva. Rivista di storia dell'arte antica e moderna* 113-114 (2004), 98-116.

Curta, Florin, "Introduction", in: Florin Curta (ed.), *Borders, Barriers, and Ethnogenesis. Frontiers in Late Antiquity and the Middle Ages*, Turnhout 2005 (Studies in the Early Middle Ages, 12), 1-9.

Curtis, Penelope, *Depth of Field: the place of relief in the time of Donatello*, Leeds 2004.

Daalder, Remmelt et al. (eds.), *Goud uit Graan. Nederland en het Oostzeegebied 1600-1850*, Zwolle 1998.

Dacos, Nicole (ed.), *Fiamminghi a Roma 1508-1608. Kunstenaars uit de nederlanden en het prinsbisdom Luik te Rome tijdens de Renaissance*, Brussels & Rome 1999.

Dahlerup, Troels, "Danish National Identity, c. 700-1700", in: Claus Bjørn et al. (eds.), *Nations, Nationalism and Patriotism in the European Past*, Copenhagen 1994, 56-67.

Damsholt, Nanna, "Tiden indtil 1560", in: Søren Mørch (ed.), *Historiens historie*, Copenhagen 1992 (Aksel E. Christensen et al. (eds.), *Danmarks historie* 10), 34-51.

Damsholt, Torben, "Den nationale magtstat 1560-1760", in: Søren Mørch (ed.), *Historiens historie*, Copenhagen 1992 (Aksel E. Christensen et al. (eds.), *Danmarks historie* 10), 61-69.

Danmarks Adels Aarbog, Dansk Adelsforening (ed.), Copenhagen 1884-

Danmarks Kirker, The National Museum of Denmark (ed.), Copenhagen et al. 1933-

Dansk Biografisk Leksikon, 1. ed., C.F. Bricka (ed.), Copenhagen 1887-1905; 2. ed., P. Engelstoft et al. (eds.), Copenhagen 1933-44; 3. ed., Sv. Cedergreen-Bech et al. (eds.), Copenhagen 1979-84.

Dansk Kvindebiografisk Leksikon, Jytte Larsen et al. (eds.), Copenhagen 2000-2001.

Das Dresdner Schloss. Monument sächsischer Geschichte und Kultur, Dresden 1992³.

Dauw, Johannes, *Der Kunst-Erfahrne curieuse, galante … Nachricht von der Edlen Schilder-Kunst*, Copenhagen 1721.

de Boor, Friedrich, "Die Bibelsprüche an den unteren Emporen der Marktkirche: In Stein gemeisselte Proklamation des reformatorischen Glaubens", in: Sabine Kramer & Karsten Eisenmenger (eds.), *Die Marktkirche Unser Lieben Frauen zu Halle*, Halle an der Saale 2004, 21-29.

de Bray, S. & C. Danckerts, *Architectura Moderna, ofte Bouwinge van onsen tyt*, Amsterdam 1631.

de Certeau, Michel, *The Writing of History*, New York 1988.

de Jong, H. M. E., *Michael Maier's Atalanta fugiens. Bronnen van een alchemistisch emblemenboek*, Utrecht 1965 (Dissertation).

de Jonge, Krista, "Architekturpraxis in den Niederlanden in der frühen Neuzeit: Die Rolle des italienischen Militärarchitekten; der *status quæstionis*", in: Günter Bers & Conrad Doose (eds.), *Der italienische Architekt Alessandro Pasqualini (1493-1559) und die Renaissance am Niederrhein: Kenntnisstand und Forschungsperspektiven*, Jülich 1994, 363-383.

de Jonge, Krista, "Le palais de Charles Quint à Bruxelles. Ses dispositions intérieures aux XVe et XVIe siècles et le cérémonial de Bourgogne", in: Jean Guillaume (ed.), *Architecture et vie sociale. L'organisation intérieure des grandes demeures à la fin du moyen age et à la Renaissance*, Paris 1994 (De Architectura 6), 107-125.

de Jonge, Krista, "Le langage architectural de Jacques Du Broeucq", in: Krista De Jonge & Marcel Capouillez (eds.), *Le château de Boussu*, Namur 1998 (Etudes et Documents, Monuments et Sites 8), 161-187.

de Jonge, Krista, "Triunfos flamencos: Felipe II y la arquitectura del Renacimiento en Flandes", in: José Martínez Millán (ed.), *Felipe II (1527-1598). Europa y la Monarquía Católica, Literatura, Cultura y Arte*, Madrid 1998, 347-369.

de Jonge, Krista, "Hofordnungen als Quelle der Residenzenforschung? Adlige und herzogliche Residenzen in den südlichen Niederlanden in der Burgunderzeit", in: Werner Paravicini & Holger Kruse (eds.), *Höfe und Hofordnungen 1200-1600. 5. Symposium der Residenzen-Kommission der Akademie der Wissenschaften in Göttingen veranstaltet gemeinsam mit dem Deutschen Historischen Institut Paris und dem Staatsarchiv Sigmaringen, Sigmaringen 5. bis 8. Oktober 1996*, Sigmaringen 1999 (Residenzenforschung 10), 175-220.

de Jonge, Krista, "'t Hof van Brabant als symbool van de Spaanse hofhouding in de Lage Landen", *Bulletin van de Koninklijke Nederlandse Oudheidkundige Bond* 98 (1999), 183-198.

de Jonge, Krista, "'Anticse wercken': la découverte de l'architecture antique dans la pratique architecturale des anciens Pays-Bas Livres de modèles et traités 1517-1599", in: Marie-Christine Heck, Frédérique Lemerle & Yves Pauwels (eds.), *Théorie des arts et création artistique dans l'Europe du Nord du XVIe au début du XVIIIe siècle. Actes du colloque international organisé les 14 et 16 décembre 2000 à Lille*, Lille 2002 (Travaux et recherches), 55-74.

de Jonge, Krista, "'Up die maniere van Brabant'. Brabant en de adelsarchitectuur van de Lage Landen (1450-1530)", in: Raymond Van Uytven (ed.), *Gotiek in Brabant. De Brabantse stad. Dertiende colloquium, Leuven 18-19 oktober 2002*, Antwerp 2003 (Bijdragen tot de geschiedenis 86, 3-4), 409-423.

de Jonge, Krista, "Vredeman de Vries as a Disseminator of Architectural Novelties", in: Heiner Borggrefe & V. Lüpkes (eds.), *Hans Vredeman de Vries und die Folgen*, Marburg 2005 (Studien zur Kultur der Renaissance 3), 83-90.

de Jonge, Krista, "Images inédites de la villégiature dans la périphérie de Bruxelles, XVIe-XVIIIe siècles. Maisons des champs et maisons de plaisance", in: Monique Chatenet (ed.), *Maisons des champs dans l'Europe de la Renaissance. Actes des premières Rencontres d'architecture européenne, Château de Maisons, 10-13 juin 2003*, Paris 2006 (De Architectura 11), 269-282.

de Jonge, Krista, "Antiquity Assimilated: Court Architecture 1530-1560", in: Krista De Jonge & Konrad Ottenheym (eds.), *Unity and Discontinuity. Architectural Relations between the Southern and Northern Low Countries (1530-1700)*, Turnhout 2007 (Architectura Moderna 5), 55-78.

de Jonge, Krista, "Le château et le jardin de 'La Fontaine' à Clausen dans leur contexte européen", in: Jean-Luc Mousset & Krista De Jonge (eds.), *Un prince de la Renaissance. Pierre-Ernest de Mansfeld (1517-1604). II. Essais et catalogue*, Luxembourg 2007 (Exhibition Catalogue), 239-262.

de Jonge, Krista, "Style and Manner in Early Modern Netherlandish Architecture (1450-1600). Contemporary Sources and Historiographical Tradition", in: Stephan Hoppe, Matthias Müller & Norbert Nussbaum (eds.), *Stil als Bedeutung in der nordalpinen Renaissance : Wiederentdeckung eine methodischen Nachbarschaft*, Cologne 2008, 264-285.

de Jonge, Kristia, "Marie de Hongrie, maître d'ouvrage (1531-1555), et la Renaissance dans les anciens Pays-Bas", in: Bertrand Federinov & Gilles Docquier (eds.), *Marie de Hongrie. Politique et culture sous la Renaissance aux Pays-Bas*, Morlanwelz 2008 ((Monographies du Musée royal de Mariemont 17), 124-139.

de Jonge, Krista & Konrad Ottenheym, "The Production Process for Architecture within the Context of the Courts (1580-1700)", in: Krista De Jonge & Konrad Ottenheym (eds.), *Unity and Discontinuity. Architectural Relations between the Southern and Northern Low Countries (1530-1700)*, Turnhout 2007 (Architectura Moderna 5), 165-208.

de Jonge, Krista & K. A. Ottenheym, "Unity and Discontinuity. Architectural Relationships between the Southern and Northern Low Countries (1530-1700)", in: Krista De Jonge & Konrad Ottenheym (eds.), *Unity and Discontinuity. Architectural Relations between the Southern and Northern Low Countries (1530-1700)*, Turnhout 2007 (Architectura Moderna 5), 111-136.

de Jonge, Krista & Marcel Capouillez (eds.), *Le château de Boussu*, Namur 1998 (Etudes et Documents, Monuments et Sites 8).

de Maegd, Chris, "Een einde en een nieuw begin: de creatie van een Hof van Plaisantie", *Monumenten & Landschappen* 17, 1 (1998), 6-44.

De Marchi, N. & H. J. Miegroet (eds.), *Mapping Markets for Paintings in Europe, 1450-1750*, Turnhout 2006.

De Vandières, S., *L'exposition universelle de 1878 illustrée. Quatre-vingt-sept belles gravures sur bois*, Paris 1879.

Deckert, Hermann, "Die lübisch-baltische Skulptur im Anfang des 16. Jahrhunderts", *Marburger Jahrbuch für Kunstwissenschaft, Kunstgeschichtliches Seminar der Universität Marburg* III (1926), 1-75.

Dedenroth-Schou, Birgitte & Jens Å. S. Pedersen, *Rådhus og Bystyre i Kolding 1500-2000*, Kolding 2001.

Degering, Hermann (ed.), *Faksimile nach der Ausgabe der Bibel von Martin Luther 1545 mit dem Bilderschmuck des in der Preußischen Staatsbibliothek befindlichen Pergamentexemplars der Ausgabe 1541, das von Lucas Cranach für den Fürsten Johann II. von Anhalt illuminiert wurde*, Berlin 1927.

Dehio, Georg, *Handbuch der Deutschen Kunstdenkmäler. Sachsen-Anhalt II. Regierungsbezirke Dessau und Halle*, Ute Bednarz et al. (eds.), Munich & Berlin 1999.

Dempsey, Charles, "*Historia* and Anachronism in Renaissance Art", *The Art Bulletin* 87 (2005), 416-421.

Den Hoed, P. M., *Iets over de cultuuraanraking van Nederland met Denemarken en Zweden. Openbare les gehouden bij de aanvaarding van het lectoraat in Zweedsche en Deensche taal- en letterkunde aan de universiteit van Amsterdam op vrijdag 27 september 1929*, Haarlem 1929.

Derrida, Jacques, "Parergon", in: Jacques Derrida, *The Truth in Painting*, Geoff Bennington & Ian McLeod (transl.), Chicago 1987.

Derrida, Jacques, *Specters of Marx: The State of the Debt, the Work of Mourning & the New International*, Peggy Kamuf (transl.), Bernd Magnus & Stephen Cullenberg (intro), New York & London 1994.

Deursen, A. Th., *De last van veel geluk. De geschiedenis van Nederland 1555-1702*, Amsterdam 2004.

Didi-Huberman, Georges, *Confronting Images: Questioning the Ends of a Certain History of Art*, Pennsylvania 2005.

Diederichs-Gottschalk, Dietrich, *Die protestantischen Schriftaltäre des 16. und 17. Jahrhunderts in Nordwestdeutschland: Eine kirchen- und kunstgeschichtliche Untersuchung zu einer Sonderform liturgischer Ausstattung in der Epoche der Konfessionalisierung*, Regensburg 2005 (Adiaphora: Schriften zur Kunst und Kultur im Protestantismus).

Diemer, Dorothea, "Giambologna in Germania", in: Beatrice Paolozzi Strozzi & Dimitrios Zikos (eds.), *Giambologna. Gli dei, gli eroi,* Florence 2006, 106-125.

Dietterlin, W., *Architectura. Von Ausstheilung / Symmetria und Proportion der Fünff Seulen*, Nuremberg 1598.

Domínguez Casas, Rafael, *Arte y etiqueta de los reyes católicos. Artistas, residencias, jardines y bosques*, Valladolid 1993.

Donath, W. & D. Schulze (eds.), *Jagdschloss Annaburg. Eine geschichtliche Wanderung*, Horb am Neckar 1994.

van Doorslaer, G., "Antoine van Oberghen, grand architecte Malinois", *Mechlinia* 2 (1923), 164-167.

Dorsman, L. J., *G.W. Kernkamp. Historicus en democrat 1864-1943*, Groningen 1990.

Douffet, Heinrich, "Erzgebirgische Bergstädte. Historische und städtebauliche Kennzeichnung", in: Dieter Dolgner & Irene Roch (eds.), *Stadtbaukunst im Mittelalter. Festschrift für Hans-Joachim Mrusek*, Berlin 1990, 182-186.

Drees, Jan, ""Die Gottorfische Kunst-Kammer". Anmerkungen zu ihrer Geschichte nach historischen Textzeugnissen", in: Bencard, Mogens et al., *Die Gottorfer Kunstkammer* (Heinz Spielmann & Jan Drees (eds.), *Gottorf im Glanz des Barock. Kunst und Kultur am Schleswiger Hof 1544-1713*, II), Schleswig 1997, 11-48.

Dreitzel, Hort, *Protestantischer Aristotelismus und absoluter Staat. Die "Politica" des Henning Arnisäus,* Wiesbaden 1970 (Veröffentlichungen des Instituts für europäische Geschichte Mainz 55, Abteilung für Universalgeschichte).

Droste, H., *Im Dienst der Krone. Schwedische Diplomaten im 17. Jahrhundert*, Berlin 2006.

Dudok van Heel, S. A. C., "The Birth of an Artists' Quarter – Pieter Isaacsz's Amsterdam Years", in: B. Noldus & J. Roding (eds.), *Pieter Isaacsz (1568-1625). Court Painter, Art Dealer and Spy*, Turnhout 2007 (Exhibition Catalogue), 75-91.

Dülberg, Angelica, *Privatporträts. Geschichte und Ikonologie einer Gattung im 16. Jahrhundert*, Berlin 1990.

Dülberg, Angelica, "'… weitaus die edelste Portalcomposition der ganzen deutschen Renaissance.' Zum Schloßkapellenportal des Dresdner Residenzschlosses", *Wallraf-Richartz-Jahrbuch* 63 (2002), 197-216.

Dülberg, Angelica, "'… weitaus die edelste Portalcomposition der ganzen deutschen Renaissance.' Geschichte und Ikonographie des Dresdner Schlosskapellenportals", *Denkmalpflege in Sachsen. Jahrbuch 2004* (2005), 52-80.

Dülberg, Angelica, Norbert Oelsner & Rosemarie Pohlack, *Das Dresdner Residenzschloss*, Berlin & Munich 2009.

Dürer, Albrecht, *Underweysung der Messung*, Nuremberg 1525 (second edition 1538).

Dürer, Albrecht, *Etliche vnderricht, zu befestigung der Stett, Schloß vnd flecken*, Nuremberg 1527.

Duerloo, Luc & Marc Wingens, *Scherpenheuvel, Het Jeruzalem van de Lage Landen,* Leuven 2002.

Duverger, Jozef, "Cornelis Floris II en het stadhuis te Antwerpen", *Gentse bijdragen tot de kunstgeschiedenis* 7 (1941), 37-72.

Duverger, Jozef & M. J. Onghena, "Beeldhouwer Willem van den Broecke alias Guilielmus Paludanus (1530 tot 1579 of 1580)", *Gentse bijdragen tot de kunstgeschiedenis* 5 (1938), 75-140.

Duvosquel, Jean-Marie (ed.), *Albums de Croÿ, VI. Comté de Hainaut III*, Brussels 1990.

Eberhardt, Jürgen, *Die Zitadelle von Jülich – Wehranlagen, Residenzschloß und Schloßkapelle – Forschungen zur Planungs- und Baugeschichte*, Jülich 1993.

Eichberger, Dagmar, "Stilpluralismus und Internationalität am Hofe Margaretes von Österreich", in: Norbert Nussbaum, Claudia Euskirchen & Stephan Hoppe (eds.), *Wege zur Renaissance. Beobachtungen zu den Anfängen neuzeitlicher Kunstauffassung im Rheinland und den Nachbargebieten um 1500*, Cologne 2003, 261-283.

Eichhorn, E. & Herman Odelberg, "Guillaume Boyen (Wilhelm Boy), peintre, sculpteur et architecte belge. Etude biographique", *Annales de l'Académie d'Archéologie de Belgique* 28 (1872), 94-132.

Eimer, Gerhard, *Die Stadtplanung im schwedischen Ostseereich 1600-1715*, Stockholm 1961.

Elkins, James (ed.), *Is Art History Global?*, New York and London 2007.

Elkins, James, "Art History as a Global Discipline", in: James Elkins (ed.), *Is Art History Global?*, New York and London 2007, 3-23.

Elkins, James & Robert Williams (eds.), *Renaissance Theory*, New York & London 2008 (The Art Seminar 5).

Ellehøj, Svend (ed.), *Christian IVs Verden*, Copenhagen 1988.

Ellenius, Allan, *De arte pingendi. Latin Art Literature in Seventeenth-century Sweden and its International Background*, Uppsala 1960.

Elling, Christian, "Philip de Lange som Søetatens bygmester", *Historiske Meddelelser om København* 1928, 375-403.

Elling, Christian, *Philip de Lange. En studie i Dansk Barokarkitektur*, Copenhagen 1931.

Elsner, Jas., "Style", in: Robert S. Melson & Richard Shiff (eds.), *Critical Terms for Art History*, Chicago & London 2003, 98-109.

Engelstoft, C. T., "Det første Forsøg paa at oprette et Stamhus i Danmark", *Samlinger til Fyns Historie og Topographie* III (1865), 117-165.

Engqvist, Hans Henrik, "Fire fynske herreborge. Nyt syn på Rygaards, Hesselagergaards, Egeskovs og Ørbæklundes bygningshistorie", *Architectura. Arkitekturhistorisk Årsskrift* 2 (1980), 55-125.

Engqvist, Hans Henrik, "Hjortesalen på Hesselagergård. Om gårdens bygningshistorie og salens genskabelse", *Architectura. Arkitekturhistorisk Årsskrift* 18 (1996), 7-23.

Erickson, Peter, "Review of Lucy Gent (ed.), *Albion's Classicism: The Visual Arts in Britain, 1550-1660*, New Haven 1995, and of Claire Farago (ed.), *Reframing the Renaissance: Visual Culture in Europe and Latin America, 1450-1650*, New Haven 1995", *Art Bulletin*, 87,4 (1996), 736-738.

Eriksen, Svend, *Om vælske gavle og andre problemer i dansk arkitektur i det 16. århundrede*, Copenhagen 1956 (Meddelelser fra Foreningen til gamle Bygningers Bevaring 7, 4).

Erler, Georg, *Die Jüngere Matrikel der Universität Leipzig 1559-1809*, 1, Leipzig 1909.

Etting, Vivian, Rodolfo Signorini & Birgitte Werdelin (eds.), *Fra Christian I's Italiensrejse 1474*, Copenhagen 1984.

van Even, Edouard, *Renseignements inédits sur la construction du refuge de l'abbaye de Herkenrode, à Hasselt (1542-1545)*, s. l. 1874.

Fabricius, K., L. L. Hammerich & Vilh. Lorenzen (eds.), *Holland-Danmark. Forbindelserne mellem de to Lande gennem Tiderne*, I-II, Copenhagen 1945.

Façade nationale belge, Brussels 1878 (Exhibition Catalogue).

Faix, Gerhard, "Heinrich Füllmaurer – Maler zu Herrenberg", *Blätter für württembergische Kirchengeschichte* 87 (1987), 153-173.

Farago, Claire (ed.), *Reframing the Renaissance: Visual Culture in Europe and Latin America 1450-1650*, New Haven & London 1995.

Farago, Claire, "Introduction", in: Claire Farago (ed.), *Reframing the Renaissance: Visual Culture in Europe and Latin America 1450-1650*, New Haven & London 1995, 1-20.

Farago, Claire, "Time Out of Joint", *The Art Bulletin* 87 (2005), 424-429.

Farago, Claire, "Review of Thomas DaCosta Kaufmann, *Toward a Geography of Art*", *Renaissance Quarterly* 53 (2005), 279-280.

Farago, Claire, "Reframing the Renaissance Problem Today. Developing a Pluralistic Historical Vision", in: Jaynie Anderson (ed.), *Crossing Cultures: Conflict, Migration and Convergence*, Melbourne 2009, 227-232.

Farago, Claire et al., *Transforming Images: New Mexican Santos in-between Worlds*, University Park (Penn.) 2006.

Federspiel, Beate Knuth, *Det gotiske Fløjalter, arbejdsgang og teknikker, Teknologihistorie*, Det Kongelige Danske Kunstakademi, Konservatorskolen, Copenhagen 1986.

Feldbæk, Ole, "Fædreland og Indfødsret. 1700-tallets danske identitet", in: Ole Feldbæk (ed.), *Fædreland og Modersmål 1536-1789*, Copenhagen 1991 (Dansk identitetshistorie 1), 111-230.

Feldbæk, Ole, "Is there Such a Thing as a Medieval Danish Identity?", in: Brian Patrick McGuire (ed.), *The Birth of Identities. Denmark and Europe in the Middle Ages*, Copenhagen 1996, 127-134.

Felix, Gilbert, *History or Culture? Reflections on Ranke and Burckhardt*, Princeton 1990.

Ferguson, Wallace, *The Renaissance in Historical Thought: Five Centuries of Interpretation*, Cambridge (Mass.) 1948.

Ferrari, Simone, *Jacopo de´ Barbari. Un protagonista del Rinascimento tra Venezia e Dürer*, Milano 2006.

Fey, Carola, Steffen Krieb & Werner Rösener (eds.), *Mittelalterliche Fürstenhöfe und ihre Erinnerungskulturen* (Formen der Erinnerung, 27), Göttingen 2007.

Fichtner, Th. & K. Wezel, "Elias Holl", in: A. Bartetzky (ed.), *Die Baumeister der "Deutschen Renaissance". Ein Mythos der Kunstgeschichte?*, Beucha 2004, 213-236.

Filarete, Antonio, *Filarete's Treatise on Architecture*, John Spencer (transl.), New Haven & London 1965.

Filarete, Antonio, *Trattato di architettura*, A. M. Finoli & L. Grassi (ed.), Milan 1972.

Fischer, Albert, *Daniel Specklin 1536-1589. Festungsbaumeister, Ingenieur und Kartograph*, Stuttgart 1996.

Fischer, Erik, with Ernst Jonas Bencard & Mikael Bøgh Rasmussen and a contribution by Marco Iuliano, *Melchior Lorck*, 1-5, Copenhagen 2009 (and forthcoming).

Fjelstrup, A., *Guldmagere i Danmark i det XVII Aarhundrede*, Copenhagen 1906.

Fleischer, Jens, "Hesselager kirkes historie", in: *Træk af Hesselager sogns historie*, Hesselager 1983, 56-68.

Foster, Hal, *The Return of the Real: The Avant-Garde at the End of the Century*, Cambridge (Mass.) 1995.

Foucault, Michel, *The Order of Things: An Archaeology of the Human Sciences*, New York 1973.

Francart, Jacques, *Premier Livre d'Architecture de Jacques Francart. Contenant diverses inventions de portes serviables à tous coeux qui desirent bastir & pour sculpteurs, tailleurs de pieres, esoriniers, maesons et autres*, Brussels 1617.

Francesca, Piero della, *De prospettiva pingendi*, I-II (text and atlante), Nicco Fasola (ed.), Florence 1942.

François, Étienne & Hagen Schulze (eds.) *Deutsche Erinnerungsorte*, 1-3, Munich 2001.

Frankl, Paul, *The Gothic: Literary Sources and Interpretations through Eight Centuries*, Princeton 1960.

Frederiksen, Hans Jørgen, "Reformationens betydning for den kirkelige kunst i Danmark", *Reformations-perspektiver, Acta Jutlandica LXII:3, Teologisk serie 14* (1987), 100-126.

Frederiksen, Niels Werner, "Nationale fjendebilleder. Rimkrøniken og de dansk-svenske relationer 1495-1613", in: Henrik Blicher et al. (eds.), *Tænkesedler. 20 fortællinger af fædrelandets litteraturhistorie. Festskrift til Flemming Lundgreen-Nielsen*, Copenhagen 2007, 25-37.

Freedberg, David, *The Eye of the Lynx: Galileo, His Friends, and the Beginnings of Modern Natural History*, Chicago 2002.

Freitag, Werner, "Die späte Reformation in der Residenzstadt Halle", in: Sabine Kramer & Karsten Eisenmenger (eds.), *Die Marktkirche Unser Lieben Frauen zu Halle*, Halle an der Saale 2004, 11-19.

Friedensburg, Walter, *Die Chronik der Cerbonio Besozzi, 1548-1563*, Vienna 1904.

Friedman, Alice T., "Did England Have a Renaissance? Classical and Anticlassical Themes in Elizabethan Culture", in: Susan J. Barnes & Walter S. Melion, *Cultural Differentiation and Cultural Identity in the Visual Arts*, Hanover & London 1989 (Studies in the History of Arts, 27), 95-111.

Friis, Astrid, *Kansler Friis' første aar*, Copenhagen 1970.

Friis, F. R., *Bidrag til dansk kunsthistorie*, Copenhagen 1890-1901.

Friis-Jensen, Karsten, "Humanism and Politics: The Paris Edition of Saxo Grammaticus's Gesta Danorum 1514", *Analecta Romana Instituti Danici* 17-18 (1988-89), 149-162.

Friis-Jensen, Karsten, "Historiography and Humanism in Early Sixteenth-century Scandinavia", in: Alexander Dalzel et al. (eds.), *Acta Conventus Neo-Latini Torontonensis*, Binghamton & New York 1991, 325-333.

Friis-Jensen, Karsten, "Introduction", in: Karsten Friis-Jensen & Peter Zeeberg (eds.), *Saxo Grammaticus, Gesta Danorum*, Copenhagen 2005, I, 37-59.

Fris, Victor, *La citadelle de Charles-Quint et le château des Espagnols à Gand*, Antwerp 1922.

Fritz, Johann Michael, *Das evangelische Abendmahlsgerät in Deutschland: Vom Mittelalter bis zum Ende des Alten Reiches*, Leipzig 2004.

Fučíková, Eliška, "Towards a reconstruction of Pieter Isaacsz' earlier career", in: G. Cavalli Björkman (ed.), *Netherlandish Mannerism,* Stockholm 1985, 165-175.

Fučíková, Eliška et al. (eds.), *Rudolf II and Prague. The Court and the City*, London 1997.

Fuhring, Peter, *Ornament Prints in the Rijksmuseum*, II: *The Seventeenth Century*, Amsterdam & Rotterdam 2004.

Fuhring, Peter & Ger Luijten (eds.), *Hollstein's Dutch & Flemish Etchings, Engravings and Woodcuts 1450-1700*, 47-48: *Vredeman de Vries*, Rotterdam 1997.

Funke, Jutta, *Beiträge zum Werk Heinrich Vogtherrs d. Ä.*, Berlin 1967 (Dissertation).

Gachard, Louis-Prosper (ed.), *Collection des voyages des souverains des Pays-Bas*, II, Brussels 1874.

Galesloot, M. A., "Le tombeau de Christian III, roi de Danemark, dans la cathédrale de Roeskilde, et celui de Gustave Wasa, à Upsala", *Annales de l'Académie d'Archéologie de Belgique* 26 (1870), 470-474.

Galland, Georg, *Geschichte der holländischen Baukunst und Bildnerei im Zeitalter der Renaissance, der nationalen Blute und des Klassicismus*, Frankfurt am Main 1890.

Galley, Nicolas, "Cornelis Ketel - a painter without a brush", in: *Artibus et historiae* 25, 49 (2004), 87-100.

Gasiorowski, Eugeniusz, "Antonis van Obbergen", *Hafnia. Copenhagen Papers in the History of Art* 3 (1976) (*Comité international d'histoire de l'art VIIe colloque international. Les Pays du Nord et l'Europe. Art et Architecture au XVIe siècle. Copenhague 1-6 septembre 1975*), 71-90.

Gatenbröcker, Silke, *Hofkunst der Spätrenaissance. Braunschweig-Wolfenbüttel und das kaiserliche Prag um 1600*, Brunswick & Prague 1998 (Exhibition Catalogue).

Gauricus, Pomponius, *Pomponius Gauricus De Sculptura (1504)*, André Chastel & Robert Klein (eds. & transls.), Genève 1969 (Hautes Études médiévales et modernes 5).

Gautier, Hippolyte & Adrien Desprez, *Les curiosités de l'exposition de 1878. Guide du visiteur*, Paris 1878.

Geissler, Heinrich, *Zeichnung in Deutschland. Deutsche Zeichner 1540-1640*, 1-2, Stuttgart 1979-80.

Gelderblom, O., *Zuid-Nederlandse kooplieden en de opkomst van de Amsterdamse stapelmarkt (1578-1630)*, Hilversum 2000.

Génard, Pierre, *Le tombeau de Christian III, roi de Danemark, dans la cathédrale de Roeskilde*, Antwerp 1880 (reprint of *Bulletin de l'Académie d'archéologie de Belgique*).

Geoseffi, Decio, *Perspectiva artificialis. Per la storia prospettiva, spigolature e appunti*, Trieste 1957 (Istituto di storia dell´arte antica e moderna 7).

Gérard, Véronique, *De castillo a palacio. El Alcázar de Madrid en el siglo XVI*, Madrid 1984.

Ghiberti, Lorenzo, *Der dritte Komentar Lorenzo Ghibertis*, Klaus Bergdolt (ed. & transl.), Weinheim 1988.

Gjessing, Nicolai, "Renæssanceårets arbejde og organisation", in: Gjessing & Vellev (eds.) 2008, 21-32.

Gjessing, Nicolai & Jens Vellev (eds.), *Renæssance 2006*, Aarhus 2008.

Glarbo, H., "Om den dansk-engelske forbindelse i Christian IV's og Jacob I's tid", *Fra Arkiv og Museum* 2, 2 (1943), 49-80.

Glotz, Samuel, *De Marie de Hongrie aux Gilles de Binche. Introduction critique aux Triomphes de Binche célébrés du 22 au 31 août 1549*, Binche 1995 (Les cahiers binchois 13).

Glotz, Samuel, *Lettre-harangue adressée à Charles Quint, par les chevaliers errants de la Gaule Belgique. Bruxelles et Binche, 1549. Un document viennois inédit*, Binche 2000 (Les cahiers binchois 17).

Godfried, Caroline, *Nederland en Denemarken – Danmark og Holland. Een expositie over de wederzijdse relaties sinds de zestiende eeuw. Een keuze uit de zestigjarige Bibliotheca Danica en een selectie uit de collecties van de Algemene Bibliotheek Universiteit van Amsterdam. Catalogus*, Amsterdam 1990.

Gombrich, Ernst, *In Search of Cultural History*, Oxford 1969.

Gonschor, Brunhilde, "Die Bilddarstellungen des 16. Jahrhunderts im Großen Hof des Dresdner Schlosses", in: *Denkmalpflege in Sachsen 1894–1994*, II, Halle an der Saale 1998, 333-375.

González, Martín & J. José, "El palacio de 'El Pardo' en el siglo XVI", *Boletín del seminario de estudios de arte y arqueologia* 36 (1970), 5-41.

González, Martín & María Angeles, *El Real Sitio de Valsaín*, Madrid 1992.

Gossman, Lionel, *Basel in the Age of Burckhardt*, Chicago 2000.

Goudeau, Jeroen, *Nicolaus Goldmann (1611-1665) en de wiskundige architectuurwetenschap*, Groningen 2005.

Gräbner, Werner, *Die Lichtenburg, eine vergessene Schloßanlage der deutschen Renaissance*, Dresden c. 1953 (unpublished manuscript, Landesamt für Denkmalpflege Sachsen, Dresden).

Græbe, Henrik, "Tøstrup kirke, Djurs Nørre herred. En kalkmaleriudsmykning fra 1582", in: Hugo Johannsen (ed.), *Synligt og Usynligt: Studier tilegnede Otto Norn på hans 75 års fødselsdag den 13. december 1990*, Herning 1990, 83-94.

Graf, Klaus, "Stil als Erinnerung. Retrospektive Tendenzen in der deutschen Kunst um 1500", in: Norbert Nussbaum, Claudia Euskirchen & Stephan Hoppe (eds.), *Wege zur Renaissance. Beobachtungen zu den Anfängen neuzeitlicher Kunstauffassung im Rheinland und den Nachbargebieten um 1500*, Cologne 2003, 19-29.

Grant O'Brien, G., "Ioannes and Andreas Ruckers. A quatercentenary celebration", *Early Music* 7 (1979), 453-466.

Grayson, Cecil, "Studi su Leon Battista Alberti", in: Paola Claut (ed.), *Ingenium*, Città di Castello 1998, 1, 245-269, 287-323.

Greenberg, Clement, *Art and Culture: Critical Essays*, Boston 1989.

Gregersen, Hans V., *Reformationen i Sønderjylland*, Aabenraa 1986 (Skrifter udgivet af Historisk Samfund for Sønderjylland LXII).

Grieten, Jan & Paul Huvenne, "Antwerpen geportretteerd", in: Jan Van der Stock (ed.), *Antwerpen, verhaal van een metropool 16de-17de eeuw*, Antwerp 1993, 69-77.

Grinder-Hansen, Poul (ed.), *The World of Tycho Brahe*, Copenhagen 2007.

Grossmann, G. Ulrich, "Die Einführung von Architekturformen der frühen Renaissance in Mitteleuropa", in: Norbert Nussbaum, Claudia Euskirchen & Stephan Hoppe (eds.), *Wege zur Renaissance. Beobachtungen zu den Anfängen neuzeitlicher Kunstauffassung im Rheinland und den Nachbargebieten um 1500*, Cologne 2003, 176-179.

Gründler, Ernst, *Schloss Annaburg. Festschrift zur Einhundertfünfzigjährigen Jubelfeier des Militär-Knaben-Erziehungs-Institutes zu Annaburg*, Berlin 1888.

Grueninger, Donat, "Die kunsthistorische Regionalisierung. Grundsätzliches zu einem neuen Forschungsansatz", *Concilium medii aevi* 7 (2004), 21-44.

Grundtvig, Joh., "Et Frieri af Kong Frederik II. i 1566-68", *Meddelelser fra Rentekammerarchivet* I (1871-1876), 100-113.

Grunsky, Eberhard, "Die ev. Hauptkirche Beatae Mariae Virginis in Wolfenbüttel. Bemerkungen zum ikonographischen Programm", *Niederdeutsche Beiträge zur Kunstgeschichte* 12 (1973), 204-228.

Guicciardini, Lodovico, *Descritione ... di tutti i Paesi Bassi, altrimenti detti Germania inferiore ...*, Antwerp 1567.

Guicciardini, Lodovico, *Description de touts les Pais-Bas, autrement appellés la Germanie inférieure, ou Basse Allemagne*, augmented French ed., Antwerp 1582.

Guiffrey, J., *Inventaire Général du Mobilier de la Couronne sous Louis XIV*, I-II, Paris 1884-1886.

Guillaume, Jean (ed.), *L'invention de la Renaissance. La reception des forms "à l'antique" au début de la Renaissance*, Paris 2003 (De Architectura 9).

Guillet, David, *Renaissance et Manierisme dans les Ecoles du Nord, Dessins des collections de l'Ecole des Beaux Arts*, Paris 1985.

Guldan, Ernst, "Die Aufnahme italienischer Bau- und Dekorationsformen in Deutschland zu Beginn der Neuzeit" in:

Edoardo Arslan (ed.), *Arte e Artisti dei Laghi Lombardi, I. Architetti e Scultori del Quattrocento*, Como 1959, 381-391.

Guldberg, Jørgen & Hans Christian Jensen, ""Kulturen af Tingene". Julius Lange og kunstindustrien", in: Hanne Kolind Poulsen et al. (eds.), *Viljen til det menneskelige. Tekster omkring Julius Lange*, Copenhagen 1999, 281-303.

Gundestrup, Bente (ed.), *The Royal Danish Kunstkammer 1737*, 1-3, Copenhagen 1991-95.

Haag-Wackernagel, Daniel, *Die Taube. Vom heiligen Vogel der Liebesgöttin zur Strassentaube*, Basel 1988.

Habich, Johannes, *Die künstlerische Gestaltung der Residenz Bückeburg durch Fürst Ernst (1601-1622)*, Bückeburg 1969.

Hafnia. Copenhagen Papers in the History of Art, 3 (1976) (*Comité international d'histoire de l'art VIIe colloque international. Les Pays du Nord et l'Europe. Art et Architecture au XVIe siècle. Copenhague 1-6 septembre 1975*).

Hahn, Peter-Michael, "Das Residenzschloss der frühen Neuzeit. Dynastisches Monument und Instrument fürstlicher Herrschaft", in: Werner Paravicini (ed.), *Das Gehäuse der Macht. Der Raum der Herrschaft im interkulturellen Vergleich. Antike, Mittelalter, Frühe Neuzeit*, Kiel 2005 (Mitteilungen der Residenzen-Kommission der Akademie der Wissenschaften zu Göttingen; Sonderheft 7), 56-74.

Hahr, August, *Die Architektenfamilie Pahr. Eine für Renaissancekunst Schlesiens, Mecklenburgs und Schwedens bedeutende Künstlerfamilie*, Strasbourg 1908 (Studien zur deutschen Kunstgeschichte 97).

Hammerich, Angul, *Musiken ved Christian den Fjerdes Hof*, Copenhagen 1892.

Hansen, Anita & Birgitte Bøggild Johannsen, „IMO LICET. Omkring Niels Hemmingsens billedsyn", in: *Kirkearkeologi og kirkekunst. Studier tilegnet Sigrid og Hakon Christie*, Øvre Eivik 1993, 181-198.

Hansen, Maria Fabricius, "Representing the Past: The Concept and Study of Antique Architecture in 15th-century Italy", *Analecta Romana Instituti Danici* XXIII (1996), 83-116.

Hansen, Maria Fabricius, "Renæssancens groteske", in: Ole Høiris & Jens Vellev (eds.), *Renæssancens verden. Tænkning, kulturliv, dagligliv og efterliv*, Aarhus 2006, 323-349.

Harasimowicz, Jan, *Treści i funkcje ideowe sztuki śląskiej reformacji 1520-1650*, Wroclaw 1986 (Acta Universitatis Wratislaviensis 819, Historia Sztuki II).

Harasimowicz, Jan, "Scriptura sui ipsius interpres. Protestantische Bild-Wort-Sprache des 16. und 17. Jahrhunderts", in: Wolfgang Harms (ed.), *Text und Bild, Bild und Text: DFG-Symposion 1988*, Stuttgart 1990 (Germanistische Symposien-Berichtsbände 11), 262-282.

Harasimowicz, Jan, "'Non minus sunt credenda, quam ipsi articuli'. La confession de foi apostolique dans la catéchèse et l'art d'église luthériens au siècle de la Réforme", in: Pierre Lacroix, Andrée Renon & Éliane Vergnolle (eds.), *Pensée, image et communication en Europe médiévale. À propos des stalles de Saint-Claude*, Besançon 1993, 237-246.

Harasimowicz, Jan, *Kunst als Glaubensbekenntnis: Beiträge zur Kunst- und Kulturgeschichte der Reformationszeit*, Baden-Baden 1996 (Studien zur deutschen Kunstgeschichte 359).

Harasimowicz, Jan, "Evangelische Heilige? Die Heiligen in Lehre, Frömmigkeit und Kunst in der evangelischen Kirche Schlesiens", in: Joachim Köhler & Gundolf Keil (eds.), *Heilige und Heiligenverehrung in Schlesien: Verhandlungen des IX. Symposions in Würzburg vom 28. bis 30. Oktober 1991*, Sigmaringen 1997 (Schlesische Forschungen 7), 171-216.

Harasimowicz, Jan, "Die Verehrung der »biblischen Heiligen« in der evangelischen Kirche Schlesiens im 16. und 17. Jahrhundert", in: Marek Derwich & Michel Dmitriev (eds.), *Fonctions sociales et politiques du culte des saints dans les sociétés de rite grec et latin au Moyen Âge et a l'époque moderne. Approche comparative*, Wroclaw 1999 (Opera ad historiam monasticam spectantia, I, Colloquia 3), 247-270.

Harasimowicz, Jan, "Sztuka jako medium nowożytnych konfesjonalizacji", in: Jan Harasimowicz (ed.), *Sztuka i dialog wyznań w XVI i XVII wieku. Materiały Sesji Stowarzyszenia Historyków Sztuki. Wrocław, listopad 1999*, Warsaw 2000, 51-75.

Harasimowicz, Jan, "Evangelische Kirchenräume der frühen Neuzeit", in: Susanne Rau & Gerd Schwerhoff (eds.), *Zwischen Gotteshaus und Taverne: Öffentliche Räume im Spätmittelalter und Früher Neuzeit*, Cologne, Weimar & Vienna 2004 (Norm und Struktur: Studien zum sozialen Wandel in Mittelalter und Früher Neuzeit 21), 413-445.

Harasimowicz, Jan, "Altargerät des 16. und frühen 17. Jahrhundert im konfessionellen Vergleich", in: Carl A. Hoffmann et al. (eds.), *Als Frieden möglich war: 450 Jahre Augsburger Religionsfrieden. Begleitband zur Ausstellung im Maximilianmuseum Augsburg*, Regensburg 2005, 210-221.

Harasimowicz, Jan, Piotr Oszczanowski & Marcin Wisłocki (eds.), *On Opposite Sides of the Baltic Sea. Relations between Scandinavian and Central European Countries*, 1-2, Wroclaw 2006.

Harbison, Craig, *The Mirror of the Artist. Northern Renaissance and its historical Context*, New York 1995.

Harris, John & Gordon Higgot, *Inigo Jones. The Complete Architectural Drawings*, New York 1989.

Haskell, Francis, *History and Its Images*, New Haven 1993.

Hassebrauk, Gustav, "Der Sturm auf Braunschweig 16.-17. October 1605", *Braunschweigisches Magazin* 7 (1901), 81-83, 93-96, 179-182.

Hassebrauk, Gustav, "Herzog Heinrich und die Stadt Braunschweig 1514-1568", *Jahrbuch des Geschichtsvereins für das Herzogtum Braunschweig* 5 (1906), 1-61.

Hassebrauk, Gustav, "Herzog Julius und die Stadt Braunschweig 1568-1589", *Jahrbuch des Geschichtsvereins für das Herzogtum Braunschweig* 6 (1907), 1-78.

Hassebrauk, Gustav, "Herzog Heinrich Julius und die Stadt Braunschweig 1589-1613", *Jahrbuch des Geschichtsvereins für das Herzogtum Braunschweig* 9 (1910), 62-108.

Heck, Kilian, *Genealogie als Monument und Argument: der Beitrag dynastischer Wappen zur politischen Raumbildung der Neuzeit*, Munich & Berlin 2002.

Heck, Kilian & Bernard Jahn (eds.), *Genealogie als Denkform in Mittelalter und Frühe Neuzeit*, Tübingen 2000.

Heckner, Ulrike, *Im Dienst von Fürsten und Reformation. Fassadenmalerei an den Schlössern in Dresden und Neuburg an der Donau im 16. Jahrhundert*, Munich 1995.

Hedicke, Robert, *Jacques Dubroeucq de Mons*, Brussels 1912 (Annales du cercle archéologique de Mons 40).

Hedicke, Robert, *Cornelis Floris und die Florisdekoration, Studien zur niederländischen und deutschen Kunst im XVI. Jahrhundert*, Berlin 1913.

Heiberg, Steffen, "Art and politics. Christian IV's Dutch and Flemish painters", in: *Art in Denmark 1600-1750*, Delft 1984 (Leids Kunsthistorisch Jaarboek 2 (1983)), 7-24.

Heiberg, Steffen, *Christian 4. Monarken, Mennesket og Myten*, Copenhagen 1988

Heiberg, Steffen (ed.), *Christian IV and Europe: The 19th Art Exhibition of the Council of Europe, Denmark 1988*, Herning 1988 (Exhibition Catalogue).

Heiberg, Steffen (ed.), *Christian 4. og Frederiksborg*, Copenhagen 2006.

Heiberg, Steffen, "Et kongeligt triumftog", in: Steffen Heiberg (ed.), *Christian 4. og Frederiksborg*, Copenhagen 2006, 28-41.

Heiberg, Steffen, "Art and the Staging of Images of Power – Christian IV and Pictorial Art", in: Baldeloch Noldus & Juliette Roding (eds.), *Pieter Isaacsz (1568-1628), Court Painter, Art Dealer and Spy*, Turnhout 2007 (Exhibition Catalogue), 231-243.

Hein, Jørgen, "Der 'Dänische Krieg' und die weitere Rolle Dänemarks", in: Klaus Bußmann & Heinz Schilling (eds.), *1648. Krieg und Frieden in Europa, Textband I, Politik, Religion, Recht und Gesellschaft, Europaratsausstellung 350 Jahre Westfälischer Friede Münster und Osnabrück 1998/99*, Munich 1998, 103-110.

Hein, Jørgen, "En trone af enhjørning-horn og løver af sølv", *Siden Saxo* 23, 2 (2006), 38-45.

Hein, Jørgen, "An unknown cameo of James I and the Order of the Garter", *The Burlington Magazine* CXLVIII (2006), 400-405.

Hein, Jørgen, "Christian 4. og Rosenborgs billedverden", in: Jørgen Hein et al. (eds.), *Christian 4. og Rosenborg*, Copenhagen 2006, 25-50.

Hein, Jørgen, *The Treasury Collection of Rosenborg Castle: Royal Heritage and Collecting in Denmark-Norway 1500-1900*, 1-3, Copenhagen 2009.

Hein, Jørgen et al. (eds.), *Christian 4. og Rosenborg 1606-2006*, Copenhagen 2006.

Heinrich Vogtherr's Kunstbüchlein, Straßburg 1472, Zwickau 1913 (Zwickauer Facsimiledrucke 19).

Heitmann, Bernhard & Renate Scholz, "Die Ebenholz-Silber-Arbeiten in der Schloßkapelle von Frederiksborg bei Hillerød von Seeland", in: Erich Schliemann (ed.), *Die Goldschmiede Hamburgs* 1, Hamburg 1985, 78-119.

Helk, Vello, *Dansk-norske studierejser fra reformationen til enevælden 1536-1660. Med en matrikel over studerende i udlandet*, Copenhagen 1987

Helk, Vello, "Den danske adels dannelsesrejser i Europa 1536-1660", in: P. Ingesman & J. V. Jensen (eds.), *Riget, magten og æren: den danske adel 1350-1660*, Aarhus 2001, 524-556.

Helk, Vello, *Stambogs-Skikken i det danske Monarki indtil 1800*, Odense 2001.

Henden Aaraas, Margarethe et al., *På kyrkjeferd i Sogn og Fjordane*, 1: *Nordfjord og Sunnfjord*, 2: *Sogn*, Førde 2000.

Hendrikman, Lars, "Portrait and Politics. Evolution in the Depiction of King Christian II of Denmark during his Reign and Exile (1531-1531)", in: Hanno Brand (ed.), *Trade, Diplomacy and Cultural Exchange*, Hilversum 2005 (Groningen Hanze Studies, 1), 186-210.

Hennaut, Eric, "Auguste Schoy (1838-1885)", in: Jean-Paul Midant (ed.), *Académie de Bruxelles. Deux siècles d'architecture*, Brussels 1989, 240-244.

Hennaut, Eric, "Saintenoy, Paul", in: Anne Van Loo (ed.), *Repertorium van de Architectuur in België van 1830 tot heden*, Antwerp 2003, 493-494.

Henriku Liivimaa krooonika (The Chronicle of Henrik of Livland), Enn Tarvel (transl. & commentaries), Tallinn 2005.

Hentschel, Walter, *Dresdner Bildhauer des 16. und 17. Jahrhunderts*, Weimar 1966.

Herbert, Robert, *Impressionism: Art, Leisure, and Parisian Society*, New Haven 1988.

van den Heuvel, Charles, *'Papiere Bolwercken'. De introductie van de Italiaanse stede- en vestingbouw in de Nederlanden (1540-1609) en het gebruik van tekeningen*, Alphen aan den Rijn 1991.

van den Heuvel, Charles, *De 'huysbou': a reconstruction of an unfinished treatise on architecture, town planning and civil engineering by Simon Stevin*, Amsterdam 2005.

van den Heuvel, Charles & Bernhard Roosens, "Los Países Bajos. Las fortificaciones y la coronación de la defensa del imperio de Carlos V", in: Carlos J. Hernando Sánchez (ed.), *Las fortificaciones de Carlos V*, Madrid 2000 (Sociedad Estatal para la Conmemoración de los Centenarios de Felipe II y Carlos V), 578-605.

van den Heuvel, Christine & Manfred von Boetticher (eds.), *Geschichte Niedersachsens*, 3, 1. *Politik, Wirtschaft und Gesellschaft von der Reformation bis zum Beginn des 19. Jahrhunderts* (Veröffentlichungen der Historischen Kommission für Niedersachsen und Bremen 34), Hannover 1998.

Hinrichs, C., "Die Idee des geistigen Mittelpunktes Europas im 17. und 18. Jahrhundert", *Jahrbuch für Geschichte des deutschen Ostens* I (1952), 85-109.

von Hintzenstern, Herbert, *Die Bilderpredigt des Gothaer Tafelaltars*, Berlin 1965.

von Hintzenstern, Herbert, "Der Gothaer Tafelaltar: Das bilderreichste Kunstwerk aus der Reformationszeit", in: Ernst Ullmann (ed.), *Von der Macht der Bilder: Beiträge des C.I.H.A.-Kolloquiums 'Kunst und Reformation'*, Leipzig 1983, 340-343.

Hipp, Hermann, *Studien zur "Nachgotik" des 16. und 17. Jahrhunderts in Deutschland, Böhmen, Österreich und der Schweiz*, I-III, Tübingen 1979 (Dissertation).

Hipp, Hermann, "Die Bückeburger "structura". Aspekte der Nachgotik im Zusammenhang mit der deutschen Renaissance", in: Georg Ulrich Großmann, *Renaissance in Nord-Mitteleuropa* I, Munich & Berlin 1990 (Schriften des Weserrenaissance-Museums Schloß Brake 4), 159-170.

Hipp, Hermann, "Die Hauptkirche Beatae Mariae Virginis in Wolfenbüttel und der protestantische Kirchenbau um 1600", in: Rainer Bürgel, Helmut A. Müller & Rainer Volp (eds.), *Kirche im Abseits? Zum Verhältnis von Religion und Kultur*, Stuttgart 1991, 181-202.

Hitchcock, H. R., *Netherlandish scrolled gables of the sixteenth and early seventeenth centuries*, New York 1978.

Hochmann, Michel, "Hans Rottenhammer & Pietro Mera, Two northern artists in Rome and Venice", *Burlington Magazine* CXLV (2003), 641-645.

Hoffmann, Cristina, *Das Spanische Hofzeremoniell von 1500 to 1700*, Frankfurt 1985 (Erlanger Historische Studien 8).

Hoffmann-Randall, Cristina, "Die Herkunft und Tradierung des Burgundischen Hofzeremoniells", in: Jörg Jochen Berns & Thomas Rahn (eds.): *Zeremoniell als höfische Ästhetik in Spätmittelalter und Früher Neuzeit*, Tübingen 1995 (Frühe Neuzeit. Studien und Dokumente zur deutschen Literatur und Kultur im europäischen Kontext 25), 150-156.

Hofmann, Werner (ed.), *Luther und die Folgen für die Kunst*, Munich 1983 (Exhibition Catalogue).

Hofmeister, Adolph, *Die Matrikel der Universität Rostock*, Rostock 1891-1895.

Hollanda, Francisco de, *Vier Gespräche über die Malerei geführt zu Rom 1538*, Joaquim de Vascuncellos (ed.), Wien 1899 (Quellenschriften für Kunstgeschichte und Kunsttechnik des Mittelalters und der Neuzeit 9 (1899)).

Hollstein, F. W. H., *German Engravings, Etchings, and Woodcuts c. 1400-1700*, Amsterdam 1949.

Holm, Henrik, "Håndbogshelvedet", in: Hans Dam Christensen & Louise C. Larsen (eds.), *Det kunsthistorike studieapparat. Hånd- og debatbog fra den videnskabelige hverdag*, Copenhagen 2004, 196-217.

Holmér, Folke, "Christianstad", in: Vilhelm Lorenzen, *Christian IVs Byanlæg og Andre Bybygningsarbejder*, Copenhagen 1937, 160-177.

Honnens de Lichtenberg, Hanne, "Christian IV and the Art of Sculpture", *Apollo* 128 (1988), 104-109.

Honnens de Lichtenberg, Hanne, *Tro, håb og forfængelighed*, Copenhagen 1989 (Renæssancestudier III).

Honnens de Lichtenberg, Hanne, "Frederik IIs kunstnere på Kronborg", *Renæssanceforum* 2 (2006), *www.renaessanceforum.dk*.

Hoppe, Stephan, *Die funktionale und räumliche Struktur des frühen Schlossbaus in Mitteldeutschland. Untersucht an Beispielen landesherrlicher Bauten zwischen 1470 und 1570*, Cologne 1996 (Veröffentlichungen der Abteilung Architekturgeschichte des Kunsthistorischen Institutes der Universität Köln 62).

Hoppe, Stephan, Matthias Müller & Norbert Nussbaum (eds.), *Stil als Bedeutung in der nordalpinen Renaissance: Wiederentdeckung eine methodischen Nachbarschaft*, Cologne 2008.

Houkjær, Ulla, "Dutch Artists in the Service of Danish History - the Kronborg Series", *Apollo* 128 (1988), 99-103.

Howarth, David, "Charles I, Sculpture and Sculptors", in: Arthur MacGregor (ed.), *The Late King's Goods. Collections, Possessions and Patronage of Charles I in Light of the Commonwealth Sale Inventories,* London 1989, 73-113.

Huizinga, Johan, *Nederland's beschaving in de zeventiende eeuw*, Haarlem 1956 (1963).

Huth, Hans, *Künstler und Werkstatt der Spätgotik*, Augsburg 1923.

Huysmans, Antoinette, "De sculptuur", in: Antoinette Huysmans et al., *Cornelis Floris 1514-1575 beeldhouwer architect ontwerper*, Brussels 1996, 70-113.

Huysmans, Antoinette et al., *Cornelis Floris 1514-1575. Beeldhouwer architect ontwerper*, Brussels 1996.

Høiris, Ole & Jens Vellev (eds.), *Renæssancens verden. Tænkning, kulturliv, dagligliv og efterliv*, Aarhus 2006

Høyen, Niels Lauritz, "Frederiksborg Slot" (1831), in: J. L. Ussing (ed.), *Niels Lauritz Høyens Skrifter*, 1-3, Copenhagen 1871-1876, 1, 161-228.

Høyen, Niels Lauritz, "Om Konstens Væsen og Opgave, særligt med Hensyn til Danmark (1851)", in: J. L. Ussing (ed.), *Niels Lauritz Høyens Skrifter*, 1-3, Copenhagen 1871-1876, 3, 1-59.

Høyen, Niels Lauritz, "Om national Konst" (1863), in: J. L. Ussing (ed.), *Niels Lauritz Høyens Skrifter*, 1-3, Copenhagen 1871-1876, 3, 160-182.

Høyen, Niels Lauritz, "Claus Berg og hans Altertavle i Odense" (1865), in: J. L. Ussing (ed.) *Niels Lauritz Høyens Skrifter*, 1-3, Copenhagen 1871-1876, 339-373.

Haastrup, Ulla, "Brugen af forlæg i Odense i 1. fjerdedel af 1500-tallet" in: Rudolf Zeitler & Jan O. M. Karlsson (eds.), *Imagines Medievales. Studier i medeltida ikonografi*, *arkitektur, skulptur, måleri och konsthandverk*, Uppsala 1983 (Ars universitas upsaliensis: ars suetica 7), 113-131.

Ilsøe, H., "Gesandtskaber som kulturformidlende faktor. Forbindelser mellem Danmark og England-Skotland o. 1580-1607", *Historisk Tidsskrift* 11, 6 (1962), 574-600.

Ilsøe, Harald, "Danskerne og deres fædreland. Holdninger og opfattelser ca. 1550-1700", in: Ole Feldbæk (ed.), *Fædreland og Modersmål 1536-1789*, Copenhagen 1991 (Dansk identitetshistorie 1), 27-88.

Imray, Jean, "The Origins of the Royal Exchange", in: Ann Saunders (ed.), *The Royal Exchange*, London 1997, 20-35.

Ingang, Gabriëlle, *Klein en toch te pronk voor de wereld. De Belgische deelneming aan de grote wereldtentoonstellingen in de negentiende eeuw*, Leuven 1986 (Master's Thesis).

Ingesman, Per, "Den danske konges repræsentanter ved renæssancepavernes hof", in: Per Ingesman & Bjørn Poulsen (eds.), *Danmark og Europa i senmiddelalderen*, Aarhus 2000, 160-182.

Ingesman, Per, *Provisioner og processer. Den romerske Rota og dens behandling af danske sager i middelalderen*, Aarhus 2003.

Ingesman, Per & Bjørn Poulsen (eds.), *Danmark og Europa i senmiddelalderen*, Aarhus 2000.

Iñiguez Almech, Francisco, *Casas reales y jardines de Felipe II*, Rome 1952 (Consejo superior de investigaciones científicas, delegación de Roma).

Irmscher, Günter, *Kölner Architektur- und Säulenbücher um 1600*, Bonn 1999.

Issleib, Simon, *Aufsätze und Beiträge zu Kurfürst Moritz von Sachsen (1877-1907)*, I, Cologne & Vienna 1989² (reprint).

Jacobs, Fredrika, "Rethinking the Divide: Cult Images and the Cult of Images", in James Elkins & Robert Williams (eds.), *Renaissance Theory*, New York & London 2008 (The Art Seminar 5), 95-114.

Jacoby, Joachim, *Hans von Aachen 1552-1615*, Munich 2000.

Jaki, Stanley L., *Uneasy Genius: The Life and Work of Pierre Duhem*, The Hague, Boston & Lancaster 1984.

Jakobsen, Tove Benedikt, *Birth of a World Museum*, Oxford 2007 (Acta Archaeologica 78, 1, suppl. VIII).

Jardine, Lisa & Jerry Brotton, *Global Interests: Renaissance Art between East and West,* Ithaca 2000.

Jensen, Frede P., "Omkring Peder Oxes fald", *Historisk Tidsskrift* 79, VI (1979), 311-337.

Jensen, Hannemarie Ragn, "Christian 4.s malerier", in: Steffen Heiberg (ed.), *Christian 4. og Frederiksborg*, Copenhagen 2006, 81-97.

Jensen, Hannemarie Ragn, "Isaac Isaacsz" in: Badeloch Noldus & Juliette Roding (eds.), *Pieter Isaacsz (1568-1625). Court Painter, Art Dealer and Spy*, Turnhout 2007 (Exhibition Catalogue), 205-217.

Jensen, Janus Møller, *Denmark and the Crusades 1400-1650*, Leiden & Boston 2007 (Barbara Crawford et al. (eds.), *The Northern World. North Europe and the Baltic c. 400-1700 A. D. Peoples, Economics and Cultures* 30).

Jensen, Janus Møller, "Humanister, korstog og kortlægningen af det yderste nord", in: Lars Bisgaard, Jacob Isager & Janus Møller Jensen (eds.), *Renæssancen i svøb. Dansk renæssance i europæisk belysning 1450-1550*, Odense 2008, 215-244.

Jensen, Jens William, "Skifte af adeligt jordegods 1400-1660", in: Per Ingesmann & Jens William Jensen (eds.), *Riget, Magten og Æren. Den danske adel 1350-1660*, Aarhus 2001, 451-477.

Jensen, Johan Møhlenfeldt, "Den rette vej til Himmeriges Rige", in: Carsten Bach-Nielsen et al. (eds.), *Danmark og renæssancen 1500-1650*, Copenhagen 2006, 242-259.

Jensen, Johannes V., *Den gotiske Renaissance*, Copenhagen 1901 (reprint 2000).

Jensen, Mette K., "Hjortesalen på Hesselagergård. Frisens restaurering", *Architectura. Arkitekturhistorisk Årsskrift* 18 (1996), 26-32.

Jerk, Flemming Oluf, *Herregårde i Danmark, 2: Fyn*, Copenhagen 1980.

Jervis, S., "Shadows not substantial things: Furniture in the Commonwealth Sale inventories", in: MacGregor, A. (ed.), *The Late King's Goods*, London 1989, 277-306.

Jespersen, Knud J. V., *A History of Denmark*, Basingstoke 2004.

Jespersen, Knud J. V., "Kappestrid uden sejrherre. Den dansk-svenske rivalisering 1563-1720", in: Janus Møller Jensen (ed.), *Slaget ved Nyborg 1659. Historie, arkæologi og erindring*, Nyborg 2009, 18-30.

Jespersen, L., "Rekrutteringen til rigsrådet i Christian 4.s tid", in: Jespersen, K. J. V. (ed.), *Rigsråd, adel og administration 1570-1648*, Odense 1980, 35-122.

Johannesson, Kurt, *The Renaissance of the Goths in Sixteenth-Century Sweden*, Berkeley & Oxford 1991.

Johannsen, Hugo, "Regna firmat Pietas. Eine Deutung der Baudekoration der Schloßkirche Christian IV zu Frederiksborg", *Hafnia. Copenhagen Papers in the History of Art* 3 (1974), 67-140.

Johannsen, Hugo, "The Graphic Art of Hendrick Goltzius as Prototype for Danish Art during the Reign of Christian IV", *Art in Denmark 1600-1750*, Delft 1984 (Leids Kunsthistorisch Jaarboek 2 (1983)), 85-110.

Johannsen, Hugo (ed.), *Synligt og Usynligt: Studier tilegnede Otto Norn på hans 75 års fødselsdag den 13. december 1990*, Herning 1990.

Johannsen, Hugo, "The Writ on the Wall: Theological and Political Aspects of Biblical Text-Cycles in Evangelical Palace Chapels of the Renaissance", in: Eyolf Østrem, Jens Fleischer & Nils Holger Petersen (eds.), *The Arts and the Cultural Heritage of Martin Luther*, Copenhagen 2002 (Transfiguration. Nordic Journal for Christianity and the Arts 4:1), 81-97.

Johannsen, Hugo, "On the Significance of Hans Vredeman de Vries for Architecture, Arts and Crafts in Denmark during the Reigns of Frederick II and Christian IV", in: Heiner Borggrefe & Vera Lüpkes (eds.), *Hans Vredeman de Vries und die Folgen*, Marburg 2005 (Studien zur Kultur der Renaissance 3), 42-49.

Johannsen, Hugo, "The Saxon Connection. On the Architectural Genesis of Christian IV's Palace Chapel (1606-1617) at Frederiksborg Castle", in: Jan Harasimowicz, Piotr Oszczanowski & Marcin Wisłocki (eds.), *On Opposite Sides of the Baltic Sea. Relations between Scandinavia and Central Europe/Po obu stronach Bałtyku. Wzajemne relacje między Skandynawią a Europą Środkową*, 2, Wroclaw 2006, 369-379.

Johannsen, Hugo, "Willem van den Blocke and his monument (1585-86) for Christoph von Dohna in the Cathedral of Odense. An Example of the Spread of the Style of Cornelis Floris in the Baltic", in: Małgorzata Ruszkowska-Macur (ed.), *Netherlandish Artists in Gdańsk in the Time of Hans Vredeman de Vries*, Gdańsk & Lemgo 2006, 111-115.

Johannsen, Hugo, "Slotskirken", in: Steffen Heiberg (ed.), *Christian 4. og Frederiksborg*, Copenhagen 2006, 133-151.

Johannsen, Hugo, "Christian IV's Private Oratory in Frederiksborg Castle Chapel", in: Badeloch Noldus & Juliette Roding (eds.), *Pieter Isaacsz (1568-1625). Court Painter, Art Dealer and Spy*, Turnhout 2007 (Exhibition Catalogue), 165-179.

Johannsen, Hugo, "Renaissance Art and Architecture in Denmark", in: Michael Andersen, Ebbe Nyborg & Mogens Vedsø (eds.), *Masters, Meanings & Models. Studies in the Art and Architecture of the Renaissance in Denmark. Essays published in Honour of Hugo Johannsen*, Copenhagen 2010, 22-31.

Johannsen, Hugo, "Dignity and Dynasty. On the History and Meaning of the Royal Funeral Monuments for Christian III, Frederik II and Christian IV in the Cathedral of Roskilde", in: Michael Andersen, Ebbe Nyborg & Mogens Vedsø (eds.), *Masters, Meanings & Models. Studies in the Art and Architecture of the Renaissance in Denmark. Essays published in Honour of Hugo Johannsen*, Copenhagen 2010, 116-149.

Judson, J. Richard & Rudolf E. O. Ekkart, *Gerrit van Honthorst 1592-1656*, Doornspijk 1999.

Jung-Köhler, Evi, "Ungebautes Imperium – Dänemarks und Schwedens Traum vom Ostseereich", in: Michael Maass (ed.), *"Klar und lichtvoll wie eine Regel". Planstädte der Neuzeit vom 16. bis zum 18. Jahrhundert*, Karlsruhe 1990, 169-179.

Jørgensen, Ellen, *Danske Dronninger*, Copenhagen 1910.

Jørgensen, Ellen, "Studier over danske middelalderlige Bogsamlinger", *Historisk Tidsskrift*, 8, IV, (1912), 1-67.

Jørgensen, Ellen, *De middelalderlige latinske Manuscripter i det kgl. Bibliotek*, Copenhagen 1927.

Jørgensen, Jesper Düring, "Introduktion til Georg Engelhard Löhneyssens ridebøger i det Kongelige Bibliotek", *Fund og Forskning* 34 (1995), 35-60.

Jørgensen, Jesper Düring, "Georg Engelhard Löhneysen fra den skrevne Bidbog til den trykte Ridebog", *Fund og Forskning* 36 (1997), 11-43.

Jørgensen, Tove, Vivi Jensen & Poul Dedenroth-Schou, *Skt. Nikolaj Kirke, Kolding*, Kolding 1987.

Kade, Reinhard, "Der Freiberger Domglöckner Johann Kröner und die kurf[ürstliche] Sächs[ische] Begräbniskapelle 1585-1625", *Mitteilungen des Freiberger Altertumsvereins* 25 (1888), 19-26.

Kähler, Ingeborg, *Der Bordesholmer Altar – Zeichen in einer Krise*, Neumünster 1981 (Studien zur Schleswig Holsteinsche Kunstgeschichte 14).

Kancelliets Brevbøger vedrørende Danmarks indre Forhold 1551-1660, C. F. Bricka et al. (eds.), Copenhagen 1885-2005.

Kappel, Jutta & Claudia Brink (eds.), *Mit Fortuna übers Meer. Sachsen und Dänemark – Ehen und Allianzen im Spiegel der Kunst (1548-1709)*, Dresden 2009.

Karker, A. (ed.), *Hieronymus Justesen Ranch, Kong Salomons hyldning …(1584)*, Copenhagen 1973.

Karpowicz, Marius, "La conquista delle corti", in: Cesare Moazarelli (ed.), *"Familia" del principe e famiglia aristocratica*, Rome 1988, 745-751.

Kaspersen, Søren, "Kirken som en have", in: Paul Svensson (ed.), *Løjttavlen. Et sønderjysk alterskab*, Herning 1983, 129-142.

Kastler, José & Vera Lüpkes (eds.), *Die Weser – Ein Fluß in Europa: Aufbruch in die Neuzeit*, Lemgo 2000, 304-311.

Kaufmann, Thomas DaCosta, "The Problem of Northern 'Mannerism': A Critical Review", in: S. E. Murray & Ruth I. Weidner (eds.), *Mannerism: Essays in Music and the Arts*, West Chester (Pennsylvania) 1980, 89-115.

Kaufmann, Thomas DaCosta, *The School of Prague. Painting at the Court of Rudolf II*, Chicago & London 1988.

Kaufmann, Thomas DaCosta, "Christian IV and Europe, The 19th Art Exhibition of the Council of Europe, Copenhagen, 1988. A Review", *Konsthistorisk Tidskrift* 58 (1989), 19-22.

Kaufmann, Thomas DaCosta, *Court, Cloister, and City. The Art and Culture of Central Europe 1450-1800*, Chicago 1995.

Kaufmann, Thomas DaCosta, "Italian Sculptors and Sculpture Outside of Italy (Chiefly in Central Europe): Problems of Approach, Possibilities of Reception", in: Claire Farago (ed.), *Reframing the Renaissance*, New Haven & London 1995, 27-66.

Kaufmann, Thomas DaCosta, "Planeten im kaiserlichen Universum. Prag und die Kunst an den deutschen Fürstenhöfen zur Zeit Rudolfs II", in: Silke Gatenbröcker (ed.), *Hofkunst der Spätrenaissance. Braunschweig -Wolfenbüttel und das kaiserliche Prag um 1600*, Brunswick 1998 (Exhibition Catalogue), 9-19.

Kaufmann, Thomas DaCosta, "La guerre de trente ans a-t-elle eu lieu? Continuities and Discontinuities during the Thirty Years' War", in: Jacques Thuillier et al. (eds.), *1648. Paix de Westphalie. L'art entre la guerre et la paix en Europe/ Westfälischer Friede. Die Kunst zwischen Krieg und Frieden. Actes du colloque organisé par le Westfälisches Landesmuseum le 19 novembre 1998 à Münster et à Osnabrück et le Service culturel du musée du Louvre les 20 et 21 novembre 1998 à Paris*, Paris 1999, 141-167.

Kaufmann, Thomas DaCosta, "National Stereotypes, Prejudice, and Aesthetic Judgments in the Historiography of Art", in: Michael Ann Holly & Keith Moxey (eds.), *Art History, Aesthetics, Visual Studies*, New Haven & London 2002, 71-84.

Kaufmann, Thomas DaCosta (ed.), *Art and Architecture in Central Europe, 1550-1620. An Annotated Bibliography*, Marburg 2003.

Kaufmann, Thomas DaCosta, "Påverkan västerifrån: nederländsk konst och arkitektur", in: Janis Kreslins, Steven A. Mansbach & Robert Schweitzer (eds.), *Gränsländer. Östersjön in ny gestalt*, Stockholm 2003, 17-41 (also published as "Letekme no rietumiem: Nīderlandes māsla un arhitektūra", in: Makslinieciska attesteba: vizuani maksla baltijas Vestur, in: *Baltija: jauns skatīums*, Riga 2003, 29-48).

Kaufmann, Thomas DaCosta, "Artistic Regions and the Problem of Artistic Metropolises: Questions of (East) Central Europe", in: Thomas DaCosta Kaufmann, *Toward a Geography of Art*, Chicago & London 2004, 154-186.

Kaufmann, Thomas DaCosta, *The Eloquent Artist. Essays on Art, Art Theory and Architecture, Sixteenth to Nineteenth Century*, London 2004.

Kaufmann, Thomas DaCosta, "Ways of Transfer of Netherlandish Art", in: Małgorzata Ruszkowska-Macur (ed.), *Netherlandish artists in Gdańsk in the Time of Hans Vredeman de Vries. Material from the conference organized by Museum of the History of the City of Gdańsk and Weserrenaissance-Museum Schloß Brake Lemgo*, Gdańsk & Lemgo 2006, 13-21.

Kaufmann, Thomas DaCosta, "The Baltic Area as an Artistic Region. Historiography, State of Research, Perspectives for Further Study", in: Jan Harasimowicz, Piotr Oszczanowski & Marcin Wisłocki (eds.), *On Opposite Sides of the Baltic Sea. Relations Between Scandinavian and Central European Countries*, Wroclaw 2006, 1, 33-39.

Kaufmann, Thomas DaCosta, "Art and the Church in the Early Modern Era: The Baltic in Comparative Perspective", in: Kodres, Krista (ed.), *Art and the Church. Religious Art and Architecture in the Baltic Region in the 13th-18th Centuries*, Tallinn 2008 (EstonianAcademy of Arts Proceedings 18), 20-40.

Kaufmann, Thomas DaCosta & E. Pilliod (eds.), *Time and Place. The Geohistory of Art,* Aldershot & Burlington 2005.

Kavaler, Ethan Matt, "Renaissance Gothic: Picture of Geometry and Narratives of Ornament", *Art History* 29 (2006), 1-46.

Kavaler, Ethan Matt, "Gothic as Renaissance: Ornament, Excess and Identity, Circa 1500", in: James Elkins & Robert Williams (eds.), *Renaissance Theory*, New York & London, 2008, 115-158.

van Keen, Mirjam G. K., "Spiritualism in the Netherlands: From David Joris to Dirck Volckertsz Coornhert", *The Sixteenth Century Journal* 33 (2002), 129-150.

Kelly, Joan, "Did Women have a Renaissance?", in: Joan Kelly (ed.), *Women, History and Theory. The Essays of Joan Kelly*, Chicago & London 1984, 19-50.

Kemp, Martin, *The Science of Art*, New Haven & London 1990.

Kernkamp, G. W., "Memoriën van ridder Theodorus Rodenburg betreffende het verplaatsen van verschillende industrieën uit Nederland naar Denemarken, met daarop genomen resolutiën van koning Christiaan IV (1621)", *Bijdragen en Mededelingen betreffende de geschiedenis der Nederlanden* 23 (1902), 189-256.

Kernkamp, Gerhard Wilhelm, *Verslag van een onderzoek in Zweden, Noorwegen en Denemarken naar archivalia, belangrijk voor de geschiedenis van Nederland op last der regeering ingesteld*, 's-Gravenhage 1903.

Kernkamp, G. W., "Memoriën van den Zweedschen resident Harald Appelboom", *Bijdragen en Mededelingen van het Historisch Genootschap* 26 (1905).

Kernkamp, Gerhard Wilhelm, *Zweedsche archivalia*, Utrecht 1908 (Bijdragen en Mededeelingen, Historisch Genootschap te Utrecht XXIX).

Kernkamp, Gerhard Wilhelm, *Baltische archivalia: onderzoek naar archivalia, belangrijk voor de geschiedenis van Nederland, in Stockholm, Kopenhagen en de Duitse Oostzeesteden*, 's-Gravenhage 1909 (Rijks geschiedkundige publication, small ser. 4).

Kerrigan, William & Gordon Braden, *The Idea of the Renaissance*, Baltimore 1989.

Khunrath, Heinrich, *Rosarium Philosophalis (Amphiteatrum Sapientiae Aeternae),* Hannover 1609.

Kiby, Ulrike, "Der Pavillon auf Säulen. Kunst zwischen Tradition und Religion", in: Ursula Härting & Ellen Schwinzer (eds.), *Gärten und Höfe der Rubenszeit. Internationales Symposium im Gustav-Lübcke-Museum der Stadt Hamm vom 12.01.2001 bis 14.09.2001*, Worms 2002 (Die Gartenkunst 14, 1, special issue), 56-64.

Kieser, Harry, *Das große Gothaer Altarwerk: Ein reiches Werk deutscher Reformationskunst*, Würzburg-Aumühle 1939 (Dissertation, Königsberg).

Klamt, J.-Chr., "Die Runde Turm in Kopenhagen als Kirchturm und Sternwarte", *Zeitschrift für Kunstgeschichte* 38 (1975), 153-170.

Klamt, J.-Chr., "The Round Tower in its Relation to Architecture of the 16th Century", *Hafnia, Copenhagen Papers in the History of Art* 4 (1976), 55-70.

Kleinschmidt, Harald, "Das kursächsische Amtshaus in Annaburg und seine Baugeschichte", in: Hans-Joachim Krause et al. (eds.), „*ES THUN IHER VIEL FRAGEN...*" *Kunstgeschichte in Mitteldeutschland. Hans-Joachim Krause gewidmet*, Petersberg 2001 (Beiträge zur Denkmalkunde in Sachsen-Anhalt 2), 187-202.

Klessmann, Rüdiger, "Eine unbekannte venezianische Venus von Hans Rottenhammer", *Niederdeutsche Beiträge zur Kunstgeschichte* 28 (1989), 131-142.

Kodres, Krista, "Church and Art in the First Century of the Reformation in Estonia: Towards Lutheran Orthodoxy", *Scandinavian Journal of History* 28 (2003), 187-203.

Kodres, Krista, "Der Vredeman de Vries-Stil als Markenzeichen Arent Passers in Reval/Tallinn", in: Heiner Borggrefe & Vera Lüpkes (eds.), *Hans Vredeman de Vries und die Folgen*, Marburg 2005 (Studien zur Kultur der Renaissance 3), 50-57.

Kodres, Krista et al. (eds.), *The Problem of Classical Ideal in the Art and Architecture of the Countries around the Baltic Sea*, Tallinn 2003 (Estonian Academy of Arts Proceedings 13).

Kodres, Krista & Merike Kurisoo (eds.), *Art and the Church. Religious Art and Architecture in the Baltic Region in the 13th-18th Centuries*, Tallinn 2008 (Estonian Academy of Arts Proceedings 18).

Körber, Martin, *Bausteine zu einer Geschichte Oesels, fünf Jahrhunderte. Von der heidnischen Vorzeit bis zum Frieden von Nystädt*, Arensburg 1885.

Körber, Martin, *Oesel einst und jetzt*, I-III, Arensburg 1887, 1899, 1915.

Koerner, Joseph Leo, *The Moment of Self-Portraiture in German Renaissance Art*, Chicago & London 1993.

Kok, A. A., *Nederlandsche bouwkunst langs de Oostzee*, E. J. Rothuizen & F. Wind (eds.), Goes 1918 (De Technische School 12).

Kollmann, Stefanie, *Niederländische Künstler und Kunst im London des 17. Jahrhunderts*, Hildesheim, Zürich & New York 2000.

Komanecky, Michael (ed.), *Copper as Canvas - Two Centuries of Masterpiece Paintings on Copper, 1575-1775*, New York 1999 (Exhibition Catalogue).

Kongsted, Ole, "Herlufsholm-samlingen: R 121-125 og danskere i Italien omkring 1600", in: John T. Lauridsen & Olaf Olsen (eds.), *Umisteligt. Festskrift til Erland Kolding Nielsen*, Copenhagen 2007, 101-118.

Kongsted, Ole, "'Jeg sender nogle nye messer...'. Om Rasmus Heinssen og repertoiret i Christian 3.s kantori i midten af 1500-tallet", *Fund og Forskning* 46 (2007), 37-55.

Kongsted, Ole, "Til Guds pris, Majestætens ære og Rigets gavn. Om Matz Hack og hans virke som kongelig sangmester ved Christian IIIs hof", in: Lars Bisgaard, Jacob Isager & Janus Møller Jensen (eds.), *Renæssancen i svøb. Dansk renæssance i europæisk belysning 1450-1550*, Odense 2008, 279-303.

Koppmann, Karl, "Zur Einholung der Prinzessin Elisabeth von Dänemark durch ihren Gemahl Herzog Heinrich Julius i.J. 1590. Auszüge aus den Rostocker Ratsprotokollen", *Jahrbuch des Geschichtsvereins für das Herzogtum Braunschweig* 3 (1904), 58-68.

Kraack, Gerhard & Nis Lorenzen, *Die St.-Nikolai-Bibliothek zu Flensburg*, Flensburg 1984 (Schriften der Gesellschaft für Flensburger Stadtgeschichte XXXV).

Kragelund, Patrick, "Olympens Guder", in: Steffen Heiberg (ed.), *Christian 4. og Frederiksborg*, Copenhagen 2006, 43-61.

Kramer, Sabine & Karsten Eisenmenger (eds.), *Die Marktkirche Unser Lieben Frauen zu Halle*, Halle an der Saale 2004.

Kratzsch, Klaus, *Bergstädte des Erzgebirges. Städtebau und Kunst zur Zeit der Reformation*, Munich & Zurich 1972 (Münchner Kunsthistorische Abhandlungen IV).

Kratzsch, Konrad (ed.), *Illuminierte Holzschnitte der Luther-Bibel von 1534. Eine Bildauswahl*, Berlin 1982.

Krause, G. (ed.), *Tagebuch Christians des Jüngeren, Fürst zu Anhalt*, Leipzig 1858.

Krause, Hans-Joachim, *Sächsische Schloßkapellen der Renaissance*, Berlin 1982 (Das Christliche Denkmal 80).

Krause, Hans-Joachim, "Zur Ikonographie der protestantischen Schloßkapellen des 16. Jahrhunderts", in: Ernst Ullmann (ed.), *Von der Macht der Bilder: Beiträge des C.I.H.A.-Kolloquiums 'Kunst und Reformation'*, Leipzig 1983, 395-412.

Krause, Hans-Joachim, "Schloß Lichtenburg und die mitteldeutsche Renaissancearchitektur", *Denkmalpflege in Sachsen-Anhalt* 1993, 129-157.

Krause, Katharina, *Hans Holbein d. Ä*, Munich & Berlin 2002.

Krauss, Rosalind, *The Originality of the Avant-Garde and Other Modernist Myths*, Cambridge (Mass.) 1985.

Kretzschmar, Hellmut, "Staatswirtschaft, konfessionelle Territorialpolitik und materieller Aufschwung im ausgehenden 16. Jahrhundert", in: Rudolf Kötzschke & Hellmut Kretzschmar (eds.), *Sächsische Geschichte*, Würzburg 1965 (reprint Augsburg 1995), 219-235.

Krieger, Martin, *Kaufleute, Seeräuber und Diplomaten. Der dänische Handel auf dem Indischen Ozean (1620-1868)*, Cologne, Weimar & Vienna 1998.

Krieger, M. & M. North (eds.), *Land und Meer: Kultureller Austausch zwischen Westeuropa und dem Ostseeraum in der Frühen Neuzeit*, Cologne, Weimar & Vienna 2004.

Kriegsbaum, Friedrich, "Hans Reichle", *Jahrbuch der Kunsthistorischen Sammlungen in Wien* new ser. 5 (1931), 199-200.

Kristensen, Marius (ed.), *Skrifter af Paulus Helie*, 1-7, Copenhagen 1932-38.

Kristiansen, Peter, "Christian 4. og det store lysthus i haven", in: Jørgen Hein et al. (eds.), *Christian 4. og Rosenborg 1606-2006*, Copenhagen 2006, 7-24.

Kruse, Anette & Karen Stemann-Petersen, "Hertug Ulrik den Ældres kiste i Roskilde Domkirke", *Nationalmuseets Arbejdsmark* 2006, 149-165.

Kryger, Karin, "Dansk identitet i nyklassicistisk kunst. Nationale tendenser og nationalt særpræg 1750-1800", in: Ole Feldbæk (ed.), *Fædreland og Modersmål 1536-1789*, Copenhagen 1991 (Dansk identitetshistorie 1), 231-424.

Kryger, Karin, "Kirkerne i Tranquebar i den danske periode 1620-1845", *Architectura. Arkitekturhistorisk Årsskrift* 29 (2007), 57-90.

Kuijpers, E., *Migrantenstad. Immigranten en sociale verhoudingen in 17de-eeuws Amsterdam*, Hilversum 2005.

Kunoth-Leifels, Elisabeth, *Über die Darstellungen der 'Bathseba im Bade'. Studien zur Geschichte des Bildthemas 4. bis 17. Jahundert*, Essen 1962.

Kurtze und doch außführliche Relation ... von gehaltenem Beylager ... Des ... Herrn Christiani II. ..., Jena 1603.

Kusche, María, "La antigua galería de retratos del Pardo: su reconstrucción arquitectónica y el órden de colocación de los cuadros", *Archivo Español de Arte* 64, 253 (1991), 1-28.

Kusche, María, "La antigua galería de retratos del Pardo: su reconstrucción pictórica", *Archivo Español de Arte* 64, 255 (1991), 261-283.

Kusche, María, "La antigua galería de retratos del Pardo: su importancia para la obra de Tiziano, Moro, Sánchez Coello y Sofonisba Anguissola y su significado para Felipe II, su fundador", *Archivo Español de Arte* 65, 257 (1992), 1-36.

Laboureur, J. le, *Histoire et relation de la Royne de Pologne*, Paris 1648.

Lacoste, Henri, "Notice sur Paul Saintenoy", *Annuaire de l'Académie royale de Belgique* 1962, 79-100.

Lademacher, Horst (ed.), *Onder den Oranje boom. Niederländische Kunst und Kultur im 17. und 18. Jahrhundert an deutschen Fürstenhöfen*, Munich 1999.

Lammertse, F. & J. van der Veen, *Uylenburgh & Zoon. Kunst en commercie van Rembrandt tot De Lairesse 1625-1675*, Amsterdam & Zwolle 2006.

Lang, Susanne, "Brunelleschi´s panels", in: Marisa Dalai Emiliani (ed.), *La prospettiva rinascimentale. Codificazioni e trasgressioni*, I, Florence 1980, 18-29.

Lange, Julius, "Nogle Sætninger om Kunstindustri i vor Tid" (1885), reprinted in: Georg Brandes & P. Købke (eds.), *Udvalgte Skrifter af Julius Lange*, I-III, Copenhagen 1900-03, III, 192-199.

Lange, Julius, "Udsigt over Kunstens Historie i Danmark", in: *Salmonsens Konversationslexikon*, Copenhagen 1895, reprinted in: Georg Brandes & P. Købke (eds.), *Udvalgte Skrifter af Julius Lange*, I-III, Copenhagen 1900-03, I, 1-87

Langenn, Friedrich Albert von, *Moritz, Herzog und Churfürst zu Sachsen*, Leipzig 1841.

Larsen, Mette Brønserud, "National identitet i dansk senmiddelalder?", *Historie* (1998) 2, 320-332.

Larsson, Lars-Olof, *Adriaen de Vries. Adrianus Fries Hagiensis Batavvs 1545-1626*, Vienna 1967.

Larsson, Lars-Olof, "Bildhaukunst und Plastik in Dänemark in der Regierungszeit Christian IV", in: *Art in Denmark 1600-1750*, Delft 1984 (Leids Kunsthistorisch Jaarboek 2 (1983)), 25-36

Larsson, Lars-Olof, "Die Brunnen auf Schloss Frederiksborg", in: *Art in Denmark 1600-1750*, Delft 1984 (Leids Kunsthistorisch Jaarboek 2 (1983)), 69-84.

Larsson, Lars-Olof, *Adrian de Vries in Schaumburg. Die Werke für Fürst Ernst zu Holstein-Schaumburg*, Ostfildern 1998.

Larsson, Lars-Olof, "Bilder i marginalen som retorisk modus", in: Kersti Markus (ed.), *Bilder i marginalen/Images in the Margins*, Talinn 2006, 12-25.

Lausten, Martin Schwarz, "Københavns Universitet i middelalderen 1479-ca. 1530", in: S. Ellehøj et al. (eds.), *Københavns Universitet 1479-1979*, I, Copenhagen 1991, 1-77.

Lausten, Martin Schwarz, *Den Hellige Stad Wittenberg. Danmark og Lutherbyen Wittenberg i reformationstiden*, Copenhagen 2002.

Lehmann, Helmut T. & Jaroslav Pelikan (eds.), *Luther's Works*, 1-55, Saint Louis 1955-1989.

Leonhardt, G., *Het huis Bartolotti en zijn bewoners*, Amsterdam 1979.

Levin, H., *The Myth of the Golden Age in the Renaissance*, London 1970.

Lieske, Reinhard, *Protestantische Frömmigkeit im Spiegel der kirchlichen Kunst des Herzogtums Württemberg*, Munich & Berlin 1973 (Forschungen und Berichte der Bau- und Kunstdenkmalpflege in Baden-Württemberg 2).

Lietzmann, Hilda, *Herzog Heinrich Julius zu Braunschweig und Lüneburg (1564-1613). Persönlichkeit und Wirken für Kaiser und Reich*, Langenhagen 1993 (Quellen und Forschungen zur Braunschweigischen Geschichte 30).

Liisberg, H. Bering, "Peter Isacksen", *Kunstmuseets Årsskrift* XI-XII (1926), 196-218.

Liisberg, H. Bering, *Christian Den Fjerde og Guldsmedene*, Copenhagen 1929.

Lillie, Louise, "Prædikestolen i Højby kirke – og om forholdet mellem kunstner, lensmand og gejstlig", in: Hugo Johannsen (ed.), *Synligt og Usynligt: Studier tilegnede Otto Norn på hans 75 års fødselsdag den 13. december 1990*, Herning 1990, 189-199.

Lillie, Louise (ed.), *Danske Kalkmalerier. Efter reformationen 1536-1700*, Copenhagen 1992.

Lindbæk, Johannes, "Dorothea, Kristiern den Førstes Dronning, og Familien Gonzaga, *Historisk Tidsskrift* 7, 3 (1900-1902), 455-512.

Lisch, G. C. Friedrich, "Katharina Hahn, Gemahlin des Herzogs Ulrik, Prinzen von Dänemark, Administrators des Bisthums Schwerin", *Jahrbücher des Vereins fur Mecklenburgische Geschichte* 23 (1858), 33-40.

Löcher, Kurt, *Barthel Beham. Ein Maler aus dem Dürerkreis*, Munich & Berlin 1999.

Löhneyss, Georg Engelhard von, *Della Cavalleria…*, Remlingen 1609-1610 (http://diglib.hab.de/wdb.php?dir=drucke/1-bell-2f-1).

Löhneyss, Georg Engelhard von, *Aulico Politica*, Remlingen 1622.

Lockhart, Paul Douglas, *Denmark, 1513-1660. The Rise and Decline of a Renaissance Monarchy*, Oxford 2007.

Lombaerde, Piet, "Dominating Space and Landscape: Ostend and Scherpenheuvel", in: Werner Thomas & Luc Duerloo (eds.), *Albert & Isabella 1598-1621. Essays*, Turnhout 1998, 173-183.

Loose, Hans-Dieter, *Hamburg und Christian IV. Von Dänemark während des Dreissigjährigen Krieges. Ein Beitrag zur Geschichte der hamburgischen Reichsunmittelbarkeit*, Hamburg 1963.

Lorenz, Sönke & Peter Rückert (eds.), *Württemberg und Mömpelgard: 600 Jahre Begegnung*, Leinefelden-Echterdingen 1999.

Lorenzen, Vilh., *Studier i dansk Herregaardsarkitektur i 16. og 17. Aarhundrede*, Copenhagen 1921.

Lorenzen, Vilh. *Haandtegnede Kort over København 1600-1660*, Copenhagen 1930.

Lorenzen, Vilh., "Nederlandse bouwmeesters en stedebouwers in Denemarken in de 17de eeuw en hun werken", *Roomsch-Katholiek Bouwblad. Veertiendaagsch tijdschrift voor bouw- en sierkunsten. Officieel orgaan der algem. Katholieke kunstenaarsvereeniging* 5 (1933-1934), 287.

Lorenzen, Vilh., *Christian IVs Byanlæg og andre Bybygningsarbejder*, Copenhagen 1937.

Luber, Katherine Crawford, *Albrecht Dürer and the Venetian Renaissance*, Cambridge 2005.

Luckhardt, Jochen & Nils Büttner (eds.), *Der Krieg als Person. Herzog Christian im Bildnis von Paulus Moreelse*, Brunswick 2000.

Ludolphy, Ingetraut, *Friedrich der Weise, Kurfürst von Sachsen 1453-1515*, Göttingen 1984.

Luha, A., E. Blumfeldt & A. Tammekann (eds.), *Saaremaa. Maateaduslik, majanduslik ja ajalooline kirjeldus*, Tartu 1934.

Luijten, G. et al. (eds.), *Dawn of the Golden Age. Northern Netherlandish Art 1580-1620*, Amsterdam 1993.

Lund, Hakon, "Palladianismus zwischen Nord- und Ostsee", in: Jörgen Bracker (ed.), *Bauen nach der Natur – Palladio: Die Erben Palladios in Nordeuropa*, Ostfildern 1997 (Exhibition Catalogue), 200-212.

Lundborg, Matheus, *Heliga Trefaldighetskyrkan i Kristianstad. Beskrivning och Historia*, Kristianstad 1928.

Luther, Martin, *Werke: Kritische Gesamtausgabe*, Weimar 1883-1983.

Lutrifonius, Paul, *Regio infanti …*, Copenhagen 1579.

Machuel, Marion Boudon, "François Dieussart in Rome: Two Newly Identified Works", *The Burlington Magazine* CXLV (2003), 833-840.

Mackowsky, W., *Giovanni Maria Nosseni und die Renaissance in Sachsen*, Berlin 1904 (Dissertation)..

MacLean, Gerald (ed.), *Re-Orienting the Renaissance. Cultural Exchanges with the East*, Houndmills, Basingstoke 2005.

Maesschalck, Alfonsine & Jos Viaene, "Het Leuvense stadhuis en de Brusselse *Aula Magna*, Brabantse gotiek of niet?", in: Raymond Van Uytven (ed.), *Gotiek in Brabant. De Brabantse stad. Dertiende colloquium, Leuven 18-19 oktober 2002*, Antwerp 2003 (Bijdragen tot de geschiedenis 86, 3-4), 283-320.

Magirius, Heinrich, "Das Renaissanceschloß in Dresden als Herrschaftsarchitektur der albertinischen Wettiner", *Dresdner Hefte* 38 (1994), 20-31.

Magirius, Heinrich, *Die evangelische Schlosskapelle zu Dresden aus kunstgeschichtlicher Sicht*, Altenburg 2009

Magnus, Johannes, *De omnibus gothorum sveonumque regibus*, Rome 1554.

Manetti, Antonio de Tuccio, *The Life of Brunelleschi*, Howard Saalman (ed.), Catherine Enggass (transl.), London 1970.

Manetti, Antonio di Tuccio, *Operette istoriche*, G. Milanesi (ed.), Florence 1887.

Marcus, Leah S., "Renaissance / Early Modern Studies", in: Stephen Greenblatt & Giles Gunn (eds.), *Redrawing the Boundaries: The Transformation of English and American Literary Studies*, New York 1992, 41-63.

Marcussen, Marianne, *Perspektiv*, Copenhagen 1984.

Marcussen, Marianne, "The Danish Art Historian Julius Lange, His Attitude to Trends in Art History in Europe and his Collaboration with Scandinavian Colleagues", in: Johanna Vakkari (ed.), *Towards a Science of Art History. J. J. Tikkanen and Art Historical Scholarship in Europe*, Helsinki 2009 (Taidehistoriallisia tutkimuksia – Konsthistoriska Studier/Studies in Art History 38), 71-83.

Marnef, Guido, *Antwerp in the Age of Reformation: Underground Protestantism in a Commercial Metropolis, 1550-1577*, Baltimore & London 1996.

Marquard, E., *Danske Gesandter og Gesandtskabspersonale indtil 1914*, Copenhagen 1952.

Marquet, Léon & Samuel Glotz, *Une relation allemande méconnue (1550) des fêtes données par Marie de Hongrie, à Binche et à Mariemont, en août 1549*, Binche 1991 (*Les cahiers binchois*, special issue).

Martens, Pieter, "Pierre Ernest de Mansfeld et les ingénieurs militaires: la défense du territoire", in: Jean-Luc Mousset & Krista De Jonge (eds.), *Un prince de la Renaissance. Pierre-Ernest de Mansfeld (1517-1604). Essais et catalogue*, Luxembourg 2007 (Exhibition Catalogue), 97-112.

Martens, Pieter & Joris Snaet, "De Mariale bedevaartskerk van

Scherpenheuvel. Een onderzoek naar dynastieke relaties en de verspreiding van ontwerpen en denkbeelden over architectuur", *Bulletin van de Koninklijke Nederlandse Oudheidkundige Bond* 98 (1999), 214-225.

Maxcey, Carl E., *Bona Opera: A Study in the Development of Doctrine in Philip Melanchthon*, Nieuwkoop 1980 (Bibliotheca Humanistica et Reformatorica XXXI).

Mbembe, Achille, *On the Postcolony*, Berkeley 2001.

McAllister Johnson, William, "On some neglected usages of Renaissance diplomatic correspondence", *Gazette des Beaux-Arts* 6, 79, 1 (1972), 51-54.

McBrien, Richard P., *Catholicism*, San Francisco 1994.

McManus, Clare, *Women on the Renaissance Stage: Anna of Denmark and Female Masquing in the Stuart Court, 1590-1619*, Manchester 2002.

McManus, Clare (ed.), *Women and Culture at the Courts of the Stuart Queens*, London 2003.

Meganck, Tine, *De kerkelijke architectuur van Wensel Cobergher (1557/61-1634) in het licht van zijn verblijf te Rome*, Brussels 1998 (Verhandelingen van de Koninklijke Academie voor Wetenschappen, Letteren en Schone Kunsten van België, Klasse der Schone Kunsten 60, 64), 52-94.

Meibom, Heinrich, *Außführlicher Wahrhaffter Historischer Bericht/ die Fürstliche Land= und Erbstadt Braunschweig/ Auch den Hertzogen zu Braunschweig und Lüneburg Wolfenbüttelschen Theils darüber habende Landesfürstliche Hoch= Obrig= und Gerechtigkeit/ auch ihre der Stadt unmittelbare angeborne schüldige Subjection und Unterthenigkeit etc. betreffend*, I-III, Helmstedt 1607-1609.

Meier, Claudia A., *Heinrich Ringerink und sein Kreis: Eine Flensburger Bildschnitzerwerkstatt um 1600*, Flensburg 1984 (Schriften der Gesellschaft für Flensburger Stadtgeschichte XXXIV).

Meijer, Bert W., *Fiamminghi e Olandesi, dipinti dalle collezioni lombarde*, Milan 2002.

Meine-Schawe, Monika, "Giovanni Maria Nosseni. Ein Hofkünstler in Sachsen", *Jahrbuch des Zentralinstituts für Kunstgeschichte* V-VI (1989-1990), 283-325.

Meine-Schawe, Monika, *Die Grablege der Wettiner im Dom zu Freiberg. Die Umgestaltung des Domchores durch Giovanni Maria Nosseni 1585-1594*, Munich 1992 (tuduv-Studien, Reihe Kunstgeschichte 46).

Meischke, R., P. Rosenberg & H. Zantkuijl, *Huizen in Nederland*, Zwolle & Amsterdam 1995.

Meldahl, Ferdinand & Fred. Skjold Neckelmann, *Denkmäler der Renaissance in Dänemark*, Berlin 1888.

Mensger, Ariane, *Jan Gossaert. Die niederländische Kunst zu Beginn der Neuzeit*, Berlin 2002.

Mensger, Ariane, "Jan Gossaert und der Niederländische Stilpluralismus zu Beginn der 16. Jahrhunderts – eine Annäherung", in: Stephan Hoppe, Matthias Müller & Norbert Nussbaum (eds.), *Stil als Bedeutung in der nordalpinen Renaissance: Wiederentdeckung eine methodischen Nachbarschaft*, Cologne 2008, 188-211.

Merback, Mitchell B., "Torture and Teaching. The Reception of Lucas Cranach the Elder's *Martyrdom of the Twelve Apostles* in the Protestant Era", *Art Journal* 57, 1 (1998), 14-23.

Michalski, Sergiusz, *The Reformation and the Visual Arts: The Protestant Image Question in Western and Eastern Europe*, London & New York 1993 (Christianity & Society in the Modern World 246).

Miedema, H., "Cover of the Amsterdam City Harpsichord", in: Badeloch Noldus & Juliette Roding (eds.), *Pieter Isaacsz (1568-1625). Court Painter, Art Dealer and Spy*, Turnhout 2007 (Exhibition Catalogue), 270.

Mielke, H., *Hans Vredeman de Vries. Verzeichnis der Stichwerke und Beschreibung seines Stils sowie Beiträge zum Werk Gerard Groennings*, Berlin 1967 (PhD-Dissertation).

Mignolo, Walter, *The Darker Side of the Renaissance*, Ann Arbor 1995.

Möller, Hans-Herbert (ed.), *Die Hauptkirche Beatae Mariea Virginis in Wolfenbüttel*, Hameln 1987 (Forschungen der Denkmalpflege in Niedersachsen 4).

Mohrat-Fromm, Anna, *Theologie und Frömmigkeit in religiöser Bildkunst um 1600: Eine niederländische Malerwerkstatt in Schleswig-Holstein*, Neumünster 1991 (Schriften des Vereins für Schleswig-Holsteinische Kirchengeschichte I, 37).

Molbech, Chr., "Historiske Bidrag til Kundskab om K. Christian den Fierdes Opdragelse og Ungdomsundervisning", *Nyt Historisk Tidsskrift* 3 (1850), 245-306.

Molbech, Christian, *Anmærkninger over nyere Tiders Architektur (…)*, Copenhagen 1855.

Moltesen, L. et al. (eds.), *Acta Pontificum. Pavelige Aktstykker vedrørende Danmark 1316-1536*, I-VII, Copenhagen 1904-43.

Montias, John M., *Art at Auction in 17th-century Amsterdam*, Amsterdam 2002.

Moran, B. T., *The Alchemical World of the German Court. Occult Philosophy and Chemical Medicine in the Circle of Moritz of Hessen (1572-1632)*, Stuttgart 1991.

Mordhorst, Camilla, *Genstandsfortællinger. Fra Museum Wormianum til de moderne museer*, Copenhagen 2009.

Morgen, Luke & Philippe Sénechal, "Introduction", in: Jaynie Anderson (ed.), *Crossing Cultures: Conflict, Migration and Convergence*, Melbourne 2009, 180-181.

Morris, Anna, *Het tijdschrift l'Emulation en de architectuurtentoonstellingen in de periode 1874-1890*, Leuven 1989 (Dissertation).

Mortensen, Erik, *Kunstkritikkens og kunstopfattelsens historie i Danmark*, 1-2, Copenhagen 1990.

Moxey, Keith, "Do We Still Need a Renaissance?", in: Jaynie Anderson (ed.), *Crossing Cultures: Conflict, Migration and Convergence*, Melbourne 2009, 233-238.

Muchembled, Robert & William Monter (eds.), *Cultural Exchange in Early Modern Europe*, I- IV, Cambridge 2006-2007.

Müller, Matthias, "Capriccio oder Politikum? Überlegungen zu ungewöhnlichen Treppentürmen an deutschen und französischen Renaissanceschlössern", in: Lutz Unbehaun, Ulrich Schütte & Andreas Beyer (eds.), *Die Künste und das Schloß in der frühen Neuzeit,* Munich & Berlin 1998 (Rudolstädter Forschungen zur Residenzkultur 1), 131-149.

Müller, Matthias, "Das Schloß als fürstliches Manifest. Zur Architekturmetaphorik in den wettinischen Residenzschlössern von Meißen und Torgau", in: Jörg Rogge & Uwe Schirmer (eds.), *Hochadelige Herrschaft im mitteldeutschen Raum (1200 bis 1600). Formen - Legitimation - Repräsentation*, Stuttgart 2003 (Quellen und Forschungen zur sächsischen Geschichte 23), 395-441.

Müller, Matthias, *Das Schloß als Bild des Fürsten. Herrschaftliche Metaphorik in der Residenzarchitektur des Alten Reiches*, Göttingen 2004.

Münster, Sebastian, *Cosmographia Universalis*, III, Basel 1554.

Muller, Frank, *Heinrich Vogtherr l'Ancien. Un artiste entre Renaissance et Réforme*, Wiesbaden 1997.

Muller, Frank, "Der Mömpelgarder und der Gothaer Altar im Lichte der politisch-konfessionellen Lage Süddeutschlands um 1540", in: Sönke Lorenz & Peter Rückert (eds.), *Württemberg und Mömpelgard: 600 Jahre Begegnung*, Leinefelden-Echterdingen 1999, 169-190.

Mulryne, J. R., Helen Watanabe-O'Kelly & Margaret Shewring (eds.), *Europa Triumphans. Court and Civic Festivals in Early Modern Europe*, 1-2, London 2004.

Murray, John F., *Vlaanderen en Engeland. De invloed van de Lage Landen op Engeland ten tijde van de Tudors en de Stuarts*, Antwerp 1985.

Musaphia, Benjamin, *Epistola regia, de maris reciprocatione ad potentissim. Daniae regim …*, Amsterdam 1642.

Møller, Henrik Sten (ed.), *The Danish Jewish Museum Daniel Libeskind*, Copenhagen 2004.

Nagel, Alexander & Christopher S. Wood, "Interventions: Towards a New Model of Renaissance Anachronism", *The Art Bulletin* 87 (2005), 403-415.

Nagel, Alexander & Christopher S. Wood, "Reply", *The Art Bulletin* 87 (2005), 429-432.

Neumann, Carsten, "Herzog Ulrich als Förderer der Künste und Wissenschaften. Gelehrte und Künstler am Güstrower Hof", in: Kornelia von Berswordt-Wallrabe (ed.), *Schloss Güstrow. Prestige und Kunst 1556 bis 1636*, Güstrow 2006, 30-37, 181-193.

Neumann, Hartwig, *Zitadelle Jülich. Grosser Kunst- und Bauführer*, Jülich 1986.

Neurdenburg, E., *Hendrick de Keyser. Beeldhouwer en bouwmeester van Amsterdam*, Amsterdam 1930.

Neurdenburg, E., "Pieter de Keyser als beeldhouwer", *Oudheidkundig Jaarboek* 9 (1940), 62-72.

Neurdenburg, E., "Hendrick de Keyser en het beeldhouwwerk aan de galerij van Frederiksborg in Denemarken", *Oudheidkundig Jaarboek* 12 (1943), 33-41.

Neurdenburg, Elisabeth, *De zeventiende eeuwsche beeldhouwkunst in de noordelijke Nederlanden*, Amsterdam 1948.

Neville, Kristoffer, "Gothicism and Early Modern Historical Ethnography", *Journal of the History of Ideas* 70, 2 (2009), 213-234.

Neville, Kristoffer, *Architecture in Sweden in the Age of Great Power*, Turnout 2009 (Architectura Moderna 7).

Nichols, John, *The Progresses … of James I*, London 1828.

Nielsen, C. V., *Perspektivens Historie*, I-V, Copenhagen 1895-99.

Niethammer, Lutz, "Maurice Halbwachs: Memory and the Feeling of Identity", in: Bo Stråth (ed.), *Myth and Memory in the Construction of Community*, Brussels 2000, 75-93.

Niitema, Vilho, *Der Kaiser und die Nordische Union bis zu den Burgunderkriegen* (Annales Academiae Scientiarum Fennicae, B 116), Helsinki 1960.

Nissen, N., *Københavns bybygning 1500-1856, visioner, planer, forfald*, Copenhagen 1989.

Noble, Bonnie-Jeanne, *The Lutheran Paintings of the Cranach Workshop, 1529-1555*, Ann Arbor 1999.

Noldus, Badeloch, *Trade in Good Taste. Relations in Architecture and Culture between the Dutch Republic and the Baltic World in the Seventeenth Century*, Turnhout 2004 (Architectura Moderna 2).

Noldus, Badeloch, "An 'unvergleichbarer Liebhaber' - Peter Spierinck, the art-dealing diplomat", *Scandinavian Journal of History* 31, 2 (2006), 173-185.

Noldus, Badeloch, "Pieter Isaacsz's Other Life – Legal and Illegal", in: Badeloch Noldus & Juliette Roding (eds.), *Pieter Isaacsz (1568-1625). Court Painter, Art Dealer and Spy*, Turnhout 2007 (Exhibition Catalogue), 151-163.

Noldus, Badeloch & Juliette Roding (eds.), *Pieter Isaacsz (1568-1625). Court Painter, Art Dealer and Spy*, Turnhout 2007 (Exhibition Catalogue).

Nopens, Christine, *Die Schloßkirche in Lichtenburg. Ein Zeugnis der Nachgotik am Ende des 16. Jahrhunderts in Sachsen*, Universität Leipzig 1984 (Diplomarbeit).

Nordstrom, Byron J., *Scandinavia since 1500*, Minneapolis 2000.

Norn, Otto, *Mester Michiels to Breve til Christian den Anden. Et Bidrag til Nederlandenes og Danmarks kunstneriske Forbindelse*, Copenhagen 1948.

Norn, Otto, "Østerholms Slotsruin på Als", *Nationalmuseets Arbejdsmark* (1956), 103-114.

Norn, Otto, "Serlio and Danmark", *Analecta Romana Instituti Danici* 1 (1960), 105-121.

Norn, Otto, *Hesselagergaard og Jacob Binck. En tilskrivning,*

Norn, Otto, "'Som David saa Bathseba i det Bad'", *Kulturminder*, N.S., V (1965), 51-70.

Norn, Otto, "Hesselagergård", in: Eva Louise Lillie (ed.), *Danske kalkmalerier. Efter Reformationen 1536-1700*, Copenhagen 1992, 94-97 (Danske kalkmalerier 7).

North, M. (ed.), *Economic History of the Arts*, Cologne 1996.

Nussbaum, Norbert, Claudia Euskirchen & Stephan Hoppe (eds.), *Wege zur Renaissance. Beobachtungen zu den Anfängen neuzeitlicher Kunstauffassung im Rheinland und den Nachbargebieten um 1500*, Cologne 2003.

Nuvoloni, Filippo, *Oratio ad Serenissium Dominum Christiernum Datiae, Norvegiae, Suetiae, Gothorum Slavorumque Regem*, (Mantua) 1474, in: Vivian Etting, Rodolfo Signorini & Birgitte Werdelin (eds.), *Fra Christian I's Italiensrejse 1474*, Copenhagen 1984.

Nystrøm, E., "Jonas Charisius' indkøb af malerier og musikinstrumenterne i Nederlandene 1607-08", *Danske Magazin* 5, 6 (1909), 225-236.

Nørregård-Nielsen, H. E., "Omkring Evert Janssen. Af Charlottenborgs Bygningshistorie", *Architectura. Arkitekturhistorisk Årsskrift* 6 (1984), 140-160.

Odelberg, Herman, "Les retables de Strengnäs (Suède)", *Annales de l'Académie d'Archéologie de Belgique* 26 (1870), 475-480.

Oettinger, Johann, *Wahrhaffte Historische Beschreibung …*, Stuttgart 1610.

Ohnesorge, Klaus-Walther, *Wolfenbüttel. Geographie einer ehemaligen Residenzstadt*, Brunswick 1974 (Braunschweiger Geographische Studien 5).

Olden-Jørgensen, Sebastian, "Sommerstuen, Slotskirken og Dansesalen", in: Steffen Heiberg (ed.), *Christian 4. og Frederiksborg*, Copenhagen 2006, 115-131.

Olden-Jørgensen, Sebastian, "Johann Damgaards Alithia (1597): Genrehistorie, teksthistorie og idehistorie: Omkring et dansk fyrstespejl til Christian 4", *Fund og Forskning* 45 (2006), 35-55.

Olsen, Rikke Agnete, "Hjortesalen på Hesselagergård. Salens Udsmykning", *Architectura. Arkitekturhistorisk Årsskrift* 18 (1996), 32-41.

Opel, Julius Otto, *Der niedersächsisch-dänische Krieg*, I-III, Halle 1872-1894.

Orenstein, N., *Hendrick Hondius*, Roosendaal & Amsterdam 1994 (G. Luijten (ed.), *The New Hollstein. Dutch & Flemish Etchings, Engravings and Woodcuts 1450-1700*).

Orgel, Stephen, *The Illusion of Power*, Berkeley 1991.

Orleans, H. de, *Inventaire de tous les Meubles de Cardinal Mazarin 1653*, London 1861.

Orr, Clarissa, *Queenship in Europe 1660-1815. The Role of the Consort*, Cambridge 2004.

Osten, Gert von der & Horst Vey, *Painting and Sculpture in Germany and the Netherlands 1500-1600*, Harmondsworth 1969 (Pelican History of Art).

Osten-Sacken, Cornelia von der, *El Escorial. Estudio iconológico*, Madrid 1984 (Libros de Arquitectura y Arte).

Ottenheym, K. A., *Pieter Post (1608-1669), architect*, Zutphen 1993.

Ottenheym, Konrad, "Fürsten, Architekten und Lehrbucher. Wege der holländischer Baukunst nach Brandenburg im 17. Jahrhundert", in: Horst Lademacher (ed.), *Onder den Oranje Boom. Das Haus Oranien-Nassau als Vermittler niederländischer Kultur in deutschen Territorien in 17. und 18. Jahrhundert*, Munich 1999, 287-298.

Ottenheym, Konrad, "Architectura Moderna. The Systematization of Architectural Ornament around 1600", in: Krista De Jonge & Konrad Ottenheym (eds.), *Unity and Discontinuity. Architectural Relations between the Southern and Northern Low Countries (1530-1700)*, Turnhout 2007 (Architectura Moderna 5), 111-136.

Ottosen, Knud, "Liturgien i Danmark 1540-1610", in: Ingmar Brohed (ed.), *Reformationens konsolidering i de nordiska länderna 1540-1610*, Oslo 1990, 258-277.

Packeiser, Thomas, "Lehrtafel, Retabel, Fürstenspiegel?", in: Sönke Lorenz & Peter Rückert (eds.), *Württemberg und Mömpelgard: 600 Jahre Begegnung*, Leinefelden-Echterdingen 1999, 191-250.

Pagden, Anthony, *European Encounters with the New World: From the Renaissance to Romanticism*, New Haven 1993.

Paludan-Müller, C., "Kong Christiern den Førstes Rejser i Tydskland og Italien i Aarene 1474 og 1475", *Historisk Tidsskrift* 5, 2 (1880-1881), 241-347.

Panofsky, Erwin, *The Life and Art of Albrecht Dürer*, Princeton 1943.

Panofsky, Erwin, *Early Netherlandish Painting*, Cambridge 1953.

Panofsky, Erwin, *Renaissance and Renascences in Western Art*, Stockholm 1960.

Panofsky, Erwin, *Perspective as Symbolic Form*, New York 1991.

Paravicini, Werner, "The Court of the Dukes of Burgundy: A Model for Europe?", in: Ronald G. Asch & Adolf M. Birke (eds.), *Princes, Patronage, and the Nobility. The Court at the Beginning of the Modern Age c. 1450-1650*, Oxford 1991 (Studies of the German Historical Institute London), 69-102.

Paviot, Jacques, "Ordonnances de l'hôtel et ceremonial de cour aux XVe et XVIe siècles, d'après l'exemple bourguignon", in: Holger Kruse & Werner Paravicini (eds.), *Höfe und Hofordnungen 1200-1600. 5. Symposium der Residenzen-Kommission der Akademie der Wissenschaften in Göttingen veranstaltet gemeinsam mit dem Deutschen Historischen Institut Paris und dem Staatsarchiv Sigmaringen, Sigmaringen, 5. bis 8. Oktober 1996*, Sigmaringen 1999 (Residenzenforschung 10), 167-174.

Pedrocco, Filippo, *Tiziano*, Milan 2000.

Peltzer, Rudolf, "Hans Rottenhammer", *Jahrbuch der Kunsthistorischen Sammlungen des Allerhöchsten Kaiserhauses* 33 (1916), 293-365.

Petersen, A. (ed.), "Frederiksborg Slots Inventarium af 1650", *Danske Samlinger* 2 (1866-67), 118-234.

Petersen, Carl S., "Danske videnskabelige Biblioteker og deres Historie", in: Svend Dahl (ed.), *Haandbog i bibliotekskundskab*, Copenhagen 1912, 1-89.

Petersen, Erling Ladewig, "Defence, War, and Finance: Christian IV and the Council of the Realm 1596-1629", *Scandinavian Journal of History* 7 (1982), 280-297.

Petersen, Erling Ladewig, "Danish Intermezzo", in: Geoffrey Parker (ed.), *The Thirty Years War*, London 1987, 71-81.

Petersen, Lorenz, "Daniel Freses 'Landtafel' der Grafschaft Hollstein (Pinneberg) aus dem Jahre 1588", *Zeitschrift der Gesellschaft für Schleswig-Holsteinische Geschichte* 70-71 (1943), 224-246.

Peterson, Jeanette & Dana Leibsohn (eds.), *Seeing across Cultures*, (forthcoming, Aldershot 2012).

Pfandl, Ludwig, "Philipp II und die Einführung des Burgundischen Hofzeremoniells in Spanien", *Historisches Jahrbuch* 58 (1938), 1-38.

Pineda, Joannes de, *De Re Salomonis …*, Mainz 1613 (Lyon 1609).

Plantenga, J. H., *L'architecture religieuse dans l'ancien duché de Brabant depuis le règne des archiducs jusqu'au gouvernement autrichien (1598-1713)*, The Hague 1926.

Plard, Henri, "Anvers dans le 'Journal de voyage aux Pays-Bas' de Dürer (1520-1521)", in: Pierre Jodogne (ed.), *Lodovico Guicciardini (1521-1589)*, Leuven 1990 (Travaux de l'Institut Interuniversitaire pour l'étude de la Renaissance et de l'Humanisme X), 237-248.

Plesberg, Katja, *Christine af Sachsen. Et eksempel på senmiddelalderlig fyrstelig fromhedspraksis,* Institut for Historie, Københavns Universitet 2001 (Master's Thesis).

Poelaert en zijn tijd, Brussels 1980 (Exhibition Catalogue), 231-237.

Poeschel, Sabine, *Handbuch der Ikonographie. Sakrale und profane Themen der bildenden Kunst*, Darmstadt 2005.

Pontoppidan, Erich & Hans de Hofman, *Den Danske Atlas*, I-IX, Copenhagen 1763-1781 (2. ed. Copenhagen 1968-1972).

Pope-Hennessy, John, *Italian Renaissance Sculpture*, New York 1985.

Porter, Roy & Mikulas Teich (eds.), *The Renaissance in National Context*, Cambridge 1992.

Poscharsky, Peter, *Die Kanzel: Erscheinungsform im Protestantismus bis zum Ende des Barocks*, Gütersloh 1963 (Schriftenreihe des Institutes für Kirchenbau und kirchliche Kunst der Gegenwart 1).

Poulsen, Hanne Kolind, *Cranach*, Copenhagen 2002.

Poulsen, Hanne Kolind, "Queen Dorothea of Denmark celebrating her dead husband – and herself!", in: Lilian H. Zirpolo (ed.), *Constructions of Death, Mourning, and Memory. Conference Oct. 27-29, 2006. Proceedings*, New Jersey 2006, 121-124.

Poulton, Diana, *John Dowland,* Berkeley 1982.

Prims, Floris, *Het stadhuis te Antwerpen. Geschiedenis en beschrijving*, Antwerp 1930.

Prinz, Wolfram & Ronald G. Kecks, *Das französische Schloss der Renaissance. Form und Bedeutung der Architektur, ihre geschichtlichen und gesellschaftlichen Grundlagen*, Berlin 1985, 1994².

(Rantzau, Henrik), *Descriptio Pompae Funebris (…) Friderici II (…)*, s.l. 1588.

Rapke, Karl, "Die Perspektive und Architektur auf den Dürer´schen Handzeichnungen, Holzschnitten und Gemälden", *Studien zur deutsche Kunstgeschichte* 39 (1902), 1-88.

Rasmussen, Carsten P., Inge Adriansen & Lennart S. Madsen (eds.), *De Slesvigske Hertuger*, Aabenraa 2005 (Skrifter udgivet af Historisk Samfund for Sønderjylland XCII).

Rasmussen, Tarald, "Innledende overveielser med europeisk perspektiv", in: Ingmar Brohed (ed.), *Reformationens konsolidering i de nordiska länderna 1540-1610*, Oslo 1990, 9-18.

Rast, Reet, "Fragmente Saaremaa sakraalsest interjöörist 17. sajandil", in: Olavi Pesti (ed.), *Saaremaa Muuseum. Kaheaastaraamat 1995-96*, Kuressaare 1997, 37-52.

Rawles, Stephen Ph. J., "The earliest editions of Nicolas de Herberay's translations of Amadis de Gaule", *The Library* 3, 2 (1981), 91-108.

Readings, Bill, *The University in Ruins*, Cambridge & London 1996.

Redworth, G. & Fernando Checa, "The Courts of the Spanish Habsburgs, 1500-1700", in: John Adamson (ed.), *The Princely Courts of Europe: Ritual, Politics and Culture under the Ancien Régime, 1500-1700*, London 1999, 47-50.

Richter, Jan Friedrich, *Claus Berg. Retabelproduktion des Spätmittelalters im Ostseeraum*, Berlin 2007.

Riegl, Alois, "Das holländische Gruppenportrait", *Jahrbuch des allerhöchsten Kaiserhauses* 22 (1902), 71-278, reed. in: *The Group Portraiture of Holland*, Los Angeles 1999.

Riis, Thomas, *Should Auld Acquaintance Be Forgot… Scottish-Danish Relations c. 1450-1701*, Odense 1988.

Rivera Blanco, Javier, "El Palacio de El Pardo entre Carlos V y Felipe II", *Reales sitios* 37 (2000), 2-15.

Roding, Juliette G., "The Myth of the 'Dutch Renaissance' in Denmark. Dutch Influence on Danish Architecture in the 17th century", in: J. Ph. S. Lemmink & J. S. A. M. van Koningsbrugge (eds.), *Baltic Affairs. Relations between the*

Roding, Juliette, "Myten om den hollandske renæssance. Christian IV's byanlæg i Skandinavien", *B. Arkitekturtidsskrift* 47-48 (1990-1991), 25-31.

Roding, Juliette G., *Christiaan IV van Denemarken (1588-1648). Architectuur en stedebouw van een Luthers vorst*, Alkmaar 1991 (PhD-dissertation).

Roding, Juliette & Lex Heerma van Voss (eds.), *The North Sea and Culture (1550-1800)*, Verloren 1996.

Roding, Juliette, "The North Sea coasts, an architectural unity?", in: Juliette Roding & L. Heerma van Voss (eds.), *The North Sea and Culture (1550-1800)*, Hilversum 1996, 96-106.

Roding, Juliette & Marja Stompé, *Pieter Isaacsz. (1569-1625). Een Nederlandse schilder, kunsthandelaar en diplomat aan het Deense hof*, Verloren 1997.

Roding, Juliette G., "Voorstellingen van vermaak in de plafonddecoratie van de grote zaal in het lustslot Rosenborg (circa 1620)", in: J. de Jongste, J. Roding & B. Thijs (eds.), *Vermaak van de elite in de vroegmoderne tijd*, Hilversum 1999, 262-287.

Roding, Juliette G., "Philip de Lange (ca.1744-1766). Het indrukwekkende oeuvre van een onbekende architect uit de Republiek in dienst van de Deense Marine", in: Leo Akveld et al. (eds.), *In het kielzog. Maritiem-historische studies aangeboden aan Jaap R. Bruiijn bij zijn vertrek als hoogleraar zeegeschiedenis aan de Universiteit Leiden*, Amsterdam 2003, 494-504.

Roding, Juliette (ed.), *Dutch and Flemish Artists in Britain 1550-1800* (Leids Kunsthistorisch Jaarboek 13), 2003.

Roding, Juliette & Marja Stompé, *Pieter Isaacsz. (1569-1625). Een Nederlandse schilder, kunsthandelaar en diplomat aan het Deense hof*, Verloren 1997.

Rodler, Hieronymus, *Perspectiua,* Frankfurt 1546.

Rodríguez Villa, Antonio, *Etiquetas de la Casa de Austria*, Madrid 1913.

Roeck, B., *Elias Holl. Architekt einer europäischen Stadt*, Regensburg 1985.

Roeck, Bernd, "Introduction", in: Herman Roodenburg (ed.), *Forging European Identities, 1400-1700*, Cambridge 2007 (Robert Muchembled & William Monter (eds.), *Cultural Exchange in Early Modern Europe* IV), 1-29.

Römelingh, J., "Christian IV and the Dutch Republic. An Introduction", in: *Art in Denmark 1600-1650*, Delft 1984 (Leids Kunsthistorisch Jaarboek 2 (1983)), 1-6.

Roethlisberger, Marcel G., *Abraham Bloemaert and his sons. Paintings and prints*, Doornspijk 1993.

Roever, N. de, "Drie Amsterdamse schilders (Pieter Isaaksz, Abraham Vinck, Cornelis van der Voort)", *Oud Holland* 3 (1885), 171-208.

Rogerson, Barnaby, "A double Perspective and a Lost Rivalry: Ogier de Busbecq and Melchior Lorck in Istanbul", in: Gerald MacLean (ed.), *Re-Orienting the Renaissance. Cultural Exchanges with the East*, Houndmills, Basingstoke 2005, 88-95.

Roggen, Domien & J. Withof, "Cornelis Floris", *Gentse bijdragen tot de kunstgeschiedenis* 8 (1942), 79-171.

Romanino. Un pittore in rivolta nel Rinascimento italiano, exhibition catalogue, Trient & Milan 2006 (Exhibition Catalogue).

Roosens, Bernhard, "Die Modernisierung älterer Festungen im niederländischen Grenzgebiet zu Frankreich und die italienischen Ingenieure (1534-1560)", in: Günter Bers & Conrad Doose (eds.), *'Italienische' Renaissancebaukunst an Schelde, Maas und Niederrhein. Stadtanlagen – Zivilbauten – Wehranlagen*, Jülich 1999, 155-165.

Roosens, Bernhard, *Habsburgse defensiepolitiek en vestingbouw in de Nederlanden (1520-1560)*, University of Leiden 2005 (PhD-Dissertation).

Ruggiero, Guido, "Renaissance Dreaming: In Search of a Paradigm", in: Gudio Ruggioero (ed.), *A Companion to the Worlds of the Renaissance²*, Oxford 2007 (Blackwell Companions to European History), 1-20.

Van Ruyven-Zeman, Zsuzsanna, Review of Antoinette Huysmans et al. (eds.), *Cornelis Floris 1514-1575. Beeldhouwer architect ontwerper*, Brussels 1996, in: *Oud Holland* 112, 4 (1998), 259-271.

Rosenthal, Earl, "The Diffusion of the Italian Renaissance Style in Western European Art", *Sixteenth Century Journal* 9 (1978), 33-45.

Rowland, Ingrid D., "Raphael, Angelo Colocci, and the Genesis of the Architectural Orders", *Art Bulletin* 76 (1994), 81-104.

Ruelens, Charles, *Le siège et les fêtes de Binche, 1543 et 1549. Deux documents publiés avec traduction, liminaires et notes*, Mons 1878 (Publication de la Société des bibliophiles belges, séant à Mons 25).

Rykwert, J., *On Adam's House in Paradise. The Idea of the Primitive Hut in Architectural History*, New York 1972.

Rylant, J. & Marguerite Casteels, "De metsers van Antwerpen tegen Paludanus, Floris, de Nole's en andere beeldhouwers", *Bijdragen tot de geschiedenis* 31 (1940), 185-203.

Rørdam, Holger Fr., "Bidrag til Sønderjyllands Kirkehistorie i 16de Aarhundrede", *Ny Kirkehistoriske Samlinger* 4 (1868), 626-732.

Rørdam, Holger Fr., *Københavns Universitets Historie 1537-1661*, 1-4, Copenhagen 1868-74.

Rørdam, Holger Fr., "Hertug Ulrik, Christian IV's Søn", *Historiske Samlinger og Studier* 8 (1896), 1-141.

Sabatier, Gérard, *Versailles ou la figure du roi*, Paris 1999.

Saintenoy, Paul, "Les architectes flamands dans le Nord de l'Allemagne au XVIe siècle", *Académie royale d'archéologie de Belgique* 5 (1907), 161-172.

Salling, Emma & Claus M. Smidt, "Fundamentet. De første

hundrede år", in: Anneli Fuchs & Emma Salling (eds.), *Kunstakademiet 1754-2004*, 1-3, Copenhagen 2004, 1, 23-117.

Sartre, Josiane, *Châteaux "brique et pierre" en France. Essai d'architecture*, Paris 1981.

Sass, Else Kai, "Kunsthistorie", in: Povl Johs. Jensen (ed.), *Det filosofiske Fakultet*, Copenhagen 1979 (Svend Ellehøj et al. (eds.), Københavns Universitet 1479-1979, XI, 4), 199-344.

Saunders, Ann, "The Building of the Exchange", in: Ann Saunders (ed.), *The Royal Exchange*, London 1997, 36-49.

Schade, Werner, "Maler am Hofe Moritz' von Sachsen", *Zeitschrift des deutschen Vereins für Kunstwissenschaft* 21 (1968), 29-44.

Schalk, F., "Das goldene Zeitalter als Epoche", *Archiv für das Studium der neueren Sprache und Literatur* 199 (1962), 85-98.

Scharfe, Martin, *Evangelische Andachtsbilder: Studien zu Intention und Funktion des Bildes in der Frömmigkeitsgeschichte vornehmlich des schwäbischen Raumes*, Stuttgart 1968 (Veröffentlichungen des Staatlichen Amtes für Denkmalpflege Stuttgart. Reihe C: Volkskunde, 5).

Schéle, Sune, *Cornelis Bos. A study of the origins of the Netherland grotesque*, Stockholm 1965.

Schepelern, H. D., *Museum Wormianum*, Aarhus 1971.

Schepelern, H. D. & Ulla Houkjær, *The Kronborg Series. King Christian IV and his Pictures of Early Danish History*, Copenhagen 1988.

Scheurleer, T. H. Lunsingh, "Silver Furniture in Holland", in: *Opuscula in Honorem C. Hernmarck*, Stockholm 1966 (Nationalmusei skriftserie 15), 141-157.

Schiebinger, Londa & Claudia Swan (eds.), *Colonial Botany: Science, Commerce, and Politics in the Early Modern World*, Philadelphia 2005.

Schildgen, Brenda Deen et al. (eds.), *Other Renaissances. A New Approach to World Literature*, Basingstoke & New York 2006.

Schilling, Johannes, "Die Wiederentdeckung des Evangeliums. Wie die Wittenberger Reformatoren ihre Geschichte rekonstruierten", in: Ludger Grenzmann et al. (ed.), *Die Präsenz der Antike im Übergang vom Mittelalter zur Frühen Neuzeit* (Bericht über Kolloquien der Kommission zur Erforschung der Kultur des Spätmittelalters 1999 bis 2002), Göttingen 2004, 125-142.

Schlegel, Johann Heinrich, *Geschichte der Könige von Dänemark aus dem oldenburgischen Stamme, Teil 2: Geschichte Christians des Vierten von 1588 bis 1629*, Copenhagen 1777.

Schlichtenmaier, Harry, *Studien zum Werk Hans Rottenhammers des Älteren (1564-1625). Maler und Zeichner mit Werkkatalog*, Tübingen 1988 (Dissertation).

Schlögel, Karl, *Im Raume lessen wir die Zeit. Über Zivilisationsgeschichte und Geopolitik*, Munich & Vienna 2003.

Schlosser, Julius von, *Präludien. Vorträge und Aufsätze*, Berlin 1927.

Schmale, Wolfgang (ed.), *Kulturtransfer*, Innsbruck 2003 (Wiener Schriften zur Geschichte der Neuzeit 2).

Schmidt, H., *Jürgen Ovens. Sein Leben und seine Werke*, Kiel 1922.

Schmidt-Voges, Inge, *De antiqva claritate et clara antiquitate Gothorum. Gotizismus als Identitätsmodell im frühneuzeitlichen Sweden*, Frankfurt 2004.

Scholten, Frits (ed.), *Adriaen de Vries 1556-1626*, Amsterdam, Stockholm & Los Angeles 1998-2000.

Scholten, Frits, *Sumptuous Memories. Studies in seventeenth-century Dutch tomb sculpture*, Zwolle 2003 (Studies in Netherlandish Art and Cultural History V).

Schoy, Auguste, "Cérémonies publiques célébrées aux Pays-Bas du XVIe au XVIIIe siècle", *Journal des Beaux-Arts et de la littérature. Peinture, Sculpture, Gravure, Architecture, Musique, Archéologie, Bibliographie, Belles-Lettres, etc.* 14 (1872), 104-105.

Schoy, Auguste, "Architecture – matériaux de construction. Façade nationale belge", in: Edmond Frederix (ed.), *La Belgique à l'exposition universelle de 1878*, Brussels, Paris, London & Leipzig 1878, 237-268.

Schoy, Auguste, *Histoire de l'influence italienne sur l'architecture dans les Pays-Bas*, Brussels 1879.

Schräpel, Werner, *Schloß Annaburg – Ein Beitrag zur Renaissance in Sachsen*, Dresden 1927 (Dissertation).

Schulting, T., "Pieter Isaacsz, Pupil of the "Artistic, sensible Mr Cornelis Ketel"", in: Badeloch Noldus & Juliette Roding (eds.), *Pieter Isaacsz (1568-1625). Court Painter, Art Dealer and Spy*, Turnhout 2007 (Exhibition Catalogue), 31-41.

Schutte, O., *Repertorium der buitenlandse vertegenwoordigers, residerende in Nederland 1584-1810*, The Hague 1983.

Schütz, Bernhard, "Das Herrenhaus Damp", in: *Kunstsplitter. Beiträge zur nordeuropäischen Kunstgeschichte. Festschrift für Wolfgang J. Müller zum 70. Geburtstag*, Husum 1984, 66-71.

Schütz, Bernhard & Christian Stocks, *Adeliges Gut Damp*, Munich & Berlin 1976 (Kleine Kunstführer 1066).

Scocozza, Benito, *Christian 4*, Copenhagen 1987.

Seklucjan, Jan, *Wybór pism*, Stanisław Rospond (ed.), Olsztyn 1979 (Literatura Warmii i Mazur w Dawnych Wiekach).

Sellink, Manfred, "Een teruggevonden *Laatste Oordeel* van Hendrick Goltzius: Goltzius' relatie met de Antwerpse uitgever Philips Galle", *Nederlands Kunsthistorisch Jaarboek/ Netherlands Yearbook for History of Art* 42-43 (1991-1992), 145-158.

Seng, Eva-Maria, *Stadt – Idee und Planung. Neue Ansätze im Städtebau des 16. und 17. Jahrhunderts*, Munich 2003.

Signorini, Rodolfo, *Opvs hoc tenve. La "architipata" Camera*

Dipinta detta "degli Sposi" di Andrea Mantegna, Mantova 2007.

Silver, Larry, "Arts and Minds: Scholarship on Early Modern History (Northern Europe)", *Renaissance Quarterly* LIX, 2 (2006), 351-373.

Silver, Larry, *Marketing Maximilian. The visual Ideology of a Holy Roman Emperor*, Princeton & Oxford 2008.

Simon, Johann, *Justa funebria … Udalrico …*, Rostock 1624.

Skafte-Jensen, Minna, "Denmark. The 16th Century", in: Minna Skafte Jensen (ed.), *A History of Nordic Neo-Latin Literature*, Odense 1995, 19-34.

Skougaard, Mette (ed.), *Gottorp - et fyrstehof i 1600-tallet*, Copenhagen 2002 (Exhibition Catalogue).

Skougaard, Mette, "Interiører" in: Steffen Heiberg (ed.), *Christian 4. og Frederiksborg*, Copenhagen 2006, 63-79.

Skovgaard, Joakim A., *A King's Architecture. Christian IV and His Buildings*, London 1973.

Skovgaard-Petersen, Karen, *Historiography at the Court of Christian IV. Studies in the Latin Histories of Denmark by Johannes Pontanus and Johannes Meursius*, Copenhagen 2002.

Skovgaard-Petersen, Karen, "Arguments against Barbarism. Early Native, Literary Culture in three Scandinavian National Histories", *Renæssanceforum* 5 (2008) 1-16.

Slothouwer, D. F., *Bouwkunst der Nederlandsche Renaissance in Denemarken*, Amsterdam 1924.

Smallman, Basil, *Schütz*, Oxford 2000.

Smed, Mette, "The Architecture of Christian IV", in: Steffen Heiberg (ed.), *Christian IV and Europe: the 19th Art Exhibition of the Council of Europe, Denmark 1988*, Herning 1988, 463-483 (Exhibition Catalogue).

Smith, David, "Herbert, Philipp", in: *Oxford Dictionary of National Biography*, 26, Oxford 2004, 714-720.

Smith, Jeffrey Chipps, *The Northern Renaissance*, London & New York 2004.

Smith, Pamela H. & Paula Findlen (eds.), *Merchants and Marvels: Commerce, Science, and Art in Early Modern Europe*, New York & London 2002.

Smith, Sophus Birket, *Kjøbenhavns Universitetsbibliothek før 1728*, Copenhagen 1882 (reprint Copenhagen 1982).

Söderlind, Solfrid, "Konsthistorieämnets förhistorie", in: Peter Gillgren, Britt-Inger Johansson & Hans Pettersson (eds.), *Åtta kapitel om konsthistoriens historia i Sverige*, Stockholm 2000, 9-38.

Söding, Ulrich, "Der Münnerstädter Altar von Tilmann Riemenschneider", in: Rainer Kahnitz & Peter Volk (eds.), *Skulptur in Süddeutschland, Festschrift für Alfred Schrädle*, Berlin 1998, 129-156.

Specklin, Daniel, *Architectura Von Vestungen*, Strasbourg 1589.

Spengler, Oswald, *Der Untergang des Abendlandes. Umrisse einer Morphologie der Weltgeschichte*, München 1918-1922, 1923 (English edition: *Decline of the West*, London 1971).

Spohr, Arne, *'How chances it they travel?' Englische Musiker in Dänemark und Norddeutschland, 1579-1630*, Wiesbaden 2009 (Wolfenbütteler Arbeiten zur Barockforschung 45).

Starke, Elfriede, "Luthers Beziehungen zu Kunst und Künstlern", in: Helmar Junghans (ed.), *Leben und Werk Martin Luthers von 1526 bis 1546. 1-2. Festgabe zu seinem 500. Geburtstag*, Göttingen 1983, 1, 531-548; 2, 905-915.

Steck, Max, *Dürers Gestaltlehre der Mathematik und bildenden Künste*, Halle 1948, 110-118.

Steenberg, J., *Rundetaarn og sneglegang*, Copenhagen 1952.

Stein, Meir, "Da muserne kom til Valby bakke…", in: Meir Stein, *Christian den Fjerdes Billedverden*, Copenhagen 1987, 9-19.

Stevin, Simon, *Materiae politicae: burgherlicke stoffen*, Leiden 1649.

Sthulmann, Adolf, *Lehrbuch der Reliefperspektive*, Hamburg 1914.

Stierhof, Horst, "Hans Schroer d. Ä. aus Lüttich. Hofmaler, Statuarius oder Monumentengießer", *Revue belge d'archéologie et d'histoire de l'art* XLIV (1975), 109-124.

Stierle, Karlheinz, "Translatio Studio and Renaissance: From Vertical to Horizontal Translation", in: Sanford Budick & Wolfgang Iser (eds.), *The Translatability of Cultures. Figurations of the Space Between*, Stanford 1996, 55-67.

Stirm, Margarete, *Die Bilderfrage in der Reformation*, Gütersloh 1977 (Quellen und Forschungen zur Reformationsgeschichte 45).

van der Stock, Jan (ed.), *Antwerpen, verhaal van een metropool 16de-17de eeuw*, Antwerp 1993.

Stopp, Frederick John, "Verbum Domini Manet in Aeternum: The Dissemination of a Reformation Slogan, 1522-1904", in: Siegbert Saloman Prawer, Richard Hinton Thomas & Leonard Forster (eds.), *Essays in German Language, Culture and Society*, London 1969 (London University Institute of Germanic Studies 12), 123-135.

Strauss, Walter, *German Single-leaf Woodcut 1550-1600*, New York 1975.

Strauss, Walter L., *Hendrick Goltzius, 1558-1617: The Complete Engravings and Woodcuts*, 1-2, New York 1977.

Stynen, Herman, *De onvoltooid verleden tijd. Een geschiedenis van de monumenten- en landschapszorg in België 1835-1940*, Brussels 1998.

Suhm, P. F., "Sanctarium Birgerianum", in: P. F. Suhm (ed.), *Samlinger til den Danske Historie* I, 3 (1780), 1-89.

Sulzer, Johann Georg, *Allgemeine Theorie der schönen Künste*, I-II, Leipzig 1771-1774.

Svanberg, Jan, "Adam van Düren. A German Stone Mason in Scandinavia in the Early Sixteenth Century", *Hafnia. Copenhagen Papers in the History of Art* 3 (1976) (Comité international d'histoire de l'art VIIe colloque international. Les

Pays du Nord et l'Europe. Art et Architecture au XVIe siècle. Copenhague 1-6 septembre 1975), 125-139.

Svaning, Hans, *Refutatio calumniarum cuiusdam Ioannis Upsalensis (…) Huic accessit Chronicon sive Historia Joannis Regis Daniæ (…) 1560*, s.l. 1561.

Syndram, Dirk et al. (eds.), *Giambologna in Dresden. Die Geschenke der Medici*, Munich 2006.

Takács, Imre (ed.), *Sigismundus Rex et Imperator. Kunst und Kultur zur Zeit Sigismund von Luxemburg 1387-1437*, Mainz 2006 (Exhibition Catalogue).

Taverne, Eduard Robert Marie, *In 't land van belofte: in de nieue stadt. Ideaal en werkelijkheid van de stadsuitleg in de Republiek 1580-1680*, Maarssen 1978.

Teuchert, Wolfgang, "Bericht über neue Ergebnisse der Bauforschung des Landesamtes für Denkmalpflege Schleswig-Holstein 1969-1984", *Nordelbingen* 54 (1985), 249-258.

Thies, Harmen, "Die Wolfenbütteler Hauptkirche Beatae Mariae Virginis von Paul Francke", in: Georg Ulrich Großmann, *Renaissance in Nord-Mitteleuropa*, I, Munich & Berlin 1990 (Schriften des Weserrenaissance-Museums Schloß Brake 4), 171-188.

Thies, Harmen, "Die Baugeschichte der Hauptkirche Beatae Mariae Virginis", in: Rainer Bürgel, Helmut A. Müller & Rainer Volp (eds.), *Kirche im Abseits? Zum Verhältnis von Religion und Kultur*, Stuttgart 1991, 203-221.

Thomson, David, *Renaissance architecture. Critics, Patrons, Luxury*, Manchester & New York 1993.

Thorlacius-Ussing, Viggo, *Billedskæreren Claus Berg*, Copenhagen 1922.

Thorlacius-Ussing, Viggo, *Claus Bergs altertavle i Sct. Knud i Odense*, Odense 1967.

Thurah, Lauritz de, *Den Danske Vitruvius*, I-II, Copenhagen 1746-1749, reedited together with a third volume, by Hakon Lund (ed.), Copenhagen 1966-1967.

Thurah, Lauritz de, *Hafnia Hodierna*, Copenhagen 1748.

Thurley, Simon, *The Royal Palaces of Tudor England. Architecture and Court Life 1460-1547*, Yale 1993.

Tielhof, M. van, *The 'Mother of All Trades': The Baltic Grain Trade in Amsterdam from the Late Sixteenth to the Early Nineteenth Century*, Leiden 2002.

Tipton, Susan, *RES PUBLICA BENE ORDINATA. Regentenspiegel und Bilder vom guten Regiment. Rathausdekorationen in der Frühen Neuzeit*, Hildesheim, Zürich & New York 1996.

Titze, Mario, "Neue Forschungen zum Vorwerk Bleesern, Ldkr. Wittenberg", *Burgen und Schlösser in Sachsen-Anhalt. Mitteilungen der Landesgruppe Sachsen-Anhalt der Deutschen Burgenvereinigung e. V.* 11 (2002), 368-383.

Tollebeek, Jo, "Renaissance and 'Fossilization': Michelet, Burckhardt & Huizinga", *Renaissance Studies* 15 (2001), 354-366.

Tomlinson, Sophie, "Theatrical Vibrancy on the Caroline Stage: *Tempe Restored* and *The Shepherd's Paradise*", in: Clare McManus (ed.), *Women and Culture at the Courts of the Stuart Queens*, London 2003, 186-203.

Topfstedt, Th., "Die 'Christianopolis' des Johann Valentin Andreae. Städtebaugeschichtliche Aspekte einer protestantischen Utopie", *Blätter für Württembergische Kirchengeschichte* 83-84 (1984), 20-33.

Trevisani, Filippo (ed.), *Andrea Mantegna e i Gonzaga. Rinascimento nel Castello di San Giorgio*, Milan 2006.

Tussenbroek, G. van, *The Architectural Network of the Van Neurenberg Family in the Low Countries*, Turnhout 2006 (Architectura Moderna 4).

Tønnes, Rikke, *Stephen Hansens palæ: Bygherren-Arkitekten Philip de Lange. Livet i og omkring et helsingørsk handelshus*, Copenhagen 1997.

Tønnes, Rikke, "Sidste blomstring", in: John Erichsen & Mikkel Venborg Pedersen (eds.), *Herregården. Menneske-samfund-landskab-bygninger*, 1-4, Copenhagen 2004-2006, 2, 225-298.

Ullmann, Ernst (ed.), *Von der Macht der Bilder: Beiträge des C.I.H.A.-Kolloquiums 'Kunst und Reformation'*, Leipzig 1983.

Unbehaun, Lutz, *Hieronymus Lotter. Kurfürstlich-Sächsischer Baumeister und Bürgermeister zu Leipzig*, Leipzig 1989.

Unnerbäck, Eyvind, *Welsche Giebel. Ein italienisches Renaissancemotiv und seine Verbreitung in Mittel- und Nordeuropa*, Stockholm 1971 (Antikvariskt Arkiv 42).

Uppenkamp, Barbara, *Das Pentagon von Wolfenbüttel. Der Ausbau der welfischen Residenz 1568-1626 zwischen Ideal und Wirklichkeit*, Hannover 2005 (Veröffentlichungen der Historischen Kommission für Niedersachsen und Bremen 229).

Uppenkamp, Barbara, "Politische Macht – Architektonische Imagination?", in: Christian Hochmuth & Susanne Rau (eds.), *Machträume der frühneuzeitlichen Stadt*, Konstanz 2006, 59-74.

van de Velde, Carl, *Frans Floris (1519/20-1570.) Leven en werken*, I-II, Brussels 1975 (Verhandelingen van de Koninklijke Academie voor Wetenschappen, Letteren en Schone Kunsten van België, Klasse der Schone Kunsten XXXVII, 30).

van de Vijver, Dirk, "L'étude de la science architecturale. Formation d'un gentilhomme architecte russe en Brabant et en Hollande (1718-1727)", *Cahiers du monde russe* 47, 3 (2006), 515-550.

Vedel, Anders Sørensen, *En Predicken som skeede udi … salige Johan Friisis begraffuelse …*, Copenhagen 1571.

Veen, J. van der, "De Delftse kunstmarkt in de tijd van Vermeer", in: Haks, D. & M. C. van der Sman (eds.), *De Hollandse samenleving in de tijd van Vermeer*, Zwolle 1996.

Venge, Mikael, *Bondekær eller tyran? Tekster til Christian II's regime, politik og personlighed*, Odense 1975.

Vermeulen, F. A. J., *Handboek tot de geschiedenis der Nederlandsche bouwkunst*, 1-3, The Hague & Gravenhage 1928-1941.

Vermeylen, F., *Painting for the Market. Commercialization of Art in Antwerp's Golden Age*, Turnhout 2003.

Verwohlt, Ernst, "Kongelige danske herolder", *Heraldisk Tidsskrift* 3, 25 (1972), 201-229.

Verzeichnus der Reise / welche die Kön. May. zu Dennemarken Norwegen Anno 1595. zu etlichen ihren Anverwandten Chur vnd Fürsten in Teutschland angestellet, Copenhagen 1595

Viator, Jean Pélérin, *De artifiali perspectiva*, Toul 1505.

Vignola, G. Barozzi da, *Regole Generali*, Rome 1602.

Vignola, G. Barozzi da, *Regole de'cinque ordini d'architettura*, Amsterdam 1617.

Villadsen, Villads, *Statens Museum for Kunst 1827-1952*, Copenhagen 1998.

Villari, Pasquale, *The Life and Times of Girolamo Savonarola*, New York 1888, reprint St.Clair Shores (Mi) 1972.

Villari, Pasquale, *The Two First Centuries of Florentine History: The Republic and Parties at the Time of Dante*, London 1905³.

Vitruvius, Pollio, *Ten Books on Architecture*, Thomas Noble Have (ed.), Ingrid D. Rawland (transl.), Cambridge 1999.

Vogtherr, Heinrich, *Ein Frembdes vnd wunderbares Kunstbüchlein*, Strasbourg 1559.

Vos, A. De, "Jacques Francart. Premier livre d'Architecture (1617). Studie van een Zuid-Nederlands modelboek met poortgebouwen", *Verhandelingen van de Koninklijke Academie voor Wetenschappen, Letteren en Schone Kunsten van België, Klasse der Schone Kunsten* 65 (1998).

Wade, Mara R., "The Politics of Splendor. Christian IV of Denmark's Hamburg Pageant", *Chloë* 23 (1995), 25-39.

Wade, Mara R., *Triumphus Nuptialis Danicus. German Court Culture and Denmark - The Great Wedding of 1634*, Wiesbaden 1996 (Wolfenbütteler Arbeiten zur Barockforschung 27).

Wade, Mara R., "Ballet in Denmark and Norway", in: Helen Watanabe-O'Kelly & Pierre Béhar (eds.), *Spectacvlvm Evropævm. Theatre and Spectacle in Europe 1580-1750. Histoire du Spectacle en Europe 1580-1750*, Wiesbaden 1999 (Wolfenbütteler Arbeiten zur Barockforschung 31), 571-575.

Wade, Mara R., "Drama in Denmark and Norway", in: Helen Watanabe-O'Kelly & Pierre Béhar (eds.), *Spectacvlvm Evropævm. Theatre and Spectacle in Europe 1580-1750. Histoire du Spectacle en Europe 1580-1750*, Wiesbaden 1999 (Wolfenbütteler Arbeiten zur Barockforschung 31), 289-297.

Wade, Mara R., "Fireworks and Entries in Denmark and Norway", in: Helen Watanabe-O'Kelly & Pierre Béhar (eds.), *Spectacvlvm Evropævm. Theatre and Spectacle in Europe 1580-1750. Histoire du Spectacle en Europe 1580-1750*, Wiesbaden 1999 (Wolfenbütteler Arbeiten zur Barockforschung 31), 743-749.

Wade, Mara R., "Opera in Denmark and Norway" in: Helen Watanabe-O'Kelly & Pierre Béhar (eds.), *Spectacvlvm Evropævm. Theatre and Spectacle in Europe 1580-1750. Histoire du Spectacle en Europe 1580-1750*, Wiesbaden 1999 (Wolfenbütteler Arbeiten zur Barockforschung 31), 465-470.

Wade, Mara R., "The Queen's Courts: Anna of Denmark and her Royal Sisters – Cultural Agency at Four Northern European Courts in the Sixteenth an Seventeenth Centuries", in: Clare McManus (ed.): *Women and Culture at the Courts of the Stuart Queens*, Basingstoke & New York 2003, 49-80.

Wade, Mara R. (ed.), *Pomp, Power and Politics Pomp, Power, and Politics: Essays on German and Scandinavian Court Culture and their Contexts*, New York & Amsterdam 2004 (Daphnis. Zeitschrift für Mittlere Deutsche Literatur und Kultur der Frühen Neuzeit (1400-1750) 32, 2003) .

Wade, Mara R., "Publication, Pageantry, Patronage: Georg Engelhard von Löhneyss' *Della Cavalleria* (1609; 1624) and His Hamburg Tournament Pageant for King Christian IV of Denmark (1603)", in: Wade, Mara R. (ed.), *Pomp, Power and Politics Pomp, Power, and Politics: Essays on German and Scandinavian Court Culture and their Contexts*, New York & Amsterdam 2004 (Daphnis. Zeitschrift für Mittlere Deutsche Literatur und Kultur der Frühen Neuzeit (1400-1750) 32, 2003),165-197

Wade, Mara R. (ed.), "Festivals in Scandinavia", in: Ronnie Mulryne, Helen Watanabe-O'Kelly & Margaret Shewring (eds.), *Europa Triumphans*, 1-2, London 2004, 237-341.

Wade, Mara R., "Witwenschaft und Mäzenatentum: Hedwig, Prinzessin von Dänemark und Kurfürstin von Sachsen (1581-1641)", in: Susanne Rode-Breymann (ed.), *Die Stadt – Ort kulturellen Handelns von Frauen in der Frühen Neuzeit*, Cologne 2007, 219-231.

Wade, Mara R., "Widowhood and Patronage: Hedevig, Princess of Denmark and Electress of Saxony (1581-1641)", in: *Renæssanceforum* 4 (2008), 1-28 (http://www.renaessanceforum.dk).

Wade, Mara R., "Dänisch-Sächische Hoffeste der frühen Neuzeit", in: Jutta Kappel & Claudia Brink (eds.), *Mit Fortuna übers Meer. Sachsen und Dänemark – Ehen ind Allianzen im Spiegel der Kunst (1548-1709)*, Berlin & München 2009, 62-69.

Wade, Mara R., "Pax Danica und die frühneuzeitliche Idee der klassischen Monarchie", in: Ulrich Heinen et al. (eds.), *Welche Antike? Konkurrierende Rezeption des Altertums im Barock*, Wiesbaden 2011 (Wolfenbütteler Arbeiten zur Barockforschung) 373-396.

Wade, Mara R., "German Theater in Denmark during the Age of King Christian IV (1577-1648)", *Thalia Germanica* (forthcoming).

Wagnitz, Friedrich, "Herzog Friedrich Ulrich, Ein glückloser

Fürst in schwerer Zeit", *Jahrbuch der Gesellschaft für niedersächsische Kirchengeschichte* 87 (1989), 51-70.

Wagnitz, Friedrich, "Ein Wolfenbütteler Fürstenschicksal im Dreißigjährigen Krieg. Würdigung von Herzog Friedrich Ulrich anläßlich des 400. Geburtstages", *Braunschweigische Heimat* 77 (1991), 5-34.

Wahrhafftige vnd kurtze Relation der Russischen … Reise … deß… Hertzog Johann deß jüngeren…, Hamburg 1603.

Wamberg, Jacob, "Ghiberti, Alberti, and the Modernity of Gothic", *Analecta Romana Instituti Danici* 21 (1993), 173-211.

Wamberg, Jacob, *Landscape as World Picture: Tracing Cultural Evolution in Images*, Aarhus 2009 (Danish ed. 2006).

Watanabe-O'Kelly, Helen, *Court Culture in Dresden. From Renaissance to Baroque*, Basingstoke 2002.

Watanabe-O'Kelly, Helen, "Festivals of the Protestant Union", in: Ronnie Mulryne, Helen Watanabe-O'Kelly & Margaret Shewring (eds.), *Europa Triumphans*, 2, London 2004, 3-118.

Watanabe-O'Kelly, Helen & Anne Simon (eds.), *Festivals and Ceremonies. A Bibliography of Works Relating to Court, Civic and Religious Festivals in Europe, 1500-1800*, London & New York 2000.

Watson, Katherine & Charles Avery, "Medici and Stuart: A Grand Ducal Gift of 'Giovanni Bologna' Bronzes for Henry, Prince of Wales (1612)", *The Burlington Magazine* 115 (1973), 493-507.

Weber, Samuel, *Institution and Interpretation*, Stanford 2001.

Weber-Karge, Ulrike, '… einem irdischen Paradeiß zu vergleichen…'. Das Neue Lusthaus in Stuttgart. Untersuchungen zu einer Bauaufgabe der deutschen Renaissance, Sigmaringen 1989.

Weilbachs Kunstnerleksikon, 1. ed., Philip Weilbach (ed.), Copenhagen 1877-1878; 2. ed., Philip Weilbach (ed.), Copenhagen 1895-96; 3. ed., Merete Bodelsen & Povl Engelstoft (eds.), Copenhagen 1947-52; 4. ed., Sys Hartmann (ed.), Copenhagen 1994-2000.

Weingart, Ralf, "Der Rotwildfries im Güstrower Schloß. Voraussetzungen und Nachfolge", *Mecklenburgische Jahrbücher* 115 (2000), 119-152.

Weinwich, Niels Henrich, *Maler-, Billedhugger-, Kobberstik-, Bygnings-, og Stempelskiærer-Kunstens Historie (…)*, Copenhagen 1811.

Weinwich, Niels Henrich, *Dansk, Norsk og Svensk Kunstner-Lexicon*, Copenhagen 1829.

Weissman, A. W., "Het geslacht De Keyser", *Oud Holland* 22 (1904), 65-91.

Weissman, A. W., "De schoonzoon van Hendrik de Keyser", *Oud Holland* 38 (1920), 155-164.

Welch, Evelyn, *Shopping in the Renaissance: Consumer Cultures in Italy 1400-1600*, London & New Haven 2005.

Wendt, Antje, *Das Schloß zu Reinbek. Untersuchungen zur Ausstattung, Anlage und Architektur eines landesherrlichen Schlosses*, Kiel 1991 (PhD-dissertation).

Werlauff, E. C., "Sophia von Mecklenburg, Königin von Dänemark …", *Jahrbücher des Vereins für mecklenburgische Geschichte* 9 (1844), 111-165.

Werlauff, E. C., *De hellige Tre Kongers Kapel (…)*, Copenhagen 1849.

Werner, Brunhild, *Das Kurfürstliche Schloss in Dresden im 16. Jahrhundert*, Leipzig 1970 (Dissertation).

Wethey, Harold, *The Paintings of Titian*, London 1975.

Wex, Reinhold, *Ordnung und Unfriede. Raumprobleme des protestantischen Kirchenbaus im 17. und 18. Jahrhundert in Deutschland*, Marburg 1984.

Wezel, Gerard W. C. van, *Het paleis van Hendrik III graaf van Nassau te Breda*, Zeist and Zwolle 1999 (De Nederlandse Monumenten van Geschiedenis en Kunst).

White, Hayden, *Tropics of Discourse: Essays in Cultural Criticism*, Baltimore 1978.

White, Hayden, *The Content of the Form: Narrative Discourse and Historical Representation*, Baltimore 1987.

White, Hayden, "Catastrophe, Communal Memory and Mythic Discourse: The Uses of Myth in the Reconstruction of Society", in: Bo Stråth (ed.), *Myth and Memory in the Construction of Community*, Brussels 2000, 49-74.

Widerberg, C. S., *Norges første militæringeniør Isaac van Geelkerck og hans virke 1644-1656: et bidrag til norske befæstningers historie*, Oslo 1924.

Wieden, Helge Bei der, *Fürst Ernst Graf von Holstein-Schaumburg und seine Wirtschaftspolitik*, Bückeburg 1961.

Wieden, Helge Bei der, *Ein norddeutscher Renaissancefürst. Ernst zu Holstein-Schaumburg 1569-1622*, Bielefeld 1994.

Wilberg-Vignau, Thea, *In Europa zu Hause - Niederländer in München um 1600/Citizens of Europe. Dutch and Flemish Artists in Munich c. 1600*, Munich 2005.

Willis, Alfred Edward, *Flemish Renaissance Revival in Belgian Architecture (1830-1930)*, Ann Arbor (Mich.) 1989 (PhD-dissertation, Columbia University, Graduate School of arts and sciences, 1984).

Wisłocki, Marcin, *Sztuka protestancka na Pomorzu 1535-1684*, Szczecin 2005 (Biblioteka Naukowa Muzeum Narodowego w Szczecinie, Seria Historia Sztuki).

Wölfflin, Heinrich, *Principles of Art History: The Problem of the Development of Style in Later Art*, London 1932.

Wörner, Martin, *Vergnügung und Belehrung. Volkskultur auf den Weltausstellungen 1851-1900*, Münster 1999.

Wolkenhauer, Anja, *Zu schwer für Apoll: Die Antike in humanistischen Druckerzeichen des 16. Jahrhunderts*, Wiesbaden 2002 (Wolfenbütteler Schriften zur Geschichte des Buchwesens 35).

Wolters, Wolfgang, *Plastische Deckendekorationen des Cinque-*

cento in Venedig und im Veneto, Berlin 1968.

Wood, Christopher, "Art History's Normative Renaissance", in: Allen Grieco et al. (eds.), *The Italian Renaissance in the Twentieth Century. Acts of an International Conference, Florence, Villa I Tatti, June 9-11, 1999*, Olschki 1999, 65-92.

Wood, Christopher S., *Forgery, Replica, Fiction. Temporalities of German Renaissance Art*, Chicago & London 2008.

Woolfson, Jonathan, "Introduction", in: Jonathan Woolfson (ed.), *Renaissance Historiography*, Basingstoke 2005 (Palgrave Advances), 1-5.

Worp, J. A. (ed.), *De Briefwisseling van Constantijn Huygens, 1608-1687*, 1-6, The Hague 1911-1917.

Zandvliet, K., *Maurits Prins van Oranje*, Amsterdam & Zwolle 2000.

Zesen, Ph. von, *Beschreibung von der Stadt Amsterdam etc*, Amsterdam 1664.

Zimmer, Jürgen, "Christoph Gertner, Hofmaler in Wolfenbüttel - Eine neu entdeckte Danaë und ein vorläufiges Werkverzeichnis", *Niederdeutsche Beiträge zur Kunstgeschichte* 23 (1984) 117-138.

Zimmermann, Paul, *Album Academiae Helmstediensis. Abt. I. Studenten, Professoren etc. der Universität Helmstedt von 1574 bis 1636*, Hannover 1926 (Veröffentlichungen der Historischen Kommission für Hannover 9), reprint Nendeln & Liechtenstein 1980.

Zorach, Rebecca, *Blood, Milk, Ink, Gold: Abundance and Excess in the French Renaissance*, Chicago 2005.

Zorach, Rebecca, "Renaissance Theory: A Selective Introduction", in: James Elkins & Robert Williams (eds.), *Renaissance Theory*, New York & London 2008 (The Art Seminar 5), 3-36.

Østergård, Uffe, "The Geopolitics of Nordic Identity – From Composite States to Nation-States", in: Øystein Sørensen & Bo Stråth (eds.), *The Cultural Construction of Norden*, Oxford et al. 1997, 25-71.

Ångström-Grandien, Inga Lena, "The Reception of the Classical Ideal in Swedish 16th Century Art and Architecture", in: Krista Kodres (ed.), *The problem of classical ideal in the art and architecture of the countries around the Baltic Sea*, Tallin 2003 (Eesti Kunstiakadeemia toimetised 13), 32-54.

INDEX

Abraham 123
Absalon, Archbishop 16, 62 f.
van Achten, Marten 111
Adolph Friedrich, Duke of Mecklenburg 246
van Aelst, Pieter Coeck 130 f.
Aeneas 175
Agerbæk, Kirsten 17
Agricola, Georgius 171
Albani, Francesco 343
Alberti, Leone Battista 93, 154, 156 ff., 161, 188
Albrecht, Duke of Prussia 165, 228, 315
Albrecht, Uwe 22, 64
Aldegrever, Heinrich 174
Alexander the Great 174, 244, 251
Alpers, Svetlana 92 f.
Anchises 175
Anderson, Benedict 71
Andreae, Johann Valentin 238
Andreæ, M. Laurentius 245
Angelico, Fra 84 f.
Anna, Duchess of Nassau 282
Anna of Denmark, Electress of Saxony 22, 63, 180, 183 f., 186 f., 189 f., 194, 200, 215
Anna of Denmark, Queen of England 47, 243, 245, 247 ff., 252 f., 255 f., 263
Anna Cathrine of Brandenburg, Queen of Denmark 237, 248 f., 254, 331 f.
Anrep, Reinholt 129, 130, 132
Achilles 62
Arcimboldo, Giuseppe 43, 46
Arnisaeus, Henning 273 f.
Arthur, King of England 62
Ascensius, Jodocus Badius 60
Assmann, Aleida 53

August I, Elector of Saxony 22, 180, 183 f., 186 f., 189 f., 194, 200, 215, 249, 256, 263, 296
Augusta of Denmark, Duchess of Schleswig-Holstein 113 f., 243, 247, 250, 254
Avery, Charles 342
von Aachen, Hans 41, 43, 46, 295, 305, 309

Bacmeister, Lucas 246
Badens, Frans 283 ff.
Baglione, Giovanni 96
Baldinucci, Filippo 96
Balfour, Michael 248
Banér, Gustav 293
Bang, Thomas 238 f.
Barbara of Brandenburg, Duchess of Mantua 54
Barbara Sophie of Brandenburg 248
de Barbari, Jacopo 156
Barberini, Carlo 338
Barnekow, Christian 287
Bartholin, Rasmus 287
Bastiaensz., Franz 285
Bathsheba 21, 138, 140 ff., 145
Baudrillard, Jean 34
Becke, Jakob 133
Beckett, Francis 17, 283, 351
Beham, Barthel 174
Belde, Henningus 245
Bellini, Gentile 167
Bencard, Mogens 25, 101
Bennett, Bonnie A. 160
van Berckerode, Balthazar Florisz. 291
Berg, Claus 17, 21, 59, 61, 152 ff., 328 ff.
Berg, Johan Adam 296
Bernini, Gianlorenzo 338 f., 343

Berrecci, Bartolommeo 37
Beyerholm, Beth 154
von Bezold, Gustav 16
Białostocki, Jan 45, 47, 75, 134
Bille, Anders 282, 287
Binck, Jacob 58 f., 62, 137 f., 203, 290, 295
Blasius, Leonard 238, 352
van den Blocke, Willem 39, 280, 349
Bloemaert, Abraham 304
Blome, Hans 208, 211
Bodin, Jean 274
Borbeck, Jacob 267
Borggrefe, Heiner 24, 306, 309
Bos, Cornelis 175
Bourré, Jean 199, 201
Boy, Wilhelm (Guillaume Boyen) 348, 352
Bozzetti 177
Brade, William 253
Brahe, Knud 214
Brahe, Otto 282
Brahe, Tycho 81, 214
Bramante, Donato 102
de Bray, Dirck 295
de Bray, Salomon 314, 320
von Bremen, Johan 119, 123
Bril, Paul 306
van den Brinck, Henri 348
Brochmand, Caspar 254
Brockenhuus, Frants 215
Broecke, Berent 283
du Broeucq, Jacques 221, 223 ff., 228
Brueghel, Jan (the Elder) 305 f.
Brueghel, Pieter (the Elder) 91, 95
Brunelleschi, Filippo 94, 153, 157, 159 f., 162
Brüggemann, Hans 162
Bryson, Norman 85
Buchloh, Benjamin 80
Buchner, Paul 190 f., 200
Buontalenti, Bernardo 322
Burckhardt, Jacob 11, 80, 84, 100
Burke, Peter 13, 56
Burman Becker, J. G. 207
de Busbecq, Ogier Ghislain 165 ff.
Bussert, Morten 62 f.
Buxhövden, Otto 130 f.
Buysser, Poulus 267
Bähr, Tekla 129
Böker, Johann Josef 158

Caesar, Gajus Julius 251
Campbell, Stephen 75
van Campen, Jacob 336
Campin, Robert 83
Carl, Duke of Mecklenburg 246
von Carlowitz, Christoph 171
Castelnuovo, Enrico 47, 75
Castiglione, Baldassare 94, 96
du Cerceau, Jacques Androuet (the Elder) 224

de Certeau, Michel 80
Chakrabarty, Dipesh 80
Charisius, Jonas 24, 236, 279 ff.
Charisius, Peder 288
Charles I, King of England 25, 303, 338, 340 f., 343
Charles V, Emperor 167, 171, 177, 219, 228, 245
Charles IX, King of France 226
Charles the Great, Emperor 236
Chatterjeee, Partha 80
Christensen, Matz 118, 207
Christian I, King of Denmark 53, 58 f.
Christian II, King of Denmark 22, 56 f., 59 f., 62, 65, 193, 227, 248 ff., 255
Christian III, King of Denmark 21 f., 40, 58, 62 f., 65, 117, 137, 200, 215, 290, 292, 295, 336, 349, 353
Christian IV, King of Denmark 13, 15 ff., 23 f., 33 f., 37 f., 41, 43 ff., 51, 53, 65, 73, 75, 102, 107, 129, 132, 194, 222, 224, 227, 235 ff., 241, 243 ff. 263 ff. 272 ff., 279, 281 ff., 287 ff., 293 ff., 301 ff., 307 ff., 313 f., 331 ff., 335 ff., 347, 353
Christian II, Duke of Anhalt 327 f., 331
Christian the Younger, Duke of Brunswick-Wolfenbüttel 264 f.
Christian, Prince Elect of Denmark 249, 254, 256
Christina, Queen of Sweden 274, 296
Christine of Saxony, Queen of Denmark 21, 56, 59, 61, 153, 155 ff., 159, 200
Claesz., Aris 280, 292 f.
Clark, T. J. 80
Clausen, Ludvig 34
Cleyn, Frantz 39 f., 338
Cocteau, Jean 34
Colantuono, Anthony 290
Colyn, Alexandre 347
Compenius, Esaias 285
van Conincxloo, Gilles 283, 285
Conrad, David 176
Conring, Hermann 274
Constantine, Emperor 266
Coornhert, Dirck 118
Cornaro, Alvise 188
Cornelissen, Willem 352
Corthoys, Peter 143
Corvinus, Matthias, King of Hungary 37
Cory, Cornelis 52 f.
Cozart, Stacey 103
Cramer, Daniel 246
Cranach, Lucas (the Elder) 59, 131, 156, 186
Culler, Jonathan 85
Cuny, Georg 349

Daems, Jan 223
Dahlerup, Vilhelm 350
Danckerts, Cornelis 314, 316 f., 320, 349
Daniel 109
Dauw, Johannes 14
David, King 21, 110, 138, 140 ff., 145, 235, 238, 284
Deckert, Hermann 156

van Delft, Claes, 293
van Delft, Herman 293
van Delft, Pieter Adriaensz. 292 f.
Derrida, Jacques 74, 77
Descartes, René 100
Didi-Huberman, Georges 19, 84 f.
Diederichs-Gottschalk, Dietrich 108
Dietterlin, Wendel 25, 321 f., 351
Dieussart, François 25, 336 ff., 341 ff.
Dolendo, Zacharias 131
Donatello (Donato di Niccolo di Betto Bardi) 157 ff., 339
Donauer, Hans 305
van der Doordt, Abraham 303
van der Doordt, Jacob 24, 302 f., 308
van der Doordt, Peter 302
Dorothea of Brandenburg, Queen of Denmark 59, 263
Dowland, John 250, 336, 341
Dubout, Marcus 285
van Duetecum, Jan 225
van Duetecum, Lucas 225
van Dyck, Anthony 44, 342 f.
Dülberg, Angelica 22
van Düren, Adam 62
Dürer, Albrecht 37, 59, 83 ff., 155 ff., 160 f., 221, 270

Eber, Paul 143
Eck, Veit 132
Edward VI, King of England 295
van Egen, Gert 280, 292
Eggers, Bartholomäus 336
Eichhorn, E. 348, 352
Eisenmenger, Karsten 105, 107
Elisabeth (Isabella) of Austria, Queen of Denmark 56, 59 f., 228, 245 ff.
Elisabeth of Bavaria, Electress of Saxony 153
Elisabeth of Denmark, Duchess of Brunswick-Wolfenbüttel 23, 243, 254 f., 263 f., 269, 272
Elisabeth of Denmark, Electress of Brandenburg 187
Elizabeth, Queen of England 223, 243, 249
Elkin, James 74 f.
Elsevier, publishers 288
Elsheimer, Adam 342
Engqvist, Hans-Henrik 140, 198 f.
von Enum, Johan 119, 123
Erasmus Roterodamus, Desiderius 60, 118
Erik of Pomerania, King of Denmark 58, 59
Erik XIV, King of Sweden 57, 63
Eriksen, Svend 146 f.
Ernest, Count of Holstein-Schaumburg 301 ff., 307 ff.
Ernst, Elector of Saxony 56, 153, 200
van Eyck, Jan 92, 154 f.
Ezekiel 236

Fanelli, Francesco 343
Farago, Claire 11, 17, 19, 101
Farnese, Alessandro 339
Fasola, Nicco 154
Fasold, Johann 190 f., 193

Ferdinand I, Emperor 165 f., 236, 295
Ferdinand II, Emperor 308
Filarete, Antonio Averlino 94, 96
Findeln, Paul 77
Fiorentino, Francesco 37
Fiorentino, Rosso 45, 224
Floris, Cornelis 39, 40, 58, 63, 223, 292, 295, 318, 336 f., 347 ff., 351
Floris, Frans 52 f.
Floris, Hans 219, 280
Foster, Hal 80
Foucault, Michel 80
Fouquet, Jean 155
Francart 320
della Francesca, Piero 154 ff.
Francis I, King of France 224
Francke, Paul 269
Francken, Frans 283
Franqueville, Pierre 43
Frans, Prince of Denmark 61
Franz I 174
Frederik I, King of Denmark 65
Frederik II, King of Denmark 16, 17, 22, 41, 43, 46, 51, 60, 63, 65, 75, 102, 128 f., 193, 207, 222 f., 227, 235, 238, 243 f., 246 f., 263, 284, 290, 292, 295, 335 f.
Frederik III, King of Denmark 239, 254, 265, 339
Frederik V, King of Denmark 14, 240, 341
Frederik of Denmark, Prince 249
Frederik Hendrik, Count of Nassau 281, 284, 286, 336
Friborg, Jørgen 14
Friedman, Alice T. 25
Friedrich the Wise, Elector of Saxony 59, 105, 153, 156 f., 184
Friedrich Ulrich, Duke of Brunswick-Wolfenbüttel 264, 269, 273
Friedrich Wilhelm, Elector of Brandenburg 336, 341 f.
Friedrich Wilhelm II of Saxony 255
Friis, Christen 282, 287
Friis, Johan 21, 63 f., 137, 139, 140, 142, 144 ff., 203 ff., 207, 215
Fuhring, Peter 225
Fuiren, Henrik 287
Fusenig, Thomas 24
Füchting, Johan 292 f.
Füllmaurer, Heinrich 108

Gabrieli, Giovanni 341
Galdendorph, Bartram 245
Galesloot, M. A. 349, 353
Gardin, Philip 290
Gauricus, Pomponius 157 ff., 162
van Geelkerk, Isaac 352
van Genten, Hermen (Hermen of Ghent) 223
Génard, Pierre 349
Gentileschi, Orazio 343
Georg II, Elector of Saxony 173
Georg, Margrave of Brandenburg-Ansbach 184
Gerhard, Hubert 337 f., 347

Gerlach, Heinrich   246
Gertner, Christoph   309
Ghiberti, Lorenzo   157, 162
Giambologna   38, 43, 339 ff.
Gilbert, Christian   255
Gilbert, Felix   80
Gilbert, Regina   255
Ginsburg, Carlo   75
Giotto   94
Girardon, François   339
Glockendon, Jørg   160 f.
von Goethe, Johann Wolfgang   95
Goldmann   350
Goltzius, Hendrick   20, 75, 117 ff., 130, 303
Gombrich, Ernst   80
Gonzaga, Ludovico   54
Gorlaeus, Abraham   282
Gossaert, Jan   59 f., 227
Gossman, Lionel   80
de Granvelle, Antoine Perrenot   224
de Grebber, Frans Pietersz   283 f.
Greenberg, Clement   80
Gresham, Thomas   223
Greyss, Johan Andreas   239
Griffel, Peder   343
Grubbe, Eiler   207, 215, 219
Grubbe, Sivert   250, 287
Guckeisen, Jacob   132
Gudewerdt, Hans (the Younger)   38
Gudonov, Boris (Tsar)   254
Guercino   343
Guicciardini, Ludovico   223
Guldan, Ernst   171
Gunnersen, Birger   61 f.
Göding, Heinrich   186, 189
Gøye, Birgitte   223

Habakuk   110
Haelwegh, Albert   280
Hagemann, H.O.   34
von Haiminsfeld, Melchior Goldast   308
Hamlet   74
Hanı, Elçi   165 f.
Hannover, Emil   351
Hans, King of Denmark   56, 57, 59, 61, 153, 187, 200
Hans, Prince of Denmark   254 f.
Hansen, Maria Fabricius   17, 19 f.
Harasimowicz, Jan   20
de la Haye, Abraham   352
Hedicke, Robert   351
Hedwig of Denmark, Electress of Saxony   22, 243 f., 248 ff., 254 ff.
Heeger, Heinrich   57
Hegel, G. W. F.   80, 95
Hein, Jørgen   239
Heinrich (the Younger), Duke of Brunswick-Wolfenbüttel   264
Heinrich Julius, Duke of Brunswick-Wolfenbüttel   23, 245 ff., 250 f., 263 f., 269, 270, 272 f., 303, 340
Heintz, Joseph (the Elder)   43, 301, 303
Helena   174
Helie, Paulus (Poul Helgesen)   57
Helk, Vello   245
van Helpen, Abel Coenders   282
Hemmingsen, Nils   129
Hendricx, Jan   316
de Hennin-Liétard, Jean   222
Henning, A.   210
Henri II, King of France   184
Henri IV, King of France   236, 339, 340
Henrietta Maria, Queen of England   338
Henriette Louise of Orange, Electress of Brandenburg   336
Henry, Prince of England   253
Henry III, Duke of Nassau   221, 226, 248
Herberay, Nicolas   224
Herbert, Philipp   252
Herbert, Robert   80
Herodes   284
de Herrera, Juan   236
Hipp, Hermann   271
Hoefnagel, Joris   47
van't Hofe, Paul   42
de Hofman, Hans   14
Hogenberg, Franz   246
Holbein, Hans (the Elder)   155, 157
Holger Danske (Ogier le Danois)   62
de Hollanda, Francisco   96
Holm, Hans J.   271
Holmér, Folke   270
Holwein, Elias   263 ff.
Hondius, Hendrick   281
Hoppe, Stephan   200
van Hornthorst, Gerrit   39, 296, 336, 341, 343
van Hornthorst, Willem   336
Howard, Henry   253
Howard, Thomas   338
von Howen, Gert   131
Hude, Kristian   352
Huizinga, Johan   335
Hume, Tobias   253
Hundermarck, Peder   282
Husen, Peter   43
Huth, Hans   158
Huygens, Christiaan   282
Huygens, Constantijn   282
Høyen, Niels Lauritz   15, 154 f.
van Haarlem, Cornelis Cornelisz.   284 f.
van Haarlem, Gerrit Cornelisz.   295

Irmisch, Hans   190 f.
Isaacz., Isaac   341
Isaacsz., Pieter   24, 39, 41, 43, 46, 280, 283 ff., 288 f., 291, 296, 301 ff., 305, 306 ff., 342
Jacobi, Petrus   127
Jakobson, Jakobson   133 f.

James I (James VI), King of Scotland and England   47, 235 f., 247 ff., 252 f., 263, 332, 338, 340
Janlet, Charles-Emile   347 f.
Janssonius, publishers   288
Jansz., Hendrick   316
Jeannin, Pierre   281
Jensen, Johannes V.   16
Jervis, Simon   332
Joachim Friederich, Elector of Brandenburg   249
de Jode, Gerard   55
Johan III, King of Sweden   40
Johann Adolf, Duke of Schleswig-Holstein   112, 247, 250 f., 255
Johann Albrecht, Duke of Mecklenburg   184, 246
Johann Friedrich, Elector of Saxony   171, 174, 183 f., 248
Johannsen, Birgitte Bøggild   12, 18, 139 ff., 147, 156, 240
Johannsen, Hugo   34, 45, 47, 52, 107, 124, 215, 238, 315, 321, 327
Johnson, Gerard   44
Jonas, Justus   112
Jones, Inigo   247, 250, 252, 316, 320, 338, 343
de Jonge, Krista   23, 37, 237, 354
Jonson, Ben   236, 247, 252
Justinianus, Emperor   236
Jørgensen, Lorentz   112
Jørgensen, Tove   119

Karaman, Ljubo   134
Karl Filip, Duke of Södermanland   331
Kaufmann, Thomas DaCosta   12, 18, 72, 75 f., 101, 103
Kavaler, Ethan Matt   74
Keldermans, Anthonis I   221
Keldermans, Rombout II   221
Kelly, Joan   25, 71
Kernkamp, Gerhard Wilhelm   350
Ketel, Cornelis   302, 303
de Keyser, Hendrick   24, 39, 271, 287, 291 ff., 313 ff., 336, 348
Khunrath, Heinrich   241
Kierkegaard, Søren   99 f.
Kierurt, Frederiq   228
Kilian, Gothofridus   123
Kiær, Søren   39
Klein, Wilhelm   349
Knieper, Hans   40, 43, 280, 295
Kodres, Krista   20 f., 75
Koerner, Joseph   19, 83 ff.
Kok, A.A.   350 f., 354
von Komerstadt, Georg   171
Konecný, Lubomír   306, 309
Krabbe, Keld   281 ff.
Kramer, Sabine   105, 107
von Kramern, Niclas   131
Krauss, Rosalind   80
Krog, A.   45
Kähler, Ingeborg   162
Königswieser, Heinrich   143
Körber, Martin   131

Lambertsz., Geraert   314
Lambrecht, Hinrich   327
Lammertijn, Passchier   282, 288
Lamoureux, Abraham-César   341
Lange, Julius   16 f., 56
Lanowiecki, Mirosław   112
Lastman, Pieter   38 f.
Laurana, Francesco   45
Leibniz, G. W.   95
Leinberger, Hans   159
Leo, Pope   94, 96
Leonardi, Giuseppe   223
Léopold II, King of Belgium   348
Liberius, Pope   266
Libeskind, Daniel   73
de Lichtenberg, Hanne Honnens   118
di Linar, Rocco   189
Lindenow, Godofredo (Godtfred Lindenov)   286 f.
Liperman, Joachim   245
Lobechius, David   246
Lockhart, Paul Douglas   54, 56
von Loehneyss, Friedrich Engelhard   274
von Loehneyss, Georg Engelhard   250 f.
Lombardi, Lambert   130
Longomontanus, Christian   238
Lorck, Melchior   14, 21, 39, 58, 165 ff.
Lorenzen, Vilhelm   352
Lotter, Hieronymus   190
Louis X, King of France   37
Louis XII, King of France   220
Louis XIV, King of France   236, 243, 274, 332, 339
Luckhardt, Jochen   264 f.
Luijten, Ger   225
Lund, F. C. 287
Luther, Martin   21, 105, 107 f., 110, 129, 131, 142 ff., 176, 187, 203
Lübke, Vera   306, 309
Lübke, Wilhelm   16
Lykke, Anna   133

Madruzzo, Christoph   175
Magnus, Duke   128
de Mancicidor, Jean   281
Mandelgreen, Nils Månsson   348
van Mander, Karel I   294
van Mander, Karel III   40 f., 131, 284, 342
Manetti, Antonio di Tuccio   94
Manners, Roger   249
Mantegna, Andrea   161
Marcus Aurelius, Emperor   339
Marcus, Leah S.   12
Marcussen, Marianne   21, 61, 154
Margaret of Austria, Regent of the Netherlands   59, 206
Markdanner, Caspar   120 f. 124
Marstand, Vilhelm   34
Marsvin, Jørgen   206
Mary of Austria, Queen of Hungary and Bohemia   219, 221 ff., 253

Masaccio 94 f.
Matthias, Emperor 308
Maurits, Count of Nassau 281 f., 286, 288, 295
Maximilian I, Emperor 25, 56, 59 f., 332
Maximilian II, Emperor 43, 46, 120, 167
Mbembe, Achille 79
Medici, Cosimo 243
da Medina, Franciscus 57
Mehmet II, Sultan 167
Meier, Claudia A. 118 f.
Melanchthon, Philip 21, 124, 146 f., 171, 176, 203
Meldahl, Ferdinand 16, 351
Melioli, Bartolomeo 58
Meursius, Johannes 287
Michelangelo Buonarotti, 25, 95 f., 319
Michelet, Jules 80
Mignolo, Walter 80
Mijnsheeren, Jan 228
Mikkelsen, Hans 244
Milner, John 95
Milner, Stephen 75
von Miltitz, Ernst 171
Mirou, Jacques 285
Mochi, Francesco 339
Moeyaert, Claes 341
Mohr, Jens 48
Molbech, Christian 15
Mont, Hans 43
de Morães, Francisco 224
Mores, Hans 25, 327, 329, 331
Mores, Jacob 25, 39, 327 f., 330
Moritz, Elector of Saxony 22, 171, 172 ff., 180, 183 f., 200, 236, 256
Moth, Poul 287
Moxey, Keith 17, 19, 101
Musaphia, Beniamin 241
Müller, Philipp 269
Münchhausen, Johannes 128
Münster, Sebastian 61
Möller, Hans-Herbert 273
Mönch, Wolf 193

Nacke, Catharina 122, 124
Nacke, Diedrich 122 ff.
Neckelmann, Frederik Skjold 16, 351
Neurdenburg, Elisabeth 313
van Neurenberg, Anna 292 f.
Neville, Kristoffer 25, 75
Newton, Isaac 95
Nicolaus, Bishop 127
Nissen, Nis 241
Noldus, Badeloch Vera 24, 306, 308 f., 353, 355
Norn, Otto 63, 138 ff., 142, 203
Nosseni, Carlo Maria 237
Nosseni, Giovanni Maria 47, 58, 189, 193, 237, 248
Novellanus, Simon 246
Nuvoloni, Filippo 53 f., 58
Nyborg, David 267, 270

Nyström, Eiler 283

van Obbergen, Anthonis 40, 43, 226 f., 280, 295 349, 351, 353
Odelberg, Herman 348, 351 f.
Oenema, Tinco 282
van Oldenbarnevelt, Johan 280 ff.
Oliver, Isaac 44
Olsen, Rikke Agnete 139 ff.
Onians, John 75
Ortwein, August 16
von der Osten, Gert 162
Ottenheym, Konrad 24, 101, 354
Overläcker, Anna 130 f.
Oxe, Peder 120

Pachs, Magnus (Mogens Pax) 245
Paciotto, Francsco 227
da Padova, Giovanni Maria (Johann Maria) 177
van Paesschen, Hans 223, 227, 280
van Paesschen, Hendrik 223
Pagden, Anthony 80
Pahr, Domenicus 43
Pahr, Baptista 58
Palaiologos, John VIII 58
Palladius, Peder 62
Paludan, Bernardus, 283, 295
Paludan, Hother 209
Panofsky, Erwin 79, 82 ff., 90, 95
Panten, Caspar 293
de Passe, Crispijn 296
de Passe, Simon 280, 296, 331
Passer, Arent 133
Payngk, Peder 237
Peacham, Henry 340
Pedersen, Christiern 55, 60 ff.
Pedersen, Poul 244
Pencz, Georg 174
Persson, Per Magnus 38
Peruzzi, Baldassare 177
le Petit, Jean Francois 282
Petrarch, Francesco 94
Petrejus, Paulus (Poul Pedersen) 245
Philip, Duke of Nassau-Saarbrücken 224
Philip II, King of Spain 219, 222, 225, 236, 295
Philip III, King of Spain 339
Philip IV, King of Spain 339
Philip Julius, Duke of Pomerania 246
Philip the Good, Duke of Burgundy 219 f.
Philipp, Landgrave of Hessen 105, 184
Piccolomini, Aenes Silvius (Pope Pius II) 53 f.
Pietersz., Aert 283
de Pineda, Johannes 236, 238
Pirkheimer, Willibald 158
Plantin, Christophe 166
Plato 62
Plinius (the Younger) 188
Pollio, Vitruvius 159 f.

Pontanus, Johannes 287, 289
Pontoppidan, Erik 14
Post, Pieter 336, 350
Poulsen, Hanne Kolind 21, 62 f.
Price, Uvedale 95
Primaticcio, Francesco 45, 224
Peter the Great, Emperor 354

della Quercia, Jacopo 158

Radzivil, Christophorus 246
de Raet, Willem 269
Ram, Giovanni 305
Ranch, Hieronymus Justesen 235
Rantzau, Gert 266
Rantzau, Henrik 63, 208
Rantzau, Josias 239
Rantzau, Peter 213
Raphael (Raffaello Sanzio) 92, 94, 96, 102
Raschy, Balthasar 131 ff.
Rasmussen, Mikael Bøgh 21 f.
Rasmussen, Tarald 134
Reichle, Hans 43, 337 f.
Reinwald, Caspar 192
Rembrandt Harmensz.-van Rijn 39
René, Duke of Anjou, Lorraine, Provence i.a. 45
Richardot, Guillaume 225
Richter, Johan 331
Riegl, Alois 81
Riemenschneider, Tilman 159, 161
Ringerinck, Heinrich 119, 123
Rodenburg, Theodoor 283, 290, 314
Roding, Juliette G. 23, 52, 263, 266, 270 f., 306, 308 f., 353, 355
Rodler, Hieronymus 161
Roland 62
Romanino, Girolamo 175
Romano, Christoforo 37
Romano, Giulio 37
Rosenkrantz, Holger 246, 287
Rosenkrantz, Jørgen 219
Rottenhammer, Hans 24, 301, 303
Rubens, Pieter Paul 44, 342, 348
Ruckers, Andreas 285
Ruckers, Hans (the Elder) 293
Ruckers, Iohannes 285
Rude, Merete 160
Rudolf II, Emperor 38, 41, 43, 46 f., 236, 244, 264, 295, 301, 306
Ruggiero, Guido 12
Rumler, Poul 235
Ruse, Henrik 352
de Rye, Anne 225

Saintenoy, Paul 349
Saly, Jacques- François-Joseph 341
da Sangallo, Giuliano 177
Sansovino, Jacopo 177

del Sarto, Andrea 45
de Saumaise, Claude 287
Savery, Rolant 47
Savonarola, Girolamo 92
Saxo Grammaticus 60, 62
van der Schardt, Jan Joris 40
van der Schardt, Johan Gregor 41, 46, 280, 336 f.
Scheffer, August 16
Schlichtenmaier, Harry 305
van Scholten, Joost 352
Schongardus, Georgius 245
Schongauer, Martin 156
Schoy, Auguste 25, 347 ff., 354
Schroer, Hans 186
Schupp, Balthasar 106
Schut, Hans 316
Schwabe, Nicolaus 337 f.
Schwarz, Georg 186
Schütz, Heinrich 176, 215, 336, 341, 343
Sehested, Claus Maltesen 133
Seklucjan, Jan 105
Sems, Johan 267 f., 352
Serlio, Sebastiano 318 f.
Sforza, Bona, Duchess of Milan 177
Siegfried 62
Sigismund I, King of Poland 177
Simon VI 304
Simon, Johann 244
Skafbo, Jens 235
Skeel, Albert 248
Slothouwer, D. F. 351 f., 354 f.
van der Sluys, Christian 267
Smith, Pamela 77
Solomon 23, 176, 235 ff.
Sophie of Mecklenburg, Queen of Denmark 246 ff., 254 f., 331
Sparr, Jens 248
Specklin, Daniel 268, 270
Speed, John 37
Speerfork, Eggert 352
Spencer, Robert 281
Spengler, Oswald 20, 91, 96
Spiering, François 284, 294, 296
Spinola, Ambrogio 281
Spranger, Bartholomeus 43 f., 47, 330
Staets, Hendrick 317
van Steenwinckel, Hans 25, 34, 39, 227, 238, 280, 287, 291, 313 ff., 320, 322, 351, 352, 353
van Steenwinckel, Lourens 25, 34, 280, 291, 313, 316, 320 f., 349
van Steenwinckel, Mayke 293
della Stella, Paolo 178
Stevin, Simon 266, 268, 282, 288
Stone, Nicholas 316
Stoss, Veit 153, 159, 161
Strauss, Walter L. 120 f.
von der Streithorst, Anton 264
Strick, Adriaan 288

Stuhlmann, Adolf 157 f.
Sture, Kristina 293
Stöhr, Michael 184
le Sueur, Hubert 340
Sulzer, Johann George 95
Sunesen, Anders (Andreas), Archbishop 72, 127
Sustris, Friedrich 41, 43
Svaning, Hans 57
Sweelinck, Gerrit Pietersz. 291
Sweelinck, Jan Pietersz. 285, 291, 296
Sweys, Lorenz Pietersz. 314 f.
Süleyman the Magnificent, Sultan 21 f., 165 ff., 236
Säre, Peeter 126, 128, 130, 132 ff.

Tacca, Pietro 43, 340, 343
Tancke, Martin 288
Taverne, Ed 270, 352
Taylor, John 301
Tendler, Christoph 184 f., 190
Tessin, Nicodemus (the Elder) 41
Thim, Reinhold 39
Thomæ, Petrus (Peder Thomsen) 245
Thorlacius-Ussing, Viggo 156
Thorndike, Lynn 92
de Thurah, Lauritz 14, 329, 348
Thøfner, Margit 20, 75
von Tiesenhausen, Margareta 132
Timm, Reinhold 293
Tintoretto (Jacopo Robusti) 305
Titze, Mario 22
Tola, Benedetto 22, 171, 175, 189
Tola, Gabriele 22, 171, 175, 189
Torrigiani, Jacopo (Jacob Twriszani) 59
Trolle, Herluf 223
Tunder, Pastor 131
Tusmer, Heinrich 127
Tzschimmer, Gabriel 175

Uffenbach, Philip 247
Ulfeldt, Jakob 24, 279, 281, 283, 285, 287, 295
Ulrich, Duke of Mecklenburg 246, 251, 254
Ulrik, Prince of Denmark 23, 243 ff., 251 ff., 273, 282
von Ungern, Jürgen 133
von Ungern, Klaus 133
Unnerbäck, Eyvind 147
Uppenkamp, Barbara 23 f.
Urbel, Emil 132
Urne, Johan 198
Urne, Lage 60, 62
Ussing, J. L. 15

van Valckenborch, Lucas 291
Valdemar II Sejr, King of Denmark 127
Valdemar IV Atterdag, King of Denmark 127
de Vandières, S. 348 ff.
Vasa, Gustav, King of Sweden 57, 353
Vasari, Giorgio 94 ff., 100, 319
Vedel, Anders Sørensen 63, 244

de Vega, Gaspar 222, 225
van Veen, Otto 283
Veneziano, Agostino 175
de Vere, Susan 252
Vermeulen, Frans André Jozef 352
Vernickel, Guillaume (Wilhelm Vernuken) 347
Veronese, Paolo Cagliari 305
del Verrocchio, Andrea 339
Viator, Jean Pélérin 160 f.
von Vietinghoff, Claus 132
da Vignola, Jacopo Barozzi 319
Villalpando, Juan Bautista 236
Villari, Pasquale 91
da Vinci, Leonardo 45, 83, 94
van der Vivjer, Dirk 16, 25
Vlnas, Vít 306, 309
Voghterr, Heinrich 173
Volkertsz., Dirck 118
van der Voort, Cornelis 236, 284
Vorstius, Adolph 287
van Vosbergen, Josias 288
Vossius, Gerard Jan 287
de Vries, Adriaen 25, 38 f., 43, 46, 295, 301, 303, 329, 336 ff., 340 ff.
de Vries, Hans Vredeman 44, 46, 130 f., 222, 224 f., 227, 269, 302, 313, 318 f., 347, 348 f., 353
de Vries, Joris 223
Vroom, Hendrick Cornelisz. 46

Wade, Mara R. 23
Wallbaum, Matthäus 25, 327
Walther, Ambrosius 186
Walther, Christoph II 192
Walther, Hans II 175 f., 178
Walther, Sebastian 193
Wamberg, Jacob 19 f., 101 f.
Warburg, Aby 82, 100
Warren, Whitney 352
Watanabe-O'Kelly, Helen 248
Weck, Anton 175
Weingart, Ralf 203
Wells-Cole, Anthony 353
Werner, Brunhild 173
Wesselofsky, Alessandro 92
White, Hayden 80
Wichmann, Henrik 34
von Wierandt, Caspar Voigt 171, 191
van Wijck, Jan 238
Wilhelm, Landgrave of Hessen 184
Wilkins, David G. 160
Willem Lodewijk, Count of Nassau 282
de Willem, Paul 288
William V, Duke of Bavaria 43, 228
William, Robert 74
Winwood, Ralph 281
de Witte, Pieter (Candid) 43, 347
Woldbye, Ole 293
Woolfson, Jonathan 12

Worm, Ole 44, 289
Wulf, Hans 301
Wölflin, Heinrich 81

Xenia of Russia, Tsarevna 254

von Zesen, Philip 286
Zorach, Rebecca 12